Britain's Moment in Palestine

"**Mandatory reading**: Michael Cohen has written a comprehensive and fair-minded account of the Palestine mandate from the antecedents of the Balfour declaration in 1917 to the consequences of the founding of the state of Israel in 1948. The dominant themes are the contradictions of British rule and the military as well as the demographic aims of the Zionists to 'make Palestine as Jewish as England was English'. His book will be used as a work of reference as well as a balanced judgment from all angles, Arab and American as well as British and Zionist. Readers will be especially interested in his interpretation of anti-Semitism, Arab collaboration with the Nazis, and the Holocaust in relation to the creation of the Jewish state. His command of archival and secondary sources establishes *Britain's Moment in Palestine* as an essential work of research and interpretation."

Professor Wm. Roger Louis holds the Kerr Chair of English History and Culture at the University of Texas, Austin, and is Editor-in-Chief of *The Oxford History of the British Empire*

In 1917, the British issued the Balfour Declaration for military and strategic reasons. This book analyses why and how the British took on the Palestine mandate. It explores how their interests and policies changed during its course and why they evacuated the country in 1948.

During the first decade of the mandate the British enjoyed an influx of Jewish capital mobilized by the Zionists which enabled them to fund not only the administration of Palestine, but also their own regional imperial projects. But in the mid-1930s, as the clouds of World War Two gathered, Britain's commitment to Zionism was superseded by the need to secure her strategic assets in the Middle East. In consequence, she switched to a policy of appeasing the Arabs. In 1947, Britain abandoned her attempts to impose a settlement in Palestine that would be acceptable to the Arab states and referred Palestine to the United Nations, without recommendations, leaving the antagonists to settle their conflict on the battlefield.

Based on archival sources and the most up-to-date scholarly research, this comprehensive history offers new insights into Arab, British and Zionist policies. It is a must-read for anyone with an interest in Israel, and the Middle East in general.

Michael Joseph Cohen was born in England, and earned his PhD under the late Elie Kedourie at the London School of Economics. He is Professor Emeritus in History at Bar-Ilan University, Israel. He has published widely on the Palestine mandate and the establishment of the state of Israel.

Israeli History, Politics and Society
Series Editor: Efraim Karsh
King's College London

This series provides a multidisciplinary examination of all aspects of Israeli history, politics and society, and serves as a means of communication between the various communities interested in Israel: academics, policy-makers, practitioners, journalists and the informed public.

1 **Peace in the Middle East**
   The Challenge for Israel
   Edited by Efraim Karsh

2 **The Shaping of Israeli Identity**
   Myth, Memory and Trauma
   Edited by Robert Wistrich and David Ohana

3 **Between War and Peace**
   Dilemmas of Israeli Security
   Edited by Efraim Karsh

4 **US–Israeli Relations at the Crossroads**
   Edited by Gabriel Sheffer

5 **Revisiting the Yom Kippur War**
   Edited by P R Kumaraswamy

6 **Israel**
   The Dynamics of Change and Continuity
   Edited by David Levi-Faur, Gabriel Sheffer and David Vogel

7 **In Search of Identity**
   Jewish Aspects in Israeli Culture
   Edited by Dan Urian and Efraim Karsh

8 **Israel at the Polls, 1996**
   Edited by Daniel J Elazar and Shmuel Sandler

9 **From Rabin to Netanyahu**
   Israel's Troubled Agenda
   Edited by Efraim Karsh

10 **Fabricating Israeli History**
   The 'New Historians', second revised edition
   Efraim Karsh

11 **Divided against Zion**
   Anti-Zionist Opposition in Britain to a Jewish State in Palestine, 1945–48
   Rory Miller

12 **Peacemaking in a Divided Society**
   Israel after Rabin
   Edited by Sasson Sofer

13 **A Twenty-Year Retrospective of Egyptian–Israeli Relations**
   Peace in Spite of Everything
   Ephraim Dowek

14 **Global Politics**
   Essays in Honour of David Vital
   Edited by Abraham Ben-Zvi and Aharon Klieman

15 **Parties, Elections and Cleavages**
   Israel in Comparative and Theoretical Perspective
   Edited by Reuven Y Hazan and Moshe Maor

16 **Israel and the Polls 1999**
   Edited by Daniel J Elazar and M Ben Mollov

17 **Public Policy in Israel**
   Edited by David Nachmias and Gila Menahem

18 **Developments in Israeli Public Administration**
   Edited by Moshe Maor

19 **Israeli Diplomacy and the Quest for Peace**
   Mordechai Gazit

20 **Israeli–Romanian Relations at the End of Ceauceșcu's Era**
   Yosef Govrin

21. **John F Kennedy and the Politics of Arms Sales to Israel**
    Abraham Ben-Zvi

22. **Green Crescent over Nazareth**
    The Displacement of Christians by Muslims in the Holy Land
    Raphael Israeli

23. **Jerusalem Divided**
    The Armistice Region, 1947–67
    Raphael Israeli

24. **Decision on Palestine Deferred**
    America, Britain and Wartime Diplomacy, 1939–45
    Monty Noam Penkower

25. **A Dissenting Democracy**
    The Case of 'Peace Now', An Israeli Peace Movement
    Magnus Norell

26. **British, Israel and Anglo-Jewry 1947–57**
    Natan Aridan

27. **Israeli Identity**
    In Search of a Successor to the Pioneer, Tsabar and Settler
    Lilly Weissbrod

28. **The Israeli Palestinians**
    An Arab Minority in the Jewish State
    Edited by Alexander Bligh

29. **Israel, the Hashemites and the Palestinians**
    The Fateful Triangle
    Edited by Efraim Karsh and P R Kumaraswamy

30. **Last Days in Israel**
    Abraham Diskin

31. **War in Palestine, 1948**
    Strategy and Diplomacy
    David Tal

32. **Rethinking the Middle East**
    Efraim Karsh

33. **Ben-Gurion against the Knesset**
    Giora Goldberg

34. **Trapped Fools**
    Thirty Years of Israeli Policy in the Territories
    Schlomo Gazit

35. **Israel's Quest for Recognition and Acceptance in Asia**
    Garrison State Diplomacy
    Jacob Abadi

36. **H V Evatt and the Establishment of Israel**
    The Undercover Zionist
    Daniel Mandel

37. **Navigating Perilous Waters**
    An Israeli Strategy for Peace and Security
    Ephraim Sneh

38. **Lyndon B Johnson and the Politics of Arms Sales to Israel**
    In the Shadow of the Hawk
    Abraham Ben-Zvi

39. **Israel at the Polls 2003**
    Edited by Shmeul Sandler, M. Ben Mollov and Jonathan Rynhold

40. **Between Capital and Land**
    The Jewish National Fund's Finances and Land-Purchase Priorities in Palestine, 1939–45
    Eric Engel Tuten

41. **Israeli Democracy at Crossroads**
    Raphael Cohen-Almagor

42. **Israeli Institutions at Crossroads**
    Raphael Cohen-Almagor

43. **The Israeli–Palestine Peace Process Negotiations, 1999–2001**
    Within Reach
    Gilead Sher

44. **Ben-Gurion's Political Struggles, 1963–67**
    A Lion in Winter
    Zaki Shalom

45. **Ben-Gurion, Zionism and American Jewry**
    1948–63
    Ariel Feldestein

46 **The Origins of the American–Israeli Alliance**
The Jordanian Factor
Abraham Ben-Zvi

47 **The Harp and the Shield of David**
Ireland, Zionism and the State of Israel
Shulamit Eliash

48 **Israel's National Security**
Issues and Challenges since the Yom Kippur War
Efraim Inbar

49 **The Rise of Israel**
A History of a Revolutionary State
Jonathan Adelman

50 **Israel and the Family of Nations**
The Jewish Nation-State and Human Rights
Alexander Yakobson and Amnon Rubinstein

51 **Secularism and Religion in Jewish–Israeli Politics**
Traditionists and Modernity
Yaacov Yadgar

52 **Israel's National Security Law**
Political Dynamics and Historical Development
Amichai Cohen and Stuart A. Cohen

53 **Politics of Memory**
The Israeli Underground's Struggle for Inclusion in the National Pantheon and Military Commemoralization
Udi Lebel

54 **Social Mobilization in the Arab/Israeli War of 1948**
On the Israeli Home Front
Moshe Naor

55 **Britain's Moment in Palestine**
Retrospect and Perspectives, 1917–48
Michael J. Cohen

Israel: The First Hundred Years (Mini Series)
Edited by Efraim Karsh

1 Israel's Transition from Community to State, edited by Efraim Karsh
2 From War to Peace? edited by Efraim Karsh
3 Politics and Society since 1948, edited by Efraim Karsh
4 Israel in the International Arena, edited by Efraim Karsh
5 Israel in the Next Century, edited by Efraim Karsh

Works by the same author

Strategy and Politics in the Middle East, 1954–1960: Defending the Northern Tier (2005)
Fighting World War Three from the Middle East: Allied Contingency Plans, 1945–1954 (1997); Hebrew edition (1998)
Truman and Israel (1990)
Palestine to Israel: From Mandate to Independence (1988)
The Origins of the Arab-Zionist Conflict, 1914–1948 (1987); paperback edition (1989)
Churchill and the Jews (1985); revised paperback edition (2003)
Palestine and the Great Powers, 1945–1948 (1982); paperback edition (1986)
Palestine: Retreat from the Mandate, 1936–1945 (1978)

Books edited

The Demise of Empire: Britain's Responses to Nationalist Movements in the Middle East, 1943–1955, with Martin Kolinsky (1998)
Britain and the Middle East in the 1930s: Security Problems, 1935–1939, with Martin Kolinsky (1992)
Bar-Ilan Studies in Modern History, vol. III (1991)
The History of the Founding of Israel, Part III, The Struggle for the State of Israel, 1939–1948, 12 volumes (1988)
The Weizmann Letters, volumes XX, XXI, 1936–1945 (1979)

Britain's Moment in Palestine
Retrospect and Perspectives, 1917–48

Michael J. Cohen

LONDON AND NEW YORK

First published 2014
by Routledge
2 Park Square, Milton Park, Abingdon, Oxfordshire OX14 4RN

and by Routledge
711 Third Avenue, New York, NY 10017

Routledge is an imprint of the Taylor and Francis Group, an informa business

First issued in paperback 2015

© 2014 Michael J. Cohen

The right of Michael J. Cohen to be identified as author of this work has been asserted by him in accordance with sections 77 and 78 of the Copyright, Designs and Patents Act 1988.

All rights reserved. No part of this book may be reprinted or reproduced or utilised in any form or by any electronic, mechanical, or other means, now known or hereafter invented, including photocopying and recording, or in any information storage or retrieval system, without permission in writing from the publishers.

Trademark notice: Product or corporate names may be trademarks or registered trademarks, and are used only for identification and explanation without intent to infringe.

British Library Cataloguing in Publication Data
A catalogue record for this book is available from the British Library

Library of Congress Cataloging in Publication Data
Cohen, Michael Joseph, 1940-author.
Britain's moment in Palestine : retrospect and perspectives, 1917–48 / Michael J Cohen.
p. cm. – (Israeli history, politics and society)
Includes bibliographical references and index.
1. Palestine – History – 1917–48. 2. Palestine – Politics and government– 1917-1948. 3. Great Britain – Foreign relations – Palestine. 4. Palestine – Foreign relations – Great Britain. I. Title.
DS126.C5316 2014
956.94'04 – dc23
2013030118

ISBN 978-0-415-72985-7 (hbk)
ISBN 978-1-138-19388-8 (pbk)
ISBN 978-1-315-85075-7 (ebk)

Typeset in Times New Roman
by Taylor & Francis Books

For Maya, Alma, Daniela, Adam and Alex

If military leaders are often castigated for preparing to fight the last war, civilians can be castigated with equal justice for trying to avoid it ... the conceptualization is inherently faulty even if understandable. One can no more avoid a war one has already been in than one can refight a conflict that is over; but ... these obvious truths rarely prevent anyone from trying.

Gerhard L. Weinberg, *A World at Arms: A Global History of World War II*

Contents

List of plates xiii
Acknowledgements xiv
Abbreviations and glossary xv

Introduction — *on a first reading...* 1

1 Britain and Zionism: The domestic context 5

2 World War One: Britain assumes the Palestine mandate 38

3 Palestine and the Near East, 1919–23 61

4 The military administration, 1918–20 75

5 Colonial Palestine 94

6 Redefining policy in Palestine 116

7 1923: The Balfour Declaration challenged 146

8 Paying for Empire in the 1920s 164

9 The Yishuv economy in the 1920s 182

10 The unravelling of the mandate, 1929–31 212

11 The Arab rebellion, I: April–October 1936 245

12 The Arab rebellion, II: July 1937–April 1939 263

13 Appeasement in the Middle East, 1937–39 287

xii *Contents*

14	World War Two: The Jews	307
15	The Allies, the Zionists and the Holocaust	335
16	World War Two: The British and the Arabs	360
17	The Arabs and Nazi Germany	382
18	The Mufti of Jerusalem in Berlin, 1941–45	418
19	Why the British left	442
20	The British lose control in Palestine	461

Conclusion 484

Bibliography 493
Index 500

List of plates

Plates (between pages 244 and 245)

1. Dr Chaim Weizmann, Sir Herbert Samuel, David Lloyd George and Frances Stevenson (Lloyd George's secretary and mistress). Circa 1920
2. Winston Churchill (Colonial Secretary), in Tel Aviv, March 1921, with the mayor, Meir Dizingoff
3. General Sir Edmund Allenby, Arthur Balfour and the High Commissioner, Sir Herbert Samuel (1920–25), Jerusalem 1925
4. Field Marshal Sir Herbert Plumer, High Commissioner from 1925–1928. Date unknown
5. Sir John Chancellor, High Commissioner from 1928 to 1931. Jerusalem, June 1930
6. David Ben-Gurion, in the uniform of the Hebrew battalions, 1918
7. Pinhas Rutenberg, 1920. Awarded the concession for the electrification of Palestine
8. Moshe Novomeysky, 1902. Awarded the Dead Sea salts concession
9. Moshe Shertok (Political Secretary of the Jewish Agency, later Sharett) with High Commissioner Sir Arthur Wauchope, 1931–38, in 1935
10. Shertok, Weizmann and Ben-Gurion at the 20th Zionist Congress, Zurich, 1937
11. Haj Amin el-Husayni, the Grand Mufti of Jerusalem, with senior Nazi officials, Berlin, 1944
12. The Mufti receiving guests in Cairo, 1946
13. Ragheb Bey al-Nashashibi, head of Arab opposition to the Grand Mufti
14. Sir Harold MacMichael, High Commissioner, 1938–44. Date unknown
15. Field Marshal Sir Bernard Montgomery ("Monty"), the CIGS, on a visit to Palestine, November 1946
16. Weizmann and Sir Alan Cunningham, the last High Commissioner, 1945–48

Acknowledgements

Earlier versions of Chapters 7 and 8 were first published in *The Journal of Israel History*, volumes 29/1, March 2010, and 30/2, September 2011, respectively. Citations from the works of Gerhard Weinberg on p. x and at the head of Chapters 14 and 15 appear by kind permission of Cambridge University Press.

I wish to thank Richard Breitman, Stuart Cohen, Tuvia Friling, Rami Ginat, Martin Kolinsky, Peter Stansky and David Stevenson for their helpful advice and comments. My special thanks are offered to Martin Cüppers of the University of Stuttgart, who shared with me documents from the German archives, and to Ami Ayalon, Meir Litvak and Esther Webman, who shared with me material on the Arabic press, and Zionist intelligence files during World War Two. And finally, my sincere thanks are due to Sarah Douglas (Production Editor) and to Holly Regan-Jones, my copy-editor, whose patience, diligence and sharp eyes saved me from many errors.

Needless to say, I alone am responsible for what follows.

I wish also to thank the archivists of the National Archives in London, Sue Donelly and Heather Dawson of the Digital Library of the London School of Economics and Political Science, Lucy McCann and Sarah Rhodes of the Bodleian Library of Commonwealth and African Studies at Rhodes House, Oxford, and Batia Leshem and Anat Benin of the Central Zionist Archives, Jerusalem.

The photographs published here appear by kind permission of the Central Zionist Archives, Jerusalem.

Arabic transliteraton: I have preferred the spellings Moslem and Husayni throughout and I have not used diacritical marks. I have not altered alternative spellings in quotations or book titles.

Abbreviations and glossary

Abwehr	German military intelligence and espionage
Aliya (Heb.)	Wave of Jewish immigration
ANZAC	Australian and New Zealand Army Corps
AZEC	American Zionist Emergency Committee
BAB	German Federal Archive, Berlin
CCS	Combined Chiefs of Staff, American
CID	Committee of Imperial Defence, British
CID	Criminal Investigation Department, British
CIA	Central Intelligence Agency, American
C in C	Commander in Chief
CIGS	Chief of the Imperial General Staff, British
COS	Chiefs of Staff, British
CZA	Central Zionist Archives, Jerusalem
DAL	Deutsche-Arabische Lehrabteilung (German-Arab Training Unit)
DGFP	Documents on German Foreign Policy
DPs	Displaced persons (unrepatriable refugees after World War Two)
Effendi	Arab notables, landowners
Fellahin	Arab peasants
GC & CS	Government Code & Cypher School, Bletchley Park
GOC	General Officer Commanding
HAC	Higher Arab Committee, Palestine
Hagana	Jewish defence organization, Palestine
Histadrut	Zionist labour union in Palestine
H.C. Deb.	House of Commons Debates (Hansard)
H.L. Deb.	House of Lords Debates (Hansard)
HST	Harry S. Truman Archive, Independence, Missouri
HUMINT	Human Intelligence
IWMA	Imperial War Museum Archives, London
JCS	Joint Chiefs of Staff, American
JRM	Jewish Resistance Movement, Palestine
IWMA	Imperial War Museum Archives, London

xvi *Abbreviations and glossary*

IZL	Irgun Zwai Leumi, Palestine ("National Army Organization" – Zionist dissident terrorist group)
LEHI	Lohamei Herut Yisrael (Stern Gang), Palestine ("Israel Freedom Fighters" – Zionist dissident terrorist group)
MELF	Middle East Land Forces, British
NA	National Archives, London
NAUS	National Archives, United States
OETA	Occupied Enemy Territory Administration (Ottoman Syria)
OSS	Office of Strategic Services, US Intelligence
PAAA	Political Archive of the German Foreign Office
Palmach	Jewish "shock troops" (commandos), Palestine
PGE	Polish Government-in-Exile, London
Poalei Zion	"Workers of Zion", major Zionist workers' party, Palestine
RAF	Royal Air Force
RM	Reichsmark
RSHA	Reich Main Security Office
SD	Sicherheitdienst – SS intelligence
SIGINT	Signals intelligence
SIS	Secret Intelligence Service, British
SMC	Supreme Moslem Council, Jerusalem
SS	Schutzstaffel (Nazi protection squadron or defence corps)
UNSCOP	United Nations Committee on Palestine
USAAF	United States Army Air Force
WA	Weizmann Archives, Rehovot
Wehrmacht	The German Armed Forces
Yishuv	The Jewish community in mandatory Palestine

Introduction

This study is a retrospective summary of the British experience in Palestine. I deal here mainly with those in the Arab, British and Zionist camps, whose decisions and actions determined Palestine's future.

In recent years, some valuable, micro social history monographs have appeared on Arab-Zionist relations in Palestine, in the workplace, and between Arab and Zionist left-wing group political groups.[1] Some social historians have criticized political histories for devoting "greatly disproportionate attention to elites and to diplomatic, political and military history, to the disadvantage of other social groups and of the social, economic, and cultural dimension … ". Important as these studies are, do they really change the political or military history of Palestine? The author of a recent monograph on relations between Arab and Jewish workers in the Palestine Railway Union has pointed out that virtually all of the Arab workers concerned were nationalists, who "strongly opposed what they regarded as Zionist encroachment on their homeland and favored an independent Arab Palestine". He concluded that Arab-Zionist co-operation at the local level could not have prevented conflict and war:

> It seems clear to me that the Zionist and Palestinian nationalist objectives were on a collision course from the very start … relations among them were profoundly affected by the dynamics of the broader Zionist-Palestinian conflict.[2]

I have attempted here to answer the following questions.

1 Why did the British government issue the Balfour Declaration in 1917, notwithstanding widespread anti-Semitism in England, and the opposition of the Anglo-Jewish establishment, even inside the Cabinet?
2 How and why did the British conquer Palestine during World War One?
3 What were the dynamics of British relations with the Arabs and the Zionists in Palestine?
4 Why did Britain cease to support the Jewish National Home during the 1930s?

5 How did World War Two affect the so-called "Palestine Triangle"[3] – Arabs, British and Jews?
6 What was the link between the Holocaust and the establishment of the state of Israel?
7 Why did the British scuttle from Palestine in 1948?

On the face of it, it is a matter for some wonder that the Zionists secured the Balfour Declaration in 1917, given the prevalence of native anti-Semitism and the hostility of the Anglo-Jewish establishment. The answer to the apparent paradox is that Britain issued the Declaration in order to serve her own interests: military and strategic in 1917, imperial after the war.

I have gone to some lengths in the first chapter to expose the genie of anti-Semitism. While it never enjoyed the state's official sanction in England, as in Nazi Germany, nevertheless, it permeated all classes of British society, workers, aristocrats, the press, Parliament, and the works of many of England's most respected literary lights. Many of Britain's leaders had prejudiced views of the Jews. Some, like Anthony Eden, were discreet; others, Churchill for instance, were less cautious, guilty of the occasional "slip". Others still, like the caustic, "undiplomatic" Ernie Bevin, who earned himself a reputation as an anti-Semite, were frankly blunt, guilty of blurting out in public what their fellow ministers kept to the inner confines of Whitehall.

I have tried to place British rule in Palestine in its wider context, as a minor, yet significant part of the British Empire. Those who determined British policy in Palestine never worked in a vacuum. The Balfour Declaration was an emergency, wartime expedient. Control of Palestine gave Britain strategic depth to the north of the Suez Canal. Thanks to the import of Zionist capital, not only was Britain able to maintain Palestine "on the cheap", without burdening the British taxpayer, but Jewish capital also subsidized some of Britain's imperial projects in the region.

During the 1920s, Palestinian Arab protests against the Zionist influx were bought off by the perquisites and patronage of office that the British showered on the clan-based leadership. But matters came to a head in 1929, with the so-called Wailing Wall riots in Jerusalem. The series of commissions and inquiries that followed persuaded the Labour government that the dual commitment to promote Zionism while preserving the rights of the native Arab population was unworkable. Jewish immigration and land purchases from the Arabs would have to be severely curtailed or halted. In October 1930, the government published a new White Paper that would have effectively halted Zionist development in Palestine. But a one-time confluence of political and economic factors (the Zionist lobby and the world-wide depression) caused the minority government to bypass its own declared policy. In a highly irregular move, the Prime Minister "re-interpreted" government policy, in a personal letter addressed to Dr Chaim Weizmann, the head of the International Zionist Movement.

But British priorities changed radically during the 1930s, when the Axis powers threatened the balance of power in Europe, and Britain's hegemony in the Middle East.

Britain's commitment to Zionism was superseded by the changing international context. With the clouds of World War Two gathering, her paramount interest became to guarantee continued access to her strategic assets in the Arab Middle East – her army and air bases and oil concessions. Policy makers determined that Britain's first priority must be to retain the friendship of the Arab states.

No British statesman ever adopted the Zionist credo that Palestine should or could absorb any significant proportion of those Jews living in the Diaspora. The diaries, letters and internal memoranda of Whitehall officials and of ordinary civilians who lived in Palestine convey something of the atmosphere and feelings of those who lived through the Palestine "experience". By 1937, there had developed an all-party consensus in Parliament that Jewish immigration into Palestine had been excessive and must be curbed, in order to assuage the justified fears of the Palestinian Arabs that their majority in the country was threatened. The Palestine White Paper of 1939, whose real purpose was to appease the Arab states, asserted that the government had already fulfilled its obligations to the Jews under the Balfour pledge.

During the first years of World War Two, from 1940 to 1942, Britain's very survival as a sovereign state hung in the balance. British policy towards the Arabs and the Zionists fluctuated wildly, with every ebb and flow of her fortunes on the battlefields of Europe and the Middle East. Appeasement in the Middle East, like that in Europe, proved rapidly to be a broken reed. As early as 1940, the Foreign Office, the principal architect of the Palestine White Paper of 1939, was forced to concede that the Arabs' allegiance could be guaranteed only by British victories on the field of battle. Rashid Ali in Iraq and Haj Amin el-Husayni, leader of the Palestinian Arabs, chose the Nazi Germany option. Egyptian support for the Axis might have developed into a full-scale revolt had the British not held a large garrison in that country and imposed their will with their battle tanks.

The experience of the Allies, the Arabs and the Jews during World War Two had a decisive impact on the denouement of the Palestine mandate. British policy towards the Jews and to Palestine didn't change in the wake of the flood of news about Nazi atrocities that reached London, and Washington, from the very earliest stages of the war. The first two provisions of the 1939 policy – the restrictions on Jewish immigration and on land sales to Jews – were adhered to strictly throughout the war. The third provision, the appointment of Palestinian ministers, was never implemented, since it would have impinged upon Britain's absolute control of Palestine.

In retrospect, it is clear that by the end of World War Two, the Arab-Zionist conflict in Palestine had become intractable. It is impossible to gauge the traumatic impact of the Holocaust on the Jewish people. The Mufti's wartime collaboration with Nazi Germany and the Allies' continuing appeasement of

4 *Introduction*

the Arabs after the war determined the Zionists to fight for a Jewish state, even before reaching a majority in Palestine.

After World War Two, the Labour government changed national priorities. Its decision to set up the Welfare State led to the evacuation of key imperial outposts, including India. With the threat of World War Three looming, this time against the Soviet bloc, the strategic role of the Suez Canal (and of Palestine) was transformed. The role of the British base in Egypt became to serve as a platform for a strategic air strike against Soviet targets, in the event of war.

After World War Two, a virtual American veto prevented the British from implementing their intention of imposing a settlement in Palestine that would be acceptable to the Arab states. During the course of one week in February 1947, the Labour government decided not only to evacuate India and to pull its troops out of Greece, but also to refer the Palestine mandate to the United Nations, without recommendations. As with India, the Attlee government decided to leave the antagonists in Palestine to resolve their conflict on the field of battle.

Notes

1 For instance, Bernstein (2000), Hillel Cohen (2008), LeVine and Shafir (2012), Lockman (1996), Shelef (2010).
2 Zachary Lockman, *Comrades and Enemies: Arab and Jewish Workers in Palestine, 1906–1948,* Berkeley: University of California Press, 1996, pp. 3, 360–61, 366.
3 Nicholas Bethell, *The Palestine Triangle: The Struggle for the Holy Land, 1935–1948,* New York: Putnam, 1979.

1 Britain and Zionism
The domestic context

Anti-Semitism in British society

> Then there is what I call quite frankly the anti-Semitic party ... those who are convinced that the Jews are at the bottom of all the trouble all over the world. Whether they are attacking an anti-Zionist ... or Zionists, or rich Jews, or poor Jews – it is the rich Jews who are all blood-suckers and the poor Jews all Bolshevists – they have that particular Hebrew mania, and they have fastened on Palestine with a view to paying off these mediaeval scores.
>
> William Ormsby-Gore (Under-Secretary of State for the Colonies), House of Commons debate, 4 July 1922

There is an apparent irony in the fact that the nation that issued the Balfour Declaration in 1917, committing Britain to help the Jews establish a National Home in Palestine, was itself deeply riddled with anti-Semitism. But the irony is only apparent, since Britain issued the Declaration entirely in pursuit of her own material interests at the time, not because of any philo-Semitism, nor any messianic belief in returning the people of the Bible to the land of the Bible.

Anti-Jewish prejudice had deep socio-economic roots in Britain, although unlike Germany, the British Parliament never passed anti-Jewish legislation as such (the Aliens Act of 1905 was prejudicial to foreign Jewish refugees; see below). Antipathy to the Jews in England was less virulent than on the continent, due to Britain's "radically different political and social setting". When Cromwell readmitted the Jews into England in 1656, they were awarded citizenship and entitlement to most of the legal rights enjoyed by native-born Englishmen.[1]

But even if the Jewish Question occupied a less prominent place in English public life than it did in continental Europe, anti-Semitism remained "a well-entrenched feature" of England's cultural and social life. It found expression in myths, public slurs and stereotypes about "Jewish difference and malevolence". Hostile and suspicious references to Jews occurred at all levels of society:

> Caricaturists, novelists and dramatists employed unflattering stereotypes of Jews in their work; preachers, politicians and journalists disparaged

Jews as sharpers, cheats, aliens and outsiders, and even as the traditional blaspheming enemies of Christendom.[2]

The case of Benjamin Disraeli is instructive. Often paraded as an example of the equal opportunities enjoyed by English Jews, his childhood baptism paved the way to his eventual entry to Number 10 Downing Street. But as an aspiring politician he was hounded continually by anti-Semites at election rallies. In 1837, he "was interrupted repeatedly by cries of 'Shylock!' ... and offers of ham and bacon, while his opponent mocked his foreign-sounding name". At another rally in 1841, members of the crowd taunted him with cries: "Bring a bit of pork for the Jew". Even after he became a national figure, *Punch* and other magazines continued to hound him about his Jewish origins, and "regularly depicted him as a Jewish old clothes man".[3]

Between 1850 and 1939, Britain's Jewish community increased tenfold. During the last decades of the nineteenth century anti-Semitic sentiment in England was exacerbated by the flood of Jewish refugees from Tsarist Russia. Jewish ghettoes, notably in London's East End, were singled out for their dirt and squalor. They increased social tensions by exerting pressures on inadequate resources. Native British labour, feeling the pinch of Britain's industrial decline, feared that the flood of Jewish immigrants was helping to sustain the "grossly exploitative sectors of the economy, in particular, the 'sweat industries', thereby weakening the [British] workers' bargaining power".[4]

A recent study of the imagery in Edwardian postcards, popular among the masses, indicates the wide dissemination of the anti-Semitic image of the Jewish immigrant in England. They usually portrayed a negative and hostile caricature of the Jew. They ridiculed their hooked noses and their Eastern European, Ashkenazi accent; they stereotyped the Jews as devious financiers, avaricious profiteers, and as pawnbrokers who charged usurious interest rates and received stolen property.[5]

In 1905, the Balfour government passed an Aliens Law that was clearly designed to assuage widespread anti-Semitic sentiment. Although the law did not contain the word "Jew", it was clearly aimed at curbing the entry of East European Jewish refugees into England. In his speech in the House of Commons defending the new measure, Balfour spoke of "the undoubted evils which had fallen upon portions of this country from an alien immigration which was largely Jewish". He declared that the Jews' natural genius had become warped by their abnormal Diaspora existence, and asserted that their refusal to assimilate deprived their hosts of the genetic benefits of intermarriage, thereby arousing anti-Semitism.[6]

Balfour went on to refer to the Jews' isolationist tendencies, and warned against the dangers of the immigration of "an immense body of persons who ... by their own actions remained a people apart", intermarrying only among themselves. While conceding that the position in England itself had not yet reached a dangerous state of affairs, he proceeded to let the anti-Semitic genie out of the bottle:

> ... some of the undoubted evils which had fallen upon portions of the country from an alien immigration which was largely Jewish, gave those of them who ... condemned nothing more than the manifestation of the anti-Semitic spirit, some reason to fear that this country might be, at however great a distance, in danger of following the evil example set by some other countries.[7]

One measure of the effects of anti-Semitism in England was the numbers of those Jews who chose to shed their Jewish identity and to assimilate. What has been called a "flight from Jewishness" was a discernible phenomenon in the Jewish communities of Western Europe. It was particularly noticeable among the Sephardi community:

> Between 1750–1830, the Sephardi community increased by no more than 200, despite the arrival of 3,000 *conversos* from the Iberian peninsula during the eighteenth century.[8]

Scores of prominent Jewish families in England assimilated between the middle of the nineteenth century and World War One. During the war, many establishment Jews became profoundly disturbed when the government began to promote Zionism as a British interest. Sir Edwin Montagu, only the second Jew to sit in the Cabinet, as Secretary of State for India, from July 1917, circulated a memorandum to his colleagues opposing the government's intention to issue the Balfour Declaration. It was entitled: "The Anti-Semitism of the present government" (see p. 50).

It has been suggested that there was some kind of continuity between liberalism and anti-Semitism.[9] Tony Kushner has suggested that:

> Within the liberal critique of Jewishness was the belief that anti-Semitism would only end when society started to tolerate Jews and the Jews in turn gave up their distinctiveness ... the corollary of the liberal critique was that the survival of anti-Semitism in a tolerant society such as Britain was due to the Jews themselves. The premise that, by refusing to integrate fully into society, the Jews were responsible for the hostility towards themselves is an example of the theory of "well-earned" anti-Semitism. Jews were attacked for refusing to integrate, for being clannish and for ultimately creating anti-Semitism.[10]

Theories about international Jewish conspiracies were rife. They appeared in England long before *The Protocols of the Elders of Zion* was published by *The Times* in May 1920.[11] One of the first to write about them was Arnold White, who published *The Modern Jew* in 1899. White accredited the Jews with a veritably incredible record. He portrayed them as a race that had "baffled the pharaohs, foiled Nebuchadnezzar, thwarted Rome, defeated feudalism, circumvented the Romanoffs, baulked the Kaiser and undermined the Third French Republic ... ". He concluded:

> ... while the engine of international finance is under Jewish control, and while public opinion is mediated by Jewish influence over the European press, the Jews will continue to be in the future, as they have been in the past, the most interesting people in the world.[12]

Authority and ideological foundation for anti-Semitism were lent by J. A. Hobson, a prolific, influential writer, journalist, historian and economist, who is perhaps remembered best for his classic, Marxist exposé of imperialism.[13] Hobson published his views extensively in the provincial press, replete with racist stereotypes. He described the Jews as: "the personification of *laissez faire* capitalism", the "cultural twins of an aggressive capitalist society ... ". On the one hand, he accused the Russian Jewish immigrant labourers of "underselling" the English working man. On the other, he accused the affluent, well-established section of the Jewish community of exploiting the situation by buying up properties in order to evict the current tenants and replace them with members of their own race, in order to exploit them at cut-rate wages.[14]

Hobson claimed that the control of international finance was passing more and more into Jewish hands and that the Jews were propagating their values via their increasing control of the London press. He observed that the major continental journals had for some time been under the control of "this active financial race" who found "newspapers convenient organs for directing foreign policy along lines favourable to the bond holding faction of the commercial community".[15]

Hobson also blamed the Jews for instigating the South African (Boer) War. In 1900, in a series of press reports, and later in a book, he claimed that the war was being fought to ensure the continued control of the Transvaal by a small group of Jewish financiers, mainly of German extraction, who had managed to concentrate in their hands that country's resources. He asserted:

> The Jews are *par excellence* the international financiers ... Primarily they are financial speculators, taking their gains not out of the genuine fruits of industry, even the industry of others, but out of the construction, promotion and financial manipulation of companies ... [16]

In 1912, theories about Jewish influence and profiteering were given apparent validation, with the publicity surrounding the so-called Marconi scandal. Although prominent non-Jewish political figures were also involved, in what was indeed a case of profiteering by insider trading in Marconi shares, the affair provoked a virulent press campaign, accompanied by increasingly anti-Semitic overtones.[17]

The bare facts of the case are as follows. In 1911, the Asquith Cabinet approved a plan for the construction of a chain of state-owned wireless stations throughout the Empire. In March 1912, Sir Herbert Samuel, the Postmaster General, awarded the contract to the Marconi Wireless Telegraph Company.[18] With the benefit of inside information, Sir Rufus Isaacs, the Attorney General, Samuel and Lloyd George (Chancellor of the Exchequer at the time), as well as the Liberal Party's chief whip, all bought shares in Marconi's American subsidiary. By the time the government's decision was made public in April 1912, the company's shares had risen to £9 – an appreciation of over 300 per cent.[19]

Two prominent literary figures of the time – Hilaire Belloc and G.K. Chesterton – initiated a public campaign against the Marconi contract. The two writers became prominent Catholic anti-Semites. Their close association earned them the sobriquet *Chesterbelloc*. The campaign was spearheaded by *The Eye-Witness*, a distributed political weekly, founded by Belloc in 1911 and edited from 1912 by Cecil Chesterton, the younger brother of G.K. Chesterton. The paper personally vilified Samuel and Sir Rufus Isaacs, making various allegations of corruption. It claimed that Isaacs had made £160,000 out of the deal, and that Lloyd George and Herbert Samuel had also profited from insider trading.[20]

On 8 August 1912, the day after the first Commons debate on the Marconi contract, the paper alleged that the contract was "a swindle, or rather theft". A further article claimed that Samuel owed his Cabinet position to bribes paid to politicians by his uncle, Lord Swaythling (Samuel Montagu, a City financier, the father of Edwin); subsequent, weekly items, several entitled "Songs of Samuel", included barbs about "the chosen – shall we say people" and "alien money-lenders".[21]

In October 1912, following widespread rumours and the *The Eye-Witness*'s allegations, the government felt obliged to appoint a Select Committee to investigate the affair. The Committee concluded that insider trading had been involved, but that neither Isaacs nor Lloyd George had committed any "dishonourable act". In the two-day Commons debate on the report, in June 1913, both Isaacs and Lloyd George denied corruption, but admitted to mistaken, bad judgement. The Liberals' majority government acquitted the two men of all charges of corruption or acting in bad faith. Samuel himself emerged from the affair with his reputation untarnished, even though he had also bought shares. This was not taken well by Lloyd George, who apparently resented the fact that he had emerged from the scandal with "shining purity". In 1914, in a private letter to a friend, he added a quite gratuitous aside, chastising Samuel as "a greedy, ambitious and grasping Jew with all the worst characteristics of his race".[22]

The affair furnished ample material for an anti-Semitic press campaign against the Jews. Such views, propagated widely by respected public figures before World War One, helped prepare the ground for the publication in *The Times* after the war of *The Protocols of the Elders of Zion*, a forged pamphlet imported into England from Russia, alleging the existence of an international Jewish conspiracy to control the world. During the war, some anti-Semitic agitators in the British right-wing press, such as Leo Maxe, editor of the *National Review* since 1893, obsessed with conspiracy theories against Britain, linked the German threat mainly with the influence of her Jews.[23]

Another example of entrenched preconceptions about the Jews among the British elite was furnished by Sir Mark Sykes, the senior official who negotiated and lent his name to the last Anglo-French colonial share-out in the Middle East: the Sykes-Picot Agreement. In June 1918, prior to the Emir Faysal's meeting at Aqaba with Dr Chaim Weizmann, the Zionist leader, Sykes briefed him on the power and influence of international Jewry. Sykes wrote that he knew that "the Arabs despise, condemn, and hate the Jews", but warned that it would be best to learn from those who had persecuted them – "the Spanish and Tsarist Russian empires" who no longer existed. Sykes advised him:

> Believe me, I speak the truth when I say that this race, **despised and weak, is universal, is all-powerful and cannot be put down** ... Jews could be found in the councils of every state, in every business, in every enterprise.[24]

Sykes promised Faysal that the Jews were not plotting to expel the Arabs from Palestine and suggested that he treat them as Prime Minister Lloyd George did, "as a powerful ally".[25]

Press incitement lead at times to outbreaks of physical violence against the Jews. During World War One, resentment at the failure of the large Russian-Jewish immigrant community to volunteer for the British war effort became an explosive issue. The Jews were accused of being "shirkers, stealing the jobs of brave British soldiers and growing rich to boot". In June 1917, a crowd of several thousands looted shops and wrecked houses in the Jewish quarter in Leeds. In September, between 2000 and 3000 Jews and Gentiles, armed with "wood logs, iron bars, and flat irons", fought a pitched battle on Bethnal Green, London.[26]

The use of the derogative nickname "Yid" for the Jews was common vogue in British intellectual circles. In early 1920, Lawrence wrote to the author Rudyard Kipling to ask him if he would read the proofs of his book *Seven Pillars of Wisdom*. Kipling replied that he would be glad to, but warned that if the proofs showed that Lawrence was "pro-Yid," he would send them back to him unread.[27]

In 1922, Hilaire Belloc published an anti-Semitic book entitled *The Jews* – which he dubbed "my admirable *Yid* book". He went over old, well-turned ground, blaming "Jewish finance" for "the drawing of Egypt into the European system, and particularly into the system of Great Britain ... [and for] the great ordeal of the South African War", which "openly and unquestionably" had been "provoked and promoted by Jewish interests in South Africa".[28]

In 1919, in his Introduction to Nahum Sokolow's *History of Zionism*, Balfour, the statesman-philosopher, wrote that Zionism would benefit Western society, by ridding it of its troublesome Jewish minorities. He postulated that the movement constituted a:

> ... serious endeavour to mitigate the age-long miseries created for Western civilization by the presence in its midst of a Body which it too long regarded as alien, even hostile, but which it was equally unable to expel or absorb.[29]

Just as enlightening is the private letter written in 1917 by Leo Amery to Sir Edward Carson, a Minister without Portfolio in the imperial war Cabinet. Amery was a genuine friend of the Zionist cause, even if the extract cited here illustrates how deeply entrenched in British society were the convictions about Jewish influence and "international conspiracies". During the summer and autumn of 1917, Amery performed a significant behind-the-scenes role in composing the final draft of the Balfour Declaration. His purpose was to persuade Carson to support a British declaration favouring a Jewish National Home in Palestine:

> Once there is a national home for the Jewish persecuted majority, the English Jews will no longer have anything to trouble about. On the other hand, an anti-Semitism which is based partly on the fear of being swamped by hordes of undesirable aliens from Russia, etc. and partly by an instinctive suspicion against a community which has so many international ramifications, will be much diminished when the hordes in question have got another outlet, and when the motive for internationalism among the Jews is diminished.[30]

Anti-Semitism occupied a significant niche in English literary discourse. Professor Endelman, the social historian of Anglo-Jewry, has noted that during the 1920s and the 1930s "both popular and serious writers – T.S. Eliot, Graham Greene, Wyndham Lewis, H.G. Wells, John Buchan, Rudyard Kipling, Dorothy Sayers, Agatha Christie, Dornford Yates – populated their books with mythic, offensive Jews". In 1935, one observer remarked that it was "unusual to find a reference to a Jewish character in English fiction which is not in the Shylock tradition". Journalists, travel writers and social commentators described Jews as "clannish, over-sexed, materialistic, averse to physical labour, alien and corrupt". Frequent reference was made to their "predatory noses".[31]

George Orwell, a radical left-wing journalist and aspiring young author, is a case in point. In 1933, he published his first book, *Down and Out in Paris and London*, at the age of 30. It featured the crudest of anti-Semitic stereotypes. Written in the first person, Orwell describes a horribly deformed "small, dark, hook-nosed man ... [who] from his appearance one could have taken him for a Jew, but he used to deny this vigorously". In another passage, Orwell fantasizes about the pleasure it would have given to him to "flatten" the nose of a "red-haired Jew", a pawnbroker, and an "extraordinarily disagreeable man". Later on, the narrator meets Boris, a Russian veteran of the Tsar's army, who tells him "what the Jews are like".

> A horrible old Jew, with a red beard like Judas Iscariot, came sneaking into our billet. "Your honour," he said, "I have brought a girl for you, a beautiful young girl only seventeen. It will only be fifty francs." "Thank you," I said, "you can take her away again. I don't want to catch any diseases." "Diseases!" cried the Jew, "*mais, monsieur le capitaine*, there's no fear of that. It's my own daughter!" That is the Jewish national character for you.[32]

Orwell's first book did not enjoy mass sales until the Penguin edition of 1940, but its anti-Semitic stereotypes were not uncommon in the British literary discourse of the 1920s and 1930s. Some of Orwell's friends were surprised that he had so many Jewish friends. Malcolm Muggeridge, a regular lunch companion, was surprised by the number of Jews who attended Orwell's funeral service, in 1950:

> Interesting, I thought, that George should have attracted Jews because he was at heart strongly anti-Semitic.[33]

T.R. Fyvel, a left-wing Jewish intellectual, a close friend and colleague of Orwell's at *Tribune*, a left-wing Labour journal, was also surprised by the number of Jews who attended the funeral. Fyvel published a warm "personal memoir" of Orwell in 1982. He recalled that Orwell had once told him that one had to distinguish between what was said about the Jews before Hitler came to power and what was said after:

> In the twenties, anti-Jewish references were not out of order. They were only on a par with the automatic sneers people cast at Anglo-Indian colonels in boarding houses.[34]

Fyvel recalled Orwell telling him that anti-Semitism had been a part of the culture in which he had grown up: "Just occasionally, the ideas of his early upbringing, in which he said that Jews featured only as objects of scorn, did come out". Fyvel refused to believe that his friend Orwell could ever have been openly anti-Semitic, but added "His ideological views concerning the assimilation into British culture of a strong Jewish ethnic minority were a different matter".[35] In 1945, Orwell would publish an shrewd essay on anti-Semitism in Britain.

Discrimination against the Jews during the interwar period was not organized, yet few Jews managed to avoid it completely. In 1932, Oswald Mosley made the only attempt to introduce the "Jewish Question" into British political life, when he established his British Union of Fascists (BUF). His party failed ever to win a seat in Parliament or on a local council and its membership never rose above 16,000. However, the violent street clashes incited by Mosley's black-shirt mobs did raise the spectre of the import into England of Nazi street brutality.[36]

In his analysis of Britain in the 1930s, Professor Endelman writes:

> Although few obstacles blocked Jewish integration into the non-commercial middle class, English culture in the broadest sense was hostile to expressions of cultural diversity. Jews and Judaism continued to be represented in negative terms in literature, drama, sermons, political debate, and other public forums ... Convinced moreover of their own superiority to other peoples and nations ... English men and women up and down the social ladder were unwilling to endorse the perpetuation of a separate Jewish culture.[37]

During the latter half of the 1930s, with Europe falling under the ominous shadow of Nazi tyranny and anti-Semitism, Balfour's turn-of-the-century argument about the Jews' resistance to assimilation reared its head again. They were blamed for the rise of anti-Semitism. In his autobiography, published in 1936, G.K. Chesterton suggested a simple explanation:

> It is often the very loyalty of the Jewish family which appears as disloyalty to the Christian state ... [38]

Winston Churchill would later earn a reputation for championing Jewish and Zionist causes. In the late 1930s, he displayed a spontaneous empathy and humanitarian concern for the Jews' suffering under the Nazis. On occasion, he was vociferous in defending their cause. Yet his impulsive reactions were rarely followed up by any substantive efforts to help. At the same time, on more than one occasion, he gave vent to anti-Semitic stereotypes – both in public speeches and in the press. The social milieu of his early childhood and his experience in the English public school system had familiarised him with anti-Semitism. He attended three different independent private schools, the third of which, from the age of 13, was Harrow. In 1945, in an essay published in *The Contemporary Jewish Record*, Orwell commented on the lot of those few Jews who entered the public school system:

> A Jewish boy at a public school almost invariably had a bad time. He could, of course, live down his Jewishness if he was exceptionally charming or athletic, but it was an initial disability comparable to a stammer or a birthmark. Wealthy Jews tended to disguise themselves under aristocratic English or Scottish names ... [39]

Jawaharlal Nehru, the Indian leader, who entered Harrow in 1905, seven years after Churchill, testified later:

> Although the Jews there "got on fairly well ... there was always a background of anti-Semitic feeling". They were "the damned Jews".[40]

In 1937, both Churchill and Lloyd George were commissioned by popular magazines to write articles on the Jewish problem. In April 1937, Lloyd George published an article in London's *Strand* magazine, entitled "What has the Jew Done?". He condemned anti-Semitism, but at the same time he charged that Jewish "separateness", self-imposed to some extent, was partly to blame.[41]

Churchill was commissioned by the American magazine *Liberty* to write an article in the same vein. The draft of his article, entitled "How the Jews Can Combat Persecution", was never published. But his repeated, albeit futile efforts to sell it indicate that he was not free of the racial prejudice embedded in English society.[42]

Churchill's article was ghost-written for him by one Adam Marshall Diston, a man with close affinities to Mosley's British Union of Fascists (BUF). Diston's text repeated the thesis that the Jews' own tendency to remain aloof from Gentile society lay at the heart of the problem (of anti-Semitism). The point was underlined by a resort to a crude stereotype:

> The Jew in England is a representative of his race. Every Jewish moneylender recalls **Shylock and the idea of the Jews as usurers**. And you cannot reasonably expect a struggling clerk or shopkeeper, paying forty or fifty per cent interest on borrowed money to a "**Hebrew bloodsucker**" to reflect that, throughout long centuries, almost every other way of life was closed to the Jewish people; or that there are native English moneylenders who insist, just as implacably, upon their "**pound of flesh**".[43]

The revelation of the article's existence in 2007 by Dr Richard Toye, a young Cambridge historian, provoked a public furor in England. Both Sir Martin Gilbert, Churchill's biographer, and the Churchill Archives rushed in to dissociate Churchill from the article. But Gilbert himself, in his official biography, had in fact written that not only had Churchill paid Diston his commission in full, but he had also sent his draft off for typing, without making any changes to the text. Needless to say, had Churchill succeeded in publishing the article, it would have appeared over his name.[44]

It is impossible to ignore the contemporary context in which the two articles were written – two years after the enactment of the Nuremberg Laws in Germany, and the looming threat over other European Jewish communities. Churchill was neither young nor inexperienced (he would be 63 years old at the end of November 1937). Nor was he a rookie journalist. As one who earned his living by journalism, he was experienced enough to know that the printed word has a habit of becoming "misconstrued" or taken "out of context". He had already been castigated more than once for his maverick, at times racist views. In claiming at this juncture that the Jews themselves were partly responsible for their own persecution, Churchill and Lloyd George were affording Hitler some measure of legitimization for his tyrannical policies towards the Jews. The fact that Lloyd George's article, published in the same year, aroused little or no fuss suggests that England of the late 1930s presented a fertile seedbed for racial incitement.

In March 1940, Churchill received an offer to publish the article, this time from the *Sunday Dispatch*. But by then, Britain was at war with Nazi Germany, Churchill held the responsibilities of office (the Admiralty) and he was just a few weeks short of inheriting the premiership. Wisely, he turned down the offer.

During the mid-1930s, the rise of Nazism, violence in Palestine and Mosley's fascist campaigns in Britain all generated unprecedented attention on the Jews. The Zionists argued that the ravages of Nazism required the establishment of a Jewish state in Palestine. Their claim was almost universally refuted by the Gentile world – on the grounds that this would be unfair to the Palestinian Arabs. In 1939, the anti-Zionist polemicist J.M.N. Jeffries published a lengthy work recommending that the Jews find themselves an "empty" territory:

> The Zionist idea of a return to the land and of establishing a polity wherein they will carry out all national work, from railway building to road sweeping, and so remove the reproach of parasitism which dogs them – that in itself is an idea which must arouse sympathy.
>
> But all that was good in it was lost when it was put into execution by the political Zionists. Like everyone else returning to the land they should have chosen a vacant plot, or chosen one which its sparse inhabitants were willing that they should occupy. Instead of this, they insisted on returning as owners to the Arabs' territory, upon the falsified plea which we know. They refused the offer in East Africa, which was the right kind of opportunity. And in the Arabs' territory the largest crop which has sprung from their spades is Tel Aviv.[45]

In effect, Jeffries negated the very concept of Jewish sovereignty. He derided the Zionists' contention that a Jewish state would stem anti-Semitism, as indicating "an entire absence of understanding of the Gentile public for the Jews". Not only that, but he repeated the broad consensus that there were "millions too many of them" to find a place in Palestine, even if they all wished to.

> It would be much better if Jews and non-Jews would recognize that Jewry has another lot in the world than to create an ordinary State or any political foundation.[46]

The research of recent years indicates that anti-Semitism ran deeper and wider, and persisted much longer in English society than had been believed previously. During a debate in the House of Commons 1942, Herbert Morrison, the Home Secretary, warned against allowing too many Jewish refugees into the country, because there was "considerable anti-Semitism under the surface in this country".[47] After the war scares of 1938, anti-Semitism was exacerbated by the belief that the Jews were responsible for the approaching war.

During the latter half of the 1930s, several extremist, patriotic bodies sprang up in England. With a shared anti-Semitic base, they were anti-Bolshevist and opposed a war with Nazi Germany. Several people joined more than one organization. One of the first was The Link, founded in July 1935 by Admiral Sir Barry Domvil. It engaged in "pro-Nazi and anti-Semitic activities". At its peak, in June 1939, The Link had some 4300 members. It was a highly decentralized body, with many, almost autonomous branches around the country, the most successful being in the London suburbs and in the Midlands. The most anti-Semitic and violently pro-Nazi branch was founded in January 1939 in Central London. Within a short period the membership of this branch grew to over 400. One of its most prominent members and speakers was Major-General J.F.C. Fuller, the noted theorist of armoured warfare (an early supporter of Mosley).[48]

General Fuller was also a member of the Nordic League, also founded in 1935, by two Nazi agents. By late 1937, the League was being described in Nazi Germany as "the British branch of international Nazism". Its branch meetings attracted audiences of between 60 to 200, drawn mainly from the upper middle classes. A *Jewish Chronicle* report of a League meeting in London's Caxton Hall on 23 May 1939 described a speech (one of the wildest) given by A.K. Chesterton (a cousin of G.K.'s), who spoke in "Oxford tones" of "greasy little Jew-boy pornographers".[49]

One of the driving forces in the Nordic League was Captain Archibald Ramsay, a Scottish Conservative MP of aristocratic descent, who married into the English aristocracy. In May 1939 he founded his own secret society that he named the Right Club (a *double-entendre*). Its members were mainly from the upper middle classes, in contrast to the populist, working-class membership of Mosley's BUF. British intelligence knew that Ramsay kept in constant touch with Mosley, and that many of the Right Club's members were also members of the BUF. Among the Right Club's membership were many aristocrats or those with aristocratic connections – for instance, Ramsay's Scottish neighbours or constituents and military officers, their wives or widows. In his memoirs, Ramsay testified that the Club's main goals had been:

> ... to oppose and expose the activities of Organized Jewry ... to clear the Conservative Party of Jewish influence ... to avert war, which we considered to be mainly the work of Jewish intrigue centred in New York.[50]

On 4 September 1939, three days after Chamberlain's declaration of war on Germany, Ramsay wrote the following poem on the House of Commons headed notepaper. It was printed and circulated among the converted. Based obviously on "Land of Hope and Glory", it reflects the cultural level of anti-Semitic prejudice at the time. An extract is reproduced here.

> Land of dope and Jewry
> Land that once was free
> All the Jew boys praise thee
> While they plunder thee ...
> Land of Jewish finance
> Fooled by Jewish lies
> In press and books and movies
> While our birthright dies[51]

Ramsay died in 1955 but it was not until 1989 that the contents of his "Red Book", a ledger containing the names (and many telephone numbers) of the Club's members, were revealed, in the safe of his former solicitors. The book listed the names of some 235 people, many of them encoded. Doubts were raised as to whether everyone on the list knew that they were included, but it appears that most were registered, dues-paying members. Although those who joined the Club in 1939 could not have been unaware of Ramsay's virulent anti-Semitism, only a small number were party to his treasonous activities in 1940.[52]

Among those whose names were deciphered were several senior Conservatives, including a large number of MPs and peers of the realm. The list included: A.K. Chesterton, who had left Mosley's BUF in 1933, because Mosley had not been anti-Semitic enough for his liking; William Joyce (Lord "Haw-Haw"), who would be executed for treason in 1946, for broadcasting Nazi propaganda during the war; the Fifth Duke of Wellington, the Duke of Westminster ("Bendor"), Lord Sempill, the Earl of Galloway and the Marquess of Graham (a future Duke of Montrose). Among the commoners was one Aubrey Lees, a colonial civil servant who had risen to the position of Deputy-Governor of the Jaffa District in Palestine, only to earn the distinction of being sent home in 1938 for uttering anti-Semitic, pro-Arab remarks. Lees, a close associate of Lord Ronald Graham, was an active member in the Link, the Nordic League and the Right Club. A Home Office report stated that he made "no secret of his great admiration for the Nazi regime" and openly criticized the government for "its failure to get rid of the Jewish menace".[53]

Although the Right Club was infiltrated by MI5 agents, its activities were never outlawed. Ramsay himself was interned from 1940 to 1944 under a special emergency law, for his association with Tyler Kent, a pro-German cypher clerk at the American Embassy in London. Being an American citizen, Kent received a relatively light sentence of 7 years imprisonment.

As noted, one of the Club's most prominent members was the Duke of Westminster, one of the richest men in Europe. His wealth derived from ownership of choice plots of real estate, in London, Rhodesia and in South Africa. He was a flamboyant character, who went through four marriages and several love affairs, notably with Coco Chanel, the French fashion designer.[54] The lavish entertainment at his country estates (including the *de rigueur* hunting) attracted senior members of the English establishment. On occasion, members of the royal family dropped in. Churchill was a close friend, and he and his wife were frequent guests at Bendor's country estates in England and France, and on board his various luxury yachts – one of which was a converted naval destroyer, serviced by 190 staff. Churchill and the Duke shared a gambling habit, the difference between them being that unlike the Duke, Churchill could not afford to lose the large sums that were at stake.[55]

Secret, closed meetings of the Right Club were held in the House of Commons. Ramsay circulated among MPs free copies of the blatantly anti-Semitic editions of *The Truth*, a paper issued by the Conservative Party, edited by a convinced anti-Semite. On 12 September 1939, the Duke of Westminster read out an anti-war statement at one of the Club's closed meetings. He claimed that the war was "part of a Jewish and Masonic plot to destroy Christian civilization". His statement was circulated to several Cabinet ministers, including Churchill and Chamberlain. Several ministers complained to Churchill about the indiscretion of his friend.[56]

On the next day, Churchill anxiously rushed off a note to the Duke, advising him that there were "some very serious and bad things" in his speech, "the full bearing of which I feel you could not have properly apprehended". Churchill did not refer to the anti-Semitic aspect of Bendor's speech, but to his opposition to the war. He warned:

> I am sure that the pursuit of this line would lead you into measureless odium and vexation. When a country is fighting a war of this kind, very hard experiences lie before those who preach defeatism and set themselves against the will of the nation.[57]

Churchill's note evidently provoked the Duke's ire for on 29 September, Churchill wrote a second letter, to reassure the Duke that he had written only "as a duty of friendship", and wished to caution him against a course which might bring him to grief. Churchill distinguished between peacetime, when people in a free country had a right to express their views about foreign policy, and wartime, when there were "grave dangers in taking a hostile line" to government policy.[58]

The author of a fine, well-documented monograph on the Right Club has warned against ascribing universal significance to the various manifestations of anti-Semitism in England which, he asserts, at the least provided "a coherent background" for many of these extremist movements.[59] The total membership of the Link, the Nordic League and the Right Club together may have been less than 10,000. However, it should be remembered that a large proportion of these men came from the pinnacles of Britain's civilian and military establishments. Their influence cannot be measured only by their numbers. These men had direct access to Cabinet ministers and, in Ramsay's case at least, they were able to circulate free copies of their pernicious publications to members of both houses of Parliament.

The hope that all anti-Jewish antipathy would dissipate during an anti-Nazi war proved to be a chimera. Anti-Semitism in Britain actually increased during World War Two. On both sides of the Atlantic, many accused their government of taking the country to war at the behest of the Jews. This accusation was exploited by Nazi propaganda, and was one of the factors that inhibited Allied leaders from taking overt actions to help those Jews trapped in Nazi-occupied Europe. Fears of being accused that they were championing "Jewish" over patriotic interests inhibited many Anglo-Jewish (and American-Jewish) leaders from protesting the apathy and inaction of Allied leaders to the Jewish tragedy. These fears lay behind the dismal fact that during the war, in Britain:

> ... there were no mass demonstrations or other pubic measures to influence the government to take active steps to rescue Jews.[60]

After World War Two, two British intellectuals, one Gentile, one Jewish, each living in a totally different social milieu, attempted to analyse the phenomenon and social repercussions of anti-Semitism in British society. The first was George Orwell, journalist, author and social outsider. The second was Professor Isaiah Berlin, a respected member of British academia, arguably the greatest British liberal philosopher of the twentieth century.

In April 1945, Orwell published his essay on anti-Semitism in Britain in *The Contemporary Jewish Record*. He had no inhibitions about deprecating the hypocrisy and incongruities of British society. He was willing to challenge conventional wisdoms and to address uncomfortable issues, including those that he himself was subject to. Some of his defenders have claimed that the mature Orwell overcame the prejudices of the young author that were evident in his *Down and Out in London and Paris*. But the later Orwell never quite shook the habit of labelling people gratuitously as Jews. Yet he did have the personal integrity to recognize the ugly truth that British society was prejudiced. Even if he was not entirely successful in ridding himself of his own prejudices, he was courageous and honest enough to admit to their existence.[61]

In Orwell's view, anti-Semitism was an inevitable manifestation of what he derided as "the disease loosely called nationalism". As such, it would never be cured until the larger disease of nationalism disappeared. In his view, anti-Semitism was a deep-rooted, irrational prejudice, insusceptible to logical argument and statistics: "one of the marks of anti-Semitism is an ability to believe stories that could not possibly be true". As he observed, the war had not only encouraged its growth, but for many, had even given it some justification:

> The theory that "this is a Jewish war" has a certain plausibility ... Jews are to be found in exactly those trades which are bound to incur unpopularity with the civilian public in war-time. Jews are mostly concerned with selling food, clothes, furniture and tobacco – exactly the commodities of which there is a chronic shortage.[62]

Orwell conceded that British society regarded anti-Semitism as "an unforgivable sin and in quite a different category from other kinds of racial prejudice". Indeed, he continued that above a certain intellectual level, people were ashamed of being anti-Semitic, and took good care to distinguish between "anti-Semitism" and "disliking Jews". He recalled a conversation with "a very eminent figure in the Labour Party" in 1940, when the government was incarcerating Jewish refugees from Austria and Germany in special internment camps. The Labour leader had told him, "quite violently": "We never asked these people to come to this country. If they choose to come here, let them take the consequences".[63]

Orwell was particularly critical of what he termed "literary Jew-baiting". He singled out Hilaire Belloc and G.K. Chesterton and their admirers, who had:

> reached an almost continental level of scurrility ... Chesterton's endless tirades against Jews, which he thrust into stories and essays upon the flimsiest pretexts, never got him into trouble – indeed Chesterton was one of the most generally respected figures in English literary life.[64]

At the same time, Orwell took the occasion to denigrate those who supported Zionism, to which he was opposed. He argued that, paradoxically, the Jews' suffering during the war inhibited the British public from giving a fair hearing to Arab claims to Palestine: "it was *de rigueur* among enlightened people to accept the Jewish case as proved ... a decision which might be correct on its own merits, but which was adopted primarily because the Jews were in trouble and it was felt that one must not criticise them". Thus he concluded with brute logic: "Thanks to Hitler ... you had a situation in which the press was in effect censored in favour of the Jews while in private anti-Semitism was on the up-grade".[65]

A different view, from a different context, was offered by Isaiah Berlin, who has been described as "a court Jew in the English aristocracy". He published a fascinating insight into the tribulations of the consummate assimilated British Jew, who in 1932, at the tender age of 23, became the first Jew ever to be elected to the college of All Souls, Oxford University. The college's dinners attracted Cabinet ministers, editors of *The Times* and leading intellectuals of the day. Berlin's election caused a sensation within the Jewish community, and brought invitations to stay at the country estates of the Jewish aristocracy. During World War Two, Berlin served as the eyes and the ears of the British government in Washington. His weekly reports were studied by Churchill. He became an ardent Zionist in 1934, after his first visit to Palestine. But he determined to make his permanent home in England, and in 1947 and in 1950, he turned down offers by Israeli leaders of senior government appointments.

Yet notwithstanding all the privileges that Oxford University had to offer, Berlin always felt an outsider, never completely at ease with his Jewishness. He was aware:

> that being an intellectual entertainer for the rich was a trap into which Jews were especially liable to fall … He always worried that a Jew should not be so emollient and accommodating. It was a central moral dilemma in his life to reconcile a sense of dignity with his eagerness to fit in. Ingratiation, he maintained, was the characteristically Jewish sin, always hoping, against the evidence, that one would "pass".[66]

In September 1951, Berlin published in the *Jewish Chronicle* a candid analysis of what has been called an "unsparing portrait of his inner experience in a Gentile society".[67] He gave his article the provocative title "Jewish Slavery and Emancipation". He maintained that the emancipation of Diaspora Jewry had been achieved only with the establishment of the state of Israel in 1948:

> Until Israel existed, no Jew was free to live a purely Jewish life, undeformed by the scrutiny, pressure and repression of non-Jews … [it] restored to Jews not merely their personal dignity and status as human beings but what is vastly more important, their right to choose as individuals how they shall live.[68]

He maintained that Jews living among the Gentiles were like anthropologists, who could prosper only by making themselves "more of an expert on the customs of the tribes than the natives". Thus the Jew's "poignant passion" for joining institutions that "admit him but do not truly allow him to belong". Berlin attributed his own social success to his "finely tuned radar", which he now regarded as a deformation:

> For they made him too eager for Gentile approval and this in itself built up a dialectic of rejection: the more sensitive he became the more his self-consciousness stuck out, the more he lay himself open to exclusion and rejection.[69]

Gentile Zionism

The very term Gentile Zionism is misleading. Gentile Zionists were not Zionists of the Gentile persuasion. They did support Zionism on occasion, but they had a quite different agenda. For Jews, Zionism was a movement of national renaissance and rescue that aimed at the Ingathering of the Exiles, in the Jews' biblical homeland. But no Gentile ever subscribed to the Zionist thesis that Palestine should, much less could provide a shelter for the ingathering of all, or even of a majority of Diaspora Jewry. This point was brought home to the Zionists in the most tragic of circumstances after World War Two. To their great dismay, very few Western statesmen supported the migration of the remnants of European Jewry to Palestine.

In the nineteenth century, a wave of Protestant millennial writers in England prophesied the return of the people of the Bible to the land of the Bible. From the mid-nineteenth century, once Russian imperialism threatened the continued hold of the Ottoman Empire over the Middle East (and involved the British in the so-called "Eastern Question"), the restoration of the Jews to the territory that had yet to be called Palestine became "a political lever for whatever government decided to get hold of it and use it for its own ends".[70] But the Ottomans, with the support of the British, survived until World War One. After the war, Gentile Zionism became an uneasy blend of an imperialism that paraded as the white man's civilizing mission, mixed with an element of Protestant missionary zeal. The Return of the Jews would constitute the repayment of a debt owed by Gentile society to a people persecuted for centuries by the Christian world.[71]

Various British statesmen have been given the accolade "Gentile Zionist" – Balfour, Churchill, Lloyd George, Leo Amery and Josiah Wedgwood, MP. But these men were never a homogeneous group. None of the first four ever joined the 7th Dominion League, a group founded in 1929 with the goal of incorporating Palestine into the British Commonwealth (see below). The author of the only monograph on the subject concluded that only Blanche ("Baffy") Dugdale, Balfour's niece, truly identified herself with the Zionists' goals. She became a member of Weizmann's inner circle of advisors, and "the truest and most intimate of all his Gentile friends".[72]

The two most high-profile supporters of the Zionist cause in the twentieth century were arguably Arthur James Balfour, namesake of the 1917 Declaration, and Winston Churchill. Ms Dugdale wrote that Zionism interested Balfour as a "political philosopher, a student of history, and a statesman". But on the whole, his attachment remained an abstract pastime, one that occupied him mainly when in opposition, relieved of responsibility.[73]

Like many other Gentile Zionists, Balfour professed to "understand" the roots of anti-Semitism, even if he did not approve of it. In February 1917, he was approached by Lucien Wolf, the anti-Zionist secretary and quasi-official Foreign Secretary of the Conjoint Committee of British Jews, the Anglo-Jewish establishment, to exert diplomatic pressure on Russia to emancipate its Jews. Balfour replied:

> The Jews were ... a "distinct race" practicing a religion that was "an object of inherited hatred". Since Jews were "numbered by millions", in

Eastern Europe, one could understand, though never justify, such persecution.[74]

Balfour was not in fact the architect of the 1917 Declaration that bore his name. Nor did he believe that the Declaration obliged Britain to assume the League of Nations mandate for Palestine. In 1919, he expressed his preference that the Americans should assume the mandate. In August 1919, Robert Vansittart, a junior Foreign Office official at the time and a member of the British delegation to the Versailles Peace conference, queried: "Not only has the mandate not been given: is it certain that we should accept it if offered? Considerations are beginning to emerge which might conceivably make it wiser for us, while supporting Zionism to the extent of our power, not to be the mandated power". Balfour (Foreign Secretary until October) responded:

> I am an ardent Zionist – But I agree with Mr Vansittart that if only our convenience is to be consulted I should personally like some one else to take the mandate. I do not however think this will happen.[75]

In contrast to Balfour, Churchill had little time for abstract philosophy. He was more the pragmatic politician, with a well-earned reputation for being an opportunist. Exceptionally for his class, he was not endowed with an independent, private income. He was compelled to harness his considerable literary talents (aided by ghost-writers) to earning his livelihood by the publication of press articles and books. As Colonial Secretary (1921–22), Churchill was a reluctant godfather to the Jewish National Home. He too shared the common belief in what has been called the "Judeo-Bolshevik bogey", which held the Jews responsible for Bolshevism, and the threat of world revolution (see next section).

In an article he published in the *Illustrated Sunday Herald* in February 1920, *before* Britain assumed the mandate for Palestine, Churchill waxed lyrical about the establishment in some distant future of a Jewish state of 3–4 millions on the banks of the River Jordan. But his first practical support for the Zionist cause was given only in May 1939, when he objected to the Chamberlain government's appeasement of the Arabs (see Chapter 13). His support for the Zionist cause ended abruptly in November 1944, with the assassination in Cairo of Lord Walter Moyne (a member of the Guinness brewing family), by Jewish terrorists. Moyne was a close friend and Churchill's appointee to the post of Minister-of-State Resident in the Middle East.[76] Until that date, Churchill had hoped that the Zionists would bring to Palestine the brains and investments needed to develop the country, and help the British hold on to it as a strategic hinterland to the Suez Canal – at little or no cost to the British taxpayer. But most of all, Churchill feared Jewish influence in Washington, and believed that Britain's sponsorship of Zionism would help secure American support, which he was convinced was vital for the survival of the British Empire.

24 Britain and Zionism

The reverse side of the Gentile Zionist coin was anti-Semitism. The same admiration for the Jews' special abilities and qualities also gave rise to fears about their powers of subversion among the nations in which they refused to assimilate. Men like Balfour and Churchill believed that the concentration of the Jews in their own "National Home" would bring to an end their Diaspora minority existence, and with it, an end to their subversive activities.

The British began to take a serious strategic interest in Palestine during the course of World War One. However, in March 1915, when Herbert Samuel first suggested to the British Cabinet that a Jewish state in Palestine, under British protection, might protect their interests to the north of the Suez Canal, his arguments were dismissed with derision. Sir Edward Grey, the Liberal Foreign Secretary queried Lloyd George's motives for supporting Samuel's scheme, noting cynically:

> He [Lloyd George] doesn't give a damn for the Jews or their past or their future ... but thinks it will be an outrage to let the Holy Places pass into the possession or under the protectorate of "agnostic, atheistic France".[77]

There is also the intriguing, eccentric case of Colonel Richard Meinertzhagen, who played a key role at a few critical junctures in the early years of Britain's mandate in Palestine. He had carried out a significant intelligence ploy before the British army's capture of Gaza and southern Palestine during the war.[78] After attending the Peace Conference in 1919, he was appointed by Foreign Secretary Curzon to the position of General Allenby's Chief Political Officer, attached to the military administration in Palestine. Prior to his appointment, Meinertzhagen penned the following curious mélange, which contains a fair dose of the classic ingredients of Gentile Zionism:

> My inclination towards Jews in general is governed by an anti-Semitic instinct which is invariably modified by personal contact. My views on Zionism are those of an ardent Zionist. The reasons which induced in me a fascination for Zionism are many and complex, but in the main were governed by the unsatisfactory state of the Jews in the world, the great sentimental attraction of re-establishing a race after a banishment of 2000 years, which is not without scientific interest, and the conviction that Jewish brains and money could, when backed by such a potent idea as Zionism, give to Palestine that impetus in industrial development which it so sorely needs after lying fallow since the beginning of the world. Neither could my mind, educated in military thought for the last 20 years, totally ignore the strategic value to the British Empire of a strong, healthy and contented Palestine under British guidance, and the resultant gratitude of the bulk of Jewry throughout the world.[79]

Meinertzhagen's report on the military's culpability for the Arab riots in Palestine in April 1920 was instrumental in persuading Lloyd George to replace the military occupation with civilian rule. General Allenby's protest cost Meinertzhagen his position. However, shortly after, he was chosen by Churchill to become his Military Advisor at the Colonial Office. In the 1930s, Meinertzhagen went on to become a Nazi sympathizer, justifying his position on the grounds that the Jews had dominated Germany in the 1920s, and that the Soviet Union posed the main threat to Europe.

The only book ever to bear the title *Gentile Zionists* does not in fact examine the ideological or religious foundations of the phenomenon, but focuses instead upon Anglo-Zionist diplomacy between the two world wars. Its author concedes that the Gentile Zionists were in fact focused on British imperial interests, which were "of no lesser importance than bringing Western civilization to the desert". Just one chapter is devoted to Josiah Wedgwood, author of a non-starter project to incorporate Palestine into the British Commonwealth, as its seventh dominion.[80]

Wedgwood, a Conservative imperialist, published *The Seventh Dominion* in 1928. Shortly after, in February 1929, he founded the Seventh (Palestine) Dominion League. His book recited the whole lexicon of Protestant empathy for the Zionist ideal:

> The link between the Protestant tradition and the Jewish renaissance; the debt owed by Gentile society for centuries of persecution; the recovery of Jewish self-respect; the civilising mission enjoyed by Gentiles and to be emulated by the Jews.[81]

But he also elaborated upon the material, strategic benefits that would accrue to Britain from a Jewish dominion in Palestine:

> Those who do settle in Palestine are likely to be of real political and commercial service to the Empire, for Palestine is the Clapham Junction of the Commonwealth. The air routes, as well as the ocean routes, east and west, and south and north, cross here, where one flank rests on the Suez Canal and the other on the port of Haifa, the natural trade base of Mesopotamia. With pipeline and railway debauching at Haifa under Carmel, the British fleet can look after the Near East in comfort and safety.[82]

There is some irony in the fact that the Conservatives never adopted the Seventh Dominion project, due to the fear that it would have confirmed universal suspicions that the League mandate was merely a subterfuge for Britain's imperial ambitions to acquire Palestine as a colony. Leo Amery favoured the project in principle, but thought it superfluous, since Britain already exercised full *de facto* sovereignty over Palestine. Most significantly, the project never gained the support of mainstream Zionists.[83]

The Judeo-Bolshevik bogey

> During the epoch of revolutionary struggle, many of the most important revolutionary leaders were Jews. Rather than relegating themselves to the periphery, Jews have always chosen to play a role at the centre of a society's industrial and ideological development.[84]

Anti-Semitism in England increased considerably as a result of the Bolshevik Revolution, owing to the prominence of Jews among the party's leadership. The Jews were stereotyped as the masterminds behind Bolshevism and world revolution. The hostility was directed not only against Russian Jewish immigrants, but also against native-born English Jews. Nor was anti-Semitism confined to the extreme right – it also pervaded the Civil Service, the military, the political elites and the press.[85]

Zionism was seen by some (Churchill, for instance) as a panacea or antidote to the perceived threat posed by world Jewry to universal world stability and order. As noted by Leonard Stein (author of the classic study of the Balfour Declaration), the events of 1917 gave birth to a new breed of Gentile Zionist, who found it:

> ... natural to turn to Zionism as a stabilizing force in the Jewish world, and to value it for its power, given a chance, to provide an antidote to the destructive mania of Jews in rebellion against their lot by offering them a healthy outlet for their frustrated energies.[86]

In early 1917, with the Americans yet to enter the war, the Allies feared that the Russian revolutionaries would remove their country's armies from the great "imperialist" war, thereby permitting the Germans to concentrate all their forces at the Western Front. The myth that the Jews controlled the Russian revolutionary movement was a key consideration in Lloyd George's decision to initiate negotiations with the Zionists in February 1917. These would bear fruit with the issue of the Balfour Declaration some 9 months later.

The "Judeo-Bolshevik bogey" smear was a mutation of the international Jewish conspiracy theory propagated by *The Protocols of the Elders of Zion*. It was not a coincidence that the agitation linking the Jews with Bolshevism peaked in 1919–20, at the very time that the British government – largely at the instigation of Churchill, then Secretary of State for War – was sending military aid to the White Guard forces in Russia, in an attempt to smother the Bolshevik revolution at birth. The White generals used the same stereotypes of the Jews to justify their pogroms against them in the Pale of Settlement.[87]

Henry Wickham Steed, editor of *The Times* from 1919 to 1922, was a classic example of this new breed of "Zionist" – an anti-Semite and Germanophobe to boot. In May 1920, Steed was the first to bring *The Protocols of the Elders of Zion* to the attention of the British public, and to endorse it, in *The Times*.[88]

Steed commented on "the disproportionate influence of the Jews upon the economy and culture of the countries in which they lived". He came to regard a home for the Jews in Palestine as a means of removing their pernicious influence.[89] He has been called the "civilized" type of anti-Semite, to be distinguished from the "paranoid Judeophobia" of some Gentile Zionists. But some of Steed's barbs against the Jews were not at all civilized! In an editorial in *The Times* on 31 July 1914, he had labelled efforts to stop the impending war as "a dirty German-Jewish international financial attempt to bully us into advocating neutrality". In another article, published on 23 November 1917, he called the Bolsheviks "adventurers of German-Jewish blood and in German pay".[90]

Under Steed's editorship, *The Times* promoted official Conservative policy on Russia – opposition to Bolshevism, support for British intervention in the civil war on the side of the White armies, and repudiation of Lloyd George's attempts to reach an understanding with the Bolsheviks. In his memoirs, Steed recorded that he had warned Colonel House, President Wilson's advisor, against the machinations of those Jews pressing for peace with the Bolsheviks:

> I insisted that, unknown to him, the prime movers were Jacob Schiff, Warburg and other international financiers, who wish above all to bolster up the Jewish Bolshevists in order to secure a field for German and Jewish exploitation of Russia.[91]

A reported conversation between Balfour and Colonel House indicates that the belief in the Judeo-Bolshevik bogey and its "antidote" was shared by men in key positions on both sides of the Atlantic. House recalled:

> [Balfour] is inclined to believe that nearly all Bolshevism and disorder of that sort is directly traceable to Jews. I suggested putting them, or the best of them, in Palestine, and holding them responsible for the orderly behaviour of Jews throughout the world. Balfour thought the plan had possibilities.[92]

The British establishment never apparently understood that those Bolshevik leaders who were Jews were what Isaac Deutscher later termed "non-Jewish Jews" – men who, like Deutscher himself, had "transcended Judaism … beyond Jewry to the highest ideals of mankind … ".[93]

The Bolshevik leaders of Jewish persuasion, most prominently Leon Trotsky (Braunstein), had little or nothing in common with and were not representative of the main body of Yiddish-speaking Russian Jewry. Their atheism and internationalism, while eschewing anti-Semitism, did not concern itself with anything Jewish *per se*, certainly not with Zionism. But attempts by

Anglo-Jewry to argue that Trotsky was not in fact "Jewish" – because he neither practised the Jewish religion, nor identified with the Jewish community – failed to dislodge entrenched preconceptions and anti-Semitic prejudice.[94]

After the war, the most prominent English politician to propagate in public the Judeo-Bolshevik bogey myth was Winston Churchill. It may be assumed that he, along with most of the Conservative political establishment, read *The Times* daily, where he would have read Wickham Steed's views.

In February 1920, while serving as Secretary of State for War, Churchill published an article in the popular *Illustrated Sunday Herald*, in which he appealed to world Jewry to choose between Bolshevism and Zionism. The article was tinted heavily with imagery from the *Protocols* and used loaded catchphrases such as the "international Jew". He warned of a "world-wide conspiracy for the overthrow of civilization". According to Churchill, the Russian Revolution was merely the latest manifestation of the "schemes" of this "sinister confederacy" of "international Jews" who were seeking to create a "world-wide communistic state under Jewish domination".

Churchill depicted an imaginary cosmological struggle between Zionism and Bolshevism "for the soul of the Jewish People", no less than a "struggle between Christ and the Anti-Christ, between 'the divine and the diabolical'". Therefore, he urged "the national Jews in every country who are loyal to the land of their adoption … [to] take a prominent part in … combating the Bolshevik conspiracy … to vindicate the honour of the Jewish name".[95]

In its issue the following Friday, the *Jewish Chronicle*, the official weekly of Anglo-Jewry, castigated Churchill severely:

> The SECRETARY OF WAR charges Jews with originating the gospel of Antichrist and with engineering a "world-wide conspiracy for the overthrow of civilisation" … It is the gravest, as it is the most reckless and scandalous campaign in which even the most discredited politicians have ever engaged … It is difficult to understand the object of this tirade, with its flashy generalizations and shallow theories.

The *Chronicle* also dismissed Churchill's mantra about the ancient virtues of the Jewish race – the Jews would not be mollified by sycophancy. His article was not:

> … rendered in any degree more tolerable by fantastic flattery of the Jews as … the most formidable and the most remarkable race which has ever appeared in the world.[96]

There is no little irony in the fact that this article has been quoted in order to demonstrate Churchill's empathy for the Jews and Zionism – by focusing exclusively on his suggestion that the Jews might set up a state of 3 or 4 millions on both sides of the River Jordan, while ignoring the first half of the article.[97]

In 1920, speculations about 3–4 million Jews settling in Palestine were sheer fantasy. Ironically, just one year later, over the protests of Dr Weizmann, it was the same Churchill, now Colonial Secretary, who removed Transjordan from the territory assigned to the Jewish National Home and handed it over to the Emir Abdullah.[98]

The *Protocols of the Elders of Zion* also reached Palestine, brought over in the baggage of officers of the British Military Mission who had served on the staff of the Grand Duke Nicholas in the Caucasus.[99] Some Palestinian Arab leaders soon became familiar with them, through the good services of British officers sympathetic to their cause. Thus in 1919, Haj Amin commented on British policy with "surprise and anger":

> The Arabs did not fear the native Orthodox Jew who was regarded as inoffensive, dependent for existence on foreign charity. But they noticed that the latest immigrants from Eastern Europe were men of a very different type, "imbued with all shades of political opinions which have **plunged Russia into a welter of anarchy, terrorism and misery during the past few years**." Nevertheless, it was the Jew as an economic competitor which really inspired "the profoundest alarm" in the minds of the native ... [100]

In August 1921, *The Times* exposed the *Protocols* as a forgery. After this, the anti-Semitic campaign in England was confined primarily to the extreme right-wing press: *The Morning Post* (a High Tory, arch-conservative morning paper, with a respectable circulation of 119,000 in 1921) and *The Britons*, a group set up for the express purpose of disseminating anti-Semitic propaganda.[101]

But Conservative opposition to the Lloyd George coalition's "Zionist policy" continued to excite public opposition from the English establishment, right up until the political coup that brought down his government in October 1922. The Conservatives' agitation, characterized by anti-Semitic stereotypes, was aired both in Parliament and in the mainstream press, from the *Express* group, owned by Lord Beaverbrook, to *The Times* and the *Daily Mail*, owned by Lord Northcliffe.

Jewish opposition to Zionism

During the first decades of the twentieth century, there developed a deep socio-economic rift inside Anglo-Jewry between, on the one hand, the native-born, established, commercial elites and on the other, the East End Jews, recent immigrants from Eastern Europe, primarily Tsarist Russia, who had poured into Britain after the pogroms that following the assassination of Tsar Alexander II in 1881.

The highly discordant public debates that took place on the "virtues" of political Zionism might have been, as has been suggested, the preserve of a few Jewish intellectuals.[102] But it would appear that these discords reflected not only doctrinal differences but also deeply entrenched personal interests. The native elites were better educated and articulate, and enjoyed easier access to the English media than did their recently arrived, East European brethren. They believed ferevently in the emancipation and assimilation of the Jews in their countries of adoption, and bitterly opposed political Zionism. They were headed by the so-called "Cousinhood", a handful of Jewish establishment families – the Rothschilds, Samuels, Montagus and Montefiores. These families had reached the economic and political pinnacles of British society. Their status rested on both their wealth and their intellect.

Their official spokesman was Lucien Wolf, the Anglo-Jewish establishment's "Foreign Secretary". In an early essay on Zionism published in 1904, Wolf pointed to the link between Gentile Zionism and anti-Semitism:

> The characteristic peril of Zionism is that it is the natural and abiding ally of anti-Semitism and its most powerful justification. It is an attempt to turn back the course of modern Jewish history, which hitherto, on its political side, has had for its main object to secure for the Jewish people an equal place with their fellow citizens of other creeds in the countries in which they dwell, and a common lot with them in the main stream of human progress.[103]

No matter what travails befell the Jews elsewhere, the assimilationist Jews in England maintained staunchly that anti-Semitism was a passing phenomenon.[104] In the spring of 1917, Wolf referred to the early phases of the revolution in Russia as a historic opportunity for the emancipation of Russian Jewry. He warned against the Zionist "solution":

> The Zionists say that the Jews are a nation. Most eagerly is this false and foolish assertion laid hold of by anti-Semites who are always eager and sympathetic Zionists. For, if the Jews are a nation, how can they be citizens of other nations? A man cannot belong to two nations. If he is a Jew by nationality, he can't be a true Russian or Englishman. Nothing must be said or done as regards Palestine and the Jews which would, or could, possibly injure the cause of the Russian Jews. Far better that no more Jews ever entered Palestine than that the emancipation of the Russian Jews be put back or hindered at this crisis in their fate.[105]

One of the more prominent members of the "Cousinhood" was Edwin Montagu. He and Herbert Samuel were first cousins. The latter, a practising Jew, was exceptional in his adoption of the Zionist cause. Both men served in Asquith's government, but they were never close friends. Samuel's biographer has asserted that Montagu was "as fundamentally estranged from Judaism and as passionate an enemy of Zionism as Samuel was its advocate".[106]

Montagu served as a junior minister at the Treasury and at the India Office, and in 1915 was appointed to the sinecure position of the Duchy of Lancaster. In August 1916, in a letter to Eric Drummond, private secretary to Foreign Secretary Grey, he wrote the following diatribe against Zionism:

> It seems to me that the Jews have got to consider whether they regard themselves as members of a religion or a race ... For myself, I have long made the choice. I view with horror the aspiration for national entity ... I regard with perfect equanimity whatever treatment the Jews receive in Russia ... Could anything be more disastrous than for Jewish Englishmen and Jewish Americans to be bracketed with the Jewish Russians, sharing the same verdict for their part in this war? ... Jewish Nationalism ... is to my mind horrible and unpatriotic ... I implore the Foreign Office ... to discountenance this pro-German anti-civilization national tendency on the part of the Jews.[107]

In July 1917, Montagu accepted Lloyd George's offer to become Secretary of State for India. In August of that year, in reaction to the Cabinet discussions of the early drafts of the Balfour Declaration, Montagu responded with his own memorandum. As noted already, he had the temerity to accuse the government of which he was a member of anti-Semitism! Perhaps more than anything else, his memorandum reflected his fears of the consequences for the Jewish establishment of a separate Jewish national entity in Palestine. Montagu protested that if that happened, he would be unable to carry out his ministerial functions, representing Britain in India – since the government's support for Zionism would make "aliens and foreigners by implication, if not at once by law, of all their Jewish fellow citizens". He also rejected the idea that Palestine was associated with the Jews or might "properly be regarded as a fit place for them to live in"[108] (see more on Montagu's opposition in the next chapter).

Montagu remained implacably opposed to the idea of a National Home for the Jews. In 1930, he published *An Indian Diary*. Beatrice Webb commented that the book reflected Montagu's persistent fury with the Balfour Declaration, and his belief that the Jewish Home was an absurdity, "a Home for a people that did not exist" and a dangerous one at that, "an outpost of Germany (read Russian Communism) on the Suez Canal".[109]

Tensions between those Jews born in England and the East End immigrants became exacerbated during the war, when the Russian Jews proved reluctant to volunteer for service in the British Army.[110] Lucien Wolf told the Foreign Office that any hostility that the Russian Jews might harbour against the Tsarist regime (Britain's ally) should not be accepted as an excuse for evading military service. The native Jewish elites feared that a poor military showing by Russian Jews would tarnish Anglo-Jewry's good name. When the government's pledge of free naturalization after the war failed to spur the Russian Jews to enlist, Herbert Samuel, now Home Secretary, announced in

Parliament in September 1917 that military service would be made compulsory.[111]

In November 1917, in reaction to the issue of the Balfour Declaration, the "Cousinhood" founded the grandiose-sounding League of British Jews. In fact, it numbered just 17 Jews. The League propagated the traditional Reform position – that the Jews were purely a religious group. It refuted the Zionist thesis that they were a nation that needed a territorial base. The League warned that Zionism might inspire anti-Semitism, and "could undermine emancipation in the West by provoking accusations of dual loyalty".[112] The League has been dismissed as "a collection of diehards, anachronistically consoling each other with memories of happier days".[113] But as with the readership of "quality" newspapers, the League's influence should be assessed not only by the length of its membership roll, but also by the status and influence of its members.

But in April 1919, the establishment Jews overshot their mark. In what became known as "The Letter of the Ten", ten of them wrote to the *Morning Post*, endorsing an editorial that the paper had published, calling on all British Jews to "dissociate themselves from a cause [Bolshevism] that is doing the Jewish People harm in all parts of the world".[114]

Written at the height of the civil war between the Red and the White armies, the letter appeared to reaffirm the anti-Semitic allegations that Russian Jews were somehow, by definition, all Bolsheviks. If recognized leaders of Anglo-Jewry could imply that their Russian brethren harboured Bolshevik sympathies, then "the *Morning Post* and the entire anti-alien camp were free to make the same allegation with impunity ... ".[115]

And indeed, the *Morning Post* seized upon the letter as a refutation of the accusations that its own statements stemmed from anti-Semitism. It repeated its argument that it was the duty of "the good Jew" to denounce acts such as attending Bolshevik meetings in London by Jews that were likely "to prejudice the Jewish community in the eyes of the British public".[116]

The articles in the *Morning Post* brought to a boiling point the rift between the minority, native elite and the Jewish masses – over 100,000 East European Jews, who were now crowded into the East End ghetto. The controversy has been seen as part of a "class struggle between the East and West Ends for control of the institutions of Anglo-Jewry". The *Jewish Chronicle* censured the Ten for having broken ranks, and for having betrayed their brother Jews, by calling them "foreign". At the end of April 1919, a meeting of the Board of Deputies of British Jews deprecated the letter, for "distinguishing between British and foreign Jews", while at the same time denying any sympathy for Bolshevism.[117]

In view of the various anti-Jewish currents at all levels of British society, including the bitter inner dissensions within Anglo-Jewry itself, it is a point for some speculation why the British Cabinet issued the Balfour Declaration in November 1917, notwithstanding and in spite of the vehement protests of the elite of Anglo-Jewry, right up to Cabinet level. After all, Britain's ruling elite socialized with and was entertained at the estates of the Anglo-Jewish establishment whereas they hardly had any idea of who exactly were the poorer immigrant classes of London's East End.

The answer would appear to be that in 1917, the majority of the Cabinet, including the influential, anti-Zionist Earl Curzon (Lord President of the Council at the time), believed that support for the Zionist cause at that juncture was vital for British interests. At the critical, final meeting of the inner war Cabinet, on 31 October 1917, Curzon agreed with Balfour: "Some expression of sympathy with Jewish aspirations would be a valuable adjunct to our propaganda".[118]

British motives for issuing the Declaration on 2 November 1917 included not only mobilizing the influence of "international Jewry" for the Allied cause and the securing of an imperial colony in Palestine – strategically situated to protect the Suez Canal, at little or no cost to the British taxpayer – but also, to some extent, the defusing of international Jewry's alleged potential for universal "pernicious subversion".

Notes

1 Todd M. Endelman, *Broadening Jewish History: Towards a Social History of Ordinary Jews*, Oxford/Portland: The Littman Library of Jewish Civilisation, 2011, pp. 78, 106–8, 205.
2 ibid, p. 106. The 1976 edition of the *Oxford Dictionary* defined a Jew as: "one of Hebrew descent; one whose religion is Judaism … (offensive) grasping person, usurer, one who drives a hard bargain". London: Book Club Associates, by arrangement with Oxford University Press, 1976, p. 450.
3 Endelman, *Broadening*, pp. 208–9. Disraeli first became Prime Minister in 1868.
4 cf. Colin Holmes, *Anti-Semitism in British Society, 1876–1939*, London: Edward Arnold, 1979, pp. 11–17, and "J.A. Hobson and the Jews", in Colin Holmes, ed., *Immigrants and Minorities in British Society*, London: George Allen & Unwin, 1978.
5 Estelle Pearlman, "The Representation of Jews on Edwardian Postcards", in Bryan Cheyette, Nadia Valman, eds, *The Image of the Jew in European Liberal Culture, 1789–1914*, London: Vallentine Mitchell, 2004, pp. 217–42.
6 cf. Michael J. Cohen, "The Churchill-Gilbert Symbiosis: Myth and Reality", *Modern Judaism*, vol. 28/2, May 2008.
7 *House of Commons Debates (H.C. Deb.)*, 4th series, vol. 149, col. 155, also Holmes, *Anti-Semitism*, pp. 19–20.
8 Endelman, *Broadening Jewish History*, pp. 7–8.
9 Bryan Cheyette, Nadia Vallman, "Introduction: Liberalism and Anti-Semitism", *The Image*, p. 22.
10 Tony Kushner, "British Anti-Semitism, 1918–45", in David Cesarani, ed., *The Making of Modern Anglo-Jewry*, Oxford: Basil Blackwell, 1989, p. 202.
11 On Wickham-Steed see the section below on the Judeo-Bolshevik bogey.
12 Arnold White, *The Modern Jew*, London: F.A. Stokes, 1899.
13 J.A. Hobson, *Imperialism: A Study*, London: Allen & Unwin, 1938, first edition, 1902.
14 Holmes, "J. A. Hobson and the Jews", pp. 127–30, 135–36, 150.
15 ibid, p. 135, citing Hobson article in *Derbyshire Advertiser*, 21 October 1892.
16 J. A. Hobson, *The War in South Africa: Its Causes and Effects*, London: publisher unknown, 1900, pp. 138–39.

17 Bernard Wasserstein, *Herbert Samuel: A Political Life,* Oxford: Clarendon Press, 1992, p. 139.
18 The chairman of British Marconi was Godfrey Isaacs, a close friend of Samuel and the brother of Sir Rufus Isaacs, the Attorney General in Asquith's government (later Lord Reading) – all three were Jews.
19 Wasserstein, *Samuel,* pp. 129–45; Bentley Brinkerhoff Gilbert, "David Lloyd George and the Great Marconi Scandal", *Historical Research,* 149, 1989, pp. 295–317.
20 Wasserstein, ibid, pp. 135–37, 145, also G.K. Chesterton: *Autobiography,* London: Hutchinson & Co., 1969 (first edition, 1936), and Hilaire Belloc, *The Jews,* Boston/New York: Houghton & Mifflin, 1922.
21 Wasserstein, ibid, p. 136.
22 ibid, pp. 143–44.
23 James Renton, *The Zionist Masquerade*: *The Birth of the Anglo-Zionist Alliance, 1914–1918,* Basingstoke/New York: Palgrave Macmillan, 2007, p. 27. Maxse's *National Review* was supported by the newspaper barons Lords Northcliffe and Beaverbrook and the editors of *The Financial News* and *John Bull.*
24 Tom Segev, *One Palestine, Complete,* New York: Metropolitan Books, 2000, pp. 110–11. My emphasis.
25 ibid.
26 Todd Endelman, *The Jews of Britain, 1656 to 2000,* Berkeley: University of California Press, 2002, pp. 185–85.
27 Kipling to Lawrence, 20 July 1920, in Thomas Pinney, ed., *The Letters of Rudyard Kipling,* vol. 5, *1920–1930,* Iowa City: University of Iowa, 2004, p. 126.
28 Belloc, *The Jews,* p. 50.
29 Nahum Sokolow, *The History of Zionism, 1600–1918,* London: Longmans Green & Co., 1919, pp. xxix, ff.
30 Cited in Cohen, *The Origins and the Evolution of the Arab-Zionist Conflict,* Berkeley/Los Angeles: University of California Press, 1987, p. 49.
31 Endelman, *The Jews,* p. 200.
32 George Orwell, *Down and Out in Paris and London,* London: Gollancz, 1933, pp. 19–20, 36–37, 161; citations are from the 1961 Harvest – Harcourt edition. George Orwell was the *nom de plume* assumed by Eric Arthur Blair.
33 Malcolm Muggeridge, *Like it Was,* London: Collins 1981, cited by T.R. Fyvel, *George Orwell*: *A Personal Memoir,* London: Weidenfeld & Nicolson, 1982, p. 178. Muggeridge was a founder member of the Fabian Society, a prominent journalist, and editor of *Punch* from 1953 to 1957.
34 Fyvel, *Orwell,* p. 181.
35 ibid, p. 179. Orwell and Fyvel first met in 1940, and became friends and colleagues, as contributors to *Tribune,* the democratic-socialist weekly.
36 Endelman, *The Jews,* pp. 202–3.
37 Endelman, *Broadening Jewish History,* p. 284
38 G.K. Chesterton, *Autobiography,* London: Hutchinson & Co., 1969, p. 75; the first edition was published in 1936.
39 George Orwell, "Anti-Semitism in Britain", *The Contemporary Jewish Record,* London: April 1945 (the article was reprinted several times in various essay collections). Leo Amery, who held several imperial ministerial posts, attended Harrow at the same time as Churchill.
40 Cited in Endelman, *Broadening Jewish History,* p. 106.
41 For this and the following, see Richard Toye, *Lloyd George and Churchill*: *Rivals for Greatness,* London, 2007, pp. 318–22.
42 *Colliers* magazine refused to release Churchill from a standing contract giving it right of first refusal on all his articles, and the *Strand* magazine turned it down, having already accepted Lloyd George's piece.

43 Toye, *Lloyd George*. My emphases.
44 ibid, pp. 209–11.
45 J.M.N. Jeffries, *Palestine: The Reality*, Westport, Conn: Hyperion Press, 1976, p. 706. First published in 1939 by Longmans, Green and Co., London.
46 ibid, p. 708.
47 Kushner, "British Anti-Semitism, 1918–45", p. 207, and Richard Griffiths, *Patriotism Perverted: Captain Ramsay, the Right Club and British Anti-Semitism 1939–40*, London: Constable, 1998, p. 21.
48 Griffiths, *Patriotism Perverted*, pp. 39–42.
49 ibid, pp. 45–47.
50 ibid, p, 122, and Archibald M. Ramsay,*The Nameless War,* London: Britons Publishing Company, 1952, pp. 103 4. Ramsay cited copiously from *The Protocols of the Elders of Zion*. On Ramsay's contacts with Mosley, see Lidell's diary entry for 21 May 1940, Nigel West, ed., *The Guy Liddell Diaries*, vol. I: *1939–1942*, London/New York: Routledge, 2005, p. 81.
51 Griffiths, *Patriotism Perverted*, pp. 169–70.
52 ibid, pp. 124–25, 143, 160, 163; in 1940, Herbert Morrison, the Home Secretary, rejected the demands of left-wing MPs to reveal the contents of the Red Book. At the time Griffiths wrote his book, all the relevant files on Ramsay, in both the British and the American archives, were still closed, more than 50 years after the end of World War Two.
53 Griffiths, ibid, p. 138.
54 Chanel was suspected of having contact with the Nazis during the war; cf. interview with Malcolm Muggeridge, who worked for MI6 in France. http://en.wikipedia.org/wiki/Malcolm_Muggeridge
55 On Churchill's gambling habit, and his extravagant lifestyle, well above his means, see Cohen, "The Churchill-Gilbert Symbiosis", notes 25–26.
56 Griffiths, *Patriotism Perverted*, pp. 31–32, 240–41, and Martin Gilbert, *Winston Churchill's War Leadership*, New York: Vintage, 2004, p. 19.
57 Gilbert, ibid.
58 Churchill to the Duke of Westminster, 13 and 29 September 1939, in Martin Gilbert, ed., *The Churchill War Papers*, vol. 1, *At the Admiralty, September 1939–May 1940*, New York/London: W.W. Norton & Company, pp. 91–93.
59 Griffiths, *Patriotism Perverted*, pp. 198–99.
60 Endelman, *The Jews*, p. 225.
61 George Orwell, "Anti-Semitism in Britain", *The Contemporary Jewish Record*, London: April 1945. http://orwell.ru/library/articles/antisemitism/english/e_antib. Also Anshell Pfeffer, "Was George Orwell an Anti-Semite?", *Ha'aretz,* 4 August 2012.
62 Orwell, ibid.
63 The fears and shock generated by the German military victories May-June 1940 created a hostile atmosphere of panic and suspicion, leading to a flurry of anti-refugee measures legislated by the Churchill government. Jewish refugees from Germany and Austria were now viewed as "enemy aliens" and interned in special camps, five of them on the Isle of Man. Some 2500 were transported to Australia, under terrible conditions.
64 Orwell, "Anti-Semitism".
65 ibid.
66 Michael Ignatieff, *Isaiah Berlin: A Life*, New York: Metropolitan Books, 1998, pp. 34, 176.
67 ibid, p. 176; one year previously, he had been turned down for membership of the St James's Club in London, as several members were "determined to have no one of Jewish extraction in the Club".

68 ibid, pp. 183–84.
69 ibid, pp. 184–85.
70 Mayir Vereté, "The Restoration of the Jews in English Protestant Thought, 1790–1840", *Middle Eastern Studies*, vol. 8/1, 1972, pp. 3–50.
71 cf. Barbara Tuchman, *The Bible and the Sword: England and Palestine from the Bronze Age to Balfour*, London: Alvin Redman, 1957.
72 Norman A. Rose, *The Gentile Zionists: A Study in Anglo-Zionist Diplomacy, 1929–1939*, London: Frank Cass, 1973, p. 221.
73 Blanche E. Dugdale, *Arthur James Balfour*, 2 vols. London: Hutchinson, 1936, p. 327; Michael J.Cohen, *Churchill and the Jews*, London: Frank Cass, first edition, 1985, revised paperback edition, 2003, pp. 14 ff; idem, *Origins*, p. 50.
74 Eugene C. Black, *The Social Politics of Anglo-Jewry, 1880–1920*, Oxford: Blackwell, 1988, p. 360.
75 Minutes of 6 August 1919, in *Documents on British Foreign Policy, 1919–1939*, First series, Vol. IV, London: HMSO, 1952, p. 345.
76 Cohen, *Churchill*, pp. 257–59.
77 Cited in Mayir Vereté, "The Balfour Declaration and its Makers", *Middle Eastern Studies*, January 1970, p. 60.
78 He deliberately dropped a haversack containing false British battle plans in the Sinai desert, where it fell into Turkish hands, thereby contributing to the surprise British attack that brought the capture of Beersheba and Gaza in 1917.
79 Meinertzhagen to Curzon, 26 September 1919, *Documents on British*, p. 425, cited in Cohen, *Churchill*, p. 17.
80 Rose, *The Gentile*, p. 74.
81 ibid, p. 75.
82 Wedgwood, *The Seventh Dominion*, p. 3, cited in ibid, p. 74.
83 Rose, *The Gentile*, pp. 78, 92.
84 Vasily Grossman, *Life and Fate*, London: Vintage books, 2006, pp. 469–70.
85 Sharman Kadish, *Bolsheviks and British Jews: The Anglo-Jewish Community, Britain and the Russian Revolution*, Frank Cass: London, 1992, pp. 7, 105.
86 Leonard Stein, *The Balfour Declaration*, London: Vallentine Mitchell, 1961, p.162.
87 Kadish, *Bolsheviks*, pp. 8, 11.
88 The publication of the *Protocols* as a booklet the previous February had aroused little attention. An article in *The Times* attributed to Steed drew a parallel "between the programme for world domination formulated by the *Protocols* and the policies of the Russian Bolshevik government". ibid, pp. 31–32.
89 Martin Watts, *The Jewish Legion and the First World War*, Basingstoke/New York: Palgrave Macmillan, 2004, p. 82.
90 Cited in Kadish, *Bolsheviks*, p.10.
91 ibid, p. 29–30.
92 Cited in Segev, *One Palestine*, p. 119.
93 Deutscher was proud to count himself among a gallery of "non-Jewish Jews" that included Heine, Marx, Rosa Luxembourg, Trotsky and Freud. See his wife's introduction to Isaac Deutscher, *The Non-Jewish Jew and other Essays*, London: Oxford University Press, 1968, Merlin paperback edition, 1981, pp. 22–23.
94 Kadish, *Bolsheviks*, pp. 4, 114.
95 ibid, pp. 140–41; Cohen, *Churchill*, pp. 55–56.
96 Cohen, ibid, p. 56.
97 cf. Martin Gilbert, *Churchill and the Jews*, London: Simon & Schuster, 2007, pp. 41–42.
98 Colonial Office files still carried the title *The Palestine and Transjordan Mandate*; the Jewish National Home was restricted to the West Bank of the River Jordan.
99 Martin Watts, *The Jewish Legion*, p.163.

100 Cited in Sahar Huneidi, *A Broken Trust: Herbert Samuel, Zionism and the Palestinians*, London/New York: I.B. Tauris & Co., Ltd, 2001, p. 36. My emphasis.
101 Kadish, pp. 32–33, 41–42.
102 Stuart Cohen, *English Zionists and British Jews: The Communal Politics of Anglo-Jewry, 1895–1920*, Princeton: Princeton University Press, 1982, p. 317.
103 Lucien Wolf, "The Zionist Peril", *Jewish Quarterly Review*, October 1904, cited in Cohen ibid, p.179.
104 Cohen, *English Zionists*, p. 181. A severe pogrom against the Jews had occurred in Kishinev, Russia, just the year before.
105 Lucien Wolf article in the *Edinburgh Review*, April 1917, cited in Kadish, pp. 168–69.
106 Wasserstein, *Samuel*, p. 224.
107 ibid.
108 ibid, pp. 224–25.
109 Beatrice Webb's entry for 4 November 1930, The Digital Library, LSE. Also Edwin Samuel Montagu, *Indian Diary*, London: William Heinemann, 1930.
110 Kadish, *Bolsheviks*, p. 217
111 Watts, *The Jewish Legion*, pp. 72–75.
112 Kadish, *Bolsheviks*, p. 132.
113 Cohen, *English Zionists*, p. 317.
114 Kadish, *Bolsheviks*, p. 121.
115 ibid, pp. 129, 134.
116 *Morning Post*, 5 May 1919, cited in ibid, pp. 124–25.
117 Kadish, ibid, pp. 127–28.
118 Minutes of the inner war Cabinet, 31 October 1917, in Cab 21/177, NA. In December 1917, the Foreign Office set up a Jewish propaganda bureau in the "Jewish Section" of the Department of Information. It was headed by Albert Hyamson, an Anglo-Jewish civil servant. His job was to convince world Jewry of Britain's earnest support for Zionism, cf. Renton, *The Zionist Masquerade*, Chapter 5.

2 World War One
Britain assumes the Palestine mandate

> ... the whole lot, Arabs, Jews, Christians, Syrians, Levantines, Greeks, etc. are beastly people and not worth one Englishman.
> Field Marshal Sir Henry Wilson (CIGS), April 1920

The colonial ethos

Imperialism has been called "as much a thought as a fact", a nation's sense of its own self-esteem and prestige:

> In the international, no less than in the personal arena prestige is sought for its own sake ... the reputation for power is valued by statesmen no less than the substance of power. Prestige is not only the sign of international success, but very often the very condition of it.[1]

Another scholar has described the ethos behind Britain's imperial mission as:

> ... the self-evident superiority of British institutions, the incorruptibility of her colonial civil and military servants, the selflessness of the British ambition to extend to ill-governed, neglected peoples the benefits of an impartial and just administration that would enable them, under appropriate guidance, to develop and flourish. That the British alone knew what would be suitable and beneficial for their imperial wards was unquestioned.[2]

Several elements of the British imperialist ethos were in evidence in mandatory Palestine. There was the condescending belief in Britain's civilizing mission, in the innate superiority of European civilization, and the concomitant "relegation of indigenous and political cultures to a position of permanent inferiority".[3] The British aristocracy's belief in its innate right to Empire rested comfortably on the conviction of its natural right to leadership over "inferior" peoples.

Britain's imperial hubris found expression even in the language that its future rulers picked up at school. The words "beastly" and "rotten" were particular favourites, when referring to "the natives". In 1920, General Congreve, the GOC Middle East, wrote in a private letter to Field Marshal Sir Henry Wilson, the CIGS, that the "Arabs, Jews and Christians in Syria and Palestine, they are all alike, a beastly people, the whole lot of them is not worth one Englishman". In his reply, Wilson threw in some of the regional nationalities for good measure: "the whole lot, Arabs, Jews, Christians, Syrians, Levantines, Greeks, etc. are beastly people and not worth one Englishman".[4] During World War Two, Churchill complained to Leo Amery, his Secretary of State for India, that the Indians were "a beastly people with a beastly religion".[5]

Britain's attitude towards her colonies derived from two main sources: first, from a conviction, firmly entrenched by the mid-nineteenth century, that her intellectual, technological and moral and therefore her social and economic achievements were the natural prerogatives of the colonial powers of north-west Europe. If this was so, then it followed that the only salvation of her colonial subjects must lie in their wholesale adoption not only of European technology but also of European laws and morals, even manners.[6]

By the twentieth century, Britain's long imperial experience had been instilled into her national mores and educational system. This produced a tradition in which most of her colonial officials conducted themselves "according to a code inculcated and reinforced from early childhood by family, school, church, and the wider society".[7]

The second source of British arrogance was fear. The officials who served in the colonies were only too conscious that they were hopelessly outnumbered by the "natives" whom they presumed to control and rule:

> Wherever Europeans found themselves in a small, privileged but vulnerable minority, all but submerged in an alien, suspicious and unpredictable community ... the price of their authority seemed to be an unbending insistence upon the outward display of subservience and conformity in the bearing and behaviour of subject peoples.[8]

Arthur Balfour, the aristocratic, liberal, philosopher-statesman, once defined the colonialist mindset as a mix of paternalism and a delicately balanced act of will:

> ... directly the native populations have that instinctive feeling that those with whom they have got to deal have not behind them the might, the authority, the sympathy, the full and ungrudging support of the country which sent them there, those populations lose all that sense of order which is the very basis of their civilization, just as our officers lose all that sense of power and authority, which is the very basis of everything they can do for the benefit of those among whom they have been sent.[9]

Ministers in Whitehall were shielded from colonial realities "in the field" by the vast distances between London and the colonial outposts. Due to the great disparity in size between the British Isles and her vast Empire, the British employed a wide array of political instruments in their colonies, reverting to "the inflexible and expensive method of direct colonial rule" only as a last resort.[10] This has been summed up neatly by one historian of the Empire: "informally if possible, formally if necessary".[11]

Whenever possible, the home country opted for indirect colonial rule, via local rulers who could be induced to co-operate, either by economic benefits or, when necessary, intimidated by the threat of or subdued by the actual use of force. The reservoir of British colonial personnel and the financial resources available were so limited that Britain was forced "to rely upon locally recruited subordinates to man its bureaucracy and security forces and to win the co-operation of the indigenous social leaders – chiefs, landowners, sultans or sheikhs", who served as proxies for British order and authority.[12]

The colonial official on the spot faced disturbing ambiguities and contradictions. Perhaps no one has described these better than George Orwell, an "outsider" who derided the so-called white man's "civilizing mission" as a cynical façade. In a memoir recalling his own five years service as a subdivisional police officer with the Indian Imperial Police in Lower Burma during the 1920s, he wrote with contempt of European colonialism:

> ... when the white man turns tyrant it is his own freedom that he destroys. He becomes a sort of hollow, posing dummy, the conventionalized figure of a sahib. For it is the condition of his rule that he shall spend his life in trying to impress the "natives" and so in every crisis he has got to do what the "natives" expect of him; he has got to appear resolute, to know his own mind ... my whole life, every white man's life in the East, was one long struggle not to be laughed at. He wears a mask, and his face grows to fit it.[13]

Orwell himself suffered acute emotional distress and mental conflict – an experience that he claimed was the common lot of the British official in India. The clash between his intellectual propriety and the uncontrollable rancour that "ruling the natives" induced in him cast him into an unbearable cognitive dissonance, which served only to exacerbate his hatred and contempt for imperialism:

> All the time I knew I was stuck between my hatred of the empire I served and my rage against the evil-spirited little beasts who tried to make my job impossible. With one part of my mind I thought of the British Raj as an unbreakable tyranny, as something clamped down ... upon the wills of prostrate peoples: with another part I thought that the greatest joy in the world would be to drive a bayonet into a Buddhist priest's guts. Feelings like this are the normal by-products of imperialism; ask any Anglo-Indian official, if you can catch him off duty.[14]

In the last resort, the survival of the Empire depended upon the ability of British forces to maintain order and suppress rebellion. However, with the exception of India, locally recruited colonial military units (usually commanded by British officers) were never powerful enough to subdue local insurrections unless backed by British forces. The ultimate sanction of colonial rule was British infantry battalions. Yet in peacetime, the home country could field only 200,000 troops, from which a "central reserve" had to be held back for the defence of England herself. The remainder were scattered in "penny packets" around the Empire. This meant that at all costs, the risk of insurrection – "by offending too many powerful groups in the indigenous society" – had to be avoided.[15]

With regard to Palestine, it is apposite to note that by the end of 1945, fully one half of the British field force – 100,000 men – was tied down there, in a futile attempt to keep the peace. This salient point will be dealt with in detail in the final chapter of this book.

By the turn of the twentieth century, Britain's Empire rested on fragile economic foundations. British industry and technology had fallen behind those of Germany and the United States. To quote a memorable turn of phrase by one historian of the Empire:

> Applause for English chemists and code-breakers cannot silence the murmur of relative economic decline.[16]

Britain remained economically viable thanks to her overseas trade and "invisible income" from services (merchant marine, banking, insurance). During the years prior to 1914, there emerged a clear consensus in Whitehall that any further expansions of Empire would weaken rather than strengthen the foundations of British power. The huge costs of World War One further eroded British confidence in the competitiveness of her industry and commerce, and augmented her sense of imperial vulnerability.

Yet during the course of World War One, unintentionally, Britain acquired huge tracts of new territory in the Middle East. She did so partly due to inertia – the need to fill the power vacuum left by the final demise of the Ottoman Empire – and partly due to a need to keep her French and Russian allies away from the main imperial routes to India, via the Persian Gulf and the Suez Canal. There was also the old drive of imperial expansion, pressed almost independently by the Indian Empire, which for years had nursed its own plans for colonizing Mesopotamia.[17]

After the war, the discrepancy between the vast expanses of recently acquired territories and the paucity of means with which to control them became acute. During the first months of the peace, the Lloyd George administration dedicated itself to a rapid demobilization of British forces – some 200,000 of whom were stationed in the Middle East – and the reduction of overseas spending to pre-war levels. Financial stringencies dictated that henceforth colonies would have to pay their own way, and not be a burden on the British taxpayer.

42 *World War One*

Yet none of these considerations aroused any doubts in Whitehall about Britain's inherent right of conquest, as due compensation for all the blood and treasure she had expended in their acquisition. The British were convinced that since their armies had played the dominant role in the conquest of the Middle East, then London should be the paramount arbiter of the region's fate after the war. This *weltanschauung* was expressed publicly by ministers. For instance, in March 1921, Winston Churchill, the newly appointed Colonial Secretary, treated a delegation of Palestinian Arabs in Jerusalem to his own nineteenth century imperial outlook:

> Britain had the right to decide the destiny of Palestine because British forces had liberated the country at the cost of 2000 lives. In response to the Palestinians' demand for self-government, Churchill replied: All of us here today will have passed away from the earth, also our children and our children's children before it is fully achieved.[18]

British military intelligence would later single out Churchill's speech as one of the factors that provoked Arab rioting in Palestine less than 2 months later, on 1 May 1921.[19] Imperial hubris was still very much in evidence 35 years later, when Anthony Eden launched the Suez war against Egypt in 1956, in secret collusion with France and Israel.[20]

Palestine was conquered during World War One, with "largely unconscious and unexamined assumptions of natural authority that pervaded the entire imperial enterprise". However, the Zionist enterprise held out the alluring prospect of a solution to Britain's own economic straits. The promise of Jewish capital to finance the development of Palestine appeared to provide a uniquely convenient solution to holding this imperial outpost "on the cheap", at little or no cost to the British taxpayer. Bankrolled by their Zionist proxies, the British would bring the benefits of Western civilization to the Arabs:

> The European [Zionist] settlers with their superior education, technological know-how, and capital, would bring material benefits to the "natives" and provide the "backward" Arabs with an example to which to aspire; the injection of the Zionist "yeast" would produce a "cake" to be shared with the Palestinian Arabs.[21]

The corollary of British support for the Zionist cause was a distinct undercurrent of contempt for the Arabs. A small, occasionally influential circle of eccentric British Arabophiles took a romantic view of the East. Their fantasies focused on the pristine, untarnished-by-Western civilization Bedouin of the Arabian Peninsula. In one sense, this was the antithesis of the West's classical "civilizing mission". Flamboyant characters like St John Philby (the father of Kim, the Soviet spy) and T.E. Lawrence ("of Arabia") were infatuated with the romance of the desert, and its nomadic inhabitants. The Bedouin were something of an anthropological find. They were admired for having preserved their pre-societal tribal culture. But the Bedouin were the exception that proved the rule.

In general, the British regarded the Arabs as technologically backward and irrational, incapable of determining their own best interests. T.E. Lawrence, for instance, whose post-war public lectures established him as a legend in his own lifetime, believed that the Hashemites – the traditional guardians of Mecca and Medina – were "the oldest, most holy, and most powerful family of the Arabs", although his attitude to them was paternalistic. He had little but contempt for the rest of the Arab world, with its outward trappings of Western civilization. He referred to the Palestinian Arabs as "stupid ... materialistic, and bankrupt" and to Auni Abd el Hadi, a member of the Arab delegation to the Versailles Peace Conference in 1919, as "more a *garçon de cabaret* than a statesman".[22]

World War One: military and strategic interests in the Middle East

The British interest in Palestine – as a defensive hinterland to the Suez Canal – dated back to the last decades of the nineteenth century. It was as old as her concern "for the defence of the short sea-route to India".[23] During the years prior to World War One, the British General Staff commissioned surveys of the Sinai Peninsula, with a view to preparing a strategic concept for the defence of the canal. The Committee of Imperial Defence (CID) suggested that the best way to meet a threat to the canal from the north would be to land four divisions at Haifa.[24] It was assumed that the Sinai desert lacked the water sources that would allow any armed force to traverse it. Any military threat to the canal from the east would require the construction of a railway across the otherwise impassable Sinai desert. But no railway was constructed there prior to World War One.

This strategic conception was shattered in February 1915, when a small Turkish force, led by German officers, successfully crossed the Sinai desert and reached the Suez Canal. Once across the canal, the Turks soon became lost in a sandstorm and the attack had no immediate military consequences. But Britain's belief that the Sinai desert constituted an impassable land buffer protecting the canal evaporated with the appearance of the first Turkish soldiers at the banks of the canal.

In March 1915, Herbert Samuel's proposal that Britain support a Zionist entity in Palestine, as a strategic asset to the north of the Suez Canal, was rejected with derision by the Cabinet.[25] But following reassessments made after the Turkish crossing, military intelligence assigned the role of strategic buffer to the canal to Palestine.[26] With the switch in strategy came a concomitant condition: to keep the French as far away as possible from the approaches to the strategic waterways under British control – not only from the Suez Canal but from the Persian Gulf also. This concept was reaffirmed in 1923, when the CID was commissioned to examine Palestine's strategic significance. Its report concluded that although Palestine itself had little intrinsic importance, Britain must remain there, if only to keep the French out of a territory so close to the Suez Canal.[27]

In this context, the Sykes-Picot Agreement of May 1916, which would have placed Palestine under international (Anglo-French-Russian) control, was an aberration, an act of carelessness by Asquith's Liberal administration, which would have brought the French perilously close to the canal.[28] The mistake would be corrected by Lloyd George, who succeeded Asquith as Prime Minister in December 1916.

Indeed, a major British motive for issuing the Balfour Declaration the following November was Lloyd George's determination to extricate his government from the Sykes-Picot Agreement. This would be achieved through the good services of the Zionists. In return for the British promise to help them build their National Home in Palestine, they agreed to do what they could to ensure British hegemony over Palestine. As noted by Professor Vereté, author of the classic study of the origins of the Declaration:

> For just as in the Declaration itself there was no guarantee yet that H.M.G. was bound to help in establishing a viable national home within the historic boundaries of Palestine, as envisaged in the Zionist programme, so there was no guarantee in it that Great Britain would alone acquire control over the country. The Zionists and the British continued to need one another after the Declaration.[29]

In 1917, the Zionists were as good as their word. Nahum Sokolov, the Russian Zionist leader, travelled to Paris at the behest of the British government. He told the French that the Zionists wanted a British protectorate over Palestine. The French realized that the British were using the Zionists to wriggle out of the 1916 agreement, but they too, like the British, believed that the Jews held the key to the Americans' entry into the war. Both allies knew that their very survival depended upon American arms.[30]

Balfour's personal share in securing the Declaration was minimal.[31] After the war, in what was possibly a flash of wise clairvoyance, he opposed a British tutelage over the Jewish National Home in Palestine. At the Paris Peace Conference, he proposed repeatedly, in vain, that the Americans be prevailed upon to take on the mandate for Palestine.[32]

The 1917 Declaration was conceived in the crisis of war. But after the war, successive governments came to appreciate the benefits of the Zionist project for Britain itself. Lord Curzon, who in 1917 expressed reservations about the Declaration, became a convert after the war. He replaced Balfour at the Foreign Office in October 1919, and was retained as Foreign Secretary by the Conservatives, who won power in October 1922. One year later, Curzon lectured an imperial conference on the material benefits that would accrue to Britain in return for her support of the Zionists:

> ... Palestine needed ports, electricity, and the Jews of America were rich and would subsidise such development.[33]

In 1928, Balfour confessed that events after the war had brought about a change of his mind. Now the grand old statesman (still holding the sinecure position of Lord President of the Council in the Cabinet), he lauded Palestine's strategic value to the Empire, as a strategic buffer to Egypt:

> Palestine ... lies at the very place where the Power primarily responsible for the security of the Suez Canal would wish to place it ... A mandated territory on the Asiatic side of the great waterway, prosperous, contented and quite impervious to Egyptian intrigue must add strength to the Empire at a point where additional strength may in the interests of the Empire and the world, be most desirable.
>
> This was not a consideration which influenced most British Zionists in 1917. It certainly did not influence me; but the trend of events since then has brought it into prominence, and the idealists – be they Jew or Gentile, are serving the interests of peace and commerce in a way which perhaps they never contemplated.[34]

British strategic interest in Palestine increased during the course of the mandate. In the 1930s, a new oil pipeline was laid from northern Iraq to the new refineries at Haifa. With the development of modern aviation, Palestine also became an important station in imperial air communications to the Far East.[35] Finally, following the signature of the Anglo-Egyptian treaty of 1936, which limited the British garrison in Egypt to 10,000 troops, Palestine acquired a new role, as a strategic annex in which to hold military reserves over and above the limit set by the treaty with Egypt, on stand-by for the defence of the canal.[36]

The MacMahon–Husayn correspondence

In the autumn of 1915, British fortunes in the Middle East sank to their nadir, following the military débâcle at the Dardanelles. Muhammad al-Faruqi, a Kurdish soldier in the Ottoman forces at Gallipoli, deserted to the British side. When debriefed at Cairo, he claimed to represent the Sharif Husayn of Mecca, and warned British officials that if the British government didn't accede to Arab demands for independence, the Arabs would switch their allegiance to the Germans. When these dire warnings were telegraphed to London, Foreign Secretary Grey authorized Sir Henry MacMahon, the High Commissioner in Cairo, to offer Husayn independent rule over a wide area, with the exception of those territories which the British had already conceded to the French, i.e. Ottoman, or Greater, Syria.[37]

Since Husayn and the British failed to reach an agreement, none was ever brought before the British Cabinet for its ratification. MacMahon himself never treated the exchange of letters seriously. With long years of service in India behind him, he possessed the traditional, colonialist mindset. When challenged in a private letter by the Viceroy of India, for having made such sweeping offers to the Sharif, he made light of the correspondence:

I do not for one moment go to the length of imagining that the present negotiations will go far to shape the future form of Arabia or to either establish our rights or to bind our hands in that country ... What we have to arrive at now is to tempt the Arab people into the right path, detach them from the enemy and bring them on to our side.[38]

No one on the British side believed that the Sharif had a mandate to represent the Arabs, or the authority or force to execute any agreement in their name. Not only that, but after the war, the British maintained that the Arabs had not fulfilled their part in the 1915 exchange – a revolt by the Arab divisions serving in the Turkish army against their masters. (The condition of an Arab revolt did not appear in MacMahon's initial offer of independence, but was added later, at the insistence of the India Office.[39])

However, all this did not prevent the British delegation to the Versailles Peace Conference from exaggerating wildly the military contribution of the Arab revolt to the defeat of the Turks, in what was a transparent attempt to finesse French claims to Syria, in favour of Britain's Hashemite clients.

In November 1918, one week after the Turkish armistice, the British and the French went yet further, in an unrealistic joint declaration, promising the Arabs independence. It was composed mainly for Western eyes – specifically those of President Wilson – with no thought for its relevance for the contemporary Middle East:

> The goal envisaged by France and Great Britain in prosecuting the war in the East ... is the complete and final liberation of the peoples who have for so long been oppressed by the Turks, and the setting up of national governments and administrations that shall derive their authority from the free exercise of the initiative and choice of the indigenous populations.[40]

Although this statement never attained the prominence of the MacMahon-Husayn correspondence, it did have the effect of raising the Arabs' hopes yet higher. But Hashemite claims to hegemony in the Fertile Crescent were not enhanced when Sharif Husayn became embroiled after the war with Ibn Saud in a war for hegemony over the Arabian Peninsula. Husayn lost the war and was forced to leave the peninsula forever. He ended his days in forced exile in Iraq, as the guest of his son Faysal. But the British, in furtherance of their own plans to control the Middle East via the Hashemite dynasty, elevated two of Husayn's sons to be the rulers of two new Arab states: Faysal to the kingship of Iraq and Abdullah to the Emirate (from 1946 the kingdom) of Trans-Jordan.

The Balfour Declaration

For many decades, popular folklore related that in 1917, the Balfour Declaration was given to Weizmann by Prime Minister Lloyd George, as a reward for his scientific contribution to the British war effort. The legend was invented some 20 years after the event, by the fertile but ageing mind of Lloyd George. In his memoirs, Lloyd George "recalled" that when Weizmann turned down his offer to accept some honour in return for his wartime services to England, he had persisted:

> But is there nothing we can do as a recognition of your valuable assistance to the country? ... He [Weizmann] replied: "Yes, I would like you to do something for my people." He then explained his aspirations as to the repatriation of the Jews to the sacred land they had made famous. That was the fount and origin of the famous declaration about the National Home for the Jews in Palestine.[41]

The myth proved robust enough to survive the denial of Weizmann himself, just over a decade later:

> His [Lloyd George's] narrative makes it appear that the Balfour Declaration was a reward given me by the Government ... for my services to England. I almost wish that it had been as simple as that, and that I had never known the heartbreaks, the drudgery and the uncertainties which preceded the Declaration. But history does not deal in Aladdin's lamps.[42]

The first serious fissure in the myth was made in 1970, by Professor Vereté. As noted already, he showed that the Declaration was the result of a British, not a Zionist initiative, issued in order to serve British interests:

> The British wanted Palestine – and very much so – for their own interests ... it was not the Zionists who drew them to the country ... had there been no Zionists ... the British would have had to invent them.[43]

In contrast to their disdainful, patronizing attitude towards the Palestinian Arabs, the British held ambiguous, exaggerated views about the alleged universal influence and power of international Jewry. They believed that the Jews were positioned strategically, close to the helm of power in the capitals of the Great Powers. For instance, Beatrice Webb, who together with her husband Sydney had lead the Fabian Socialists before the war (see Chapter 10), noted in her diary in 1930:

> At the time of the Balfour Declaration, the one and only consideration was the relative power to help us to win the war of the international Jewish financiers on the one hand, and on the other the Arabs in revolt against the Turkish Empire.[44]

At the beginning of 1917, Lloyd George initiated the negotiations in London with the Zionists, due primarily to military exigencies. The situation of the allies on the battlefield was in desperate stalemate, and Britain's population was gradually starving, as British vessels carrying food imports were sunk at an ever-increasing rate by German submarines. The British and the French believed that American military intervention was required if they were to prevail over the Germans. They also believed that Jewish influence inside the White House could be critical in persuading President Wilson to enter the war. Even if the Americans declared war on Germany in April 1917, nearly 7 months before the Balfour Declaration was published, the American Zionists were able to demonstrate their influence on two occasions prior to 2 November.

On the first occasion, in July 1917, Weizmann succeeded in heading off a mission by presidential envoy Henry Morgenthau Sr, to persuade Turkey to sign an early, separate peace. The American initiative, in its initial form, would have left Turkey in possession of its Asian territories, including Greater Syria (which included what would become Palestine), down to the Egyptian border. The British and the Zionists shared a mutual interest in not allowing this to happen.

Morgenthau had served as American ambassador in Constantinople, until the summer of 1916, when he returned to the United States to help President Wilson in his election campaign. Morgenthau had been very outspoken against the Turkish massacre of the Armenians, and had raised considerable sums for their relief. However, despite the Young Turks' indifference to Morgenthau's pleadings for them to stop the massacres, he retained an inflated, totally unrealistic belief in his own personal influence with the Turkish leaders. In 1916, he made a rash, totally unfounded claim that "he could buy Palestine for the Jews through his personal contacts".[45] In May 1917, he suggested to the State Department that he use his personal contacts with the Turks to negotiate a separate peace agreement with them. The President, Colonel House (his senior advisor) and Secretary of State Lansing all agreed to his proposal, even if the latter doubted whether it had any more than a 50–50 chance of success.

Morgenthau's mission had some of the characteristics of an *opéra bouffe*, although its potential for harming vital British and Zionist interests was enormous. Curiously, Foreign Secretary Balfour, who was in Washington at the time, did not immediately grasp the significance of the mission. When asked by the State Department for his opinion, he replied: "Speaking off hand and without consultation with my Government, I could see no objection". The American Zionists, who were close to President Wilson, felt unable to oppose his quest for a separate peace with the Turks.

But Zionist (and Armenian) leaders in London were alarmed at the possibility of a separate peace that would leave Turkey-in-Asia intact. Weizmann, while stressing his own absolute loyalty to Britain, warned the Foreign Office repeatedly about German approaches to the Zionists "with a view to coming to terms". The Foreign Office was itself having second thoughts. When the British asked the Americans to drop the plan, they refused. But given their dependence on the Americans, they could hardly refuse to co-operate with Morgenthau.

The British and the Americans agreed that on his way to meet the Turks, Morgenthau would stop off at Gibraltar to meet British and French representatives. The British appointed Weizmann as its representative to the talks and accepted his condition that no arrangement with Turkey would be agreed to "unless Armenia, Syria and Arabia are detached". It took just two days of talks, on 4–5 July, for Weizmann to persuade Morgenthau to break off his mission. It soon became apparent that Morgenthau did not even know the basic facts about the current situation in Turkey. Weizmann's persistent questioning failed to elicit from him any coherent plan of action. In his face-saving report to the State Department, Morgenthau wrote that the time was not yet ripe for negotiations with the Turks, who would regard an Allied approach as a sign of weakness. In his autobiography, he blamed Weizmann for his failure.

It is highly doubtful whether Morgenthau could have persuaded the Turks to make a separate, early peace – certainly not on the condition of ceding their Middle Eastern possessions (Greater Syria was still in their hands – the British had yet to conquer Gaza). But Morgenthau's own weaknesses doomed his mission. His flights of fancy were revealed as just that, without foundation. His interlocutors perceived that he was "incapable of continuity of thought or effort". Opposite him, Weizmann proved himself a masterful diplomat and negotiator and the British credited him with derailing the mission. Weizmann's standing soared, not only within the Zionists' ranks but also in the eyes of the British government, whose officials in London were then working on the drafts of what would soon be published as the Balfour Declaration.

The second occasion on which Weizmann was able to demonstrate his own influence and that of the American Zionists came during the autumn of 1917. The British needed the approval of President Wilson for the Balfour Declaration, which involved the acquirement by the British of a new colony in Palestine. The British and the French never revealed to Wilson their partition of the Middle East (the Sykes-Picot Agreement of 1916). Without the Zionists' intervention, it might have proved difficult, if not impossible to secure his agreement to the annexation of Palestine by Britain, which ran counter to Wilson's Fourteen Principles. On this vital issue, Weizmann again acted as Britain's broker. He forwarded various drafts of the proposed Declaration to Louis Brandeis, urging him to secure the President's approval. Brandeis, a leading figure in the American Zionist movement, became a close friend of President Wilson, after he helped in his 1912 presidential election campaign. In January 1916, the president rewarded him with a nomination to the US Supreme Court.[46]

Weizmann was particularly concerned to mobilize the support of American Jewish leaders for the Declaration, following the harsh opposition to it raised inside the British Cabinet by Edwin Montagu, Secretary of State for India since July 1917. When the Zionist formula (asking the government to recognize Palestine as "a National Home for the Jewish People") was debated by the Cabinet on 3 September 1917, Montagu opposed vigorously, and it was decided to defer a final decision while the draft was sent to President Wilson for his approval.[47] Wilson's reply was non-committal.

On 19 September 1917, Weizmann cabled to Brandeis a draft of the Declaration that had been approved by the Foreign Office and the Prime Minister, and had been submitted to the Cabinet. Weizmann added that it would help greatly if the President and he would approve. On 24 September, Brandeis replied: "From talks I have had with the President and from expressions of opinion given to closest advisers, I feel I can answer you that he is in entire sympathy with the declaration quoted in yours of the 19th".[48]

When the draft Declaration was discussed by the Cabinet on 4 October, two weighty objections were raised. The first was Montagu's claim that British support for a Jewish National Home in Palestine would threaten the civil and political rights of Jews living in other countries. Montagu made the lightly veiled assertion that Whitehall was under the control of the Zionists, an organization run by "men of enemy descent and birth". He insisted that the true views of the indigenous Anglo-Jewish community were represented by "**his** kind". The Zionists were worried also by the practical objections to the Declaration voiced by Lord Curzon, a veteran statesman, a former Viceroy of India, now Lord President of the Council, with a seat on the inner war Cabinet. Curzon was the only Cabinet minister who had actually visited Palestine. He described the country as "barren and desolate" for the most part and asked how was it proposed to get rid of the existing Moslem majority and introduce the Jews in their place, and how were the latter supposed to earn their living? He concluded "a less propitious seat for the future Jewish race could not be imagined".[49]

The Cabinet was presented with a revised draft of the Declaration which, taking into account Montagu's opposition, added a guarantee of "the rights and political status enjoyed in any other country by Jews who are fully contented with their existing nationality". But once again, instead of reaching a decision, the Cabinet decided to consult President Wilson.[50]

Montagu, hinting at resignation, composed a semi-hysterical plea to Lloyd George:

> It is a matter of deep regret to me ... that you are being ... misled by a foreigner, a dreamer, an idealist ... who sweeps aside all practical difficulties with a view to enlisting your sympathy on behalf of the Zionist cause ... If I were to resign now ... a match would have been put to the Indian fire.
>
> It seems almost inconceivable that I should have to give it up [his office] for something wholly unconnected with India at all, and yet what am I to do? I believe firmly that if you make a statement about

Palestine as the national home for the Jews, every anti-Semitic organization and newspaper will ask what right a Jewish Englishman, with the status at best of a naturalized foreigner, has to take a foremost part in the Government of the British Empire. Palestine is not now British. It belongs to our enemies. At the best it can never be part of the British Empire.[51]

In reply to the Cabinet secretary's request for his view of the latest draft of the Declaration, Weizmann replied acidly with an attack on "those Jews who by education and social connections have lost touch with the real spirit animating the Jewish people".[52]

On 10 October Weizmann cabled to Brandeis this latest draft, together with a plea that he and the American Zionists exert pressure on the White House to support it. Brandeis would not get to see the President until 18 October. Meanwhile, on 13 October, Wilson consulted with Colonel House about a public speech that he intended making to warn against German peace feelers. He told House that he would also announce that the future disposition of Turkey should be left to the peace conference. House, who still favoured leaving Turkey-in-Asia intact, was against any presidential statement, but he persuaded Wilson to change this part of his speech to "Turkey must not be partitioned among the belligerents, but must become autonomous in its several parts according to race". Curiously, the two men did not apparently speak specifically about the British Declaration.

On 16 October, after returning to his home in New York, Colonel House received a letter from the President informing him that he concurred with the British Declaration. On the same day, perhaps still unaware of the President's decision, Rabbi Stephen Wise and Jacob de Haas, two American Zionist leaders, were received by House. It remained for him only to inform them of Wilson's decision, and to ask them not to publicize the President's agreement.[53]

On 18 October, Brandeis cabled Weizmann that he had seen the President, who had informed that he had already advised the British government that he was in favour of the Declaration. He asked Weizmann not to publicize his own involvement.[54]

It appears probable that Brandeis played a key role in persuading the President to give the British a green light for issuing the Balfour Declaration. It may be assumed that Weizmann never missed any opportunity to embellish Brandeis' role when discussing with the British the political influence of the American Zionists.

In 1917, the government also believed that the Jews controlled the revolutionary movement in Russia. It believed that a public declaration promising to support the establishment of a Jewish National Home in Palestine would persuade the revolutionaries, allegedly led by Jews, not to pull Russia out of the "imperialist" war – a nightmare contingency that would enable the Germans to concentrate all their forces on the Western Front.

The Zionists used the government's belief in the international power and influence of world Jewry as one of their key negotiation cards in London. Weizmann also played on British fears that the Germans would pre-empt them with their own pro-Zionist Declaration. This fear of a pre-emptive German "Zionist" declaration was the first argument employed by Balfour at the final, decisive Cabinet meeting at the end of October 1917.[55]

This enduring British fear of the Zionist lobby in Washington is illustrated strikingly by a Cabinet memorandum written by Winston Churchill some 22 years after the event, on Christmas Day 1939. Churchill, First Lord of the Admiralty at the time, appealed to the Chamberlain Cabinet not to implement the Land Regulations of the 1939 White Paper on Palestine, because of mounting protests by American Jewish Zionists. He gave his colleagues his own analysis of why the government had issued the Declaration in 1917:

> ... it had not been for light or sentimental reasons that Lord Balfour and the Government ... made the promises to the Zionists which have been the cause of so much subsequent discussion. The influence of American Jewry was rated then as a factor of the highest importance, and we did not feel ourselves in such a strong position as to be able to treat it with indifference. Now ... I should have thought it was more necessary, even than in November 1917, to conciliate American Jewry and enlist their aid in combating isolationist and indeed anti-British tendencies in the United States.[56]

The twice-promised land

In both cases – the correspondence with the Arabs in 1915, and the 1917 promise to the Jews – British manoeuvres appear to fall neatly into the category of what has been called by Barbara Tuchman the "March of Folly".[57]

In the case of the Arabs, the Foreign Office was persuaded by its officials in Cairo that if they didn't accede to Husayn's demands for independence, the Arab nationalists – with an illusory mass following throughout the Fertile Crescent – would rebel against them, and transfer their allegiance to the Germans. At the time, no one bothered to check or verify the size or extent of the Arab national movement, and no evidence has been unearthed since to indicate that the Arabs intended or would have been able to carry out a revolt of any kind against the Turks.

In public, British ministers and officials would consistently deny that Palestine had been included in the area delineated by MacMahon's letter of 24 October 1915. But within the confines of Whitehall it was conceded that Palestine *had* been included. Early in 1922 (while Churchill was still Colonial Secretary), Lloyd George commissioned a confidential study of the government's respective obligations towards the Arabs and the Zionists. John Shuckburgh, head of the Middle East department at the Colonial Office, was commissioned to prepare it. He conceded, unequivocally:

World War One   53

> ... geographically Palestine **is included** in the area within which Britain was to acknowledge Arab independence.[58]

But no British official would ever admit as much in public. To have done so would have been to concede the Arab accusation that Britain had promised Palestine twice. Shuckburgh advised that it would be politically unwise to reopen this particular Pandora's box. In a letter to High Commissioner Samuel, he explained that the Colonial Office was against "making any further public announcements on this troublesome question ... it seems that our best policy is to let sleeping dogs lie as much as possible".[59]

The official British line (until 1939) became that they had given to the Palestinian Arabs much more than their fair due and therefore, they owed them no more. In 1923, Churchill's successor at the Colonial Office, the Duke of Devonshire, advised the Cabinet:

> Whatever may be thought our case is based on the exact wording of the MacMahon letter ... What we promised was to promote Arab independence throughout a wide area. That promise we have already substantially fulfilled ... Considering what they owe us, they may surely let us have our way in one small area [Palestine], which we do not admit to be covered by our pledges.[60]

In comparing the MacMahon offer with the Balfour Declaration, Devonshire explained that the British were not legally bound to the Palestinians in any way. He reminded his colleagues that no treaty had ever been signed with the Sharif of Mecca, and that the correspondence had been "rather long and inconclusive", leaving many issues unresolved:

> It should also be remembered that Sir H. MacMahon's offer, whatever may have been its precise scope, was made, not to the Arabs of Palestine, but to the Sharif of Mecca. Unlike the Balfour Declaration, it was not made public at the time and did not, in fact, become known to the Arabs of Palestine until after the war.[61]

Devonshire next distinguished between the Sharifians (the Hashemites), who had fought on the British side in the war, in the Arab revolt, and the Palestinians, who had not:

> There is no question of our having induced them [the Palestinians] to fight for us by giving them an undertaking from which we have since receded. In point of fact, practically none of them did fight for us ... The main burden of complaint comes, not from the Sherifian family, to whom our promises were given and who fought by our side in the war, but from the Palestinian Arabs (or a certain section of them), to whom we gave no promises and who did not fight at all ... It may be too much to hope that

we can ever satisfy the Palestinian Arabs; but so long as the general body of Arab opinion is not against us, the dangers arising from local dissatisfaction ought not to be serious. The task of reconciling the local Arabs to the Zionist policy would have been much easier if political exigencies had not made it necessary to sever all connection between Syria and Palestine.[62]

When delving into Britain's motives for issuing the Balfour Declaration, one may discern traces of both the *Protocols of the Elders of Zion* and the "Bolshevik bogey" syndrome. A recent study into the mindset of the Whitehall officials asserted that the British issued the Declaration as a propaganda tool in order to win the support of world Jewry. This was because:

… those behind the Balfour Declaration imagined Jewry to be a hostile international power, which was thought to be conspiring with the enemy forces of Germanism and Bolshevism.[63]

The officials' failure to appreciate the true nature of the Bolshevik movement in 1917 is little short of astounding: first, for believing, quite erroneously, that a majority of Russian Jews favoured Zionism and second, for failing to understand that those Bolshevik leaders who were Jewish by birth were "non-Jewish Jews", who cared little or nothing for the Jewish, let alone the Zionist cause.[64] The belief, fostered by the British ambassador at St Petersburg, that the Jewish leaders of the Bolsheviks would keep Russia in the war if they promised to support the establishment of a Jewish National Home in Palestine was misguided wishful thinking.

The United States has been described as "the pre-eminent battlefield in the Allies' global propaganda conflict with the Central Powers".[65] The British (and French) belief in the influence of the Jews in Washington was not without foundation. Two instances have been noted already. But it appears that in 1917, the Cabinet was concerned most about the Russians making an early peace with the Germans.

There is no evidence to indicate that in October 1917, any member of the war Cabinet took the time to consider the long-term implications of the Balfour Declaration for Britain's future position in the Arab world. This is confirmed by Sir John Shuckburgh who, in a private conversation in 1923, recalled the wartime considerations of the Cabinet:

The War Cabinet also considered the effect on German-Jewish mentality both in the USA and in Germany. We had outbid the Germans who had prepared their own Balfour Declaration. But apparently what weighed more heavily with the Cabinet was the effect on Russia. It was known there was Jewish influence behind the Bolshevist movement. It was hoped to keep the Russian Government firm and steady in the cause of the Allies. It was not realized that Russia was really finished as far as fighting was concerned. In short the War Cabinet was fighting blindly in the dark for immedate advantages and could hardly be expected to think of the ulterior consequences. At the date of its publication the Balfour Declaration had a universal and briliant reception. It was at the time a master-stroke and was worked to the limit of its propaganda value.[66]

Once adopted by the Cabinet, British support for Zionism took on a momentum of its own. From being a "carrot" intended to keep the Russians fighting, and to lure the United States into the war, it became very much "a question of British self-interest and a matter of competition with the Central Powers".[67]

After the war, the Lloyd George administration rebuffed Arab accusations that it had promised Palestine twice.[68] But of course, politicians rarely air their private thoughts in public. Perhaps nowhere was the contrast between private and public positions so sharp as with the case of Balfour. In August 1919, in one of the last memoranda he wrote as Foreign Secretary, he deplored the numerous, conflicting commitments with which Britain had burdened itself in the Middle East during the war:

> ... so far as Palestine is concerned, the Powers have made no statement of fact which is not admittedly wrong, and no declaration of policy which, at least in the letter, they have not always intended to violate.

But Balfour set aside the Arabs' claims in favour of those of the Jews, whom he regarded – along with the Greeks – as one of the most gifted of the ancient races:

> Zionism ... was rooted in age-long traditions ... and of far profounder import than the desires and prejudices of the 700,000 Arabs who now inhabit that ancient land.[69]

The "private" Balfour was not in evidence when he spoke in the House of Lords nearly 3 years later, in June 1922, during a key debate on Palestine. The Lords passed a motion condemning the government's support of the Jewish National Home in Palestine. Balfour, recently elevated to an earldom but out of office, protested vehemently against what he condemned as the Palestinians' unfounded, unjustified pretensions. His speech evoked the traditional, nineteenth-century imperial ethos:

> Of all the charges made against this country, I must say that the charge that we have been unjust to the Arab race seems to me the strangest. It is through the expenditure largely of British blood, by the exercise of British skill and valour, by the conduct of British generals, by troops brought from all parts of the British Empire – it is by them in the main that the freeing of the Arab race from Turkish rule has been effected. And that

we, after all the events of the war, should be held up as those who have done an injustice; that we, who have just established a King in Mesopotamia, who had before that established an Arab King in the Hejaz, and who have done more than has been done for centuries past to put the Arab race in the position to which they have attained; that we should be charged with being their enemies, with having taken a mean advantage of the course of international negotiations, seems to me not only most unjust to the policy of this country, but almost fantastic in its extravagance.[70]

Balfour's speech became an ideological prop for the Conservative administration that took office in October 1922. But most of the officials whose job it was to deal with the routine administration of the mandate would come to regard the 1917 Declaration as one of the greatest mistakes of Britain's imperial history.[71] In April 1923, Shuckburgh told a colleague:

[he] had a sense of personal degradation. He had always had this feeling during the two years he had been at the Colonial Office. The British policy in Palestine was built on this ambiguity and the Middle East Department suffered from it. He could not go on, they could not go on, feeling this sense of equivocation. It was personally degrading and unworthy of the British Government. **It was of course a result of the War, an evil result and furnished an explanation but not a justification for prolonging it**.[72]

In 1917, no one could have foreseen how events in Palestine would play themselves out. The British had trapped themselves in a cul-de-sac in Palestine, even if unwittingly. In October 1930, the socialist Beatrice Webb, whose husband, Lord Passfield, was Colonial Secretary at the time, wrote the following prescient assessment in her diary:

The man on the spot gave promises to the Arabs, the British Cabinet gave promises to the Jews, always qualifying the promise of a Jewish Home by the perfunctory condition of the well-being of the Arab inhabitants. After ten years it is clear to all who study the question that these promises were and are incompatible ... Owing to the superior wealth and capacity of the Jews, it is the Arab who has suffered damage during the last ten years ... Today they [the Zionists] are furious with the expressed intention of the British Government to protect the Arab cultivator from being expropriated and becoming a landless proletariat. This protection of the Arab is not only justified, on grounds of justice, but on the ground of expediency. Unless Great Britain is prepared to keep an army of occupation in Palestine indefinitely she cannot prevent the old and new [Zionist] settlements from being periodically raided by the neighbouring Arab States as well as by the resident Arabs. The British have also to consider the Mohammedans of India, not to mention of Egypt.

Probably future governments will be only too glad to have had the ice broken and the Jews forced to be more considerate and reasonable. What seems to me probable is that when the Jewish authorities realise the anti-God and communist character of the new settlers they will gradually give up the idea of a Palestine Jewish State and possibly even of a Jewish cultural home.[73]

The Balfour Declaration put Britain on a collision course with the Arabs. Its virtual cancellation in 1939 would put them on a collision course with the Zionists also.

Notes

1. A.P. Thornton, and H.J. Morgenthau, quoted in Stuart A. Cohen, "Prestige and Policy in British Imperialism before 1914: The Case of Mesopotamia", *Bar-Ilan Studies in History,* Ramat-Gan: Bar-Ilan University Press, 1978, p. 195.
2. John Darwin, *Britain and Decolonisation*, London: Macmillan, 1988, p. 15.
3. ibid, p. 10.
4. Congreve-Wilson correspondence of April 1920 in HWW 2/52A/16, Imperial War Museum Archives, London (IWMA).
5. Madhusree Mukerjee, *Churchill's Secret War: The British Empire and the Ravaging of India during World War II*, New York: Basic Books, 2010.
6. Darwin, *Britain*, p. 11.
7. A. J. Sherman, *Mandate Days: British Lives in Palestine, 1918–1948*, New York: Thames & Hudson, 1998, pp. 14, 30–31.
8. Darwin, *Britain*, p. 10.
9. Cited in Sherman, *Mandate Days*, p.32.
10. Darwin, *Britain*, p. 7.
11. John Gallagher, cited in David Reynolds, *From World War to Cold War: Churchill, Roosevelt, and the International History of the 1940s*, Oxford: Oxford University Press, 2006, p. 58.
12. Darwin, *Britain*, p. 30.
13. George Orwell, *Shooting an Elephant, and Other Essays,* New York: Harcourt Brace, 1950 (first published in 1945), p.8.
14. ibid, p. 4.
15. Darwin, *Britain*, pp. 30, 32.
16. Edward Ingram, *The British Empire as a World Power,* London: Frank Cass, 2001, p. xi.
17. cf. Sherman, *Mandate Days*, p. 14; on the imperial aspirations of the India Office, Briton Cooper Busch, *Britain, India and the Arabs, 1914–21*, Berkeley: University of California Press, 1971, and Cohen, "Prestige and Policy", pp. 179–95.
18. Bernard Wasserstein, *Herbert Samuel: A Political Life*, Oxford: Clarendon Press, 1992, pp. 255–56.
19. cf. Michael J. Cohen, *Churchill and the Jews,* revised paperback edition, London: Frank Cass, 2003, p. 91.
20. cf. David Carlton, *Britain and the Suez Crisis*, Oxford: Blackwell, 1988, and W. Scott Lucas, *Divided We Stand: Britain, the US and the Suez Crisis*, New York: Hodder & Stoughton, 1991.
21. Barbara J. Smith, *The Roots of Separatism in Palestine: British Economic Policy, 1920–1929*, Syracuse: Syracuse University Press, 1993, p. 7.

22 Quotes from David Garnett, ed., *The Letters of T.E. Lawrence*, London: Jonathan Cape, 1938, p. 267, Lawrence minute of 25 February 1921, FO 371/6375, E2354, and notes: "Syria: The Raw Material", in Yale Report, 25 February 1918, all cited in Cohen, *Churchill*, pp. 76–77.
23 Yaacov Herzog, *A People that Dwells Alone: Speeches and Writings of Yaacov Herzog*, Misha Louvish, ed., London: Weidenfeld & Nicolson, 1975, p. 193.
24 ibid, and Mayir Vereté, "The Balfour Declaration and its Makers", *Middle Eastern Studies*, January 1970, pp. 50–51.
25 cf. Wasserstein, *Samuel*, p. 210.
26 Douglas Duff, *Palestine Picture*, London: Hodder & Stoughton, 1936, pp. 270–71.
27 Cabinet memorandum by the Colonial Secretary, the Duke of Devonshire, CP 351(23), 23 July 1923, Cab 24/162, NA. See also Chapter 7.
28 When the Bolsheviks seized control of Russia in November 1917, they seceded from the tripartite agreement.
29 Mayir Vereté, "The Balfour Declaration and its Makers", *Middle Eastern Studies*, January 1970, p. 66.
30 cf. Michael J. Cohen, *The Origins and Evolution of the Arab-Zionist Conflict*, Berkeley: University of California Press, 1987, pp. 45 ff.
31 ibid, p. 50.
32 Balfour minute of 6 August 1919, in *Documents on British Foreign Policy, 1919–1939*, vol. IV, London: HMSO, 1952, p. 330, cited in Cohen, *Churchill*, p. 86.
33 Cited in Thomas Jones, *Whitehall Diary*, vol. I: 1916–1925, Keith Middlemass, ed., London: Oxford University Press, 1969, p. 246.
34 Balfour memorandum for Cabinet, recommending a British guarantee for a Zionist Loan, March 1928, CP 71, in Cab 24/193, NA.
35 cf. Bernard Lewis, "Epilogue to a Period", in Uriel Dann, ed., *The Great Powers and the Middle East, 1919–1939*, New York/London: Holmes & Meier, 1988, pp. 419–25; and Smith, *The Roots*, p. 5.
36 Michael J. Cohen, "The Egypt-Palestine Nexus, 1935–1939", in *Bar-Ilan Studies in History*, vol. III, Michael J. Cohen, ed., Ramat-Gan: Bar-Ilan University Press, 1991, pp. 67–79.
37 For this and following, see Cohen, *Origins*, Chapter 1. In 1915, the India Office supported the candidacy of Ibn Saud over that of Husayn for leadership of the Arabs. It is interesting to note that in February 1939, Ibn Saud, who was courting Germany, told Hans Grobba, the German ambassador to Jidda, that during the First World War, the British had offered him the caliphate and the title of king; cf. Grobba to the German Foreign Ministry, 18 February 1939, in *Documents on German Foreign Policy*, p. 808.
38 MacMahon to Viceroy Hardinge, 5 December 1915, in Elie Kedourie, *In the Anglo-Arab Labyrinth*, Cambridge: Cambridge University Press, 1976, p. 120.
39 Cohen, *The Origins*, Chapter 2. The entire correspondence is in George Antonius, *The Arab Awakening*, London: Hamish Hamilton, 1938.
40 Antonius, ibid, appendix E.
41 David Lloyd George, *The Truth about the Peace Treaties*, London: Victor Gollancz Ltd., 1938, vol. I, p. 349. Lloyd George completed his memoirs when he was 71 years old. Weizmann discovered a new chemical process for the production of acetone – a material of which there was a great shortage – needed in the manufacture of cordite explosive propellants, which were critical to the Allied war effort. On the production of acetone, cf. Jehuda Reinharz, *Chaim Weizmann*, vol. II, *The Making of a Statesman*, New York/Oxford: Oxford University Press, 1993, Chapter II. Weizmann became a wealthy man from the royalties he was paid for the patents on his discoveries. idem, pp. 60–67.

World War One 59

42 Chaim Weizmann, *Trial and Error*, New York: Schocken Books, 1949, p. 150. On the persistence and continuing dissemination of the myth. cf. Reinharz, ibid, pp. 68, 433, note 207.
43 Vereté, "The Balfour Declaration", p. 50.
44 Diary entry of 26 October 1930; Digital Library of the London School of Economics and Political Science (LSE). At the time, her husband, elevated to the peerage as Lord Passfield, was Colonial Secretary.
45 This section on the Morgenthau mission is based mainly on Reinharz, *Weizmann*, pp. 160–66.
46 Brandeis' nomination proved to be so controversial that it took a then-unprecedented 4 months between Wilson's nomination and the Senate's final confirmation.
47 For this and following, cf. Cohen, *The Origins*, pp. 52–53.
48 Brandeis to Weizmann, 26 September 1917, Weizmann Archives (WA), also *The Letters and Papers of Chaim Weizmann*, Leonard Stein, ed., Jerusalem: Israel Universities Press, 1975, pp. 505–6.
49 cf. Reinharz, *Weizmann*, pp. 196–97.
50 ibid, p. 196.
51 ibid, p. 198.
52 ibid, p. 199.
53 Reinharz, *Weizmann*, pp. 200–201. British-born de Haas was secretary of the First Zionist Congress in 1897. He moved to the United States in 1902, where he assumed the leadership of the fragmented American Zionist movement. He converted Brandeis to Zionism in 1912.
54 Brandeis to Weizmann, 19 October 1917, WA.
55 Cohen, *Origins*, Chapter 2.
56 Cohen, *Churchill*, p. 195.
57 Barbara Tuchman, *The March of Folly*, New York: Macmillan, 1962.
58 Sahar Huneidi, "Was the Balfour Declaration Reversible? The Colonial Office and Palestine, 1921-23", *Journal of Palestine Studies*, vol. 27/2, Winter 1998, p. 34, my emphasis.
59 Shuckburgh to Samuel, 7 November 1922, ibid, p. 34.
60 CP 351, supra.
61 ibid.
62 ibid. The Arab historian A.L. Tibawi has claimed that the first group of Palestinian Arabs was recruited for the Arab revolt in July 1918; he asserts that some 125 volunteered, but does not ascertain if they reached the battlefield before the end of the war. During the reign of the Sharif's son Faysal at Damascus, from October 1918 to July 1920, the Palestinians identified themselves as residents of southern Syria, and sent representatives to the Arab Congress in Damascus; many occupied senior positions in Faysal's short-lived administration. cf. Abdul Latif Tibawi, *Anglo-Arab Relations and the Palestine Question, 1914 – 1921*, London: Luzac, 1977, and Cohen, *Origins*, pp. 27–28.
63 James Renton, *The Zionist Masquerade: The Birth of the Anglo-Zionist Alliance, 1914–1918*, Basingstoke/New York: Palgrave Macmillan, 2007, p. 3.
64 Isaac Deutscher, *The Non-Jewish Jew*, London: Oxford University Press, 1968, pp. 22–23, 40–41, 49.
65 Renton, *The Zionist*, p. 5.
66 Conversation between Shuckburgh and Sydney Moody, cited in Evyatar Friesel "British Officials on the Situation in Palestine, 1923", Middle Eastern Studies, Vol. 23, No. 2 April 1987, p. 207. Moody served as District Officer of Safed under the military administration in Palestine, and continued under the civil administration of Herbert Samuel; in 1923, he was attached for 1 year to the Colonial Office in London; he returned to serve in the Palestine Secretariat in Jerusalem until 1939; he concluded his career as Colonial Secretary of Mauritius.

67 Eugene C. Black, *The Social Politics of Anglo-Jewry, 1880–1920*, New York: Blackwell, 1988, p. 36.
68 On the inclusion of Palestine in MacMahon's offer of 24 October 1915, cf. Cohen, *Origins*, pp. 18–23.
69 Balfour memorandum of 19 August 1919, "Syria, Palestine and Mesopotamia", in *Documents on British*, p. 345.
70 Balfour speech in the House of Lords, 21 June 1922, cited in Devonshire memorandum, CP 351(23), supra.
71 Elizabeth Monroe, *Britain's Moment in the Middle East, 1914–1956*, London: Chatto & Windus, 1964, p. 43.
72 Friesel, "British Officials", p. 200. My emphasis.
73 Diary entry of 26 October, 1930, LSE.

3 Palestine and the Near East, 1919–23

> The countries that do belong to us are England, Ireland, Egypt, the lower part of Mesop [sic] and India. The countries that do not belong to us are the plebiscite areas, Constantinople, Palestine, all Persia and the greater part of Mespotamia ...
>
> Field Marshal Sir Henry Wilson (CIGS), December 1920

The military against the "new provinces"

After World War One, the Liberal consensus was that the great age of imperial expansion had come to an end and further imperial accretions would only weaken, rather than strengthen Great Britain. In 1922, one-third of all government expenditure was still being spent on the service of the government's war debt.

After the war, Lloyd George decreed that military expenditures must be cut back to pre-1914 levels. But the need for economic stringency did not lead him to abandon Palestine; nor did it deter him from insisting that Britain support Greek aspirations to Smyrna (on which, see p. 63). The military chafed at the economic retrenchments imposed. Field Marshal Sir Henry Wilson, Chief of the British Imperial Staff (CIGS), held the Liberal politicians in utter contempt, referring to them derisively as the "frocks". In June 1921, he confided to his diary: "A more hopeless, ignorant, useless lot of men I have never seen". Wilson's own preoccupation with internal security and the Irish problem, together with his impatience with what he regarded as the "dithering and lack of judgement" of the politicians, led him also to denigrate the dispersal of reduced British forces across the highly volatile Middle East.[1]

While required by the government to reduce expenditures drastically, the military were also expected to maintain order in the vast new territories just conquered in the Middle East. The military protested strongly against retaining what they referred to disparagingly as the "new provinces" – those territories that had comprised former Ottoman Syria: Mesopotamia (Iraq from 1924), Palestine and Trans-Jordan.[2]

As commander of an army that now felt that it had more Empire than it could cope with, Wilson believed that the conquest of the "new provinces" had been a mistake. He complained that they constituted an excessive burden, that they had never been and should not be allowed to become an integral part of the Empire. At the end of December 1920, in response to complaints about the huge expenditures involved in the repression of the summer's 4-month-long revolt against British rule in Iraq, Wilson wrote to General Sir Aylmer Haldane, GOC Mesopotamia (1920–22), defining which were, in his view, the integral parts of the Empire and which were not:

> The countries that do belong to us are England, Ireland, Egypt, the lower part of Mesop [sic] and India. The countries that do not belong to us are the plebiscite areas, Constantinople, Palestine, all Persia and the greater part of Mespotamia ... I think that this same cry for retrenchment will take us out of Palestine, except possibly for a very small force, and will also in the course of the coming year take us out of Constantinople. Personally, I am all in favour of coming out of Persia, of Mesop [sic] – except Basra and the oil-fields country – of Palestine, and of Constant [sic] ... I am entirely opposed to the present Cabinet plan of backing the Greeks against the Turks.[3]

Wilson earned a reputation for being a man of poor judgement, with a proclivity for going out on a limb. But his minister, Winston Churchill, Secretary of State for War (January 1919 to February 1921), supported his opposition to the retention of Britain's wartime conquests in the Middle East. Churchill agreed that neither Palestine nor northern Iraq held any strategic or economic value for the Empire, and both should be returned to the Turks.[4]

Few men personified Britain's colonial hubris more than Winston Churchill, the perennial nineteenth-century imperialist. After World War One, first as Secretary of State for War and next as Colonial Secretary (1921–22), he had to deal with an Arab revolt in Iraq, Egyptian nationalist disturbances in Egypt, and two waves of Arab riots in Palestine (1920, 1921). During his visit to Egypt and Palestine in March 1921, he experienced at first hand the intensity of Arab opposition to Zionism. But when he met the Palestinian Arab leaders in Jerusalem, he warned them that neither they nor their children's children would reach independence, and that even if he was empowered to do so, he would not rescind the Balfour Declaration.

Four months later, in a House of Commons debate, he treated his fellow MPs to a lecture on the relative merits of Britain's Empire in black Africa, and of the "new provinces":

> In the Middle East you have arid countries. In East Africa you have dripping countries. There is the greatest difficulty to get anything to grow in the one place, and the greatest difficulty to prevent things smothering and choking you in their hurried growth in the other.
>
> In the African colonies you have a docile, tractable population, who only require to be well and wisely treated to develop great economic

capacity and utility; whereas the regions of the Middle East are unduly stocked with peppery, pugnacious, proud politicians and theologians, who happen to be at the same time extremely well armed and extremely hard up.[5]

Whereas Churchill and Wilson shared the same views about "the new provinces", they parted ways over India. Wilson fumed at Churchill's all-consuming passion for economic retrenchment, as mandated by Lloyd George. His heated reaction to Churchill's proposal to cut back on expenditures in India brought out his contempt for "the frocks":

> There were more ridiculous notes from Winston about greatly reducing the garrison in India ... Winston, regardless of safety and hoping that any disasters may come after he has left office, is trying to gain credit and make a name by saving money. He certainly won't do so with my approval nor without a very clear definition from the Cabinet of those who will bear the responsibility.[6]

The Palestine-Smyrna nexus

From 1919 to 1922, Palestine was a secondary (even if related) problem, compared to that presented by the appearance of a renascent Turkish nationalism, led by the charismatic, gifted Turkish general Mustafa Kemal.[7] In August 1919, Kemal rebelled against the regime of the Turkish Sultan and repudiated Allied attempts to dismantle the Ottoman Empire. The opposition of the British military to holding on to the "new provinces" was increased by the military challenge now posed by Kemal, who threatened to reverse Britain's wartime conquests in the Middle East.

In August 1920, the Allies secured the signature of the Turkish Sultan to the Treaty of Sèvres, which was supposed to have marked the formal end of the First World War in Asia Minor, and reduce Turkey to a minor, European state. The treaty assigned eastern Thrace and the millet of Smyrna to Greece. But Kemal Pasha, who would become the father (Attatürk) of modern Turkey, determined to push the Greeks out of Smyrna. Lloyd George regarded the rise of Kemalist nationalism as a "reincarnation of Ottoman imperialism". He wanted instead to create a "moderate, pacific and compliant Turkish state, confined to Anatolia".[8]

Churchill, together with CIGS Wilson, opposed Lloyd George's anti-Turk policy vigorously, and repeatedly advocated appeasing Kemal. Churchill became obsessed with the fear of further hostilities with the Turks, convinced that the danger was greatest in Smyrna. He shared Wilson's dread that a Greek collapse in Asia Minor would be followed by a Kemalist attack on the reduced Allied garrison at the Straits. But Lloyd George, supported by Foreign Secretary Curzon, overrode the military's objections and managed to mobilize a majority of the Cabinet in support of his policy on Smyrna. This was achieved by reassurances that "the task of defeating Kemal in the field" would be achieved by "Greek, not British armies".[9]

From late 1919, the Turkish and Bolshevik problems became interlocked in Churchill's mind. He feared that Kemal's renascent Turkey would join forces with the Red Army in a combined military sweep across the Middle East. This would wreak humiliation and defeat upon the British Empire, and wipe out all of Britain's territorial acquisitions in the Middle East.

Churchill felt increasingly isolated in the Cabinet, at loggerheads with Lloyd George over two major, connected issues: the first, British support for the Greeks in Smyrna; the second, Lloyd George's opposition to sending any further support for the White against the Red armies in the Russian civil war.

At the beginning of December 1920, in a private letter to Lloyd George, Churchill hinted that their differences might lead to his resignation:

> We seem to be becoming the most anti-Turk and the most pro-Bolshevik power in the world: whereas in my judgement we ought to be the exact opposite.[10]

In August 1922, the Turks routed the Greek army in Smyrna and completed the conquest of the province – British support notwithstanding. The Turkish victory was accompanied by a large-scale massacre of the Greek Orthodox Christian population.[11]

In view of the military's opposition to retaining the "new provinces", and in reaction to the crises in the Near and Middle East between 1919 and 1921, Churchill wrote a series of private letters to Lloyd George, urging him to withdraw all British forces from the Middle East and relinquish all British claims to the region. His letters do not support Churchill's reputation as a life-long supporter of the Zionist cause, a reputation that has proved remarkably robust, surviving the test of both time and historical criticism.[12] This anomaly has much to do with the disparity between his private positions and his public utterances. Those close to him were quite aware of his real position. For example, Maxwell Coote, Churchill's temporary ADC at the Cairo conference in March 1921, thought it curious to hear Churchill give:

> a tremendously pro-Zionist speech ... when one knows he is really not in sympathy with the Zionist cause.[13]

Churchill pleaded with Lloyd George that Britain should evacuate Palestine and the French do likewise with the Lebanon and Syria. He sent the last of these private appeals to the Prime Minister in June 1921 when, as Colonial Secretary, he held direct ministerial responsibility for Palestine.

In October 1919, Churchill presented to Lloyd George the military's view that the partition of the Ottoman Empire had been a mistake, which would involve expenditures for the construction of military establishments and development work far in excess of anything that Britain might hope to recover in return. He described the incendiary state of affairs in the Middle East in apocalyptic terms, against the context of the government's commitment to the Greeks:

> Venizelos and the Greeks he represents (in whose future we have so great a interest) may well be ruined as a result of their immense military commitment in the Smyrna Province. The French are about to over-run Syria with hordes of Algerian troops and will soon be involved in a protracted and bloody struggle with the Arabs who are defending their native land.[14]

In somewhat contrived terms, as if the Turks represented the acme of Western liberalism, he claimed that the partition of their Empire would be a "crime against freedom", which would lead to accusations that they [the British] had abetted "the conquest of the Arabs by the Turks ... deserting, and, it will be alleged, betraying those Arabs who fought bravely with us in the war". He pleaded that Britain already had much more Empire than she could possibly develop for several generations, and argued that they might succeed in compelling "other Powers to give up their exploitation claims against Turkey" only if they set an example:

> The Greeks should quit Smyrna, the French should give up Syria, we should give up Palestine and Mesopotamia, and the Italians should give up their sphere.[15]

Churchill also warned against the government's support for the Zionists:

> Lastly, there are the Jews, who we are pledged to introduce into Palestine and who take it for granted that the local population will be cleared out to suit their convenience.

In a further private letter to the Prime Minister, sent in June 1920, Churchill elaborated upon the expense and risks entailed in the government's support for the Zionists:

> Palestine is costing us 6 millions [pounds sterling] a year to hold. The Zionist Movement will continue to cause friction with the Arabs. The French ensconced in Syria with 4 divisions (paid for by not paying what they owe us) are opposed to the Zionist Movement & will try to cushion the Arabs off on to us as the real enemy.

He predicted:

> The Palestine venture is the most difficult to withdraw from and one which certainly will never yield any profit of a material kind.

In December 1920, still smarting at public criticism of the outlay of £40 millions that it had cost to put down the rebellion in Iraq, Churchill wrote again to Lloyd George:

> I deeply regret and **resent** being forced to ask Parlt [sic] for those appalling sums of money for the new Provinces ... They [the military] disapprove of the policy against Turkey and do not care about Mesopa [sic] or Palestine ... all the extra expense of Army estimates arises from this evil combination.[16]

On 1 January 1921, at a New Year's Eve party at the home of Sir Philip Sassoon (a wealthy Jewish magnate), Churchill was persuaded by Lloyd George to take over the Colonial Office. He agreed to the move on condition that the jurisdiction of his new department be expanded to include the Middle Eastern mandates, and Egypt. Lord Curzon, the Foreign Secretary, successfully resisted Churchill's demand for Egypt.

It is doubtful whether Churchill considered the Colonial Office to be a promotion, but rather he saw it as a stepping stone to a higher position. But Lloyd George had other ideas, and their relations remained volatile. Within a month of Churchill assuming his new post, they sank to a nadir. In March 1921 (while Churchill was visiting Jerusalem), Lloyd George passed him over for the vacated position of Chancellor of the Exchequer, a position considered to be a stepping stone to the premiership, one that Churchill believed was rightfully his.[17]

At the Colonial Office, Churchill's main concern was with the urgent need to reach an agreement on the Middle East with Kemal Pasha's Turkey. Churchill believed that Palestine was an integral part of the Asia Minor problem, whose future, he was convinced, was contingent upon a final settlement with Kemal. By mid-1921, the Greeks were facing their nemesis in Smyrna.

At a special Cabinet meeting held on the morning of 31 May 1921, CIGS Wilson reported that the Greek army was on the point of collapse and was about to fall back on the port of Smyrna. If that happened, and Kemal then turned north, the small British force at the Straits would become vulnerable. Wilson advised the immediate evacuation of this force. At a second meeting that same afternoon, Churchill reminded his Cabinet colleagues about the still unsatisfactory situation in Palestine, and warned that Britain's tenure of the country was conditional upon there being no Turkish aggression.[18]

On the next day, 1 June, a meeting of the special Cabinet sub-committee on the Turkish crisis concluded that a Turkish occupation of Constantinople would be a great moral blow to Britain, "unacceptable except as the purchase-price of peace". Further, the committee was warned by the military that if the Turks did retake Constantinople, it would become almost impossible to hold on to Palestine and Mesopotamia. In a private letter to Lloyd George the next day, Churchill proposed "substantive negotiations" with the Kemalists, and the dispatch of an ultimatum to the Greek leader, Venizelos, making continued British support contingent upon his withdrawal first to the Smyrna coast, and ultimately, on a total evacuation by all Greek forces of Asia Minor.[19]

While these critical events in Asia Minor were demanding the Cabinet's urgent attention, Palestine had suffered a new round of internecine strife. On 1 May 1921, an outbreak of Arab disorder had required the urgent dispatch of reinforcements from Egypt. In a further private appeal to Lloyd George, in the middle of the riots, Churchill seized the opportunity of the delay in the ratification of the Palestine mandate by the League of Nations to urge Lloyd George yet again to give up the Middle Eastern mandates, in order to appease Mustafa Kemal:

> I now learn that the League of Nations wish to postpone the Mandates for Palestine and Mesopotamia until the Americans are satisfied ... I ought to warn you that if this course is followed, and if at the same time the Turkish situation degenerates in a disastrous manner, **it will be impossible for us to maintain our position either in Palestine or in Mesopotamia and the only wise and safe course would be to take advantage of the postponement of the Mandates and resign them both and quit the two countries at the earliest possible moment**, as the expense to which we shall be put will be wholly unwarrantable.[20]

But Lloyd George ignored all of Churchill's entreaties, as well as the protests of the military. He enjoyed Lord Curzon's support, on both Smyrna and Palestine. Curzon's world outlook was determined by his term as Viceroy of India (1899–1905), the "jewel" in the imperial crown. During the war, he became convinced that Palestine was of vital strategic importance for the Empire, as a defensive buffer to the north of the Suez Canal – the imperial shortcut to India.

Whereas Curzon had expressed strong reservations about the Balfour Declaration during the Cabinet discussions in October 1917, at the decisive Cabinet meeting at the end of the month, he agreed to its issue, mainly for propaganda reasons. During the following year, Curzon came to appreciate the strategic virtues of the Declaration. He was appointed by Lloyd George to chair the Cabinet's influential Eastern Committee, charged with determining Britain's post-war policy in the Middle East. In December 1918, he told the committee that the Balfour Declaration afforded Britain a legitimate right to remain in Palestine, which experience had shown was a strategic asset:

> Had not the whole history of the war shown us ... that Palestine is really the strategic buffer of Egypt and that the Canal, which is the weak side of Egypt, if it has to be defended in the future, it will have to be defended – as it has been in the war – from the Palestine side? We were tempted into Palestine by our position upon the Canal and by the threat of a Turkish invasion that inevitably drew us forward upon the Canal, drew us across

the Sinai Peninsula, and involved us in Palestine itself. Therefore, from the strategic point of view there is a close interest between Palestine and Egypt.[21]

Curzon's views reflected a general consensus within the Lloyd George administration that Palestine had to be Britain's strategic buffer to the Suez Canal, since in contrast to the Sinai desert, it was an inhabitable territory in which a military garrison could be stationed permanently. Thus Palestine became indispensable for a defence of the canal against a potential attack from the north.

Even Edwin Montagu reconciled himself after the war to British sponsorship of the Jewish National Home in Palestine. An "intransigent anti-Zionist" who had bitterly opposed the issue of the Balfour Declaration in 1917, Montagu now treated it as a *fait accompli*, a pledge that the government was duty bound to honour. In 1922, in a private letter to his cousin, Sir Herbert Samuel, who since July 1920 was serving as the first British High Commissioner for Palestine, he wrote:

> As you know, I regarded the Balfour declaration with strong opposition and disapproval, and even today would give anything that it should not have been made in the interests of the British Empire and of our race. But it seems to me that conflict of opinion on the basis of the policy must have ended when the declaration was announced and endorsed and any view held as to its advisability is only of historic interest. It is almost a platitude to say that Great Britain's promises in regard to the East particularly, and indeed elsewhere, ought to be kept and honoured without hesitation, and made as successful as human effort can make them.[22]

The Balfour Declaration under attack

After the war, the government's support for a Jewish National Home in Palestine excited fierce and bitter opposition, both in Britain and in Palestine. In Britain, the anti-Zionist campaign was infused with anti-Semitic prejudice, an accepted part of the nation's public discourse of the time. On the one hand, the Jews were stereotyped as "wealthy and powerful" and on the other, as the masterminds behind the Bolshevik revolution, the agents of universal social upheaval.

Indeed, many of the British establishment, including Cabinet ministers, harboured anti-Jewish prejudices. Their views were aired both in Parliament and in the press. In Parliament, the campaign was spearheaded by the Conservative opposition, in particular by the so-called "Tory die-hards", who in 1916 had elected to remain outside the Lloyd George coalition. The theme that the Jews were the masterminds of the Bolshevik movement was a prominent one in political circles during the 1920s.[23]

Parliamentary debates on Palestine were laced with anti-Semitic vitriol. In June 1921, in a Commons debate on the Colonial Office vote, Esmond Harmsworth – nephew of Lord Northcliffe, the press baron – resorted to anti-Semitic stereotypes, in an outburst that did not apparently evoke any protest in the House:

> I do not pretend to be either a Zionist or an anti-Zionist ... I say that it is a mistake that the taxpayers of this country should be asked to pay for a national loan to the Jews. **The Jews are a very wealthy class, and should pay for their own national home if they want it**. I have never yet met one who would go and live there, but, if they want their national home, after all, **they are the richest nation in the world, and let them pay for it**. As representing a portion of the British taxpayers, I do protest most strongly that any money of theirs should be thrown away in Palestine to provide for that home.[24]

Just over a year later, William Ormsby-Gore MP (a future Colonial Secretary) asserted in the Commons that the opponents of British policy in Palestine belonged to a long tradition of native anti-Semitic prejudice:

> Then there is what I call quite frankly the anti-Semitic party, that is to say those who are convinced that **the Jews are at the bottom of all the trouble all over the world ... it is the rich Jews who are all blood-suckers and the poor Jews all Bolshevists** – they have the particular Hebrew mania, and they have fastened on Palestine with a view to paying off those mediaeval scores.[25]

Parliamentary opposition to Zionism was supported by the right-wing press. It has been suggested that for this section of the press, "Zionism represented an invasion of the Holy Land by godless Bolsheviks". On 23 November 1917 (3 weeks to the day after the issue of the Balfour Declaration), *The Times* published an article repeating the calumny that the Bolsheviks were "adventurers of German-Jewish blood and in German pay".[26] The anti-Zionist campaign was motivated in part by the personal animosity of the Conservative press barons – Lord Northcliffe, owner of the influential *Times* and *Daily Mail*, and Lord Beaverbrook, who controlled the mass-circulation *Express* group – against Lloyd George, whom they regarded as "the dominant and malign political force" in the country. Their papers accused the government of wasting taxpayers' money in order to finance the establishment of a national home for Zionist Jews in Palestine. The Jews were stereotyped as "foreign, powerful, wealthy, money-grubbing, arrogant and pushy".[27]

In February 1922, Lord Northcliffe visited Palestine for 1 week. On 14 February, on his way back home, he held a press conference in Cairo. It was duly reported in *The Times* the next day, under the headline "Palestine Dangers. Arrogance of Extremists. 'A Second Ireland'". Northcliffe avowed that he was himself an "old supporter of Zionist ideals", but admonished that the "natural apprehension [and] alarm felt by the overwhelming Muslim and Christian majority" was due entirely to the public declarations of the "Zionist extremists". He warned that unless greater consideration was shown for the rights of the native population, Palestine might become a second Ireland.[28]

Two days after his Cairo press conference, a *Times* editorial reflected the ambivalent feelings of not a few of the English upper class towards the Jews and Zionism:

> We have strongly supported the Zionist ideal, which seemed to us to afford an opportunity of releasing the Jews from the ambiguous and anomalous position that they occupy in many countries, and to enable them to recover a natural equilibrium by a progressive affirmation of their natural individuality ... Yet it is a task of the utmost difficulty and delicacy to import into modern Palestine, with its quiet, easy-going Muslim and Christian population, the dreamers of the ghettoes of Eastern Europe.
>
> They [the Jews] come with the marks of bitter racial and party conflict upon them. They come with disturbing, often with revolutionary, ideas and habits ... they condemn and criticise, often unjustly and unfairly, with a peculiarly irritating asperity, everything that conflicts with their preconceived ideal.[29]

Upon Northcliffe's return to London, *The Times* adopted a distinctly anti-Zionist position. It became one of the most outspoken public voices against the government's Palestine policy, and sponsored publications against what Northcliffe termed "extremist Zionism".

At the same time, it should be emphasized that whereas government officials and ministers could not have failed to be aware of the anti-Semitism that fuelled much of the opposition to Zionism, none could ignore the existence of very serious problems in the relations between the Arabs, Zionists and British in Palestine. These problems could not simply be ignored, no more than the public agitation in Britain could be dismissed as only empty, racist bigotry.[30]

Some scholars have claimed that when the Conservatives took office at the end of 1922, they were on the point of abrogating the Balfour Declaration. Bernard Wasserstein, one of Sir Herbert Samuel's biographers, has credited the High Commissioner with rescuing the Zionist cause single-handed:

> ... seldom had Britain's policy in Palestine seemed less of a *chose jugeé* than during the first half of 1923, when the entire government seemed occupied with delving into its very foundations.
>
> The weakness of the Zionists in 1923 both in Palestine and in British politics was such that a British decision to abandon the Jewish National Home might have aborted the Zionist enterprise. That the Cabinet

decided otherwise was not the least of the services rendered by Samuel to Zionism – although it was little recognized by Zionists then or since.[31]

Wasserstein argued that Samuel's warning that a final decision on future policy in Palestine could not be postponed any longer, due to the unsettled security situation in Palestine, was the decisive factor.[32] This argument is something of a *non sequitur*. The Cabinet hardly needed Samuel to remind it of the need for haste. Had the government given over-riding priority to Samuel's argument – the need to staunch the prolonged agitation in Palestine by appeasing the Arabs – its logical conclusion would have been to abandon Zionism and the Balfour Declaration, not the opposite!

In contrast, Dr Sahar Huneidi, an Arab scholar, has asserted that Chaim Weizmann deserves the main credit for the government's decision to adhere to the Declaration, due to his all-pervasive influence over John Shuckburgh, head of the Middle East Department at the Colonial Office:

> Weizmann had only to threaten to resign from the Zionist Organisation, thus leaving the movement in the hands of the "extremist elements", for Shuckburgh to bend over backward to give him his way.[33]

Echoing the *Protocols*, Huneidi concluded that Shuckburgh was:

> … without doubt manipulated by Weizmann, whose omnipresence at the Middle East Department promoted the Zionist cause and influenced British officials.[34]

Walid Khalidi, the noted Palestinian scholar, added his own embellishment, to the effect that Shuckburgh seems to have been "mesmerised by Chaim Weizmann".[35]

The claim that the British were on the point of abandoning the Zionist cause rests also on the contention that the Committee of Imperial Defence (CID) decided that "Palestine was not as important strategically as once thought", and that the General Staff ruled that the country was no longer essential for the defence of the Suez Canal.[36]

Dr Huneidi credits Weizmann with the remarkable feat of surmounting even this obstacle, single-handed:

> Weizmann had managed to convince British statesmen and politicians that the Balfour Declaration, which many had come to regard as a political mistake, meant much more than was originally intended, and that abandoning the Palestine mandate and the Zionist policy would lead to a severe loss of prestige and ethical stature for the British Empire. **Weizmann was able to do this despite the fact that the Committee of Imperial Defence had decided that Palestine was of no strategic importance to the British Empire.**[37]

In reality, the fate of the Jewish National Home in Palestine never hung on the word of either Weizmann or Samuel. The Conservative government's reassessment of its Palestine policy during the first half of 1923 was determined largely by two senior British officials: the first was Lord Curzon, the Foreign Secretary; the second was Brigadier General Sir Gilbert Clayton, a senior British official in Egypt and, from June 1922, the Chief Secretary-designate to the Palestine administration. General Clayton's expert military opinion on Britain's need of Palestine as a strategic buffer to the Suez Canal served as a useful counter to the negative voices emanating from the COS (see Chapter 7).

Notes

1 Wilson's diary quote in *Field Marshal Wilson, Bart, His Life and Diaries*, vol. II, ed., Sir Charles Edward Callwell, London: Cassell, 1927, p. 293.
2 cf. Michael J. Cohen, *Churchill and the Jews*, revised paperback edition, London: Frank Cass, 2003, p. 62.
3 Wilson-Haldane, 28 December 1920, in Martin Gilbert, *Winston S. Churchill*, companion vol. IV/3, Houghton Mifflin, Boston, 1978, pp. 1275–76; Wilson's reference to leaving "lower" Mesopotamia, except for "Basra and the oil-fields country" arouses the suspicion that his knowledge of the country was not all that might have been expected. The main oil reserves of that country lay primarily in the northern region of Mosul.
4 Churchill to Lloyd George, 4 December 1920, and Churchill to Cabinet meeting of 13 December 1920, cited in Cohen, *Churchill*, p. 70.
5 Churchill speech on 14 July 1921, *House of Commons Debates* (*H.C. Deb.*), 5th series, vol. 144, col. 1626.
6 Wilson diary entry, 1 May 1920, in Gilbert, *Winston S. Churchill*, companion volume IV/2, p. 1078.
7 Mustafa Kemal had commanded the Turkish forces that trounced the British at Gallipoli in 1915; Churchill, as First Lord of the Admiralty, had been the principal sponsor of the abortive British attempt to force the Dardanelles with naval forces alone and seize Constantinople.
8 Cohen, *Churchill*, p. 63.
9 ibid, pp. 65–66.
10 Churchill to Lloyd George, 4 December 1920, Gilbert, *Winston S. Churchill*, companion volume IV/3, pp. 1260–62.
11 Over 1 million Greek Christians were displaced; most were resettled in Attica and the newly incorporated Greek territories of Macedonia and Thrace. They were exchanged with some half a million Turkish Moslems displaced from Greek territories.
12 cf. Martin Gilbert, *Churchill and the Jews*, London: Simon & Schuster UK, 2007; also review by Michael J. Cohen, "The Churchill-Gilbert Symbiosis: Myth and Reality", *Modern Judaism*, vol. 28/2, May 2008, pp. 204–28.
13 Maxwell Coote diary entry of 29 March 1921, cited in Richard Toye, *Lloyd George & Churchill: Rivals for Greatness*, London: Macmillan, 2007, p. 219. The speech Coote referred to was apparently delivered in Jerusalem, where Churchill stayed for a week after the Cairo conference.
14 For this and following, cf. Churchill to Lloyd George, 25 October 1919, in Gilbert, *Winston S. Churchill*, companion volume IV/2, pp. 937–38.
15 For this and following see Gilbert, *Winston S. Churchill*, companion volume IV / 1, pp. 484–85.

Palestine and the Near East, 1919–23   73

16 Gilbert, *Winston S. Churchill*, companion volume IV /3, pp. 1260–62. Emphasis in original.
17 Churchill cut short his visit to Palestine and rushed back to London in quest of the office – much to the disappointment of his Zionist hosts. cf. Cohen, *Churchill*, pp. 72, 89; on Churchill's relations with Lloyd George, see Toye, *Lloyd George & Churchill*.
18 For this and following, cf. Cohen, *Churchill*, pp. 93–97.
19 ibid, p. 95; the war in Smyrna dragged on for another year; in September 1922, having defeated the Greeks in Smyrna, Kemal's Turkish forces moved north to the Straits, posing a threat to the small Anglo-French force stationed near Canakkale (Chanak) where they were guarding the Dardanelles neutral zone. The handling of the crisis by Prime Minister Lloyd George, supported now by Churchill – when a battle against a superior Turkish force was avoided only because the local British commander refused to obey government orders – was a major factor leading to the downfall of his government; on the Chanak crisis, cf. idem, p. 326.
20 Gilbert, *Winston S. Churchill*, companion volume IV /2, pp. 1489–91. My emphasis.
21 Cited in David Lloyd George, *The Truth about the Peace Treaties*, vol. II, London: Victor Gollancz, 1938, p. 1147.
22 Bernard Wasserstein, *Herbert Samuel: A Political Life*, Oxford: Clarendon Press, 1992, p. 259.
23 On the respectability of anti-Semitism in England during the early decades of the twentieth century, cf. Peter Stansky's perceptive *Sassoon: The Worlds of Philip and Sybil*, London/New Haven: Yale University Press, 2003, pp. 207 ff.; see also Chapter one of this book.
24 *H.C. Deb.*, 5th series, 14 June 1921, vol. 143, col. 332. My emphases.
25 ibid, 22 July 1922, vol. 156, col. 264, my emphasis; Ormsby-Gore served as Under-Secretary of State for the Colonies from October 1922 to January 1924, and from November 1924 to August 1925, and as Colonial Secretary from 1936 to 1938.
26 cf. David Cesarani, "Anti-Zionism in Britain, 1922-2002: Continuities and Discontinuities", *Journal of Israeli History*, vol. 25(1), 2006, p. 136; quote from *The Times* in Kadish, *Bolsheviks*, p. 10.
27 Cesarani, ibid, p. 134. For Lloyd George's account of Northcliffe's hostility to himself and to his government, cf. Lloyd George, *The Truth About,* vol. I: pp. 265–70, 558–60. Alfred Harmsworth, the first Lord Northcliffe (1905), was the founder of modern journalism in England; he became owner of *The Evening News* (1894), *Daily Mail* (1896), *Daily Mirror* (1903) and *The Times* (1908). Canadian-born Max Aitken, Lord Beaverbrook (1917), was the founder of modern, mass-circulation newspapers in England; he bought the *Daily Express* in 1916, and the *Sunday Express* 2 years later.
28 Cohen, *Churchill*, p. 137.
29 *The Times*, 17 February 1922.
30 Evyatar Friesel, "British Officials on the Situation in Palestine, 1923", *Middle Eastern Studies*, Vol. 23, No. 2, April 1987, p. 201.
31 Wasserstein, *Samuel*, 1992, pp. 241, 264. Wasserstein states that it was clear that Samuel's meeting with the Cabinet committee set up in 1923 to determine policy in Palestine would be "crucial" but apart from noting that Samuel defended his policy "brilliantly", he does not elaborate further; cf. Bernard Wasserstein, *The British in Palestine: The Mandatory Government and the Arab-Jewish Conflict, 1917–1929*, London: Royal Historical Society, 1978, pp. 125–26.
32 Wasserstein, *The British*, p. 75.
33 cf. Sahar Huneidi, "Was the Balfour Policy Reversible? The Colonial Office and Palestine, 1921–23", *Journal of Palestine Studies*, vol. 27/2, Winter 1998, pp. 30–31.

John Shuckburgh founded the Middle East department at the Colonial Office in February 1921, and headed it until 1931.
34 Sahar Huneidi, *A Broken Trust: Herbert Samuel, Zionism and the Palestinians*, London/New York: I.B. Tauris & Co. Ltd, 2001, p. 237.
35 Foreword to ibid, p. x.
36 cf. Huneidi, "Was the Balfour", p. 35, and *A Broken Trust*, p. 74; also Gideon Biger, *An Empire in the Holy Land: Historical Geography of the British Administration in Palestine – 1917–1929*, New York: St Martin's Press, Inc., 1994, p. 73.
37 Huneidi, *A Broken Trust*, p. 76. My emphasis.

4 The military administration, 1918–20

> I dislike them all equally, Arabs, Jews and Christians in Syria and Palestine, they are all alike, a beastly people ...
> General Congreve (GOC Palestine) to CIGS Wilson, 1 April 1920

Preservation of the *status quo*

The British conquest of Greater Syria from the Turks began in 1917, with General Allenby's conquest of Gaza and Beersheba (October and November) and Jerusalem (December). It was completed 1 year later, on 1 October 1918, when Allenby's forces occupied Damascus, the Syrian capital, without a battle (the Turkish army had fled northwards several days before).[1] World War One in the Middle East was at an end.

In December 1917, Allenby set up a "provisional" military regime in Palestine. In April 1918, in anticipation of the rout of Turkish forces in the Middle East, an Occupied Enemy Territory Administration (OETA) was established for what had been Ottoman Syria. Palestine was designated OETA South.[2]

Most of the senior personnel of the military administration were professional soldiers, with little or no prior training or experience for the job at hand. The administrative and personal skills required were not taught at military staff colleges. The general impression created was that of "a collection of unqualified amateurs haphazardly thrown together by the war and told to run a country".[3] Ronald Storrs, who served as the first British military governor of Jerusalem (1917 to 1921), recorded in his memoirs that the administration had included:

> a cashier from a bank in Rangoon, an actor-manager, two assistants from Thos. Cook, a picture-dealer, an Army coach, a clown, a land valuer, a bo'sun from the Niger, an organist, an Alexandria cotton-broker, an architect ... a Junior Service London postal official ... a taxi driver from Egypt, two schoolmasters and a missionary.[4]

This motley collection, which in civilian life had "been engaged in virtually every occupation but colonial administration",[5] ruled Palestine from late 1918 to the end of June 1920. The military administration in Palestine was a unit of the Egyptian Expeditionary Force (EEF), under the supreme command of General Allenby in Cairo, which came under the purview of the War Office.

The formal and legal assignment of OETA in Palestine was to preserve the *status quo,* until the country's political future was decided by an appropriate international body. The Hague Convention of 1907 had determined that no occupying power had the right to legislate new laws "unless they were clearly necessary for the welfare of the population". Neither could existing laws and customs be annulled. For as long as the military ruled, no physical changes were permitted, except those deemed necessary for military purposes. In the case of Palestine, since the *status quo ante* had been Turkish military rule during most of the war, and prior to that, retrograde Ottoman rule, strict passivity meant leaving the country without any reasonable transportation system, without either public education or health systems, and without government aid to agriculture, commerce or industry.[6]

The military refused to act on proposals for economic development, regardless of whether they were initiated by British experts or by the Zionists. Even when it became clear that the British would continue to rule Palestine, its economic development was left to the future civil administration. Most of OETA's actions were taken to serve the interests and needs of the army. One sphere in which the military administration did invest heavily was the construction of an extensive network of roads, to facilitate the transfer of military personnel and matèriel across the country.[7]

As noted in the previous chapter, the British General Staff were against Britain assuming control of the Middle East mandates. But issues of high policy were determined by the Foreign Office (until February 1921, when the Colonial Office took charge), which leaned on the advice of its own man-on-the-spot, the "Chief Political Officer".[8]

However, it proved impossible to separate military from political issues. British assistance to the Jewish National Home, as promised by the Balfour Declaration, was regarded by the military as a violation of the *status quo.* Inevitably, the military did not follow Foreign Office instructions to avoid all involvement in "politics".[9] The military's over-riding concern – to avoid or reduce to a minimum any conflict with the Arab world – determined their opposition to Zionism.

The military conceded that the Balfour Declaration had been a wartime necessity, but insisted that it would be folly to continue to adhere to it after the war. They warned that continued support for the Zionists endangered Britain's vital interests in the Arab and Moslem worlds. They pleaded incessantly with London for the revocation of the government's Zionist policy. They rejected Zionist claims that Arab opposition to Zionism was artificial, or that it could be contained by firm British resolve. They insisted that the Declaration could be imposed only "at the point of British bayonets".

There was also a lack of personal chemistry between the Zionists and the officers of OETA. The latter were not accustomed to having the "natives" look them in the eye and answer back – especially not when they were Jews. Major General Sir Louis Bols, who in 1919 succeeded Major General Sir Arthur Money as Chief Administrator of Palestine, confessed to being "sick and tired of receiving orders from those subservient to him". He was not so much motivated by politics as offended by a lack of due respect. Following the riots of April 1920, he sent the following tirade against the Zionists to GHQ Cairo:

> The Zionist Commission did not loyally accept the orders of the Administration, but ... adopted a hostile, critical and abusive attitude ... With one or two exceptions, it appears impossible to convince a Zionist of British good faith and ordinary honesty ... they seek not justice from the military occupant, but that in every question in which a Jew is interested, discrimination in his favour shall be shown.[10]

The military preferred the local Arabs, with their "veneer of 'cringing' good manners", to what some officers referred to as "the hordes of Jews from Eastern Europe", with their "terrifying brilliance at chess".[11] Ronald Storrs later wrote a reasonably detached description of the position in Palestine:

> The British officer, work as he might, felt himself surrounded, almost opposed, by an atmosphere always critical, frequently hostile, sometimes bitterly vindictive and even menacing ... when I revisited Palestine in 1931, and found the British Administration fully convinced that in any future crisis, while the Arabs might be their enemies, the Jews certainly would be, I could not help asking how far these wild, derisive indignations could be said to have furthered the cause of Zion.[12]

In March 1918, Dr Chaim Weizmann, the Zionist leader, arrived in Palestine at the head of a Zionist Commission (renamed the Palestine Zionist Executive in 1921). The Commission derived its authority from article four of the draft mandate, which was approved by the Cabinet in November 1920 and submitted to the League of Nations. The article included the following declaration:

> An appropriate Jewish Agency shall be recognized as a public body for the purpose of advising and co-operating with the Administration of Palestine in such economic, social, and other matters as may affect the establishment of the Jewish National Home and the interests of the Jewish population in Palestine, and, subject always to the control of the Administration, to take part in the development of the country.
>
> The Zionist Organization and constitution, so long as its organization and constitution are in the opinion of the Mandatory appropriate, shall be recognized as such an agency.[13]

The Zionist Commission's terms of reference included overseeing the practical implementation of the government's support for the establishment of the

Jewish National Home – subject to General Allenby's authority. The Commission was supposed to have acted as a liaison between the Yishuv (Jewish community in Palestine) and the British authorities on the one hand and the Arabs on the other.

But relations between the Commission and OETA deteriorated and became strained. With some justification, the military feared that the Commission was undermining their authority, by promoting Zionist affairs in Palestine to the point of "provoking Arab hostility and usurping functions proper to the government".[14] They were infuriated by the powers that some Commission members presumed to arrogate to themselves, and by their arrogant attitude towards British officers. They were exasperated more than anything else by the apparent ease with which some members of the Commission were able to go over their heads to mobilize ministerial, parliamentary and public pressure in London.[15] Ronald Storrs reflected the general consensus in his memoirs:

> Leading Jews in England were known to have the immediate ear of more than one Cabinet Minister: no Arab had.[16]

As with most of the myths about Jewish influence in the corridors of power, this one was a gross exaggeration. But Storrs rested his case on no less an authority than the semi-official *Survey of British Commonwealth Affairs*:

> ... one further inequality. This was the inequality of access to the ear of British democracy. Jewry was represented in every layer of English society – in the Lords and the Commons, in powerful capitalistic organizations and in the Labour Party, in the press and in the Universities.[17]

Official co-operation between OETA and the Commission deteriorated steadily and eventually died out. British officers objected to the Commission's pressure to lift the ban on Jewish immigration and refused to reopen Palestine's doors to the Jews – all in the name of the preservation of the *status quo*; they permitted the return only of some of the pre-war Jewish inhabitants of Palestine who had been deported by the Turks during the war; OETA also objected to Zionist pressures to provide full employment for the Jews in the public services. Some of the Commission's members managed to arouse the antagonism even of leaders of the Yishuv, who resented their foreign brethren's haughty, at times patronizing attitudes. The Arabs regarded the Zionist Commission, with its quasi-official status, as the embryo of a Jewish government, the instrument with which London intended to set up a Jewish state in Palestine.

OETA prohibited the publication of the Balfour Declaration in Palestine, on the grounds that it would provoke public disorder (the Declaration was in fact readily accessible through the Egyptian press, copies of which were regularly available in Palestine). The military also banned the playing of the Jewish National Anthem (*Hatikvah* – the Hope) on public occasions, and all land sales. The laying of the foundation stone for the Hebrew University in Jerusalem was held up until 1925 when symbolically, Lord Balfour attended the ceremony as guest of honour.[18]

Many of the British officials who served in Palestine during the mandate would have agreed with Storr's final verdict:

> ... a people [the Jews] can be at once bitterly wronged and yet withal so maddeningly tiresome as sometimes to annihilate surprise, though never regret for their suffering.[19]

What London regarded as a question of high policy – the fulfillment of the Balfour promise to the Jews – was seen by the military as a military issue. They pleaded with London to force the Zionists to modify their plans for large-scale immigration and land settlement, to cease their provocative talk of a Jewish state in Palestine, and to behave less arrogantly towards the local Arabs. They warned of the dire consequences for British imperial interests should the government continue to support the Zionist cause:

> ... practically all Muslims and Christians of any importance in Palestine are anti-Zionist and bitterly so ... if we mean to carry out any sort of Zionist policy we must do so with military force and adopt a strong policy against all agitators in the country ... We must also be ready to risk disorders in the Muslim world at large and be prepared for the propaganda that is certain to be made with regard to Jews taking possession of the Holy Places and the Holy Land.[20]

The military's mindset

As with other parts of the Empire, the British brought to the Middle East an innate sense of their own superiority, with its attendant prejudices. This was evident at the most senior levels of the army, from the CIGS in London to General Congreve, GOC the Egyptian Expeditionary Force from 1919 to 1922, down to the junior officers in charge of day-to-day affairs in Palestine.

The views and opinions of the British in Palestine about the Jews reflected those *à la mode* in the home country. As noted already (Chapter 1), during the first decades of the twentieth century, anti-Semitism was an accepted part of the cultural norms of English society, a regular ingredient of public discourse.

Cairo was the centre of British anti-Zionist and anti-Jewish sentiment in the Middle East. During the war, the Arab Bureau had fostered the Arab revolt against the Turks, and many senior officers there felt committed to an Arab-British alliance. The publication of the Balfour Declaration in 1917 aroused profound misgivings. Six weeks after its issue, Brigadier General Clayton, chief of British intelligence in Egypt from 1914 to 1917, wrote to Mark Sykes, warning of dire consequences:

I am not fully aware of the weight which Zionists carry, especially in America and Russia, and the consequent necessity of giving them everything for which they ask, but I must point out that by pushing them as hard as we appear to be doing, we are risking the possibility of Arab unity becoming something like an established fact and being ranged against us.

He next resorted to a worn anti-Semitic stereotype:

The Arab ... finds that the Jew with whom he comes into contact is a far better business man than himself, and **prone to extract his pound of flesh**.[21]

Anti-Semitic comments appeared frequently in the intelligence reports that the Army GHQ at Cairo sent to London. One particular source of friction between the army and the Jews was the Jewish Legion, which Lloyd George had agreed to mobilize in 1917.[22] General Allenby and his staff feared that the political aspirations of the Legion's three battalions were in direct conflict with British interests in the Middle East. The military were concerned above all with the post-war challenges to British rule posed by the forces of Arab nationalism in the region: Saad Zaghlul's nationalist movement in Egypt, and the rebellion which raged in Iraq through the summer of 1920. London's support of Zionism was regarded by the military as a "superfluous fly in the ointment".

A GHQ intelligence report of January 1918 was particularly derogatory about the question of the conscription of Russian and Polish Jewish *émigrés* in England. As with most documents pertaining to the Jews, the report went beyond strictly military issues. It derided "this monied and artful race" for their success in avoiding conscription, "through medical deception and the manipulation of the special tribunals". The report concluded with a condemnation of:

... the grabbing propensities of the Jewish tribe for buying up businesses on the cheap where forced sales were made by Englishmen who had been called up.[23]

After the war, Lt Colonel Eliezer Margolin, the Jewish commander of the 39th battalion, wrote a stinging, even if subjective indictment of OETA's treatment of the Jewish Legion:

Everything has been done to hamper, damp down and suppress Jewish effort, both civil and military, in Palestine. This anti-Semitic policy even went so far as to attempt the elimination of the Jewish units ... This anti-Jewish attitude filtered down through all channels ... men were made to feel that they were the "despised race" ... No stone was left unturned in order to discredit us in every way.[24]

When Arab riots against Zionist immigration broke out in Palestine on 1 April 1920 (see p. 85ff.), General Congreve sent his personal assessment direct to CIGS Wilson. He began with a frank admission of the military's sympathies for the Arabs and their fears of a Zionist takeover. He reassured Wilson that: "Everyone has accepted the Government adoption of Zionism loyally and there have been no acts which can be interpreted as hostile to it". But inevitably, his colonialist hubris and racial prejudice raised their heads:

> To people living amongst the Jews in Palestine it is difficult to dissociate the theory of Zionism with the actual man on the spot who is anything but attractive and **when you add … the centuries of aversion to Jews born in us it is hardly expected that private feeling can be pro-Jew** … But I dislike them all equally, Arabs, Jews and Christians in Syria and Palestine, they are all alike, a beastly people, **the whole lot of them is not worth one Englishman**.[25]

Congreve would hardly have allowed himself such an outburst to a superior officer had he not known his correspondent well. Sure enough, CIGS Wilson replied in kind, identifying himself fully with Congreve's views:

> I quite agree with you that the whole lot, Arabs, Jews, Christians, Syrians, Levantines, Greeks, etc. are beastly people and not worth one Englishman.[26]

The majority of the officers of OETA South – Palestine – were no less bigoted. Their preconceptions about the Jews were reinforced by the contents of the *Protocols of the Elders of Zion,* which some brought with them to Palestine in their kitbags.[27]

The views of Major General Sir Arthur Money, the first "Chief Administrator" of OETA South, were not atypical. Money was somewhat exceptional in having a colonial background. His family had served for generations in India. He himself had prior experience of the military administration of an occupied territory – Mesopotamia. It has been suggested that he brought with him to the Middle East, as part of his mental baggage, "much of the social and political outlook of the world of [Forster's] *A Passage to India*".[28]

In November 1918, in an official report on Palestine for the General Staff, Money derided the Jews as a class that "were inferior morally and intellectually to the bulk of the Muslim and Christian inhabitants".[29] The very fact that the commander of OETA included such comments in official dispatches speaks for itself. However, he confined his most disparaging comments about the Jews to the privacy of his personal diary. His entrenched prejudices about the Jews were confirmed for him in Palestine, almost at first sight. Shortly after his arrival, he entered a crude, bigoted reference to the religious Jews of Jerusalem in his diary: " … dirty idle wasters … their women more prostitutes than the rest of the population put together".[30] A few months later, in a personal letter to a friend, Money repeated the sentiments that he had already placed on official record: "I've always found the Mohammedans out there (the better class at any rate) much straighter than the Jews and Christians, who speaking generally are a pretty low lot".[31] Had such comments been published, they would have raised not a few blushes at Whitehall, and would possibly have precipitated Money's dismissal. In any case, he stayed in Palestine for barely a year, leaving the country at the end of July 1919, feeling unable to carry out the Zionist policy dictated by London. In a private letter written a month before his departure, he cast aspersions against those Jews whom he alleged held sway over the heads of government in London: "I am the more inclined to go since I see every prospect of the edifice I have built with some labour being pulled down by Messrs. Balfour, Lloyd George and their long-nosed friends".[32]

The high regard in which members of the British community in Palestine held the OETA officers indicates shared cultural values. One example was Charles Ashbee, a British architect who worked in Jerusalem for a short period as a government consultant. Ashbee had a clear preference for things Arab, for the "beauty and dignity" of timeless tradition. For example, he made great efforts to save Hebron's glassblowing craft from extinction. In contrast, he abhorred "the squalid ugliness and disharmony" which he believed the Zionists were bringing with them from the cities of Eastern Europe and the United States.[33]

Ashbee wrote of the British officers in Palestine:

> I have met that finer something in many of the officers, an idealism among the men, a dream of a nobler life in which the army is a finely tempered instrument.[34]

He admired General Money in particular: "with his clear, blue, sympathetic eyes". For Ashbee, Money was the epitome of the consummate English gentleman and officer:

> They couldn't have put a better man here – if he has the nerve to carry things through, and the means to his right hand.[35]

When Money left Palestine, Ashbee wrote a eulogy for him, which to some extent reflects the social mores and the insularity of the British elite in Palestine at the time:

> We saw General Money off today. I think we were all sorry to lose him ... He was not a great administrator, but he had something that made up for it. He was a loveable, conscientious, and honourable English gentleman whom everybody could trust – and what a long way that goes.[36]

Ashbee himself left Palestine in umbrage in July 1922, following a breakdown in a local government sewage project in Jerusalem's religious quarter. The resulting flood of sewage spilled over into the affluent Wadi Joz residential area in which he (and the Mufti of Jerusalem) lived. In his memoirs, Ashbee vented his spleen, dredging up familiar aspersions about the Jews' international influence:

> The best Muslim residential area in the city has now been flooded with the drainage of *Meoscheorim* [sic], and a pool of liquid sewage lies, at the moment of writing, in the lovely valley between the Grand Mufti's house and ours. For us it means that we shall probably not be able to return to our house. The property owners, all Muslims, are very angry. They have sent in petition after petition and all have been ignored ... Had the situation been reversed and the drains of a Muslim slum voided into the best Jewish quarter there would have been such a cry in Israel as would have moved Wall Street and Park Lane.[37]

Ashbee was far from sanguine about Palestine's future:

> Had he [Money] not been tired, and sick for home, or had he been ten years younger, many of the great things we have planned in the last two years might have been put through, but now – the outlook is cloudy. There are too many Anglo-Indians about.[38]

On the eve of his departure, General Money told friends that he had asked many people, in England and elsewhere, "why had England capitulated to the Zionists?"; if it was not for money, then what was it? But no one had been able to give him an answer.[39] The reason then current in Palestine, as reported by Ashbee, was an extravagant version of the myth about Lloyd George having promised Palestine to Weizmann as a reward for his having invented a new chemical process for the production of acetone during the war:

> [Weizmann] in the nick of time invented some ultra-Teutonic deadliness of gas and bombs capable of destroying no end of Germans and incidentally Jews.[40]

In Cairo, General Congreve shared the military's consensus about Jewish influence over the government in London. After meeting him in June 1921, one Colonial Office official noted:

> ... he [Congreve] and all his officers were certainly under the impression that H.M.G. were in the hands of the Zionist Organization, and that no matter what we said we were really pursuing an unfair policy in favour of the Jews.[41]

The military's convictions about Jewish influence in the corridors of power owed much to the general belief that the Jews had been the masterminds behind the Bolshevik revolution, which now threatened to engulf the world. This obsession with the Jews' universal machinations, the "Judeo Bolshevik myth" or "Judeo Bolshevik bogey", has been referred to in Chapter 1.[42]

In April 1920, General Congreve wrote to CIGS Wilson about "the complicity of the Jews in Bolshevism". A year later, he called the Zionists "Bolshevists very thinly disguised".[43] Following the riots of April 1920, General Bols wrote to Allenby a long letter of complaint about the Zionists. He drew upon a document written by a British official, "Some features of political Zionism", which appeared to have been inspired by the *Protocols*. He referred to "the undoubted existence of a ruling ring of Zionist Bolsheviks", and to the Jews' "destructive, tyrannical, and anti-Christian aims ... their insidious and unscrupulous methods and their domineering methods". Bols had no doubts about his "facts":

> The existence of this ruling ring is undoubted. They are Bolshevik in ideas; they are anti-British in every sense of the word ... The Jew should not be given any powers of government over Palestine ... To permit the Jew to govern the other peoples would be cruel to the extreme.[44]

One curious lacuna persists in our knowledge of the period – that is, the role played by Winston Churchill, Secretary of State for War for most of the period of the military administration in Palestine, and as such, their political sovereign. So far, no records have come to light on Churchill's attitude to the bigotry of the military administration in Palestine, not even in the voluminous official biography. We know little or nothing of Churchill's reactions to the numerous manifestations of the officers' anti-Semitism, and their frequent demands that London abandon its Zionist policy. In later years, notwithstanding his own occasional anti-Semitic *faux pas*, Churchill repeatedly accused the military of being infused with anti-Semitism. For instance, in 1942, when the military command in the Middle East protested against Zionist appeals to raise a Jewish force, he responded:

> ... it may be necessary to make an example of these anti-Semitic officers and others in high places. If three or four of them were recalled and dismissed, and the reasons given, it would have a very salutary effect.[45]

Senior British officers who had had no direct contact with either Zionism or Palestine also displayed an innate anti-Semitism at times. A case in point is a private letter written in 1941 by Air Marshal Sir Arthur Harris, who would earn notoriety as "Bomber" Harris. In a report from Washington complaining about how difficult it was to deal with the Americans, he included an entirely gratuitous jab at the Jews:

> ... when one is dealing with a people so arrogant as to their own ability and infallibility as to be comparable only to the Jews and the Roman

Catholics in their unshakeable conviction that they alone possess the truth.[46]

When writing his war memoirs in 1948, Churchill wanted to include the following charge about the military and members of his wartime administration:

> All our military men disliked the Jews and loved the Arabs ... General Wavell was no exception. Some of my most trusted Ministers like Lord Lloyd, and, of course, the Foreign Office, were all pro-Arab, if they were not actually anti-Semitic.

Sir Norman Brook, Attlee's Cabinet secretary, who also served Churchill as an advisor on his memoirs, persuaded him to delete this particular passage. Brook explained that he was not disputing the validity of Churchill's charges, but he feared that they would be taken out of context and exploited in the current political controversies over Palestine.[47]

Stereotypes about the Jews' international influence proved difficult, if not impossible, to eradicate. For instance, in 1982, an officer who had served in the Palestine police wrote in his official history of the force: "For a hundred years Jews held high places in the Intelligence systems of world powers".[48]

The 1920 riots – the dismissal of OETA

In 1920, many Palestinians, encouraged by some of the senior officers of OETA, still hoped for a cancellation of the mandate, or at least for the annulment of British patronage of the Jewish National Home. Until the summer of 1920, when the French routed and exiled King Faisal from Syria, many Palestinian Arabs hoped for the reabsorption of Palestine into Greater Syria, as it had existed before its division by the French and the British.[49] Some OETA officers believed that they could finesse the home government's commitment to the Zionists by extending the Hashemite hegemony from Syria to Palestine. They behaved as if they were quite ignorant of official Foreign Office policy, which in 1911 had publicly promised Syria to the French.

On 14 January 1920, Colonel Waters-Taylor (Chief of Staff, OETA, 1919–20) met with the Emir Faisal in Beirut and, without any authorization, encouraged him to demand an "undivided Syria", in which Britain would recognize him as "overlord of the entire Fertile Crescent, while maintaining British military administrations in Mesopotamia and Palestine".[50]

On 7 March 1920 Faisal was proclaimed king of an independent Greater Syria, by the Syrian Congress in Damascus. This induced intense excitement in Palestine, and sparked off a series of demonstrations calling for reunion with Syria, under Faisal's rule. General Bols (supported initially by Allenby) sent a series of telegrams to the Foreign Office urging Britain to recognize Faisal as "overlord of Palestine". The unrest in Palestine was exacerbated by one of the worst storms in the history of Jerusalem, and by food shortages.[51]

On 4 April 1920, Arab riots broke out in Jerusalem, following the traditional procession that marked the annual Nebi Musa pilgrimage.[52] The military administration had received advance indications of disorders, but had shrunk from banning what had always been a strictly religious event – not wishing to infringe the religious *status quo*. After the pilgrimage, masses of incited Arabs from all over the country swept into Jerusalem. Faisal's portrait was paraded in the streets, to wide acclaim. Initial attacks on Jewish passers-by soon developed into full-scale rioting. Ironically, the Arabs' principal target was the religious, anti-Zionist Jews who lived in the Old City of Jerusalem. Looting and killing raged for the next four days, the majority of the victims being old men, women and children. Total casualties were nine people killed, five of them Jews, and 244 wounded, 211 of them Jews.[53]

On the morning of 4 April, Ze'ev Jabotinsky and Pinhas Rutenberg visited Storrs, as representatives of the nascent Jewish defence force, the Haganah. The two stated that they had trained, armed men on standby, and demanded permission to deploy them to protect the defenceless Jewish quarter in the Old City. Storrs refused.

The British believed that the Jews must be disarmed, in order to avoid provoking the Arabs. Their premise was that they had no option but to reject all Zionist demands to carry arms. Accession to Jewish demands would have contradicted one of the most fundamental of imperialist axioms – that the colonial power must have an absolute monopoly over the means of coercion, and that there could be no questioning its ability to assert and preserve order. The Jews were hardly familiar with this type of logic nor with the rigours involved in ruling a worldwide colonial Empire. Inevitably, they took the British refusal as conclusive proof of their anti-Semitism.

But the British themselves failed to protect the Old City. In mid-1919 there had been only 22 Jewish policemen in Jerusalem; by the time of the riots in April 1920, that number had risen to 27, compared with 156 Arab police. When the riots erupted, there wasn't a single British police constable inside the city. This situation had come to pass notwithstanding the clear Jewish majority in the city, and the known unreliability of the Arab members of the police force – most of who joined the rioters on 4 April.[54] With the wisdom of hindsight, the historian of the Palestine police noted later:

> ... the Palestine Police were simply never going to get Arab or Jewish recruits who could be expected to divorce themselves from such sacred and incompatible causes, and here the problem was acute. Even if a Palestinian police officer was luke warm in political, religious and racial beliefs, he could not afford to appear impartial because he had to live with the community as did his wife and children.[55]

OETA had to fall back on the army. Yet rather than attempt to disperse its troops throughout the labyrinthine alleys of the Old City, the army deployed outside the city walls, in the hope of preventing additional rioters from entering Jerusalem. The troops outside the city did possibly prevent the riots from developing into a full-scale pogrom. However, they did nothing to prevent or halt the arson and acts of violence that proceeded unchecked inside it.[56]

Notwithstanding Storr's orders, Jabotinsky organized a desperate and rudimentary Jewish self-defence unit. But he and his men were arrested by British troops on their way into the Jewish quarter. A member of the Zionist Commission trying to take in food and medical help was also arrested.[57]

The army and the Palestine police were two, virtually separate, almost insulated authorities. After the event, Edward Horne, the official historian of the Palestine police, laid the major part of the blame for the riots on the Zionists, specifically on Jabotinsky.[58] He alleged that the Arabs were incited to riot by the young Jewish immigrants that Jabotinsky organized in a parade of the streets of Jerusalem, campaigning for the mobilization of a Jewish defence force. Horne held stubbornly to his Machiavellian assertion about Jabotinsky, even if he conceded that no concrete evidence was ever produced. He insisted that Jabotinsky's actions had been a "serious contributory factor" and conjectured:

> ... only the administration seemed astonished at the violence ... Some of the ex-Turkish police officers were not a bit surprised ... These men knew what could happen during *Nebi Musa* unless one took precautions. Jabotinsky was no fool, he clearly knew too; and one is left with the thought that he deliberately set out to incite the Arabs in order to claim the need for Jewish protection.[59]

Horne makes no mention of the sponsorship of the Greater Syria idea by senior British army officers as a factor that incited the Palestinian Arabs against the mandate; nor the fact that Arab policemen joined the rioters; nor does he note that the demonstrations took place despite a warning given to Arab nationalist leaders by General Bols on 12 March that he was prohibiting all further demonstrations.

In fact, Horne confuses the 1920 riots with those of 1921! His assertion that the Palestinians were protesting against Jewish immigration was correct for the second round of Arab riots, in May 1921, but *not* for April 1920, when the Arabs focused their attack against the non-Zionist, religious Jewish community of the Old City of Jerusalem.[60]

In the wake of the riots, the Foreign Office set up a committee of inquiry composed of three military officers, headed by Major General P. C. Palin, the GOC Palestine.[61] The committee's report, which was never published, was submitted to the Foreign Office on 1 July 1920 – the very day on which General Bols handed over control of Palestine to the incoming High Commissioner, Sir Herbert Samuel. The report, which faithfully reflected the views of the military, was sharply critical of the Zionists, whom it accused of exacerbating Arab anxieties, by their "impatience, indiscretion and attempts to force the hands of the Administration". However, the report also criticized the poor operational functioning of the military command – specifically for withdrawing all troops from Jerusalem early in the morning of 5 April, and for the undue length of time it took the army to regain control once martial law was proclaimed.

OETA's downfall was brought about largely by Colonel Richard Meinertzhagen, the Chief Political Officer. As noted already, Meinertzhagen was something of an anomaly, a British officer who supported Zionism, notwithstanding some deeply entrenched anti-Semitic traits. After meeting Weizmann, whose lifelong friend he became, he described him in terms reminiscent of the "Bolshevik bogey" myth at its wildest: "An enemy of society, and his real aims go further than Zionism for they encompass the destruction of all society which hinders revolutionary ideas".[62]

Perhaps his preference for the Zionists owed something to his imperious, derisive dismissal of the Arabs: " ... an admirable looter and jackal among mortals ... decadent, stupid, dishonest and producing little beyond eccentrics influenced by the romance and silence of the desert".[63] In a long letter to the Foreign Office, written less than a week after the end of the riots, Meinertzhagen vented his accumulated spleen against the military. He accused them of negligence before the riots and of laxity in not suppressing them more quickly. He overlooked the fact that he himself had reported to the Foreign Office four days before the riots that he did "not anticipate any immediate trouble in Palestine".[64]

When apprised of Meinertzhagen's accusations, General Allenby was furious. He accused him of insubordination and demanded his dismissal. Meinertzhagen duly lost his post, but the damage had been done. His report reached Lloyd George at a critical juncture, during the San Remo conference, where the British and the French were dividing up the Middle East between them.

The two colonial powers continued to act as if they were still living in the nineteenth century. They were able to do so since President Wilson had already been shunted to the sidelines of history – his vision of a new world order of internationally negotiated peace agreements had been rejected by the American people. Lloyd George secured French acquiescence to British rule over Palestine and, with Curzon's reluctant concurrence, decided on the summary dismissal of OETA. It was to be replaced by a civil administration headed by a high commissioner, with his official residence in Jerusalem.

The establishment of a mandatory regime in Palestine, *ad hoc*, involved the brushing aside of a number of legal niceties. Britain had yet to secure a formal peace treaty with Attatürk's resurgent Turkey, therefore the premature disposition of occupied Turkish territory prior to a formal peace treaty might be adjudged invalid under international law.[65] Further, the League of Nations – the body that was supposed to award the mandates over former Ottoman territories, and from which the mandatory powers would derive their authority to administer their new gains – had yet to be formally instituted. The League's official award of the Palestine mandate to Britain still lay some 18 months in the future.

Lloyd George's choice for Palestine's first high commissioner was Herbert Samuel, a Jew. Samuel had held three junior ministerial positions in Asquith's Liberal government (1909–14), and had served for less than a year as Home Secretary in his 1916 coalition. Once out of office, he drew close to the Zionists, and in 1919 served as an advisor to their official delegation to the Versailles Peace Conference. In January 1920, the government dispatched him on a 2-month study visit to Palestine. It was assumed that Samuel would become the first head of a civil administration in Palestine after the termination of the military regime. However, during his short stay in Palestine, he was taken aback by the strength of Arab opposition to Zionism, and developed doubts about the wisdom of his appointment. Near to the end of his visit, he confided presciently to his son Edwin:

> The more I see the conditions here the more I am confirmed in my original opinion that it would be inadvisable for any Jew to be the first Governor. It would render more difficult, I am inclined to think, and not more easy, the fulfillment of the Zionist programme ... With a Jew as Governor, many measures would be viewed with suspicion and would provoke antagonism which would be accepted without much question at the hands of a non-Jewish British Governor.[66]

Unsurprisingly, some of the senior British officers in Palestine and Cairo were expressing similar concerns about Samuel's appointment. Their comments reflected their entrenched prejudices. On 7 May, General Bols wrote to Allenby:

> By British government the people of the country understand a non-Jewish Government, because they know that a British Jew is a Jew first and a Britisher afterwards ... I fear that British Christian officers will not be found to take service under a Jewish Governor.[67]

Bols' views served as the basis for an apocalyptic warning telegraphed by Allenby to Foreign Secretary Curzon, who still held ministerial responsibility for Palestine:

> I think that appointment of a Jew as first Governor would be highly dangerous ... They [the Palestinian Arabs] will regard appointment of a Jew ... even if he is a British Jew, as handing the country over at once to a permanent Zionist Administration ... I anticipate that when news arrives of appointment of Mr. Samuel general movement against Zionists will result, and that we must be prepared for outrages against Jews, murders, raids on Jewish villages, and raids into our territory from East if no wider movement.[68]

Curzon told Samuel that he would not back down, but suggested by way of compromise an "interim Christian Governor" for one year. But Lloyd George would not hear of any delay in Samuel's appointment. Samuel himself was hesitant. He wanted to learn first what the Jewish community in Palestine thought. A delegation of the Yishuv then in London, fearing a continuation of the OETA administration, pleaded with him to take up the position forthwith.[69]

Samuel decided not to take any final decision until he had consulted with Weizmann. The latter formed a poor initial impression of Samuel: "weak, frightened and trembling, altogether too cautious". But perhaps this very same assessment led Weizmann to believe that he would be able to control him, once he was ensconced at the high commissioner's residence. Indeed, it has been suggested that once Samuel took up office, Weizmann treated him as if he were a member of his own staff. In any case, the Zionists could hardly reject the Jewish nominee of a British Prime Minister. Moreover, they were still in a state of shock after the April riots, and filled with anxiety lest military rule continue.[70]

In April 1920, on his way back from a holiday in Florence, Samuel visited Lloyd George at San Remo. Weizmann was there also, lobbying for the Zionist cause. Lloyd George and Balfour formally offered Samuel the position of high commissioner. Samuel's emotions prevailed over his reservations, and he allowed Weizmann to persuade him to take up the offer. Lloyd George urged him to expedite his departure for Palestine.

Frances E. Newton, an Englishwoman who lived for some 50 years in Palestine, commented caustically in 1948 that the real reason why the military government was changed to a civilian one in 1920 was:

> Since it had not been possible to induce the soldier administrators as a body to become tools of Zionist policy, the Military Administration was abolished, and a Government, euphemistically called "Mandatory" was set up, which could enforce obedience from its employees.[71]

Britain's military occupation of Palestine, like all other regimes of its kind, was never intended to be anything other than transitional. But the circumstances of its precipitate demise, like many other aspects of British policy in the Middle East during this period, was not the product of a considered policy, but almost a whim of Lloyd George's own personal fancy.

Sir Herbert Samuel arrived in Palestine on 30 June 1920, and took over the reins of government from General Bols the next day. The civil regime that assumed control over Palestine remained under the jurisdiction of the Foreign Office until February 1921, when it was transferred to the Colonial Office, under Winston Churchill.

Even after the military occupation rule of Palestine came to an end, questions of policy and security in the country remained inextricably intertwined. Following a second round of Arab rioting in May 1921, the military again pressed the government in London to end its pro-Zionist policy in Palestine. At the end of May 1921, General Congreve warned Churchill that if the government continued to implement the Balfour Declaration:

> ... sooner or later the whole country will be in a state of insurrection and the only way of enforcing the policy and legislation will be by military force ... I must make it quite clear to you that the forces at my disposal in Palestine are not sufficient in case of organized insurrection.[72]

The War Office retained responsibility for security in Palestine until December 1921, when British imperial policy in the region was reorganized. A new strategy was introduced, which it was hoped would enable the British to control the vast desert expanses of the Middle East with reduced, less expensive forces. It was decided to deploy Air Force patrols to control the region. The new strategy was a lesson learned from Britain's failure to suppress the 1920 rebellion in Iraq with small, isolated army garrisons.[73]

As part of this general reorganization, responsibility for the security of Palestine was transferred to the Air Ministry, with headquarters in Iraq. This anomaly persisted until September 1936, when the Cabinet decided to dispatch a full division to Palestine to crush the first phase of the Arab rebellion. Military responsibility for Palestine was returned to the War Office, which was given the authority to proclaim martial law in the country, if required.

Notes

1. On the occupation of Damascus, cf. Elie Kedourie, "Faisal's Entry into Damascus, 1918", *Middle Eastern Studies*, vol. 1/1, 1964.
2. Bernard Wasserstein, *The British in Palestine: The Mandatory Government and the Arab-Jewish Conflict, 1917–1929*, London: Royal Historical Society, 1978, pp. 18–20.
3. ibid, p. 19.
4. Ronald Storrs, *Orientations*, London: Nicholson & Watson, 1937, p. 360.
5. A. J. Sherman, *Mandate Days: British Lives in Palestine, 1918–1948*, New York: Thames & Hudson, 1998, p. 42.
6. Gideon Biger, *An Empire in the Holy Land, 1917–1929*, New York: St Martin's Press, 1994, p. 92.
7. ibid, pp. 77, 92.
8. Wasserstein, *The British*, p. 18.
9. ibid, p. 20.
10. Fritz Liebrich, *Britain's Naval and Political Reaction to the Illegal Immigration of Jews to Palestine, 1945–1948*, London: Routledge, 2005, p. 30.
11. Storrs, *Orientations*, pp. 420, 432; Tom Segev, *One Palestine, Complete*, New York: Metropolitan Books, 2000, pp. 94–96.
12. Storrs, ibid, pp. 427–28. After serving as Military Governor of Jerusalem from 1918 to 1921, Storrs served as Civil Governor from 1921 to 1926, when he was appointed Governor and Commander-in-Chief of Cyprus.
13. Cited in Wasserstein, *The British*, p.133.
14. ibid, p. 66; the Zionist Commission was composed of several English Zionist Jews, headed by Dr Chaim Weizmann, and Nahum Sokolov, the Russian Zionist

leader; Major William Ormsby-Gore (a future Colonial Secretary) and James de Rothschild, a Jew, were attached as Political Officers; M. Sylvain Lévy, a non-Zionist, was attached as a representative of the French Government.
15 Wasserstein, *The British*, pp. 27, 53.
16 Storrs, *Orientations*, p. 415.
17 ibid, p. 419, note 5. *The Survey of British Commonwealth Affairs* was published by Oxford University Press in 1937 by the Royal Institute of International Affairs.
18 Wasserstein, *The British*, pp. 41–42.
19 Cited in Howard Sachar, *The Emergence of the Middle East, 1914–1924*, New York: Alfred Knopf, 1969, pp. 388–89.
20 ibid. p. 390.
21 Clayton to Sykes, 15 December 1917, cited in ibid, p. 23. My emphasis. Clayton and General Money resigned their positions in Palestine in July 1919.
22 Martin Watts, *The Jewish Legion and the First World War*, Basingstoke/New York: Palgrave Macmillan, 2004. In 1917, with the Balfour Declaration being considered by the inner war Cabinet, Lloyd George was interested more in garnering the support of American Jewry than with the potential military contribution of the Jewish battalions. The Legion played a small part in the battle for Megiddo (September 1918), but its significance was more symbolic than military; idem, p. 239.
23 ibid, p. 129.
24 ibid, p. 184. Margolin, born in Russia, had been a pioneer in Palestine before emigrating to Australia; during World War One, he served with the Zion Mule Corps at Gallipoli in 1915, and then with Australian forces in France, where he gained a commission and was awarded the DSO; he returned to Australia when the Jewish battalion was formally disbanded, after the 1921 riots in Palestine; idem, pp. 160, 234.
25 General Congreve to CIGS Wilson, 1 April 1920, the private papers of the CIGS, Field Marshal Sir Henry Wilson, HWW 2/52A/16, Imperial War Museum Archives, London. (hereafter, IWMA).
26 CIGS Wilson to General Congreve, 26 April 1920, HWW, 2/52A/17, IWMA.
27 Many of the officers were transferred to Palestine after serving on the staff of the Grand Duke Nicholas in the Caucasus; cf. Watts, *The Jewish Legion*, p. 163.
28 Wasserstein, *The British*, p. 22. Mesopotamia came under the purview of the India Office; it was conquered by British-officered Indian forces in 1918.
29 ibid.
30 Entry for 9 September 1918, ibid.
31 Entry for 16 October 1918, ibid.
32 Private letter of 9 June 1919, ibid, p. 48; see also A. J. Sherman, *Mandate Days: British Lives in Palestine, 1918–1948*, New York: Thames & Hudson, 1998, p. 53.
33 Segev, *One Palestine*, p. 167.
34 Charles R. Ashbee, *A Palestine Notebook, 1918–1923*, New York: Doubleday/Page and Company, 1923, p. 88.
35 ibid, p. 30.
36 ibid, p. 88.
37 ibid, pp. 205–6. *Meoscheorim*: Mea She'arim (one hundred gates) – the Ultra-Orthodox quarter.
38 ibid, p. 88.
39 ibid, pp. 90–91.
40 ibid. On the myth of Weizmann being rewarded for his invention of acetone, see Chapter 2.
41 Note of talks in Colonial Office, 16 June 1921, in Wasserstein, *The British*, p. 107.
42 ibid, p. 11.

43 General Congreve to CIGS Wilson, 1 April 1920, HWW, 2/52A/16, and 18 May 1921, HWW 2/25A/21, IWMA.
44 General Bols to General Allenby, 21 April 1920, in Wasserstein, *The British*, p. 67.
45 Churchill to Lord Cranborne, the Colonial Secretary, 5 July 1942, in Prem 4/51/9, NA.
46 Letter in the Harris collection at the RAF archives, Hendon, cited by Max Hastings, *Winston's War: Churchill 1940–1945*, New York: Alfred A Knopf, 2010, p. 150.
47 David Reynolds, *In Command of History: Churchill Fighting and Writing the Second World War*, London: Penguin: 2005, p. 191.
48 Edward Horne, *A Job Well Done: A History of the Palestine Police Force, 1920–1948*, Sussex: The Book Guild, 2003, p. 32. The book was first published in 1982 by the Palestine Police Force.
49 The French took over the Lebanon and Syria, the British, Palestine and Trans-Jordan.
50 Wasserstein, *The British*, pp. 60–61.
51 ibid.
52 Nebi Musa (the prophet Moses); regarded as the most important Moslem pilgrimage in Palestine, from Jerusalem to the alleged tomb of Moses, at a site near Jericho.
53 Wasserstein, *The British*, pp. 64–65.
54 ibid, pp. 47, 197.
55 Horne, *A Job Well Done*, p. 46.
56 Sherman, *Mandate Days*, p. 53.
57 Wasserstein, *The British*, pp. 64–65.
58 Jabotinsky was a veteran of the Zionist Mule Corps who saw action at Gallipoli in 1915, and later an officer in the Jewish battalions.
59 Horne, *A Job Well Done*, pp. 29–30.
60 As noted, OETA allowed the return of only a trickle of the pre-war Jewish community that had been deported from Palestine by the Turks during the war.
61 After OETA was disbanded, General Palin acted in London as an unofficial consultant to the various Palestinian Arab delegations that came to lobby the government. Wasserstein, *The British*, p. 116, note 6.
62 Cited in ibid, p. 52.
63 ibid.
64 Meinertzhagen to Foreign Office, 14 April, and 31 March 1920, ibid, p. 71.
65 Bernard Wasserstein, *Herbert Samuel: A Political Life*, Oxford: Clarendon Press, 1992, p. 242.
66 Samuel to son Edwin, 22 February 1920, ibid, p. 243.
67 Bols memorandum of 7 May 1920, Wasserstein, *The British*, p. 83.
68 ibid, p. 82.
69 ibid, p. 83
70 Wasserstein, *Samuel*, pp. 242–44, and Segev, *One Palestine*, p. 149.
71 Francis Emily Newton, *Fifty Years in Palestine*, Wrotham: Coldharbour Press, 1948, p. 142.
72 General Congreve to Churchill, 30 May 1921, cited in Wasserstein, *The British*, pp. 106–7. When the second wave of Arab riots erupted in Palestine on 1 May 1921, the government was forced to rush in troop reinforcements.
73 Cohen, *Churchill*, pp. 80–83. On the Cairo conference, see Aaron Kliemann, *Foundations of British Policy in the Arab World: The Cairo Conference of 1921*, Baltimore: Johns Hopkins Press, 1970.

5 Colonial Palestine

> It is quite true that a great many, I might say almost all, of the British Officials in Palestine, are not sympathetic to a Zionist policy which would be detrimental to the Arabs ... But if the whole of the present Staff were changed and replaced by others chosen by yourself, in six months the newcomers would hold precisely the same view.
>
> High Commissioner Samuel to Weizmann, August 1921

Social mores

The British concocted a convenient formula for carrying out their unique imperial mission in Palestine – the dual obligation to the Zionists, by virtue of the Balfour Declaration, and to the Palestinian Arab "natives", whose well-being the Declaration had promised not to harm. The plan was to encourage an influx of Western-educated Zionist settlers who "with their superior education, technological know-how, and capital, would bring material benefits to the 'natives' and provide the 'backward' Arabs with an example to which to aspire".[1]

Apparently, it never occurred to the British colonial mind (nor to most Zionists) that the material benefits brought by the Zionists to Palestine might disturb the socio-economic fabric of an essentially rural society, and that consequently they would *not* be welcomed by the "natives".

However, as will be seen in Chapter 7, another factor appealed equally, if not more to the imperial mind in London: the apparition that the cornucopia of Zionist-generated capital would enable a virtually bankrupt island-with-an-Empire to retain its strategic foothold in Palestine at little or no cost to the British taxpayer.

The British were quite certain that not only was their rule over non-Europeans part of the natural order of things, but that it would benefit them. This innate sense of mission and ascendancy served to stiffen British resolve and to sustain morale in Palestine for more than two decades. However, by the final years of the mandate, the officials' confidence in this divine order had all but evaporated.[2]

Once a civilian administration was established in Palestine in 1920, the country's moderate climate enabled officials to bring out their wives and children. The latter remained in the country until old enough to go to school – back in England, of course. The British tried to recreate in Palestine a microcosm of the society with which they were familiar back home – along with all of its trappings. They lived largely within the social confines of their own small community, which functioned according to English social norms that emphasized "decorum, deference and the avoidance of shame".[3]

Most officials were concerned "not to let the side down" and were moved by a burning ambition to move up the social and administrative ladders:

> They and their wives moved in a carefully choreographed round of official and unofficial entertaining, always with a keen eye to prize postings and advancement ... the game of relative advantage was played in offices, clubs, dining rooms and on occasion in bedrooms ... the salaries of all ranks were published, and everyone ... knew precisely which officers had private means to supplement official emoluments.[4]

With the arrival of the wives and families, there arose that quintessential symbol of British social status – the officers' club – for sports and social intercourse. The English class system was adhered to strictly. The ranks – police, soldiers and NCOs – were excluded from the officers' clubs. They frequented their own canteens, pubs and brothels. As elsewhere in the Empire, the "natives" were not allowed into the officers' clubs, except as guests of British members.[5]

The British also brought tennis to Palestine. One anecdote tells that when Lord Milner, the Secretary of State for the Colonies (1919–21), visited the country, he had tea with the Governor of Hebron and then enjoyed a game of tennis. Two Arab prisoners, complete with leg irons, were summoned to act as ball boys.[6]

In Palestine, as elsewhere in the Empire, the old boy school and university networks continued to function. Old Etonians and Oxford and Cambridge men all held their own reunion dinners. The clubs provided a respectable social venue for relatives and visitors, especially for the young and unattached. For instance, a young spinster might:

> ... extend her social circle and above all escape from the all too alien local colour into the comfortable English predictability.[7]

There were also many unofficial, informal social occasions: "dinners and lunches, tea parties, tennis matches, amateur theatricals, recitals, and 'at homes'". Officials loved to invite each other over for what they happily referred to as a "do". Frequently, they had invitations printed for the event, which were delivered by hand.

Considerable effort was invested in making officers feel at home. For instance, the main purpose of a road that the British paved between Latrun and Ramallah was to serve officers on their weekend family picnics.[8] At the initiation of a police inspector who missed his fox hunting back home, a hunting club was established near Ramle. Palestine had no foxes, so they made do with jackals, which were chased on horseback across cactus-strewn fields; members could buy especially tailored red coats, complete with buttons emblazoned with the insignia "Ramle Vale Jackal Hounds". In the Galilee, officers "took advantage of the open countryside to explore the pleasures of hunting and riding", much as they might have done in other corners of the Empire, or at home. Police ponies were used for polo matches, and on occasion, grouse hunts were held in the grounds of Government House, the High Commissioner's official residence.

But when the security situation deteriorated, especially from the mid-1930s, the British were forced to restrict or give up their various outdoor fun and sports activities.[9] Nonetheless, British sang-froid and the stiff upper lip remained the order of the day. Keeping up appearances in front of the "natives" was critical. Social calendars were adhered to even if curfews restricted some evening activities. In letters home and in conversation, British understatement was *de rigueur*. Entrenched public school jargon coloured letters home:

> Military confrontations and other incidents were consistently referred to as "shows"; random, sometimes murderous violence was played down as "riots" or "brigandage"; and long, seldom successful searches for guerilla bands in the countryside were described in terms of rough public-school games of hide and seek, with the police tracker dogs lending the proceedings an improbable sporting atmosphere that reminded some participants of hunting in the English countryside.[10]

The civil administration

Palestine was not a standard Crown colony, nor was it formally a part of the Empire. After World War One, nineteenth-century colonialist conceptions were revamped in the spirit of Wilsonian principles of self-determination. The League of Nations, the brainchild of President Wilson, produced a new term for colonial trusteeship – the "mandate". The official mission of the mandatory powers was to prepare peoples that had never enjoyed self-rule for independence. But once the United States opted out of international affairs, Great Britain and France resumed colonial "business as usual". They shared out between themselves the mandates over the newly created Arab states, the progeny of 400 years of Ottoman rule. They declared their good intention of training their new subjects for independent rule. As one historian put it:

> This new form of colonialism was said to incorporate international law, as well as the principle of democracy and justice, and respect for the

wishes of the inhabitants of each country ... Mandates could, theoretically, be revoked.[11]

But the League never revoked a British or any other mandate. The British were required to report annually to the League's Permanent Mandates Commission, whose official task was to ensure that the mandatory power adhered to the principles prescribed by the League, a body that proved too impotent to impose its will. In the absence of the United States, imperial Britain was the single most powerful member of the League, and until 1939 no one ever seriously questioned the way she ruled Palestine. In the summer of that year, the Zionists appealed to the League against the Palestine White Paper of the previous May, claiming that it was in breach of Britain's mandatory obligations to them. But World War Two intervened before the League's General Assembly could consider the issue at its annual assembly in September.

Palestine was ruled as a colonial autocracy. Its high commissioners, unfettered by any constitutional machinery, were answerable only to the government in London and, theoretically, to the League's Permanent Mandates Commission. All appointments, budgets and other decisions required London's approval. The home government determined whether to extend or shorten the length of each high commissioner's term of office. Sir Herbert Samuel (1920–25) was allowed just one 5-year term. Two high commissioners were relieved of or left their position in the wake of "disturbances" in Palestine: Sir John Chancellor's term was limited to just 3 years (1928–31), following the rejection of his policies after the Wailing Wall riots in 1929 (Chapter 10); General Sir Arthur Wauchope (1931–38), who enjoyed a very successful first 5-year term, had his second term cut short for failing to deal firmly enough with the second, more deadly stage of the Arab rebellion.[12]

As noted already, in February 1921, responsibility for the administration of Palestine was transferred from the Foreign to the Colonial Office. Due to the frequent changes of Colonial Secretaries (19 between 1919 and 1948), the permanent officials in London and the High Commissioner in Jerusalem were frequently the real arbiters of policy.[13] This continued for the first 15 years of the mandate, until the advent of the series of crises that presaged World War Two. When the Arab rebellion engulfed Palestine in 1936, the Foreign Office assumed effective control of policy, and for the first time sanctioned the intervention of the Arab states in the affairs of Palestine.[14]

The High Commissioner was also the commander-in-chief, with the power of veto over decisions taken by the GOC. The latter assumed effective command only during the handful of short-lived periods of martial law. The judicial system in Palestine, nominally independent, was in the last resort also dependent upon the High Commissioner and the government in London. On one rare occasion, in 1936, when Chief Justice MacDonnell criticized an administrative decision in public, the Colonial Office, on the recommendation of the High Commissioner, had him removed. This was not so easy, since colonial judges, like their colleagues in England, enjoyed tenure for life.

MacDonnell turned down an initial offer of another colonial Chief Justice position, ostensibly on the grounds of ill health. Ultimately, in return for agreeing to leave Palestine, he was made an offer he could not refuse – a full pension plus 2 months paid leave (in order to pack up his household effects), although he was still 8 years away from the official retirement age.[15]

The rule of high commissioner has been described as:

> ... a benevolent dictatorship, its officials attempting doggedly to undertake the impossible task of continuing to favour, or at least permit, burgeoning Zionist development while somehow simultaneously accommodating Arab opposition.[16]

Although the British in Palestine were caught between a rock and a hard place, the appellation "benevolent" is hardly appropriate. As noted already, one of Britain's primary motives for retaining Palestine until the mid-1930s was its need for the import of Zionist capital to pay for the upkeep of the country.

Sir Herbert Samuel, the first High Commissioner, was a liberal by ideology and a Liberal by political affiliation. He arrived in Palestine with the mission of "civilizing" the country – with the aid of Jewish capital and brains. He applied "a Gladstonian parsimony of attitude to the balancing of budgets" and opposed "excessive state control or intervention". He did not want Palestine to become "a land flowing with licensed milk and registered honey".[17] This led to a situation that was described cynically by Charles Ashbee, a British architectural consultant in Jerusalem, as follows:

> The Administration ... is often forced into the illogical position of adopting methods of constructive socialism where Jewish affairs are concerned, but of preaching a serene and cold *laissez faire* when the interests are non-Jewish.[18]

Samuel was neither impartial nor detached when he took up his post. He was a practising Jew and a Zionist. As noted already, he accepted the appointment only after serious misgivings, against his better judgement. No one ever doubted his personal integrity, but he aroused in the Jews and the Arabs respectively exaggerated hopes and fears. His reactions to the second wave of Arab riots, in May 1921 (see Chapter 6), gave the Zionists cause to regret having urged him to take on the job. They were unable to comprehend the fact that he saw himself first as a servant of the British Crown, and only second as a Jew and Zionist. Samuel's hypersensitivity to his own delicate position between the Arabs and the Jews in Palestine caused him at times to adopt what today would be called a policy of affirmative action – in favour of the former.

Leonard Stein, an Anglo-Jewish barrister and one of Weizmann's inner circle, served as political Secretary of the World Zionist Organization from

1920 to 1929. In 1923, he wrote what was probably one of the milder, balanced Zionist verdicts on Samuel:

> I always felt that, just because he was a Jew, his very high-mindedness and scrupulous sense of propriety would, from our point of view, weaken his hands in carrying out the policy of the Mandate. He could not, or was bound to feel that he could not, do what a non-Jewish High Commissioner could. Consequently, from first to last, his regime has inevitably been a series of apologies and explanations. All this is part of the price we have to pay for a Jewish High Commissioner, in whom so many Zionists saw an invaluable asset.[19]

During the first 3 years of the mandate, the government made repeated attempts to establish legislative or advisory councils that would include Arab and Jewish representatives, in numbers vaguely proportionate to each race's percentage of the whole population. The Arabs consistently rejected all British initiatives, because each contained built-in guarantees for continued Jewish immigration and development. Arab participation would have meant acceptance of Britain's mandate and collusion with its patronage of the Jewish National Home (paragraph 4 of the Mandate for Palestine).[20]

In 1925, his last year in office, Samuel sought London's approval for yet another constitutional initiative – nation-wide municipal elections. The ensuing debate inside the Colonial Office reflects the anomalies produced by Samuel's almost obsessive attempts to introduce some of the trappings of Western democracy into Palestine. In contrast to Samuel, the Colonial Office had given up all hope of introducing any form of representative rule into the country. The department had lost patience with the High Commissioner, and blamed him for having led them into previous Arab snubs. The officials concluded that it would be neither "wise nor dignified" to give the Arabs a further opportunity of administering a humiliating rebuff to the government.[21]

But this was not the only reason for rejecting Samuel's proposal out of hand. New elections in Jerusalem would have jeopardized the policy of maintaining the *status quo ante* between the rival camps of Arab notables and the Jews. By 1925, the demographic balance in Jerusalem had altered in favour of the Jews, whereas the mayoralty remained an Arab fiefdom. The Colonial Office noted the anomalies and contradictions of this situation:

> It is probable that there are actually more Jewish than Arab electors in Jerusalem and the result of an election would almost inevitably be the appearance of a Municipal Council with a Jewish majority; the Jews would naturally demand a Jewish mayor and this would not only upset the whole Arab population of the country, but would also particularly annoy the "big" families.
>
> It is clearly out of the question to allow some municipalities to elect their own Councils and not allow the capital to do so; and the Colonial

Office do not feel satisfied that it would be possible for Jerusalem to do so without precipitating a serious Arab-Jewish conflict.

Neither do they feel convinced that a genuine demand for the institution of Municipal elections exists in Palestine except among that small class which would use such elections solely for the purpose of promoting anti-Government feeling ... in any case no final decision should be reached until the new High Commissioner has had an opportunity of reviewing the whole situation.[22]

Samuel's belief that he could introduce liberal institutions into Palestine while at the same time pursuing the Balfour Declaration policy was naïve, detached from the local reality. Most colonial officials appreciated that Western institutions were not relevant to the more traditional social fabrics prevalent in the Levant, especially not in the context of the Arab-Zionist conflict. As many of the permanent officials in Whitehall realized, there was never any chance that the various experiments in "constitutional carpentry" could have succeeded in reconciling the Palestinian Arab nationalists to British sponsorship of the Jewish National Home.

Whereas Palestinian Arabs and Jews had no influence upon the determination of policy in Palestine, many did accept office as civil servants in the British administration. In July 1921, Colonial Office figures listed 1388 Christian Arab, 719 Moslem Arab and 514 Jewish employees in government service. Roughly 20 per cent were Jews, at a time when they comprised approximately 11 per cent of the total population. By 1929, approximately 32 per cent of government officials were Jews, whereas they had now reached 19 per cent of the population.

In general, the Christian Arabs were more urbanized and better educated than the Moslems. They possessed a higher degree of professionalism and had a better knowledge of Western languages. This led to a disproportionate number of Christian Arabs in most government departments, and to an absolute majority in the civil service as a whole. This situation generated tensions between the Christian and Moslem sections of the Arab community. The number of Arab officials differed from department to department. Since the Zionists set up their own independent educational network, nearly all the teachers in the Department of Education were Arabs; since there were very few Arab engineers, hardly any of the senior officials in the Department of Public Works were Arab.[23]

The British never entrusted any senior positions of responsibility to the Arabs. No Arab was ever appointed as a head of department or as a district commissioner. Samuel's administration began with some 2500 employees.[24] By 1947 this number had burgeoned to over 30,000. Their salaries swallowed up 75 per cent of Palestine's annual budget.

The disproportionate number of Jews in the administration, in particular the strong Anglo-Jewish element during Samuel's term, symbolized for the Arabs the Anglo-Jewish axis. At one point, Churchill considered imposing a *numerus clausus* on Jewish appointments. Whereas Samuel opposed "fixing a definite number or ... imposing a residential qualification", he agreed with Churchill that "too large a proportion of British Jews in the Administration" would be "politically undesirable".[25] One colonial official commented cynically:

> An English Jew [official] needs more faith, courage, and imagination, and less sensitiveness and vanity than ordinary mortals, because he will often find himself in a pro-Jewish or a pro-Arab atmosphere: and he would find it difficult to say which was more offensive to him, to be disliked as a Jew or liked as a brother by the Yemenites.[26]

For the first 15 years of the mandate, the readiness of thousands of Arabs to work for the administration lent British rule a degree of legitimacy, and weakened the Arab national movement. Indeed, the British took on many Arab officials for that very reason. One of the first acts of the Arab nationalist leaders in 1936 would be to call a general strike of all Arab civil servants – a call which went unanswered. The civil service in Palestine did not produce any *esprit de corps* between Arabs and Jews. The divided loyalties of each race remained an ever-present "spoiling factor".

No one seriously believed that a single homogeneous Palestinian nationality would ever emerge, even if all permanent residents were granted Palestine passports. Both communities reserved their first loyalty for their own people, and only second to the British. The Christian Arab minority, always at pains to prove its patriotism, was frequently at the forefront of the Arabs' national struggle, especially in the increasingly influential Arab press, dominated by Christian Arab publishers.

The British and the Zionists

The Yishuv in Palestine initiated and developed its own social and political institutions. In contrast, parallel institutions for the Arab community, when developed at all, were initiated by the British from above. The British hoped that social and economic progress would help reconcile the Arabs to the Jewish National Home. But Arab institutions and communal progress lagged way behind that of the Jews, not least because the British remained reluctant to expend their taxpayers' money on Palestine, and the Arabs had no external resources comparable to those of the Yishuv. Thus instead of reconciling the two communities, as the British had hoped, their separate institutions only drove them further apart.

The Jews that the British encountered in Palestine presented a totally novel challenge. They were unlike any of the "natives" with whom they had traditionally interacted across the Empire. The Jews were not deferential, nor were they endowed with an innate, subservient charm comparable to that of the Arabs. They were rough-grained and didn't invest too much effort in trying to be affable. The Jews who migrated to Palestine from Europe were frequently better educated than the British officials they negotiated with. They were too clever and too stubborn by far for the liking of the average colonial official (or British officer). Colonial officials were not accustomed to being answered back, much less to being out-argued or outwitted. The Jews refused to be impressed or intimidated, even when the British official confronting them literally held the power of life and death over them, by virtue of emergency regulations. Even Weizmann thought that the Palestinian Jews "suffered delusions of grandeur".[27]

The Yishuv's self-confidence derived also from the fact that it was not dependent upon British economic subsidies. Not only that, but until the mid-1930s, they could be confident that the Jewish National Home enjoyed the official support of the home government, by virtue of the Balfour Declaration. Under Samuel, the Yishuv developed into a largely autonomous society, subsidized by funds mobilized by the world Zionist movement. Its social and political institutions were forged into a largely homogeneous, albeit insular "state-in-the-making". In October 1920, Samuel sanctioned the establishment of an elected Jewish representative assembly (Asefat Nivcharim) whose executive body, the national council (Va'ad Leumi), presided over all Jewish communal affairs. In December 1920, a national federation of Jewish Labourers (Histadrut) was founded, which not only organized and protected labour but also built up a community-wide social welfare network that included health care, education and housing. Lastly, in 1920, the Haganah, an underground Jewish defence force, was established, under the purview of and funded by the Histadrut.

The Yishuv was quite aware of the officials' preference for the Arabs. Its leaders drew up a detailed strategy for advancing closer relations with British officials, through social and sporting encounters. They tried to lure British officials to live in Jewish residential areas, by offering lower, subsidized rents. They even built tennis courts for their convenience. But all the Jews' efforts were in vain – the British simply preferred to live in Arab neighbourhoods.[28]

In July 1921, by which time Samuel had been in office for a year, Weizmann complained to him about the hostile attitude of his officials. In reply, Samuel quashed any idea that the Zionist might expect better treatment from a different set of people. He wrote presciently:

> It is quite true that a great many, I might say almost all, of the British Officials in Palestine, are not sympathetic to a Zionist policy which would be detrimental to the Arabs, and are not prepared to carry out with any goodwill a Policy which is likely to result in a regime of coercion. But if the whole of the present Staff were changed and replaced by others chosen by yourself, in six months the new-comers would hold precisely the same view.[29]

The officials' preference for the Arabs and their antipathy to the Jews are alluded to frequently in the diaries of Owen Tweedy, an English journalist who served in the British army in the Middle East during World War One, and later became a freelance journalist, working for some of the major London papers. In 1927 he visited Palestine in order to collect material for a series of articles on the country. His private diaries are replete with stereotypes of the Jews, and with the bitter, racist, anti-Zionist views of the British officials he interviewed. He spoke with "a Manchester Jew boy named Epstein", also a Dr Kohn, "a Jew and a German ... very dirty and slobbery". He found Yitschak Ben-Zvi, a leader of the Zionist labour movement and a future president of Israel, " not very clean". Siegfried Hoofien, director of the Anglo-Palestine Bank, impressed Tweedy with his "organized mind and logical explanations", although he added that Hoofien "had a hard mouth and is, I bet, a hard lender". He wrote of a visit to the Wailing Wall: "I left through lanes of mendicant Jews of all ages and stages of decay and got away feeling dirty". He found Tel Aviv no better. He fled the town – "pursued by a horrid little Yid waiter". In contrast, he found George Antonius, the Christian Arab intellectual who worked in the administration, as "helpful and as nice as ever".[30]

The problems created for the British by their open identification with the Arabs may be illustrated by two examples, each one indicating different aspects of their dilemma in Palestine.

The first case is that of Norman Bentwich, a British Jew, a barrister by profession, who first came to Palestine as a legal counsellor to OETA. Samuel promoted him to the sensitive position of Attorney General, the chief law officer in Palestine. As such, Bentwich served as a lightning rod for much of the Arabs' frustration with the administration. Although his integrity and loyalty were never in doubt, he, like many other Jewish civil servants, found himself in an impossible position, his personal loyalties strained and his every action subjected to criticism by one side or the other.[31]

Bentwich was finally hounded out of Palestine, largely due to a campaign mounted against him by Sir Michael McDonnell, the Chief Justice in Palestine, who openly supported the Arabs. McDonnell's scurrilous campaign prompted High Commissioner Chancellor to complain to the Colonial Office about his and his wife's prejudices:

> ... in connection with the action taken by the Chief Justice ... both he and Lady McDonnell are devout Catholics and like all Latins in Palestine are strongly anti-Semitic.[32]

Although the Colonial Office officials never doubted the personal integrity of Bentwich, many were inclined to accept the Chief Justice's criticism of him. Bentwich's alleged influence was inflated to levels that would not have embarrassed the authors of the *Protocols*. A widespread belief developed that he was the government's instrument for executing the Balfour Declaration. Sir Henry Grattan Bushe, the legal advisor of the Colonial Office, commented:

> It is not only the Arabs who hold these views; I have heard them from many British officials. Mr Bentwich is known as "the uncrowned king of Palestine", and it is universally believed that it is he who dictates the policy of the Government. I do not believe for a moment that he would consciously give any advice which was biased ... but his views are so extreme that I think he is unconsciously biased and at any rate there is a general belief to that effect which from the point of view of efficiency is almost as bad as though it were true. Moreover his whole life is wrapped up in the ideal of an independent Palestine, and he has not and will not accept the actual position. Over and over again his advice is tainted from this circumstance.[33]

Not only Bentwich's race, but his known espousal of Zionism worked against him. The universal belief that he was biased – quite regardless of the decisions he took on each individual case – made his position untenable. In 1929, he declined High Commissioner Chancellor's "invitation" to leave the country. The Arabs, lead by the Mufti of Jerusalem, threatened a general strike if he wasn't removed. Chancellor gave way to Arab protests, and told Bentwich that in future, all cases involving Arabs would have to be dealt with by the Solicitor-General. In November 1929, Bentwich was shot and wounded lightly in the knee. He recovered quickly, but the attack provided Chancellor with a pretext on which to remove him. In late 1930, Bentwich returned to London for a vacation, hoping to clear his name. But when he persisted in his refusal to resign, he was informed that Lord Passfield, the Colonial Secretary, had decided to terminate his appointment. He was "compensated" with a 1-year appointment to a Chair of International Relations at the Hebrew University, Jerusalem.[34]

Bentwich's "opposite number" was the Arabophile Ernest Richmond, a British architect, who identified himself openly with the Palestinian Arab cause. Richmond first came to Palestine at the invitation of his friend Ronald Storrs, in order to supervise the restoration of the Dome of the Rock in Jerusalem. On Storrs' recommendation, Samuel appointed him as his assistant Civil Secretary, with responsibility for Arab affairs. From this position, Richmond arrogated to himself the role of spokesman for Arab public opinion. Initially it was a role fully recognized and approved of by the beleaguered Samuel.

Richmond's virtues were extolled by Charles Ashbee, a fellow architect. Ashbee was the consummate example of a British citizen who formed his impressions on the basis of a short stay in Palestine. He had no real conception of, much less any interest in the government's international commitments to or its wider interest in supporting Zionism. He failed to understand the government's obstinate support for the Zionists, despite open Arab opposition. In 1923, upon his return to England, he published an "instant" record of his 3 years in Jerusalem. He conveyed his own views through a fictitious character pointedly named Mercutio. At one of Mercutio's meetings – with a

Zionist Ashbee called "Funkelstein" – Mercutio argued that Richmond was in fact the Zionists' saviour:

> Richmond is the sheet anchor of Zionism in Palestine ... and it is to the supreme credit of Samuel and his administration that he has not bent to the pressure of people like you to have him sent home ... You Zionists make me mad. You are so blind. Can't you see that it is he, and he alone that gives the Arabs confidence in an administration that for them would otherwise be wholly Zionist. The fact that there is an Englishman ... wholly devoted to Arab interests, an Englishman too of fearless and outspoken honesty ... is for them a standing sign of the impartial justice of the British Raj ... if it weren't for Ernest Richmond you'd be having your throats cut, and don't you make any mistake about that.[35]

Initially, Samuel would have agreed with Ashbee's estimation of the value of Richmond's services. He rebuffed all Zionist attempts to have him removed, and confided in Shuckburgh, head of the Middle East Department at the Colonial Office:

> ... in the absence of any Arab in the higher ranks of the Administration, Richmond, who is in close and sympathetic touch with the Arabs, acts as a most useful intermediary. If he were to go there is no one to take his place.[36]

Richmond's role as a counter to officials like Bentwich is epitomized by his role in the curious episode of the appointment of Haj Amin el Husayni as Mufti of Jerusalem (see p. 110). The appointment reflects Samuel's acute sensitivity to his own position as a Jew, and confirms his initial dependence on Richmond as the unofficial voice of the Arab community. Samuel deferred to Richmond's advice to appoint Haj Amin as Mufti, although he had placed only fourth in the Ottoman elections for the position. In doing so, Samuel went against legal convention, and against the advice of his two most senior officials – Bentwich, Legal Secretary at the time, and Colonel Wyndham Deedes, the Civil Secretary. Richmond dismissed the validity of Bentwich's advice on the ground that he was a Jew. He advised Samuel that it was generally believed that the Jews had opposed Haj Amin's election, that they had "fixed" the elections so that he would not be elected, whereas "the vast majority of the people" desired his appointment. This was hardly borne out by the election results, but Richmond added a decisive, racial argument:

> ... no opinion emanating from the Legal Secretary or his entourage or from anyone dependent in any degree on the favour of his Department will at the present time be regarded as other than suspect by a very large majority of the people in this country.[37]

Not only did Richmond presume to know what the Palestinian Arab consensus was, but he also presumed to be *au fait* with the nefarious machinations of the Zionist movement. In June 1922, he went over the head of Deedes, his superior, and sent to the Colonial Office a warning, flavoured with overtones of the "Judeo-Bolshevik" bogey, entitled "Tendencies and Dangers of the Jewish Labour Movement in Palestine". He asserted:

> The Zionist movement may be described in its local manifestation as a movement with a decidedly Communistic bias ... There can be little doubt that in the eyes of the Arab inhabitants (Muslim and Christian) what is actually happening is that Palestine is being made the seat of a social and political experiment affecting all classes of the population and abhorrent to the deepest convictions of the majority ... the Jewish movement includes interference with the social structure and national life of other communities, an interference prompted as they believe by a desire to disintegrate other communities.[38]

But Samuel turned against Richmond in 1923, as the latter's opposition to official policies became more flagrant and virulent. Relations between the two men became marred by animosity and personal affronts. Richmond accused Samuel of carrying out the government's policy dishonestly. He asserted that Samuel's racial origin was an obstacle, and urged the establishment of an administration whose personnel, rightly or wrongly, could not be accused of partiality.

In March 1924, Richmond resigned, moved to do so by the promotion over his head of another man to the recently vacated post of Civil Secretary. He was unable to reconcile himself to what he regarded as the government's support for Zionism. In an emotional letter to Samuel, turning down a dinner invitation, he condemned official policy in almost neurotic terms:

> I have been led gradually and most reluctantly, but definitely to a conviction that the Zionist Commission, the Middle East Department of the Colonial Office and this Administration are dominated and inspired by a spirit which I can only regard as evil, and that this spirit is ... acting in a manner that is not only unwise and impolitic but evil ... While forming part of this machine I have tried to alter it. I have completely failed ... Since things are so, I must go.[39]

The subject of Jewish influence and control of affairs in Palestine was a frequent topic of discussion inside the administration, one that caused Gentile officials great concern. Richmond's extremist views were shared by a great number of officials. They regarded the inclusion of Jews in the administration, by definition, as impolitic, if only because the Palestinian Arabs regarded it to be so. Brigadier General Sir Gilbert Clayton, who succeeded Deedes as Civil Secretary, shared Richmond's views. In March 1924, Clayton wrote a private letter to a friend decrying "an intangible 'something' behind everything, an unseen influence". In tones of desperation and resignation that echoed Richmond's, he concluded:

> Frankly, unless the place is to be run by Englishmen on British lines, I am off and that within a few months ... You cannot have Jews – however upright and honourable – in control, and hope to convince the Arabs that they are going to get a fair run.[40]

On the day after Clayton wrote this letter, Humphrey Bowman, the Director of Education, confided to his diary his belief that Samuel's religion disqualified him from holding the position of high commissioner. Notwithstanding the British Jews' legal emancipation, the civil liberties that they enjoyed, their rise to the peaks of British society and their proven integrity, Bowman still believed that they were not British enough:

> I believe he [Samuel] is perfectly honest, as far as he can be in his position: but he is not English, and therefore he is the wrong man for the job ... I do not see how any good can come to this country, until the Administration is British at the top and until the preferential clauses in the Mandate are changed.[41]

In 1927, Richmond, who had converted to Catholicism in 1926, returned to Palestine. He was required to give a commitment that he would not become involved in local politics, and he assumed the ostensibly apolitical post of Director of Antiquities (1927–37). His appointment was facilitated by Samuel's departure from the country in 1925, and by the appointment of a Gentile successor, Field Marshal Plumer. The British never again appointed a Jew to the position of High Commissioner for Palestine, or to any senior positions in the Palestine administration.

The British and the Palestinian Arabs

The British never hid their preference for the Arabs. William Ormsby-Gore, a senior Whitehall official, once commented:

> One can't help noticing the ineradicable tendency of the Englishman who has lived in India or the Sudan to favour quite unconsciously the Muslim against the Christian and Jew.[42]

Another example is Beatrice Webb, whose husband Sydney (Lord Passfield) was the Labour Colonial Secretary from 1929 to 1931. In October 1930, she noted in her private diary:

> Why is it that everyone who has dealings with Jewry ends by being prejudiced against the Jews? Sydney started with a great admiration for the

Jew and a contempt for the Arab, but he reports that all the officials, at home and in Palestine, find the Jews – even many accomplished and cultivated Jews – intolerable as negotiators and colleagues.[43]

In contrast to the Jews, the Arabs fitted into a familiar colonial mould, one that the British felt comfortable with – ignorant, suppliant natives, with "cringing good manners",[44] who could usually be relied upon to welcome the "benefits" of British rule. The British attitude to the Arab *fellahin* (peasantry) was typically one of paternalistic, condescending disdain. But they were grateful for the Arabs' "natural courteous deference to social and official superiors". However, British Arabophiles preferred the desert Bedouin. They epitomized the romantic image of the pristine, unspoiled-by-the-West authentic Arab, whose attributes included:

> ... chivalric virtues prized in the English public school, the testing place of physical hardship, tribal loyalties and intense male camaraderie.[45]

In contrast, the Palestinian Arabs were stereotyped as degenerate Levantines, of mixed race and questionable character.[46] One of the more benign assessments of the Palestinians was that of Douglas Duff, a naturalized Briton, who served in the Palestine police from 1922 to 1932. In his short book on Palestine, he reflected on the ambiguities of British sentiment towards them:

> For some queer conservative reason, the average Englishman's sympathies seem to fly towards the Arab ... Certainly he is picturesque in his medieval virtues, as he is terrible in his ancient vices and treacheries. His houses, his clothes, his appearance, perhaps the fact that we believe he is being harshly treated, as the weaker of the two protagonists ... tend to make so many of the British race espouse his cause. But even if you love the Arab, as I confess I do, you must admit his bad points – his laziness and dilatoriness, his contempt of keeping faith with anyone who is not of the religion, his fanaticism and his crass, willful ignorance.[47]

In a speech before an imperial conference in June 1921, Colonial Secretary Churchill explained why the British were not granting the Arabs the benefits of self-rule. With what has been called his own "brand of condescending, 'white man's burden' imperialist outlook", Churchill stated:

> There is no doubt that these turbulent peoples are apt to get extremely bored if they are subject to a higher form of justice and more efficient administration than those to which they have for centuries been accustomed. At any rate, we have reverted perforce, and by the teaching of experience, to more primitive methods.[48]

Churchill's sentiments were common currency at the Colonial Office. In November 1921, after months of frustrating, fruitless negotiations with the Palestinian Arab delegation in London, John Shuckburgh advised Churchill:

> It is submitted that the time has come to leave off arguing and announce plainly and authoritatively what we propose to do. Being Orientals they will understand an order, and if once they realize that we mean business, may be expected to acquiesce.[49]

In 1925, Humphrey Bowman wrote the following objection to a proposal for giving locally elected bodies more control over the education of their own children:

> The dangers of going too far or too fast in the matter of educational devolution can hardly be exaggerated ... In Europe the virtues of honesty, of truth, of straight and honourable dealing, of clean living, are taught in the home as well as at school. In Palestine, as in most Oriental countries, the inculcation of such virtues is left by the parent for the most part to the teacher.[50]

British citizens living in Palestine typically adopted a condescending attitude to the "natives". In October 1919, Ms E.P. Emery, the English headmistress of a high school for girls in Jerusalem, noted in her private diary:

> Nothing but a thorough-going despotism for a hundred years will pull this country together, for there is no section of the community which you could trust to rule at all, and the country has lived for so long under the Turks, that it will take ages to instill into the people any idea of public service, or truthfulness, or cleanliness.[51]

Her views were echoed by the wife of a British official in Jerusalem, who looked back to the Ottoman period with evident nostalgia. In April 1936, with the Arab rebellion raging, she compared the ruthlessness of the Turks – who had controlled the country with an iron hand with a mere handful of armed gendarmerie – with the lax attitude of Sir Arthur Wauchope, the fourth High Commissioner:

> H.E. is (we think) being much too lenient & inclined to talk to these blackguards instead of shooting them.[52]

British contempt for the Palestinian Arabs was matched by that of many Zionist leaders. Chaim Weizmann told General Money that it was pointless to try to negotiate with the Palestinians as they were a "demoralized race". He asserted that there was "a fundamental difference in quality between Jew and native", although he reassured him that the Zionists had no "desire to turn out Mohammed in order to put in Mr Cohen as a large landowner". He warned Balfour that the British should keep an eye on "the treacherous Arabs, lest they stab the Army in the back".[53]

In March 1923, Colonel F.H. Kisch, chairman of the Palestine Zionist Executive, blamed Samuel's "liberal" policies for the constitutional impasse with the Arabs:

> This situation cannot be expected to improve until the government puts its foot down ... In my opinion the present lamentable situation is the direct result of the application of the methods of English liberal administration to the government of an Eastern and backward people, accustomed to the strong hand of Turkish misrule.[54]

In the absence of any constitutional progress, Samuel adopted standard colonial procedure – making alliances with the native Arab elites. This policy has been called one of "personal rewards coupled with institutional changes that made the positions of their allies within the indigenous community seemingly inviolable".[55] In making the position of the indigenous notables dependent upon themselves, the British instilled in the Arabs a vested interest in their continuing to support British rule. In Palestine, the Colonial Office referred to the Arab clans as "the big families". Samuel secured the benevolent neutrality of the two major clans in Palestine – the Husaynis and the Nashashibis – by awarding each its own power and patronage base.

Soon after arriving in the country, Samuel issued a general pardon to all the Arabs whom the military administration had indicted for their role in the April 1920 riots. Among the pardoned was Haj Amin el Husayni, the younger scion of the Husayni family. Of the 13 mayors of Jerusalem since the incorporation of the city in 1864, six had been Husaynis. In 1921, elections were held for the post of the Mufti of Jerusalem. During the election campaign, Haj Amin accused the Nashashibi and Jarallah families of co-operating with the Jews to defeat him. He circulated pamphlets against the Jarallah candidate which read: "If Jarallah becomes the Mufti he would assist the Jews by selling to them the Waqf property" including that which included the Western (Wailing) Wall.[56]

Notwithstanding the fact that Haj Amin came only fourth in the Ottoman-style elections, Samuel appointed him as the Mufti of Jerusalem. He thereby broke the custom of choosing the winner from the three candidates who had secured the most votes. The British later gave Haj Amin the title "Grand Mufti", a post unknown during the Ottoman period.[57]

In January 1922, at a ceremony in Government House presided over by Chief Secretary Deedes, the Supreme Moslem Council (SMC) was established. The government gave the Council control over all Moslem *waqfs* (lands held in religious trust) and the courts of Islamic law (the *shari'a*). Again, with the government's support, Haj Amin was chosen as president of the new body – over the vigorous opposition of Ragheb Nashashibi, head of the rival clan.

Haj Amin became undisputed religious head of the Moslem community in Palestine, largely by virtue of his control of the huge patronage at the disposal of the SMC.[58] With British support, Haj Amin became the most powerful political figure in the Arab community. During the 1920s, he occupied himself with building up his own power base. A large part of the SMC's budget was disbursed in salaries to men who were almost exclusively members or supporters of the Husayni clan. From 1921 to 1931, the SMC's budget rose by 20 per cent, from £50,000 to £60,000. The British paid the bill, but relinquished all rights of audit or supervision.

Concurrent with Haj Amin's appointment as Mufti, Ragheb Nashashibi was appointed mayor of Jerusalem, replacing the Husayni mayor, who had been implicated in the riots earlier that year. Ragheb had represented Palestine in the Ottoman Parliament before the war, and would serve as mayor of Jerusalem from 1920 to 1934. Samuel also appointed as many Arab notables as he could to government positions. Haj Amin's political dominance was disturbed only briefly by a temporary setback in the 1927 municipal elections. He overcame this by leading a religious crusade against alleged Zionist designs on the Holy Basin in Jerusalem (Chapter 10).

The SMC was the only institution of Arab self-rule in Palestine, yet it was never subjected to any process of democratic election. In 1931, in return for the Husaynis' acquiescence in the government's retreat from the 1930 White Paper, the government agreed to the indefinite postponement of the electoral reform of the SMC, thereby relieving Haj Amin of the need to stand for re-election as its president.

A sympathetic biographer of Samuel has called his faith in Haj Amin: "a profound error of personal and political judgement". But his assertion that Samuel failed to perceive the Mufti's "bloated ambition to become leader of the entire Arab world" seems to be unmerited.[59] The Mufti's pan-Islamic ambitions developed only after Samuel's departure from Palestine, and except for a brief, violent interval in 1929, he remained outwardly subservient to the British until 1936.

It is a moot point whether Samuel or anyone else could have foreseen in 1925 the Mufti's later, nefarious career. The Mufti *had* been implicated in the 1920 riots, but Samuel evidently singled him out – in what appeared to be a smart move at the time – as a key Palestinian leader whose allegiance was worth purchasing. In 1923, Samuel told a Cabinet committee that he had appointed Haj Amin as president of the SMC so that he would serve as an intermediary between the British and the Moslem community. He congratulated himself that his move had proved to be a success. In view of the Mufti's future record, there is no little irony in Samuel's praise of him and his personal friends, as being:

> … always active in times of political crisis … in preventing people getting too excited and too violent.[60]

In historical perspective, Samuel's policy of winning (buying) over the Palestinian Arab notables enjoyed only an ephemeral success. It was a routine imperial gambit, employed when the Empire was at the zenith of its power. But allegiance to the British lost its allure for the Arabs during the 1930s, as they compared Britain's visible weakness and decline with the rise of Fascism and Nazism. Britain's alignment with the Husaynis unravelled with the Arab rebellion that began in 1936. In 1937 the Peel Royal Commission blamed the government for having allowed the SMC to become an *imperio in imperium*. By the time that the government dissolved the SMC in late 1937, the Mufti was already deeply involved in the organization of a terror campaign against the Zionists and the British administration.

Samuel's policy succeeded in holding the Palestinian national movement at bay for nearly a decade, during its incubation period. Samuel had never contemplated granting the Palestinian Arabs majority rule. It was self-evident that given half a chance, the Arabs would halt all further Jewish immigration and the development of the Jewish National Home, to whose progress the government remained officially committed, until 1939.

At the personal level, there was little social contact between the British and the Arabs, even if at the individual level, the British reveled in the Arabs' "exquisite courtesy and generous hospitality". As noted by one British officer of the Jewish faith, they found the Arabs – whether they "whine, or threatened, cajoled or protested ... always picturesque, ingratiating, sympathetic".[61] Ralph Poston, Wauchope's personal aide from 1931 to 1938, recalled that there had been virtually no socializing with either community. Very few of the British knew Arabic or Hebrew, whereas most of the Yishuv leaders knew English.[62]

Some of the British elite did socialize with a select minority of the Arab elite, the educated intelligentsia. Of particular note is the celebrated *salon* presided over in the mid-1940s by Mrs Katy Antonius, widow of the respected Christian Arab historian, George Antonius. Mrs Antonius was born into the Egyptian elite, daughter of Dr Faris Nimr Pasha of Alexandria, an Arabic expert and owner of the Egyptian newspaper, *Al-Muqadam*. Katy was fluent in several languages, and her *salon* became a "watering-place" not only for the elite of British society in Palestine, but also for "Western politicians, journalists, artists, notables from around the world" and many Arab leaders.[63] Richard Crossman, the British journalist and politician, who spent a few months in Palestine in 1946 as a member of the Anglo-American Committee of Inquiry, left the following description of one of her soirées:

> Evening dress, Syrian food and drink, and dancing on the marble floor ... It is easy to see why the British prefer the Arab upper class to the Jews ... This Arab intelligentsia has a French culture, amusing, civilized, tragic and gay. Compared with them the Jews seem tense, *bourgeois*, Central European.[64]

While the Yishuv developed the autonomous institutions – social, political and military – of a "state-in the-making", the Arabs, still dominated by their feudal clans, failed to develop any parallel institutions. Nonetheless, their overwhelming numerical superiority constituted an existential threat to the Yishuv. One scholar has noted the vulnerability of the Zionist enterprise during the first two decades of the mandate:

> The Jewish National Home, although a product of Jewish brains, Jewish sweat, and Jewish money, was in this period utterly dependent for its existence on British rule in Palestine.[65]

There is no way more fitting to close this chapter than with an extract from a personal description of Palestine written in 1934 by Sir Isaiah Berlin. Berlin, son of Russian *émigrés*, was brought to England by his parents in 1921 at the age of 11. In 1932, before his 24th birthday, he became the first Jew ever to be elected to a post at All Soul's College, Oxford University. In 1934, he visited Palestine and became an instant convert to Zionism. However, having reached the privileged, secluded pinnacle of English academia, and having been feted by the Anglo-Jewish establishment for his rare achievement, he had no intention of leaving his charmed life for the harsher clime of Palestine. His detached, ironic description of the country was written through the prism of "English eyes and through the filter of some very English metaphors".[66] His description of the Zionists contained an element of self-dislike, but also some home truths. He compared Palestine to an English public school:

> The High Commissioner was the headmaster; the Colonial Office was the Board of Governors; the school itself was divided into the Arab house and the Jewish house. Most of the masters liked the Arab house, because its pupils were "gay, affectionate, high spirited and tough, occasionally liable to break out and have a rag and break the skulls of a few Jews or an Englishman perhaps". The Jewish house, Berlin said, was full of able and rich boys, "who were allowed too much pocket money by their parents, rude, conceited, ugly, ostentatious, suspected of swapping stamps unfairly with the other boys, always saying they know better, liable to work too hard and not play games with the rest".[67]

Notes

1 Barbara J. Smith, *The Roots of Separatism in Palestine: British Economic Policy, 1920–1929*, Syracuse: Syracuse University Press, 1993, p. 7.
2 A. J. Sherman, *Mandate Days: British Lives in Palestine, 1918–1948*, New York: Thames & Hudson, 1998, p. 33, and Tom Segev, *One Palestine, Complete*, New York: Metropolitan Books, 2000, p.8.
3 Sherman, ibid, pp. 33, 48.
4 ibid, pp. 33–34.
5 ibid, p. 59, also Segev, *One Palestine*, p. 8.
6 Segev, ibid.
7 Sherman, *Mandate Days*, p. 59.
8 ibid, p. 51; Segev, *One Palestine*, pp. 8, 82.

9 Segev, ibid, p. 344; Sherman, *Mandate Days*, pp. 52, 67.
10 Sherman, ibid, p. 98.
11 Segev, *One Palestine*, p. 118.
12 Michael J. Cohen, "Direction of Policy", *Middle Eastern Studies*, vol. II/3, October 1975. When he completed his term, Samuel's request to settle down in Palestine was vetoed by his successor, Lord Plumer.
13 A notable example was the so-called "Churchill" White Paper of 1922, which in fact was drafted by Samuel and Sir John Shuckburgh, head of the Middle Eastern department at the Colonial Office.
14 See Cohen, *Direction,* p. 244; for the effect of the international crises on Palestine, cf. Michael J. Cohen, "British Strategy in the Wake of the Abyssinian Crisis, 1936–39", in Michael J. Cohen, Martin Kolinsky, eds, *Britain and the Middle East in the 1930s*, London: Macmillan, 1992, pp. 21–40.
15 Cohen, "Direction", pp. 248–52.
16 Sherman, *Mandate Days*, p. 63.
17 Bernard Wasserstein, *The British in Palestine, The Mandatory Government and the Arab-Jewish Conflict, 1917–1929*, London: Royal Historical Society, 1978, p. 87.
18 Charles R. Ashbee, *A Palestine Notebook, 1918–1923*, New York: Doubleday/Page and Company, 1923, pp. 269–70.
19 Stein to Kisch, 10 April 1923, quoted in Wasserstein, *Herbert Samuel: A Political Life*, Oxford: Clarendon Press, 1992, p. 261.
20 On the failure of the various constitutional initiatives in Palestine, see Wasserstein, *The British*, pp. 93, 122–29, 144.
21 Colonial Office memorandum, CO 733/110/260, NA. Previous "rebuffs" were the Arab boycott of the elections to a legislative council in 1922, and their veto of an advisory council, in 1923.
22 Ibid. The British permitted municipal elections in 1927.
23 Wasserstein, *The British*, pp. 167–69.
24 Memorandum by the Duke of Devonshire, the Colonial Secretary, CP 351 (23), 27 July 1923, in Cab 24/161, NA.
25 Samuel to Churchill, 13 August 1922, CO 733/24/335, NA.
26 Minute by Sydney Moody, 12 March 1923, cited in Wasserstein, *The British*, p. 215.
27 cf. Sherman, *Mandate Days*, p. 30, Weizmann's views cited in Fritz Liebrich, *Britain's Naval and Political Reaction to the Illegal Immigration of Jews to Palestine, 1945–1948*, London: Routledge, 2005, p. 25.
28 Segev, *One Palestine*, p. 345.
29 Samuel to Weizmann, 10 August 1921, WA, cited by Evyatar Friesel, "Through a Peculiar Lens: Zionism and Palestine in British Diaries, 1927–31", *Middle Eastern Studies*, 29/3, 1993, p. 437.
30 Tweedy's diary notes of 2 May 1927, cited in ibid, p. 424, and note 16. Between April 1927 and February 1931 Tweedy made five visits to Palestine; he wrote for the *Daily Telegraph* and the *Financial Times*.
31 Wasserstein, *The British*, p. 47.
32 Chancellor letter of September 1929 cited in ibid, p. 212. In 1936, McDonnell's public criticism of the military action against the Arab rebels, sanctioned by the High Commissioner, prompted the latter to demand his removal from Palestine.
33 Minute by H.G. Bushe, 4 October 1929, in ibid, p. 212.
34 Wasserstein, ibid, pp. 209–15.
35 Ashbee, *A Palestine*, pp. 238–39. Mercutio was a character in Shakespeare's *Romeo and Juliet*; neither a Montagu nor a Capulet, though friendly with the Montagus, he was one of the few in Verona able to associate freely with both houses. Ashbee's view of Palestine as part and parcel of the British Raj is also worth noting.

Colonial Palestine 115

36 Wasserstein, *The British*, p. 145.
37 ibid, pp. 99–100 and 145.
38 Richmond to Shuckburgh, 30 June 1923, ibid, pp. 143–44.
39 Richmond to Samuel, 13 March 1924, ibid, p. 145.
40 General Clayton to Walford Selby, 3 March 1924, ibid, p. 148.
41 Bowman diary entry for 4 March 1924, cited in Sherman, *Mandate Days*, p. 56.
42 Cited in Segev, *One Palestine*, p. 154. Ormsby-Gore was Under-Secretary of State at the Colonial Office from 1922 to 1929, and Colonial Secretary from 1936 to 1938.
43 Entry for 30 October 1930, Mrs Webb's private diary, in the Digitalised Library, the London School of Economics, London (LSE).
44 "Cringing good manners" is the term used by Ronald Storrs, Military Governor of Jerusalem from 1918 to 1921, in his memoirs, *Orientations*, London: Ivor Nicholson & Watson, 1937, p. 420.
45 Sherman, *Mandate Days*, pp. 25, 28
46 Wasserstein, *The British*, p. 12.
47 Douglas Duff, *Palestine Picture*, London: Hodder & Stoughton, 1936, p. 195. After World War Two, Duff became a successful author, mainly of boy's adventure books, of which he published over 100.
48 Sherman, *Mandate Days*, pp. 78–79.
49 Cited in Wasserstein, *The British*, p. 115.
50 ibid, pp. 184–85.
51 Diary entry, 26 October 1919, in Sherman, *Mandate Days*, p. 34.
52 ibid, p. 96.
53 Segev, *One Palestine*, p. 110.
54 Colonel Kisch to the Zionist Executive, 13 March 1923, Wasserstein, *The British*, p. 123.
55 Joel S. Migdal, ed., *Palestinian Society and Politics*, Princeton: Princeton University Press, 1980, p. 20.
56 cf. Nasser Eddin Nashashibi, *Jerusalem's Other Voice: Ragheb Nashashibi and Moderation in Palestinian Politics, 1920–1948*, Exeter: Ithaca Press, 1990, pp. 126–27.
57 During the Ottoman period, all Islamic affairs in Palestine, including the payment of salaries to religious officials, were administered from Istanbul. On Samuel's appointment of Haj Amin as Mufti, see Elie Kedourie, "Sir Herbert Samuel and the Government of Palestine", *Middle Eastern Studies*, 5/1, January 1969, pp. 44–68; also Yehoshua Porath, *The Emergence of the Palestinian-Arab National Movement, 1918–1929*, London: Frank Cass, 1974, pp. 188–207.
58 The SMC paid the salaries of all personnel working for religious institutions, from the Mufti himself, to *shari'a* judges, to the cleaning staff in the mosques. It also retained the sole prerogative of hiring and dismissal.
59 Wasserstein, *Samuel*, p. 266.
60 ibid, p. 132.
61 ibid, p. 28.
62 Sherman, *Mandate Days*, p. 60.
63 ibid, p. 25. George Antonius wrote the first history of Arab nationalism, *The Arab Awakening*, London: Hamish Hamilton, 1938. It was reprinted numerous times and became a classic.
64 Segev, *One Palestine*. When he returned to England, Crossman published an "instant" pro-Zionist book on the Committee's work. See Chapter 19.
65 Wasserstein, *The British*, p. 138.
66 Michael Ignatieff, *Isaiah Berlin: A Life*, New York: Metropolitan Books, 1998, p. 79.
67 Cited in ibid. In 1950, Prime Minister Ben-Gurion offered Berlin the directorship of the Israeli Foreign Office. Berlin turned down the offer politely.

6 Redefining policy in Palestine

> I agree that a point might be reached when we should have to declare that we had failed, and that we were not justified in demanding further sacrifices from the British taxpayer.
>
> Winston Churchill, Colonial Secretary,
> Commons debate on Palestine, June 1921

The 1921 riots

On 1 May 1921, during the course of May Day celebrations, street fights broke out spontaneously between Jewish Communists and Socialists on the Tel Aviv-Jaffa border. The clashes soon escalated into Arab-Jewish brawls. Arabs began attacking the Jews in Jaffa and looting their shops. Their main target became the immigrant hostel, the first stop for all Jewish arrivals. The hostel was burned to the ground, and those Jews who tried to flee the carnage were shot.

Edward Horne, the official historian of the Palestine police, grossly understated the number of fatalities during the riots: 27 Jews and three Arabs. This contrasts with the contemporary estimate made by British intelligence – 40 Jewish and 18 Arab fatalities. The Zionists put their own fatalities at 47 – 45 of whom were burned to death or shot at the Jaffa hostel. Horne all but exonerated the Arab members of the Palestine police who joined the rioters, shifting the blame onto one individual police constable, Adib Khayal. The latter was indicted for the killing of 13 Jews, including women and children, for which he received a 5-year prison sentence.[1]

During the night of 1–2 May some 30 Jewish soldiers – the rump of the dismantled Jewish battalions – rushed to Tel Aviv, without informing their officers. Their Jewish commander, Colonel Margolin, went after them and secured permission from the Governor of Jaffa to organize his men in the defence of the helpless Jews in Jaffa. However, the arming of these Jewish ex-servicemen, who appeared in British uniform, served only to heighten tensions further.

Initially, Samuel believed that the riots were a local affair, confined to Jaffa. But as they spread to other towns, he was forced on 3 May to accede to the army's demand to impose martial law – albeit for Jaffa only. Scheduled troop withdrawals from Palestine were held up. On 4 May, Samuel sent an alarmed request for the urgent dispatch of British warships to Jaffa and Haifa – as a demonstration of strength and a precaution against further outbreaks. Because so many of the Arab police had turned their weapons on the Jews, all the Arab police were disarmed, as were the Jewish soldiers.[2]

The rioting assumed a momentum of its own and spread beyond Jaffa. On 5 May, Arab rioters attacked the Jewish townships of Petah Tikva, Kfar Saba and Rehovot, and the area to the north of Tulkarm. The British rushed in troops and aircraft bombed the Arab rioters from the air. A crowd of Arabs that had gathered to attack the Jewish township of Hadera was driven off by aerial bombardment. Within 2 days, British forces managed to restore order.[3]

The 1921 riots constituted a defining event in the history of the mandate. Those of the previous year had not led to any serious review of policy. They had been all but dismissed as insignificant, attributed to the mishandling of the situation by the military administration. Those of 1921, under Samuel's benign rule, came as a quantum shock. Samuel himself was disabused of his initial optimism, and made a radical reassessment of his previous beliefs. He concluded that the continued progress of the Jewish National Home would require, if not the Palestinian Arabs' blessing, then at least their acquiescence. His biographer noted:

> Samuel's self-delusion of the previous ten months as to the readiness of the Arabs to accept Zionism in return for the benefits of an honest, efficient, uncorrupt, and fair-minded *Pax Britannica* now gave way to a much more realistic and pessimistic view.[4]

The British passed the blame for their own lack of foresight on to the Zionists. They accused them of having overstated their case and of having brought to Palestine too many immigrants, without due consideration for Arab sensitivities.[5]

Samuel concluded that the Arab riots were protests against Zionist immigration. On the sixth day of the riots, he announced the suspension of all further Jewish immigration, until further notice. Samuel was motivated partly by his fear for the immediate safety of those already *en route* to Palestine. He asked the Zionists to hold up for the time being the dispatch of any further immigrants; he asked General Allenby, now High Commissioner of Egypt, to furnish temporary accommodation in Egypt to those Jews already on the high seas. Allenby, fearing nationalist protests in Egypt, turned down Samuel's request. Notwithstanding Zionist protests in London and Jerusalem, three boatloads of Jewish immigrants (many of whom had fled pogroms in the Ukraine) were returned from Egypt to their ports of embarkation.[6]

Wyndham Deedes, the Civil Secretary (later styled Chief Secretary, 1920–23), arrived in Palestine as an enthusiastic Zionist supporter. He had his reservations about Samuel's suspension of Jewish immigration at the height of the riots – which he regarded as appeasement of the Arabs. But he concurred with Samuel that any further development of the Jewish National Home would require the Arabs' acquiescence. The onus for conciliating them would fall on the Zionists.[7]

Samuel also had pragmatic reasons for suspending Jewish immigration. Hitherto a member of the Zionists' inner councils, he was privy to their financial problems, to their inability to finance large-scale immigration, or to find useful employment in Palestine for all of the new arrivals. Samuel knew that the Zionists themselves had approached the Foreign Office in London in confidence, asking the officials not to grant any more immigration visas to Jewish applicants in Europe. Samuel believed that the riots provided an opportune moment to "kill two birds with a single stone": by suspending immigration he could assuage the Arab rioters, and at the same time ease the Zionists' financial exigencies. He argued in vain with the latter that if he had not suspended immigration, they themselves would have appealed to him to do so.

But Samuel's timing was bad, his decision lacked political acumen. His suspension of Jewish immigration sent out a message that Britain's policy in Palestine was susceptible to pressure. It was seen as a capitulation to Arab violence. In these circumstances, the Zionists could not publicly give up their rights, as enshrined in the Balfour Declaration.[8] Samuel had established an unfortunate precedent – henceforth, each wave of Arab violence would be rewarded with a government inquiry that reopened the basic premises of British policy on Palestine.

In London, the Colonial Office was preoccupied with the fear that the unrest in Palestine and Samuel's request for a delay in troop withdrawals would jeopardize planned spending cuts. Colonial Secretary Churchill, ever budget conscious, asked Samuel how many military units he wanted to retain, and for how long. He queried rhetorically whether this would not involve a considerable increase in the costs of the garrison and warned that any additional costs would have to be borne by locally generated revenue. Hubert Young, a Colonial Office official, told a Zionist representative that Samuel's reports had made it quite clear that the Palestinian Arabs had rioted "in order to show the British taxpayer that the policy of the Jewish National Home would require the use of considerable force". Young reassured his interlocutor that the government would not be deterred by acts of violence. But at the same time, he warned that if any additional troops were needed in Palestine, the British taxpayer would not approve the extra costs involved.[9]

Several British officials in Palestine lamented the confusion and chaos that Britain's support for Zionism had got them into. They regarded Britain's position as fundamentally unjust, and feared that the current crisis was exacerbated by Samuel's being a weak-kneed, Jewish High Commissioner. This was the opinion of Charles Ashbee (whom we have met already in Chapter 4):

> The Administration is in one of its recurrent states of nervous collapse. That is to say, being an essentially timid Administration, with an uneasy Protestant conscience, it is arming itself cap-a-pie and shaking to its knees: route marches, demonstrations in the streets, displays of Indian soldiery, armoured cars, and all for the sake of the Mandate and this unhappy "*Wa'd* Balfour" which we should be so much better without.[10]

Samuel's appeasement of the Arabs shattered his hitherto harmonious relations with the Zionists. They regarded his decision to suspend immigration as a strategic error, a clear signal that Britain's support for Zionism was not final and might be changed by violence. On 3 June 1921, Dr David Eder, chairman of the Zionist Executive in Palestine, addressed that body in apocalyptic terms:

> We have gone through the gravest crisis in our movement since the declaration of war in 1914 ... With this concession to mob violence, we may expect at any moment further outbreaks ... The High Commissioner's liberalism amounts to a premium on violence – to which he bows ... Many people are trying to put the blame on his advisers, or upon the military. As regards his advisers and staff, I think I know their faults and weaknesses. I pointed them out a year ago. As the High Commissioner did not listen then, and as he claims to know all about them, I contend the responsibility must rest entirely with the High Commissioner, who after all has chosen his own officers.[11]

Many Zionist leaders favoured breaking with Samuel and demanding his dismissal. Weizmann toyed with the idea of asking the government to replace him with Major General George MacDonogh, Director of Military Intelligence, a man known to be sympathetic to the Zionist cause. Weizmann discussed the idea with Colonial Office officials, but soon realized that the Zionists could not depose a Jewish High Commissioner without rendering grave injury to their own cause. In Palestine, the entire Zionist Commission and Va'ad Leumi threatened to resign. But they quickly withdrew the threat, when warned that their resignations would be countered by those of Samuel, Deedes and Bentwich – the main British supporters of the Zionist cause in Palestine.[12]

Faute de mieux, calmer counsels prevailed. Leonard Stein, after rehearsing Samuel's weaknesses ("the price we have to pay for a Jewish High Commissioner"), concluded soberly:

> Whatever his weaknesses may have been, and however severely he may have been criticized in many parts of the Jewish world, I am sure that H.E.'s presence in Palestine is still a great moral asset in the eyes of the entire Zionist public, and that the loss of that asset would produce serious

depression in Zionist ranks. When all is said and done, H.E.'s presence in Palestine has become a symbol.[13]

The 1922 "Churchill" White Paper[14]

Colonial Secretary Churchill was not committed to a British Palestine. In private, he referred to the mandates for Palestine and Mesopotamia as inherited liabilities that the government was now unable to turn its back on. From the summer of 1921, he devoted his energies to the negotiation of a treaty with Eire. His primary interest in Palestine was to cut down British costs to an absolute minimum. In the absence of a committed, involved minister, Samuel and the senior officials at the Colonial Office were given considerable leeway in the determination of British policy in Palestine. Senior Cabinet ministers were concerned more with considerations of *realpolitik* than with the merits of the respective sides to the conflict.[15]

The dissonance between Churchill's public and private views led him into contradictions. While paying lip service to official policy, his private anxieties leaked out at times. During a Commons debate on 14 June, marked by mounting opposition to the government's Zionist policy, he shared his concerns with members of the House. On the one hand, he argued that any retreat from the promises to the Zionists would be tantamount to accepting that "the word of Britain no longer counts throughout the East and the Middle East". But on the other, he insisted that there must be a limit to Britain's obligations in Palestine:

> I agree that a point might be reached when we should have to declare that we had failed, and that we were not justified in demanding further sacrifices from the British taxpayer.[16]

He quickly reassured the House that they had not reached that point yet. However, it is worth recalling that just 2 weeks before, he had sent a private note to Lloyd George, pleading with him to give up Britain's Middle Eastern mandates – including Palestine – and return them to the Turks.[17]

The 1921 riots shattered Samuel's initial illusion that unlimited Jewish immigration would be accepted placidly by the Palestinian Arabs. But he never really shed his naïve, "orientalist" belief that they (the "natives") could be induced to accept the trappings of Western democratic institutions (along with the material benefits that the Zionists would bring) – even if they were debarred from discussing, let alone limiting the Zionists' privileged position.

Samuel was due to make a public statement in Jerusalem on 3 June, the occasion of the King's official birthday. He took the opportunity to reassure the Arabs on two central issues: first, that the government intended to establish institutions of self-government in Palestine, as provided for by the mandate; and second, that when Jewish immigration was resumed, the government would regulate and limit it. Churchill blocked Samuel's intention of announcing the introduction of elective institutions, on the grounds that Britain could hardly do so until the mandate was ratified by the League of Nations. Although Churchill favoured constitutional progress, he did not think it politic to offer concessions so soon after the riots. Samuel was forbidden to use the words "elected" or "representative" in his speech, but he was authorized to make the nebulous announcement that the Colonial Secretary was "giving his closest attention to the question of ensuring a free and authoritative expression of popular opinion".[18]

In 1921, the most burning issue was Jewish immigration. The Palestinian Arabs had frequently complained about the influx of "the least desirable elements of Eastern Europe", i.e. Communists. Samuel's promise to monitor the Jewish immigrants for any subversive affiliations was seized upon eagerly by Churchill, known for his antipathy to the Bolsheviks, and the connection he had made between them and the Jews (Chapter 1). He wrote to Samuel:

> Communist elements and tendencies among the Jewish immigrants will prove a very real and serious danger which it would be imprudent to under-rate even at this stage. I hope you will endeavour at once to purge the Jewish colonies and newcomers of communist elements and ... have all those who are guilty of subversive agitation expelled from the country.[19]

In a speech before the Commons in March 1922, Churchill reported that Jewish immigration had been "most strictly watched and controlled". Still apparently obsessed with the "Judeo-Bolshevik bogey", he concluded, with a considerable dose of hyperbole:

> We cannot have a country inundated by Bolshevist riffraff, who would seek to subvert institutions in Palestine as they had done with success in the land from which they came.[20]

Churchill's extravagant claims proved to have little or no substance. Subsequently, an official British investigation revealed that no more than 2 per cent of the Jewish immigrants were in fact "suspected Bolsheviks". In July 1923, the Duke of Devonshire, the Conservative Colonial Secretary, reported to the Cabinet:

> The common allegation that the Jewish immigrants are all "Bolsheviks" is ... wide of the mark ... the worst of the undesirables who entered the country during the early years have been got rid of.[21]

After the trauma of the May riots, Samuel determined that all Jewish immigrants would in future be screened, and that men without their own private means would be allowed in only if they had a job waiting for them.

Samuel's Birthday Speech contained the main elements of the 1922 White Paper, a statement of policy that would remain the law in Palestine until 1937.[22] Although Samuel said nothing specifically about constitutional progress, he did promise to take immediate steps to ensure closer consultation on administrative matters with "responsible persons who speak on behalf of all sections of the population". He announced the resumption of Jewish immigration, but reassured the Arabs that conditions in Palestine would not permit the mass migration of Jews. He stated that some Jews:

> ... should be enabled to found here their home ... within the limits which are fixed by the numbers and interests of the present population ... in order to help by their resources and efforts to develop the country to the advantage of all its inhabitants.[23]

His speech infuriated the Zionists, whose leaders once again considered mass resignation, boycotting the administration and severing all contact with the High Commissioner. But an appeal to Churchill revealed that he stood behind Samuel on the new immigration policy. The Zionists realized that any sanctions would be self-defeating – for they could hardly expect better treatment from a new high commissioner, who would inevitably be a Gentile.

Unknown to the Zionists, General Congreve, the GOC of the Egyptian Expeditionary Force, had telegraphed to Samuel to admonish him that his Birthday Speech had not gone far enough. Congreve warned that unless the Palestinian Arabs were given concrete reassurances about Jewish immigration and about the limits of Britain's commitment to the Balfour Declaration, Palestine was likely to be reduced to a state of general insurrection, a situation that the forces at his disposal would be unable to handle. Congreve's warning added more authority to Samuel's position, and he passed it on to the Colonial Office.

The consensus at the Colonial Office was that they were faced with two incompatible, irreconcilable obligations in Palestine, which left them with two, equally distasteful alternatives:

> ... either the abandonment of the Zionist policy in anything like the form the Jews hope and expect to see it; or stifling the local [Arab] aspirations to an extent which is repellant to our traditions, with possibly military and financial commitments beyond our means.[24]

Major Young, the author of this assessment, proposed that if the Arabs proved to be "incurably anti-Zionist", Britain should abandon both the Balfour Declaration and the mandate. As will be seen in the next chapter, this option was considered and rejected in 1923 by a special Cabinet committee set up by the Conservative government.

Weizmann learned of Samuel's Birthday Speech while in the United States, where he was on a fund-raising tour for the Zionist cause. He was enraged by what he regarded as Samuel's betrayal of the Balfour Declaration. A nineteenth-century diplomat by disposition, Weizmann decided to go over Churchill's head, and to appeal to two of the architects of the Balfour Declaration – Balfour himself and Prime Minister Lloyd George. Shortly after his return to Britain, Weizmann persuaded Balfour to convene a private meeting at his house to sort out matters. Churchill and Lloyd George were also invited. On the face of it, this was a major diplomatic coup for Weizmann. But Balfour was already past his prime, now holding the dubious status of elder statesman.[25]

Churchill tried to head off the meeting at Balfour's house, by inviting Weizmann to a private meeting ahead of it. Weizmann later described their meeting as "a very long argument … which lasted one hour and a half." He accused Churchill of having manoeuvred the Zionists into a vicious circle:

> On the one hand they complain about Zionism being a burden on the British taxpayer, and when we desire to lighten this burden by developing Palestine and so increasing the wealth and productiveness of the country, they refuse to let us go on with our work because they fear an Arab outburst.[26]

Weizmann employed the same argument at the meeting of ministers at Balfour's house, on 22 July 1921. Churchill found himself in a minority of one. He was forced, reluctantly, to toe the line taken firmly by the senior ministers.

Weizmann opened by attacking Samuel's Birthday Speech, as a negation of the Balfour Declaration, which, Weizmann claimed, had anticipated an ultimate Jewish majority. Churchill dissented from his assertion, but both Balfour and Lloyd George affirmed that they had always understood that the 1917 Declaration had meant the eventual possibility of a Jewish state. Churchill himself had not been a member of the inner war Cabinet that had decided on the issue of the Declaration. But the fact is that nothing had been said at the decisive Cabinet meeting nor written into the protocol about a Jewish state.

When Weizmann asked rhetorically why Samuel had raised the question of self-government in Palestine, Churchill replied lamely that the same policy was being adopted in Mesopotamia (Iraq) and Trans-Jordan. Weizmann retorted cynically that their actions in those Arab countries were merely a camouflage for a British retreat, and the "representative" character of government under Arab chiefs was a "mere farce". Weizmann baited Churchill: "Why don't you give representative government to Egypt?". Near to the end of the meeting, Lloyd George turned to Churchill and told him bluntly: "You mustn't give representative government to Palestine". Finding himself in a minority, and unwilling to carry the personal responsibility, Churchill grumbled that if that was the case, the entire Palestine issue would have to be reconsidered by the Cabinet.[27]

Churchill felt that he was trapped in an insoluble paradox. He saw the logic in Samuel's plea that some measures of self-government must be given to the

Palestinian Arabs – not only because the British were granting similar measures to the Arabs in Trans-Jordan and in Iraq, but also because their mandate from the League required them to do so. However, as he told Shuckburgh, head of the department's Middle East section, any measures providing for elective institutions had also to include guarantees that the government would carry out its pledges to the Zionists. This required that the key issue of Jewish immigration must remain *ultra vires*.[28]

The meeting at Balfour's house was ostensibly a triumph for Weizmann and a humiliation for Churchill. But Weizmann left the meeting feeling depressed. He knew that the Colonial Office, rather than Balfour or Lloyd George, was charged with the day-to-day administration of Palestine, and it would determine the Zionists' fate. Weizmann felt that he could not rely on Churchill, a volatile, unpredictable man. He told one of his close confidants that he "never knows where he has Churchill".[29] Eight days after the meeting at Balfour's house, he warned Deedes, the civil secretary of the Palestine administration, that he would probably have to resign his position as head of the Zionist movement:

> Of the Balfour Declaration, nothing is left but mere lip-service ... We were able to get little truth out of Churchill, he supported the officials' views and everything said by Samuel, whom he quoted constantly.[30]

Inside the Colonial Office, there was consternation among the senior officials when they learned that Lloyd George had contradicted the position taken by Churchill, in support of Samuel. Colonel Meinertzhagen, Churchill's military advisor, vilified the department's officials as:

> ... almost 100% hebraphobe ... the worst offender being Shuckburgh ... Hubert Young and little Lawrence do their utmost to conceal their dislike and mistrust of the Jews but both strongly support the official pro-Arab policy of Whitehall and frown on the equally official policy based on the Balfour Declaration.[31]

Nor was Lloyd George's commitment to the Zionists consistent or engraved in stone. In February 1919, he had written to Philip Kerr, his private secretary: "If the Zionists claim that the Jews are to have domination of the Holy Land under a British Protectorate, then they are certainly putting their claims too high".[32]

But given the Prime Minister's official *diktat* in 1921 that there would be no retreat from the government's commitment to the Zionists, the Colonial Office officials now treated the Palestine problem as one of tactics rather than strategy: "to offer both Jews and Arabs inducements that would keep them happy for the time being". They tried to do this at a series of meetings with an official Arab delegation that was in London, and with the Zionists.

The Arabs' refusal to accept the Balfour Declaration was met by Zionist recitals of the Jews' long history and their historic right to Palestine. When

Deedes, Weizmann's former friend and supporter, added his voice to those pressing for the deletion of article 4 of the mandate (which referred to support for the Jewish National Home), Weizmann replied in apocalyptic, millennial terms:

> You speak of co-operation between the Administration of Palestine and the Zionist Organization. I am afraid this co-operation is being rendered illusory – but not by us ... It is quite true that the Zionist ideals may have upset some Arabs and some British anti-Semites, but these are the very ideals which have been sanctified by thousands of years of martyrdom. For the sake of these ideals we have gone through torture all over the world, and these ideals are the very lifeblood of Zionism. Take them away, or water them down and Zionism ceases to exist ... I cannot ask the Zionist Organization to commit suicide. I have always preached and taught that there is an identity of interests between a British and a Jewish Palestine, but this policy is being systematically destroyed.[33]

In view of the intransigence of the Arab delegation, the Colonial Office proposed a compromise deal with Weizmann. In return for his agreement to the establishment of a part-elected, part-appointed advisory council, that would be barred from discussing Jewish immigration, and similarly, the government's restriction of immigration to those who could be absorbed into the economy, Weizmann was offered a string of British concessions: a commitment that all anti-Zionist officials would be removed from the Palestine administration and that Palestine would be detached from the military command in Egypt. In addition, the franchise for the supply of electricity to Palestine and Trans-Jordan would be granted immediately to Pinhas Rutenberg, a Russian Jewish immigrant; a purely Jewish police reserve would be established and the Arab villages indicted for their part in the May riots would be punished.[34]

On 12 August, at a meeting with the Arab delegation, Churchill lost any hope that he may have still had that the Palestinians might relent on their demand that the British cancel the Balfour Declaration. They insisted on the establishment of a national government, responsible to a parliament elected by "those natives of Palestine who lived in the country before the war".

On 18 August 1921, the Cabinet discussed the situation in Palestine. Churchill circulated a pessimistic survey of the situation:

> The whole country is in ferment. The Zionist policy is profoundly unpopular with all but the Zionists. Both Arabs and Jews are arming, ready to spring at each other's throats.

He warned that the Palestine garrison would probably need to be increased, rather than reduced, and complained that the annual cost of holding on to Palestine – £3,319,900 – was due almost entirely to their Zionist policy. He made his own position quite clear: if the government nonetheless wished to proceed with the Zionist policy, the whole Cabinet would have to take responsibility:

> I have done and am doing my best to give effect to the pledge given to the Zionists by Mr Balfour on behalf of the War Cabinet ... I am prepared to continue in this course, if it is the settled resolve of the Cabinet.[35]

Churchill's demand that the full Cabinet take responsibility for its Palestine policy may be understood in the context of the disastrous Dardanelles campaign, which 5 years previously had cost him his seat in the Cabinet. He added a further warning that if the Arab delegation returned home without having secured the "withdrawal of Balfour's pledge", another round of violence would sweep Palestine. He presented the Cabinet with two radical, diametrically opposed alternatives, a reflection of his own and his officials' sense of desperation. The first was to refer the mandate back to the League of Nations, set up an Arab National Government and curtail or halt Jewish immigration; the second was to help the Zionists build up their own armed forces to the point where they could defend themselves, after which the government would withdraw the British garrison.

The Cabinet rejected both of Churchill's proposals, and endorsed Lloyd George's assertion that Britain's honour and international standing were bound up with its commitment to the Balfour Declaration. An aimless, academic discussion ensued. On the one hand, the inevitable outcome of the current policy was stressed: the contradictions of attempting to pursue a Zionist policy while at the same time preserving the rights of the Arab population would result only in estranging them both. On the other hand, the British justified the Zionists' right to develop the country with their skills and capital, given the Arabs' failure to have done so. Churchill himself, with a characteristic touch of imperialist hubris, asserted:

> ... the Arabs have no prescriptive right to a country which they had failed to develop to the best advantage.

The Cabinet took no decision. With the negotiations with the Arabs and the Zionists at an impasse, Churchill occupied himself with another issue closer to home – the negotiation of a treaty with the Irish. His mood and barely concealed wish to scuttle the British mandate over Palestine may be gauged from a private letter he wrote to Balfour on 10 October 1921:

> We are committed in Palestine to the Zionist policy against which nine-tenths of the population and an equal proportion of the British officers are marshalled ... I shall simply have to carry on as well as I can in harmony with the Mandate and allow events to tell their own tale. We obviously cannot keep these turbulent countries year after year in our

charge because the League of Nations is unable to come to any decision in regard to them.[36]

In the meantime, the Colonial Office made two concessions to the Zionists; it awarded the concession for the electrification of Palestine and Trans-Jordan to Pinhas Rutenberg, and separated Palestine from the Middle East Command in Cairo. However, the "anti-Zionist officials" whose removal had been demanded by the Zionists remained in Palestine.

On two separate occasions in November 1921, Churchill was scheduled to address a joint meeting of Arabs and Zionists, but backed out at the last minute. Both parties were puzzled by his behaviour. The Zionists were distressed by his apparent neglect of their cause. They were convinced that the Palestinian Arabs would never compromise, confident in the knowledge that the majority of British officials opposed the Balfour Declaration. The Zionists managed to block an initiative by the officials in Palestine to delete article 4 of the draft mandate. This, together with article 6 – instructing the Palestine administration to co-operate with the Jewish Agency in encouraging the "close settlement by Jews on the land" – would be approved by the League in July 1922. These articles established a legal basis for the activities of the Palestine Zionist Executive to function as a quasi-government of the Yishuv.[37]

It was left to the Colonial Office officials to keep both Arabs and Zionists in play – due to the fear that the Arabs' return to Palestine empty-handed would ignite yet another round of riots. At the end of December 1921, Shuckburgh finally drew up a draft constitution that contained the main elements of the 1922 White Paper. It consisted of four basic proposals:

1 Policy in Palestine would continue to be guided by the Balfour Declaration.
2 The rights of the Palestinian Arabs would be guarded.
3 Jewish immigration would be allowed up to the "economic absorptive capacity" of the country.
4 A legislative council would be set up, with 17 elected and ten officially appointed [British] members.

The draft was handed to the Arabs and the Zionists in February 1922. The Arabs rejected it out of hand. They refused to countenance the inclusion of the Balfour Declaration in the mandate, and refused to accept the legislative council as proposed – a body that by definition would not be allowed to pass any ordinance that infringed Britain's patronage of the Zionists. The Arabs also opposed what they referred to as the "excessive powers" granted to the High Commissioner over the proposed council. Samuel would control 14 of the proposed 27 votes on the council, and hold the power of veto over all of its decisions; he would also have been empowered to prorogue or dissolve the council at will; any ten members would have constituted a quorum – enabling the government to control it with the ten appointed British officials.

The government told the Arabs again that Britain regarded herself as bound by the Balfour Declaration, which had preceded the League of Nations covenant. Therefore, she would not allow the development of a constitutional situation that would not allow Britain to fulfil that pledge. Shuckburgh insisted that the issue of Jewish immigration would have to be excluded from the purview of the proposed legislative council. Notwithstanding the Arabs' absolute rejection of the scheme, it appeared in the 1922 White Paper.

On the issue of Jewish immigration, Shuckburgh offered the Arabs the disingenuous reassurance that it would be controlled "within the limits fixed by the numbers and interests of the present population". But as noted, the British had their own interest in the continuation of Jewish immigration: any significant interruption would have dried up the infusion of Zionist capital into Palestine, without which the British could not have maintained their hold on the country.

On 4 July 1922, Churchill was called upon to defend the government's policy in Palestine in the House of Commons, in a debate on the Colonial Office vote. Just 2 weeks before the debate, the House of Lords had passed a motion introduced by Lord Islington, to the effect:

> That the Mandate for Palestine in its present form is inacceptable to this House, because it directly violates the pledges made by His Majesty's Government to the people of Palestine ... and is, as at present framed, opposed to the sentiments and wishes of the great majority of the people of Palestine.[38]

Fearing that the Arabs might think that the Lords' vote represented a British volte-face, the government turned the Colonial Office vote into one of confidence. One of the main issues of contention was the Rutenberg electricity concession, a monopoly that was attacked not only by the opponents of Zionism, but also by MPs concerned to protect British industrial interests (on the concession, see Chapter 9).

The debate in the Commons was charged with emotion. Typical was an outburst by Sir William Joynson-Hicks, a Conservative opponent of the coalition's support for Zionism:

> The real trouble is the way in which the Zionists have been permitted by the Government, or with the connivance of the Government, practically to control the whole of the Government of Palestine. They naturally say, "This High Commissioner may be an Englishman, but, in addition to being an Englishman, he is a Zionist, and he cannot be expected to hold the scales fairly between us and the Jewish population".[39]

William Ormsby-Gore, a future Colonial Secretary, was moved to state:

> Then there is what I call quite frankly the anti-Semitic party, that is to say, those who are convinced that the Jews are at the bottom of all the

trouble all over the world. Whether they are attacking an anti-Zionist like the Right Hon. gentleman the Member for Cambridge County (Mr. Montagu), or Zionists, or rich Jews, or poor Jews – it is the rich Jews who are all blood-suckers and the poor Jews all Bolshevists – they have that particular Hebrew mania, and they have fastened on Palestine with a view to paying off these mediaeval scores.

The campaign which has been engineered against the Balfour Declaration and against the policy of His Majesty's Government in Palestine, where it is not anti-Semitic, is anti-British. It is contrary to British interests.

Churchill did not conceal his own misgivings about the Balfour Declaration. He reminded the House that he had not been a party to the Cabinet's decision in 1917, and that the Declaration had been issued in order to promote British war interests. He harangued the opposition:

You have no right to say this kind of thing as individuals; you have no right to support public declarations in the name of your country in the crisis and heat of the War, and then afterwards, when all is cold and prosaic, to turn around and attack the Minister of the Department which is faithfully and laboriously endeavouring to translate those perfervid enthusiasms into the sober, concrete facts of the day-to-day administration.

Churchill maintained that he was only trying to carry out his duty. He then mentioned by name 12 MPs who in 1917 had supported the Declaration in public, but now opposed it. His next remark might well have been aimed also at his senior colleagues in the Cabinet:

We really must know where we are. Who led us along this path, who impelled us along it? I remained quite silent. I am not in the "Black Book". I accepted service on the lines laid down for me. Now, when I am endeavouring to carry it out, it is from this quarter that I am assailed.

The final draft of the White Paper stated that the Jews were in Palestine "as of right and not on sufferance". Jewish immigration would be subject to the "economic absorptive capacity" of Palestine to absorb the new arrivals. The White Paper denied that the government had ever supported the Zionists' aspiration to "make Palestine as Jewish as England was English"[40] and reassured the Arabs that the government had never:

... at any time contemplated, as appears to be feared by the Arab Delegation, the disappearance or the subordination of the Arab population, language or culture in Palestine ... The terms of the [Balfour] Declaration ... do not contemplate that Palestine as a whole should be converted into a

Jewish National Home, but that such a Home should be founded in Palestine.[41]

The White Paper's definition of the "Jewish National Home" inclined towards that of Ahad Ha'am (the father of "spiritual" or "cultural" Zionism)[42] – the establishment in Palestine of a Jewish spiritual centre. Humphrey Bowman, for instance, went on record that many of his colleagues were impressed by "spiritual Zionism" – "the revival of the language, the establishment of the University ... ". But they opposed political Zionism, "since it threatened the status of the Arabs"[43] The White Paper endorsed this concept:

> When it is asked what is meant by the development of the Jewish National Home in Palestine, it may be answered that it is not the imposition of a Jewish nationality upon the inhabitants of Palestine as a whole, but the further development of the existing Jewish community, with the assistance of Jews in other parts of the world, in order that it may become a centre in which the Jewish people as a whole may take, on grounds of religion and race, an interest and a pride.[44]

Weizmann, as Herzl had been before him, was a "political Zionist". Both aspired to secure a national entity, initially under the protection and patronage of a Great Power, but eventually independent and sovereign. But in 1922, the Zionists, even the radical Jabotinsky, had no alternative but to acquiesce in the new policy. They were warned that if they rejected the new White Paper, the government would return the mandate to the League. They were especially upset by and protested in vain against Churchill's severance of Trans-Jordan from the area originally opened up to the Jewish National Home. Some 25 years later, Weizmann would note in his memoirs:

> The Churchill White Paper was regarded by us as a serious whittling down of the Balfour Declaration. It detached Trans-Jordan from the area of Zionist operation, and it raised the subject of a legislative council. But it began with a reaffirmation of "the Declaration of November 2 1917. ... [and] it established the principle of "economic absorptive capacity".[45]

At their fifth national congress, convened in Nablus in August 1922, the Palestinian Arabs rejected the new White Paper. The British could not threaten them with abandoning the mandate. More legislative and advisory council schemes would be floated in later years, all to no avail. As noted by one scholar:

> In these circumstances there were few realistic political proposals which British officials in Palestine could have made to their masters in London which could have dented the British imperial shield sheltering the Jewish National Home.[46]

No elected assembly was ever convened during the period of the British mandate over Palestine. The country would be governed by the High Commissioner, advised by various councils of British officials, acting as rubber stamps. The long-term effect was to reinforce the alienation and estrangement of Jews and Arabs in Palestine, and to accelerate their development into:

> ... more and more separate political, social and economic entities, bound together by no ties other than the political will of the British Government.[47]

The 1922 White Paper was the first attempt to clarify the meaning of the Balfour Declaration. Given that it had been issued originally in order to serve British war interests, and that the clash of Arab and Zionist interests in Palestine had quickly proved unbridgeable, the new policy could only aspire to pull off that quintessential diplomatic goal: to appear to give each side what it wanted.

The new policy failed to settle any of the underlying, fundamental problems in Palestine. The Zionists were able to live with and at times managed to circumvent the immigration restrictions. Fortunately for them, the Palestinian Arabs boycotted the elections to the legislative council, so they were not faced with the choice of sitting as a minority on an elected body. Arab national aspirations were discounted and brushed aside. However, as will be seen in the next chapter, those senior Cabinet ministers who ultimately determined "high policy" were concerned more with Britain's "place in the sun" – her international standing, and her strategic and imperial need for Palestine. The officials who had to administer Palestine on a daily basis were reduced to despair. Many would resign.

In later years, Churchill would take pride in what he would call "his" White Paper – even though his was a nominal, ministerial paternity. As happens so often, the new policy would appear in retrospect in a far more favourable light than it did at the time. It would take the Arab revolt of 1936–39, and Britain's urgent need of the support of the Arab states on the eve of World War Two, to force the British to revise the 1922 policy and retreat from the Balfour Declaration.

Churchill's official biographer has summarized his term at the Colonial Office with the following *apologia*:

> While publicly he had often emerged as their [the Zionists'] champion, in the daily administration of his department he had allowed decisions to be reached, often by others, which were to their disadvantage.[48]

Jewish immigration

At the time of the British conquest of Palestine in 1918, there were some 56,000 Jews living in the country – they comprised about 10 per cent of the total population. From 1920 to 1948, the Jewish population increased more than tenfold, to over 600,000. Nearly half a million of these were immigrants.

In the name of preservation of the *status quo*, the military administration had urged the government not to permit Jewish immigration until Palestine's political future was settled. But quietly and unofficially, a trickle of Jewish immigrants arrived, notwithstanding official restraints. Among these were many former residents who had been deported by the Turks during the war, now encouraged to return by the Balfour Declaration. By July 1920, when the administration passed into civilian hands, the Yishuv had grown to 61,000.[49]

When Samuel took office as High Commissioner, he authorised the issue of 16,500 immigration labour certificates. Jewish labourers would be allowed entry according to their prospect of finding gainful employment. Together with their families, this quota represented a potential increase of up to 70,000 souls. "Capitalist" immigrants – those with personal assets worth at least P£500 (later increased to P£1000) – would be admitted without restriction.

Initially, control of immigration was left in Zionist hands. No criteria were set and Palestine was inundated by a flood of young men and women, full of ideals but sadly lacking in practical know-how or skills. By October 1920, the Zionists' financial resources became so depleted that they approached the Foreign Office, in confidence, to ask that the 16,500 quota be reduced to a mere 1000 per year.[50]

The generous immigration quota issued by Samuel was never filled. From the beginning of Samuel's term until the Arab riots of May 1921, only 10,652 Jews arrived; the monthly average during the last 6 months of 1921 was a mere 550. The total number of Jews admitted during 1922 was 7884. The British census of 1923 indicated that of a total population of 756,000 in Palestine, 589,000 were Moslems, 83,000 were Jews and 73,000 were Christians.[51]

Jewish immigration would remain a contentious issue between the British and the Zionists for the duration of the mandate. Whereas the British tried to apply the economic absorptive capacity principle to the entire population of Palestine, the Zionists insisted that it be applied only to the Yishuv. The Colonial Office agreed to negotiate the biannual quotas with the Zionist executive. The Zionists put in their requests for certificates based upon their estimates of employment opportunities during the next 6 months. Their forecasts were then debated and whittled down in talks with officials of the Palestine administration.

Wide divergences between Zionist and British estimates became routine. Without exception, Zionist estimates were reduced by the British.[52] The Zionists exploited the new immigration formula as a political instrument, and were not above "bending the rules". In the Diaspora, they had learned to use "wily, manipulative, innovative, and calculating methods to survive".[53] Their over-riding goal was to increase the size of the Yishuv – which could not be done by "proving" that new labour immigrants would be gainfully employed. Unskilled labourers were brought in under the guise of professionals, and Jewish employers signed guarantees for immigrant labourers to whom they had no intention of offering employment. In retrospect, the Colonial Office estimated that for the period 1 December 1921 to 1 March 1922, some 40 per cent of the Jewish immigrants should not have been granted entry visas.[54]

The Zionists blamed the administration for focusing too much on the agricultural sector, whereas the industrial and commercial sectors held out the greatest economic promise. The Zionists based their projections on the long-term effects of capital imports and human skills, which they expected would create additional absorptive capacity. They rejected the officials' static concept of Palestine's economic potential, arguing that it was expanding continually, as new capital and new production techniques were introduced.[55]

Between 1922 and 1939, the total population of Palestine doubled, from 750,000 to 1,500,000. This was due not only to the Arabs' natural increase, but also to the immigration of some 335,000 Jews as well as to the immigration of tens of thousands of Syrian Arabs from the Hauran region.[56] When the mandate ended in 1948, Palestine was supporting a much larger population – both Arab and Jewish – at a much higher standard of living than it had in 1920. This belies the scurrilous remark of Sydney Webb, the Fabian Socialist Colonial Secretary, who said in 1929: "There is no room to swing a cat in Palestine".[57]

However, long-term economic projections could not save the Yishuv from short-term economic crisis and depression. During the first 10 years of the mandate some 100,000 Jews entered Palestine, but nearly one-quarter left – leaving a net increase of 75,000. Initially, many found employment with the administration, especially in the building of strategic roads undertaken by the British in the early 1920s for their own needs. Once these roads were finished, the number of Jewish unemployed increased sharply.[58]

Between 1924 and 1926, a large immigration wave (the fourth *aliya*) of Polish Jews arrived. They had been left with no alternative to Palestine after the United States closed its doors to immigrants in 1924. A significant proportion of the newcomers were bourgeois middle class, most of whom settled in Tel Aviv. The total inflow of Jewish capital during these 3 years was over P£17 million – more than eight times Palestine's domestic product in 1923.[59] Much of the initial economic boom that they created derived from the construction and affiliated trades. In Tel Aviv, 48 per cent of all workers were engaged in the building trade. The increased demand that they brought spread to all branches of the economy, stimulating employment and new investment.

However, the large numbers of new immigrants in proportion to the existing Yishuv could not be absorbed. In 1925, the number of new arrivals was the highest immigration ratio ever recorded, over one-third of the existing Jewish population: 34,386 new arrivals, into a Jewish community that numbered some 95,000.[60] From 1926, the proportion of "capitalist" immigrants fell, and the capital inflow also fell. In addition, the financial resources of the new immigrants were depleted substantially by a rapid depreciation of the Polish zloty. The initial boom was followed by a depression. It began in the construction sector and spread rapidly to others. Tel Aviv, the centre of the construction boom, was the centre of the bust. This town alone, with 40 per cent of its labour force out of work, accounted for 50 per cent of Palestine's total unemployed. As the numbers of unemployed swelled, immigration came to a virtual halt, and the number of emigrants increased: in the second half of 1926 they exceeded the number of immigrants. Of the 7365 Jews who left Palestine in this year, 95 per cent were recent immigrants who had been in the country for between 1 and 3 years.[61]

T.I.K. Lloyd, the Colonial Office official dealing with Palestine, offered the following, incisive analysis of the depression:

> Almost every immigrant of independent means who settles in Tel Aviv first builds a house, thereby exhausting, or nearly exhausting his capital; and then he has to rely on the arrival of more immigrants with capital to purchase his goods (if, as in many case, he opens a shop) or otherwise provide him with employment.

The performance of the Jewish economy during the 1920s gave the clearest possible indication of the divergence of the Arab and Jewish communities. The economic crisis reinforced the Conservative government's view that the principle of economic absorptive capacity should not apply to the Palestinian Arabs, that it should mean "not absorption into a monolithic Palestinian economy but simply absorption into the Yishuv".[62]

Learning the "lessons" of the mid-decade depression, the government restricted immigration more stringently between 1926 and 1929. At the same time, faced by wide-scale unemployment, the Zionists reduced their demands for immigration visas. For the period April–September 1927, the government conceded only 500 of the 1500 immigration visas requested by the Zionists. During the following 12 months, Jewish immigration was suspended completely, as a temporary measure.[63]

In effect, legal restrictions proved to be irrelevant, since few Jews wanted to immigrate into Palestine during the troughs of the economic slowdown. There was a rapid economic recovery from 1928 and substantial growth over the following 3 years. However, the world Depression that followed the Wall Street Crash of 1929, and the Wailing Wall riots in the same year, combined to deter any significant new immigration.[64]

During the 1920s the government concerned itself almost exclusively with the economic aspects of Jewish immigration, with little thought for changes in the country's demographic balance, and the obvious political repercussions. That would change in 1929. The minority Labour government (June 1929 to August 1931) would be the first to take into account the political ramifications of Jewish immigration. In 1937, the Peel Royal Commission report gave official recognition to the evident fact that not only economic, but also political conditions must be taken into account. The Commission coined a new formula for Jewish immigration – a "political high ceiling".

Land sales

Professor Kenneth Stein, author of the pioneering study of the sale of Arab lands to the Zionists during the mandatory period, has claimed that these transactions, for the most part carried out clandestinely, were a more significant factor in the emergence of Jewish statehood than Jewish immigration – which occurred usually in the glare of daylight, with high-profile publicity. Stein claims that it was the Arabs' willingness to continue selling off their lands to the Zionists that gave the latter confidence that they would eventually attain sovereignty.[65]

I would suggest that the purchase of land and Jewish immigration were joint, mutually dependent pillars of the Zionist endeavour. The government gave priority to curbing immigration, suspending it several times. The Yishuv doubled its numbers during the first decade of the mandate, and then again during the first 5 years of the 1930s. Large-scale Jewish immigration, especially during those 5 years, aroused more Arab opposition than land transfers. The Palestinian Arabs realized that if Jewish immigration continued at the same rate, they would soon find themselves in a minority.

The willingness of Arab landowners to sell off their lands grew with the Zionist demand, as Jewish immigration increased. In the 1920s, the largest volume of lands was sold by absentee landowning *effendi*. But in the 1930s, thousands of Arabs, resident *fellahin* from every social and ethnic sector, sold off smaller plots to the Zionists, due to personal economic straits. A new class of Arab land brokers made a nice living from the trade. Other Arabs sold the Zionists information about available lands, investigated who owned the title deeds when ownership was unclear, and helped to convince unwilling owners to sell. Arab collaborators, sometimes with the help of thugs, drove off trespassers who had squatted on sold lands, in the hope of receiving compensation.[66] All parties involved in the land transactions, including the British by-standers, colluded in a conspiracy of silence.

The Zionists paid the full market price for the lands they bought. From 1920 to 1927, 82 per cent of the Arab lands they purchased were from absentee Arab landlords, mostly from the Lebanon and Syria. In 1918, with the Anglo-French partition of Ottoman (or Greater) Syria, these *effendi* had become foreigners overnight. They did not want the complications of administering lands across the border, most of which were uninhabited. Where the plots were inhabited, the *effendi* had little or no concern for the Palestinian *fellahin* who leased and tilled them. Indeed, the market price decreased if the lands had sitting tenants. Tenancy and leasehold agreements were usually made for the short term, concluded orally with illiterate peasants, renewable at the end of each season. Many owners didn't even register their ownership, fearing the taxation that this would incur.

The military regime closed the land registers for Palestine in 1918, due to the financial chaos and the severe indebtedness of the peasantry brought about by the war. They were reopened in 1920 when the civil administration took office. The economic situation had not improved much, but the new administration decided that the closure of the land market was preventing economic growth and discouraging capital investment.[67]

Arab land sales to the Jews did not arouse too much opposition during the 1920s. Over 60 per cent of the lands bought by the Zionists were from absentee owners of large plots. But both the volume and character of the sales changed during the 1930s. Most of the lands sold to the Zionists were by resident, smaller landowners, forced by indebtedness to sell off small plots. It has been estimated that from 1932 to 1945, 65 per cent of the lands bought by the Zionists were from small, indebted, resident landowners. A combination of objective conditions impelled them to sell; drought, plague and a worldwide overproduction of cereals – some of which was dumped in Palestine – depressed the prices of local produce. The government was forced to remit tithes on a large scale. But nonetheless, many small landowners fell victim to moneylenders and were forced into default.[68]

The increased Zionist demand for land generated by mass Jewish immigration during the first half of the 1930s and the lure of a market in which land prices were forever on the rise were too much to resist. As a result, a large class of agricultural labouring tenants emerged. Zionist land purchases did not cause the proletarianization of the Arab peasantry, the *fellahin*, but they did accelerate it.

Disputes between Jewish buyers and former Arab tenants became more frequent, and the eviction of Arab tenants, even if they were few, increased fears of a Zionist takeover. But throughout the entire period of the mandate, Arab protests against land sales to the Jews were limited, since, as one study has noted, the leaders of the nationalist campaigns against the sales were themselves involved in the market:

> Pressure for change from Arab leaders was sporadic and muted because many of them were landowners and their interests did not necessarily coincide with those of the peasantry.[69]

Organized demonstrations and protests against Arab land sales to the Zionists merely drove the market further underground and pushed up prices even more. The Arab press featured frequent articles inveighing against the sales, and there were occasional references to the involvement of members of the SMC and the Arab Executive. But all the parties involved – Arabs, British and Zionists – colluded in keeping the identity of the Arab sellers secret. The Zionists took every care to protect the identity of those from whom they bought land – frequently through the agency of second or third parties.[70] The sales would become a major political issue in the 1930s, one of the major issues dealt with by the 1939 White Paper (see Chapters 10, 13).

The *fellahin* had an ancestral attachment to their land, but over 25 per cent of them managed to eke out only a bare subsistence. Their plots might have supported more people had they been tilled more scientifically – for instance, irrigation would have raised the yields. The *fellahin* were also burdened by oppressive taxation. The purchase of their lands by the Zionists was facilitated by the conservative nature of the colonial administration, which was:

> … unwilling to contemplate any thoroughgoing land reform or land redistribution that would have upset the social and political status quo by directly challenging the economic position of the landowning class.[71]

The Arab *effendi* could not resist the lure of quick profits in the continually rising market. They denied their tenants the use of their lands (fallow lands were not taxed), and sold off parcels to the Zionists, in order to maintain their lifestyle and prestige. Throughout the entire mandatory period, the Zionists always found Arabs who were willing to sell off their lands.

The British legislated several land transfer ordinances to protect the *fellahin*, but as noted by one scholar:

> Once the tenants were ready to take financial compensation and quit the land for the tempting lights of the neighbouring towns, no legislation could be effective.[72]

The number of land sales fell temporarily during the Arab rebellion that began in 1936, especially during its second stage, from late 1937. This was due to the physical threats against Arab landowners by the armed gangs, who also murdered some of those known to be involved. The Arabic press initially printed warnings to all those involved in the sales, including the speculators and the brokers, and later began to expose those involved, by publishing their names. But some Arabic newspapers criticized the harsh measures taken by the gangs, and the leaders' failure to find alternative compensation for the penurious peasants. The land sales to the Jews picked up again in 1939, after the rebellion had been crushed. The sellers were no longer described as "traitors who must be punished". Instead, the press referred to the harsh reality in which the Palestinian Arabs found themselves. On 25 October 1939, *Al-Karmil* printed a long article on the sales:

> The problem of the land sales has resumed its former status and even worsened. The reasons for the increase in sales are the prevailing insecurity, the economic hardships … and the Jews' wish to exchange money for land, since the currency devaluation is causing them concern.[73]

During the latter stages of the rebellion, the Arabic press, intimidated and virtually controlled by the Husayni armed gangs (see Chapter 17), added vitriolic attacks against the Jews to their campaign against the land sales.

These reeked of anti-Semitism and included allegations of Jewish conspiracies that would not have shamed the *Protocols of the Elders of Zion*. On 29 November 1937, *Al-Karmil* printed the following diatribe:

> If a handful of Jews in Iran and Egypt succeeded in ruling these countries unhindered, how will the Arab State defend itself from the Jewish State? The Jews are a destructive element everywhere. They defeated Tzarist Russia and brought bolsehvism to the east. They fomented the [civil] war in Spain.

On 15 December, *Al-Difa'* asserted: "the Jews' greediness is undermining the peace and quiet of Palestine". Several papers reported on Jewish plots against the Palestinians, both in Lebanon and in Egypt. *Al-Jami'a al-Islamiyya* printed frequent slanderous articles against Jews, including a report of a speech by the Catholic Arab Bishop Hajjar, to the effect that he saw no possibility of any Arab-Jewish compromise, due to "Jewish treachery, selfishness and prevalent permissiveness".[74]

In contrast to the restrictions on Jewish immigration, the land ordinances lacked real teeth. They were easily circumvented in a market where the paucity of Zionist funds was the only real obstacle to sales. The first ordinances required the sellers to leave sufficient land for the subsistence of tenant occupants and their families. However, the Land Protection Ordinance of 1929 cancelled this provision, replacing it with a more lenient one that obliged the seller to give his tenant 1 year's notice of sale, and to pay compensation for the disturbance of the tenant's tenure and for any improvements that he had made. A Protection of Cultivators Ordinance, enacted in 1933, was castigated in 1941 by the Palestine administration as "contentious, uniformly unsatisfactory, consistently evaded, and an obstacle to [economic] development".[75]

Whereas British estimates of Palestine's economic absorptive capacity were always lower than those of the Zionists, their estimates of the amount of land required for an Arab family's subsistence were always higher than those of the Zionists. The British based their calculations on the *status quo* – the primitive techniques used by the Arabs. Zionist estimates, based on the use of modern techniques, were as much as 50 per cent higher than those of the British.[76]

Jewish immigration and land settlement had disruptive effects on the social fabric of Arab society in Palestine, which had been based on village identity, kinship and personal connections. Traditional, hierarchic ties were strained and severed. The vast majority of Palestine's Arabs was "illiterate and unsophisticated peasantry that had no interest in political involvement [and] was not cognizant of its legal rights ... ". When required to pay rents and heavy government tithes, they were driven into the unrelenting hands of the moneylenders.[77]

The Zionists' claim that their innovations would bring about a rise in the Arabs' standard of living never materialized. The Palestinian Arabs never

Redefining policy in Palestine 139

reached the levels of modern irrigation and scientific methods used by Jewish farmers. Mechanized agriculture required skills, knowledge and capital beyond the limits of the average Arab peasant. A switch from the dry farming of cereals to the cultivation and marketing of crops that required intensive irrigation would have required a complete change of cultivation habits, "greater daily attention than did the leisurely annual disposal of cereal crops in day-to-day farming".[78]

It did not help matters that Arab lands were concentrated inequitably in the hands of a minority of wealthy, landowning *effendi*. These families were content to see the Zionists buying at any price. National protests against the sales drove up prices still further. In October 1935, Afif I. Tannous, a Palestinian intellectual, wrote:

> ... the *fellah* until recently has been the subject of oppression, neglect, and ill treatment by his own countrymen and the old political regime. The feudal system played havoc in his life, the *effendi* class looked down upon him, and the old Turkish regime was too corrupt to be concerned with such a vital problem.[79]

Measures to prevent the redistribution of lands in Palestine were never seriously provided by the British. The home government was unwilling to go beyond face-saving ordinances to protect the small Arab cultivator. Even if it had been willing to invest the necessary funds for land reforms and if the administrative staff had been available, it is unlikely that many Arabs, traditionally suspicious of all intervention by the authorities, would have co-operated. Both the Arab sellers and the Zionist buyers found ready ways to bypass legal ordinances.

It has been estimated that from 1922 to 1924, the mandatory regime spent a mere 1 per cent of its budget on lands administration, in contrast with over 50 per cent on building up strategic infrastructures (mainly roads). The government appreciated that any real land reform, i.e. prohibition of land transfers to Jews, would have meant a reduction in much-needed taxes. It has been estimated that in 1928 the Yishuv – 17 per cent of the total population at the time – was paying 44 per cent of the total taxes collected. When a concrete proposal was made in 1930 to invest in improvements to the Arabs' cultivating techniques, the Treasury vetoed the investment of the sums required (see Chapter 10).[80]

In the wake of the August 1929 disturbances, the government appointed two commissions of inquiry: the first, the Shaw Commission, to investigate the causes of the riots; the second, a one-man commission of inquiry, by Sir John Hope-Simpson, to investigate land settlement, immigration and development (details in Chapter 10). Hope-Simpson concluded that almost 30 per cent of Arab rural families – 86,980 – were landless, and 29.4 per cent homeless. He blamed Zionist land purchases for the situation, without providing any proof of how many Arab landholders had been deprived of their lands by the Zionists. In his assessment of the amount of cultivable lands still available, Hope-Simpson referred only to those lands to which the Zionists had either laid claim or which they already occupied; he made no mention of the fact that 70 per cent of all state lands had been allocated to the Arabs. He also glossed over the Arabs' poor exploitation of the soil, the excessive tax burden imposed by the British, and the natural disasters – drought and plague – that had reduced agricultural yields.[81]

The widespread sale of Arab lands to the Zionists during the mandatory period wrought changes in the Palestinian demography and landscape. There was a mass migration of Arabs from village to town. Entire Arab villages disappeared because of land sales.[82] A Zionist land expert reported in the 1930s:

> ... some villages in the Nablus area had been almost emptied, their inhabitants having moved to the city. In the towns, the former *fellah* was confronted by the unfamiliar hardships of inflation and unemployment.[83]

In 1933, Christopher Eastwood, one of High Commissioner Wauchope's private secretaries, confessed that he was becoming more and more pro-Arab as he observed the inexorable process by which the Arabs were losing their patrimony. He noted in his diary the continuous sale of lands by Arabs to Jews, and the Jews' readiness to pay "fantastic prices" for land. He recognized the fact that in these conditions, no individual Arab, no matter how "patriotic", could be expected not to sell.[84]

In public, Arab leaders protested about the land sales to the Jews, making maximum political use of each dispute. But behind the scenes, most of the traditional, landowning leadership were selling off parcels of their own lands, unable to resist the temptations of the rising market. The shadowy land market, in which the Arabs were selling off their national birthright, became a serious factor in the radicalization of the Arab masses and their alienation from their traditional leaders. Many drew the conclusion that the British would not protect them and that their own leaders were inadequate and deceitful. Many young villagers, torn from their ancestral rural homes, found solace in city pleasures: alcohol, card clubs, cinema and prostitutes.

For many Arabs, frustration and anger found their outlet in open rebellion against the Yishuv and the British. Many Arab attacks during the 1936–39 rebellion were against areas of intensive Zionist settlement.[85] But Arab land sales to the Zionists continued during the entire course of the rebellion, even if the intra-Arab terror campaign brought a reduction of some 30 per cent in the sales, compared to the previous 4 years.[86] The Zionists' knowledge of Arabic enabled them to analyse the strengths and weaknesses of the Palestinian Arabs. During the rebellion, and more especially after the Peel Commission had allotted the Arab-populated Galilee to the prospective Jewish state, Zionist land purchasing agencies began to identify "lands necessary for the

Redefining policy in Palestine 141

consolidation of Jewish-held regions, for the creation of territorial depth, and for geo-political requirements".[87]

World War Two broke out less than a year after the end of the Arab rebellion. The economic crisis during the first years of the war, the desire to have cash in hand for emergencies, and the cessation of intra-Arab terror all led to a renewed flourishing of the land sales. Most of those who had conducted the punitive campaign against the sales were in exile, fugitives from British justice. Veteran Arab collaborators thrived and new ones entered the market. They helped not only to register acquired lands, but also to persuade reluctant sellers. Sales via second or third parties allowed the sellers to believe that they were selling their land to other Arabs, although had they chosen to know, it was quite obvious who was buying their land. Village *mukhtars* across the country helped; at times they even initiated sales. The extra income helped them to shore up their political and social standing. Lawyers and government officials facilitated the conclusion of "under the table" deals. The only obstacle to the sales was the Land Regulations clause of the 1939 White Paper. Zionist lawyers found loopholes. Indebted landowners were allowed by law to sell off part of their holdings in order to pay off their debts. Would-be sellers "borrowed" money from the Jewish National Fund, failed to repay, and were then "forced" by the courts to sell. It was clear to all concerned that these were in fact "fixed", voluntary transactions.[88]

After World War Two, several extremist religious-nationalist Arab groups sprang up to oppose the growth of the Jewish National Home. One of them, the "Arab Blood Society", which was active in the Jaffa and Tulkarm areas, was formed specifically for the purpose of intimidating and even killing Arab land brokers. A number of Arab land brokers were murdered. There were also several acts of extortion, intimidation and violence against merchants who were thought to be involved in land sales to the Jews.[89] An Arab historian has summarized the phenomenon:

> The suspicion, mistrust, cynicism, resentment, antagonism, and demoralization that was engendered at all levels of Palestinian Arab society by land sales cannot be over-emphasized ... It continued throughout the mandate and formed an ongoing basis for conflict.[90]

The Zionists benefited from the lack of national cohesion that characterized Arab society – the hierarchy of a narrow class of notables and a peasant majority that was largely illiterate. The Zionists knew that the amount of Arab land on sale would always exceed the limits of their budget. They discerned the lack of national unity in what was basically a feudal society, catapulted into the twentieth century by the European colonial powers, after 400 years of regressive Ottoman misrule.

The British failed to meet the expectations of the dispossessed Arabs, or to restore their lands to them. A true remedy to the Arabs' predicament – had they been willing to accept one from the British – would have involved:

142 Redefining policy in Palestine

> ... an agrarian policy that provided credit facilities, agricultural tax reform, modernization of agricultural methods, and more efficient land use.[91]

None of these measures was ever seriously considered by the British. They had neither the political will nor the financial resources, much less the trained personnel. The first attempt to implement Eastwood's solution to the problem, "to remove this fear of eventual submergence", would be made by the Peel Commission in 1937.

Notes

1. cf. Edward Horne, *A Job Well Done: A History of the Palestine Police Force, 1920–1948*, Sussex: The Book Guild, 2003 (first published by the Palestine Police in 1982), p. 43; Bernard Wasserstein, *The British in Palestine: The Mandatory Government and the Arab-Jewish Conflict, 1917–1929*, London: Royal Historical Society, 1978. p. 102; and Michael J. Cohen, *Churchill and the Jews*, revised paperback edition, London: Frank Cass, 2003, p. 99.
2. Wasserstein, ibid, pp. 101–2; Cohen, ibid, pp. 99–101.
3. ibid, ibid.
4. Bernard Wasserstein, *Samuel: A Political Life*, Oxford: Clarendon Press, 1992, p. 257.
5. Jewish immigration during the first 10 months of Samuel's term reached only a small fraction of the initial quota that he had authorized.
6. Details in Wasserstein, *The British*, pp. 103–4.
7. ibid, p. 141.
8. cf. Cohen, *Churchill*, p. 100; Michael J. Cohen, *The Origins and the Evolution of the Arab-Zionist Conflict*, Berkeley: University of California Press, 1987, pp. 81–82.
9. Churchill telegrams to Samuel, 4 and 12 May 1921 (Churchill had planned the reduction of the Palestine garrison from 25,000 to 7000 troops); also Young and Landman conversation, in Z4/302/4A, CZA.
10. Diary entry for 11 July 1922, Charles R. Ashbee, *A Palestine Notebook, 1918–1923*, New York: Doubleday/Page and Company, 1923, pp. 206, 221. *Wa'd*: Arabic for promise.
11. Cited in Wasserstein, *The British*, p. 110. Dr Eder, an Anglo-Jewish psychoanalyst, served as chairman of the Palestine Zionist executive from 1920 to 1925.
12. ibid, pp. 111–12. MacDonogh's sympathies for the Zionists derived largely from his first-hand acquaintance with the valuable wartime intelligence provided to General Allenby in Syria by the Jewish spy group, NILI.
13. Stein to Brigadier Kisch, 10 April 1923, cited in Wasserstein, *Samuel*, p. 261.
14. White Papers were draft statements of government policy, named after the colour of the paper on which they were printed; they were circulated to MPs in advance of the debate and vote on the proposed new policy.
15. Note of Churchill's private luncheon with Thomas Marlowe, editor of the *Daily Mail*, on 30 May 1921, in Cohen, *Churchill*, p. 104.
16. ibid, p. 109. Unless otherwise noted, citations are from my book.
17. On Churchill's appeals to Lloyd George to give up the Middle Eastern mandates, cf. ibid, pp. 62–63, 66, 70, 75, 96, 104.
18. ibid, pp. 103, 106.
19. Churchill to Samuel, 12 May 1921, CO 733/23742, NA.
20. Speech of 9 March 1922, in *House of Commons Debates* (*H.C. Deb.*), 5th series, vol. 151, col. 1548. Churchill's remarks were made in response to a vicious

campaign by the Northcliffe press against the entry into Palestine of what he termed undesirable, "Bolshevist" Jews.
21 Colonial Secretary's memorandum, CP 351 (23) Cab 24/161. NA.
22 In 1937, the regulation of immigration according to the 1922 formula of "economic absorptive capacity" was buried by the Peel Royal Commission, which determined that political factors, i.e. Arab opposition, also had to be taken into account. After that, immigration was limited to the nebulous "political high level" recommended by the Royal Commission.
23 Samuel's speech in Cohen, *Churchill*, pp. 104–5.
24 Minute of 10 June 1921 by Major Hubert Young, Assistant Secretary, ibid, p. 108.
25 In October 1919, Lloyd George moved him from the Foreign Office to the sinecure post of Lord President of the Council.
26 Cohen, *Churchill*, p. 114.
27 ibid, pp. 114–15.
28 ibid, pp. 108–9.
29 Letter of Miriam Sacher, cited in Martin Gilbert, *Winston S. Churchill*, vol. IV, Boston: Houghton Mifflin, 1975, p. 639.
30 Weizmann to Deedes, 31 July 1921, Cohen, *Churchill*, pp. 115–16.
31 ibid, p. 98. Meinertzhagen's mother was Georgina Potter, a sister of Beatrice Webb, wife of Sidney Webb, the Labour Colonial Secretary from 1928 to 1931 – see Chapter 10.
32 Lloyd George to Kerr, 15 February 1919, in the Lothian papers, in James Renton, *The Zionist Masquerade: The Birth of the Anglo-Zionist Alliance, 1914–1918*, Basingstoke/New York: Palgrave Macmillan, 2007, p. 153.
33 Weizmann to Deedes, 13 December 1921, in Wasserstein, *The British*, pp. 134–35.
34 For this and the following passages, cf. Cohen, *Churchill*, pp. 116–18. On the economic and political ramifications of the Rutenberg concession, see Chapter 8.
35 ibid, pp. 117–18.
36 ibid, p.123.
37 Wasserstein, *The British*, p. 135.
38 Debate of 21 June 1922, *House of Lords Debates* (*H.L. Deb.*), 5th series, vol. 50, col. 994.
39 The debate on 4 July 1922, and all quotations from it, are in *H.C. Deb.*, 5th series, vol. 156, cols 221–343.
40 The phrase was Weizmann's – an unguarded slip of the tongue, when asked at the Versailles Peace Conference what he meant by a "Jewish National Home". Weizmann pleaded with Samuel not to include his remark in the final draft of the White Paper, but Samuel insisted on leaving it in.
41 Cited in Wasserstein, *The British*, p. 118.
42 Ahad Ha'am (Heb. one of the people) was the *nom de plume* of Asher Ginsberg, a leading figure in the movement for spiritual or cultural Zionism, and a mentor to Weizmann. In 1907, he moved to London to work as a sales agent of Wissotzky, the Russian tea company. In 1922, he moved to Palestine, where he lived for the remaining 5 years of his life.
43 Quoted in Tom Segev, *One Palestine, Complete*, New York: Metropolitan Books, 2000,p. 154.
44 Wasserstein, *The British*, p. 118.
45 Chaim Weizmann, *Trial and Error*, New York: Schocken Books, 1966, p. 290 (the first edition was printed in 1949).
46 Wasserstein, *The British*, p. 157.
47 ibid, p. 130; on the Arabs' successful boycott of the elections to the legislative council in 1922 and on the failure of later constitutional initiatives, see idem, pp. 119–24, 127–29.

48 Gilbert, *Winston S. Churchill*, vol. IV, p. 662.
49 Gideon Biger, *An Empire in the Holy Land, 1917–1929*, New York: St Martin's Press, 1994, pp. 221–22.
50 Moshe Mossek, *Palestine Immigration Policy under Sir Herbert Samuel: British, Zionist, and Arab Attitudes*, London: Frank Cass, 1978.
51 Cabinet memorandum by Lord Devonshire, CP 351 (23), 27 July 1923, in Cab 24/161, NA.
52 Barbara J. Smith, *The Roots of Separatism in Palestine: British Economic Policy, 1920–1929*, Syracuse: Syracuse University Press, 1993, pp. 68–69; the total inflow of Jewish capital into Palestine between 1920 and 1947 has been estimated at P£178 million, the major part of which was Jewish donations; see Nadav Halevi, "The Political Economy of Absorptive Capacity", *Middle Eastern Studies*, 1983, vol. 19/4, pp. 456–69.
53 Kenneth W. Stein, *The Land Problem in Palestine, 1917–1939*, Chapel Hill: University of North Carolina Press, 1984, p. 214.
54 Smith, *The Roots*, pp. 68–71.
55 ibid, pp. 72–73.
56 The British were aware that tens of thousands of Syrian Arabs entered Palestine during the course of the mandate. The Arab governor of the Syrian Hauran estimated that over 35,000 Hauranis entered Palestine in 1934 alone. The British treated the Syrian Arabs as Palestinians and never recorded their numbers in their official reports; cf. Fritz Liebrich, *Britain's Naval and Political Reaction to the Illegal Immigration of Jews to Palestine, 1945–1948*, London: Routledge, 2005, pp. 30–32.
57 Cited in Halevi, "The Political Economy", p. 467
58 Biger, *An Empire*, pp. 224–25.
59 Halevi, "The Political Economy", p. 463.
60 ibid, p. 224; also Smith, *The Roots*, pp. 80–81.
61 Halevi, supra, and Smith, ibid, pp. 78–81. The Zionists asked for 16,500 certificates for the 6-month period from October 1925 to March 1926 but for the following 6-month period, April to September 1926, they asked for only 2500, and for the period after that, October 1926 to March 1927, they asked for just 1500 certificates; Smith, *The Roots*, p. 82.
62 Smith, ibid, pp. 76.
63 ibid, p. 82.
64 Cohen, *Origins*, pp. 82–85.
65 For this and following, cf. Stein, *The Land*, and Yehoshua Porat, *The Palestinian Arab National Movement: From Riots to Rebellion, 1929–1939*, London: Frank Cass, 1977, especially Chapter 4. Dr Stein's pioneering research was based on the *Tabu*, the Ottoman land registries, which the British used, and Israel continues to use.
66 Hillel Cohen, *Army of Shadows: Palestinian Collaboration with Zionism, 1917–1948*, Berkeley/Los Angeles: University of California Press, 2008, pp. 32–34.
67 Smith, *The Roots*, p. 91.
68 Wasserstein, *The British*, pp. 91–93, 115; Stein, *The Land*, pp. 19, 178–80; and Charles S. Kamen, *Little Common Ground: Arab Agriculture and Jewish Settlement in Palestine, 1920–1948*, Pittsburgh: University of Pittsburgh, 1991, p. 256.
69 Smith, *The Roots*, p. 115.
70 Stein, *The Land*, p. 30, calculated that of the 89 Arabs who served on the Arab Executive from 1920 to 1928, at least one quarter profited by land sales to the Jews. A full list of Arab leaders, including members of both the Husayni and Nashashibi families who sold lands to the Zionists, is given in his appendix, pp. 228–38. On references in the Arabic press, cf. Porat, *The Palestinian*, p. 38. In his evidence before the Peel Commission in 1937, Gilbert MacKereth, the British

Redefining policy in Palestine 145

Consul in Damascus, stated that a check in the Palestine Land Registry would reveal that the Mufti himself had acted as a broker in Arab sales to the Zionists; FO 371/20804, NA.
71 Wasserstein, *The British*, pp. 14, 115, and Smith, *The Roots*, pp. 109, 115. In 1913, more than 90 per cent of the Turks' direct income from Palestine came from taxes on land and crops.
72 Porath, *The Palestinian*, p. 297.
73 cf. Mustafa Kabha, *The Palestinian Press as a Shaper of Public Opinion, 1929–1939: Writing up a Storm*, London: Vallentine Mitchell, 2007, pp. 225–26, 266. *Al-Karmil* (named after the Carmel mountain, Haifa) was an Arabic weekly founded by Arab Christians, whose platform was opposition to Zionist colonization. Its first issue appeared in 1908.
74 Quotes in ibid, pp. 237–38. Bishop Hajjar, a resident of Haifa, was head of the Arab Catholic community in Palestine.
75 Stein, *The Land*, pp. 190–91.
76 Kamen, *Little Common Ground*, pp. 28, 259.
77 Smith, *The Roots*, pp. 109, 256; Stein, *The Land*, pp. 5, 217.
78 Stein, ibid, p. 101.
79 ibid, p. 26.
80 ibid, Chapter 2.
81 ibid, pp. 108–10.
82 ibid, p. 216.
83 ibid, p. 216; Segev, *One Palestine*, p. 354.
84 Diary entry, 14 April 1933, in Sherman, *Mandate Days*, p. 88.
85 Porath, *The Palestinian*, p. 297.
86 Cohen, *Army*, p. 189.
87 Stein, *The Land*, pp. 207–8, 215. In 1931, 2216 Palestinian Jews had a fluency in Arabic, compared with just 21 Muslims and Christian Arabs who knew Hebrew. From 1936 to April 1940, the volume of lands owned by the Jewish National Fund in the Galilee soared from 103 to 54,873 dunams.
88 Cohen, *Army*, pp. 189, 190–92.
89 Issa Khalaf, *Politics in Palestine: Arab Factionalism and Social Disintegration, 1939–1948*, Albany: State University of New York Press, 1991, p. 99.
90 ibid, p. 235.
91 Stein, *The Land*, p. 215.

7 1923: The Balfour Declaration challenged

> Given Oriental mentality, it is not surprising that the Palestine Arabs should entertain strong hopes of a reversal by the present Cabinet and Parliament of their predecessors' policy.
>
> Colonial Office Cabinet memorandum, February 1923

The Conservatives under siege

From October 1922, the new Conservative government engaged in much soul-searching over the Palestine question. But Prime Minister Bonar Law took no concrete steps to improve the situation. In the face of his procrastination, the public campaign against the Balfour Declaration intensified.

The change of administration in London appeared to have opened up for the Palestinian Arabs the real prospect of a reversal of Britain's policies in Palestine. On the face of it, as the new government was only too well aware, the Palestinians had good reason for hoping so. The vigorous parliamentary and public opposition to the Balfour Declaration policy during the previous 2 years had come mainly from the Conservative benches, and the right-wing press.

Four days after the general election, the *Daily Express*, owned by Lord Beaverbrook, asked: "Who was this 'Mysterious Chaim' [Weizmann]", who had "inveigled the innocent and unsuspecting British into the mire of the Middle East".[1] The Palestinian Arabs circulated copies of the MacMahon-Husayn correspondence to *The Morning Post, The Times*, and *The Daily Mail.*[2]

In January 1923, J.M.N. Jeffries published a series of articles in *The Daily Mail*, owned by Lord Northcliffe. They called for "an evacuation from Palestine and the abolition of the Balfour Declaration". In a book he published in 1923, Northcliffe, owner of the *Mail,* expressed his contempt for the people of Palestine:

> All lie profusely; the Muslim outrageously, the Zionist artistically, the Orthodox Jews the bitterest of all.[3]

On 23 February 1923, the *Mail* published a report headed: "Palestine waste and Bolsheviks. Incessant arms smuggling. Lord Northcliffe's remedy: stop the immigration". Later in the year, the paper published a 72-page "Daily Mail Enquiry", a booklet written by Jeffries, whose title – *The Palestine Deception* – gave away its content.[4]

On 11 February 1923, Beaverbrook's *Sunday Express* asserted:

> British troops had died to establish a Jewish despotism over Christians and the "subsidised" importation of Jews from Russia.

The article went on to accuse the government of having established in Palestine, at the expense of the British taxpayer: "a Zionist Government, with a Jewish Governor".[5]

In the House of Lords, the anti-Zionist campaign proceeded without abatement. On 1 March 1923, Lord Sydenham, one of the leaders of the opposition in the Lords to the Lloyd George coalition's support of the Zionists, demanded that the MacMahon-Husayn correspondence be published, claiming that "the public has the right to know exactly how our national obligations stand with regard the Arabs". He recited the history of the "MacMahon pledges" in great detail, with long quotations from the correspondence itself. But the Colonial Secretary, the Duke of Devonshire, announced that "much to his regret", the government could not make the correspondence available to the public, on the grounds that "passages not relating to the controversy could be detrimental to the public interest".[6]

On 27 March, Sydenham even attributed the fall of the Lloyd George coalition to its pro-Zionist policy, and by corollary, accredited the election of the current Conservative administration to its opposition to the coalition's Palestine policy. He hypothesized that:

> ... many gentlemen today occupying quite prominent positions in HMG who were last year and the year before among the most active and vehement assailants of Zionist policy in Palestine. ... [this] would constitute a strong ground for early consideration of the whole policy.[7]

Such was the impact of the agitation that in February 1923, Devonshire circulated a Cabinet memorandum to his colleagues, pressing the need for a clear government statement on whether or not they intended to change its Palestine policy:

> The present state of suspense is fair to nobody. It is not fair to allow the Jews to go on collecting money for their projects in Palestine if there is any question of non-fulfillment of the pledge on which these projects are based. It is not fair to the Arabs, if we mean to maintain our policy, to allow them to continue agitation which may develop into action for which they will suffer in the long run.[8]

148   1923: The Balfour Declaration challenged

Devonshire warned "there could be no doubt" that the change of government in England had revived the hopes of the Arab politicians. He reminded his colleagues: "the newspapers which had espoused the Arabs' cause were in the main those that displayed special hostility to the Coalition Administration". He concluded:

> Given Oriental mentality, it is not surprising that the Palestine Arabs should entertain strong hopes of a reversal by the present Cabinet and Parliament of their predecessors' policy.[9]

Devonshire believed that they had just two options left: either "complete evacuation" or stay on and honour Balfour's pledge. But he warned that if they chose the former:

> We certainly should stand convicted of an act of perfidy from which it is hardly too much to say that our good name would never recover.[10]

Considerations of higher policy and of the potential injury to Britain's good name were of little or no consolation to those officials charged with the day-to-day administration of the mandate. As one scholar has observed:

> The tangle of British diplomatic commitments in the area, traditional socio-political attitudes of the "official mind", and first-hand perception of the profundity of the Arab-Jewish schism in Palestine, all inclined British officials to consider their task distasteful, if not impossible.[11]

Many officials, saddled with executing a policy that they could not fulfil with a clear conscience, became demoralized. A rare insight into their anguish is provided by the transcript of a private conversation in April 1923 between Sir John Shuckburgh, founding head of the Colonial Office's Middle East department, and Sydney Moody, a Palestine government official.[12] Shuckburgh confessed to:

> ... **a sense of personal degradation**. He had always had this feeling during the two years he had been at the Colonial Office. The British policy in Palestine was built on this ambiguity and the Middle East Department suffered from it. He could not go on, they could not go on, feeling this sense of equivocation. It was personally degrading and unworthy of the British Government. It was of course a result of the War, an evil result and furnished an explanation but not a justification for prolonging it ...
>
> We might logically rule Palestine as a conquered country, but after all could we, ought we, to force on the Arab population of Palestine a mass of alien immigrants mostly Russian and Polish? However good it might be for Palestine the Arabs did not want it, were bitterly opposed to it and deeply resented the treatment ...

The High Commissioner's new suggestion for an Advisory Council, reserving from discussion controversial points of policy, and all our shuffling, scrambling, accommodating, hedging tricks to alter the Order in Council in order to fit the circumstances were unworthy of a great nation and seemed to be an attempt to smuggle in by guile what we could not straightforwardly carry through. The elections were a farce and a failure.[13]

Shuckburgh despaired of ever finding a solution to the *imbroglio* between Arabs and Jews in Palestine. He had no faith in the government's policy of trying to reconcile the Arabs to Zionism. Since the only course left was to impose Zionism by force – something that the British electorate would never tolerate – he wished that Britain could divest herself of the Balfour promise.[14]

Charles Ashbee, whom we have already met in previous chapters, adopted the same line as Jeffries' "Deception" pamphlet, concluding:

1 The policy of the Balfour Declaration is an unjust policy as understood and as sometimes practised in Palestine, is based upon a fundamental injustice and therefore dangerous both to civilization and to Jewry.

2 Our British attitude is unintelligent. Such plan as we have is not thought out. As a consequence our administrators risk lending themselves to something that is disingenuous and that will have to be reconsidered and re-evalued.[15]

The Cabinet sub-committee on Palestine

It was not until June 1923, following the resignation of Prime Minister Bonar Law due to serious illness, and his replacement by Stanley Baldwin, that the government took any concrete steps in respect of Palestine.[16]

One of Baldwin's first decisions was to appoint a special Cabinet sub-committee "to examine Palestine policy afresh and to advise the full Cabinet whether Britain should remain in Palestine and whether, if she remained, the pro-Zionist policy should be continued". The sub-committee was chaired by Devonshire, but its most influential member was the Foreign Secretary, Lord Curzon, one of the few ministers who retained his office when the Conservatives replaced the Lloyd George coalition. Curzon set the tone of the committee's deliberations and crafted its final report.[17]

Dr Weizmann learned about the establishment of the new sub-committee belatedly, on the eve of the Cabinet's discussion of its report. He reacted in a characteristically hysterical fashion. Shuckburgh reported that Weizmann had visited him greatly agitated, fearing that more concessions would be made to the Arabs, which would "further whittle down the Balfour Declaration and the privileges of the Jews in Palestine". Weizmann warned that if this happened, it would break up the Zionist Organization and kill Zionist activity in Palestine. On the next day he warned Devonshire:

> ... a readjustment involving the abandonment of vital principles, would be a shattering blow which might well prove fatal to Zionism.[18]

During the sub-committee's month-long deliberations, the opponents of Zionism in the House of Lords stepped up their agitation; in the Commons, 100 Conservative MPs signed a petition, demanding of the sub-committee that:

> ... the DEFINITE pledges given to the Palestine Arabs be fulfilled ... the whole population of Palestine, with its 93 percent Arabs, should be consulted, and a form of government agreed upon in harmony with their wishes ... to impose on an unwilling people ... the dominating influence of another race is a violation of natural rights condemned in the covenant of the League of Nations.[19]

Palestine as a strategic asset

The committee first examined Palestine's strategic significance for the Empire. The military – like politicians of different persuasions – rarely spoke with a single, united voice. Debates on strategy were usually marked by inter-service rivalry, with each branch of the armed forces trying by special pleading to increase its own share of the military budget.

It should also be recalled that in 1923, the navy, not the army, was the senior and the most important of Britain's three armed services. Without the fleet, Britain could not have maintained its overstretched Empire. Most of the British establishment would have concurred with Churchill's *obiter dictum* that without its Empire, "Great Britain" would be reduced to "Little England".

Note needs to be taken also of the ambitions of the up-and-coming Royal Air Force (RAF), whose full potential still lay in the future. The RAF had already fixed its eyes on Palestine as a major imperial staging post for aircraft flying to India and to Britain's Far Eastern imperial outposts.[20]

Some scholars have claimed that the British General Staff dismissed Palestine's strategic importance. One study has asserted that as early as 1920, it was made clear to the government that "the occupation of Palestine fulfilled no strategic need".[21] Another study concluded, more specifically, that in 1923, the General Staff dismissed Palestine as being "of no strategic value in defending the Suez Canal".[22]

Indeed, given the General Staff's reticence about "the new provinces", it is not surprising that in 1923, they contended:

> **Palestine is not of strategic importance for the primary task of defending the Suez Canal** ... it might well prove a weakness by increasing our commitments and making calls upon the garrison in Egypt.[23]

However, the army did concede that any estimate of Palestine's strategic value depended upon the decision about which of three alternatives would serve as the best defence line for the canal: (a) the northern frontier of Palestine; (b) an intermediate position in Palestine itself, or (c) the Sinai desert. They chose the third option, from Rafah in the Sinai Peninsula, with Britain's main force based in Egypt.[24]

They continued that whereas there were certain advantages to holding off an enemy attack at a distance from the canal, i.e. in northern Palestine, in practice, any advantage would be more than offset by "the dissipation of forces and effort resulting from a longer line of communications and the rearward services which these entail". Further, they warned that "any advantages possessed by a forward position" might be more than offset by disturbances in the rear of the area of operations. For this same reason, they also dismissed the admittedly promising potential of Haifa as a deep-water port.[25]

En passant, one might note that the General Staff's warning about "disturbances in the rear of the area of operations" could be, and indeed was, argued both ways. The General Staff's conclusions were disputed by Brigadier General Sir Gilbert Clayton, an officer with long experience in the Middle East, who had served in a series of senior official positions in Egypt.[26] Clayton would have a key influence on the deliberations of the Cabinet's sub-committee on Palestine.[27] The Colonial Office, which in June 1922 appointed him to the position of Chief Secretary in Palestine, used him as an *ex officio* military advisor. During the early stages of the strategic debate, Clayton asserted that the volatile position in Egypt in fact tended to *increase* the strategic value of Palestine. Britain could not have gone so far as she had in Egypt [in repressing Saad Zaghlul's national movement] had she not been in secure possession of Palestine.[28]

The General Staff argued that Rafah (at the southern limit of the Gaza Strip) was still some 120 miles from the canal – a considerable distance (in 1923), even for air action. However, the idea that any significant military base could function in the Sinai desert – "thanks to improvements in communications during World War One" – was purely fanciful, even when the project was revived, ephemerally, in the early 1950s.[29]

However, notwithstanding their deprecation of Palestine's strategic value, the General Staff did *not* recommend evacuation. They insisted that Britain must hold on to Palestine, if only to prevent any potential enemy from moving into the resulting vacuum that her evacuation would leave.[30] The COS warned that a British withdrawal would result in a domino-like deterioration of "Britain's entire strategic position in the Middle East", and would "result ultimately in the resumption of Turkish rule over Palestine, including Trans-Jordania". If this occurred, the French position in Syria would be compromised, and the chances of Turkey retaking that country would increase; a return of the Turks to Syria would in turn undermine Britain's own position in Iraq. The COS concluded that for as long as Britain's relations with Angora (the capital of modern Turkey, Ankara, from 1930) remained uncertain, and for so long as "conflicting Arab aspirations are in a state of flux":

> ... our control of Palestine exerts an influence **the loss of which would be to our detriment strategically**.[31]

By coincidence, on 24 July 1923, 1 week before the Cabinet's final decision on Palestine, Britain and her allies signed the Treaty of Lausanne with the Turks; this replaced the defunct Treaty of Sèvres and was supposed to settle all differences with Kemal Attatürk.[32] But the agreement, upon which the ink had barely dried, did not even rate a mention during the Cabinet's deliberations on Palestine.

The conquest of Palestine during the last months of the war had also opened up the irresistible prospect of a strategic link between northern Iraq (with Mosul's huge oil reserves) and a terminal on the Mediterranean coast, in Palestine. The General Staff conceded that in that eventuality, "Palestine, with its port of Haifa, would become of greater importance". The Colonial Office added that the development of this "trans-desert route", whether by rail and/or by oil pipeline, would require "our retention of Palestine" or, at a minimum, "a friendly Palestine"; the navy, with its oil-burning fleet, naturally added its support.[33]

The General Staff also conceded Palestine's potential as an important "link in the air route to Baghdad". However, when the Air Staff had the temerity to claim that Palestine would be an important station in the construction of a world-wide chain of imperial air bases, the General Staff retorted cynically:

> ... if we are to hold and garrison increasingly broad areas of the earth's surface in order to confine foreign aerodromes to a safe distance from our own territories, we shall presently, as the range of aircraft increases, have to control most of the world.[34]

The Naval Staff opposed the army's dismissal of Palestine as a strategic buffer to the Suez Canal. They began with a reminder of the canal's logistical significance: the sea route from Britain to the Empire in the East, to Singapore, was 11,600 miles via the Cape route, but only 8000 miles via the canal. They warned that if Palestine's ports were to fall into hostile hands, this would constitute:

> ... a grave menace to the Mediterranean approaches to the Canal, and would probably necessitate the establishment by Great Britain of a naval base on Cyprus.[35]

But in any case, the views of the General Staff were not accepted by Cabinet ministers. At the decisive CID meeting on Palestine on 12 July 1923, Sir Samuel Hoare, the Secretary of State for Air, insisted:

... it was not merely the defence of the Canal, but the broad air strategy of the Empire which required the retention of Palestine.[36]

The military's contempt for Cabinet ministers was reciprocated in kind by Whitehall. On one occasion, Shuckburgh dismissed a statement by a War Office "expert" that "Palestine was rather a source of weakness than of strength", observing:

> But of course you cannot set overmuch value on official military opinion because it is usually conflicting and even if not conflicting it varies every six months.[37]

In its final report, the Cabinet sub-committee reproduced verbatim a Shuckburgh memorandum of 2 July 1923, which summed up neatly the military consensus:

> Although the strategic value of Palestine is rated by the Imperial General Staff less highly than it has been placed by some authorities, yet none of us can contemplate with equanimity the installation in Palestine of another Power.[38]

Lord Curzon's views are of especial significance. His experience as a former Viceroy of India and as one who had held ministerial responsibility for both Egypt and Palestine made him especially sensitive to the nexus between the two countries. He never wavered in his conviction, conceived during the war, that Palestine was an essential strategic buffer for the Suez Canal. Immediately after the war, he formulated a doctrine before the Cabinet's Eastern Committee that became Cabinet orthodoxy:

> Has not the whole history of the war shown us ... that Palestine is really the strategic buffer of Egypt, and that the Canal, which is the weak side of Egypt, if it has to be defended in the future, it will have to be defended – as it has been in the war – from the Palestine side?[39]

While Curzon proffered some lofty words about the mandate for Palestine being allotted to either the United States or to Great Britain, he left no doubt about his own determination that the Britain should keep it for herself. But this did not make Curzon into an advocate of a Jewish state. He favoured some form of a Jewish entity within the wider frame of the Empire.[40]

During the 1923 debates on Palestine, the Colonial Office case for retaining the mandate and for adhering to the Balfour Declaration leaned heavily on the briefs of Brigadier General Clayton, who during the war had developed a "personal commitment to the Anglo-Arab alliance".[41] Initially, he believed that through the instrument of the 1922 Palestine White Paper, Britain's Arab policy could be reconciled with its sponsorship of Zionism. He became acquainted with and learned to respect Sir Herbert Samuel, the first High Commissioner to Palestine, and he believed that the White Paper had put that country back "on the right track". From his Egyptian perspective, Clayton was convinced of Britain's strategic need for Palestine. Indeed, it has been claimed that he went to Palestine in 1923 "with the hope that there he would again be at the centre of Britain's imperial strategy in the Middle East".[42] For a time, in 1925, he was even considered the favourite to succeed Samuel as High Commissioner – not least because his candidacy was supported by the Zionists.[43]

Like Curzon, Clayton came to appreciate Britain's need to adhere to the 1917 pledge to the Zionists, if she wanted to hold on to Palestine. Clayton's influence on the Cabinet's sub-committee on Palestine is reflected in the fact that their final report cited him several times as an authority – once, as a corrective to Samuel's naive optimism about the situation in Palestine:

> Sir H. Samuel, in his recorded evidence, placed before us his estimate of the future of Palestine ... These estimates may turn out to be unduly sanguine; already they have to some extent been checked by the less rosy forecast of Sir G. Clayton.[44]

Clayton's lengthy analysis of Palestine's importance as a strategic hinterland to Egypt was reprinted almost verbatim in both of the key memoranda on Palestine that the Colonial Office submitted to the Cabinet in 1923, in February, and in the memorandum printed as an annex to the Cabinet sub-committee's final report.

The sub-committee's final report also cited and adopted Clayton's conclusion: "there is no ground whatever for advocating the abandonment of the Zionist policy or relinquishing the Mandate", as well as his recommendation that an answer to Palestinian Arab objections might be found "by modifying objectionable Articles in the Mandate, or at least by removing all possible grounds for any charges of partiality or bad faith, to dissipate the present fear and distrust of the Arabs".[45]

The Colonial Office *tour d'horizon* on Palestine's importance as a strategic buffer to the Suez Canal, presented to the CID in July 1923, is worth quoting at length:

> Previous to 1914 and during the critical phases of the Great War, Egypt was the essential link between Europe and our Eastern possessions. The Suez Canal assumed an importance which rendered its defence of vital consequence. Nevertheless the Turk reached the Canal, and at one point [February 1915] succeeded in crossing it ... **The geographical defence of Egypt, namely, the Sinai Desert, had proved itself inadequate in modern warfare, and still more apparent would this become in any future war.**
>
> As the Great War developed and military operations in the Middle East expanded, it soon became apparent that **not only Egypt but Palestine**

rose in importance in the political and strategic world. Palestine ... **assumed the proportion of a strong enemy base, both naval, military and air, whose occupation became necessary for our security in the East and Mediterranean.**

... Many as were the advantages of defending Egypt along the lines of the Suez Canal, a line some 80 miles long, and with a desert glacis stretching to the east, there were disadvantages. The line was too attenuated except for a large body of troops. Any strategic counter-attack was impossible owing to a lack of water in the Sinai Desert ... The bombing of Cairo was undertaken by the Turk in days when aeronautics were in their infancy. To remove this menace a methodical advance was undertaken by us across Sinai and the Turkish army was defeated in Palestine.[46]

Britain's economic interest

A major taunt in the public campaign against the government's support for Zionism was the alleged waste of the British taxpayers' money. One typical article, published in the mass-circulation *Daily Express* in February 1921, castigated the government's squandering of British resources "in the arid wastes of the Middle East at a time when the British people were already crushed by taxation, oppressed by restricted trade and widespread unemployment".[47]

In 1922, one-third of all government expenditure was still going to service the national debt. Given that the British wanted to retain control of Palestine, and that no government would willingly spend taxpayers' money on the Zionist enterprise (who would?), the obvious solution lay in the pockets of the Jews, allegedly the "richest nation on earth".

By 1923, no British official disputed the fact that without the continued import of Jewish capital and enterprise into Palestine, not only would the pace of development in that country slow down drastically or even come to a halt but any expenses incurred in its routine administration and control would fall on the British taxpayer. Such a prospect was pure anathema to all post-war British governments.

Lord Curzon had discovered a "solution" to his earlier fears of fostering unrealistic hopes of a large-scale Jewish immigration into an undeveloped country. At an imperial conference in October 1923, after reiterating his views on Palestine's strategic importance, he explained how the Jews themselves were going to finance the development of the country:

We cannot now recede [from Palestine]. If we did the French would step in and then be on the threshold of Egypt and on the outskirts of the Canal. Besides **Palestine needs ports, electricity, and the Jews of America were rich and would subsidize such development**.[48]

156 1923: The Balfour Declaration challenged

The pragmatic, imperialist viewpoint was never stated more candidly than by Sydney Moody, in his private conversation with Shuckburgh in April 1923:

> I have no fervent belief in the fulfilment of prophecy by the return of the Jews to the Holy Land. The historical and sentimental arguments left me cold. It is time to [recognize] that Palestine is under-populated and underdeveloped and suffering from the neglect of centuries and that **the Jews are the only people who are capable of rebuilding it because they have the necessary money, enthusiasm and manpower.**[49]

In 1923, the need for Jewish capital to finance the development of Palestine was one of the key planks in the Colonial Secretary's case for retaining the mandate. He began by correcting the "gross exaggeration" upon which much of the public campaign against the government's "Zionist policy" had been based – that it was costing the British taxpayer a lot of money. He informed the Cabinet that the actual cost to the British taxpayer of holding Palestine had been just over £2 millions in 1922–23, and it was planned to reduce this sum to £1½ million. However, the Zionists had already spent £5 millions developing the country, and were ready to invest much more. He then reiterated a few "home truths" about Britain's need of Jewish investment in Palestine:

> It is they alone who are both able and willing to supply capital enterprise and additional labour. Palestine is a poor country and unlikely to attract capital from the outside world on its own merits. The Zionists have a special incentive, unconnected with calculations of profit and return, to devote their brains and resources to the development of the country.

In complete contrast to Moody's private cynicism, Devonshire concluded his case for the Cabinet with the worn "civilizing mission" cliché:

> It may well be argued that by giving them [the Jews] the opportunity of doing so, we are serving the interests of civilization as a whole, quite apart from any sentimental considerations about restoring a scattered people to its ancient fatherland.[50]

The sub-committee's final report reiterated the need for Zionist capital to develop Palestine:

> ... it [the Balfour Declaration] has been the basis upon which Zionist co-operation in the development of Palestine has been freely given and upon which very large sums of Jewish money have since been subscribed.
> ... **we do not want to staunch the flow of subscriptions from the Jewish world, which are still essential for the continued existence of the colonies in Palestine, and secondarily for the future development of Palestine as a**

whole ... the best hope for the relief of the British taxpayer lies in improving the economic conditions of the country.[51]

The international commitment

For England, a small island kingdom that did not have a significant land army, but controlled an empire scattered across the globe by means of its fleet, the need for continental land alliances was obvious. The importance of honouring promises was much more than just another item in the cultural baggage of the consummate English gentleman. It was regarded as a *sine qua non* for the conduct of the nation's foreign affairs. On countless occasions, English statesmen argued that if the word of the government could not be relied upon, how could they ever hope to persuade other states to enter into alliances with Britain?

The general consensus, led by Curzon, was that the Balfour Declaration was one of England's binding commitments.[52] But perhaps no British statesman gave better expression to this principle than Winston Churchill. Even though he had initially opposed the retention of Britain's Middle Eastern conquests, when called upon to defend the 1922 White Paper in the House of Commons, he argued:

> I appeal to the House of Commons not to alter its opinion on the general question, but to **stand faithfully to the undertakings which have been given in the name of Britain, and interpret in an honourable and earnest way the promise that Britain will do her best to fulfil her undertakings to the Zionists.**[53]

The Palestine sub-committee's final report also dwelt at length on the need to honour the Balfour pledge:

> ... it is often represented that the Zionist policy was a mere fad of the late Government and (to quote Lord Sydenham's words) "one of the many legacies of evil which the coalition has 'bequeathed'". This view cannot possibly be sustained. The policy is a legacy, not of Mr. Churchill or of the Coalition, but of the Great War. The Balfour Declaration was a war measure, taken by the War Cabinet ... after full deliberation at a time when the military situation was exceedingly critical, and designed to secure tangible benefits which it was hoped would contribute to the ultimate victory of the Allies. These benefits may or may not have been worth securing, and may or may not have been actually secured; but the objections to going back on a promise made under such conditions are obvious. The Jews would naturally regard it as a matter of baseness if, having appealed to them in our hour of peril, we were to throw them over when the danger was past ... **The policy of the Balfour Declaration was**

accepted by the Principal Allied Powers ... We are in fact committed to the Zionist policy before the whole world in the clearest and most unequivocal fashion.[54]

In presenting the sub-committee's report to the Cabinet on 31 July, Curzon reiterated yet again the potential harm to Britain's international reputation and integrity, should she renege on the Balfour Declaration:

> ... it is well nigh impossible for any Government to extricate itself without a substantial sacrifice of consistency and self-respect, if not of honour. Those of us who have disliked the policy are not prepared to make that sacrifice. Those of us who approved the policy throughout would, of course, speak in much less equivocal terms.[55]

On 31 July 1923 the Cabinet rubber-stamped the sub-committee's report. It adopted Curzon's proposal that Arab grievances against the Zionists' privileged position should be assuaged by the creation of an analogous Arab Agency, that would have "a position in regard to the question of immigration" identical to that of the Jewish Agency.[56]

The dual commitment to Arabs and Zionists

It will be recalled that in March 1923, Lord Sydenham had asked Colonial Secretary Devonshire to publish the MacMahon-Husayn correspondence, so that the public might be informed of where Britain stood in respect of its obligations to the parties concerned. In the Lords debate, Devonshire had adroitly side-stepped the issue.[57] Devonshire's reply was given after the Colonial Office itself had reviewed Britain's wartime commitments to the Arabs and the Jews. In a frank memorandum circulated by Devonshire to his Cabinet colleagues, he revealed the true nature of Britain's duplicitous stance on the Palestine question.

He reviewed four alternative policy options for future policy in Palestine – the first three of which would have involved giving up the mandate:

1. They could decide that if they felt bound to maintain the wartime coalition's promise to the Arabs, which had preceded that given to the Jews, then they would have to "declare the Jewish pledge to be null and void".
2. They could determine that not only was the language used in the pledge to the Arabs "inconclusive", but the pledge to the Jews provided not only for a National Home for them – but also for the "maintenance of the civil and religious rights of the non-Jewish communities in Palestine". Since experience had already shown that the two parts of the pledge were "wholly incompatible", they could decide against proceeding any further with "the experiment".

3. They might decide that whatever may or may not have been given to the Arabs and to the Jews, the commitments incurred are "more than we are able to discharge", and they had no alternative other than "to abandon the task".
4. They might continue the policy of the previous government: that nothing that was said to the Arabs during the war precludes "the due fulfillment of the Balfour Declaration", and regard the 1922 White Paper as "adequately safeguarding both parts of the Declaration".[58]

Devonshire asserted that the public promise made to the Jews was more significant than the secret correspondence with the Hashemite Sharif Husayn of Mecca (not with the Palestinians), which in any case had been broken off inconclusively:

> We should be placed in an intolerable position after breaking a promise made to the Jews in the face of the whole world ... We should, indeed, stand convicted of an act of perfidy, from which it is hardly too much to say that our own good name would never recover.[59]

The conclusion drawn by the Conservative government in 1923 was in line with what it perceived to be Britain's own imperial interests at the time. It is appropriate to leave the last word to John Shuckburgh, the *éminence grise* at the Colonial Office, who since February 1921, as founder-director of the department's Middle Eastern section, had sat at the fulcrum of day-to-day policy making on Palestine.[60] When asked by Moody in April 1923 if he thought that Britain had "got her money's worth" from the Balfour Declaration, he replied:

> He thought not, but pointed out that it was nevertheless a bargain into which we had entered and from which we had expected certain advantages. Whether we had actually got our money's worth did not affect the binding nature of the bargain.[61]

Until the mid-1930s, Britain treated Palestine as *sui generis*, and rebuffed all attempts by the Arab states to intervene in its affairs. But from 1936 – with Italy breathing down her neck in the Middle East and the European balance threatened by Hitler's revanchist Germany – Britain gave the highest priority to retaining at least the benevolent neutrality of the Arab states. By the late 1930s, British officials had come to see the Balfour Declaration in a quite different light – as a wartime deviation that must not be repeated in the next war. In 1944 one official referred to it as the cause of all of Britain's problems in the Middle East:

> ... that fateful mental aberration known to history as the Balfour Declaration.[62]

Notes

1. Article of 28 October 1922 cited in Norman Rose, *A Senseless, Squalid War: Voices from Palestine, 1945–1948*, London: The Bodley Head, 2009, p. 27.
2. On the delegation's activities, and the press articles, see Sahar Huneidi, "Was the Balfour Declaration Reversible? The Colonial Office and Palestine, 1921–23", *Journal of Palestine Studies*, vol. 27/2, Winter 1998, pp. 33–34.
3. Lord Northcliffe had included Jerusalem in his world tour; his book, *My Journey Round the World, 1921–1922*, is cited by Nasser Eddin Nashashibi, *Jerusalem's Other Voice: Ragheb Nashashibi and Moderation in Palestinian Politics, 1920–1948*, Exeter: Ithaca Press, 1990, p. 120.
4. ibid, p. 34; also Michael J. Cohen, *Churchill and the Jews*, London: Frank Cass, first edition, 1985, revised paperback edition, 2003, pp. 136–38; J.M.N. Jeffries later published a full-length book, *Palestine: The Reality*, London: Longman's, 1939; on Jeffries' book, see also Chapter 8.
5. Article of 11 February 1923, in David Cesarani, "Anti-Zionism in Britain, 1922–2002: Continuities and Discontinuities", *The Journal of Israeli History*, vol. 25/1, pp. 134–35; also Sahar Huneidi, *A Broken Trust: Herbert Samuel, Zionism and the Palestinians*, London/New York: I.B. Tauris & Co., Ltd, 2001, p. 57.
6. Huneidi, "Was the Balfour", p. 34.
7. ibid, p. 32. In May 1923, Sir L. Worthington-Evans, one of the more prominent opponents of Zionism, was appointed Postmaster-General in Baldwin's new government.
8. CP 106 (23), 17 February 1923, in Cab 24/159. NA.
9. ibid, and report of Palestine sub-committee, 27 July 1923, CP 351 (23), Cab 24/161, also in T160/44. NA.
10. ibid.
11. Bernard Wasserstein, *The British in Palestine: The Mandatory Government and the Arab-Jewish Conflict, 1917–1929*, London: Royal Historical Society, 1978, p. 15.
12. The following is based on Moody's record of their conversation on 13 April 1923, in the Moody collection at Rhodes House, Oxford, in Evyatar Friesel, "British Officials on the Situation in Palestine, 1923", *Middle Eastern Studies*, Vol. 23, No. 2, April 1987, pp. 194–210. Sydney Moody first came to Palestine to serve with the military administration that governed Palestine from 1918 to 1920; he continued to serve under the civil administration from July 1920. He began as a District Officer in Safed, was seconded for a year to the Colonial Office in London in 1923, and returned to work in the Secretariat of the Palestine government until 1939.
13. Friesel, ibid, p. 200. My emphasis.
14. Compare Bernard Wasserstein, *Herbert Samuel: A Political Life*, Oxford: Clarendon Press, 1992, p. 262, with the record of Shuckburgh's private conversation with Moody, ibid.
15. Charles R. Ashbee, *A Palestine Notebook, 1918–1923*, New York: Doubleday/Page & Company, 1923, p. 267. Ashbee, a Fellow of the Royal Institute of British Architects, was in charge of overseeing building projects and the protection of historic sites and monuments.
16. In May 1923, Bonar Law was diagnosed with terminal cancer – he died later the same year. Baldwin took office as Prime Minister on 23 May 1923.
17. Other members of the sub-committee were the Secretaries of State for India, War and Air, the First Lord of the Admiralty, the President of the Board of Trade, and the Financial Secretary to the Treasury, Sir William Joynson-Hicks; cf. Minutes of Cabinet meeting on 23 June 1923, Cab 23/46, and T160/44. Joynson-Hicks was leader of the right-wing Tory faction that had opposed Zionism; in July 1922, he

1923: The Balfour Declaration challenged   161

proposed a vote of non-confidence in the Commons on the government's Palestine policy. cf. Sahar Huneidi, "Was the Balfour", p. 34; Wasserstein, *The British*, p. 126.

18 Weizmann–Shuckburgh meeting on 25 July 1923, and Weizmann letter of 26 July, in Huneidi, ibid, p. 37.
19 The full text of the petition is in CP 60 (23) in CO 733/58, and in Cab 24/158, NA.
20 The RAF built three major air bases in Palestine during the 1940s – Ramat David in 1942, Lydda in 1943, and Hatzor in 1945.
21 Gideon Biger, *An Empire in the Holy Land, 1917–1929*, New York: St Martin's Press, 1994, p. 73.
22 Huneidi, "Was the Balfour", p. 35.
23 CID 199-C, 18 June 1923, in Air 5/586, NA. My emphasis.
24 ibid.
25 ibid. During the late 1930s, the Arab rebellion in Palestine would indeed tie down forces earmarked for the defence of the canal. But on the other hand, after Britain signed the Anglo-Egyptian Treaty in August 1936 – which imposed a ceiling of 10,000 troops on the size of the British garrison in Egypt – she was left with no alternative but to station in Palestine all forces required for the defence of the canal above the treaty limit. Without the absolute freedom to use Palestine as a staging-base for an unlimited number of troops, Britain would have been unable to prepare adequately for the defence of Egypt. See Michael J. Cohen, "The Egypt–Palestine Nexus: 1935–1939", *Bar-Ilan Studies in History*, vol. 1, Ramat-Gan: Bar-Ilan University Press, 1991, pp. 67–79.
26 Brigadier General Sir Gilbert Clayton served as private secretary to Sir Reginald Wingate, commander of Egypt's army and governor general of the Sudan, 1910–14; Director of Intelligence, Egypt, 1914–17, in which capacity he headed the Arab Bureau at Cairo; Chief Political Officer, under General Allenby, to the Egyptian Expeditionary Force that ruled Palestine, 1917–19; and advisor to the Egyptian Ministry of the Interior, 1919–23.
27 In June 1922, Clayton accepted the post of Chief Secretary to the Palestine administration following the resignation of the former incumbent, Colonel Wyndham Deedes. He did not take up his new post until April 1923; cf. Huneidi, *A Broken Trust*, pp. 109–10.
28 Clayton cited in CP 351 supra; also Friesel, "British Officials", p. 202.
29 At the beginning of the 1950s, when the British faced the prospect of having to evacuate Egypt, the General Staff prepared detailed feasibility studies for the construction of an alternative military base in Sinai, centred on the Gaza Strip; the plans were dismissed out of hand by the government – even if communications were considerably better than they had been in 1923; see Michael J. Cohen, *Fighting World War Three from the Middle East*, London: Frank Cass, 1997, pp. 147–60. In July 1948, when the General Staff circulated their first contingency plan for a defence line against a possible attack by the Soviets against the Suez Canal, they opted for the "intermediate position in Palestine", the so-called "Ramallah Line", running from Tel Aviv via Ramallah to Jericho; idem, pp. 167, 199–200.
30 Wasserstein, *Samuel*, p. 264.
31 CID 199-C, supra. My emphasis.
32 The Lausanne conference opened on 21 November 1922. The Treaty was signed by Britain, France, Italy, Japan, Greece and Romania – and the Turks, after 8 months of crisis-ridden negotiations. The independent republic of Turkey was proclaimed on 29 October 1923.
33 Colonial Office memorandum, 14 May 1923, CO 537/869, NA. Haifa's importance as an egress to the Mediterranean remained a constant in British strategy,

1923: The Balfour Declaration challenged

even if in 1926 the CID ruled it out as a port for the navy – on the grounds that it was vulnerable to land attack. Alexandria was the preferred choice for a refuelling base in the eastern Mediterranean. Report on the strategic importance of Mediterranean ports, CO 537/869, NA.

34 CID 199-C, 18 June 1923, supra.
35 Naval Staff appendix to CID 199-C, Air 5/586, NA.
36 35th meeting of the CID, 12 July 1923, in CO 537/869. NA. An independent Air Ministry was established in January 1917; it was absorbed by the War Ministry in January 1919; in May 1923, it became an independent ministry again – although its minister was not included in the Cabinet until 1924.
37 Friesel, "British Officials", p. 202. Shuckburgh referred to a debate in the Lords on 27 March 1923, in which Lord Raglan had expressed doubts about the Zionists' frequent claim that Palestine held great strategic value for the British; *House of Lords Debates (H.L. Deb.)*, 5th series, vol. LIII, p. 699.
38 CP 351 supra, NA; see also Shuckburgh minute, 2 July 1923, in CO 733/58, NA.
39 Curzon speech on 5 December 1918, cited in David Lloyd George, *The Truth about the Peace Treaties*, London: Gollancz, 1938, p. 1147.
40 ibid; also John Fisher, *Curzon and the British Empire in the Middle East, 1916–1919*, London: Frank Cass, 1999, pp. 211–214.
41 Wasserstein, *The British*, pp. 22–24.
42 cf. Dennis Edward Knox, *The Development of British Policy in Palestine, 1917–1925: Sir Gilbert Clayton and the "New Eastern Question"*, PhD dissertation, Michigan State University, pp. 150–51, 370, 387.
43 Wasserstein, *The British*, p. 151.
44 Palestine sub-committee report, CP 351, supra; on Samuel's naiveté, see Wasserstein, *Samuel*, pp. 256–57, 266.
45 CP 351, supra.
46 Colonial Office paper for CID, "The Strategic Importance of Palestine", 2 July 1923, CID 199-C, in CO 537/869. NA, my emphases. Also CP 351 ibid.
47 Article of 5 February 1921, cited by Huneidi, *A Broken Trust*, p. 57.
48 Cited in Keith Middlemass, ed., *Thomas Jones, Whitehall Diary*, vol. 1. *1916–1925*, London: Oxford University Press, 1969, p. 246, my emphasis.
49 Friesel, "British Officials", p. 204. My emphasis.
50 CP 351 supra.
51 ibid. My emphasis.
52 Wasserstein, *The British*, p. 55.
53 Commons debate on 4 July 1922, in *H.C. Deb.*, 5th series, vol.156. Churchill's speech is in cols 327–42. My emphasis. In May 1939, Churchill would speak in very similar terms against the 1939 White Paper (comparing it to the Munich Agreement), as a breach of Britain's undertaking to the Zionists. cf. Cohen, *Churchill*, pp. 182–83.
54 Palestine Committee report, CP 351supra. NA. My emphases.
55 ibid, my emphases; cited also in Wasserstein, *The British*, p. 127.
56 Cabinet minutes in Cab 23/ 46, NA. The Arab Agency, like previous constitutional offers to the Arabs, also proved to be a "non-starter"; Wasserstein, ibid, pp. 62, 127–29. The Palestinian Arabs insisted on a power of veto on Jewish immigration, not an equal say with the Jews, with the ultimate veto remaining in the hands of a British High Commissioner.
57 In 1938, ahead of the Round Table conference on Palestine, scheduled for February 1939, George Antonius published the entire correspondence, as an annex in his *The Arab Awakening*, London: Hamish Hamilton, 1938.
58 For this and following, see CP 106 supra.
59 ibid; the "perfidy" phrase was also picked up by Curzon.

60 Shuckburgh, together with Samuel, was the real author of the so-called "Churchill" White Paper of 1922; cf. Cohen, *Churchill*, pp. 142–43, Wasserstein, ibid, p. 118.
61 Friesel, "British officials", p. 207.
62 Norman Rose, *A Senseless*, p. 31.

8 Paying for Empire in the 1920s

> I am still far from satisfied that it is desirable [and] in the taxpayers' interest to guarantee a loan to Palestine ... any Bill for that purpose ... would receive violent opposition ... You would get united against the Bill the anti-Expansionist party and the anti-Semite party ...
>
> Sir William Joynson-Hicks, August 1923

Imperial financing

By the end of the nineteenth century, Britain had fallen behind her two major rivals – the United States and Germany – both economically and industrially. The British Empire survived until World War Two thanks to the "invisible income" generated by invested capital and the services it provided (the goods carried by its merchant navy, banking and insurance), which filled the gap in its trade balance. But the immense costs of the 1914–18 war eroded Britain's self-confidence. She emerged in 1918 owing a huge debt to the United States. The punitive reparations imposed by the victors upon Germany and her allies were designed to cover the debts. But the vertiginous inflation of the German mark in the 1920s emasculated the reparations in real terms and put paid to any hopes of a quick economic recovery in Britain.

Since the closing decades of the nineteenth century, the British had expected their colonies to be self-supporting. One study of British imperialism has described the "classical objectives of Victorian imperialism" as follows:

> ... the creation of a compliant local regime which would preserve Britain's political and strategic interests while relieving her of the trouble and expense of ruling directly over an alien and unpredictable society.[1]

But during World War One the Empire had expanded to its zenith, due mainly to the un-planned conquest of huge territories in the Middle East. The costs of the war made it quite apparent that the mother country could not sustain any further increase in her imperial burdens.

Britain's imperial doctrine now stipulated that the empire should be a source of income, not expense for the home country. She arrogated to herself the right to control the economies of her various colonies. She prevented the erection of tariff walls behind which local industries might develop, and barred discrimination against British goods. Without protective tariffs, there was little chance that colonial economies would free themselves from dependence upon European manufactures, to be paid for, hopefully, by locally produced primary commodities.[2]

There was a huge discrepancy between the vast, largely arid expanses of Britain's newly acquired territories in the Middle East, and the paltry means at her disposal to control them. The military's estimates of the troop levels that would be required to hold on to the new territories were dismissed out of hand by the home government. The Cabinet accepted without question Lloyd George's decree that the budget of the armed forces must be reduced to pre-war levels.

Palestine itself was basically a poor country, lacking growth potential. Apart from a limited reserve of minerals in the Dead Sea, it had no known natural resources (i.e. metals, oil), no significant agricultural potential or local consumers' market, and no obvious outlets for British capital investment. Customs duties – considered to be a tax on the wealthier urban population – did not reach the usual two-thirds of colonial governments' total revenue until the end of the 1920s. Income tax was not introduced until September 1941.[3]

Sir Herbert Samuel, the first British High Commissioner, believed that government aid to Jewish enterprise would stimulate the industrialization of Palestine on modern European lines. But Samuel's initiatives were quashed by the Colonial Office. The country was flooded with imported goods that were "dumped" at very low prices on to a domestic market unprotected by tariff walls.[4]

Britain's primary interest in Palestine was strategic. But thanks to the Zionists, she came into a unique windfall – large imports of Jewish capital, donations to the development of the Jewish National Home. During the entire period of the mandate, the Palestine administration's entire annual budget never reached the level of Jewish capital imports. During the first 10 years of British rule, these totaled P£44 million, about twice the government's own expenditure. Some 73 per cent of this capital was private.[5]

The British Treasury retained strict control of Palestine's currency. The country benefited from the prestige and stability that came with the backing of the pound sterling, a recognized international currency. There were never any foreign exchange shortages, and no barriers to large imports of capital. But the local banking system consisted primarily of short-term deposits, as the large inflows of capital were usually spent immediately on Zionist colonization and the establishment of new businesses. There were no controls over or direction of investment, nor any restraint on the re-export of profits. Under British law, all capital reserves were held in Britain by the Crown Agents for the Colonies. These constituted a virtual loan to the British Treasury.[6]

The Palestine loan

Since Palestine had been a part of Ottoman Syria until World War One, it remained under the nominal control of the Foreign Office until February 1921, when the country was transferred to the jurisdiction of the Colonial Office.

In 1918, when General Allenby conquered the country, Palestine was a rural, neglected Ottoman backwater. Allenby had to pave a series of military roads for his army.[7] When Samuel arrived, he embarked upon a series of projects to establish basic infrastructures, i.e. road construction, swamp drainage, improvements to water supplies, irrigation and urban sewage systems and a telephone network. Given that the Palestine administration itself was legally unable to issue government bonds to fund these projects (until the League of Nations awarded the mandate to Britain, in September 1922), Samuel went into deficit spending, to the tune of some £2 million. Until 1922, Whitehall exercised no real budgetary control over expenditures in Palestine. In 1925, a Colonial Office official recalled the anarchy that had prevailed during the first 2 years of the mandate:

> The actual fact is that the approval of the Colonial Office was in those days neither sought nor given for expenditure on capital account and the result was that the Palestine Government succeeded in spending more than a [£] million and a half of money before the Colonial Office woke up to the true facts and succeeded in applying the brake.[8]

Given the home government's determination not to spend British taxpayers' money, the Palestine administration had to raise a loan on the international money markets. This was needed not only to cover the deficit already incurred, but also for future development and capital expenses (to which Britain's own imperial projects in the area would be added). Since Palestine itself was unable to offer sufficient security to raise a loan, the administration was forced to fall back on the government in London to provide an imperial loan guarantee. Until the loan could be floated, Palestine's deficits had to be covered by the British Treasury, which drew the funds from the reserves held by the Crown Agents for the Colonies. Negotiations to finalize the terms of the loan guarantee would take just over 5 years to complete.[9]

Britain's need for Zionist capital to finance the maintenance of Palestine has been described in the previous chapter. Chaim Weizmann never failed to seize any opportunity to remind the British of this need. For example, in October 1928, in a letter to William Ormsby-Gore, Under-Secretary of State for the Colonies, he argued that Haifa harbour should be built exclusively by Jewish labour:

> The harbour works are being financed from the proceeds of the Palestine Loan. It is no exaggeration to say that Jewish colonisation has been

largely instrumental in placing Palestine in a position to raise a loan of these dimensions on the strength of its taxable capacity, as measured by its financial record during the past few years. Similarly, the revenues on which the service of the loan is charged may fairly be said to be revenues which are directly or indirectly dependent to a considerable degree on the development of Jewish enterprise and the influx of Jewish capital; it is self-evident that if Jewish activity came to a standstill, or suffered a serious check, the security for the loan (apart from the British guarantee) would be materially impaired.[10]

Weizmann would hardly employ such arguments with American Jewish donors, during his fund-raising tours of the United States! Diaspora Jewry was mobilized to donate funds to the Jewish National Home – not for the welfare of the Palestinian Arabs, and hardly in order to relieve the British taxpayer of the costs of Empire. It is also to be doubted if the American Jews appreciated the extent to which they were helping to finance British strategic projects in the region: the construction of a network of strategic roads in Palestine,[11] the deep-water port at Haifa, and the railway/oil pipeline link that would be built between Kirkuk and Haifa during the early 1930s.

But the import of Jewish capital into Palestine was always a contentious issue. Zionist leaders claimed that their capital and skills would benefit all the inhabitants of Palestine – even if only indirectly. Initially, their claim received support from the Colonial Office, which adopted a patronizing policy towards the "native" Palestinian Arabs. But many British eyebrows were raised when in September 1921, Pinhas Rutenberg was awarded the electricity concession for most of mandatory Palestine and Trans-Jordan – excluding Jerusalem (see Chapter 9).[12] In January 1922, the head of the Colonial Office asked John Shuckburgh why the government should agree to the electrification of Palestine's railways, when France and Great Britain still used steam locomotives. He explained:

> The Rutenberg concession has always been regarded as the more practical example of the policy of setting up the National Home for the Jews. It is so regarded by the Zionists themselves. We are always trying to divert the attention of the Zionists from political to industrial activities, and preaching to them from the text that their best chance of reconciling the Arabs to the Zionist policy is to show them the practical advantages accruing from the Zionist enterprise.[13]

Imported Jewish capital, invested exclusively in Jewish enterprises, did create numerous jobs for Arab workers (at bargain wages). However, the Histadrut (the Zionist labour union) policy of pressuring Jewish employers to hire only Jewish labour actually led to job losses among the Arabs.[14]

The Arabs never conceded the claim that they too would benefit from the Zionists' largess. From the outset, they protested that the Jewish National

Home was the main, if not the sole beneficiary of Jewish capital. They asserted that most of the new roads were paved to serve the Jews and that the unprecedentedly high taxes levied by the British were needed to maintain a bloated administration that was required to serve the expanding Jewish population.

Colonial Office officials also failed to take into account the interests of British industrialists and bankers. While opposed to the expenditure of taxpayers' money on the Empire, the latter regarded the contracts for colonial development schemes as their natural and exclusive prerogative. At the very least, they expected all concessions in Palestine to be issued as public tenders.

Herbert Samuel, formerly privy to the Zionists' inner councils, believed that his own *laissez faire* economics meshed in with British imperial doctrine:

> The liberal approach of non-intervention in economic matters, and the retention of traditional socio-economic structures (primarily in the rural Arab community) fitted in well with the colonialist posture of maintaining socio-economic stability in colonized areas and encouraging their continued concentration on the production of primary products, thereby providing for colonial economic activity complementary to (and not competing with) the industrial "mother country".[15]

Samuel believed that in lieu of government subsidies, wealthy Jews could be persuaded to finance the building of the Jewish National Home. At a meeting with Jewish magnates and Zionist leaders in June 1920, on the eve of his own departure for Palestine, Samuel was reassured that they would help to raise a Palestine loan. One of Samuel's biographers has returned an acerbic verdict on his initial euphoria, asserting that after lengthy legal and technical delays had been overcome:

> ... the awful truth was revealed: the Zionists had been guilty of what amounted almost to a confidence trick in which they had deceived themselves as well as others. The "leaders of Jewish finance", it turned out, were not at all eager to perform the role assigned to them by Samuel and Weizmann.[16]

This oversimplifies a complex issue. Many Anglo-Jewish notables did oppose Zionism and refused to contribute to the cause. But others were pro-Zionist and willing to help to raise a Palestine loan. However, there were numerous problems involved, many of which resulted from the conflicting interests and intentions of the British and the Zionists. The following extract from a lengthy, confidential memorandum sent in 1924 by Samuel to J.H. Thomas, the Colonial Secretary, represents the most generous limits of British imperial thinking on Palestine. The memorandum, complaining of the excessive financial burdens imposed by the home government on Palestine, is worth quoting at length:

> I feel, indeed, that I have a dual capacity. I have to act as the spokesman of the people of Palestine with H.M.G ... At the same time I am an official of the British Government, and one who is fully conscious of the urgent need for the utmost economy on its part in all forms of expenditure that are not essential ...
>
> In our case a Loan is needed in order to repay the temporary borrowings from the Crown Agents, who have advanced monies deposited with them that belong to various Colonies; it is needed to enable an Agricultural Credit Bank to be established for the assistance of cultivators; to provide stud farms for the improvement of stock, and to supply other agricultural requirements; to complete the cadastral survey of the land; to allow the further development of the road system, of swamp drainage and other anti-malarial works, of water supplies and irrigation, of the telephone system, and of other works of improvement.
>
> It is true that a considerable amount of capital is being introduced into Palestine by the Zionist Organization, and allied bodies and individuals. But these funds are almost all spent upon the development of Jewish agriculture, Jewish industries, and the Jewish quarters of the towns. They do not supply, to any large extent, the purposes that have been enumerated. Indeed, from a political point of view, they make it all the more necessary for Government works to be undertaken, since such works will principally benefit the Arabs because they form the great majority of the population.[17]

Samuel's views were far too liberal for Whitehall, yet fell way short of Zionist expectations. The latter would not have agreed with his contention that the Palestine loan was needed to finance public works that would "principally benefit the Arabs". They asserted that the National Home clauses of the mandate required the government to provide the Yishuv with services commensurate with the revenues collected from it. Whereas the League mandate stipulated legal and administrative equality between Arabs and Jews, its article two required the Mandatory to place Palestine:

> ... under such political, administrative and economic conditions as will secure the establishment of the Jewish National Home.[18]

Those Jewish financiers who were willing to help float the loan were clearly motivated by Zionist sentiment. Had they not wanted specifically to help build up the Jewish National Home, they could have found more lucrative and safer avenues of investment. At the same time, they treated their investment in Palestine as a strictly business enterprise. They were not about to risk their capital on an unknown entity, especially not in the early, uncharted first years of the mandate. Until the end of July 1923, no one could guarantee that Britain would even remain in Palestine, let alone predict for how long. They were willing to receive a lower return on their investment in Palestine than that which they could have secured elsewhere, but they expected it to be guaranteed. As such, a loan that the British government itself was unwilling to guarantee could not be regarded as a sound business proposition.

The British Treasury was equally wary of guaranteeing a Palestine loan, and unwilling to commit the British taxpayer to repaying it after the end of the mandate. The Treasury insisted that the loan be treated as a liability of Palestine's – not of the Mandatory. In July 1922, 2 months before the League of Nations awarded the mandate to Britain, a Treasury official noted:

> The great difficulties of a loan are that Palestine has no certain political future. Even if a final mandate were given to this country, which has not yet been formally done, that mandate might come to an end at any moment, which would leave the holders of a prospective loan without any security ... a purely Palestine loan would not be a trustee security.[19]

The Colonial Office objected to the Treasury's inflexibility on the loan guarantee. The department had its own anxieties – that without the loan, the administration and security of Palestine would become too dependent on Jewish capital. The Treasury's parsimony towards Palestine during the 1920s would spark frequent clashes between the two departments. These tensions peaked during the second Baldwin administration (1924–29), when Leo Amery, a Zionist supporter, and Winston Churchill, a professed supporter, headed the Colonial Office and the Treasury respectively.

In February 1923, Colonial Office and Treasury officials met with the heads of the recently formed Economic Board for Palestine (EBP), a body set up by the pro-Zionist Jewish industrialist and financier Sir Alfred Mond,[20] and a council of prominent British Jews. The meeting was convened by the government, in the hope that the EBP would persuade Jewish banking houses – in London, New York, Amsterdam and Paris – to join the British Crown Agents in launching the Palestine loan. A pall of doubt hovered over the meeting, since the Cabinet had yet to determine if Britain would retain the mandate.

Mond offered to form a syndicate to take over the whole of the Palestine loan. But this did not suit the Colonial Office, which feared that a purely Jewish syndicate would only intensify Arab hostility and increase Zionist interference in the Palestine administration. Treasury officials and representatives of the Crown Agents for the Colonies then explained the difficulty of granting a government guarantee for a loan to a country over which Britain's tenure was temporary and indefinite.[21]

Leonard Cohen, a member of the EBP executive, explained that the loan's prospectus as it stood would only discourage investors, that "no private financial house of repute would undertake the issue of the Loan". Mond conceded that most of the large financial houses, both in Britain and in the United States, were "definitely anti-Zionist". However, he added, no Jewish investor would contemplate investing in Palestine until the doubts about the government's future policy were cleared up:

... the Mandate represented the policy of the late government, but not necessarily that of their [Conservative] successors. Unless the government publicly stated that they intended to continue the policy of their predecessors the issue of the Loan would be impracticable.[22]

When asked by Shuckburgh if the loan might be floated successfully should the Treasury agree to restore the government guarantees, Mond remained sceptical. He believed that the most fundamental problem was the persisting doubt about Britain's future policy in Palestine. Not only that, but there was no indication whether the proceeds of the proposed loan would be devoted to capital works that would appeal to the Zionists.

Mond believed that the Rothschild bank would be the most suitable agency for raising the loan as a private issue.[23] But the Colonial Office feared opposition if the loan was entrusted to a Jewish financial house:

> By entrusting the whole issue to a Jewish house we would afford critics of Zionism a loophole for an attack on our present policy in Palestine on the score that the Jews are making profits out of the Loan at the expense of the British taxpayer. For this reason alone it was of great importance that the issue should not be of a purely Jewish character, and in order to avoid this it was, in his opinion, essential that the Loan should be issued by the Crown Agents.[24]

The consensus among the Jewish magnates was that first there had to be a clear government declaration that it would adhere to the conditions of the League mandate, i.e. continue to pursue the policy of the Balfour Declaration; and second, they would require the government to give a clear assurance that it would "assume responsibility for the protection of the interests of the bondholders during the whole currency of the Loan" (i.e. in the event that the British relinquished the mandate before the term of the loan expired).[25]

As noted, at the end of July 1923, the Baldwin Cabinet decided to retain the Palestine mandate. The Colonial Office now reminded the other ministries concerned that Britain herself stood to gain from the successful issue of the Palestine loan; first and most important, the loan was essential in order to enable the Palestine administration to repay to the Crown Agents the £2 million that it had already spent; second, the loan would enable the Palestine administration to borrow money on the markets at a lower rate than previously and, with the extra revenue, it would be able to administer the mandate with a reduced grant-in-aid from London.[26]

But the Treasury remained unwilling to involve the British taxpayer in any financial commitment to Palestine. As noted already, the Conservative right wing had been among the most vociferous and violent opponents of the Lloyd George coalition's support for Zionism. They habitually had resort to anti-Semitic stereotypes. One of the most vociferous leaders of the Opposition in 1922 was Sir William Joynson-Hicks, whose public speeches since 1908 had earned him notoriety as an anti-Semite.[27] At the time of the parliamentary debates on the 1922 White Paper, he had played a key role in opposing the government's policy, both in the Commons and in the press. In particular, he attacked the government's decision to award the electricity concession to Rutenberg, rather than to a British company (see Chapter 9).

Fate would have it that during the summer months of 1923, Joynson-Hicks held an influential position in the first Baldwin administration, as Financial Secretary at the Treasury. In May, when Chancellor of the Exchequer Baldwin replaced Bonar Law as Prime Minister, Joynson-Hicks became acting Chancellor, until the end of August.[28] Much of consequence had happened since the Conservatives' 1922 campaign. The 1922 Palestine White Paper had been passed into law, and in September 1922, the League of Nations had awarded the mandate for Palestine to Britain. The Conservatives had no intention of giving up the mandate, but Joynson-Hicks remained opposed to any financial commitment to Palestine by Britain. He cautioned that pending some "effective settlement of the Arab versus Jew question", he would be reluctant to assume responsibility for piloting through Parliament a Bill for the Palestine loan guarantee:

> I am still far from satisfied that it is desirable [and] in the taxpayers' interest to guarantee a loan to Palestine. I am, however, certain, that any Bill for that purpose, would, at the present time, receive violent opposition in the House of Commons, probably from the Liberal Party, the Labour Party and certainly from the right wing of the Tory [Conservative] Party. You would get united against the Bill the anti-Expansionist party and the anti-Semite party and the Government might find itself in a very awkward position.

Nor had he forgotten the injury to British industrial interests:

> It will not be forgotten that the Rutenberg concessions are being exploited for the benefit of German and other industrialists and the English taxpayer would rightly be furious if a loan guaranteed by him was spent at Krupps ...
>
> If the Loan is to be guaranteed, I would make it up to five millions and clear off the whole of Palestine's debts and give her money to develop, but it would, of course, be a condition that the development money other than labour, should be expended in Great Britain.[29]

It was left to the short-lived Labour government (January–November 1924) to approve the imperial loan guarantee – although not before the Treasury and the Colonial Office had haggled at length about how much debt it was fair or possible to impose on Palestine.[30]

In April 1924, the Treasury agreed to increase the original sum of the loan, from £2.5 to £4 million. The increased amount was calculated to enable the government to recoup the debt of £2 million already incurred by the Palestine administration, and in addition, to enable it to pay for the construction of a deep-water harbour at Haifa (£1 million), and to repay the French an additional £1 million for the fixed capital assets (railways and rolling stock) that they had left behind in Palestine.[31]

Although the Colonial Office feared taking on the extra debt, it agreed to the increase. Recouping what were called "book debts" was a paramount consideration for the Treasury. At times, this involved some complicated book-keeping. For instance, the Treasury offered to increase Palestine's annual civil grant-in-aid, in order to enable the administration to repay its debts more quickly. The Colonial Office baulked at the prospect of increasing Palestine's budgetary deficit still further. However, the department jumped at the Treasury's offer of a further "sweetener" – to reduce Palestine's debt if the country made an immediate cash payment to the government from the proceeds of the loan. This opportunity was deemed by the Colonial Office to be "too good to refuse offhand". Since the extra cash payment would require a paring down of the Palestine budget, the Colonial Office adjured Samuel to balance his books by reducing expenditures, including those on services such as health and education:

> We must in fact make up our minds that Palestine is too poor a country to be given public services of the scale and standard we should like to see established.[32]

London took it for granted that the colonies could not expect to enjoy the same standard of living as the home country. In the period preceding World War Two, the Palestine administration spent 10–12 per cent of its budget on health and education – largely on the Arab population. This proportion was comparable to Britain's other colonies, but not to the amounts spent by British governments at home, where an estimated 66 per cent of their budgets went on social services. In the period 1918–45, the British built only five Arab schools in Palestine. Due to the Arab-Zionist conflict, they spent some 60 per cent of the Palestine budget on security, compared to roughly 11 per cent at home.[33]

In November 1924, Winston Churchill was appointed Chancellor of the Exchequer (1924–29). A vigorous defender of the 1922 White Paper, he was now in a unique position to improve the fortunes, or at least to alleviate the economic misfortunes of the Jewish National Home during the last 3 years of his tenure, when the Palestine economy sank into recession.

From 1920 to 1923 Jewish immigration into Palestine was fairly stable, at an annual rate of about 8000. But in 1924 immigration from Poland (over half of all the new immigrants) surged, due both to restrictive economic policies in Poland, and to new restrictions on immigration enacted by the American government. The largely middle-class Polish Jews concentrated in Tel Aviv, whose population mushroomed from 2000 in 1920, to 20,000 in

1924, and to 40,000 in 1925. In 1925, more than 70 per cent of all investment in Palestine was spent on the construction and associated trades.[34] But in 1926 the construction "bubble" burst and the Yishuv entered an economic recession, whose main feature was high unemployment (see details in Chapter 9).

Churchill was preoccupied exclusively with revitalizing the British economy, still in a post-war depression. Britain's most serious problem was mass unemployment. Churchill's efforts at solving Britain's economic problems were not an unmitigated success. His decision to return the pound sterling to the Gold Standard proved to be a mistake. It led to a steep rise in the value of the currency, which crippled British exports and hampered any economic recovery.[35] In addition, in 1926, when the British trade unions declared a general strike, that also covered the British press, Churchill was appointed editor of the weekly propaganda bulletin that the government issued in defiance of the unions. In July 1945, British workers would remember his role in defeating the strike, when they voted at the "khaki" elections.[36]

Churchill adhered rigidly to the imperial orthodoxy that the colonies must be self-supporting. His veto on all expenditures on imperial development projects – including Palestine – had a direct and prejudicial effect on the Jewish National Home. Under Churchill, the Treasury imposed on Palestine a change from "public investment and deficit financing ... to fiscal conservatism".[37] Churchill was responsible for holding up the government guarantee for the Palestine loan for a further 3 years, despite the fact that it was needed as much by the British Treasury as by Palestine. One scholar of Britain's economic policies in Palestine during the first decade of the mandate concluded:

> ... the overriding reason for guaranteeing the loan was to enable Palestine to repay its "debts" to HMG and to satisfy the Imperial need for a deep-water harbour at Haifa ... [38]

Initially, Churchill tried to argue that the Labour government's agreement to guarantee the Palestine loan was not binding on the Conservative government. He was soon corrected by Leo Amery, the Colonial Secretary, who pointed out that on 2 July 1924, Lord Arnold, the Labour Under-Secretary of State for the Colonies, had already announced the government's agreement to grant the loan guarantee in the House of Lords. Any reversal now, Amery warned, would incur "very grave charges of a breach of faith". He also reminded Churchill that it would be impossible to raise the Palestine loan without the British guarantee, and that it was needed:

> ... in the first instance to pay off the advances made to her by the Crown Agents for the Colonies. These advances represent the money of various Crown Colonies and Protectorates lent to Palestine ... in anticipation of the Palestine Loan ... [its] issue to enable the advances to be repaid became absolutely necessary.[39]

The Treasury and the Colonial Office haggled further over the size of Palestine's debt. Churchill criticized as "exceedingly liberal" his predecessor's agreement to reduce by 50 per cent the amount due for the payment of the capital assets left in Palestine – from just over £2 to £1 million. Field Marshal Sir Herbert Plumer, the High Commissioner (1925–28), criticized the government for making Palestine pay for railways that had been built in 1918 to meet the requirements of the British conquest, but did not meet the country's industrial and agricultural needs. The Treasury insisted that the roads built by the army would be of permanent benefit to Palestine.[40] Churchill also demurred at his predecessor's agreement to accept the payment of the proposed loan in bonds, rather than in cash. In addition, he refused to waive interest payments for a further 5 years, but directed that if Palestine was not in a position to begin the repayment of interest immediately, then the equivalent sum would be added to the principal of the loan. That would mean an addition of some £12–15,000 to the annual payments, when they began after 5 years.

Amery rejected Churchill's proposals, refusing to "impose a liability on Palestine" that the country would be unable to meet. He proposed that they return to the original "book debt" of £2,106,864. He advised that Palestine would begin repayments as soon as her finances permitted, which, he warned, might not be until the distant future.[41] Further to another reassessment of Palestine's debt to the Treasury, the sum of the loan was increased yet again – to £4,740,000.

Once at the Treasury, Churchill saw Palestine in a different light from that which he had seen when justifying the electrification concession to Rutenberg in 1922. When he finally approved the government guarantee, he appended the condition proposed by Joynson-Hicks in 1923 – all contracts for development projects in Palestine financed with the proceeds of the loan must be awarded to British companies.

This condition of Churchill's caused yet another contretemps between the two ministries. Amery objected that article 18 of the mandate stipulated that there should be "no discrimination in Palestine against nationals of any State Member of the League of Nations". He added that in practice, British companies would enjoy some advantage over their foreign competitors. But Churchill insisted that the fact that the British were guaranteeing the loan placed them in a special position.

They agreed to refer the issue to the government's law officers. The latter chose to ignore the relevant articles of the League mandate and gave their opinion that: "the attachment to the British guarantee ... of a formal condition that non-local expenditure should be in the United Kingdom would not be inconsistent with the terms of the Palestine and East African Mandates". On 3 March 1926, the Cabinet approved the loan guarantee together with the appended condition that development contracts would be awarded to British companies. The Palestine loan stock issue, now set at £4,740,000, yielding a 5 per cent interest per annum, was published in *The Times* some 18 months later, on 30 November 1927. It was fully subscribed immediately.[42]

Palestine subsidizes Trans-Jordan

In 1926, Palestine's budget was in healthy surplus, to the tune of £1.5 million. At the same time, the Yishuv economy was in decline and unemployment on the rise. But Churchill rejected the High Commissioner's requests to spend any of the surplus on local public works projects, to relieve unemployment. Churchill had other ideas on how to spend the surplus – in order to cover Trans-Jordan's deficits. Ever since Churchill had created the desert emirate east of the River Jordan in 1921, the British Exchequer had been forced to keep it afloat with an annual subsidy. At the end of 1926, in order to reduce this annual subsidy, Churchill directed that Palestine's budget surplus should be used to meet one-half of Trans-Jordan's administrative costs. Amery demurred, but bowed to the persuasive powers of the influential Montague Norman, Governor of the Bank of England since 1920.

But High Commissioner Plumer refused to bow to London's diktat. With Palestine's economy in recession (see Chapter 9), he treated the Colonial Office to a long sermon on the inequity of subsidizing Trans-Jordan from Palestine's budget:

> I hold the view that it is neither just nor politic to regard Trans-Jordan as a dependency of, or an annex to Palestine, and to levy contributions from the latter in support of the former ... I gather that HMG ... consider that Palestine has a material interest both in the preservation of order in Trans-Jordan and in its economic development ... In that case it is a matter for careful consideration to what extent it is justifiable, and how far it is to their interest to mulct the taxpayer of Palestine for what may be described as an "insurance" in the one case and an "investment" in the other ... As regards "insurance" ... Palestine ... is practically secure no matter what may happen in Trans-Jordan and other adjoining territories ... Natural expectation of Palestine is that any surplus balances of revenue would be expended on services which would be of value to the people of the country ... It has been found necessary to curtail the funds allotted to Extraordinary Public Works and to postpone several important services. The public are aware of this and it is certainly not the time to incur avoidable extraneous expenditure.[43]

But Churchill remained adamant. Matters came to crisis point in 1928, when he insisted that Palestine also cover half of the costs of maintaining the recently formed Trans-Jordan Frontier Force. In comparison, when the Palestine gendarmerie had been set up in 1922, the Palestine administration had had to meet the entire cost of the force. The new Frontier Force, which would eventually become the Arab Legion, was established mainly in order to patrol the emirate's vast desert expanses.[44]

Since the Force was regarded formally as an imperial unit for service in both Palestine and Trans-Jordan, Plumer proposed that each country pay one-half of its costs. Since Trans-Jordan would clearly be unable to pay its share, Plumer applied to London for an imperial grant-in-aid to cover it, on the grounds that:

> ... it would be quite unjust on the Palestine taxpayers to call on them to pay for the security of Trans-Jordan by requiring them to meet the cost of the Frontier Force.[45]

Not only did the Treasury dismiss Plumer's request for the imperial grant-in-aid for Trans-Jordan, but it also rejected his suggestion that each country cover half the costs of the Force. Instead, the Treasury insisted that Palestine pay not only two-thirds of the costs of the Force, but also half of Trans-Jordan's third, i.e. 5/6ths of the total costs! Plumer fought a rearguard action. He conceded the demand that Palestine pay two-thirds of the cost of the Force, but he drew the line at Palestine being required to pay one-half of Trans-Jordan's share. But again the Treasury remained adamant. Eventually, Amery bowed to the senior department, in return for yet another accounting compromise with the Treasury. He justified his decision on the grounds that the extra payment required of Palestine was a kind of insurance premium against disorder in either territory. He justified the five-to-one ratio of their respective payments by arguing that Palestine's revenues were roughly ten times those of Trans-Jordan.[46]

Plumer feared that under existing economic conditions, Palestine's current budget surplus could not be maintained, and that she would be unable to subsidize Trans-Jordan indefinitely. He regarded the home government as ultimately responsible for the security of both territories, and insisted that Palestine had no need of the Trans-Jordan Frontier Force. He not only rejected the London agreement on the financing of the Force, but demanded that by the end of 1928 Palestine be relieved entirely of the costs of maintaining it.[47]

But the Treasury officials had no more respect for the elderly (71 years old in 1928) field marshal's knowledge of finances than they had had for Herbert Samuel's. In January 1928, in protest at the rejection of his demands, Plumer offered his resignation:

> ... to impose on the taxpayers of Palestine the burden of the cost of the Trans-Jordan Force would be unjust. I am certain that the people themselves will so regard it. I cannot acquiesce in a policy which I believe to be unjust, and have therefore no alternative but to ask the Government to appoint some one to take my place.[48]

The threat of a high commissioner resigning – in protest at his own government's policy – was a rare, if not unique event in the annals of British colonial history. It prompted something close to panic at the Colonial Office. With the Colonial Secretary abroad on an imperial tour, William Ormsby-Gore, his Under-Secretary, took the unusual step of appealing over Churchill's head direct to the Prime Minister, with a copy to the Treasury. He warned of the serious domestic political consequences should the High Commissioner resign. But Churchill refused to waive Palestine's share of the costs of the Trans-Jordan Force.

When Amery returned to London, he took up the issue in person with Churchill, asking him to waive at least the charge on Palestine of £30,000 that the two had already agreed to, towards the costs of maintaining British troops in Trans-Jordan. He warned that the government's opponents might exploit any political crisis in Palestine. This would be particularly inopportune at a time when they were about to embark on the railway/pipeline project from Kirkuk to Haifa – another imperial asset that was to be subsidized by the Palestine budget.[49]

Churchill paid scant attention to either the moral considerations raised by Plumer or the domestic political issues raised by Amery. He was preoccupied with preparing the new budget. He replied to Amery that the £30,000 he was asking for was already included in his budget estimates and he could not at this late stage add a supplementary one. There is some irony in the fact that when Churchill presented his budget to Parliament on 24 April 1928, he announced with evident gratification that he had been fortunate in receiving two unanticipated windfalls: one was the repayment of loans by Kenya and Palestine to the tune of £4.5 million.[50]

Amery had little choice but to bow again to the senior department. He switched his powers of persuasion to Plumer, appealing to his conscience not to resign. He warned him that this would make public property of the government's internal dissensions, thereby supplying ammunition to the enemies of Zionism. His appeal might well have been drafted by the Zionists:

> The Beaverbrook-Rothermere press would joyfully seize the occasion for a renewed attack on the whole Mandate and urge us to clear out of Palestine altogether ... Palestine would lose far more than the amount now at issue. Arab agitation would naturally fasten upon your resignation to make trouble in general, and more particularly to put out that all this military expenditure imposed on Palestine is only in order to force Zionism on an Arab world struggling to be free and united.
>
> You have done such a splendid Imperial service in Palestine ... I do most earnestly implore you not to let your very natural dissatisfaction and disappointment prompt you into doing something at this moment which can only harm the cause for which we both care in Palestine itself and elsewhere, and add greatly to my own difficulties in the continuous struggle I have to wage to secure any kind of consideration for Imperial interests at this time of great financial stress at home.[51]

One final attempt by Amery to secure some gesture from Churchill was rebuffed. The latter remained unmoved by the High Commissioner's resignation threat. Plumer stayed on for 4 more months and resigned in August. The official reason given for his premature departure was ill health. No official receptions were held in his honour.

British Imperial dogma, that no colony should be a burden on the mother country, did not prevent the Treasury from raiding the surplus of one colony – Palestine – in order to relieve Britain of the burden of subsidizing another – Trans-Jordan. Nor did his stint at the Treasury inhibit Churchill from later vaunting in public his own role in the creation of the desert emirate back in 1921. In March 1936, in a speech in the House of Commons, upon his return from a private visit to the Middle East (on the yacht of Lord Moyne), he stated:

> The Emir Abdulla is in Transjordania [sic], where I put him one Sunday afternoon at Jerusalem. I acted upon the advice of that very great man Colonel Lawrence, who was at my side in making the arrangements.[52]

Ironically, Churchill also expressed his satisfaction with the tranquil state in which he had found Palestine – just 3 weeks before the outbreak of the Arab rebellion there.

Notes

1 John Darwin, *Britain, Egypt and the Middle East: Imperial Policy in the Aftermath of War, 1918–1922*, London: Macmillan, 1981, p. 221.
2 John Darwin, *Britain and Decolonisation*, London: Macmillan, 1988, pp. 9–14. Most of Britain's white dominions and India were granted tariff autonomy after World War One.
3 An early study of the economics of Empire, which focuses on Britain's fiscal policies towards the dominions, makes no mention either of Palestine or of the Middle East; Ian M. Drummond, *British Economic Policy and the Empire, 1919–1939*, London: George Allen & Unwin Ltd, 1972.
4 Barbara J. Smith, *The Roots of Separatism in Palestine: British Economic Policy, 1920–1929*, Syracuse: Syracuse University Press, 1993, p 176.
5 Diary entry of Henry Gurney, Chief Secretary of the Palestine administration, 15 April 1948, cited in A. J. Sherman, *Mandate Days: British Lives in Palestine, 1918–1948*, New York: Thames & Hudson, 1998, pp. 228–29; Tom Segev, *One Palestine, Complete*, New York: Metropolitan Books, 2000, p. 262.
6 Smith, *The Roots*, pp. 28–30, 38. On 1 November 1927, a Palestine Order-in-Council tied the Palestine pound to the English pound sterling, at the rate of one to one.
7 It has been estimated that between 1920 and 1929, Britain spent over £9 million – nearly half of mandatory Palestine's annual budget – in order to maintain the military garrison in Palestine; Segev, *One Palestine*, p. 72.
8 Unsigned, undated note, March 1925, CO 733/110/260, NA.
9 Smith, *The Roots*, pp. 32 ff.
10 Weizmann to Ormsby-Gore, 9 October 1928, Pinhas Ofer, ed., *The Letters & Papers of Chaim Weizmann*, vol. XIII, 1926–29, Jerusalem: Transaction Books/ Rutgers University/Israel Universities Press, 1978, p. 499. The construction of Haifa harbour, begun in 1930, was the main example of Palestine being made to pay for British imperial interests; the harbour served as the terminal for the trans-desert

oil pipeline and railway from Kirkuk, and served as an entrepôt for British commercial interests; cf. Smith, *The Roots*, p. 49.
11 British records show that the few main roads built by the British in Palestine were for strategic purposes, and that the majority of second- or third-class roads were built to connect Jewish settlements with the main roads. Zionist-generated capital funded as much as three-quarters of the costs of the latter; Smith, ibid, p. 58.
12 Jerusalem, still subject to an Ottoman concession, was not hooked up to the grid until 1928.
13 Shuckburgh to Masterton-Smith (Permanent Under-Secretary at the Colonial Office), 17 January 1922, CO 733/29, NA.
14 Jacob Metzer, *The Divided Economy of Mandatory Palestine*, Cambridge: Cambridge University Press, 1998, p. 7, and Smith, *The Roots*, p. 159. Jewish employers were intimidated and deterred from hiring Arabs by the Histadrut.
15 Metzer, ibid, p. 177.
16 Bernard Wasserstein, *Herbert Samuel*, Oxford: Oxford University Press, 1992, p. 254.
17 Samuel to J.H. Thomas, 8 February 1924, in T160/44, NA.
18 Metzer, *The Divided Economy*, pp. 4, 188.
19 Initialled note by Treasury official, 9 July 1922, in T160/44, NA.
20 Sir Alfred Mond visited Palestine for the first time in 1921 with Chaim Weizmann; he became an enthusiastic Zionist, and a good friend of Churchill's.
21 For this and following, cf. Smith, *The Roots*, pp. 33 ff.
22 Meeting of British officials with EBP, 26 February 1923, Treasury files, T160/44, NA.
23 Lionel de Rothschild and his brother Anthony were joint managing partners of the famous banking house. In May 1923, Lionel informed a Treasury official that his bank did not wish to be associated in any way with a Palestine loan; see Norman to Niemeyer, 2 May 1923, ibid.
24 Meeting of 26 February 1926, ibid.
25 ibid, and letter from Sir Robert Waley-Cohen to William Ormsby-Gore, 13 March 1923, ibid, NA. Waley-Cohen came from a prominent Anglo-Jewish family, one of a small group that had built up the Royal Dutch Shell oil conglomerate.
26 cf. Cabinet memorandum by Colonial Secretary Amery, 17 February 1926, CP (26)71, in Cab 124/178, NA.
27 William Joynson-Hicks, a solicitor, was first elected to Parliament on behalf of the Conservative Party in 1900. He supported the Aliens Act of 1908, which was aimed primarily against Russian Jews seeking asylum in England. In the 1908 by-election for Manchester North-West, he defeated Churchill, a Liberal at the time.
28 When Baldwin became Prime Minister in May 1923, he stayed on nominally as Chancellor until the end of August. In order to relieve himself of the burden of the two posts during this interim, Joynson-Hicks effectively replaced him as Chancellor, with a seat in the Cabinet. At the end of August 1923, Neville Chamberlain was appointed Chancellor and Joynson-Hicks Minister of Health.
29 Memorandum by Sir William Joynson-Hicks, 17 August 1923, T160/44, NA.
30 Correspondence in ibid.
31 John Meikle (Treasury) to the Under-Secretary of State for the Colonies, 17 August 1925, ibid.
32 ibid.
33 Metzer, *The Divided Economy*, p. 180; Segev, *One Palestine*, p. 171.
34 Metzer, ibid, p. 67; Segev, ibid, p. 237. From 1924 to 1925, the net Jewish immigration into Palestine was 22,000, from 1926 to 1927, 2,220 and from 1928 to 31, 2,546; Metzer, p. 71.

35 The Nobel laureate economist Paul Krugman has commented: "The hard right often favors hard money – preferably a gold standard": *New York Times*, 12 January 2011.
36 The Conservative majority of 432 seats in the House of Commons was reduced to 213. The Labour Party increased its share from 154 to 393 seats.
37 Metzer, *The Divided Economy*, p. 178.
38 Smith, *The Roots*, p. 35.
39 Churchill to Amery, 4 December 1924, and Amery to Churchill, 22 December 1924, in T160/44, NA.
40 Smith, *The Roots*, p. 48.
41 ibid.
42 Cabinet memorandum by Amery, CP 71(26), 17 February 1926, in Cab 24/178, Cabinet discussions on 3 February and 31 March 1936, also Amery to Churchill correspondence in T160/44, and notes in CO 733/124, NA.
43 Plumer to Amery, 27 October 1926, CO 733/117, NA.
44 cf. Smith, *The Roots*, p. 47.
45 Minutes of February 1928, in CO 733/151/1, 57155, NA.
46 Churchill agreed to waive Palestine's payment of half of Trans-Jordan's administrative costs, in return for which Palestine would pay 5/6ths of the costs of the Frontier Force indefinitely, and in 1927–28, pay an additional £30,000 towards the costs of stationing British troops in Trans-Jordan; Michael J. Cohen, *Churchill and the Jews*, London: Frank Cass, revised paperback edition, 2004, p. 154.
47 Minutes and correspondence in CO 733/151/1, 57155, NA.
48 Plumer to Ormsby-Gore, 8 January 1928, in ibid.
49 The Kirkuk-Haifa oil pipeline was completed in 1934. The Haifa oil refineries, which became operational in 1940, were capable of supplying the entire needs of Britain's Mediterranean fleet; cf Steven Morehead, *The British Defence of Egypt, 1935–1940*, London: Frank Cass, 2005, p. 23.
50 Cohen, *Churchill*, p. 156.
51 Amery to Plumer, 13 April 1928, ibid, p. 157.
52 *House of Commons Debates* (*H.C. Deb.*), fifth series, vol. 310, col. 1114, 24 March 1936. On the circumstances in which it was decided to carve out a separate emirate of Trans-Jordan from the Palestine mandate, cf. Cohen, *Churchill*, pp. 80–82, 87–90; on Churchill's inflated admiration for T.E. Lawrence, see idem, pp. 75–76.

9 The Yishuv economy in the 1920s

> There is no excuse whatever for Palestine being a burden on the Exchequer of this country ... I cannot understand why the idea of keeping Palestine in a dole-fed condition at the expense of our taxpayer attracts you.
> Churchill to Leo Amery, 30 April 1927

The Zionist loan

From 1922 to 1929, the total volume of Palestine trade increased three times, total revenues six times. Clearly, the increases were due to the large inflows of Jewish capital brought in by Jewish immigrants, and donations to the Zionist cause.[1]

But in 1926, the Yishuv economy declined into an economic recession. The short-lived economic boom of the fourth *aliya*, fuelled by a steep rise in Jewish immigration, largely from Poland (from 7000 in 1923 to 33,000 in 1925), had been based precariously on the construction sector, primarily in Tel Aviv. The recession was triggered by a steep decline in Jewish immigration from Poland (and in the amount of capital they brought with them), a poor harvest and cattle disease. The construction industry declined by 60 per cent in 1926, and by a further 56 per cent in 1927. The number of Jewish unemployed more than doubled in 1 year, from 3000 in 1925 to 8000 in 1926. At the peak of the crisis, during the first 8 months of 1927, one-third of the entire Jewish labour force was unemployed – over half of that number in Tel Aviv alone.[2]

The Palestine administration found itself in an anomalous situation. Its budget was in healthy surplus, due to revenues derived primarily from the Zionists' enterprise, but the Treasury was unwilling to channel any of the surplus to relieving their unemployment. High Commissioner Plumer felt guilty for having allowed in too many new immigrants during the previous few years, for not having "resisted the insistent demands of the Zionist Executive and the specious pleadings of Jewish supporters all over the world". His "solution" was to encourage Jewish emigration. The officials at Whitehall were quite aware that the very concept of re-emigration was anathema to the Zionists, whose very *raison d'être* was to encourage Jewish immigration to

Palestine. Not only was Jewish re-emigration uneconomical, but it was quite obviously bad for morale. But the Colonial Office supported Plumer's proposal that unemployed immigrants should return to their countries of origin. The department proposed that the administration stop paying unemployment benefits, that Plumer direct the Jews to hard manual labour, and that any who refused should be "encouraged" to leave the country. In 1926 and in 1928, the number of Jews who emigrated from Palestine exceeded the number that arrived.[3]

The Zionists were quite aware of the government's reticence about spending British revenues on Palestine. They also appreciated that the Palestine loan was not going to be spent solely, or even mainly on their own colonization projects. Weizmann confessed to his colleagues that the current unemployment in the Yishuv was a very difficult disease to cure without a large loan. Therefore, at the end of 1927 he tried to raise a £2 million Zionist loan on the international money markets. The money was to be spent on projects designed specifically to alleviate Jewish unemployment. Once again, international securities would be required. The Zionists hoped that the British would put up part of the international guarantee required, under the auspices of the League of Nations.

In late 1927, Weizmann sounded out European statesmen to take on a part of the proposed loan guarantee. In January 1928, he met with Raymond Poincaré, the French Prime Minister, and secured from him a commitment to guarantee up to £250,000 of the loan, provided that Britain took the initiative with the League of Nations.[4]

In February 1928, Weizmann submitted to the Colonial Office an official request for a government guarantee for the Zionist loan, explaining that it was needed to promote further Jewish colonization. He discussed the project several times with Ormsby-Gore and Shuckburgh. Both men expressed sympathy, but doubted if the Treasury would agree to pledging a government credit, unless the Zionists themselves could provide sufficient security. Weizmann confessed to his colleagues that this would be very difficult, since they could not "offer any security of a bankable nature".[5] But he told the Whitehall officials that the real justification for their loan lay in their mutual interest in the continuation of Jewish immigration and development, since the current depression also meant a drop in government revenues. He warned that both the Zionists and the government needed to initiate a new period of Zionist colonizing activity as soon as possible.

In March, Weizmann departed for several months to the United States on a fund-raising campaign. During this visit he would initiate moves to raise a Zionist Loan on Wall Street, to be launched by several American Jewish magnates and Alfred Mond (now Lord Melchett) from England. The goal was to establish a Zionist settlement company with a share capital of $2–3 million, to be subscribed half by non-Zionist American Jews and half by non-Zionist Jews around the world, including Edmund de Rothschild. The directors of the new settlement company were scheduled to meet in London in

June. The new company would raise double the amount of the proposed League loan, under a British or League guarantee.[6] However, the main purpose of the meeting of the Jewish magnates in London was to apply pressure on the government to return to full support of the Jewish National Home. Weizmann believed that the meeting would:

> ... assure the British Government that the American non-Zionist Jews would be ready to produce a considerable amount of capital for the upbuilding of Palestine if the Government would on its side carry out the Mandate in the spirit as well as in the letter.[7]

The British, not for the first or the last time, found themselves in an insoluble paradox over Palestine; on the one hand, faced with local Arab opposition, they had been in retreat from the 1917 Declaration, but on the other, those officials concerned with the administration of Palestine knew that Jewish immigration held the key to the economic welfare of the country. In 1928, T.K. Lloyd, the Colonial Office official in charge of Palestine, noted in an internal memo:

> The Jews have contributed disproportionately to the revenues [of Palestine]. Immigration of Jews and increase in revenues are in direct ratio. Surplus balances have only been accumulated owing to Jewish capital, as the High Commissioner has admitted. Loans, similarly, have been made possible by Jewish influence and activities.[8]

The officials also conceded, in confidence, that Britain herself was partly to blame for the current economic recession in Palestine; she had not drawn up a well-considered fiscal policy, she had failed to make land available for colonization and had not yet revised the oppressive Ottoman land taxation system.[9] Lloyd anticipated an improvement in the Palestine economy within the next 2–3 years and he drew up a series of proposals for helping out the Zionists in the interim: a programme of public works (including the expedition of plans to build the harbour at Haifa), preferential treatment for Jewish workers, and a revision of the Turkish land taxation heritage.[10]

However, as noted in the previous chapter, colonial orthodoxy ruled out the expenditure of government revenues on unemployment benefits, and the Treasury imposed a veto on providing work for the unemployed. When Churchill learned of Colonial Office plans to subsidize public works to employ Jews, he sent the following, hand-written irascible note to Amery:

> There is no excuse whatever for Palestine being a burden on the Exchequer of this country. It is quite capable of paying its own way in every respect as most Crown Colonies. I cannot understand why the idea of keeping Palestine in a dole-fed condition at the expense of our taxpayer

attracts you. I should have strained every nerve to secure solvency and independence at the earliest possible moment.

There is no credit in making one country swim at the expense of the other. The credit is to make it self-supporting.[11]

Churchill was applying double standards. As noted in the previous chapter, he had no compunction about making Trans-Jordan "swim" at the expense of Palestine.

Nonetheless, some efforts, financed largely by Zionist funds, were made to ease the plight of the Jewish unemployed. The Zionist Executive managed to secure Plumer's agreement to the construction of a road from Jaffa to Petah Tikva. The government did not put out the project for open tender and the road was built exclusively by Jewish labour. The administration's official report for 1928 recorded the expenditure of some P£76,500 on public works.[12]

But as already seen, the Treasury was against any expenditure on welfare in Palestine. Its official line was articulated by A.J. Harding, a member of the Palestine Currency Board. In a memorandum that totally disregarded the contribution of imported Jewish capital to the country's economic well-being, he wrote:

> ... the theory that Jewish immigrants in Palestine have the right without any effort of their own to look to the Palestine Government and failing them to His Majesty's Government to provide work for them, to establish hospitals and schools for them and their children and, in short, to provide all the amenities of western civilization and to spend money on the "modernization" of a country which, though backward is not more so than its neighbours. The Mandate does not place any such obligation on His Majesty's Government nor have they ever imposed such a policy on the Palestine Government.[13]

Even if some Colonial Office officials harboured some empathy for the Zionists' economic plight, none supported the issue of a government guarantee for the proposed Zionist loan. This was due to two fundamental reasons.

First, they had doubts about the Zionists' financial stability – would they be able to meet the annual interest payments on the loan, to be repayable over the next 40 years? The collateral offered by the Zionists was the annual donations to the Zionist Organization – an unpredictable entity. The fact that two large British banks had recently turned down the Zionists' requests for a loan of £400,000 did not help their case. Why should the Treasury step in where large commercial banks feared to tread? Officials were also cynical about the Zionists' own forecasts of Palestine's economic potential, demonstrably skewed by their own political interests. The current recession provided a ready-to-hand object lesson. Lloyd recalled that in 1926 the Zionists had claimed:

> ... the essential fact is that the Jewish urban population, by one means or another is making a living in its own way and is absorbing without serious difficulty a growing volume of immigration.[14]

Lloyd observed that within a few months of this forecast, the number of Jewish unemployed in Palestine had soared to 8000, proving that "the volume of immigration in 1925 had outrun the economic capacity of the country". Moreover, he observed cynically, "human nature being what it is", Jewish donations would fall off once the £2 million loan had been raised.[15]

But the second and most important reason, self-evident to all the officials who had anything to do with the Palestine administration, was that Britain could not permit any outsider to learn of the extent to which Britain was dependent upon the import of Jewish funds, not only for her administration of the country but also for financing her own imperial projects. This spectre was raised by the possibility that the Zionists might default on the loan. If they failed to meet their interest payments, other powers would be highly critical, not only of them but also of the British. This might lead to demands for an investigation into Palestine's finances and a demand that all income from taxation derived from the Zionists and their colonies should be set aside and remitted directly to the international debtors. The Colonial Office, which had fought a futile battle against the Treasury's use and misuse of revenues from Palestine, was acutely aware that their financial practices would not stand up to international scrutiny. Not only that, but any kind of international involvement might also lead to Zionist pressure that all revenues originating from Zionist sources be used exclusively for the benefit of the Yishuv. Lloyd warned:

> I can imagine no better lever than an internationally guaranteed loan for the Z[ionist] O[rganisation] to use in exercising pressure on H.M.G. and on the Palestine Government to obtain concessions and privileges which have not yet been given to them.[16]

In view of the opposition of the Colonial Office, there was little need for the Treasury to launch its own campaign against the Zionist loan guarantee. Sir James Grigg, Churchill's principal private secretary at the Treasury, reassured him that in any case, there was no chance that the League would agree to guarantee a Zionist loan. That body intervened only in the "most urgent and exceptional cases", where loans were:

> ... part of general schemes for the financial and monetary reconstruction of countries likely, without League support, to fall to pieces.[17]

It is quite clear that there was never any real chance that the Zionists would receive a British guarantee for their loan. There was an across-the-board consensus on this among all the officials in the relevant government departments. But their ministers were concerned about the potential damage that Zionists' American lobby might cause to Anglo-American relations if the government rejected the loan guarantee out of hand.

The Zionists' request for the loan guarantee did in fact reach the Cabinet. This was due largely to the initiative of Arthur Balfour, namesake of the 1917 Declaration. He was now the grand old man of English politics, still a member of the Cabinet, albeit without any specific ministerial responsibilities. In January 1928, Weizmann mobilized him – as he had done in July 1921 – to sponsor the Zionist cause. Balfour agreed to raise the issue in the Cabinet and prior to that, to convene another private meeting of the ministers concerned at his home – as soon as Colonial Secretary Amery returned from his imperial tour.[18]

The conference at Balfour's home took place on 27 February 1928. Apart from Weizmann and Amery, Churchill attended in his capacity as Chancellor of the Exchequer. The Colonial Secretary and the Chancellor were not about to discuss with Weizmann (or with Balfour, for that matter) their fears of an international scrutiny of Britain's accounting methods in Palestine. But they were concerned to encourage Weizmann before he left for his American tour. Amery had just had first-hand experience of the Zionist lobby during his trip to Canada.

The question of the American Zionists' criticism of British policy in Palestine was the first issue raised by the British ministers at Balfour's house. Weizmann conceded that the Jews were wont to exaggerate, but he insisted that they had legitimate grounds for complaint.[19] He reminded the meeting of the inconvenient fact that whereas the Palestine government currently enjoyed a surplus of P£1.5 million, the Yishuv was going through an economic and social crisis, which the administration was making no effort to relieve. He also reminded those present that whereas both Iraq and Palestine had been charged for the costs of the British military occupation regimes that had ruled them following the defeat of the Turks, Iraq had since been relieved of her share of the debt, whereas Palestine was still burdened with £30,000. Amery and Balfour affirmed the justness of Weizmann's claims. Churchill made a vague comment that Palestine's post-war debt might be adjusted. When Churchill agreed with Balfour's remark that Palestine was becoming even more important to the Empire than Iraq, Weizmann interjected "if Palestine was so important, then why was it being penalized and overburdened financially?".

Churchill explained that he feared that the grant of a government guarantee for the Zionist loan might stimulate anti-Semitic feeling in the Commons. However, he surmised that the guarantee might secure parliamentary approval if the loan was presented as a League initiative. Those present agreed that the loan should be presented as a measure for financing definite constructive projects, not just to tide over current problems (i.e. Jewish unemployment). It was decided first to secure the Cabinet's approval in principle, before taking the issue to the League. Balfour undertook to prepare a memorandum for the Cabinet.

Weizmann emerged from the meeting convinced that Balfour, Churchill and Amery would all support the loan guarantee. He reported to a Zionist colleague in Paris that the meeting had been "most successful".[20] But Colonial Office officials were alarmed at how forthcoming and encouraging Churchill had been. Amery regretted that the Chancellor had adopted "an exceedingly encouraging tone, to the extent of leading Weizmann to believe that he had a real chance of securing a government guarantee".[21]

Churchill's behaviour can be readily explained by his belief that American Jewry played a critical role in the formation of policy in Washington, and that the Zionists were able to turn the White House against Britain at their will.[22] Simply put, Churchill wanted to gain time, to reassure Weizmann of the government's benign intentions before he left for the United States. Weizmann, long aware of his American "trump card", did not hesitate to use it. Ten days prior to the meeting at Balfour's house, he had told Shuckburgh that one of the main reasons he was seeking an early governmental approval of the loan guarantee was that he was leaving shortly for the United States and would be able to report to his colleagues there that their request for a guarantee was progressing and had been submitted to the Cabinet. This is precisely the result that the ministers achieved at Balfour's house.

The first of three Cabinet meetings on the loan guarantee was held on 13 March 1928. The discussion centred on a long memorandum circulated by Balfour, although he was unable to attend the meeting in person, having fallen critically ill. His paper claimed that any impartial investigation of Britain's record in Palestine would reveal a lack of British generosity:

> Far from being the spoilt child of the mandatory system Palestine has been its Cinderella.[23]

It went on to reiterate Weizmann's claim that whereas Iraq had been relieved of its share of the Ottoman debt, Palestine – "a country far smaller and poorer" – was the only country of the former Ottoman empire that was still required to bear a share.[24] It continued that Palestine was unique among Britain's colonial possessions, in that it lacked neither capital nor settlers, both of which were supplied by the Zionists. Balfour then stressed the strategic importance of Palestine for the Empire:

> Palestine ... lies at the very place where the Power primarily responsible for the security of the Suez Canal would wish to place it ... A mandated territory on the Asiatic side of the great waterway, prosperous, contented and quite impervious to Egyptian intrigue must add strength to the Empire at a point where additional strength may, in the interests of the Empire and the world, be most desirable.

Balfour's paper asserted that it was only the Zionists' resources that enabled Britain to retain Palestine. Those resources might do nothing "to relieve the

British taxpayer" but their effects, indirectly, both morally and materially, must be beneficial. He concluded with the recommendation that the government approve the loan guarantee, from a statesman's point of view – even if, on purely financial criteria, it might not be approved by a banker or an accountant.

Amery opened the Cabinet debate. While refuting the charge that Britain had neglected Palestine, he supported the Zionists' request for a government guarantee under the auspices of the League. With oblique reference to the Zionists' influence in the United States, Amery pressed upon his colleagues the urgency of the matter:

> Dr Weizmann was leaving this week for America and hoped to have some indication of the Cabinet's policy before sailing.[25]

Austen Chamberlain, the Foreign Secretary, warned that a League guarantee would involve a certain amount of control over Palestine's finances. Amery interjected that the guarantee was for a loan to the Zionists, not to Palestine. Significantly, Churchill remained silent. The Cabinet concluded that it didn't have enough information, and asked Amery to circulate a memorandum for the next meeting (the Colonial Office paper had been held up due to a technical mistake).

Churchill believed apparently that once Weizmann left for the United States he would remain ignorant of the top-secret Cabinet proceedings. But the Zionist leader was kept privy to the Cabinet's proceedings by "Baffy" Dugdale (Balfour's neice and Weizmann's close advisor), who had her own sources inside the Cabinet. On the day after the first Cabinet meeting, she sent to Weizmann her own prescient assessment:

> In his [Balfour's] absence your affair has gone badly ... Of course the technical advisers were all against it – as we knew they would be. I have reason to think that A [mery] did his best to counteract their arguments, but single-handedly I suppose he was not enough. I fancy the other person who was present at your lunch party [Churchill] cannot have extended himself. We must remember of course that just at this time of year he has tremendous decisions on his mind [the Budget] ... Not that I consider this a sufficient excuse ... as things stand, its prospects are considered practically hopeless.[26]

The accuracy of Dugdale's assessment is confirmed by Amery, who vented his spleen in the confines of his private diary:

> ... also the proposed Zionist loan for which Balfour and Winston in their enthusiasm had let me in for but which obviously **Winston has now ratted on** and Austen [Chamberlain] turned down on Foreign Office grounds. However, they were postponed in order to spare poor old Balfour a shock while he is ill.[27]

The next and decisive Cabinet meeting took place some 3 weeks later, on 4 April. Balfour was still too ill to attend. The Zionists' request for the loan guarantee was rejected. Amery remained the only minister in favour. He suggested that the first step should be to approach the French, Italian and other governments, to mobilize their support for raising the issue at the League headquarters in Geneva. But Churchill had circulated a memorandum to the Cabinet that effectively destroyed all chance of the government agreeing to the guarantee. He cited an expert's report that there was no prospect of the loan being issued under the auspices of the League.[28] He next reminded his colleagues that they had "just got rid of the incubus of guaranteed loans" for the development of their own trade and warned: "to open the door again to such concessions ... would be disastrous". He ridiculed the Zionists' request:

> The Zionist Organization claims to have a steady income of nearly £700,000 per annum. With such resources it is absurd to pretend that they could not raise a loan of £2,000,000 privately, without the assistance of the League or from His Majesty's Government. Indeed, with so large an income, it is by no means clear that further provision by way of a loan is really necessary.[29]

Churchill also dismissed Balfour's claim that Iraq had received preferential treatment to Palestine; he protested that only the year before the government had approved the guarantee for a Palestine loan. Finally, he warned that to guarantee a loan for one particular section of the population in Palestine would be bound to arouse "vigorous criticism". No serious debate took place. However, in deference to the still-absent Balfour, it was decided to defer the formal rejection of the loan guarantee until he was well enough to attend the Cabinet.[30]

Weizmann, still touring the United States, was again kept apprised of the Cabinet proceedings by Mrs Dugdale. He was disappointed with Churchill and even with Amery. His reply to Dugdale indicates that he totally misread the balance of power inside the British Cabinet and he still hoped, anachronistically, that the invalided Balfour might yet save the day:

> I am afraid that Winston has not lived up to his promise, and I wonder whether Amery has been supporting our case with the vigour which was required. However, I am still hopeful that when Lord Balfour returns it may be possible to obtain a satisfactory decision.[31]

On 20 June, at the third and final Cabinet meeting on the loan guarantee, the Zionist request was formally rejected. One additional imperial consideration was raised. The government could not consider committing credits to the Zionists before it had worked out the financing for another impending imperial project involving Palestine – the construction of the railway and oil pipeline from Kirkuk to Haifa. Churchill did not speak at the meeting.

However, ever sensitive about and fearful of the Zionist lobby in the US, the Cabinet employed subterfuge with the Zionists. Amery was instructed to tell them that there were "very grave difficulties" in granting the guarantee and that without finally rejecting their request, the government was unable to support it for the present. At the same time, he was to tell them that the government was eager to do all it could "towards the support and development of Palestine".[32]

Balfour was the first to break the news to Weizmann. He too chose the path of subterfuge. He said that the Cabinet had been sympathetic to the loan guarantee, and that he, Amery, Churchill and Birkenhead had all favoured granting it. However, whereas all the financial objections had been swept aside, the issue had been deferred for the present, due to considerations of foreign policy. He advised Weizmann that the alternative they were considering – a British loan – would not secure parliamentary approval.

On 20 June Weizmann met Amery, who promised to help in every possible way. Weizmann was unable to resolve the paradox – if there had been so much support in the Cabinet, then why was its decision so negative? He informed Amery that the American Zionists had undertaken to raise a loan of £600,000, if the English Zionists raised £300,000–400,000 in the UK. The total of £1 million or so would enable them to place their financial institutions on a solid footing.[33]

Weizmann's efforts to establish a sound financial base for the Jewish National Home would wait until August 1929, when he succeeded in establishing an enlarged Jewish Agency that included non-Zionists.

Amery's altercations with Churchill over Palestine and his frustration with his veto on his various schemes for imperial development opened up a wide chasm between the two men. Amery became so exasperated that in April 1929 he warned Prime Minister Baldwin that Churchill would be a handicap for the party at the general elections, due the next month. He advised that if Churchill was replaced at the Exchequer by Neville Chamberlain, it would be worth "twenty or thirty seats at least". He confided to his private diary that only an electoral defeat "would free the Party from that incubus at the Treasury".[34]

The Zionists were privy to the Amery-Churchill feud. In April 1928, before the Cabinet officially "buried" their loan guarantee, Weizmann described it in a report to the Zionist Executive:

> ... I think that Amery is rather jealous of Churchill. When Amery returned from his Imperial Tour he had a great many projects, which were of course dependent on the consent of the Treasury for their realization. Churchill turned all of them down, and Amery was very much surprised when he saw that Churchill agreed in principle to our Loan.[35]

By the mid-1920s, two of the main architects of the 1917 Declaration, Lloyd George and Balfour, were political has-beens. Lloyd George now headed an emasculated Liberal Party[36] and the invalided Balfour held a symbolic, sinecure seat in the Cabinet.

Two Cabinet ministers exerted a key influence over Palestine from 1924 to 1929: Leo Amery and Winston Churchill. Amery had been one of the midwives at the birth of the Balfour Declaration[37] but at the Colonial Office, he was checkmated at every turn by Churchill, the senior minister. In 1922, as Colonial Secretary, Churchill had waxed eloquent about the achievements of the Zionist settlers at Rishon Le'Zion and had pushed the Palestine White Paper through Parliament, against vigorous opposition. But at the Treasury, his parsimony towards the Empire was applied nowhere with more severity than with the Jewish National Home in Palestine. He remained impervious to the special pleadings of Balfour and Weizmann, to the protests of Leo Amery, and even to Plumer's resignation. Churchill would win his Zionist laurels much later, in 1939.

The protracted negotiations that took place from 1920 to 1928 between British officials, Zionist leaders and wealthy Jewish magnates are instructive of Britain's attempts to run her Empire "on a shoestring". They illustrate the way in which, notwithstanding the pious intentions embedded in the Balfour Declaration, Britain expropriated the flow of Zionist-generated Jewish capital into Palestine for her own imperial purposes. The Zionists' ability to mobilize considerable amounts of capital would prove to be the determining factor in the government's decision to give them the two major economic concessions awarded by the British government in Palestine during the 1920s.

The Rutenberg electrification concession

The grant of commercial concessions to foreign industrial consortia to develop Palestine's natural resources was a legacy from the Ottomans. Their object had been to enrich the Ottomans' depleted coffers without investing their own funds. Few of the pre-World War One concessions were in fact exploited, due to the onset of the war. In 1919, the peace conference determined that all Ottoman concessions granted prior to the war remained legally valid. The British were unable either to abrogate or alter them without the assent of the concessionaire. At times, this proved to be a protracted process, as the concessionaires, with few exceptions, had no intention of investing in or exploiting their awards, but treated them as a useful instrument for extorting money from the British Mandatory.[38]

During the first years of the mandate, the Colonial Office hoped to gain accolades for the government's support of the Zionists. The grant of economic concessions to the Zionists would demonstrate the government's practical support for the Jewish National Home. While the concessions did not usually yield a quick return of the capital invested, they were of huge political and economical significance for the Zionists. The latter would be thankful for the preferential treatment, the concession would demonstrate to the Arabs the material benefits of the Jewish National Home, and the opposition at home would be persuaded that the government's policy was bringing material advantages to Palestine. Most of these naïve hopes were soon dashed.

Two Russian-born Zionists received major economic concessions from the British in the 1920s: in September 1921, Pinhas Rutenberg was awarded the concession for the production and distribution of electricity to Palestine and Trans-Jordan, and in 1927, Moshe Novomeysky was offered the concession to extract the salts and minerals (potash and bromide) of the Dead Sea. The concessions indicated a clear bias towards a community that remained a minority for the duration of the mandate. They aroused a hornets' nest of opposition – from the Palestinian Arabs, from anti-Zionist and anti-Semitic quarters in Britain, and last but not least, from British commercial and industrial interests.

Rutenberg, a Russian-Jewish mining engineer, was involved in both of the Russian revolutions, in 1905 and in 1917. During World War One, he was active in efforts to create a Jewish armed force to fight for a Jewish Palestine. In 1919, having secured promises of financial support from the Rothschild family for his scheme for the electrification of the Palestine, he emigrated there from Paris. The electrification concession gave him (and the Zionists) an extraordinary degree of influence over Palestine's economic future. Novomeysky used his experience in extracting salts from the lakes of Siberia and China to establish the chemical industry in Palestine.

The Colonial Office negotiated the terms of the electrification concession with Rutenberg in secret, in order not to jeopardize his chances of raising the required capital. In 1921, the government published the award as a *fait accompli*, without either publishing it as a tender or giving Parliament an opportunity to debate and approve the decision. The concession gave Rutenberg unusually advantageous terms, well in advance of the League's approval of Britain's mandate over Palestine. The government tried to explain the benefits of the concession for Palestine, but public opinion in Britain did not understand why it had not been issued as a public tender, according to regular commercial practice.[39]

The award produced a storm of protest in the national press and in Parliament. The major criticism was that British industrial interests had not been considered. The press campaign included xenophobic, anti-Semitic insinuations. In May 1922, a *Daily Sketch* editorial asked why, if the government had paid out £3.1 million for Palestine the year before:

> ... the monopoly concession had been handed over to "a gentleman bearing the fine old English name of Rutenberg", who had made Palestine "a land fit for Fritzes to plunder".[40]

At the end of May, Sir William Joynson-Hicks, a Conservative MP and lawyer, published a cynical, acerbic protest in *The Times*, one of the main organs of the Conservative opposition:

Now we see what we conquered Palestine for; now we know what our soldiers died for, and what our taxpayers are now spending £300,000 a year for; and a suggestion that any man exploiting Palestine should purchase his goods in Britain is a flagrant violation of the whole principle of mandates. If this is so, the sooner we get rid of the mandates the better.

The matter cannot stand where it is. No wonder the Arabs are sullen to the verge of revolt. If the House of Commons has any spirit at all, it must insist on a full discussion of the whole matter.[41]

Two days later, *The Times* published an editorial entitled "Rutenberg monopoly". It asserted that the concession was highly unusual, if not unique in the annals of the British Empire:

The disquieting feature of the Rutenberg scheme is that by it a monopoly is created on behalf of interests that are not British. Since Great Britain is responsible for the political control of Palestine, why has a step been taken which signifies the transference to other hands of such a large share in the economic control of the country? From all accounts of the scheme ... it is clear that the British administration in Palestine is placing itself in the very ambiguous position of transferring to others the essence of power while retaining an embarrassing responsibility.[42]

The Rutenberg concession and the new Palestine White Paper were discussed in the Commons debate on the Colonial Office vote, on 4 July 1922. As noted already, the vote was made into one of confidence. Joynson-Hicks led the attack against the concession, protesting that British industrial interests had been excluded from Palestine, calling it the "most astonishing" that he had ever seen in his life:

The real trouble is the way in which the Zionists have been permitted by the Government, or with the connivance of the Government, practically to control the whole of the Government of Palestine ... there is no provision whatever for any benefit for the manufacturers of Great Britain. There is no Clause providing that any orders should be placed in Great Britain ... We have spent millions of money in Palestine, and sacrificed thousands of English lives, and after all this no benefit is to come to England, and we are to go on spending our money keeping the British Army in Palestine.[43]

Sir John Butcher, a Conservative QC (the first Baron Danesfort, 1924), also expressed his "amazement" at the terms of the concession. He dissected and exposed the unusual privileges that it contained. By its terms, Rutenberg was to receive the exclusive right to use the waters of the River Jordan, and its tributaries, and of Lake Tiberias for the storage of water and the generation of power, as well as the right to construct dams on the River Jordan for water storage. By the terms of the concession, the High Commissioner was bound, upon Rutenberg's request, "to expropriate any individual from his land, his buildings and his property, which are to be handed over to the company, on compensation". The company would enjoy tax relief and, whenever it proved unable to pay its shareholders a 6 per cent annual dividend, free of tax, the company would be relieved of all taxation in Palestine.

Butcher protested on two grounds: first, on behalf of the native Palestinian Arabs:

> Is that fair to the inhabitants of Palestine, or to the interests of the Arabs? If that is how you preserve the rights of the Arabs in your Mandate, it is a novel Mandate. It is unknown outside of Palestine.

and second, on behalf of British industrial interests:

> We are in Palestine as a conquering nation. Heaven knows we spent enough blood and treasure in liberating the people of that country. Would it not be reasonable, would it not be fair to our own people, when we are granting this great concession, that we should at least say to British workmen and British manufacturers, "You shall have a chance in the development of this country?". It is a very misplaced sentimentalism and a deplorably mistaken policy.[44]

Rutenberg was also subjected to personal attack. He was accused of being a Communist who had been involved in the assassination of the Tsar. In the Commons, Churchill tried in vain to refute the aspersions, by reminding the House that Rutenberg had been thrown out of Russia by the Bolsheviks in October 1917. But the slurs stuck. In a book published in 1948 by Frances Newton, a long-time British resident of Jerusalem, she charged that Rutenberg had been a:

> … ruthless revolutionary, responsible to a great extent for the elimination of the cousin of our King George V from the throne of Russia.[45]

But the most serious criticism of the concession was that it had not included conditions guaranteeing that British economic interests would benefit. Indeed, it was reported that Rutenberg had already placed his first order with a German company. Churchill did not address this issue in 1922 but, as we have seen in the previous chapter, he did not repeat the mistake when he was the minister responsible for granting the British guarantees for the Palestine loan.

In defence of the concession, Churchill adopted the paternalistic line of the Colonial Office that prevailed at the inception of the mandate. He asserted that the introduction of Zionist immigrants into Palestine would bring material benefits to all concerned, and the native Arabs would be grateful.

Churchill also made one of the first public admissions that Britain needed Jewish capital to build up the country:

> At the same time that this pledge [the Balfour Declaration] was made to the Zionists, an equally important promise was made to the Arab inhabitants in Palestine – that their civil and religious rights would be effectively safeguarded, and that they should not be turned out to make room for new comers. If that pledge was to be acted upon, it was perfectly clear that the newcomers must bring their own means of livelihood, and that they, by their industry, by their brains, and by their money, must create new sources of wealth on which they could live without detriment to or subtraction from the well-being of the Arab population. It was inevitable that, by creating these new sources of wealth, and bringing this new money into the country, they would not only benefit themselves, but benefit and enrich the entire country among all classes and races of its population.

His next comment, on the Palestinian Arabs, was routine colonialist hubris:

> I am told that the Arabs would have done it themselves. Who is going to believe that? Left to themselves the Arabs of Palestine would not in a thousand years have taken effective steps towards the irrigation and electrification of Palestine. They would have been quite content to dwell ... in the wasted sun-scorched plains, letting the waters of the Jordan continue to flow unbridled and unharnessed into the Dead Sea.

Finally, Churchill deployed his considerable talent for flowery rhetoric and dismissed the criticism of the concession as merely anti-Jewish prejudice:

> I come to Mr. Rutenberg himself. He is a Jew. I cannot deny that. I do not see why that should be a cause of reproach, at any rate on the part of those who have hitherto supported the Zionist policy. It is hard enough, in all conscience, to make a New Zion, but if, over the portals of the new Jerusalem, you are going to inscribe the legend, "No Israelite need apply", then I hope the House will permit me to confine my attention exclusively to Irish matters.

The government secured a large majority for the Colonial Office vote: 292 against 35 votes. But over half of the MPs were either absent or abstained.

The Palestinian Arabs never appreciated the benefits of Zionist capital, most of which, in any case, was directed into the Jewish sector of the economy. They vigorously opposed the award of monopolies of Palestine's natural resources to Jewish immigrants. At first, their leaders opposed the connection of the electric grid to Arab towns and villages. Not only would this be taken as Arab assent to Rutenberg's monopoly, but they feared that it would make the Arab economy dependent upon Zionist electricity. However, some Arab towns were lured by the novelty of modern street lighting. In 1923, Jaffa, a mainly Arab town, relented and agreed to be linked up to the grid. One of the key factors in the town's change of mind was the payment of a bribe of P£1000 to one of the town council's more influential members. Haifa, another mainly Arab town, followed in Jaffa's wake.[46]

Opposition to the concessions came also from British Arabophiles, a small class of British romantics, some of whom settled in the region. They nurtured quixotic visions of the Middle East – of endless desert dunes and camel-mounted Arab Bedouin riding into the sunset. Not a few of the British officers who served in the Middle East during the first decades of the twentieth century identified with the Arabs, even if their attitude to them was patronizing. A few of them, notably T.E. Lawrence (of Arabia) and Harry Philby of Arabia (father of Kim, the spy), enjoyed significant, even if peripheral influence on British policy. Another influential Arabophile, Ms Gertrude Bell, had a considerable influence on British imperial policy, especially in Iraq, due to her skills and contacts. She has been described as a writer, traveller, political officer, administrator, archaeologist and spy. With T.E. Lawrence, she helped establish the Hashemite dynasties in Iraq and Trans-Jordan. Like Lawrence, she never married.

One Arabophile settled in Palestine – Ms Frances Newton. Palestine became her adopted country, her second home. She settled there in 1899 and lived there for most of her life – some 50 years. She spent most of World War One in London, where she became secretary of the Syria and Palestine Relief Fund. During this period she became acquainted with T.E. Lawrence and King Faysal. The latter visited her after the war at her home on Mount Carmel, Haifa. She was something of an eccentric, whose virulent opposition to Zionism was tainted with anti-Semitism. A supporter of the Palestinian Arab cause, Ms Newton was one of the major campaigners against the Rutenberg concession.[47]

Ms Newton remained an incorrigible admirer of the Mufti and blamed the British for having forced him into the arms of the Nazis.[48] Her attack on the Rutenberg concession drew its inspiration from J.M.N. Jeffries' *Palestine: The Reality*, a polemic that went through several editions.[49] She and Jeffries regarded the concession as part of an international Jewish conspiracy, whereby Jewish capital would be used to industrialize and control the world.

Jeffries castigated the terms of the concession, for giving Rutenberg the right not only to build "factories, works and undertakings" that might be needed for producing material or machinery, but also to erect such factories and undertakings that would be "able to utilize large quantities of electrical energy". The Zionists' goal was:

> ... to make of Palestine a land of industrialism, linked with the centres of industrialism about the globe.[50]

Jeffries wrote disparagingly that whereas the Zionists publicized "attractive pictures of sunburnt young Jewish haymakers", the "real emblem of the National Home should be a clerical worker or a shopkeeper at his Tel Aviv counter". The Zionists' main aim, he concluded:

> ... was to master Palestine, whether it paid or not, to turn it into a business-land, whether the business were good or not.[51]

Ms Newton accused the Western powers in the Middle East, and the Zionists in Palestine, of destroying the ancient, pastoral calm of traditional societies. She alleged that the Jewish drive to industralize Palestine was transforming forever the rustic landscape of the country. Nothing illustrates her *weltanschauung* better than the following passage:

> The Western State had no business whatever to try and force upon the Arabs the Western style of existence, which roughly is the making of profits in order to spend them on the alleviations of life. The Eastern idea that is ingrained in Palestine is the making of a subsistence ensuring life itself.[52]

While conceding that Rutenberg's hydro-electric project was a "great engineering feat", Ms Newton called it "none the less a horrible blot on a lovely landscape". It was the incarnation of Western capitalism, which would obliterate a biblical, pastoral serenity:

> "Cheap power" was the secret lever by which an industrial revolution in Palestine would come into operation and change the character of the country from its peaceful oriental aspect to that of one where – as has already happened in certain areas – the noisy rattle of machinery takes the place of grazing cattle and sheep, and the hustling, bustling crowd of factory workers replaces the thrifty farmers busy with their ploughs ... The industrializing of the country would mean a compete *bouleversement* of the character of the Holy Land as portrayed in the New Testament.[53]

Ms Newton repeated Jeffries' assertion that the Rutenberg concession was just a part of an insidious, international Zionist conspiracy. The industrialization of Palestine was part of a wide-ranging scheme to increase the economic absorptive capacity of Palestine, thereby enabling significant Jewish immigration and eventually, the creation of a Jewish state, since, she claimed: "in an industrialized country, the control of the main natural sources meant political power".[54]

Again echoing Jeffries, Ms Newton saw the electrification concession as part of a world-wide Jewish conspiracy, in a typical regurgitation of the *Protocols of the Elders of Zion*:

It would be interesting to know what other companies producing light, heat and power are entitled to build, set up and carry on factories so as to ensure the consumption of large quantities of the commodity they produce. These clauses surely show that the devisers of the Rutenberg scheme intended to make of Palestine a land of industrialism linked with centres of industrialism about the globe.[55]

Ms Newton and Jeffries were perhaps fringe figures, of marginal importance. She was certainly eccentric. But their influence, both in Britain and in Palestine, should not be under-estimated. Jeffries' book, which has been called the most comprehensive statement of the Palestine problem from the Arab point of view, went through several editions. Ms Newton influenced and was influenced by the Palestinian Arabs, with whom she lived for several decades. She also mixed socially with British officials.

For their part, the Zionists consciously maintained a low profile on the Rutenberg concession. The critics' conspiracy theories about taking over world capitalism were without a shred of foundation, but the accusation that the concession was one of the instruments whereby they proposed to take over Palestine was not so exaggerated. In 1921, Rutenberg himself wrote in a secret report:

Palestine will be Jewish only if the entire work relative to the building up of Jewish life will be carried out by Jewish workers ... the rebuilding of Palestine by Arab labour would result in the creation of an Arab and not a Jewish Palestine.[56]

Rutenberg drew up secret plans for the protection of his power stations by Jewish colonists, and in 1925 he approached the Colonial Office with a proposal to extend his concession to provide for the establishment of factories all over Palestine, to be run by the electricity he produced, equipped with machines that he would be allowed to import duty-free, operated exclusively by Jewish labour. Inevitably, his scheme was turned down by the government.[57]

The Novomeysky Dead Sea concession

Palestine had few known natural resources, the major one being the mineral deposits in the waters of the Dead Sea, which included potash. During World War One, the Germans had controlled a virtual monopoly of the world's short supply of potash, leading to a steep inflation in its price. Therefore the potash known to be found in the waters of the Dead Sea assumed a distinct strategic value. The Dead Sea attracted considerable attention, not only from Novomeysky, but also from British chemists and engineers.

Novomeysky's own interest in the Dead Sea went back to 1906, when he met with fellow scientist and Zionist Otto Warburg.[58] The latter showed him a Zionist-sponsored report on the Dead Sea prepared by a German geologist,

Professor Blankenhorn. Novomeysky immediately saw similarities between the chemical composition of the Dead Sea and that of the Siberian lakes he was familiar with. In 1907, he applied to the Ottoman authorities for permission to extract salts from the Dead Sea. They were not granted. He visited Palestine in 1911 to carry out his own research, to test the climate of the area, and the practicability of constructing evaporation pans.

But Novomeysky faced competition from two British groups who had approached the British government before him. The first group to study the Dead Sea was headed by W.H. Tottie, a merchant banker from London, director of the Canadian Merchants and General Trusts. Tottie was the head and financial sponsor of a group comprising R.H. Bicknell, a London consultant engineer, and Dr Annie Homer, a research chemist. The Tottie-Bicknell group studied the commercial exploitation of the Dead Sea salts from as early as 1916, seeing the possibility of breaking the Germans' monopoly. In 1918, they presented a comprehensive scheme to the government. In October of that year, Mr Bicknell made a formal application for permission to send out a group of engineers and scientists to Palestine, to produce a study that would satisfy their financial sponsors.[59]

In 1918, Major Thomas G. Tulloch, another British engineer, who had served in Palestine during the war, approached the government. He too advised that the Dead Sea salts could break the German monopoly on potash. The government sent him out to Palestine to inspect the area with one Major Brock, a Canadian geologist. Brock reported back that the Dead Sea contained vast amounts of potassium chloride, from which potash could be extracted. In 1922, a report by the geological advisor to the Palestine administration suggested that the market value of the Dead Sea salts might be in excess of £8 billion.[60]

Novomeysky emigrated to Palestine in 1920, and bought some land on the northern shore of the Dead Sea, near Jericho. In the meantime, the Tottie-Bicknell group had run into trouble finding financial sponsors. The Colonial Office clearly preferred the Tulloch proposal to Novomeysky's, but it realized that he would be unable raise the considerable financial support required. On the assumption that the Zionists *could* raise the capital, the department suggested to Tulloch that he team up with Novomeysky. The two negotiated terms and signed an agreement in 1923.[61]

In 1924, with the official backing of the Zionist Department of Trade and Industry, Novomeysky founded the Palestine Mining Syndicate. With the High Commissioner's permission, he continued with his geological surveys of the Dead Sea, together with a British geologist, George Stanfield Blake. In 1925, he sent one of his managers to the Dead Sea, where he spent 2 years surveying and running tests on the extraction of potash from its waters. During this time, Novomeysky devoted his own time to mobilizing financial backing for the project.

In 1921, the government's award of the electrification concession to Rutenberg had held out little prospect of immediate commercial gain, given that there were few if any electrical appliances in Palestine at the time. In contrast, by 1925, the government was fully apprised of the strategic value of the Dead Sea for the Empire and of the potential profits to be made from the minerals in its waters. Inevitably, Novomeysky's struggle to secure the concession would be more difficult and protracted. Politically, given the precedent of the fierce protests against the award of the Rutenberg concession, the Colonial Office was not going to award the concession without first putting it out to open tender.[62]

The government published the tender in May 1925. Four applications were received, three of them serious. One large company of alkali manufacturers soon pulled out, fearing that it was impracticable to compete with the Germans. The three other groups submitted their offers to the government in December 1926. One was from the Novomeysky-Tulloch group; another from an American industrial consortium, comprising General Motors, Du Pont and Standard Oil;[63] and the third was from the Tottie-Bicknell group.

The American consortium also withdrew its offer, soon after. The Tottie-Bicknell tender was considered to be the best, but in February 1927, the group informed the government that its financial guarantees had been withdrawn and they would have to seek others. The group never submitted a new offer, since Tottie died suddenly in April 1927. Despite several initially optimistic reports, the Colonial Office officials came to the concludsion that due to technical problems, no significant profits were to be expected from the Dead Sea waters in the short term. Therefore, there was no imperative to give preference to British interests.[64]

In April 1927, High Commissioner Plumer offered the concession to the Novomeysky-Tulloch group. In May, Leo Amery, the Colonial Secretary, announced the award in the House of Commons. The government's offer was conditional upon reaching agreement with the concessionaire on suitable terms and conditions, and subject to the group producing satisfactory financial guarantees. Negotiations were begun with the British Crown agents in September of that year.[65]

In order to prepare for the anticipated opposition in Parliament, Novomeysky mobilized Lord Melchett, in his capacity as President of the Economic Board of Palestine. Melchett had become a significant figure in British politics and industry. He had entered Parliament as a Liberal in 1906 and switched to the Conservatives in 1926. In 1928 he was elevated to the peerage as Baron Melchett, with a seat in the House of Lords. During this time he built up his father's industrial interests (mainly in the nickel industry). In 1926, he formed a merger of four different companies to create Imperial Chemical Industries (ICI), one of the world's largest industrial conglomerates at the time.

Melchett's response to Novomeysky's request for help reflects the ideological priority that the Zionists bestowed upon the concession:

> You will readily understand that the matter is of more than industrial significance. The Dead Sea represents the only important mineral wealth

of Palestine, and those of us who are interested in establishing there a National Home for the Jews cannot contemplate with equanimity the control of this passing into the hands of the American group, who are not interested in the economical development of the country.[66]

At one point, Melchett himself offered to finance the concession. But his negotiations with Novomeysky broke down over Melchett's refusal to agree that preferential treatment be given to Jewish labour. But Melchett continued to support the Dead Sea concession, which the Zionist movement adopted as a national project of the Jewish people.[67]

Novomeysky secured financial support from James de Rothschild,[68] Isaac Naiditch, a Russian Zionist resident in Paris, and several Zionist colonial funds. The finances of the house of Rothschild and the political influence of Melchett and Weizmann were undoubtedly critical in securing the concession for Novomeysky. However, the government's announcement that the award was being offered to what was regarded as a Zionist group stirred up a hornets' nest in both Houses of Parliament. The fact that the terms of the concession had yet to be finalized, and that Novomeysky failed to raise all of the funds required until late in 1928, allowed the "patriotic" party in Parliament to press for exclusive British control of the mineral assets of the Dead Sea.

The concession was debated in the Commons on 30 November 1927. Colonel Howard Bury, Conservative, introduced a motion asking the Prime Minister if, in view of the value of the Dead Sea concession to the British Empire, he would ensure that a British company received the concession, and that control remained in British hands. He warned that this was necessary in view of the fact that Germany currently held a monopoly of the world's potash supply, whereas the potash deposits in the Dead Sea area alone were worth £14 million (during the following 6 months, Colonel Bury asked no less than 26 questions about the concession). William Ormsby-Gore, the Under-Secretary of State for the Colonies, replied on behalf of the Prime Minister. He asserted that Bury's estimate of £14 million was "astronomical" and informed the House that whereas negotiations with the concessionaires were still under way, the government had no intention of securing a controlling interest in the concessionary company.[69]

The Commons discussed the concession again 2 weeks later, on 15 December 1927. Orsmby-Gore reviewed the replies to the government tender. Four definite applications had been received, all of which had been "carefully compared and examined in detail". He reminded the House of what he had told them the previous May, that the final award of the concession to the Tulloch-Novomeysky group was conditional upon reaching agreement on "suitable terms and conditions ... and subject to their giving satisfactory financial guarantees". At the close of this short exchange, Colonel Josiah Wedgwood asked rhetorically whether the Under-Secretary could state "whether most of the opposition to this concession comes from the usual anti-Semitic sources?" Orsmby-Gore did not reply.[70]

The House of Lords debated the concession on 23 May 1928.[71] Opposition to the Novomeysky concession was led by Lord Islington, the Speaker of the House, a former Under-Secretary of State for the Colonies and for India during World War One. Islington had led the opposition to the government's support for the Zionists after the war. He moved a motion requiring that the concession should go to a British consortium and remain under British control. Behind this argument remained the enduring memory of the German potash monopoly during World War One, which, he reminded the House, had sent the cost of potash in Britain spiralling from a pre-war price of just over £9 to approximately £80 per ton. Islington protested at the Zionists' involvement, and insinuated that Novomeysky was a Russian Jew who might have German connections. This slur would stick to Novomeysky throughout the parliamentary debates.

The Lords debate was marred by anti-Zionist and anti-Semitic overtones. Lord Islington referred to "the unfortunate experiment which is known as the Zionist Home in Palestine". He reminded the Lords that the current population of Palestine was 87 per cent Arab and 10–12 per cent Jewish. He adjured that as the Mandatory, Great Britain was obliged to "mete out even justice and equity in all matters and interests, political, social or economic, to the people of Palestine as a whole, and not to any minority or section within the confines of that territory". Not only that, but he pointed out that half of the area that fell under the Dead Sea concession lay outside of Palestine, in Trans-Jordan – a territory in which Britain's commitment to the Zionists did not apply. Islington's next comment raised yet again the spectre of the *Protocols*:

> There would appear to be, I do not know why, some organized practice on the part of His Majesty's Government to conceal by evasion, subterfuge, and every means in their power the identity of this anonymous group that stands behind the names of Mr. Novomeysky and Major Tulloch ... An increasing number of people are asking why there is this mystery about the group. What occult reasons can there be for secrecy ... regarding the names and constitution of a group which is to operate an undertaking of first-class national and Imperial importance?

No one ever probed into the identity of the financial sponsors of the other groups. The Duke of Buccleuch, one of Britain's richest landowners, pursued Islington's trail. "I have noticed that a certain number of people seem to think that Jews have a historical right to Palestine. I have always imagined that the only part to which they had any historical right was Judea, which is a comparatively small portion of Palestine."

In the name of the government, the Earl of Birkenhead, the Secretary of State for India, remarked that the Lords' remarks about Tulloch and Novomeysky were unfair, given that these gentlemen had no right of reply, whereas the Lords' aspersions were protected by parliamentary privilege. Yet Birkenhead's next comment revealed, perhaps unwittingly, his own aristocratic insularity. Referring to the Duke of Buccleuch's comments, he stated:

The noble Duke who spoke last animadverted unfavourably upon Mr. Novomeysky's name. It is not a name with which I am particularly enamoured or which I desire to bear, but the only argument which the noble Duke used was in the first place that he was a Jew.

Islington's motion was narrowly defeated, by 38 to 25 votes. Constitutionally, the House of Lords had no real power to block legislation by the Lower House. But had Islington's motion passed, it would have forced the government to turn the Commons vote on the Novomeysky concession into one of confidence – as it had done in similar circumstances with the Colonial Office vote in July 1922.

However, notwithstanding all of Parliament's protests, Novomeysky was the only concessionaire who succeeded in mobilizing the substantial funding required for the project. In September 1928, he acquired the last of the funding he needed, when Supreme Justice Louis Brandeis and Judge Julian Mack, two leading American Zionists, promised to raise $1 million for the concession, $300,000 of which they promised for 1 November.[72]

Nonetheless, one further, last-ditch debate on the concession took place in the House of Lords on 20 March 1929.[73] It was again marked by xenophobic allusions to undisclosed foreign financial interests who were about to take control of an important imperial resource, one that the British should keep for themselves. Viscount Templeton introduced a motion asking the government to retain control of the Dead Sea concession. He linked the concession to the Rutenberg concession awarded 7 years earlier. Templeton's veiled allusions to the influence wielded by international Jewry lifted yet another page from the *Protocols*:

> The Rutenberg Concession, which gave a Russian Jew a stranglehold on the economic life of Palestine and Transjordania for 70 years, in spite of determined protests in both Houses of Parliament, indicates the undue influence of Zionists and international financiers. In the question of the Dead Sea, which, owing to its vast wealth and power, is the key of the Middle East, the same undue influences are at work.

Templeton insisted that the British group's tender for the Dead Sea concession remained the best, even if its financial sponsors had withdrawn. He complained that instead of offering the concession to Novomeysky, the government should have "waited a reasonable time for the British group to negotiate elsewhere for financial guarantees" (he was apparently unaware that Tottie had died in April 1927, nearly 2 years earlier).

Lord Danesfort[74] feared that the Dead Sea monopoly might fall into the wrong hands, protesting that the government did not even know the identity of Novomesky's sponsors. He claimed that Major Tulloch was merely a cover – "nothing but a mere name". He demanded to know, since Novomeysky himself was obviously unable to raise the finances required, who was the real power behind the concession. Otherwise, he suggested, there was grave danger that this substantial supply of potash would fall into the hands of a monopoly, like that which the Germans had enjoyed during World War One. He insisted that the terms of the mandate did not prevent the government from keeping the concession under British control. Other speakers also pressed the government to reveal the names of Novomeysky's sponsors.

Lord Melchett spoke next. He had an obvious interest in deflating what he asserted were the grossly exaggerated estimates of the mineral wealth of the Dead Sea, and of the dangers of a German monopoly. He portrayed himself as one with professional knowledge of the chemical industry, and warned that it was most dangerous to make statements in the Lords which might be used later "by company promoters and groups of financiers, some of them none too scrupulous, to lure unwary investors into the idea that there is a golden fortune in Dead Sea potash". He surprised the House by asserting that contrary to the conventional wisdom, there was in fact a large surplus of potash in the world. He informed the Lords that he had discussed the Dead Sea salts with many international experts – and there did not exist a single important group of financiers in the whole world that thought it worth while applying for the concession. In this last claim, he was evidently quite right.

Melchett next took issue with Viscount Templeton's aspersions about Jewish influence, which with due decorum he referred to as "rather unfair". Melchett gave his own personal testimony about Rutenberg, as a member of the Palestine Mining Syndicate's board of directors:

> Why was that concession given to that gentleman? It was given because he happens to be a very competent electrical engineer, who applied for it. The noble Viscount cannot know the years of difficulty we had to find the necessary capital, and cannot know how Mr Rutenberg was thanked by three successive High Commissioners. I think he [Templeton] might withdraw the kind of expression he used. Might I ask whether no Palestinian subject is to have a concession in Palestine, because both Mr. Rutenberg and Mr. Novomeysky are Palestinian subjects? To have a concession in Palestine you must apparently be a subject of another nation. Surely such a claim cannot be substantiated. It is time people recognized that there is such a thing as a Palestinian nation. It is not true to say that Mr. Rutenberg is a Russian Jew. He is a Palestinian Jew. I must enter a protest against the endeavour to create prejudice against men who have gone to develop Palestine, and who have become Palestinian subjects.

The Earl of Plymouth, as Parliamentary Under-Secretary of State for Dominion Affairs, replied on behalf of the government. He stated that the terms of the League mandate required that there should be no discrimination in the "exercise of commerce and industry" against the nationals of any other states that were members of the League, or of Palestinian nationals (article

18). He advised that negotiations with the Novomeysky group were now reaching their conclusion, and the government would not entertain any alternative offers unless and until those negotiations proved to be abortive. He added that the British group had lost their financial backing because of the sponsor's doubts about the prospects of producing potash profitably.

Both the Colonial Office and Novomeysky were alarmed by the extent and nature of the opposition to the concession in the House of Lords. The department had promised to reveal the names of Novomeysky's investors, and now feared having to disclose the fact that three of the four subscribers to his company were Jews. Novomeysky agreed to a Colonial Office request to set up an entirely new company, with a majority of British directors. In April 1929, the second Earl of Lytton was persuaded by Weizmann to accept the position of chairman of the board (Weizmann's first choice, Lord Allenby, had turned down the offer). Lytton was eminently acceptable to the Colonial Office. He had an impeccable political "pedigree" and was related by marriage to Balfour.[75]

The government signed the final agreement with Novomeysky on 22 May 1929 and awarded the concession to him officially in 1930. The agreement included the conditions that the chairman of the board of directors must always be a British subject and that British or Palestinian subjects should always form the majority on the board. The concession was to last for 75 years, after which Novomeysky would have the first option on any extension. Novomeysky undertook to hire a "reasonable proportion of Arab labour".[76]

The new company, the Palestine Potash Company, completed its first bromine plant in February 1931, and its first potash factory began production in November 1931. All the chemicals were exported to Britain.[77] Notwithstanding the compromise with the government, the company remained essentially a Zionist enterprise. The large majority of its directors were Zionists, and nearly 70 per cent of its original capital was provided by the Zionist Jewish Colonial Trust and the Palestine Economic Corporation. Roughly three-quarters of the company's employees were Jewish. Although the company returned a trading profit of £23,000 from as early as 1932, no dividends were distributed throughout the entire period of the mandate.[78]

Opposition to Novomeysky's concession persisted in Palestine itself. One of his opponents was Ms Frances Newton, who had her own commercial plans for the Dead Sea. She had dreams of making her fortune by the discovery of oil in the same area. Her plans for drilling for oil in the Dead Sea area were not exactly consistent with her professed concerns about preserving the pastoral landscape of the country.

In 1934, Ms Newton and her sister tried to secure an economic concession for the exploration and production of oil in the Dead Sea. She and her sister travelled to Amman, where they secured the approval of the Emir Abdullah. But on their return to Jerusalem, they discovered that the issue had been referred to the direct purview of the Colonial Office in London. The British government did not believe in the existence of oil shales in commercial quantities in the Dead Sea area. Ms Newton complained that the government preferred to exploit Iraqi oilfields in the Mosul area – which required a 700-mile long pipeline to bring the oil to the Haifa refineries – rather than developing an oilfield in the Dead Sea area, some 75 miles from the Gaza coast.[79] Ms Newton's naïve plans were overtaken by the realities of World War Two.

With Britain fighting for her survival, and with a spiralling need for oil for military purposes, the search for oil became the preserve of the major oil conglomerates, which had the necessary vast resources for drilling and exploration.

When Ms Newton's plans came to naught, she found two ready-to-hand scapegoats – the vast oil conglomerates and Novomeysky. In her memoirs, she unearthed a new conspiracy plotting to control the world:

> ... an action brought in the Courts of America against the Standard Oil company has revealed that purely commercial interests, amount in reality to being vast economic super States, that control the destinies of nations ... Those who control the oil supplies of the world are the rulers of the nation's destinies.[80]

The two major economic concessions discussed in this chapter illustrate one of the major paradoxes of the Palestine mandate. Whereas successive British governments recognized their dual obligation in Palestine, both to "facilitate" the establishment of the Jewish National Home *and* to protect the native Arab population, their unwillingness to spend British money on the country left them dependent upon Zionist-imported capital, not only to finance their own administration, but also for the development of Palestine's infrastructures.

At the outset of the mandate, some Colonial Office officials believed that the Rutenberg concession would persuade the Arabs of the Zionists' ability to bring material benefit to the country. At the same time, it would focus the Zionists' efforts in the economic and commercial fields, diverting them from their vexatious meddling in politics.

The grant of the concession to exploit the minerals of the Dead Sea to the Novomeysky group aroused protracted public protests, overlaid with ant-Zionist and anti-Semitic overtones, both in the press and in both Houses of Parliament. But the prospective sponsors of the rival concessionaires remained unconvinced of the Dead Sea's potential to yield quick profits. Within the corridors of power, British officials realized that only the Zionists, with their strong ideological commitment to Palestine, were willing to invest the huge amounts required to build up the country's infrastructures, without the prospect of short-term profits. As noted already, in 1923, Foreign Secretary Curzon had told an imperial conference: "Palestine needs ports, electricity, and the Jews of America were rich and would subsidize such development ... ".[81] In the case of the Dead Sea concession, patriotic sentiment was appeased by the government's insistence that Novomeysky award the majority of the seats on his company's board of directors to British citizens.

The economic concessions awarded to the Zionists in the 1920s developed into significant pillars of the future Jewish state. Even if they were not particularly profitable (especially not the Rutenberg scheme) in the short term, certainly not enough to attract disinterested foreign capital, they raised the Zionists' political prestige and furthered their national aspirations.

The Palestinian Arabs regarded the concessions as tangible evidence that with British connivance, the Zionists were taking over the country. On 15 May 1930, the Arab newspaper *Filastin* asserted:

> Of late, the Colonial Office has robbed us of our treasures and signed without any reluctance the charter of our economic bondage to the Zionists ... The Electricity Scheme; the Salt enterprise; the Haifa harbour, Tiberias hot baths and then the Dead Sea Concession. All these have been usurped by the Zionists.[82]

Notes

1. cf. Roger Owen, "Economic Development in Mandatory Palestine", in George T. Abed, ed., *The Palestinian Economy*, London/New York: Routledge 1988, p. 25.
2. The wealth of the Jewish middle class in Poland was emasculated by the erosion of the value of the Polish zloty and new government restrictions on cash transfers; cf. Jacob Metzer, *The Divided Economy of Mandatory Palestine*, Cambridge: Cambridge University Press, 1998, p. 68; also Barbara J. Smith, *The Roots of Separatism in Palestine: British Economic Policy, 1920–1929*, Syracuse: Syracuse University Press, 1993, p. 81; and note by T.K. Lloyd, 13 February 1928, CO 733/150/5, NA.
3. Smith, ibid, p.153. Of the 7365 Jews who emigrated from Palestine in 1926, 95 per cent had been in the country for between 1 and 3 years; idem, p. 81.
4. Weizmann to Leonie and Alfred Landsberg, 3 January 1928, Pinhas Ofer, ed., *The Letters and Papers of Chaim Weizmann*, [WL] vol. XIII, Jerusalem: Rutgers University, Transaction Books, 1978, p. 338. Raymond Poincaré, a veteran French politician, was serving his third term as Prime Minister, from July 1926 to July 1929.
5. Weizmann to Arthur Ruppin, 14 February 1928, p. 371, and to Sir Alfred Mond, 21 February 1928, pp. 380–81, ibid.
6. Weizmann (New York) to the Zionist Executive, 14 April 1928, ibid, p. 436,
7. Weizmann to Blanche Dugdale, 17 April 1928, ibid, p. 439. The conference of Jewish magnates was scheduled originally to meet in London on 10 June 1928. It was postponed until the official establishment of the Jewish Agency for Palestine (which included non-Zionists), at the 16th Zionist Congress, held in Zurich from July to August 1929.
8. Lloyd note, 8 February 1928, CO 733/150/5, NA. Lloyd was an assistant principal secretary at the Colonial Office.
9. The regressive Ottoman land and buildings taxes (*werko*) were replaced by a new urban property tax in 1929, and a new rural property tax in 1935; whereas a general progressive income tax was introduced in 1941, import duties remained the largest single source of revenue throughout the mandatory period; cf. Metzer, *The Divided Economy*, pp. 181–82.
10. Lloyd note of 8 February, supra.

11 Churchill to Amery, 30 April 1927, in Martin Gilbert, *Winston S. Churchill*, companion volume V/1, Boston: Houghton and Mifflin, p. 995. Dole was the term commonly used for unemployment benefits. In his *Churchill and the Jews*, London/New York: Simon & Schuster, 2007, Gilbert devotes less than one page (90–91) to Churchill's 5-year term at the Exchequer. He has nothing to say about the government guarantee for the Palestine loan, and writes, quite misleadingly, that Churchill favoured granting a government guarantee for the Zionist loan.

12 Zionist subsidizing of the costs of the Jaffa–Petach Tikva road was via an indirect payment of the unemployment benefits of many Jewish unemployed. In 1922, the Zionist Executive had loaned the administration some E£22,000 for the construction of the Bet Dajan–Rishon Le'Zion–Rehovot road; Smith, *The Roots*, pp. 150–52. Lloyd had estimated that it would cost the administration E£200,000 to finance a public works programme that would keep 1000 Jews at work for a year.

13 Note by A.J. Harding, 26 April 1928, CO 733/158, NA. The Palestine Currency Board, under Colonial Office supervision, governed the issue of Palestine's currency.

14 Note by Lloyd, 8 February 1928, supra.

15 Note by Lloyd, 27 February 1928, CO 733/150/5, NA.

16 ibid.

17 Note of 27 March 1928, CO 733/150/4, NA.

18 cf. Cohen, *Churchill*, pp. 113–16. In 1928 Balfour held the sinecure Cabinet post of Lord President of the Council; he was an ageing invalid, approaching his 80th birthday. He died in 1930.

19 For this and following, see records of the meeting by Sir John Shuckburgh, 27 February 1928, in CO 733/150/5, NA; and by Chaim Weizmann, in S50/5, Central Zionist Archives (CZA), reprinted in *Weizmann Letters*, XIII, p. 387.

20 Weizmann to Isaac A. Naiditch, 27 February, and Weizmann to Manka Spiegel, 18 March 1928, *WL* XIII, pp. 387, 408.

21 Shuckburgh note, 5 April 1928, CO 733/150/4, NA, also Amery diary note, 27 February 1928, John Barnes and David Nicholson, eds, *The Leo Amery Diaries*, vol. 1, *1896–1929*, London: Hutchinson, 1980, p. 538. Leo Amery was born of a Jewish mother and therefore, by Jewish law, was Jewish. During his "wilderness years" out of government, he was appointed to the board of governors of several large companies, including Marks and Spencer.

22 On Churchill's belief in the influence of American Jews on American foreign policy, cf. Cohen, *Churchill*, pp. 113, 146, 186–203, 328.

23 For this and following, CP 71, 5 March 1928, in Cab 24/193. NA. Balfour's memorandum reads as if the Zionists drafted it for him.

24 In February 1924, Samuel estimated that the annual repayments of the Ottoman debt would come to roughly £180,000, which amounted to about one-seventh of Palestine's annual revenue from taxes; he added that this charge was not balanced by any assets left behind by the Ottomans; Samuel to Colonial Secretary Thomas, 8 February 1924, T160/44, 1401/01/02. Colonial Office officials later conceded that Palestine was the only territory detached from the former Ottoman Empire that had not defaulted on its repayments of the Ottoman debt; note by Lloyd, 8 March 1928, CO 733/150/4, NA.

25 Minutes of the Cabinet debate on 13 March 1928, in Cab 14 (28), Cab 23/57, NA.

26 Dugdale to Weizmann, 5 April 1928, Weizmann Archives. She indicated that her source was "M.H." – probably Douglas M. Hogg, the Lord Chancellor.

27 Diary entry for 4 April 1928, *Amery Diaries*, p. 541. My emphasis. There were doubts whether Balfour would survive his illness.

28 Foreign Office memorandum, 29 March 1928, CP 110 (28), and Treasury memorandum, 2 April 1928, CP 114(28), Cab 24/194, NA; the expert opinion was written by Sir Otto Niemeyer (Financial Controller at the Treasury, and a

Director of the Bank of England), which concluded "both the Financial Committee and the Council of the League would find great difficulty in regarding the Zionist case as a proper subject for their intervention".

29 Amery attached to his Cabinet memorandum a paper in which the Zionists argued "a substantial and growing income is in itself no substitute for the capital without which the orderly execution ... of a systematic plan of colonization presents serious difficulties". Appendix to Colonial Office memorandum, CP 85 (28) 15 March 1928, Cab 24/193, NA.
30 Cabinet meeting on 4 April 1928, Cab 20(28) cab 23/57, NA.
31 Weizmann to Dugdale, 17 April 1928, *WL* XIII, p. 438.
32 Meeting on 20 June 1928, Cab 33(28) in Cab 23/58, NA.
33 Weizmann report to Zionist Executive, 21 June 1928, Weizmann Archives (WA).
34 Amery to Baldwin, 27 April 1929, in Gilbert, *Churchill*, companion vol. V/1, p. 1469, and Amery diary note, 20 June 1928, *Amery Diaries*, p. 536. At the general elections held on 30 May 1929, the Conservatives lost over 150 seats, dropping from 419 to 260. Labour formed a minority government.
35 Weizmann to Zionist Executive, London, 4 April 1928, *WL* XIII, p. 425.
36 In the general elections of October 1924, the Liberal party had been reduced from 159 to 40 seats in the Commons.
37 Amery, an assistant secretary to the Cabinet in 1917, had drawn up the final draft of the Declaration.
38 Gideon Biger, *An Empire in the Holy Land, 1917–1929*, New York: St Martin's Press, 1994, pp. 94–95.
39 Smith, *Roots*, p. 121.
40 *The Daily Sketch*, undated, in CO 733/40, NA.
41 *The Times*, 29 May 1922.
42 ibid, 31 May 1922.
43 For this, and all quotes from the Commons debate on 4 July, cf. *House of Commons Debates* (*H.C. Deb.*), 5th series, vol. 156, cols 221–343.
44 ibid, cols 315–20.
45 Frances Newton, *Fifty Years in Palestine*, Wrotham: Coldharbour Press, 1948, p. 221. Rutenberg was involved in the Socialist-revolutionary movement in Russia in 1905, and was forced to flee the country after the abortive revolution of that year. He returned in July 1917, as an adherent of the Socialist-revolutionary Kerensky government. When the Bolsheviks seized control after the October revolution, they forced him to leave the country again, this time for good.
46 Biger, *An Empire*, p. 237; Smith, *The Roots*, pp. 117, 122, 132; on the bribe in Jaffa, see Hillel Cohen, *Army of Shadows: Palestinian Collaboration with Zionism, 1917–1948*, Berkeley/Los Angeles: University of California Press, 2008, pp. 39–40.
47 See diary of Owen Tweedy, May 4, 1927, St Anthony College, Oxford, Middle East Centre. In 1938, Ms Newton was deported from Palestine for publishing two pamphlets that accused the British of committing atrocities against the Palestinian Arabs. She was not allowed to return until after World War Two. In 1946, she founded the Anglo-Arab Friendship Committee in London, whose aim was to combat Zionism. She was created a Dame of Justice of the Venerable Order of St John of Jerusalem, and made a Fellow of the Royal Geographical Society and of the American Geographical Society.
48 Newton, *Fifty Years*, p. 293.
49 J.M.N. Jeffries, *Palestine: The Reality*, Westport, Conn: Hyperion Press, 1976. The book was first published in 1939 by Longmans, Green and Co. and next in 1969 by the Beirut Institute for Palestine Studies. Jeffries dedicated his book to his "Colleagues in the Arab Centre".
50 ibid, pp. 436–37; chapters xxv and xxvi are devoted to his critique of the Rutenberg concession.

The Yishuv economy in the 1920s 211

51 ibid, p. 437.
52 Newton, *Fifty Years*, p. 210, citing Jeffries, p. 440.
53 ibid, p. 205.
54 ibid, pp. 203, 207.
55 ibid, p. 202.
56 Cited in Smith, *The Roots*, pp. 119–21.
57 Internal Colonial Office correspondence, March 1925, CO 733/107, NA.
58 Otto Warburg was a German botanist and a noted industrial agriculture expert. He was an active Zionist and served as president of the Zionist Organization from 1911 to 1921.
59 On the Bicknell-Tottie group, see Dr Annie Homer (a graduate of Cambridge University), "The Dead Sea Concession: The History of an Application", *The Chemical Age*, issue 17, December 1927: http://cosmos.ucc.ie/cs1064/jabowen/IPSC/php/art.php?aid=152076
60 See CO 733/46, NA, cited in Smith, *Roots*, p.126. Potash is the name for the various salts that contain potassium in water-soluble form. Potash is used mainly as a fertilizer, but also for numerous industrial purposes.
61 Memorandum of October 1922, in CO 733/46, NA, cited in Smith, *Roots*, p. 127.
62 cf. M.A. Novomeysky, *Given to Salt: The Struggle for the Dead Sea Concession*, London: Max Parrish, 1958.
63 For details, see Smith, *The Roots*, pp. 126–29. Standard Oil had begun marketing the first leaded petroleum that required a bromine derivative to prevent damage to the engine's cylinders.
64 Smith, ibid, p. 127.
65 Statement in the Commons by William Ormsby-Gore, Under-Secretary of State for the Colonies, 15 December 1927, in *H.C. Deb.*, vol. 211, cols 2503–4.
66 See article in http://chemistry.org.il/booklet/16/pdf/novomersky.pdf
67 Smith, *Roots*, p. 128.
68 James de Rothschild, born in France, was the son of Baron Edmund de Rothschild, head of the international banking dynasty and a Zionist. James was naturalized, and became a British politician and philanthropist.
69 *H.C. Deb.*, vol. 211, cols 496–98.
70 ibid, cols 2503–4. In February 1929, Wedgwood would found The Seventh [Palestine] Dominion League. see Chapter 1.
71 *House of Lords Debates* (H.L.Deb.), vol 71, cols 262–93.
72 Smith, *Roots*, p. 128.
73 For this and following, see H.L. Deb., 20 March 1929, vol. 73, cols 731–758.
74 As Sir John Butcher, Danesfort had played a prominent role in the opposition to the Rutenberg concession in the House of Commons.
75 Details in Smith, *Roots*, p. 129. Lytton had held various positions in the Admiralty, was a former governor of Bengal and for a short period, the Viceroy of India.
76 ibid.
77 *Jewish Daily Bulletin*, 21 August 1932.
78 Details in Smith, *Roots*, p. 130.
79 Newton, *Fifty Years*, p. 226.
80 ibid, p. 228.
81 Cited in Keith Middlemass, ed., *Thomas Jones, Whitehall Diary*, vol. 1. *1916–1925*, London: Oxford University Press, 1969, p. 246.
82 CO 733/185, NA.

10 The unravelling of the mandate, 1929–31

> It has emerged quite definitely that there is at the present time and with the present methods of Arab cultivation no margin of land available for agricultural settlement by new immigrants.
> Official Report by Sir John Hope-Simpson, October 1930

The Wailing Wall riots: 1929

During the decade between 1929 and 1939, all the premises that had guided the 1923 decision to retain the Palestine mandate were superseded by more urgent considerations. Two major waves of Arab violence swept Palestine – in 1929, and from 1936 to 1939. As happened after the 1921 riots, each wave of violence brought a new commission of inquiry and recommendations that involved a fundamental revision of policy. But it should be stressed that Britain's retreat from her commitment to Zionism from the mid-1930s was *not* due to events in Palestine itself, but to the threats posed to Britain's Middle Eastern hegemony by the rise of revisionist, fascist regimes in Germany and in Italy. Italy's brutal conquest of Abyssinia (1935–36) and Hitler's occupation of the demilitarized Rhineland in 1936 (an infringement of the Versailles Treaty) affected Britain's ability to maintain its strategic interests in the Middle East. With insufficient forces to impose her will by force, she resorted to the appeasement of the Arab world.

The 8-year hiatus between the riots of 1921 and of 1929 was a period of relative tranquillity for Palestine. In retrospect, it is clear that this was an outward calm before the storm. The officials at Whitehall wanted to believe that Samuel's policy of "buying over" the traditional notable rulers had worked, as it had in other parts of the Empire. In any case *realpolitik*, Britain's own interests, dictated continuing with the *status quo*. Arab quiescence was maintained, to some extent, by their belief that the economic crisis that the Yishuv experienced during the second half of the 1920s presaged the end of the Zionist "experiment".

British security forces were depleted during the 1920s, as if the Arab-Zionist conflict had been solved. The British garrison that had numbered 25,000 in 1920 was reduced by May 1921 to 7000. A mere 18 British officers commanded them. A Palestine gendarmerie of some 500 Arabs and Jews under British officers was mobilized in 1921. Its primary task was to secure the country's long borders with Syria and the Lebanon and only secondarily to aid in keeping order inside Palestine. After the May 1921 riots, this scheme for a mixed Arab-Jewish defence force was dropped. It was replaced in 1922 by a British gendarmerie, composed of some 700 former Black and Tans.[1] They were veterans of World War One, heavy drinkers and violent. Edward Horne, the official historian of the Palestine Police, recalled that these "rowdy and eccentric Irishmen" had brought a peace to Palestine that she had not seen for centuries and has not seen since.[2] One of their ranks, Douglas Duff, recorded his own personal "joys" when quelling a disorderly crowd: "Once again I experienced that strange and utterly sublime ecstasy of 'going berserk', as my barbarian forefathers had done. I had no consciousness of what I was doing as I sprang at the crowd".[3]

But in 1926, the British and Palestinian gendarmeries were dissolved, due to financial stringencies, and the last regiment of British cavalry was transferred out of Palestine. Some 200 Black and Tans joined the British Section of the Palestine Police. But by 1928, many of them had had enough and chose to return home, either to join the army or to seek adventure elsewhere. A few of those who remained rose to senior positions in the Palestine Police, for example, Douglas Duff, who became Police Inspector for Jerusalem, and Raymond Cafferata, who became a district commander in Haifa.[4]

As noted already, following the calm that came with the 1922 White Paper, the military command of Palestine was transferred to RAF Middle East, whose headquarters was in Iraq. In 1928, the GOC Palestine had at his disposal just a handful of aircraft, six armoured cars and the personnel required to maintain them. All British units were at least 25 per cent under strength, and most of the men were due home for a 2-month leave. Of a total police establishment of some 1500 men to cover the entire country, just 292 were British. The great majority of the force was Arab, with a smaller number of Jews, all under British command. Yet the British were quite aware that neither race could be relied upon to keep order impartially in any situation of intercommunal strife, least of all to fire upon their own kinsmen. In sum, in the event of disturbances, Palestine was dependent upon the quick arrival of reinforcements from Egypt. In August 1929, when the Wailing Wall riots erupted, the reinforcements arrived too late to prevent wide-scale destruction and murder.

From 1925, this superficial calm was presided over by the second High Commissioner, Field Marshal Sir Herbert Plumer. A World War One hero, he possessed an unruffled, self-confident, nineteenth-century imperialist disposition. His very presence commanded authority. Unique among British holders of the post, he adopted a neutral, apolitical attitude to his job. Unlike Samuel, Plumer was not troubled by any emotional or spiritual ties to either race in Palestine. He had no intellectual interest in or knowledge of Zionism and he opposed all constitutional initiatives. He was concerned solely with the preservation of the *status quo* and the maintenance of law and order – all at a minimal cost to the British taxpayer.

Plumer impressed upon his officials the importance of security, and refused to address political problems. He admonished his district commissioners to stop sending him political reports: "There is no political situation – don't create one!". He remained unmoved by hints of Arab willingness to co-operate, just as he was not intimidated by threats of renewed violence.[5] Norman Bentwich recalled that an Arab delegation had warned Plumer that if he did not allow them to organize a demonstration (against the French) they would be unable to take responsibility for the preservation of order. Plumer had replied:

> ... he never asked them or expected them, to take this responsibility ... he himself would assure security.[6]

Plumer left Palestine in July 1928, after only 3 years in office (on the reasons for his early departure, see Chapter 8). He was not replaced for 6 months, until December of the same year, when Sir John Chancellor arrived. Chancellor was a 25-year veteran of the colonial service, having served as governor of several minor British colonies. But he had no experience of the Middle East, or of Palestine. He arrived in the country believing that the Balfour Declaration had been a "colossal blunder", unfair to the Arabs and harmful to the best interests of the Empire. He was temperamentally unable to cope with the inter-racial strife in which he was shortly plunged and thoroughly disliked his tenure as High Commissioner. He failed to establish good working relations with the Whitehall officials, who rejected his demands to expand the police force. Nor were his personal relations with his officials in Jerusalem too good. One of them described him as:

> ... a discontented, self-pitying, lonely, suspicious man, aloof towards his subordinates and hypersensitive to criticism.[7]

Although Chancellor favoured the Arabs over the Zionists, his relations with them were also troubled. In a letter to his son, he described cynically a meeting with the Arab Executive at Government House:

> I told them that I had heard that they had passed a resolution to the fact that I was not a fit person to be High Commissioner & that they were going to ask the Sec. of State to recall me. I said that I was not disposed to contradict them as to that; but that I was of the opinion that under present conditions I knew of no one who would be a good High Commissioner of Palestine except God.[8]

It was his misfortune to arrive on the eve of one of the country's cyclical "explosions". There is some irony in the fact that the fuse that ignited the

1929 riots may be traced back to Samuel's policy of rewarding the Arab notable clans with the bounties of British patronage. The Mufti of Jerusalem, Haj Amin el-Husayni, had used the budget of the SMC to reward his own clan, to the virtual exclusion of his rivals, notably the Nashashibis. All religious posts, even the most menial, were awarded to Husayni followers; likewise, funds for the building or renovation of mosques and other religious institutions were channelled to Husayni strongholds. The resulting frustration and anger of the other clans lay behind the significant gains registered by the opposition groups in the municipal elections of 1927. Following this setback, the Mufti planned a campaign to re-establish his hegemony by inciting the faithful against the Zionists. Playing on Moslem religious sentiment, he claimed that they planned to seize the Moslem's holy sanctuary, the Haram as-Sharif. The Mufti aspired to gain recognition not only as the supreme leader of the Palestinian Arabs but also as the champion and defender of Islam.

The Yishuv provided the Mufti with a ready pretext, at the Western or "Wailing" Wall in Jerusalem, where Jewish and Moslem religious interests overlapped and clashed. The Wall was a remnant of Herod's Temple, and as such was regarded by the Jews as a sacred site. The Moslems called the same area the Haram as-Sharif, which was the third holiest place in Islam, after Mecca in Saudi Arabia and Karbala in Iraq. The compound included the site of the seventh-century al-Aqsa Mosque and the Dome of the Rock. The holiness of the Western Wall for the Moslems derived from it being the place to which Muhammad is alleged to have tethered Buraq, his miraculous horse, before ascending to Heaven.[9]

Since 1922, the Jews had brought a separating screen and chairs to the Wall on Yom Kippur, the most sacred day in the Jewish calendar. When they did so in September 1928, the British police removed them forcibly, as they had done in previous years. As usual, the police action provoked a storm of Jewish protest. But in 1928 the Mufti harnessed the issue to his own purposes. He began a public campaign that accused the Jews of encroachment and designs upon the Moslem holy places. He asserted that the annual Jewish infringements of the *status quo* at the Wall were evidence of their "unlimited greedy ambitions". He initiated a press campaign against "Zionist ambitions" and appealed to Indian Moslems to help save the Wall. He began to mobilize international Moslem opinion, in order to secure a British guarantee of Moslem rights in the Wailing Wall area (see p. 240 for the Moslem Congress convened in Jerusalem at the end of 1931).

During the following months the Arabs began to harass the Jews during their prayers at the Wall. They opened a new entrance at one end of the precinct, transforming what had been a cul-de-sac into a narrow passage. Mules were driven through, and their excrement defiled the areas where the Jews prayed; the noise of construction work, falling bricks and the turned-up volume of the muezzin (the Moslem public crier who calls the faithful to prayers four times daily) all added to the Jews' discomfort and bitterness, and to their grievances against the British, who failed to intervene to restore the *status quo ante*.[10] Their sense of victimization transformed the Wall into a symbol of the Zionist struggle, even for secular Jews. The Va'ad Leumi lobbied the government to expropriate the Wall and hand it over to the Jews. Right-wing Zionist groups began their own press campaign and set up a committee for the defence of the Wall. These moves merely confirmed Arab fears.

One of Chancellor's first acts in Palestine, in January 1929, was to inform the Arabs that he was prepared to consider the establishment of a legislative assembly. A tentative agreement on its composition was reached, even if its powers were left vague. Such an assembly would have suited the Nashashibi opposition, given its recent gains in the 1927 municipal elections. But the Mufti had his own political agenda – to rally the Arab masses to his own leadership, with his campaign to rescue the Wailing Wall from the Zionists. The occasion of Yom Kippur in August 1929 provided him with his opportunity. Arab-Jewish clashes in the vicinity of the Wall were followed by 8 days of riots and pogroms. These derailed negotiations for local autonomy, even if Chancellor became even more determined to secure more self-government for the Palestinian Arabs.

The events leading up to the outbreak of the mass violence may be reviewed here briefly. On 14 August, 6000 Jews demonstrated in Tel Aviv, brandishing banners inscribed: "The Wall is Ours". That same evening, some 3000 Jews held prayers at the Wall itself. The next day, large numbers of orthodox Jews gathered to pray at the Wall, accompanied by some 300 brawny youths with staves, members of a right wing youth group. After shouting slogans, they all dispersed. On the following day thousands of Moslems flocked to the Wall, listened to sermons, burned Jewish prayer books and removed the notes that pious Jews habitually pushed into the crevices in the Wall.

The spark that began the conflagration was ignited on Saturday 17 August, the birthday of the prophet Muhammad. Minor brawls between Arabs and Jews in Jerusalem ended with the death of one Jewish youth and many injured. On the following Friday, a series of Arab murders of Jews began in Jerusalem and spread to other parts of the country. In 1929, as in 1920, the historical community of Orthodox, non-Zionist Jews bore the brunt of Arab attacks – this time in the towns of Hebron and Safed. In Hebron, a single British policeman tried in vain to halt the pogrom. Some 133 Jews and 116 Arabs were killed and 198 Jews and 232 Arabs were injured. Most of the Arab casualties were shot by British reinforcements.

The riots exposed the total inadequacy of British security forces in Palestine. The British garrison needed substantial reinforcements and the Palestine police force had to be reorganized. Troop reinforcements were summoned immediately, but they arrived by sea, too late to avert the waves of violence. The COS dismissed the riots as a security issue, "a lack of adequate preventive forces".[11] Sir Hugh Trenchard, Chief of the Air Staff and as such responsible for security in Palestine, reiterated this line in a letter to the Colonial Secretary:

> ... the element of "danger" is largely conditioned by our ability to suppress disturbances in their incipient state ... When disorder broke out in August, there were no military forces at all in Palestine.[12]

The riots occurred when the High Commissioner and the Zionist leadership were abroad, and the police chief, Arthur Mavrogordato, was on leave. The Zionists were attending their biannual congress in Zurich. Chancellor had travelled to Geneva to present Britain's annual report on Palestine to the League's Mandates Commission. He proceeded from Geneva to London, for consultations. On receiving news of the riots, he rushed back to Palestine. He was disgusted by Arab atrocities against the older, orthodox Jewish communities. After a visit to Hebron, he confided to his son:

> I do not think that history records many worse horrors in the last few hundred years. I am so tired and disgusted with this country and everything connected with it that I only want to leave it as soon as possible.[13]

On 1 September, he issued a strongly worded public proclamation, condemning:

> ... the atrocious acts committed by bodies of ruthless and bloodthirsty evildoers; of savage murders perpetrated against defenceless members of the Jewish population, regardless of age or sex, accompanied, as at Hebron, by acts of unspeakable savagery.[14]

Special, single-judge courts were set up to mete out swift justice to those involved in the atrocities. These tried over 700 Arabs for offences connected with the riots; 55 were found guilty of murder and 25 of them were condemned to death. Following appeals to the High Court in Palestine and nationalist appeals for clemency, Chancellor reprieved all but three. Their death sentences were commuted to prison terms; a further 150 Arabs were convicted of looting and arson, and 219 for minor offences. Over 160 Jews were tried; two were found guilty of murder but were reprieved; seven Jews were found guilty of looting, and nine of minor offences.[15]

But Arab atrocities did not convert Chancellor to Zionism – the opposite was the case. His disgust with the Arabs' cruelties against helpless civilians did not make him forget where Britain's imperial interests lay. He believed that a continued British tenure of Palestine depended upon the assent of the Arabs – still the vast majority of the population. The 1929 riots finally dispelled any lingering British doubts about the unbending antagonism of the Palestinian Arabs to the Jewish National Home, and shattered any remaining delusions that the two races might meld into a single Palestinian nation. In December 1929, Ernest Richmond, now Director of Antiquities, expressed the general consensus among British officials when he told Owen Tweedy, a British journalist:

> The Jews came to Palestine in order to live as Jews and not as Palestinians, integrated in an Arab region. The only way to maintain Zionism against the Arabs was by force.[16]

At the High Commissioner's request, the home government set up a four-man commission of inquiry to investigate the immediate cause of the disturbances. It was headed by Sir Walter Shaw, a retired colonial judge, whose last post had been Chief Justice of Singapore. Lord Passfield (Sidney Webb), the Colonial Secretary, reassured Lord Melchett privately:

> ... the present Commission has been deliberately kept down to an immediate quasi-judicial investigation of the outbreak itself, to the exclusion of matters of high policy.[17]

In order to allay persisting Zionist apprehensions, Prime Minister MacDonald announced in the Commons in December 1929 that the fundamental principles of the mandate were "clearly outside the terms of reference" of the new commission.[18]

But this was precisely what Chancellor had in mind – a reopening of the fundamental principles of the mandate and a drastic constitutional change. The Labour government's tortuous reactions to the 1929 riots present a classical case of the civil servants – in this case, the Colonial Office establishment – dictating policy to a newly incumbent government (Labour took office in June 1929), whose ministers were not fully cognizant of the international complications involved in Britain's commitment to Zionism.

On 17 January 1930, Chancellor sent a long memorandum to Lord Passfield about the situation in Palestine. Passfield circulated it to the full Cabinet on 27 March. Chancellor proposed no less than the abrogation of the Balfour Declaration, by removing all those provisions in the mandate that gave the Jews "a privileged position in Palestine over the indigenous population".[19]

Chancellor asserted that the 1929 disturbances had not been motivated by either religious agitation or a lack of faith in Britain. He claimed to discern "a considerable growth of nationalist feeling within the Arab community" which had led to the recent "outburst of enmity towards the Yishuv". The Arabs did not accept the government's interpretation of either of its wartime promises – the MacMahon-Husayn correspondence or the Balfour Declaration (see Chapter 2). Chancellor could conceive of only two possible courses of action:

1 to withdraw the Jews' privileged position in Palestine, and to grant a measure of self-government to the people, or
2 to continue the present policy, supported by military forces to protect the Jews.

Chancellor dismissed the second option out of hand, as being:

> ... altogether repugnant to modern sentiment, and no palliative ... for a situation which had become a menace to the Empire.

He proposed the following practical measures: the government should issue a statement declaring that all the cultivable lands in Palestine were already occupied, and none of those in the possession of the indigenous population could be sold to the Jews without creating a class of landless Arab cultivators. With regard to the future of Jewish immigration, Chancellor was aware of Palestine's need for the capital brought in by the Zionists. Therefore, he made the anomalous proposal that the government should limit Jewish immigration, "to a degree that would safeguard the continued influx of Jewish funds".

Initially, the Colonial Office rejected Chancellor's proposals. John Shuckburgh, who had set up the Middle East section in the department in 1921, had been privy to all the 1923 Cabinet debates on Britain's need to hold on to the Palestine mandate – her strategic requirements, her need to honour international commitments and last but not least, her need for Jewish capital and revenues to maintain and develop the country. In 1929, he feared that any dilution of Britain's support for Zionism might lead the Jewish Agency to abandon the Jewish National Home, which would reduce Britain's "excuse for remaining in Palestine" to little more than the protection of the holy places. The department decided to keep Chancellor's recommendations secret, not wishing to pre-empt or influence the Shaw Commission's findings. This proved to be a futile exercise, as Chancellor met with the Commission's members during their stay in Palestine and had a key influence on their report – it contained striking similarities to Chancellor's own proposals of January 1930, which eventually became the basis of the Labour government's policy throughout 1930.[20]

The Shaw commission stayed in Palestine from October to December 1929 and delivered its report in March 1930. It found that the riots had begun with unprovoked Arab attacks against the Jews. A majority of the commission concluded that the outbreak had not been premeditated and exonerated the Mufti of the Zionists' charge of incitement – although it did criticize him for not having restrained his followers. One member of the commission, Labour MP Harry Snell, wrote a dissenting opinion, indicting the Mufti for having incited the disturbances. Chancellor conceded that Snell had assessed the Mufti's role more accurately than the rest of the Commission. Many of the senior Colonial Office officials agreed with Snell, but fear of an Arab backlash dictated a discreet silence:

> ... it is our private opinion in the Office that the Mufti and some of his supporters were probably very much more responsible for some of the deplorable incidents in Palestine than the majority of the Shaw Commission appear to think ... Since we have no definite facts supported by

unimpeachable evidence which we can bring forward in a contrary sense ... I do not see what use we can make of it unless it was sufficient to enable us to take definite action against the Grand Mufti, which is obviously impossible. He is much too wily a bird to give us a chance ... a public statement would, of course, have unfavourable reactions in our negotiations with the Arabs.[21]

The Shaw report determined that most of the Arab casualties had been caused by the British reinforcements rushed in from Egypt.[22] However, in defiance of its terms of reference, the commission reopened the fundamental premises of the mandate. Influenced by Chancellor, it reiterated his conclusion that the underlying cause of the riots had been:

... widespread hostility towards the Jews, based on the fear that continuing Jewish immigration and land purchases in Palestine would block any progress towards national self-determination, and ultimately transform the Arab population of the country into a landless minority.[23]

The Commission drew far-reaching political conclusions. It determined that the conflict in Palestine stemmed from differing Arab and Jewish interpretations of Britain's promises to them, and from:

... [the Arabs'] feeling of animosity and hostility towards the Jews consequent upon the disappointment of their political and national aspirations and fear for their economic future.[24]

The report determined that there had been excessive Jewish immigration in 1925 and 1926, and recommended that the government redefine its policy for Palestine, and that until another commission of inquiry reported back with its recommendations, all further immigration should be suspended. It also recommended the introduction of new methods of cultivation, in order to stimulate the growth and increase the productivity of the Arab agricultural sector.

The 1930 (Passfield) White Paper

The second Labour government in history (1929–31), headed by Ramsay MacDonald, was, like its predecessor in 1924, a minority administration, dependent upon the support of the Liberals.[25] Labour's past record on Palestine was ambiguous. On the one hand, in August 1917, it had committed itself to a "Jewish return" to Palestine. But in 1918, the final version of the party's War Aims Memorandum had called for the "effective protection" of "natives in all colonies and dependencies ... against the excesses of capitalist exploitation".[26]

One scholar has claimed that Britain's radical left, even when critical of the Zionists, displayed a "special affinity for the socialist achievements of the

Jewish labour movement in Palestine [which] preserved the socialist humanistic traditions of the Labour movement in their attitude to Zionism".[27] This conclusion rests on the unfounded assumption that Labour's traditions would lead a Labour government to side with the Zionists, rather than with the native Palestinian Arabs. But the British left's genuine admiration for the Zionists' socialist endeavours and for their collective settlements (*kibbutzim*) did not lead the Labour government to support Zionism – especially not when British interests were imperilled. On the two occasions when Labour held the reins of power (1929–31 and 1945–51), the government did not support the Zionist cause.

The Zionist labour movement nurtured close ties with senior members of the Labour Party. The party's support for Zionism derived in some measure from the belief that the Jews in Palestine were realizing a socialist utopia. Ramsay MacDonald had visited Palestine in 1922 as a guest of the Histadrut labour federation. Initially he supported the Zionists, first, due to his belief in the Jews' historical connection with the Holy Land and second, because in contrast to the Arabs, who he believed were unable to develop the country's resources, he was impressed by the Zionists' achievements. But MacDonald's belief in the justice of the Zionist cause was shattered by the 1929 riots.

MacDonald's Colonial Secretary was Lord Passfield. As Sidney Webb, he had been a leading socialist intellectual over the previous four decades. He had helped to establish the London School of Economics and served there as Professor of Public Administration from 1912 to 1927. Together with George Bernard Shaw, Webb founded the Fabian Socialists in 1884, a prominent intellectual society that advocated gradualist, democratic reform during the decades prior to World War One. The Fabians laid the intellectual foundations of the Labour Party, which Webb and his wife joined in 1914. In 1892, Webb had married Beatrice Potter, a liaison that was predominantly a meeting of minds, welded by shared intellectual and ideological values. Mrs Webb's ideological dedication is illustrated by the fact that when her husband was elevated to the House of Lords in 1929, taking the title of Lord Passfield, she refused to allow anyone to address her as Lady Passfield.[28]

Once Colonial Secretary, Passfield treated his wife most evenings to graphic reviews of his day at the office. Their conversations covered the vast complex of imperial problems that came within the purview of the Colonial Office, including Palestine. Beatrice kept a detailed diary, in which she recorded social and political events and gossip, as well as her opinions on the inequities of capitalist society and British imperialism. Given the decades-long intellectual partnership she had enjoyed with her husband, both in politics and in their joint writing projects, it may be assumed that her diary also reflects his views.[29]

The Labour government took office barely 10 weeks before the outbreak of the Wailing Wall riots. Ministers had no time to familiarize themselves with the complexities of British interests and international commitments in Palestine. The Shaw commission's report asserted that any additional Jewish immigration into Palestine would create a class of expropriated, landless Arabs. MacDonald did not like the report ("far too pro-Arab for the P.M.'s taste", Mrs Webb noted in her diary). He asked Passfield to convene a lunch with the Zionist leaders, after which he and Passfield met privately with Baldwin, Lloyd George and Samuel, the first High Commissioner. Initially, MacDonald decided to appoint General Smuts, a known Zionist supporter, to lead another inquiry. But he soon had second thoughts, due to Smuts' known bias. He agreed to Passfield's recommendation to appoint Sir John Hope-Simpson, an agrarian expert, to report on land settlement development and immigration into Palestine. All of this was done before the Shaw report was even submitted to the Cabinet.[30]

Hope-Simpson's private letters are tinged with anti-Semitism and it is clear that he reached his conclusions about there being "no available land in Palestine for additional Jewish settlement" well before he arrived in the country. During his visit, he became close personal friends with Chancellor, whose views he adopted wholesale.[31] His report would shatter any lingering beliefs that Labour ministers might have still entertained about the benefits and progress that the Zionists were bringing to the Palestinian Arabs.

Hope-Simpson visited Palestine in May 1930. He carried out a cadastral survey of the country from the air, which served to confirm his preconception – that with the Arabs' current methods of cultivation the remaining reserves of land in their hands were insufficient for the subsistence of their progeny. He conceded that Zionist land purchases had been legal, made with the full knowledge of the government, at inflated prices. He acknowledged also that they had paid large sums in compensation to the displaced Arab cultivators, something that they were not legally obliged to do (the exiled Arab *effendi* who sold off their lands paid no compensation to the dispossessed *fellahin*). But he insisted that the existing legislation was not preventing the creation of a class of landless Arabs. Not knowing how many Arabs had owned land previously, and without accusing the Zionists, he concluded that 30 per cent of the Arab population was now landless:

> ... at the present time and with the present methods of Arab cultivation no margin of land is available for agricultural settlement by new immigrants, with the exception of such undeveloped land as the various Jewish Agencies hold in reserve ... Without development, there is not room for a single [Jewish] settler.[32]

In a private letter to Passfield, Hope-Simpson castigated both Whitehall and Jerusalem for not having initiated any serious steps to develop the country and for being "inactive spectators of the communities' development, intervening only at times of crisis". He accused the Zionist labour movement of turning the country into "a place of social experiment of the communist type on the greatest scale". His conclusions reiterated those of Chancellor:

... either the existing area must be rendered capable of supporting more ... or the admission of Jews must be prevented ... The government must either shoulder the burden or surrender the mandate.[33]

In a secret, unpublished annex to his official report (delivered to the government at the end of July), Hope-Simpson made a malicious attack on the Yishuv leaders. The Zionist economy, he charged, rested on shaky foundations, being dependent upon donations from abroad. The Zionists were deliberately trying to buy up all of the country, leaving the Arabs without a living; he blamed the Zionists for the wretched condition of the Arabs, because they employed only Jews in their enterprises. The Zionists countered that if they did not employ any Arabs (which was not in fact true), then how would a halt to Jewish immigration benefit them?

Hope-Simpson asserted that a programme of modern agrarian reforms would take years to effect, after which only 20,000 more families would be able to settle in Palestine. He introduced a new interpretation of the 1922 principle of "economic absorptive capacity" – not of the Jewish sector alone, but of the entire Palestinne economy. He called for a reduction, even a total suspension of Jewish immigration – so long as there remained any Arab unemployed in the country.

The Zionist argument that industry would play an increasingly significant role in the economy, creating additional economic absorptive capacity for increased immigration, carried little or no weight with colonial officials. They assumed a static, rural Arab society, which for the foreseeable future would continue to cultivate their lands with their traditional methods. In the meantime, not only were the Zionists buying up so much Arab land that none would be left for the current owners' children, but the leasing conditions of the Zionist land settlement agencies – by allowing only the hiring of Jewish labour – barred the Arabs from working on the lands purchased.[34] Not only that, but the Zionists' policy of hiring only Jewish labour also excluded the Arabs from the growing industrial sector.

There was a clear ideological gap between MacDonald and Passfield, even if the Prime Minister initially adopted Hope-Simpson's report. This gap widened during the spring and early summer of 1930, when Passfield was preoccupied with another issue – the treatment of the black natives in East Africa by British white settlers. Lord Lugard, the Passfields' house guest in August 1930, spoke of "the naively barbaric capitalism of the [British] White Settlers" in Kenya and in other British colonies. In June 1930, Passfield published a White Paper on "Native Policy in East Africa". It defined Britain's duty under their mandate as the promotion of the "social progress of the inhabitants", and determined that "the interests of the African natives must be paramount".[35]

The Kenya White Paper was published shortly after Hope-Simpson delivered his report on Palestine which, as noted, concluded that the Zionists were pursuing a deliberate policy of trying to create a class of landless Arab proletariat in the country. For Passfield, it was a logical step to identify the Zionist settlers in Palestine with the white settlers in East Africa. The only difference was that, together with Hope-Simpson, he did not regard the Zionists as naïve.

Passfield disregarded the international ramifications of Britain's commitment to Zionism. He was not convinced that the Zionists were bringing benefits to the Palestinian Arabs and he adhered to the principle just applied to East Africa – that the natives' (in this case, the Palestinian Arabs') rights must be paramount. Such ideas persisted inside the Labour Party until well after World War Two. George Orwell, a party member, was an astute social critic and a confirmed anti-Zionist. After the war, he told a friend and colleague that the Zionists in Palestine were like "the white rulers in India and Burma".[36] Passfield's initial attempts in 1930 to reassure the Zionists that the government would fulfil its obligations to both races in Palestine at first lulled Weizmann into believing that he would support their cause.[37]

Passfield's entrenched preconceptions, identifying the Zionists with the white colonists in Kenya, are confirmed by the frequent references in his wife's private diary. For instance, in September 1930, she wrote in her diary:

> I admire Jews and dislike Arabs. But the Zionist Movement seems to me to be a gross violation of the right of the native to remain where he was born and where his father and grandfather were born ... this process of artificially creating new communities of immigrants, brought from any part of the world, is rather hard on the indigenous natives! The white settlers in Kenya would seem to have as much right, on this assumption, to be where they are, as the Russian Jews in Jerusalem![38]

The Webbs shared some of the common stereotypes of the day about why the British had become beholden to the "all-powerful Jews" in 1917. In late October 1930, following Zionist protests against the latest White Paper on Palestine, Mrs Webb vented her spleen in her diary:

> At the time of the Balfour Declaration, the one and only consideration was the relative power (to help us to win the war) of the international Jewish financiers on the one hand and on the other the Arabs in revolt against the Turkish Empire ... Owing to the superior wealth and capacity of the Jews, it is the Arab who has suffered damage during the last ten years ... An additional touch of irony to this ill-fated episode lies in the fact that the Jewish immigrants are Slav Mongols and not Semites and the vast majority are not followers of Moses and the prophets, but of Karl Marx and the Soviet Republic.[39]

Four days later, on the day the White Paper was published, she described her husband's views of Weizmann:

Weizmann, Sidney admires as a remarkable and, in a way, an attractive personality. ... **But he is a champion manipulator – and uses arguments and devices, regardless of accuracy, straightforwardness, or respect for confidence ... a clever devil** ... [40]

Passfield was discreet in his dealings with the Zionists, writing to Weizmann to deplore the Arab attacks in Hebron as "bloodthirsty and ruthless".[41] But his wife, unburdened by the responsibilities of office, spoke her mind freely. In reply to Weizmann's description of the week-long slaughter in Palestine, she retorted insensitively:

> I can't understand why the Jews make such a fuss about a few dozens of their people killed in Palestine. As many are killed every week in London in traffic accidents, and no one pays any attention.[42]

Passfield's antipathy to the Zionists was fanned by the Colonial Office officials and those of the Palestine administration, by Chancellor especially. Chancellor's antipathy towards the Yishuv was, almost inevitably, tinged with anti-Semitism. He wrote to his son: "truly the Jews are an ungrateful race". Like most of the British in Palestine, he favoured the Arab over the Jews. At the same time, he adopted a typically patronizing attitude to them, confiding to his son "they are like children, and very difficult to help".[43]

Like Samuel before him in 1922, Chancellor was arguably the main architect of the Passfield White Paper, which adopted wholesale his memorandum of January 1930. At the end of May 1930, in response to Chancellor's plea to suspend all further immigration, the government authorized him to freeze the issue of the biannual immigration quota of 2350 certificates that had already been approved. The government announced also its intention to curtail the authority of the Jewish Agency, and to prepare new land ordinances that would "prevent the dispossession of the [Arab] agricultural population".

But following a wave of international Jewish protests, notably in Poland and in the United States, the new land ordinances were put on hold. On 7 July, Passfield called in Weizmann in an effort to appease him. He reassured him, somewhat disingenuously, that the government wanted to encourage the development of the Jewish National Home, and had no intention of impeding Jewish immigration or restricting Jewish land purchases. However, he pleaded that the government must issue "an authoritative reply to Arab accusations". He promised Weizmann that he would release the suspended immigration certificates soon (he didn't do so until early November, when just 1500 of the 2350 were issued). Weizmann – perhaps overconfident because of Labour's political vulnerability – harangued Passfield:

> The Government ought to be clear on the point that we were not interested in building up a country for the Arabs ... our conception of the

Jewish National Home was that of a great settlement. To that end we should seek to pack as many Jews into Palestine as was at all possible.[44]

But MacDonald soon realized that he had a crisis on his hands: not only with the fierce domestic and international Jewish backlash, but also with the Conservatives, with his Liberal "allies", and even with his own frustrated MPs – in particular with the 25 trade union MPs whom Ernest Bevin controlled. If these all combined against him, his minority government would be defeated. Nonetheless, Hope-Simpson's report was devastating, and initially, he went along with Colonial Office policy.

Like his predecessors, MacDonald was troubled by the Zionists' ability to spoil Britain's relations with the United States. A recent, revisionist study of the Balfour Declaration has noted:

In the years prior to the [first world] war, the image of the influential Jewish plutocrat, the cosmopolitan, wire-pulling financier, attempting to influence politics, press and government policy, had come to prominence in British culture.[45]

These fears burgeoned after the Wall Street Crash of October 1929, and the formation of the enlarged Jewish Agency in August 1929, which several non-Zionist American Jewish magnates had joined.

The United States was plunged into an economic depression (called by MacDonald "an economic blizzard"), and began to press for the repayment of debts owed her from World War One. MacDonald became furious with the Jews for holding public demonstrations and mobilizing the Zionist lobby in the United States against Britain. In May 1930, he received a Zionist delegation headed by Weizmann, and reassured them that he was standing firm against the heavy pressure of the Arab delegation then in London, who demanded a halt to Jewish immigration and land purchases and the establishment of a legislative council (with an Arab majority that would try to stop Jewish immigration). But then MacDonald inveighed against the "incitement by American Jews against the British government".[46]

MacDonald was lobbied also by Harold Laski, one of Britain's outstanding Marxist intellectuals and a new recruit to the Zionist cause. Laski had been mobilized by Louis Brandeis and Felix Frankfurter, close friends since his teaching days at Harvard and Yale. MacDonald told Laski that he was angry with the Zionists for "exerting pressure on him through American Jewry".[47]

During the late summer of 1930, Britain's own economic troubles deepened. The Americans' tariff war against foreign imports spread to Europe. In Britain, unemployment rose from 1,204,00 in March 1929 to 1,700,000 by March 1930. In April 1930, Chancellor Snowden's budget, supported by all parties, raised taxes to 25 per cent and cut the salaries of all state employees. But foreigners still continued to withdraw their capital from London, and it was feared that Germany would default on her loan repayments. The run on the pound continued. By 19 September 1930, Britain's foreign credits were exhausted and the pound had fallen in value by 25 per cent. An emergency act suspending the Gold Standard passed through Parliament in two days.[48]

This latest phase of the economic crisis occurred during the Cabinet's final debates on its new Palestine policy, and made any substantial financial commitment to Palestine unthinkable. This ruled out any chance of implementating the very foundation of the Hope-Simpson report – the need for agricultural reform in the Arab sector (i.e. a rearrangement of holdings, the introduction of irrigation). Yet only the modernization of the Arabs' methods of cultivation could have increased productivity, thereby increasing the number of families that could subsist on the same plot of land.

When the Cabinet met on 15 September, Chancellor Snowden stated that Hope-Simpson's figure of £6–8 millions was much higher than had been anticipated and could not be met. The Treasury's veto effectively destroyed any attempt at a balanced policy in Palestine. The Cabinet appointed a sub-committee of experts (including Hope-Simpson) to study the issue. The committee realized that in the current economic circumstances, any proposal to spend many millions on the settlement of the Jews and the Arabs in Palestine would meet with serious opposition in Parliament and in the country. Their report was as much a political as an economic statement. It concluded that the terms of the mandate did not oblige Britain to provide financial assistance to the Jewish National Home:

> ... the settlement of the Jews on the land for the purpose of the Jewish National Home must be regarded as completed and it was questionable whether an expenditure upwards of £10 million, largely at the charge of the British Taxpayer, in order to enable Palestine to maintain an artificial flow of immigration is justified either by the terms of the Mandate or on economic grounds or with reference to the needs of other parts of the Empire.[49]

However, the committee understood that it would be "politically impracticable" to issue such a statement. Further, the committee warned that if the government's policy fell "seriously short of Jewish expectations", the import of Jewish capital "for social and other services on behalf of the Jewish population in Palestine" might be reduced. The government would then be left with the responsibility for some of those services, which would have to be curtailed.

But the committee concluded that Britain **was** "morally, if not legally bound" to make provision for those Palestinian Arab families that had been dispossessed of their lands. It proposed that the government guarantee a much lower loan, of £2.5 millions, for the resettlement of an estimated 10,000 dispossessed Arab families.

The Zionists were to be allowed to continue to settle the reserve of lands in their possession – at their own expense. The committee estimated that these reserves would suffice for all the Zionists' immigration requirements for the next 5 years – an estimated 5000 families (in fact, nearly 200,000 more Jews immigrated to Palestine between 1931 and 1935). In order to pre-empt any future Zionist demands, the committee recommended that the Palestine administration should immediately prohibit all further land sales to Jews (in order to allow the assimilation of dispossessed Arabs on the lands they now held), and restrict Jewish immigration drastically to those who could be absorbed on the lands the Jews already had, or those who could be absorbed into the non-agricultural sector.

The committee's report was laid before the Cabinet on 19 September 1930. The White Paper was revised accordingly and approved by the Cabinet on 24 September. It was published on 21 October, together with the Hope-Simpson report – from which the development scheme had been deleted.[50]

The new White Paper elevated the issue of Arab land sales to that of Jewish immigration. The preamble to the new policy reiterated the government's commitment to both races in Palestine, as laid down by the mandate, and argued that they were in no sense irreconcilable. But paradoxically, it went on to portray the clash of interests between the Arabs and the Zionists. The new policy revived the 1922 legislative council scheme, as requested by Chancellor. On the question of land sales, the White Paper adopted Hope-Simpson's conclusion:

> It can now be definitely stated that at the present time and with the present methods of Arab cultivation there remains no margin of land available for agricultural settlement by new immigrants, with the exception of such undeveloped land as the various Jewish agencies hold in reserve.[51]

The White Paper also endorsed Hope-Simpson's criticism of the Zionists' policy of employing only Jewish labour, and for the first time, asserted that the issue of immigration certificates would be determined according to the *total* number of unemployed in the country instead of, as hitherto, according to the number of job opportunities for Jewish immigrants:

> The economic capacity of the country to absorb new immigrants must therefore be judged with reference to the position of Palestine as a whole in regard to unemployment. ... Article 6 of the Mandate directs that the rights and position of the other sections of the population shall not be prejudiced by Jewish immigration. Clearly, if immigration of Jews results in preventing the Arab population from obtaining the work necessary for its maintenance, or if Jewish unemployment unfavourably affects the general labour position, it is the duty of the Mandatory Power ... to reduce, or, if necessary, to suspend such immigration until the unemployed portion of the "other sections" is in a position to obtain work.[52]

The MacDonald "black" letter

The Passfield White Paper was never enacted into law. In February 1931, it was simply by-passed by a letter from the Prime Minister to Dr Weizmann, which "reinterpreted" it.

Three major factors brought about this reversal, which constituted a capitulation to Zionist demands. The first was the government's lack of internal cohesion and its vulnerability as a minority administration. MacDonald learned immediately that both the Conservative opposition and his parliamentary allies, the Liberals, would oppose the new policy. The second factor was the deep economic depression that spread from the United States to Britain. This crippled the government's ability to invest in land reforms in Palestine – upon which Hope-Simpson's entire report depended. The third factor, linked directly to the second, was the government's heightened fear of the Zionists' ability to spoil Anglo-American relations.

The new White Paper came as a complete shock to the Zionists. They regarded it as a flagrant breach of Britain's obligations under the Balfour Declaration and the 1922 White Paper. It threatened to end all further Zionist development in Palestine. The government, instead of investigating those guilty of inciting the 1929 riots and bringing the murderers to justice, had reopened fundamental political issues, which the Zionists had believed to be a *chose jugée*.

After receiving an advance copy of the White Paper, Weizmann called a press conference on the eve of its publication, at which he announced his resignation as President of the Zionist Organization and of the Jewish Agency. His resignation, published in *The Times*, was followed by those of Lord Melchett, chairman of the Jewish Agency Council, and Felix Warburg, a prominent American banker and since September 1929 leader of the non-Zionist section of the enlarged Jewish Agency. No president was elected to replace Weizmann until the Zionist Congress of mid-1931. His position as Jewish leader remained *de facto* the same.

Demonstrations against the government's new policy were organized in London, New York, Palestine, South Africa and Warsaw. *The Times* published rumours that plans were being discussed in New York to bring "economic and political pressure to bear on Britain".[53] At a meeting in late October, Laski had warned MacDonald of the harm that his Palestine policy was doing to Anglo-American relations. But MacDonald rebuffed all his entreaties to mitigate the new policy. MacDonald was still infuriated by what he regarded as a campaign of incitement against Britain organized by prominent American Jews.[54]

The Labour government, a house divided, was not equipped to face the political storm that greeted its new Palestine policy. In August 1930, Mrs Webb had already noted "the rot" within the party and heaped scorn upon its ministers:

> The Cabinet is made up of men who are either too old, too thoroughly comfortable, too snobbish or too genuinely sceptical about the practicability of their assumed creed, to be keen about social reform.[55]

In 1930, Weizmann was unable to mobilize senior Cabinet ministers against the Colonial Office, as he had with Balfour and Lloyd George in 1921. But he found willing allies not only in the Conservative and Liberal parties, but also within the ranks of the Labour Party. He met with opposition leaders and he and his advisors helped to draft the letters that they published in the national press.

When leaders of the opposition began a public campaign against the new policy, MacDonald and his senior ministers took fright and performed an ungraceful volte-face. Passfield was made the scapegoat of the whole affair. During the first week of November, MacDonald disowned the policy that he himself had just voted for in the Cabinet. Weizmann was content to conclude that MacDonald had been duped by the Colonial Office. He commented in his memoirs: "It was curious how little the Prime Minister seemed to realize the inconsistency of the new course [the 1930 White Paper] with the letter and spirit of the Mandate".[56]

It required only a couple of articles in *The Times* to produce panic among Labour's leading ministers. Two days after the publication of the White Paper, three leading Conservatives, Stanley Baldwin, Austen Chamberlain and Leo Amery, published a letter in *The Times*. Drafted by Blanche Dugdale, Weizmann's confidante, the letter claimed that the new policy was in conflict with the spirit of the Balfour Declaration and with statements made by successive governments over the previous 12 years. Two days later, *The Times* featured a speech by Lloyd George, in which he had called the new policy "a breach of national faith ... a revocation of ... a solemn pledge given at a most solemn moment". He warned that England would be chastised throughout the world as "Perfidious Albion".

But the step that perhaps frightened the government most was a further letter in *The Times*, published on 4 November by two respected legal authorities, Lord Hailsham (Conservative) and Sir John Simon (Liberal), both former Attorney Generals. Their letter questioned the legal validity of the new White Paper and argued that the government should not attempt to implement it before obtaining the approval of the International Court at The Hague.[57]

The Hailsham/Simon letter shook Foreign Secretary Henderson, who had taken part in the League's discussions during the Cabinet's deliberations on Palestine. He asked MacDonald to convene the Cabinet immediately. It met 2 days later. All the senior ministers capitulated. Henderson told the Cabinet that he was alarmed at the prospect of having to defend the new policy at the League of Nations. Since it was already evident that the new White Paper had no chance of securing a majority in the Commons, the Cabinet decided to appoint a special sub-committee to consult with the Zionists – "in the most politic and tactful manner possible" – in order to reach an agreed "reinterpretation" of the new policy. MacDonald informed the Cabinet that he was about to meet Weizmann right after the meeting (at a lunch already arranged by his son Malcolm).[58]

At the lunch, MacDonald admitted to Weizmann that mistakes had been made, but regretted that formally, the White Paper could not now be revoked. But he reassured Weizmann that "clarifications and amendments would annul it in practice". In the meantime, no ordinance under the current White Paper would be executed in Palestine. MacDonald complained about how tired he was, and blamed Passfield for the current situation – "he was too old, very efficient in some ways, but with the mind of a German professor and a blind belief in the Colonial Office officials". At the end of the meeting, Weizmann told MacDonald that he would need to secure the agreement of his American colleagues to enter new talks with the government. MacDonald urged him to do so right away, adding that he personally had taken over Anglo-American relations from Henderson, since he "feared that the influential American Zionists, led by Louis Brandeis, could damage these relations". It is unclear whether MacDonald had discovered that Henderson had already advised Harold Laski to urge the Americans to exert political pressure through the British Embassy in Washington. After the meeting, Weizmann informed Warburg by telegram that the Prime Minister had invited him to meet the Cabinet in order to settle the terms of a new White Paper.[59]

MacDonald selected Henderson to head the special Cabinet committee to consult with the Zionists. At Weizmann's request, Malcolm MacDonald, the Prime Minister's son, was appointed as Henderson's "personal assistant". Since the 1929 riots, Malcolm had become his father's indispensable point man with the Zionists. His real task on the committee was to relay to his father all of Weizmann's requests. Hope-Simpson claimed later that Malcolm had composed the final draft of the Prime Minister's letter to Weizmann.[60]

But Weizmann faced opposition to further talks with the government, both from the American Zionist leaders and those of the Yishuv, such as Pinhas Rutenberg (head of the Va'ad Leumi). They all insisted on the retraction of the White Paper as a precondition for any talks. But the Marquess of Reading, an eminent British jurist and one of Weizmann's mentors, convinced him that this was an impractical demand, and pressed him to pursue the negotiations immediately, since the government might fall soon, even within weeks.[61] Weizmann reported to Warburg on the urgency of the situation:

> There is a possibility Government may fall about New Year essential seize opportunity offered which may never recur ... Month's postponement fatal ... also for counter pressure Arabs, also effect on carefully built up British opinion.[62]

Weizmann lobbied without success to have responsibility for Palestine transferred to the Foreign Office. The Zionists believed that the Foreign Office officials were "infinitely more intelligent" and had "a wider view than the rather parochial C.O. officials". But Henderson refused to take on Palestine, even if he did accept MacDonald's invitation to chair the new Cabinet committee. In fact, this met Weizmann's demands.[63]

Weizmann recalled later that Passfield and the Colonial Office had done everything that they could to block an agreement between the sides. By corollary, Passfield felt humiliated and lamented to Chancellor that all of his proposals had been rejected by the committee. In fact, Passfield was excluded from the inner circle of decision makers on Palestine. Hope-Simpson, a personal friend of Passfield, reported to Chancellor that the Colonial Secretary's relegation to ordinary membership of the committee had been "a most undignified position" for him, the man "principally, indeed solely, concerned" with Palestine. Henderson reported to the Zionists that he had silenced Passfield unceremoniously on several occasions.[64]

Negotiations between the Zionists and the Cabinet sub-committee dragged on until the beginning of February 1931.[65] At the end of December 1930, Weizmann cautioned Malcolm MacDonald that from the purely British point of view, a visit by him to the United States might be most useful to the government. At the same time, he warned of a Zionist financial collapse – until and unless he was able to produce a concrete achievement, in the form of the neutralization of the White Paper. Until then he would be unable to guarantee even minimal funding for their enterprise in Palestine. He reminded Malcolm that a Zionist financial collapse would have disastrous results not for only for them, but also for the Palestine government.[66]

Meanwhile, the government was forced to confront the opposition in the Commons. The debate on Palestine took place on 17 November 1930, on the afternoon of the Cabinet committee's first meeting with the Zionists. Given that Lord Passfield sat in the House of Lords, it was left to his undersecretary to defend the new policy in the Commons. The debate itself was an unmitigated disaster for the government. It reflected not only a widespread sympathy for the Zionist cause but, more seriously, the government's precarious tenure on power.[67]

The White Paper was not introduced as a motion to be voted upon, as was usually the case with a statement of a new government policy. This was because Labour knew that there was no chance of the new policy being approved as it stood. That is why they had already authorized negotiations with the Zionists, with a view to reaching a "reinterpretation" of the White Paper that would be acceptable to them.

The Commons was treated to the unedifying spectacle of a schism between the Prime Minister and his Colonial Secretary. Rumours, which MacDonald did nothing to dispel, were circulated that the new policy was a Colonial Office production. Passfield's wife noted the "long continued conversations of the Prime Minister and other Labour leaders with Lloyd George and his group of followers, in and out of the House of Commons ... a definite concordat against the Left".[68]

David Lloyd George opened the debate. He had been Prime Minister of the government that had issued the Declaration in 1917. Now 67 years old, he was "father" of the House, its longest serving member, and leader of the rump of the once-great Liberal party. Had there still been any lingering doubts about the chances of the White Paper securing a majority, he soon dispelled them. He chastised the government for having produced a "one-sided document, biased ... utterly stupid", which read as if "it had been written by an anti-Semitic official".[69] He speculated whether MacDonald had even been consulted before the White Paper was issued – adding quickly that he did not want an answer. When MacDonald spoke later in the debate, he didn't refer to this aspersion, leaving the impression that the latest White Paper was indeed a Colonial Office "putsch".

Passfield had already tried to cover himself. On the day after the decisive Cabinet meeting on 6 November, he gave an interview to the New York Jewish paper, the *Daily Forward*, in which he asserted that the whole Cabinet had approved the White Paper. Leo Amery, who led the Conservative attack on the White Paper, referred to Passfield's "astonishing remark" in the interview: "It is not my document; it is the Cabinet's ... I am only technically responsible". Of course, constitutionally, this was perfectly true. But Passfield failed to stifle the pernicious rumours that the White Paper was his personal creation – a situation with which MacDonald was only too content.

Hope-Simpson's critique of the Zionists' exclusivist economic policies were cited during the debate: "the persistent and deliberate boycott of Arab labour in the Zionist Colonies" was not only contrary to article 6 of the mandate, but was also "a constant and increasing source of danger to the country".[70]

Lloyd George mocked this section of the report – had Labour never heard of workers giving "preference to members of their own union"? He ridiculed the government's proposals on land sales and Jewish immigration, asserting that if Arab lands were developed they could support many more people (in fact, this was exactly Hope-Simpson's argument). He continued that most of the lands bought by the Jews were in any case "swampy and malarial" or "sand dunes" that had required heavy expenditure to make them habitable. He continued that had there been any development policy in Palestine, twice as many Arabs could have been living off the lands they now occupied:

> You are using the fact that you are doing nothing for the Arabs as an excuse for forbidding the Jews to do something for themselves. That is a policy which is utterly stupid.

Leo Amery lead the Conservative opposition to the new policy. In 1917, as a member of the Cabinet secretariat, he had helped to compose the final draft of the Balfour Declaration. He was privy to the considerations that in 1923 had led the Baldwin Cabinet to decide to retain the Palestine mandate (Chapter 7) and had served as Colonial Secretary from 1924 to 1929. Amery retained a long-term personal attachment to the Zionist project. Both Amery and Lloyd George spoke as if the reservation in the Balfour Declaration about protecting the rights of the Arabs no longer existed.[71] Amery adopted a typically imperialist line, the very antithesis of Passfield's "natives first" doctrine:

Unless you insist at the outset that the race with the higher standard of living shall be prepared to undertake every task, from the humblest, you soon get a tradition established under which one race becomes the hewers of wood and drawers of water and the others the capitalists and the skilled artisans.

Amery cited the letter of Hailsham/Simon in *The Times*, asking rhetorically whether the new White Paper was not in direct conflict with the terms of the mandate. He asserted that the policy now proposed left the impression that Jewish development should take place only on lands that the Zionists had already bought and that Jewish immigration should be severely restricted so long as a single Arab was out of work. He concluded: "No wonder that there has been an outcry all over the world". He ridiculed the report stating that MacDonald had reassured General Smuts that "everything is as it was before":

Unfortunately, everything is not as it was before ... Arab and Jewish feeling has again been strained ... Moslem feeling all over the world is being mobilised against the Mandate itself, not against the details of its application. Jewish feeling all over the world has been mobilised against this country. Is not that a disaster which a little prudence and forethought, a little psychology and a little tact, might have averted?

MacDonald did his best to reassure the Commons that the government intended to carry out its obligations to both communities in Palestine. He protested that there was no justification for the propaganda attacks to the effect that the Government wished to halt or curtail immigration, according to the number of unemployed Arabs. But he all but gave away the government's intention to retreat from the White Paper, when he announced that they were consulting with Zionist representatives in order to clear up "misunderstandings". He added disingenuously that he would be "only too glad to keep in similar touch with the Arabs".[72]

Labour had already been given a painful reminder of the need to accommodate the Zionists. On 6 November, the Party suffered a second by-election defeat to the Conservatives, following that of the previous May. As chance would have it, Harry Gosling, the Labour MP for Whitechapel, in London's East End, died on 24 October 1930. This necessitated a third by-election, which was scheduled for 3 December. Labour needed desperately to hold on to every single seat in the Commons. Its candidate for Whitechapel was a member of the executive of the Transport and General Workers Union (TGWU), whose 25 MPs were controlled by Ernest Bevin, head of the Union. His influence inside the Party was growing.

Over one-third of Whitechapel's voters were Russian-Jewish immigrants, mostly Zionists, affiliated to the Poalei Zion workers' party in Palestine. Bevin warned MacDonald that his 25 MPs would not support the party unless the government corrected the unfavourable impression created by the White Paper.[73] In response, the government released part of the immigration quota that it had suspended earlier in the year, and leaked a statement to the effect that it was about to improve the position of the Zionists "materially". Labour scraped through to victory in the by-election, but with 40 per cent fewer votes.[74]

The spectacle of the government wooing its Jewish voters was a rare event in British politics. But contrary to many accounts, the Whitechapel by-election was not the breaking-point that caused MacDonald's volte-face. He had capitulated 4 weeks previously, at the Cabinet meeting on 6 November. On 14 December, Mrs Webb commented on the widening rift between her husband and MacDonald:

> The P.M. is cross about Palestine: the Shaw Commission and Hope-Simpson with his report, both nominees of Sidney's, have been too pro-Arab; a White Paper (which the P.M. saw and approved) was "tactless" – indeed he allowed Lloyd George in his virulent attack on the White Paper, to assert that "the P.M. has not seen it" – which was mean of MacDonald ... The P.M. lets Sidney know that he thinks him "fussy" ... Sidney would like to retire but ... it would be taken as a victory for the Jews over the Arabs and might lead to trouble in Palestine.[75]

The Colonial Office officials washed their hands of the Palestine problem. They noted their minister's demoralization and his effective exclusion from the decision-making process. From Jerusalem, Chancellor warned that severe consequences would follow in Palestine if there was any retreat from the new policy – any remaining Arab moderates would join the extremists. His request that the new policy include the establishment of a legislative council scheme was rejected out of hand by the Cabinet committee.[76]

On 5 February 1931, the full Cabinet confirmed the final draft of the letter to Weizmann, and agreed to issue it as a new White Paper. But the barrage of protest by the colonial officials forced MacDonald to retreat, in an effort not to enrage the Arabs too much. Instead, it was decided to address an official letter to Weizmann that would "reinterpret" the White Paper of October 1930. However, the conundrum of determining the exact legal status of the letter would still cause the Prime Minister some awkward moments in the Commons.

First, there was a minor crisis over the question of who would sign the letter. Passfield feared that if the Foreign Secretary, as chair of the committee, signed it, that would signal the government's capitulation to Weizmann's demand that jurisdiction over Palestine be transferred to the Foreign Office. Passfield knew that he personally was *persona non grata* with the Zionists and therefore debarred from signing it. Therefore, he insisted that the Prime Minister himself sign the letter.[77] Ironically, this gave the letter more legal stature than it might otherwise have had.

On 11 February, the status of the letter generated the following exchange in the Commons. Ormsby-Gore asked Dr Drummond Shiels, the Under-Secretary of State for the Colonies, whether the discussions between the government and the Zionist representatives were concluded, if it was proposed to transfer the supervision of Palestine from the Colonial to the Foreign Office, and if he had any announcement to make regarding instructions that were to be sent to the High Commissioner in Palestine regarding the various questions raised in the Hope-Simpson report. Dr Shiels replied that the Prime Minister himself would reply to the question about the discussions with the Zionists and he denied that supervision of Palestine would be transferred to the Foreign Office. MacDonald was put on the spot when Austen Chamberlain, a former Conservative Foreign Secretary, asked him if he would not lay his letter to Weizmann before the House as a new White Paper. MacDonald made the following, convoluted reply:

> I think under the circumstances that we had better let it go as a letter which will be ... presented as a Parliamentary paper ... the White Paper which was published in October lays down the policy of the Government ... I am very unwilling to give this [letter to Weizmann] the same status as the dominating document ... In the body of the letter it will be made quite clear that **it is to be read as the authoritative interpretation of the White Paper on the matters with which the letter deals**. There will be no doubt as to the official character of the letter. It will be communicated as an official document to the League of Nations.[78]

But this did not satisfy Weizmann, who wanted an unambiguous commitment that MacDonald's letter would over-ride existing policy. On hearing of the Zionists' objections, MacDonald himself telephoned to Weizmann that same evening, to ask what he could do to set matters right. Weizmann insisted:

> We want to make it clear that the letter to me containing the authoritative interpretation of the White Paper shall be the basis of the law in Palestine. Unfortunately, Lord Passfield still imagined that nothing had happened or changed since the publication of the White Paper. He is causing trouble all the time. If a question is put to you in the House tomorrow, then you can still put matters right.[79]

The issue was discussed by the Cabinet committee and the Zionists the next day, at their final meeting. Henderson promised that MacDonald would confirm the authoritative nature of the letter in the Commons. On the morrow, the morning of MacDonald's speech in the Commons, Henderson met in private with Weizmann, who asked that the letter be laid before the Council of the League of Nations as an official document and be dispatched to the High Commissioner as an official Cabinet instruction. MacDonald complied and later that same day, he read his letter to Weizmann into the protocols of the Commons. It was "published with the Votes", thereby according it the status of official government policy.[80]

MacDonald's letter confirmed the Jews' right to exclude Arab labour from their enterprises and promised that "Jewish workers would be given a share of public works commensurate with Jewish contributions to revenue", rather than a share commensurate with the percentage of the Jewish population in Palestine. It made no mention of the legislative council and, as requested by the Zionists, it reaffirmed the government's commitment to the Jewish people as a whole, not just to the Yishuv. The letter reversed two key injunctions of the Passfield White Paper: it reaffirmed that Jewish immigration would depend upon the economic absorptive capacity of the Jewish sector alone, not on that of the entire economy, and stated clearly that no restrictions on land transfers would be imposed:

> His Majesty's Government did not prescribe and do not contemplate any stoppage or prohibition of Jewish immigration in any of its categories ... [and] did not imply a prohibition of acquisition of additional land by Jews ... nor is any such intended.[81]

The 1930 White Paper had brought considerable, but only ephemeral relief to the colonial officials dealing with Palestine. MacDonald's letter to Weizmann wreaked despair and demoralization among them. In February 1930, Chancellor had threatened to resign if the government succumbed to Jewish pressure. He stayed on in Palestine only long enough to accumulate his full pension rights. He left Palestine at the end of October 1931, 3 years to the day after taking up his post as High Commissioner.[82] Passfield told Hope-Simpson that he too would have resigned, but he had not wanted to embarrass the government. He affirmed his determination to leave the government by the end of July 1931, at the latest.[83] Sir John Shuckburgh, the long-serving head of the Middle East department, was so distraught that he too considered retirement – but he discovered that he could not afford to do so, since he was not yet eligible for a full pension.[84]

Since his very first days in Palestine, Chancellor complained that it was impossible to govern the Jews, who enjoyed free access to the Prime Minister and to the Cabinet. After the publication of MacDonald's letter, he told Owen Tweedy that he was "tired and bitter", that "he loathed the Jews and regarded them as his personal enemies".[85] In a letter to his son, he put MacDonald's retreat down to his fears of the Jews' international power:

> MacDonald was intimidated by the Jews ... the world economic crisis requires special caution; who would want at this juncture to mess with "World Jewry?"[86]

Hope-Simpson, who had first-hand experience of British politics (as a Liberal MP from 1922 to 1924) and became a personal friend of both Chancellor and

Passfield, put the government's volte-face down to party politics. He wrote to Chancellor:

> The whole thing is only explicable by political considerations. Whitechapel was in question and they wanted the Jewish vote. Also there is a considerable party of members, who are either Jews themselves, Christian Zionists, or dependent to some extent on Jewish subscription and Jewish votes, who might make the position of a minority government untenable. These are the considerations that influence policy – not considerations of right or wrong. I personally am becoming disgusted with party politics. The Conservatives are just as bad as anyone else. So are the Liberals. So are Labour.[87]

The 1930 White Paper was bypassed as if it had never existed. It was committed to the archives, until its reincarnation, in another format, in 1939. The method used to annul official government policy, by means of a letter written by the Prime Minister to a private individual, is probably unique in the annals of the British constitution. The fact that no one at the time seriously challenged the probity of MacDonald's behaviour reflects the broad consensus favouring the Zionists, as well as the anomalies of party politics at the time. Notwithstanding MacDonald's semantic acrobatics, it was clear to all that his letter to Weizmann was now the law of the land in Palestine. Hope-Simpson referred to it bitterly as "the revised White Paper".[88] In June 1937, William Ormsby-Gore, now the Conservative Colonial Secretary, was asked in the Commons about the government's policy in Palestine. He replied that the government had made it clear, on more than one occasion, that until the publication of the Peel (partition) report, it could not stray from official policy as laid down by MacDonald's letter to Weizmann of February 1931.[89]

A unique combination of extraneous factors led to the Labour government's retreat, against the consensus of the entire colonial establishment. However, for those who held responsibility for the day-to-day administration of Palestine, the writing was on the wall. It was only a matter of time (5 years) before a new Arab uprising, in a radically transformed international context, would cause the British government to revive the basic principles of the 1930 White Paper.

For the Zionists, MacDonald's letter represented a triumph over the government's challenge to their land settlement policies and its intention to change the regulations defining the limits of Jewish immigration. They succeeded in repudiating the charge that they were creating a class of landless Arabs. The letter provided a critical 5-year window of opportunity for the further expansion and development of the Yishuv. Jewish land acquisitions and immigration proceeded virtually unlimited during the years when Nazism cast its long shadow across Europe, reaching record levels in 1934 and 1935. Between 1931 and 1936 the Yishuv more than doubled in size, from 164,000 to 370,000.[90]

Weizmann was held in unique respect, even awe, by British ministers. But MacDonald's letter to him was his last diplomatic triumph, second only to the Balfour Declaration, an achievement in which he rightfully took pride.[91] Weizmann was aware that he had benefited from the opposition's zeal to humble a beleaguered minority administration that had acted in a particularly clumsy fashion. His resignation in October 1930 was symbolic, and it had the desired effect – of frightening the British. Until the end of the mandate, Weizmann remained their preferred, favourite Zionist.

For the Arabs, MacDonald's letter (they soon dubbed it the "Black Letter") was a key turning point in their relations with the British, the end of any hopes they may have still harboured about getting fair treatment from London. The letter served as irrefutable proof of the influence wielded in London by the Zionists and world Jewry, and their ability to turn parliamentary opinion against the advice of the Colonial Office experts. A statement issued by the Palestinian Arab Executive in 1931 expressed their bitter disillusion:

> Let us leave this Government to flatter the Jews as much as they desire and let us seek help from ourselves and the Arab and Islamic World ... Mr MacDonald's new document has destroyed the last vestige of respect every Arab had cherished toward the British Government.[92]

On the issue of land sales, there is some irony in the fact that in the early 1930s, when the Palestine government carried out three separate enquiries into the number of Arabs who had been made landless by the Zionists, both the Arab Executive and the Jewish Agency kept the submission of claims to a minimum. The Arabs were interested in keeping their own complicity a secret; the Zionists wanted to refute Hope-Simpson's (in fact Chancellor's) claim that Zionist settlement was creating a class of landless Arabs. In April 1932, the final report of Lewis French, Director of the Palestine Land Development Department, concluded that just 570 Arab families had been made homeless due to land sales to the Zionists. A later report, based on "the narrowest definition of what constituted a landless Arab", found that during the years 1931–39, less than 900 Arab families had been displaced. Of these, only 74 were eventually resettled, at a cost of some P£84,000, spent mostly on land purchases. The Palestine government's healthy surplus, P£4.7 million in 1935, would be used up mostly on the suppression of the Arab rebellion from 1936 to 1939.[93]

The Colonial Office officials were right in fearing grave repercussions in Palestine. The fact that their predictions of wide-scale Arab violence were delayed until 1936 was due to internal dissensions within the Palestinian Arab community. During the first half of the 1930s, the Arabs' protests were muted, vitiated by internal divisions between the moderates, who proposed an economic and political boycott of the Jews but continued negotiation and co-operation with the government, and a rising, younger generation of radicals who urged a campaign of non-co-operation with the Mandatory.[94]

Until 1936, the Mufti refrained from any anti-British activity. His acquiescence in British rule was purchased by a "sweetener" – by British agreement to relieve him of the need to stand for re-election for the presidency of the SMC, as required by the Council's constitution. In fact, the 1929 riots had helped the Mufti restore his prestige, not only as a Palestinian national but also as a pan-Islamic leader. In 1930, using his position as president of the SMC, he invited Moslem leaders from the Arab states and India to attend a world Islamic congress in Jerusalem. It convened in December 1931. Over 700 delegates from various Moslem countries attended. The congress resolved that a permanent General Islamic Congress would convene every 2 years in Jerusalem, organized by a permanent executive committee, of which the Mufti was appointed president. The congress resolved not only to defend the Moslem holy places in Jerusalem against the Zionists, but also to condemn all land sales to the Jews, to set up an Arab company to pre-empt the sales, and to condemn imperialism in all forms.[95]

The British realized that the Zionists' campaign in London had undermined the authority of the High Commissioner in Jerusalem. There was a consensus in Whitehall that their influence must be curbed, to prevent not only the erosion of British authority in Palestine, but also the attrition of her prestige in the Arab world.[96] But the inherent merits of the Palestinians' cause were never sufficient on their own to determine Britain's high policy. British priorities would change in the mid-1930s, as the clouds of World War Two gathered. Then London's over-riding concern became to retain the fealty of the Arab states.

The historic significance of Weizmann's achievement – in providing a window of opportunity for Zionist immigration into Palestine during the early years of the rise of Nazism – was not appreciated by the other Zionist parties at the time. He was attacked by the leaders of American Zionism and by Jabotinsky's right-wing Revisionist Party. At the 17th Zionist Congress held in Basle in June 1931, the Revisionists demanded an official British endorsement of their own platform – the establishment of a Jewish state on both banks of the River Jordan. Weizmann pre-empted his critics. In his opening address to the Congress he resigned as president of the World Zionist Organization. He would be re-elected to the presidency of the movement in 1935.

Notes

1 Bernard Wasserstein, *The British in Palestine: The Mandatory Government and the Arab-Jewish Conflict, 1917–1929*, London: Royal Historical Society, 1978, p. 158. The Black and Tans were an auxiliary police force that the British had used to suppress the rebellion in Ireland from 1919 to 1921.
2 Edward Horne, *A Job Well Done: A History of the Palestine Police Force, 1920–1948*, Sussex: The Book Guild, 2003, p. 97.
3 Wasserstein, *The British*, p. 158, and Douglas V. Duff, *Bailing with a Teaspoon*, London: John Long, 1953, pp. 176–78.
4 Wasserstein, ibid, pp. 158–59, Duff, ibid, and Charles Jeffries, *The Colonial Police*, London: Max Parrish, 1952; Martin Kolinsky, "Premeditation in the

Palestine Disturbances in 1929", *Middle Eastern Studies*, vol. 26/1, January 1990, pp. 22–23.
5 cf. A.J. Sherman, *Mandate Days: British Lives in Palestine, 1918–1948*, New York: Thames & Hudson, 1998, pp. 75–78; Wasserstein, *The British*, pp. 151–53.
6 Norman Bentwich, *England in Palestine*, London: K. Paul, Trench, Trubner & Company Limited, 1932, p. 144.
7 Wasserstein, *The British*, p. 155.
8 Sherman, *Mandate Days*, p. 85.
9 For this and following, see Wasserstein, *The British*, pp. 217–35, also Yehoshua Porath, *The Emergence of the Palestinian-Arab National Movement, 1918–1929*, London: Frank Cass, 1974, Chapter 7.
10 The government's law officers advised that all matters pertaining to the Haram were in the sole purview of the SMC, and the government was unable to intervene.
11 Sherman, *Mandate Days*, pp. 27, 83; Kolinsky, "Premeditation", pp. 18, 27.
12 Trenchard to Lord Passfield, 29 December 1929, CO 733/180/1, NA.
13 Cited in Tom Segev, *One Palestine, Complete*, New York: Metropolitan Books, 2000, p. 327.
14 Cited in Yehoshua Porath, *The Palestinian Arab National Movement*, vol. two, *From Riots to Rebellion, 1929–1939*, London: Frank Cass, 1977, p. 1.
15 Kolinsky, "Premeditation", pp. 30–31.
16 Richmond conversation with Owen Tweedy cited in Evyatar Friesel, "Through a Peculiar Lens: Zionism and Palestine in British Diaries, 1927–31", *Middle Eastern Studies*, 29/3, 1993, p. 427.
17 Kolinsky, "Premeditation", p. 20.
18 *House of Commons Debates* (*H.C. Deb.*), 23 December 1929, vol. 233, col. 1902.
19 For this and the following, see Chancellor to Passfield, 17 January 1930, CO 733/183/77050, NA, cited in Gabi Sheffer, "Intentions and Results of British Policy in Palestine: Passfield's White Paper", *Middle Eastern Studies*, vol. 9/1, January 1973, pp. 44–45.
20 ibid, pp. 45, 52; Kolinsky, "Premeditation", pp. 29–30.
21 Note by O.G.R. Williams, cited in Pinhas Ofer, "The Commission on the Palestine Disturbances of August 1929", *Middle Eastern Studies*, vol. 21/3, July 1985, p. 356.
22 cf. Kolinsky, "Premeditated", p. 22. Subsequent research leaves little doubt that the Mufti was personally involved. His public tirades throughout the previous year against an alleged Zionist conspiracy to buy up the Haram compound had incited the Arabs to a religious frenzy.
23 *The Shaw Commission Report on the Disturbances of August 1929*, Cmd 3530, London: HMSO, 1930; and Sherman, *Mandate Days* p. 83.
24 *The Shaw Report*, ibid.
25 In the general elections held on 30 May 1929, Labour won 288 seats, the Conservatives 260; on 5 June, Ramsay MacDonald was appointed Prime Minister after he secured the support of the Liberal Party's 59 MPs.
26 The Palestine plank of the party's platform was drafted by Sidney Webb. cf. Paul Keleman, "Zionism and the British Labour Party: 1917–39", *Social History*, vol. 21/1, January 1996, pp. 72–74; Keleman referred to the two Labour administrations as "*contre-courant*" to the party's record. For a study of relations between Poalei Zion (the Yishuv labour party) and Labour, based mainly on Zionist documents, cf. Joseph Gorny, *The British Labour Movement and Zionism, 1917–1948*, London: Frank Cass, 1983.
27 Gorny, ibid, p. 233.
28 In 1913, the Webbs, together with George Bernard Shaw, founded the *New Statesman*, a left-wing weekly.

29 A four-volume edition of her diaries first appeared between 1982–85; I have on occasion used volume 4, *The Diary of Beatrice Webb, 1924–1943*, "The Wheel of Life", edited by Norman and Jeanne MacKenzie, London: Virago, in association with the LSE, 1985. But when possible, I have preferred the digitalized version, made available online at the beginning of 2012 by the Library of the LSE. This version includes some highly sensitive entries left out of the published version.
30 Mrs Webb's diary entry for 30 March 1930, in *The Diaries*, vol. 4, p. 212. Hope-Simpson, formerly of the Indian Civil Service, had most recently been deputy chairman of a League of Nations commission for the settlement of refugees in Greece.
31 For example, Hope-Simpson to Chancellor, 26 June 1930, Chancellor papers, 16/6, cited in Friesel, "Through a Peculiar Lens", p. 430 and note 52; Sheffer, "Intentions and Results", p. 51.
32 *Hope-Simpson Report on Immigration, Land Settlement and Development*, Cmd 3686, London: 21 October 1930, Chapter XI, Conclusion, p. 141.
33 Hope-Simpson to Passfield, 18 August 1930; his letter was circulated to the Cabinet by Passfield as CP 301(30), September 1930, NA; Sheffer, "Intentions and Results", p. 51.
34 Keleman, "Zionism", p. 76.
35 Memorandum on Native Policy in East Africa, Cmd 3573, June 1930. Lord Lugard was the British representative on the Permanent Mandates Commission at the League of Nations; cf. Mrs Webb's diary entry, 13 August 1930, LSE.
36 T.R. Fyvel, *George Orwell: A Personal Memoir*, London: George Weidenfeld & Nicolson Ltd, 1982, p. 142. The conversation took place some time during the winter of 1945–46.
37 Keleman, "Zionism and the British Labour Party", p. 75
38 Entry of 2 September 1930, *The Diary*, Mackenzie, p. 190.
39 Entry of 26 October 1930, LSE.
40 Entry of 30 October 1930, ibid, my emphases. This entry is not included in the published selection.
41 Passfield to Weizmann, in Gorny, *The British*, p. 56
42 Chaim Weizmann, *Trial and Error*, New York: Schocken Books, 1972, p. 331; Weizmann gives no date for the meeting. Mrs Webb's descriptions of the Jews of London's East End in the 1880s contained "explicitly anti-Semitic pronouncements"; Gorny, ibid, p. 76. On her anti-Semitic tendencies in general, see also Joseph Gorny, "Beatrice Webb's Views on Judaism and Zionism", *Jewish Social Studies*, vol. 40, spring 1978, pp. 95–116.
43 Friesel, "Through a Peculiar Lens", pp. 429; also Wasserstein, *The British*, p. 155, and Sherman, *Mandate Days*, p. 77, 85, 253
44 Norman Rose, *The Gentile Zionists*, London: Frank Cass, 1973, pp. 12–14; Weizmann's record of the July meeting is cited on p. 14.
45 James Renton, *The Zionist Masquerade: The Birth of the Anglo-Zionist Alliance, 1914–1918*, Basingstoke/New York: Palgrave Macmillan, 2007, p. 24.
46 Gorny, *The British*, p. 79.
47 ibid, p. 80. Harold Laski was Professor of Political Science at the LSE from 1926 to 1950; he lectured at Harvard and at Yale from 1916 to 1920. While there, he befriended Frankfurter and Brandeis. In July 1930, the group led by Brandeis had returned to the leadership of the American Zionist Movement. Laski later served as chairman of the Labour Party, 1945–46.
48 cf. Robert Skidelsky, *Politicians and the Slump: The Labour Government of 1929–31*, London: Macmillan, 1967, Penguin, 1970. A European banking crisis in May 1931 led to a balance of payments crisis and a financial crash in Britain. By 1932, unemployment in Britain rose to 3.75 million, 25 per cent of the total workforce.

The unravelling of the mandate, 1929–31   243

49 Cabinet meetings of 15 September, Cab 23/65, and Snowden report in CP 309, 23 September 1930, Cab 24/215/9, NA. The committee's professional members included Hope-Simpson and O.G.R. Williams of the Colonial Office, also Sir Basil Blackett (Chair), and Sir John Campbell; for their report, see Cab 24/215, NA.
50 Minutes of meeting in Cab 23/65, Cab 23/65/6/ NA; and *Palestine: Statement of Policy*, Cmd 3692, London: HMSO, 20 October 1930. After the Passfield White Paper was put into cold storage, the Cabinet whittled down Britain's "contribution" to Arab agricultural development to a paltry £50,000. In August 1931, the Arabs duly rejected this sum, realizing also that acceptance would imply their recognition of the British mandate, with its sponsorship of the Jewish National Home.
51 Cmd 3692, ibid.
52 ibid.
53 Rose, *Gentile*, p. 17.
54 Laski met MacDonald twice at the end of October; cf. Gorny, *The British*, pp. 98–99. Louis Brandeis, a Justice of the Supreme Court until 1939, and Felix Frankfurter, a Roosevelt appointee to the Supreme Court in 1938, had close connections to the American establishment; Felix Warburg took part as an American observer at the meetings of the Cabinet sub-committee; on his copious correspondence with Weizmann, cf. Dresner, editor, *Weizmann Letters* [*WL*], vols XIV, XV.
55 Diary entries of 3 and 8 August; Mrs Webb described MacDonald as "a snob with aristocratic tendencies". Prime Minister MacDonald, nearly 64 years old, was ageing and plagued by ill health; Foreign Secretary Henderson was nearly 67 years old, and Passfield had just celebrated his 71st birthday. These were advanced ages for those times.
56 Weizmann, *Trial*, p. 333.
57 *The Times*, 23, 25 October and 4 November 1930; also Sheffer, "Intentions and Results", p. 54.
58 Cabinet meeting of 6 November 1930, Cab 66/30, in Cab 23/65, NA; also Weizmann report to Oskar Wasserman, 13 November 1930, in *WL*, vol. XV, Dresner, pp. 39–42.
59 cf. Gorny, *The British*, pp. 79, 97–98, 99–101, and Weizmann to Felix Warburg, 6 November 1930, *WL*, vol. XV, pp. 34–35. Passfield's mental decline is confirmed by his wife's diary entry, 2 September 1929, LSE.
60 Weizmann – Wasserman report, *WL*, vol. XV, supra.
61 ibid, p. 41, and *WL*, vol. XV, pp. ix-xi, 32–36. Lord Reading (Rufus Isaacs) had held the positions of Attorney General in Asquith's Liberal government and Lord Chief Justice of England from 1913 to 1921. He served as British ambassador to the United States from 1918 to 1919, as Viceroy to India from 1921 to 1926, and for a brief period in 1931, he succeeded Henderson as Foreign Secretary.
62 Weizmann to Warburg, 8 November 1930, in ibid, pp. 35–36.
63 Rose, *Gentile*, pp. 11, 20–22; also Sir John Hope-Simpson to Sir John Chancellor, 26 February 1931, the John Chancellor papers, file 6, folios 56–59, Rhodes House Library, Oxford.
64 Rose, ibid, p. 25; Weizmann, *Trial*, p. 334; and Gorny, *The British*, p. 100. As well as Henderson (chairman) and Passfield, the other members of the sub-committee were A.V. Alexander, First Lord of the Admiralty, and Thomas Shaw, Secretary of State for War.
65 Rose, ibid, pp. 23–27, and p. 35, footnote 138.
66 Weizmann to Malcolm MacDonald, 30 December 1930, WA.
67 The debate is in *H.C.Deb.*, 5th series, vol. 245 cols 77–210, from which all the following quotations are taken. Curiously, earlier scholars hardly referred to the debate, if at all; Gorny and Rose do not even mention it; Kolinsky refers to it only *en passant*.
68 Entry of 12 February 1931, in *The Diary*, MacKenzie, p. 238.

69 Some of the opposition speakers may well have been briefed by the Zionists; Ben-Gurion had called the White Paper "a document permeated with anti-Semitism from beginning to end", cited in Gorny, *The British Labour*, p. 89.
70 The passage from the Hope-Simpson report was cited by Major Elliott, Conservative.
71 The relevant passage in the Declaration read: " ... it being clearly understood that nothing shall be done which may prejudice the civil and religious rights of the existing non-Jewish communities in Palestine ... ".
72 MacDonald had already published a letter to that effect in *The Times* on 15 November 1930. The talks with the Arab delegation that had visited London at the end of March 1930 reached an impasse in mid-May, after the government rejected their demands for the prohibition of and a halt to all further Jewish immigration. The Arabs attributed the failure of the talks to the influence of the Zionists; cf. *The Times*, 14 May 1930.
73 Bevin went on to serve as a Labour minister in Churchill's wartime coalition. After the war, he served as Foreign Secretary in the Labour government, in which post he earned the reputation in Zionist eyes as an anti-Semite.
74 In the May 1929 general elections, the Labour candidate for Whitechapel won 13,701 votes; in the 3 December by-election, the Labour candidate received 8544 votes, the Liberal (a Jew) 7445, the Conservative 3417 and the Communist candidate 2106 votes; cf. Rose, *Gentile*, pp. 37–40, notes 1, 12.
75 Entry of 14 December 1930, LSE.
76 Porath, *The Palestinian*, p. 33.
77 Rose, *Gentile*, p. 26.
78 *H.C.Deb.*, vol. 248, cols 388–90. My emphasis.
79 Rose, *Gentile*, pp. 26–27.
80 ibid, p. 27; for MacDonald's statement in the Commons, see *H.C.Deb.*, vol. 248, cols 751–57.
81 *H.C.Deb*, ibid; also Barbara J. Smith, *The Roots of Separatism in Palestine: British Economic Policy, 1920–1929*, Syracuse: Syracuse University Press, 1993, p. 16.
82 Kenneth W. Stein, *The Land Problem in Palestine, 1917–1939*, Chapel Hill: University of North Carolina Press, 1984, p. 85.
83 Hope-Simpson to Chancellor, 26 February 1931, supra. Passfield remained in office until August 1931, until MacDonald formed a "National Government" with the Conservatives.
84 Shuckburgh joined the India Office in 1900; in 1931, he was relieved of direct responsibility for Palestine and promoted to Deputy Permanent Under-Secretary at the Colonial Office, where he served until his retirement in 1942.
85 Tweedy diary note, 14 February 1931, cited in Friesel, "Through a Peculiar Lens", p. 433, and note 69.
86 Cited in Segev, *One Palestine*, p. 337.
87 Hope-Simpson to Sir John Chancellor, 26 February 1931, supra.
88 ibid.
89 Debate of 9 June 1937, *H.C.Deb.*, vol. 324, cols 746–47.
90 cf. Stein, *The Land*, p. 81.The number of Jewish immigrants soared from 4075 in 1931, to 37,337 in 1933, to a record 62,000 in 1935.
91 cf. Weizmann, *Trial*, p. 335.
92 Porath, *The Palestinian*, p. 34.
93 Stein, *The Land*, pp. 110, 117, 157. On the landless Arab enquiries, cf. idem, Chapter 5.
94 Porath, *The Palestinian*, pp. 9–12, 34–36.
95 ibid, pp. 295–96.
96 MacDonald-Passfield correspondence, and Shuckburgh minutes of July 1931, cited in Friesel, "Through a Peculiar Lens", p. 434 and notes 71–74.

Plate 1 Dr Chaim Weizmann, Sir Herbert Samuel, David Lloyd George and Frances Stevenson (Lloyd George's secretary and mistress). Circa 1920.

Plate 2 Winston Churchill (Colonial Secretary), in Tel Aviv, March 1921, with the mayor, Meir Dizingoff.

Plate 3 General Sir Edmund Allenby, Arthur Balfour and the High Commissioner, Sir Herbert Samuel (1920–25), Jerusalem 1925.

Plate 4 Field Marshal Sir Herbert Plumer, High Commissioner from 1925–1928. Date unknown.

Plate 5 Sir John Chancellor, High Commissioner from 1928 to 1931. Jerusalem, June 1930.

Plate 6 David Ben-Gurion, in the uniform of the Hebrew battalions, 1918.

Plate 7 Pinhas Rutenberg, 1920. Awarded the concession for the electrification of Palestine.

Plate 8 Moshe Novomeysky, 1902. Awarded the Dead Sea salts concession.

Plate 9 Moshe Shertok (Political Secretary of the Jewish Agency, later Sharett) with High Commissioner Sir Arthur Wauchope, 1931–38, in 1935.

Plate 10 Shertok, Weizmann and Ben-Gurion at the 20th Zionist Congress, Zurich, 1937.

Plate 11 Haj Amin el-Husayni, the Grand Mufti of Jerusalem, with senior Nazi officials, Berlin, 1944.

Plate 12 The Mufti receiving guests in Cairo, 1946.

Plate 13 Ragheb Bey al-Nashashibi, head of Arab opposition to the Grand Mufti.

Plate 14 Sir Harold MacMichael, High Commissioner, 1938–44. Date unknown.

Plate 15 Field Marshal Sir Bernard Montgomery ("Monty"), the CIGS, on a visit to Palestine, November 1946.

Plate 16 Weizmann and Sir Alan Cunningham, the last High Commissioner, 1945–48.

11 The Arab rebellion, I
April–October 1936

> ... tho' force can quell the riots and sabotage in time, it cannot kill feeling ... it is obvious to all of us that unless immigration is reduced to a trickle from the present flood, troubles in one way or another will continue.
>
> Diary entry of Humphrey Bowman, Director of Education, June 1936

Strategic exigencies[1]

The Arab rebellion against the British began in April 1936. It had two phases: the first, from April to October 1936; the second, from September 1937 to April 1939.

British reactions to the rebellion cannot be comprehended without a prior survey of the geo-strategic changes that swept Europe and the Middle East from the mid-1930s. In 1936, facing unprecedented threats from the rising Fascist powers, the Foreign Office usurped the traditional hegemony of the Colonial Office over Palestine, and assumed *de facto* control of policy in the country. The Foreign Office formulated a new doctrine for the Middle East: Palestine could no longer be treated in isolation, since Britain's actions there would affect her relations with the entire Arab and Moslem worlds. For the first time, the British granted the Arab states a *locus standi* in Palestinian affairs.

In October 1935, Italian forces invaded Abyssinia. Over the course of the following 8 months, they completed the brutal conquest of the country, employing all the weapons of modern warfare – including aerial bombing and mustard gas – against barefoot native warriors. The conquest presented the British with the spectre of an Italian land attack against Egypt and the Suez Canal – the imperial conduit to India – "the jewel in the Crown". With the opening of hostilities in Abyssinia, Britain mobilized and dispatched her main fleet to the Eastern Mediterranean. Only three ships were left in home waters to fend off a possible German attack. None at all were stationed in the Far East to defend Singapore, Britain's main base in the East. In March 1936, the Germans took advantage of Britain's preoccupation with Italy to reoccupy the demilitarized Rhineland – in flagrant violation of the Versailles Treaty.

The Arab rebellion, I

At the League of Nations, Britain led a campaign to mobilize Italy's Balkan neighbours to impose sanctions on her. But none of them were willing to risk war with Italy. Britain herself, unwilling to fight Italy on her own, shied away from closing the Suez Canal to Italian shipping, which carried essential oil supplies and arms to the Italian forces. The failure to impose sanctions against Italy was a mortal blow to the League of Nations, an institution that had been designed to guarantee international order.[2] The Arabs regarded the League's failure as Britain's. As the British themselves were only too aware, their failure to stop Mussolini's Italy raised doubts about their ability to protect their Empire.

Britain was forced to reassess her strategic priorities. For more than a decade after World War One, her armed forces had been reduced drastically under the so-called Ten Year Rule. This guideline, adopted by the Cabinet in August 1919, instructed the Chiefs of Staff (COS) to draw up the services' budgets on the assumption that the Empire would not be engaged in any major war during the coming 10 years.[3] In 1928, Chancellor Churchill persuaded the Cabinet to make the Ten Year Rule self-perpetuating. It was abandoned just 4 years later, in 1932 (the year after the Japanese invaded Manchuria), with the caveat that the services must bear in mind the country's grave financial and economic situation.

In 1931, Sir Frederick Field, the First Sea Lord, Commander of the Royal Navy, informed the influential Committee of Imperial Defence (CID) that in the event of war, the navy would be unable to protect British trade on the high seas, that no port in the Empire was adequately defended, and that if the fleet was moved to the Far East to protect British imperial possessions, there would not be enough ships left to protect the British Isles and its trade. This contingency materialized in 1935, when the fleet was moved to the Eastern Mediterranean.

In 1936, Britain faced three potential enemies: Germany, Japan and Italy, in that descending order of menace. In February, the Cabinet decided that Britain could not fight all three simultaneously. After years of paring down defence budgets, the military were unable even to assess accurately their requirements for mounting an adequate deterrent to Germany and Japan. The CID pleaded the case for a new two-power naval standard – against Germany and Japan, enough at least to counter Japanese aggression along the eastern circumference of the Empire. The navy was determined not to permit any temporary breach with Italy to derail its priorities for imperial defence. It refused to countenance any proposal to divert military resources to the Middle East or to Mediterranean bases such as Malta or Cyprus.[4]

The COS and the Chamberlain Cabinet, apart from Foreign Secretary Eden, drew the conclusion that Italy must be appeased.[5] Eden came to the Foreign Office in December 1935, fresh from leading Britain's abortive campaign at Geneva to impose League sanctions on Italy. The Middle East ambassadors quickly apprised him of the need to restore Britain's prestige in the Arab world. No one in London could really be sure about Mussolini's future intentions, but many feared that he had grandiose plans to revive the historic Roman Empire. Mussolini's Abyssinian adventure had in fact left his armed forces overextended and the Italian economy tottering. But some officials feared that the very desperation of his position would make the Italian dictator go for a rash, "mad dog" attack on Egypt – exploiting his theatre dominance in the Mediterranean, in an attempt to snatch a quick victory before Britain could bring in reinforcements.

In June 1936, the month after the completion of the Italian conquest of Abyssinia, and with the Arab rebellion in Palestine at its height, Eden warned the Cabinet of a possible Italian attack against Egypt. The COS dismissed his fears with the assertion that Italy would not move unless sure of Germany's support. But the chiefs insisted on a return to tranquility in the Middle East, which could be achieved only by restoring friendly relations with Italy. That summer, the government officially recognized the Italian conquest of Abyssinia, and withdrew the main fleet back to home waters. During the winter of 1936–37, the CID immersed itself in a study of Britain's strategic priorities. In February 1937, the Cabinet endorsed its conclusion that hostilities with Italy must be ruled out.

Britain's failure to stop the Italian conquest of Abyssinia left a profound impression on the Arab world. The Arabs compared the evident impotence of Britain and France, the old colonial powers, with the dynamic policies and military and diplomatic triumphs of the resurgent Fascist powers – Germany and Italy. In 1936, a wave of disorders and protests against the *status quo* swept the Middle East. In January, a general strike in Syria demanded independence from the French; in April, the Arab rebellion erupted in Palestine and in August, the Egyptians extracted from the British a new treaty that promised British evacuation in 20 years. The new treaty set a 10,000 ceiling on the number of troops Britain was allowed to hold in Egypt, and determined that all her military forces should be confined to Britain's military Base in the Canal Zone.[6]

In April 1937, shortly before the second and most violent phase of the Arab rebellion erupted in Palestine, Eden pleaded again that British prestige in the Middle East must be restored, by preparing for a possible war with Italy. But he was over-ruled by the service chiefs. They were supported by Neville Chamberlain, the powerful Chancellor of the Exchequer, shortly to become Prime Minister. Chamberlain insisted that a unilateral war with Italy was "unthinkable". At the time, he was putting the final touches to a new, 5-year rearmament budget, at a total cost of £1500 million, which made no provision for a war with Italy. The new budget was approved by the full Cabinet in June 1937, with Chamberlain now in the Prime Minister's seat.

Chamberlain made the search for an accommodation with Italy one of the central pillars of his foreign policy.[7] The corollary to this was the appeasement of the Arab states. During the winter of 1937–38, Eden, supported this time by the Prime Minister, would lead the battle at Whitehall to reverse its support for the Peel Partition Plan (Chapter 13).

With the expansion of Japanese-Chinese hostilities in Manchuria during the summer of 1937, the dual threat of Germany and Japan materialized. No one challenged the strategic priority of the Far East over the Mediterranean and the Middle East. The chiefs determined that in the event of war, the Mediterranean would have to be abandoned (or left to the French to defend), until Britain had triumphed in the main theatres of war. Sir Ernle Chatfield, the new First Sea Lord, warned that the loss of the Far East would constitute no less than the "the start of the break-up of the Empire". A strategic appreciation by the CID in February 1938 concluded:

> ... the UK and Singapore must be defended first ... no danger in the Mediterranean could be allowed to interfere with the dispatch of the Fleet to the Far East.[8]

It was against this context that the main source of local opposition to Britain's support of the Jewish National Home in Palestine – Sir Miles Lampson, Britain's influential ambassador to Egypt – must be considered. Lampson pleaded incessantly with London the need to abandon Zionism and to appease the Arabs. His major concern was that the troops sent out to defend the Suez Canal, now "on loan" to Palestine to put down the Arab rebellion, would become bogged down there. Lampson was also the primary voice warning London about Britain's loss of face in the Arab world, for having failed to stand up to Italy. In March 1937 he warned that Britain's position in the Middle East now depended upon "fair dealing" in Palestine:

> While I do not suggest that we should swallow whole the Arab case against Zionism, it is essential that it should not appear to the Arab and Egyptian Governments ... that our weight is thrown definitely on the Zionist side ... A combination between Egyptians and Arabs which began with a challenge to Zionism might end with a challenge to our military position in the Middle East. ... we should carefully analyse – and Palestine is very much a case in point – whether if we antagonize the Arabs we can cope with them and the Italians at the same time.[9]

The rebellion: April–October 1936

On 19 April 1936, sporadic outbreaks of violence by Arabs against Jews in Palestine began. By the end of the day nine Jews had been killed and ten wounded. The following night, two Arabs were murdered, probably by Jews, as an act of revenge. There followed a series of wanton terrorist outrages, which included the indiscriminate murders of Jewish civilians. The British imposed a general curfew and declared a state of emergency. The violence escalated into what would become known as the Arab rebellion.[10]

The Arabs were emboldened by their view that Britain was an imperial power in decline. They saw their own position in Palestine as critical. First and foremost, there was the huge influx of Jewish immigration from 1932 to 1935 – nearly 200,000 Jews, doubling the numbers of the Yishuv. Many of the new immigrants were German Jews, who by special arrangement with the Nazi government brought with them German-made machinery and equipment, "bought" with their financial assets, which had been expropriated by the Germans (see Chapter 17).

In 1935, the Arabs had petitioned High Commissioner Wauchope with three demands: the cessation of Jewish immigration, a prohibition of land transfers to the Jews, and the grant of independence. The government refused to limit immigration, but accepted Wauchope's plea to try out the legislative council scheme once again. The Zionists would be represented on the new council in proportion to their percentage of the total population – just over one-third. Wauchope announced the government's agreement to the scheme in December 1935. But it was rejected by Parliament in March 1936, following a vigorous campaign against it by the Zionist lobby. The Palestinians were particularly disillusioned by the defeat of the scheme, similar to the one that the government had offered them in 1922, and again in 1930.

It confirmed their belief that the Zionists controlled the government in London. They concluded that only violence might change Britain's policy – an option now seen as feasible, in view of the government's recent display of impotence against Italy.

On 25 April, the major Arab political parties set up a Higher Arab Committee (HAC), which assumed the political leadership of the rebellion. On 15 May, following the Syrian precedent, the HAC declared a nationwide general strike of all Arab workers and businesses, to be continued until the Arabs' three demands were met.

An anomalous situation emerged: the HAC, under the Mufti's presidency, was leading the strike but the SMC, also under his presidency, continued to function. The Mufti decided on a partial strike of the SMC: he closed all the organization's offices but the religious courts (the *shari'a*), the *waqf* foundations, the mosques and the poor relief services all continued to function. Traditionally, the SMC supplied alms and aid to the poor and needy but in practice, Haj Amin diverted some of these funds (as well as financial aid that he received from the Italians and Germans), to supplying the rebel gangs with food, ammunition and weapons. The HAC issued a decree ordering all Arabs to cease paying taxes unless the government changed its policy of support for Zionism. But the decree had little effect, since most of the government's revenue came from indirect taxation. A proposal that all Arabs working for the government go on strike was abandoned. All senior Arab government officials were allowed to continue working, on condition that they signed a pledge expressing their solidarity with the strikers, and paid 10 per cent of their salaries in to the strike fund. At times, the "contributions" were obtained under threat. The government took no action, preferring to turn a blind eye.[11]

In the towns, public vilification, threats and actual violence were employed against Arab strike breakers. Businesses and shops that opened were picketed and their owners' names were published in the Arabic press; vegetable and fruit suppliers and hawkers who tried to continue business were beaten up and on occasion murdered. By the beginning of May, the strike had all but paralysed urban commerce. Arab transportation (including Arab taxis) was all but halted; Jewish transport was sabotaged – by the strewing of nails on the roads, sniping and grenades. On two major arterial roads, Jaffa to Haifa and Haifa to Jerusalem, the Jews armed their cars and travelled in convoys. The Arabs began to attack British installations – government offices, police stations and army bases. From 10 to 13 May the main railway line from Palestine to Egypt was sabotaged.

The main centre of violence during the first months of the rebellion was in Jaffa. The town's citadel afforded an ideal base for snipers and bomb throwers. The town's tortuous narrow streets and alleys provided an ideal refuge for terrorist fugitives. Small terrorist bands shot at British police and military patrols almost nightly, and threw bombs at police headquarters and government buildings. Wauchope acceded to the army's demand to demolish a large section of the old town and to widen its streets, in order to facilitate the movement of military vehicles and to deprive the rebels of easy retreats. His official announcement gave the pretext that the demolitions were required for "public health" reasons. His announcement earned him the censure of the British Chief Justice in Palestine (on which, see p. 254). The demolitions were begun on 16 July and lasted for 2 weeks. Jaffa was brought under army control shortly thereafter.[12]

Violent acts against Jews and their property became a major feature of the strike. The first attacks by Arab peasants against Jewish rural settlements and isolated police and army units began on 10 May, simultaneously with a wave of bomb throwings in the towns. During the second half of May armed peasant bands were organized. The leaders of the rural bands were peasant youth with a high school education, who had worked for the government and later returned to the countryside. But the poorer *fellahin* (peasants) did not strike – they could hardly afford to. Although those Arabs who tried to sell their produce to Jewish settlements were assaulted, no one really expected them to cease tilling their lands, from which they barely eked out a living. The HAC did not have the resources to compensate them, or to feed and maintain the Arab masses.

By June 1936, with the urban centres largely under British control, the rebellion's centre of gravity moved to the rural areas. The most lawless region was the remote hilly area of Samaria, with Nablus at its centre. This region suited guerilla warfare. It had few roads and many of its villages were inaccessible to motor vehicles. The rebel gangs were able to rely on the local villages for food and information, if not willingly given, then by coercion. The gangs' most frequent targets were the IPC oil pipeline (from Mosul to Haifa), road and railway bridges, and isolated Jewish colonies, where cattle were slaughtered, crops and trees burned, and civilians murdered. British troops were unfamiliar with the terrain, and not accustomed to coping with guerilla warfare. The Arab bands were able to retreat with impunity to the hills or to inaccessible villages. The campaign of individual terror reached its peak in August, by which time some 80 Jews had been killed and 400 injured.[13]

In late August, the rebellion assumed new proportions, with the arrival on the 22nd of the month of Fawzi el-Qawukji, a Syrian Arab who had served as a captain in the Ottoman army, and later as an instructor in an Iraqi military school. Fawzi brought with him some 200 Iraqi, Syrian and Trans-Jordanian volunteers. They installed themselves in northern Samaria. On 2 September, Fawzi convened a meeting of the commanders of six of the main Palestinian bands, who agreed, formally, to recognize him as their supreme commander.

The bands' operational skills soon improved, due mainly to the experience of the foreign volunteers. But the Palestinian fighters had no experience of open battle against a regular army with air support. The first set battle between the British and a mixed force of Palestinians and foreign volunteers took place on 3 September. The Arab forces held out for 6 hours and succeeded in shooting down one British airplane before breaking ranks. But mutual recriminations followed. The Palestinians and the foreign volunteers each accused the other of retreating first. Fawzi didn't conceal his disappointment with the Palestinians' performance, and the latter didn't hide their mistrust of him. The Husaynis spread rumours that Fawzi was in British pay. Fawzi returned the compliment by accusing the Mufti of acting secretly for the British. Fawzi acted as if the HAC didn't exist and flouted the authority of the Husayni notables. Fawzi's short-lived intervention in the rebellion sabotaged the efforts of the HAC and of its president to establish their position as the undisputed leaders of the rebellion.

From the outset, the Palestinian forces suffered from internal dissensions and disunity. Their commanders could not agree to unite, and the Palestinian fighters refused to recognize the supreme authority of a foreign command, even if Arab. In addition, the long-standing dissensions between the Husaynis and the Nashashibis sharpened the more the rebellion progressed. Fawzi didn't hide his preference for the Nashashibis. Attempts at mediation by the Emir Abdulla of Trans-Jordan (who also favoured the Nashashibis) only made matters worse. These internecine frictions would degenerate into internecine terror in 1937, when the clans clashed over the Peel Commission's Partition Plan.

In September 1936, with the rebellion posing a severe challenge to British forces, the Cabinet decided to send out a full division of troops, and to give them freedom of action under martial law. The additional division doubled the number of British troops in Palestine, who now accounted for some 40 per cent of the total British field force.[14] However, before the army could deploy its full force, the Palestinian Arabs signalled their readiness to call off the rebellion. An appeal by the Arab kings to the Palestinians was organized, to which the HAC acceded. The haggling over terms dragged on until October.

In the meantime, the army chafed at the bit, frustrated by the last-minute attempts to appease the Arabs, thereby depriving the army of a decisive victory. On 6 October, General Sir John Dill, the new GOC Palestine (1936–37), who arrived in late September as commander of the extra division, appealed to the War Office:

> ... am anxious as is also the High Commissioner that parleys with Arab kings should come quickly to an end. Appreciate political issues involved with Arab kings, etc. which are causing delays, but militarily it is highly desirable that 1st Division having arrived with great flourish of trumpets, strong action should immediately follow. The role of paper tiger for the army is neither dignified or effective. Shall be grateful for anything you can do to force the pace, because unless greatly mistaken martial law will in any event be necessary to restore order here.[15]

Much to Dill's chagrin, the military showdown that he wanted so much was averted. The Arab kings issued their appeal to the Palestinian Arabs, and on 12 October Wauchope was able to report to London that all acts of violence had ceased.

The first phase of the rebellion in 1936 had been contained, but not crushed. The gangs disbanded, but were not broken or disarmed. They stored their arms in secret caches, ready for use on another day. The British made no attempt to seek out their stores. In June 1937, on the eve of the Cabinet debate on partition, British military intelligence warned presciently about the consequences of not having crushed the rebels the year before:

> The last rebellion was mainly raised and controlled by the Higher Arab Committee led by a gentleman called the Grand Mufti. The fact that the rebellion was not suppressed by military action and the institution of martial law, and that no direct measures were taken against the Grand Mufti and Committee has left them with their power and prestige largely unimpaired.[16]

The Arabs suffered 197 killed and nearly 1000 wounded, mainly at the hands of British security forces. Arab terrorist bands had committed many acts of brutal murder against unarmed Jewish civilians, including women and children.

The Arab general strike had unintended side effects. It catalysed the Yishuv economy towards self-autonomy. By 1936, there were some 400,000 Jews in Palestine, 30 per cent of the total population. But the Jewish sector already constituted the main base of Palestine's economy. The Arabs resided mainly in the rural areas; the Jews constituted a majority in Haifa, Palestine's main industrial centre, in Tel Aviv, which overtook Jaffa as the country's main commercial centre, and in Jerusalem, the country's administrative capital.[17]

Jewish agriculture already supplied most of the Yishuv's food requirements and the Jews owned the country's main industries, including, significantly, the country's electricity grid. Jewish production was mainly for Jewish consumption and export. The only Arab industry for which there was a Jewish market was stone quarrying – the Jewish construction sector was dependent on gravel supplied by the Arabs. The general strike brought all Jewish construction to a halt. There was also a shortage of fresh vegetables, but makeshift solutions were readily found by importing goods from Egypt and Syria.[18]

In work places where Arab labourers went on strike, the Yishuv leadership made efforts, not always successful in the long term, to ensure that Jews replaced them.[19] Haifa port never closed down, and most of its Arab dockers stayed on the job. When Jaffa port went on strike, the Jews built a wharf at Tel Aviv, and secured a government licence to unload goods there. At the end of the first phase of the rebellion, an Arab appeal to the government to revoke Tel Aviv's licence was turned down.

For the Palestinian Arabs, the rebellion's most significant achievement was political – the mobilization of the Arab states to their cause. The Palestine conflict was transformed into a pan-Arab issue. With every additional deterioration in the international situation, the closer the Arab states came to attaining a virtual power of veto over British policy in Palestine. The writing was already on the wall – even if the government left it to the Peel Royal Commission to read it out.

The British response: negotiation and appeasement

At first, many British residents in Palestine failed to take the rebellion seriously. Perhaps going on past experience, they did not believe that the Arabs constituted a credible military force. Some civilians referred to the hunts for guerilla bands as some new form of blood sport, and failed to register the full gravity of targeted killings and random murders by bombs and bullets, or the extent of extortion and intimidation within the Arab community. For many Britons, keeping up appearances and the outward display of sang-froid remained paramount. The following letter from a British housewife to her parents, written during an early stage of the rebellion, even if not necessarily representative, indicates a certain detachment, even isolation from reality:

> It is one long story of snipings and pottings and ineffective bombs ... Yesterday was the King's Birthday, and we stopped the war for an hour to have a birthday parade for Edward VIII ... We were all dressed in our best bib and tucker and sat under marquees. All very fine and debonair like.[20]

Senior officials empathized with the Arabs' alarm at the accelerating rate of Jewish immigration and understood their motive for rebellion. Humphrey Bowman, the veteran director of education (1920–36), defined accurately the heart of the problem in his diary:

> ... tho' force can quell the riots and sabotage in time, it cannot kill feeling: and that will continue until the *cause* is settled ... immigration:

and it is obvious to all of us that unless immigration is reduced to a trickle from the present flood, troubles in one way or another will continue.[21]

From the outset, British policy was torn between two conflicting strategies on how to deal with the rebellion: on the one hand, the army's demand to impose martial law and crack down on the rebels; on the other, the determination of High Commissioner Wauchope to end the rebellion by negotiation and concessions. His prime concern was not to jeopardize the achievements of his first 5 years in office. He feared that the adoption of harsh measures on a wide scale would leave behind an "embittered people ready to rise at any moment against the British administration".[22]

Yet when Wauchope did concede the army's demands, he found himself pilloried from an unexpected quarter – by the British judiciary in Palestine. The administration's reaction to the rebellion was subjected to severe criticism by the courts. They challenged the emergency regulations and regularly handed down light sentences to rebels convicted of crimes such as arson, intimidation and the sabotage of roads. Sir Michael MacDonnell, the British Chief Justice of Palestine from 1927 to 1936, held strong pro-Arab views, and did not bother to conceal them. It was widely believed that his views influenced his judicial decisions. As president of the Court of Criminal Appeals, he frequently quashed convictions handed out by the lower courts. During this first stage of the rebellion some 300 people were killed and 1300 injured. Not a single death sentence was imposed.

The lenience of the courts did not make the High Commissioner's position easier and the light sentences that they handed down did little to inspire confidence in the deterrent power of British law in Palestine. When an Arab appeal against the Jaffa demolitions came before the High Court, MacDonnell took the opportunity to berate the administration in public – for using the pretext of a "public health necessity" to justify the demolitions. He challenged the integrity of the administration:

> It would have been more creditable if the Government, instead of endeavouring to throw dust in people's eyes by professing to be inspired with aesthetic or other quasi-philanthropic motives ... had said, frankly and truthfully, that it was primarily for defensive purposes.

In his summing-up, MacDonnell called the demolitions "a glaring case of evasiveness" and accused Wauchope of having displayed "a singularly disingenuous lack of moral courage". His fellow judge on the Bench, the recently arrived Justice Manning, rebuked the High Commissioner for pursuing a policy of "deceit, circumlocution and blunder".[23]

The Chief Justice's Jaffa judgement was published by the HAC in several languages. Wauchope estimated that the Arabs printed 10,000 copies of it. MacDonnell's censure of the administration was his most notorious, but also his last act against the British administration. Wauchope pressed the Colonial Office to take the unprecedented step of forcing him to take an early retirement. Wauchope warned London that the judgement would have a seriously detrimental effect on security in Palestine, and would be taken as an incentive to resist the government's measures to restore law and order. He feared that it would encourage Arab members of the judiciary to join the Arabs' general strike, and would weaken the government by bringing it into disrepute just at a time when it needed fortifying. After protracted negotiations, the right formula was found to induce the Chief Justice to take an early retirement and leave Palestine. On the eve of his departure, the HAC held a farewell party for him, at which the Arabs expressed their appreciation of his efforts. His case was probably unique in British colonial history.[24]

During this first phase of the rebellion, Wauchope's advice was usually followed by the Colonial Office. This was due to the fact that the outbreak of violence found the incumbent Colonial Secretary, J.H. Thomas, preoccupied with his own personal troubles (a scandal over leaked Budget secrets) to assert any control over policy. Thomas soon elected to resign, and was replaced at short notice at the end of May 1936 by William Ormsby-Gore.[25]

In mid-1936, the government took the unprecedented step of allowing the Arab states to intervene in the affairs of Palestine. This departure brought the Foreign Office, the senior department, into direct, daily involvement with Palestine. The department's paramount concern was to avoid alienating the Arab states. It shared the Palestinian Arabs' anxiety about the accelerated rate of Jewish immigration into Palestine during the first half of the decade. While paying lip service to the unfortunate predicament of European Jews, at the same time, the department also accused them of "forcing the pace". The permanent officials expected the Jews to understand Britain's own problems. They expected the Zionists to help Britain to appease the Arab states, lest she be forced to abandon Palestine – leaving the Yishuv to the whims of a different, less amenable power.

The negotiations between various agents of the British and Arab governments during the summer of 1936 will be described here in some detail, because they mark the beginning of two historical processes: the imposition of Foreign Office control over policy in Palestine, and the transformation of the Arab-Zionist conflict in Palestine into a pan-Arab issue.

From the end of April 1936, the British were approached by a procession of Arab rulers, whom the Palestinians had asked to act on their behalf. After initial reservations, the government agreed to Arab demands to stop Jewish immigration, in return for the Arabs stopping their acts of violence. But negotiations faltered on a question of tactics: which side would make the first move? The government could not afford to appear to be giving in to violence again, and it refused to halt immigration until after the Palestinians had called off the rebellion. The Palestinian leaders had similar concerns – they were unwilling to call off the rebellion until they could show their people some tangible British concessions.[26]

At the end of April, the Mufti asked Ibn Saud, King of Saudi Arabia, to intervene with the British. The Saudi ruler was told by the Foreign Office that the government would not be moved by threats of violence and that he could serve Palestinian interests best by persuading them to stop their rebellion. The British agent at Jidda persuaded the Saudi ruler to steer clear of Palestinian affairs. On 1 May, the Palestinians turned to Abdullah, the Emir of Trans-Jordan – regarded throughout the Middle East as a British puppet. They asked him to intervene with the government in London, to secure their three demands. They told him that their main interest was to have Jewish immigration stopped. Abdullah, acting as an unofficial British spokesman, advised them to send a delegation to London. When the Palestinians approached him once more, on 6 June, he told them to stop their terrorist acts, in order to allow a Royal Commission of Inquiry to go out to Palestine and begin its work.

The decision to send out a Royal Commission to Palestine had been taken by the Cabinet on 18 May. Its terms of reference were to:

> ascertain the underlying causes of the disturbances which broke out in Palestine in the middle of April; to enquire into the manner in which the Mandate for Palestine is being implemented in relation to the obligations of the Mandatory towards the Arabs and the Jews respectively; and to ascertain whether, upon a proper construction of the terms of the Mandate, either the Arabs or the Jews have any legitimate grievances on account of the way in which the Mandate has been or is being implemented; and if the Commission is satisfied that any such grievances are well-founded, to make recommendations for their removal and for the prevention of their recurrence.[27]

But the government refused to announce the appointment of the Royal Commission until the Palestinians stopped their rebellion. The Palestinian leadership felt unable to do this. Therefore, the announcement of the Commission's appointment was delayed until July 1936.

When three Arab kings – of Saudi Arabia, the Yemen and Iraq – proposed their mediation, the Foreign Office favoured acceptance. Aware of the continuing Hashemite-Wahhabi rivalry, Trans-Jordan was excluded from the initiative, in order to prevent a clash between Abdullah and Ibn Saud.[28] The department emphasized the importance of Iraq for imperial communications, and described the delicate position in which the three kings – all allies and friendly to Britain – now found themselves as a result of the rebellion in Palestine. It warned that "any extension of Italian influence in Saudi or Yemeni territory" must be prevented.[29] Most significantly, the department proposed offering the Arab rulers the cessation of Jewish immigration as a trump card for use in their mediation with the Palestinians.

But the Colonial Office stood firm – no concessions could be made before the Palestinian Arabs called off the rebellion. The most that Ormsby-Gore would agree to was the stoppage of immigration for the duration of the Royal Commission's stay in Palestine. However, since it had been agreed that the Commission would not leave for Palestine until the disorders had ceased, the Cabinet deferred a decision about immigration until a later date.

The turning point in the negotiations came on 3 July when, during further consultations at the Foreign Office with the Saudi Minister in London, the officials accepted his proposal to mobilize the kings of Iraq and Yemen in a joint effort to mediate with the Palestinians. The Saudi Minister stated that the Palestinians were now willing to call off the disorders on three conditions: that all Arab prisoners convicted for acts of violence were released, that the communal fines imposed recently on villages harbouring rebels were cancelled, and that all Jewish immigration was suspended forthwith.

The Foreign Office reply was non-committal, but the Arab Kings now forced the issue. The Imam of the Yemen declared that he was prepared to appeal to the Palestinians to cease the violence if the government promised first to suspend immigration. King Ghazi of Iraq went yet further, suggesting that the kings open immediate talks on the three demands of the Palestinians. The Saudis themselves pointed out the impropriety of these proposals, since the Royal Commission had been appointed to examine precisely these issues. But they all pressed for an immediate government announcement on the suspension of immigration, pending the Commission's report. On 15 July, the Cabinet decided, over the opposition of the Foreign Office, to reject the Arab rulers' latest proposal – that the government inform them in advance of its intention to suspend immigration once the Commission set out for Palestine.[30]

But informal negotiations continued. By 29 July, the Cabinet felt that enough progress had been made in order to authorize the Colonial Secretary to make a formal announcement on the appointment of the Royal Commission. Ormsby-Gore did so in the Commons that same day and outlined the Commission's terms of reference.[31]

By mid-August, with public security in Palestine deteriorating, the War Office, frustrated by Wauchope's refusal to declare martial law and give the army its head, added its voice to those demanding further political concessions. It proposed that the government announce that the three kings had proposed the suspension of immigration, and that the government had accepted their proposals. Unsurprisingly, the proposal was supported by the Foreign Office.

The only remaining obstacle to reaching a deal with the Arabs was Wauchope himself, who was anxious to preserve the prestige of his administration. But during the last week of August, his resolve also broke and he agreed to make concessions – in confidence – before the violence was called off. Further talks between Abdullah, the Palestine administration and the Palestinian leaders produced yet another version of the old formula. The High Commissioner would give his word that immediately, or one week at the most after the strike and the disorders were called off, he would suspend immigration until the government determined future immigration policy, on the basis of the Royal Commission's recommendations. The Colonial Secretary agreed to ask the Cabinet to confirm a suspension of immigration from 1 October, the date on which the Commission was due to leave for Palestine.

But even this understanding was sabotaged by the arrival in Jerusalem on 21 August of Nuri al-Said, the Foreign Minister of Iraq. Nuri stayed as Wauchope's house-guest in Jerusalem, and soon usurped the role of chief negotiator.[32] He had his own agenda – the promotion of his pet project for the creation of a Hashemite-led Arab Federation, to include Iraq, Trans-Jordan and Palestine. His interest in Palestine was increased by the fact that the Mosul–Haifa (IPC) oil pipeline had become operational in January 1935. But Nuri al-Said's intervention did not suit the Saudis. The British understood all too well that Ibn Saud was determined to thwart any Hashemite expansionist plans. The Iraqi-Saudi feud would remain a constant obstacle to attempts by the Arab rulers to intervene in Palestine.

With Wauchope fully in the picture, Nuri al-Said opened a new set of talks with the HAC. He quickly reached an agreement whereby the Palestinian executive would agree to end the strike and the disorders, in return for which Nuri himself would negotiate with the British "to guarantee the Palestinians' legitimate demands". In his desperation, Wauchope recommended that the government accept this formula. He now favoured even a temporary suspension of Jewish immigration, to allow Nuri Said to conclude his mediation successfully.

But this time Orsmby-Gore decided to stand firm. He instructed Wauchope that only the Cabinet had the authority to approve Nuri al-Said's initiative. He personally might agree to Nuri appearing before the Royal Commission, but he could never agree to granting Iraq a permanent *locus standi* in Palestine. He warned Wauchope against saying or doing anything that might commit the government to a suspension of immigration.

The Foreign Office had its own reasons for alarm. Its officials realized that Nuri al-Said was using the Palestine issue in order to further his own and Iraq's ambitions. He was arrogating to himself a role that the British had already refused to give to Ibn Saud. If Nuri al-Said now had his way, it could reignite the Hashemite-Wahhabi conflict, with the British caught in the crossfire. Indeed, the British learned that while Nuri al-Said was in Jerusalem, Yasin Pasha, the Iraqi Prime Minister, had told the Saudi Minister in Baghdad that the Saudi initiative had failed because the British did not trust them.

The British had lost control of the confused, convoluted negotiations with the leaders of the three Arab states, each of whom saw in the Palestine imbroglio an opportunity to further his own interests in the pan-Arab arena. The British were saved from the morass of conflicting Arab rivalries only by the guile of the Zionists who, aided by inside information, leaked details of the government's negotiations to the press.[33]

On 1 September 1936, one day before the key Cabinet meeting on Palestine, the *Palestine Post* published an accurate draft of an alleged agreement between Nuri al-Said and the HAC. It contained three points: a general amnesty for all Arab offenders, an immediate suspension of Jewish immigration, to continue until the Royal Commission delivered its report, and the recognition of the Iraqi government as representative of the Palestinians before the Commission. When Weizmann confronted Ormsby-Gore with the article, the latter had no choice but to issue a categorical denial: no such terms had been agreed to by any British representative and no promises had been given to Nuri al-Said, either with regard to the suspension of immigration or with respect to his own status on Palestine.

The exposure of the secret negotiations effectively ruined any remaining chance of reaching a deal with the Arabs. The British were furious with the Arabs, whom they suspected, wrongly, of having leaked the information to the paper. Ormsby-Gore was forced to adopt a harsher line, and to declare that the Royal Commission would not leave for Palestine until the violence in Palestine stopped.

The Cabinet meeting on 2 September made a volte-face from the prior policy of appeasing the Arabs. The Foreign Office, still in favour of concessions, found itself in a small minority. The Cabinet decided to dispatch a full division of troops to Palestine. Military command of Palestine was transferred from the air force to the army. The new policy was published on 7 September, and the necessary legislation enacted by the Privy Council and gazetted at the end of the month. As noted, the execution of the new policy was delayed for nearly a month, in part due to legal uncertainties and in part due to Wauchope's last-minute efforts to avert an armed suppression of the rebellion. That would have entailed the almost complete abdication of his own authority as High Commissioner.

The Palestinians had no illusions that they could hold out against the reinforced British army. The guerilla bands had been severely mauled by the British, thanks to aerial bombings. The very threat of martial law brought about a drastic reduction in violent acts. By September, donations to the strike funds had fallen off and the HAC was no longer able to support the strikers. It was anxious lest the rebellion collapse. The strike had proved to be an economic disaster for many, and the land-owning notables and the Arab middle class were anxious to call it off. Strong pressure was exerted by the citrus grove owners – anxious to have workers available for the orange picking season, due to begin at the end of September.

It remained only to provide the HAC with a ladder with which to climb down. Wauchope agreed readily to the HAC's request to approach the Arab kings to appeal to them to end the rebellion. The HAC made a few token efforts to extract further concessions, but appreciated that they had no choice now but to bow to *force majeure*. The Colonial Office noted:

> ... we could have a settlement almost at once if we are prepared to pay the price ... The [Arab] Committee say so in so many words that they will do what the Arab kings tell them to do ... Ibn Saud is ready to move but

he must have a concession (an amnesty for those imprisoned during the disturbances).[34]

The HAC asked the Saudis to try to extract from the British promises not only of a general amnesty for all Arab offenders, but also that all Jewish immigration would be stopped pending the report of the Royal Commission. But the government in London now stood firm against the grant of any concessions, apart from allowing the Arab rulers to appear before the Royal Commission.

The HAC drafted the text of the appeal which the Arab kings were to address to them. It stressed the national ties of the Arab rulers to Palestine and promised implicitly the fulfilment of the Palestinians' demands. Their draft was duly issued by the Arab kings, and published in Palestine on 10 October. The salient part read:

> ... we appeal to you to restore tranquillity in order to prevent further bloodshed, relying on the good intentions of our friend the British Government and their declared desire to see that justice is done. Be assured that we shall continue our endeavour to help you.[35]

On the same day the HAC published its agreement to call off the strike and the disorders. General Dill issued an order of the day to the army announcing: "the strike and armed rebellion had been called off unconditionally by the HAC". He added that this was due in large measure to "the resolute and energetic action of the three services". But Wauchope vetoed its publication in the local press, in order to save the Palestinians' face.

On 12 October, the Arab bands were given a week's grace to disband. Most of them did so, except for Fawzi's band of 200 volunteers. They were surrounded by British forces in northern Samaria. But following appeals by Palestinian leaders, Wauchope ordered General Dill to cancel the operation planned against Fawzi's men, for fear that it would "probably result in a recrudescence of rebellion on the part of the villagers". Fawzi and his men were allowed to slip away quietly to Trans-Jordan, and thence to Iraq.[36]

In a dispatch to London at the end of October 1936, Dill commented sourly:

> An opportunity had, in fact, been missed of re-establishing British authority in the country.[37]

In his memoirs, published in 1937, Sir Ronald Storrs reflected from a distance on this first phase of the rebellion. He surmised:

> ... the immediate adoption of the [Legislative] Council might have proved cheaper, and could not have proved dearer, in treasure, prestige and blood – British as well as Jewish and Arab – than its rejection.[38]

Had it been only a question of counting casualties, Storrs may possibly have been right. But he had left Palestine in 1926. Writing his memoirs 11 years later, he contemplated with equanimity the permanent freezing of the Yishuv's status at a minority of one-third in Palestine. For the Zionists this would have been tantamount to signing the death warrant of the Jewish National Home. In contrast, in September 1937, on the eve of the second phase of the rebellion, with the wisdom of hindsight, Ormsby-Gore, still the Minister responsible for the day-to-day administration of an intractable colony, drew different conclusions about the way the British had handled the 1936 phase of the rebellion:

> I bitterly regret that we did not give the rebels an effective taste of martial law before the leaders called off the strike and disturbances. Our actions or inactions appear to the world to have been weak. I realize I was myself to blame in not pressing for more vigorous repressive action then.[39]

Notes

1. cf. Michael J. Cohen, "British Strategy and the Palestine Question, 1936–39", *Journal of Contemporary History*, vol. 7/3–4, July-October 1972, pp. 157–83, and idem, "British Strategy in the Wake of the Abyssinian Crisis, 1936–39", in Michael J. Cohen, Martin Kolinsky, eds, *Britain and the Middle East in the 1930s*, London: Macmillan, 1982, pp. 21–40.
2. The League's demise began in 1931, when it failed to stop the Japanese invasion of Manchuria.
3. As a result of the Ten Year Rule, defence spending was slashed from £766 million in 1919–20, to £189 million in 1921–22, to £102 million in 1932.
4. Lawrence Pratt, "The Strategic Context: British Policy in the Mediterranean and the Middle East, 1936–39", in Uriel Dann, ed., *The Great Powers in the Middle East, 1919–1939*, New York: Holmes & Meier, 1988, pp. 12–15.
5. For this and following, cf. Cohen, "British Strategy in the Wake", pp. 24–26.
6. The British base in Egypt, the largest military complex in the world, comprised 11 air and 16 army bases. At the end of World War Two, the Egyptians demanded that the British evacuate. When the Egyptians' appeal to the UN yielded no results, they abrogated the 1936 treaty unilaterally, in October 1951.
7. Eden never reconciled himself to the appeasement of Italy, and resigned from the government when Chamberlain sent an envoy to Rome in February 1938.
8. cf. minutes of Cabinet meeting, 23 February 1938, in Cab 23/92. NA.
9. Lampson to Eden, 1 March 1937, ME (O) 223, Cab 51/9, NA.
10. cf. Yehoshua Porath, *The Palestinian Arab National Movement, vol. two, From Riots to Rebellion, 1929–1939*, London: Frank Cass, 1977.
11. ibid, pp. 168 ff.
12. Had Wauchope authorized the demolitions on grounds of security, he would have had to seek the prior permission of the courts; he had every reason to fear that they would deny permission. cf. ibid, p. 80, and Michael J. Cohen, "The Direction of Policy", *Middle Eastern Studies*, vol. 11/3, October 1975, pp. 238–61.
13. One estimate, based on Zionist sources, claimed that from 1936 to 1939 the Arabs destroyed some 200,000 trees on Jewish-owned land. During the same period, the Jews planted about 1 million trees; cf. Howard M. Sachar, *Europe Leaves the Middle East, 1936–1954*, London: Allen Lane, 1974, p. 93.

14 Norman A. Rose, *The Gentile Zionists: A Study in Anglo-Zionist Diplomacy, 1929–1939*, London: Frank Cass, 1973, p. 110.
15 Dill to War Office, 9 October 1936, cited in Michael J. Cohen, *Palestine: Retreat from the Mandate, 1936–1945*, London/New York: Paul Elek/Holmes and Meier, 1978, p. 29.
16 Lecture by MI2, Military Intelligence, 22 June 1937, WO 106/1594B, NA.
17 45,000 Jews and 40,000 Arabs lived in Haifa; 40,000 Arabs and 10,000 Jews lived in Jaffa, and 70,000 Jews and 40,000 Arabs lived in Jerusalem.
18 cf. Barbara J. Smith, *The Roots of Separatism in Palestine: British Economic Policy, 1920–1929*, Syracuse: Syracuse University Press, 1993, pp. 178–80.
19 Once peaceful conditions were restored, many Jewish employers preferred to take back Arab labourers, who were usually better workers, for lower wages. On the issue of "Hebrew Labour", see Anita Shapira, *The Failed Struggle*, Tel Aviv: Kibbutz Hame'uchad with Tel Aviv University, 1977 (in Hebrew), and *Land and Power: The Zionist Resort to Force, 1881–1948*, translated by William Templer, Oxford: Oxford University Press, 1992.
20 Letter of 24 June 1936, cited in A.J. Sherman, *Mandate Days: British Lives in Palestine, 1918–1948*, New York: Thames & Hudson, 1998, p. 99.
21 Bowman diary, 7 June 1936, in ibid, p. 100.
22 cf. Porath, *The Palestinian*, vol. two, p. 195. Wauchope was the only High Commissioner (1931–38) to be rewarded with a second 5-year term; but he was relieved of his post due to what was regarded as his poor handling of the Arab rebellion. His departure, explained officially as being due to poor health, paved the way for a major army crackdown against the rebels from the autumn of 1938.
23 The judgement of 5 July 1936 was printed in the London *Times* the next day. Quotations in Cohen, "Direction", p. 250.
24 Like all British judges, MacDonnell enjoyed security of tenure for life and there was no precedent for the removal of a colonial judge. He exacted an exorbitant price for agreeing to retire early. ibid, pp. 250–51, and Porath, *The Palestinian*, vol. two, pp. 197–98.
25 Thomas elected to resign before an Exchequer Court of Enquiry delivered its report – which found him innocent of having sought any personal gain. Cohen, ibid, p. 243.
26 For details of the negotiations, cf. Cohen, *Palestine*, pp. 18–24.
27 The Peel Royal Commission report, July 1937, Cmd 5513, London: HMSO.
28 In 1924, the Wahhabi Emir Ibn Saud had defeated the Hashemite Emir Husayn, in their struggle for hegemony over the Arabian Peninsula. Husayn was ousted from the Arabian Peninsula, which was renamed Saudi Arabia. Husayn spent the rest of his life as the guest of his son Faysal in Iraq, where the latter was elevated by the British to the kingship in 1921.
29 Porath, *The Palestinian*, vol. two, p. 205.
30 Cabinet meeting of 15 July 1936, in Cab 23/85, NA.
31 Cohen, *Palestine*, pp. 34–38; Porath, *The Palestinian*, vol. two, p. 221.
32 Nuri al-Said was flown from Iraq to Jerusalem in an RAF plane.
33 One of the Zionists' sources of inside information was Blanche "Baffy" Dugdale; she passed on to the Zionists inside news from Cabinet meetings, which she received from her lover, Walter Elliott, Minister of Agriculture, Health, and then Minister at the Scottish Office, 1936–40.
34 Cohen, *Palestine*, p. 28.
35 Porath, *The Palestinian*, vol. two, p. 214.
36 ibid, p. 215.
37 ibid.
38 Ronald Storrs, *Orientations*, London: Nicholson & Watson, 1937, p. 441.
39 Porath, *The Palestinian*, vol. two, pp. 215–16.

12 The Arab rebellion, II
July 1937–April 1939

> ... the situation was such that civil administration and control of the country was, to all practical purposes, non-existent.
> Report for August–October 1938, Lt Gen Haining, GOC Palestine

Strategic exigencies

During the summer of 1937, in addition to Britain's growing European and Far Eastern concerns, her position in the Middle East deteriorated further. Italy poured large numbers of troops into Libya. Not only the Middle East commanders but the COS in London were alarmed. Whereas Italy would be no match for Britain in a general war, she enjoyed local logistical advantages over Britain in the Mediterranean. Italy had a six-to-one local superiority in the air, and operated along shorter lines of communications. She had several air bases on the southern tip of the Italian peninsula and on her Mediterranean islands – all within easy flying distance of Egypt. Even if Britain could spare troop reinforcements for Egypt, they would need to travel over 2000 miles by sea along the short Mediterranean route – which was now exposed to Italian air and submarine attack.

The COS were unable to offer any real hope of relief, but they and the CID agreed that British possessions in the Middle East could not be left dependent upon vulnerable lines of communication. A compromise of sorts was found. The chiefs agreed to the Middle East Command's appeal that Egypt and the Suez Canal be reinforced with enough forces to make her self-sufficient during the early stages of a war. It was decided to send a Middle East Reserve of two brigades to Egypt. It was hoped that this force, together with the 10,000 troops already stationed there, would be enough to hold the canal base until additional reinforcements could be brought from other theatres.

The Middle East Reserve was dispatched to Egypt in August 1938, at a time when Britain faced concurrent crises in Europe and in Palestine. In Europe, Chamberlain was trying to avert war with Germany by satisfying Hitler's demands on Czechoslovakia. In Palestine, the administration had all but lost control of the southern half of the country and feared that Jerusalem itself would be taken over by the rebels. While the Reserve was on the high seas, headed for Egypt, both Sir Harold MacMichael (High Commissioner, 1938–44) and Lt General Robert Haining (GOC Palestine 1938–39) sent urgent appeals to London for immediate reinforcements of an extra division. In retrospect, Haining wrote:

> The rising tide of rebellion in the southern and virtually unoccupied part of the country during August made it essential to ask for more troops ... this was made increasingly urgent by rapid deterioration, amounting almost to disintegration, of the Arab section of the Palestine Police, some 1,500 in number ... Arab section was disarmed, some of the weaker and strategically insecure posts were evacuated; all possible Arab constables were withdrawn to the towns for employment on traffic control, office duties and similar work.[1]

The Cabinet agreed to divert the Middle East Reserve, while still at sea, from Egypt to Palestine. But in early September, as the Czech crisis became acute, war with Germany became a real possibility and the main fleet was mobilized. A special meeting of ministers ordered the Middle East Reserve to change course again, back to Egypt. The ministers decided that if war did break out, the Palestine Partition Plan (see Chapter 13) would be suspended summarily, and all Jewish immigration stopped. This was because no troop reinforcements would then be available for Palestine, as all available shipping would be required for the war effort.[2]

After the Munich Agreement (at the end of September), the Middle East Reserve was transferred back to Palestine to deal with the last phase of the rebellion, which was crushed finally in early 1939. In July 1939, one brigade of the Reserve was returned from Palestine to Egypt; the second was retained in Palestine, on standby for transfer to Egypt, the moment hostilities with Italy appeared to be imminent.

The concept of the Middle East Reserve was based on the premise that limited forces would be able to hold on to an essentially friendly Middle East. But unless the friendliness, or at least the "benevolent neutrality", of the Arab states was forthcoming, substantial increases in the Middle East garrison would be required. Therefore, the restoration of peace in Palestine became a *sine qua non* of British strategy for the Middle East.

A special Middle Eastern sub-committee of the CID was appointed in order to draw up financial and economic inducements that would secure the loyalty of the Arab states. The CID endorsed the sub-committee's report in January 1939. The preface reiterated what by now had become dogma – that a settlement of the Palestine problem acceptable to the Arab states was a *sine qua non* for assuring their friendship:

> We feel it necessary to point out at the outset, as an essential part of our report, the strong feeling which exists in all Arab States in connection with British policy in Palestine. It is evident that by far the most

important measure which could be taken to influence the Arab States in favour of the United Kingdom would be our Palestine policy. We assume that, immediately on the outbreak of war, the necessary measures would be at once taken ... in order to bring about a complete appeasement of Arab opinion in Palestine and in neighbouring countries ... if we thus fail to retain Arab goodwill at the outset of a war, no other measures which we can recommend will serve to influence the Arab States in favour of our country.[3]

The sub-committee proposed the establishment of a secret slush fund for buying the friendship of local Arab sheikhs, in the event of hostilities. The amounts proposed were determined arbitrarily, according to the committee's estimate of the recipients' importance. In Trans-Jordan, the British Resident would be supplied with £10,000 – for "payments" to Abdullah, to tribal sheikhs and newspapers; Ibn Saud would receive a "gift" of £200,000 and the ambassador at Jedda would receive an additional £25,000 to "influence" Saudi officials. Likewise, the British agent at Bushire[4] would receive £4000 – for what was termed euphemistically "intelligence" matters. In addition, Iraq would be granted a loan to compensate her for the loss of oil royalties and given an unspecified amount of arms.

The reaction to partition in Palestine

In June 1937, the Cabinet approved the Royal (Peel) Commission's report and published it on 7 July 1937.[5] The Commission concluded that the inter-racial conflict in Palestine was irresoluble, and that only a "surgical operation" – the partition of the country into Arab and Jewish states – held out any hope. It proposed that the Arab state be annexed to Trans-Jordan, and set aside strategic enclaves to protect British interests. In the interim period prior to the establishment of the Arab and Jewish states, the "economic absorptive capacity" regulation for Jewish immigration would be replaced by a "political high level" of 12,000 per annum.[6]

The Yishuv divided down the centre over the Partition Plan, across party lines. The majority, headed by Ben-Gurion and Weizmann, accepted the plan in principle while making it clear that they would demand more territory for the Jewish state. Typically, Ben-Gurion advised his colleagues that they must not allow the British to think that they were doing them a favour. The 20th Zionist Congress, convened in Zurich in August 1937, passed a resolution to the effect that the Partition Plan delineated by the Peel Commission was unacceptable, but authorized the Zionist Executive to negotiate an improved one.

The Palestinian Arabs also divided in their reaction to the Partition Plan, along the rift line of the two major clans, the Husaynis and the Nashashibis. Both clans had built up power bases with the perquisites granted them by British patronage – the Mufti through his control of the SMC and Ragheb Nashashibi with the municipal assets of Jerusalem.

During the first decade of the mandate, the Zionists had made vain efforts to nurture an Arab opposition to the Mufti. Many Zionists denied the authenticity of nascent Palestinian Arab nationalism. They believed that it was a propaganda tool used by the land-owning *effendi* against Zionism. Their belief was based upon a misplaced Marxist hypothesis that Arab opposition to Zionism was confined to the exploitative *effendi* and the urban elites, who feared that the Arab working class, the peasantry (*fellahin*), would align itself with the Zionist labour movement. This hypothesis materialized, on a very modest scale, more than 20 years later, when Arab workers co-operated with the Zionists in a joint railways union.[7]

At the inception of the mandate, the Zionists believed that they would be able to finance "a propaganda machine of [Arab] newspapers and writers" that would persuade both the British and the Arab *fellahin* that they would benefit from collaboration with the Yishuv. Many of the "initiatives" of the Arab collaborators during the 1920s, including their protest telegrams to London against the Palestine Arab Executive, were in fact initiated, written by and paid for by the Zionists.[8]

Zionist initiatives reached their zenith after the 1929 riots. In reaction to the wave of commissions of inquiry and experts sent by the British to Palestine, the Zionists set up and funded an Arab "United Bureau", whose goal was to "prove" to the British that a large body of Palestinian Arabs welcomed Zionist immigration. The Jewish Agency drafted a petition that challenged the legitimacy of the SMC, highlighted the material benefits brought to Palestine by Zionist settlement, and inflated the extent of domestic opposition to the Husaynis. Dozens of Arabs were persuaded to sign the petitions, which were sent to the Shaw Commission. But they did not influence the Commission's report. The majority of its members were not persuaded that the Mufti had incited the riots.

The Zionists' main effort was devoted to the so-called "farmers' parties" that formed mainly in a group of villages in the vicinity of Jerusalem. These formed ostensibly to protect the villagers' interests against those of the urban elites. In 1930, the Zionists initiated and allocated funds for a convention of village *fellahin*, to protest the visit of an official Arab delegation to London. But the convention broke up amidst harsh recriminations, when members of the Arab Executive Committee appeared on the scene and spoke out against dividing the nation. When members of the Executive disclosed that the Zionists were behind the initiative, the assembly broke up in turmoil. Two years later, in 1932, Abd al-Qadar Shibli, an attorney from Acre, approached the Zionists and offered to organize a second convention, promising that there would be no resolutions against their interests. In return, Shibli asked the Zionists for P£30 for his own expenses, and a commitment to buy 16,000 dunams of land from his father. This initiative was an even greater failure than the first. Instead of the 400 peasants promised by Shibli, only a few dozen turned up. After more than a decade of effort, this bitter lesson convinced the Zionists to abandon their strategy of artificially promoting an alternative, rural Arab leadership. The Zionists' strategy, "based on false assumptions", had proved futile.[9]

Fundamental social changes in Palestinian Arab society gathered momentum during the 1930s. The formation of new political parties by a new generation of Arab middle-class intellectuals reflected their frustration with the barren negotiations of the traditional elites with the British. Grim economic conditions forced an increasing number of indebted Palestinian peasants to sell off parcels of their land in order to pay their bills. The increased volume of land sales played a significant role in the disintegration of the old hierarchical system. The acceleration of Arab urbanization during the latter half of the decade signalled a change from a barter economy to a commercial one, with a new awareness of goods that only money could buy. Many Arabs, frustrated by their leaders' futile diplomacy and disillusioned with the British, turned to acts of violence:

> ... the Zionists' success at neutralizing the threats posed to its development confirmed to some Arab leaders and fellahin just how empty, insincere, and ineffective British promises and actions were.[10]

In 1937, a new opportunity and a new strategy for winning over Arab supporters presented itself to the Zionists, when the Husaynis and the Nashashibis clashed over partition. Ragheb Nashashibi let it be known that he would co-operate in the implementation of the Partition Plan. He preferred the annexation of a part of the country under the rule of the Emir Abdullah to the Mufti's tyranny over a unified Palestine. The Nashashibis' Defence Party resigned from the HAC in the same month that the Peel Report was published.

The reaction to partition of many Palestinian Arabs was determined not so much by patriotism or by clan allegiance as by where they happened to live. The Nashashibi mayors of Jaffa, Ramleh and Nablus – all allotted to the proposed Arab state – spoke out publicly in favour of the plan. But many Arabs who resided in towns allotted to the Jewish state, e.g. Acre, opposed partition on personal grounds. The Christian Arabs of the Galilee closed ranks with their Moslem brethren, in protest at their inclusion in the proposed Jewish state. Christian civil servants, who feared losing their jobs in a Jewish state, also opposed partition, as did Arab merchants who feared that the Jews would take over their trade.[11]

But Ragheb Nashashibi was taken aback by the unexpected opposition to partition of both Iraq and Saudi Arabia, allegedly Britain's allies. This led him and many others to suspect that Britain herself was not really committed to the Peel plan. Ragheb was accused of having resigned from the HAC in order to be free to campaign for partition. After receiving several murder threats, he made a volte-face and published a letter to the High Commissioner rejecting partition.

The leaders of the Arab states did not speak out with one voice on the future of Palestine. Abdullah of Trans-Jordan, who had long cherished an ambition to annex Palestine to his unviable desert emirate, was unable to contain his enthusiastic support for the Peel plan. He regarded the absorption of Palestine's West Bank as the first step towards the realization of his own Greater Syria scheme – a union of Trans-Jordan, Syria and Palestine. Ragheb Nashashibi's public reversal on partition brought him and Abdullah into conflict. Ragheb accused Abdullah of acting too hastily and the latter accused Ragheb of cowardice and a lack of conviction.

Abdullah's well-known ambitions were enough to cause the other Arab states to oppose the Peel plan. Abdullah's plans clashed with Nuri al-Said's plans to annex Palestine as part of his Fertile Crescent federation. Ibn Saud automatically opposed any plan that would benefit the Hashemites – whether Abdullah or the royal Hashemite house of Iraq. In the 1930s, Egypt was too preoccupied with the British occupation to concern herself with Palestine, although she, like Trans-Jordan, had a long common border.

The Husaynis' opposition to partition was due not only to Haj Amin's refusal to give up any part of Palestine, but also to his fear of losing his hegemony to Abdullah. The Husaynis regarded the end of hostilities in 1936 merely as a temporary truce, pending the report of the Peel Commission. Following their disillusion with the Partition Plan, the HAC mobilized extensive support for armed resistance. On 8 September 1937, a pan-Arab conference on Palestine was convened at Bludan, in Syria. Some 400 Arab delegates attended, mostly from Palestine and Syria. The conference condemned the Partition Plan and vowed to pursue the struggle until Arab sovereignty over all of Palestine was achieved. During their stay in Bludan, the Palestinian guerilla leaders met with some of the Syrian volunteers who had joined the rebellion the previous summer, in order to co-ordinate plans for the next phase of the rebellion.

The second phase of the rebellion

In September 1937, the HAC, without the Nashashibis, initiated the second phase of the rebellion. Their clear goal was to force the British to retreat from the Partition Plan. Their opening move was the assassination of L.A. Andrews, the acting British District Commissioner for the Northern District of Palestine, as he was leaving church after Sunday prayers. The unprecedented (for Palestine) murder of a senior British official indicated not only the Husaynis' disdain for British rule, but also their opposition to the inclusion of the Galilee, with its large Arab majority, in the Jewish state. London regarded the assassination as a declaration of war against the Empire, and as such (with the Egyptian precedent of 1924 in mind), decided to react harshly.[12]

The Colonial Office was filled with remorse that the government had not allowed the army to crush the rebels the year before. It was not about to allow the Mufti to derail the Partition Plan – regarded by the department as a golden opportunity to divest itself of the Palestine problem. There was ample evidence that Haj Amin had used SMC funds to finance acts of terror. Not only that, but British intelligence had evidence that at the time of the Italian conquest of Abyssinia (1935–36), they had invested money on propaganda in Palestine, and had made direct payments to Haj Amin (see Chapter 17).

In mid-July 1937, well before the assassination of Andrews, in anticipation of the Mufti's rejection of partition, the Colonial Office agreed to Wauchope's demand for his arrest. But Haj Amin took refuge in the Haram al-Sharif area adjacent to the Al Aqsa mosque, a holy sanctuary that the British dared not violate. The Colonial Secretary, Ormsby-Gore, remembered the evidence that Haj Amin's incitement had been instrumental in leading to the Wailing Wall riots. With the hindsight that the government had missed the opportunity to defeat the rebels in 1936, he vented his spleen:

> ... I still feel that we shall never get on top of this murder campaign and its inevitable consequence of counter-murder by the Jews who we are unable to protect, until we have eliminated the Mufti and his gang. He was the *fons and origo* of the murders in 1929, and as long as we appear to funk dealing with this black-hearted villain and allow him to disseminate anti-British propaganda throughout the Islamic world, and organize terrorism of any Arabs in Palestine not subservient to him and his Supreme Muslim Council, we cannot hope to maintain law and order or even be the *de facto* government of Palestine.[13]

The killing of Andrews removed all prior British inhibitions about arresting the Mufti. The government was also smarting from the Peel Commission's rebuke that it had allowed him to build up the SMC into an *imperio in imperium*. It decided to hold the Husayni leadership collectively responsible, and to remove them from the offices in which Samuel had installed them 15 years before. On 1 October, the Palestine administration divested the Mufti of his posts as president of the SMC and chairman of the *Wakf* funds committee, and issued arrest warrants for him and the other six members of the HAC. The Cabinet authorized the Colonial Secretary to declare martial law at his discretion. Five members of the HAC were arrested and deported to the Seychelles islands. The sixth, Jamal el-Husayni, the Mufti's cousin, escaped to Syria. The British placed a police guard on every exit of the Haram al-Sharif. But on the night of 12 October, the Mufti eluded the siege and escaped to the Lebanon, disguised as a Bedouin. He settled in Junieh, a coastal city 10 miles north of Beirut.[14]

The French granted the Mufti asylum and refused British demands to intern him or restrict his freedom of action.[15] The Mufti continued to control the rebellion in Palestine. Shortly after his arrival, he called for a resumption of hostilities and established a Central Committee for the Jihad, with its headquarters in Damascus. Under the Mufti's direction, the Committee functioned as the rebellion's headquarters. It dealt with the collection of intelligence, propaganda, fund-raising, arms purchases and the dispatch of volunteers to Palestine. The internecine terror campaign began to take a heavy toll. In October 1937, British intelligence sources reported that the Mufti was using donations to distress and relief funds to support the terrorist gangs and for the purchase of arms and ammunition. They confirmed that he was behind a wave of assassinations that occurred in the Jerusalem area during the autumn. In May 1938, High Commissioner MacMichael asserted that there was a general consensus in Palestine and in the Arab world that the Mufti was "the most dangerous and subtle" of Britain's enemies, who supplied "the inspiration of every fresh move of the terrorists". He pressed the government to have the Mufti removed from the Lebanon, and proposed that if the French would not comply, they should close all of the frontier crossings between Palestine, the Lebanon and Syria.[16]

But the French refused to act against the Mufti. Not only did they fear adverse Arab reactions in their own colonies, but their officials in Syria took satisfaction in repaying the British for having given shelter in 1925 to those Druze leaders who had fled to Palestine at the time of the Druze rebellion. However, with the outbreak of World War Two, old colonial scores had to give way to common Anglo-French strategic interests. In October 1939, after the Mufti had fled the Lebanon for Baghdad, a French liaison officer in Cairo made a frank confession to his British counterpart about his country's machinations and reassured him that they now had the measure of the Mufti:

> ... El Haj Husseini is a dangerous man, ready to play any role, whatever its aspect. England's enemy today, he may quite easily become ours tomorrow. His protestations of friendship are suspicious and show, to say the least, self-interest. If his presence in Syria has been of use to us, it would appear to be with the greatest circumspection that we should employ him for our own political ends.[17]

British intelligence learned that the corrupt French director of the Syrian Police, a M. Columbani, had taken a £500 bribe for allowing the Mufti to slip away.[18]

This second phase of the rebellion was the most violent and extensive – in terms of both Arab attacks on British and Jewish targets and internecine Arab terror. By mid-October 1937, the violence had surpassed anything known in 1936. Jewish settlements and buses came under attack, and the toll of murdered Jews soared. British installations, including Lydda airport, railroad rolling stock and the Mosul–Haifa oil pipeline, were sabotaged. In contrast to their lenient attitude in 1936, British courts now routinely handed down harsh sentences and punishments on captured rebels. By the end of 1937, over 800 Arabs had been arrested and a number had been executed. When "military control" was imposed in October 1938, the military courts would impose still harsher sentences.

Perhaps the most significant feature of this stage of the rebellion was the Husaynis' campaign of threats, intimidation and the elimination of any Arab who dared to support partition. Husayni terror became a deterrent stronger even than British law. Prominent, wealthy Arabs who had shown sympathy for the Jews or the British were either intimidated into silence or coerced into support for the rebel gangs, on pain of abduction or assassination.

During this period, the Arabic press lost much of its credibility as a reliable source of information. It proved unable to withstand the dual, conflicting pressures of the British censor on the one hand, and the violent intimidation of the Arab gangs on the other. As noted by the Arab historian of the Arabic press in Palestine:

> More than one newspaper published news items that they were later forced to alter or completely retract under pressure from the censor, or they were forced to repeat the initial version a day later under pressure from the armed bands. In such circumstances the reliability of the press was questioned, and readers' trust diminished.[19]

Public appeals were made to the press "to present a more reliable picture". But the threat of Arab terror increased following the publication of the Peel Partition Plan in July 1937. Most of the Arabic newspapers now toed the Mufti's line. A notable example was the newspaper *Filastin*, which had traditionally led the press opposition to the Mufti. After the publication of the Partition Plan, the paper supported the Mufti in glowing terms, affirming that he was the Palestinians' only leader, that "his acts embodied the wishes of the Palestinian people". On 18 October 1937, *Filastin* published an article stating:

> When speaking of the Palestinian problem there are no moderates or radicals. We have rejected the partition plan and we will fight any idea or attempt to propose partition, as partition is a national disaster.[20]

But 'Issa al-'Issa, the paper's Christian Arab editor, was unable to compromise himself indefinitely. He was among a number of Arab editors who chose to flee the country rather than surrender to the dictates of the peasant gangs. Considering themselves to be members of the urban elites, they felt that capitulation to the violence of the gangs was an insult to their "honour and status".[21]

The rebels used extreme brutality against anyone whose nationalism was suspect. The Nashashibis took no part in the new wave of violence against the British and the Jews. Occasionally, villages and groups of peasants tried to organize themselves into self-defence groups against the gangs. The Nashashibis co-operated with British forces, handing over to them the names of several gang leaders.[22] The hatred and blood feuds generated by the internecine terror campaign would plague Palestinian society for years to come.

The Husayni terror engulfed Arabs who had sold lands to Jews, Arab police officers who remained loyal to the British and anyone whose loyalty to the national cause was suspect. Under the cover of ostensible patriotism, many Arabs seized the opportunity to settle personal accounts. Estimates of the number of Arabs from rival clans killed by the Mufti's henchmen between 1937 and 1939 vary from 900 to 3000.[23]

During this second phase of the rebellion, the differences between the poor, rural Arabs and the more prosperous city dwellers sparked open conflict. Many villagers had been reduced to poverty by the general strike of the previous year, and rebelled now against the Husaynis' campaign of violence and extortion. The beginnings of an authentic peasant revolt became apparent. In August 1938, MacMichael regarded it as significant enough to report it to London:

> ... something like a social revolution is beginning. The influence of the landlord-politician is on the wane. He has done nothing but talk (and pay): others have taken risks, and these others are disposed to take a line of their own.[24]

Nearly 80 per cent of the leaders of the Arab gangs were peasants, angry and frustrated by the notables' apparent impotency in the face of what appeared to be a Zionist takeover of their country, under British auspices. The gangs were most active in those areas adjacent to the main concentrations of Jewish settlement – the coastal plain, the Haifa–Acre bay area and the Jezre'el valley. Here, the Arabs had felt the direct impact of Zionist settlement.[25]

In those towns where Arab rebel forces took control, notably Jaffa and the Arab sections of Haifa and Jerusalem, some of the gangs took up the cause of the Arab poor against the propertied classes. They imposed a moratorium on the repayment of debts, and reduced or cancelled rental payments. In some places, notably Haifa, the notables fled when the rebels took control.

The British crush the rebellion

By the summer of 1937, Arab terrorism had sapped the empathy that many British officials in Palestine had previously held for the Arabs. The security forces, frustrated by the failure of the courts to mete out what they considered to be adequate justice, began taking the law into their own hands. During village searches, British forces assaulted Arabs at random and destroyed property gratuitously. In December 1937, a British policeman wrote home about "acts of casual brutality":

> The military courts started off well but as we expected are being too lenient and want too much evidence to convict on, so any Johnny Arab who is caught by us now in suspicious circumstances is shot out of hand ... Most accidents out here are caused by police running over an Arab the same as a dog in England except we do not report it.

In 1938, a British solider wrote home:

> If you run over an Arab make sure you kill him, even if you have to reverse over him. If you injure him you've got to pay his hospital bills.[26]

Ragheb Nashashibi regarded the Mufti's flight to the Lebanon as a golden opportunity for him to take over as leader of the Palestinian Arabs. Once the Mufti was shorn of his offices and became a fugitive from British law, Ragheb sought to secure the presidency of the SMC for the opposition. He was willing to take drastic steps, and to seek Zionist aid to achieve his goals. He asked Moshe Shertok of the Jewish Agency to fund his leadership campaign. In return, he offered to agree to any policy proposed by the Jewish Agency, in a three-way partnership with the British.[27] Zionist intelligence learned of a secret meeting Ragheb had held in September 1937 with British officials and officers. Ragheb, accompanied by four personal bodyguards, explained the extent of the Mufti's continuing influence in Palestine, via the religious establishment. He reported that there was not a Moslem village in Palestine in which the religious officials, all in the pay of the SMC, did not advocate the Mufti's line – any who dared to oppose him were dismissed. Ragheb proposed that the British appoint a "temporary manager" for the SMC, that they determine a transition period during which its affairs would be "cleaned up", after which new elections should be held.[28]

But none of Ragheb's plans ever got off the ground. Even in the Mufti's absence, his supporters were still able to intimidate and terrorize the Arab community. The rebel gangs extorted food and money from both the urban and rural Arab populations to fund their operations. Anyone who rejected their demands or expressed support for partition was branded a traitor and punished cruelly: "Muggings and robberies in the name of the rebellion became daily events". The rebels mobilized a special "purge force" to eliminate all informers and political opponents. The murders of Arabs suspected of supporting partition, of suspected Zionist informers, and of Arab policemen became "a nation-wide phenomenon". All open dissension from the Mufti's line was stifled.[29]

In 1938, Ragheb fled to the safer clime of Egypt. His place as leader of the Nashashibis was taken by his nephew Fahkri, who continued to support partition. With the outbreak of World War Two, Fahkri fled to Baghdad, where he was assassinated in November 1941, by an agent of the Mufti.[30]

At the same time that the government in London was developing a policy of appeasing the Arab states, it decided to adopt a harsh policy against the Palestinian rebels. In March 1938, Sir Harold MacMichael replaced Wauchope as High Commissioner. Wauchope's "soft" policy against the rebels in 1936 was regarded by many as having set the scene for the renewed outbreak of terrorism in September 1937 (Wauchope had blocked the army's planned offensive against Qawukji in October 1937). Unlike Wauchope, MacMichael was not burdened with the fear of spoiling his past civilian record. He arrived in Jerusalem as the country was sinking into anarchy. He was a seasoned colonial administrator, who has been described by one of his colleagues as:

> ... a loveable bit of inhumanity ... [with] a lack of imagination which was often so deadly that it could be mistaken for active wickedness.[31]

In his self-imposed isolation inside Government House, MacMichael remained something of an unknown entity, even from his own officials. During his term as High Commissioner, there was a significant increase in the mutual distrust between the British and the indigenous population.

Soon after MacMichael's arrival, new counter-insurgency measures were initiated. The most significant project was to block the roads between Palestine and Syria, which afforded ready access to the transit of terrorist gangs. This was done between May and July 1938, with the construction of a 9-foot high barbed-wire barrier along the entire northern frontier between Palestine and French-mandated Lebanon and Syria, at a cost of some £200,000. The fence was designed by Sir Charles Tegart, a senior police officer and engineer, with an impressive record of combating terrorism in India. Initially, seven police fortresses were built into the fence; by the end of 1938, 20 pillboxes were added. The fence had a dual objective: to prevent the infiltration of the rebel gangs, and to facilitate military engagements in its vicinity. It was patrolled by a mounted frontier division. In September 1938, the Palestine Police were subordinated to the army and began to share patrol duties along the fence. Although individual rebels still managed to penetrate the northern fence, it severely hampered the movement of entire gangs. With the completion of the fence, the rebels switched the focus of their operations to the south of the country.[32]

After a lull during the spring of 1938, the rebellion surged again in the summer. Some 15,000 local guerillas, together with volunteers from neighbouring countries, were now engaged in subversive activity. By August 1938, the gangs' activities, centred around Jerusalem, had brought about a near paralysis of the civil authority. Most banks and post offices had to be closed, many roads became unsafe to travel on, train services were severely disrupted, and telephone lines were cut. Several outlying British police stations were conquered by the rebel gangs, providing them with a ready source of arms and ammunition. By mid-October, the rebels were in virtual control of the south of the country, including the Old City of Jerusalem.

The gangs also wreaked extensive damage on Jewish farms – to their crops and citrus groves. Isolated or small groups of Jews caught working their fields or travelling on the roads were murdered. This provoked revenge attacks by Jewish terrorists, such as the planting of bombs in busy Arab markets. The outrages fed a rising crescendo of inter-racial violence.

In June 1938, Sidney Burr, a British policeman, wrote home to his family:

> Sitting at home by the fire in England you cannot visualize a country only the size of Wales, under British rule, where there is absolutely no law and order. Police and troops are powerless and our only object out here seems to be clearing up after the crime has been committed ... Even at the best of times Palestine is as dull as ditch water but what with curfews and people walking about with the fear of death in them it's like living in a cemetery.[33]

His views were echoed by Sir William Battershill, Chief Secretary to the Palestine Government from 1937 to 1939. Battershill returned to Palestine in October 1938, after a 3-month leave in England. He referred in his private diary to the "unbelievable contrast" between the situation when he had gone on leave in July and that when he returned:

> To say that the Civil Government runs this country would be an untruth. The gangs rule the country. No D[istrict] C[ommissioner] can go outside his headquarters unless accompanied by a considerable force ... The Government has evacuated several places, notably Beersheba and Jericho ... Jaffa is more or less in a state of siege ... Arabs are abducted in broad daylight.[34]

The army became anxious about losing control. General Robert Haining, GOC Palestine 1938–39, recalled later:

> ... the situation was such that civil administration and control of the country was, to all practical purposes, non-existent.[35]

By the middle of October 1938 the rebels were virtually in control of the Old City of Jerusalem. Numerous Arab civil servants purchased their lives by turning over secret British documents to the rebels. The army was obviously undermanned. But the Munich crisis, a *force majeure*, had required the transfer to Egypt of the reinforcements on their way to Palestine. A "terrible mess" had ensued. Battershill was even more shocked by the irascibility of General Haining than he was by the army's loss of control. He believed that Haining had lost his nerve: "he freely criticized to me not only the civil administration but also people at home ... Of no one did I hear any good, not even of his own officers in Palestine". Battershill noted that the general was "irritable, touchy, and not to put a fine point on it unbalanced". He suspected that what Haining really wanted was to oust the High Commissioner and assume absolute control. But MacMichael held on to his position, "in spite of the intrigues to get him out of the post".[36]

In London, the Colonial and War Offices agreed on a face-saving compromise for the division of authority in Palestine. It was intended to mollify MacMichael, himself a former general. They called it "military control", a formula that avoided the unsavoury connotations of martial law, always distasteful to high commissioners. However, with the police now under the army's command, there was little doubt about who was in charge.[37]

After the Munich Agreement, the British were able to rush troop reinforcements to Palestine: part of the Middle East Reserve from Egypt, and three battalions from India. By the end of October there were two divisions and three RAF squadrons in Palestine – a total of 20,000 troops and nearly 3000 police. A newly promoted major general – Bernard Law Montgomery – was sent out to command the newly formed 8th Division, charged with restoring security in the North. He was a strong-headed, haughty, short-tempered officer, with no intention of concerning himself with the finer points of the Arab-Zionist conflict. He dismissed out of hand the administration's claim that the rebels represented an authentic national movement. In his first order of the day to his troops, he stated that they were facing:

> ... gangs of professional bandits and terrorists ... Our first and primary task, therefore, is to hunt down and destroy these armed gangs.[38]

The army was given virtually a free hand, and went over to the offensive. The Arab gangs were pursued back to their hideouts in the hills and into those villages that still offered them shelter. Severe reprisals were taken against villages that resisted British troops or continued to offer shelter to the rebels.

British forces resorted to tactics reserved for those colonies that could be hidden from international scrutiny. Army discipline frayed under the strains and frustrations of combating irregular forces. Many soldiers were incensed by what they regarded as the undue leniency of the military courts, their punctiliousness and insistence on the legal niceties requiring due evidence. The troops became fatigued and disheartened by the seeming futility of trying to pin down the elusive guerilla bands. In February 1938, one soldier wrote home:

> After being in the hills all day we are called out continuously at night to colonies which are being shot up. This week I have been under fire six times & seen my opponents only once ... I am absolutely fed up with the life here now as we have no time for recreation at all ... If things go on like this much longer I am going to resign as I am not at all interested in the cause we are fighting for.[39]

The official historian of the Palestine police recalled:

> ... throughout 1938 the stories of heroism, frustrations and disasters still poured in, and the strain of it all began to show upon the faces of the men. Constant patrolling and constant vigilance was required to perform the simplest task. Disturbed sleep with turn-outs every night so that men slept for days in their clothes, brought a grim atmosphere to every police mess. It also brought a binding comradeship and an *esprit-de-corps* which had a remarkable effect upon the force. It never lost its pride.[40]

Some of the security forces began to take the law into their own hands. They committed gratuitous acts of violence and looted or destroyed Arab property at random. For many of them, a toxic mix of frustration, rage and contempt reduced the Palestinian Arabs in their eyes to the level of animals. If captured alive, suspect rebels were subjected to vicious interrogation, humiliation and torture (on their genitals and flagellations on the soles of the feet). The physical abuses spread so much that in November 1938, General Haining ordered his divisional commanders to take "exemplary" action against soldiers who indulged in "unnecessary violence, vindictiveness [and] killing in cold blood".[41]

More and more rebel leaders, including several of the top commanders, were killed or jailed. Many thousands were held without trial in overcrowded detention camps with poor sanitation, without recourse to international scrutiny or protest. The British employed other colonial "practices" (from India) – they burned the bodies of dead terrorists, in order to prevent the funerals turning into mass demonstrations, and used Arabs as human targets at the head of convoys, to deter the terrorists from sabotaging and mining the roads and railways.[42]

The year 1938 was the most costly in human lives. It has been estimated that some 9–10,000 Arabs took part in the rebellion; 1500–2000 full-time regulars and some 6000 part-time fighters – townsmen and peasants who were mobilized from time to time. The number of rebels captured was more than ten times the number of the two preceding years. After 3 years of sporadic fighting, the rebellion had cost nearly 7000 casualties – some 3700 Arabs, 2400 Jewish, and 600 British.

A key role in the defeat of the rebellion was played by Orde Wingate, a young British army captain, who introduced new, unorthodox, controversial tactics. He proposed a "government gangs" strategy, using the terrorists' own operational and tactical methods against them.[43] To this end, from June 1938 he began to mobilize and train Jewish commando units into "special night squads" (SNS). Wingate's millennial, Old Testament fundamentalism made him into a natural convert to the Zionist cause. Under his unorthodox training, the SNS specialized in night ambushes and pursued the gangs back to their hideouts. During the last months of 1938, the rebels were systematically combed out of the hills and the villages in which they sought refuge. The SNS chalked up dramatic military successes and by December the army had regained the initiative. Wingate's night squads all but snuffed out the gangs' almost nightly sabotage of the Mosul to Haifa oil pipeline (he was awarded the DSO for his work).

However, once relative calm was restored, the British "remembered" that one day the Jews might turn their arms against them and try to achieve their goals by force. At the beginning of 1939, as London prepared to appease the Arab states at one last round-table conference in London, the SNS were reduced in size and phased out. In May 1939, on the eve of the publication of the White Paper, Wingate was transferred back to England, on suspicion of passing on military secrets to the Zionists.[44]

Arab opposition to the Husaynis

Since the summer of 1938, the leaders of the Palestinian Arab opposition had been preoccupied with their own survival. Several attempts were made by the rebel gangs to murder religious leaders who opposed them. The Jewish Agency obtained a Husayni "hit-list" that promised a reward of P£500 for the killing of opposition leaders. The list included Ragheb Nashashibi, Suliman Tuqan and Hussam al-Din Jarallah. The last named had been designated by the opposition to assume Haj Amin's post as president of the SMC. At the local level, countless blood feuds cried out for revenge.[45]

The leaders of the Yishuv had an interest in encouraging Arab opposition to the Mufti's gangs. Ben-Gurion offered to fund the establishment of opposition military units, later called "peace bands". In March 1938, Fahkri Nashashibi took up the offer. The bands were organized mainly for self-defence against the gangs' attacks, but only occasionally did they engage them in open battle. In the autumn of 1938, Fahkri initiated a media campaign (also funded by the Jewish Agency) sharply critical of the Mufti. Countless Arabs had noted how the Husaynis had taken advantage of the rebellion for their own personal gain, by "plundering, blackmailing, and robbing ... ". Fahkri was able to mobilize the support of numerous villages, whose headmen had lost prestige and status when their villagers had been humiliated and intimidated by the gangs. In December 1938, Fahkri succeeded in assembling two reportedly large meetings of supporters from villages in the Hebron-Jerusalem-Ramallah area. At the end of the year – by which time the rebel gangs had already lost the initiative to the British army – the Hagana supplied Fahkri with "crates of weapons".[46]

The British authorities were divided among themselves about how to treat the Nashashibi opposition. The High Commissioner and the CID Palestine were against taking sides in what appeared to them to be an Arab civil war. They didn't believe in Fakhri's ability to impose the hegemony of the Nashashibis. In contrast, the army was eager to crush the Husayni-led rebellion as quickly as possible, using all means available. They supported the peace bands with money and arms. In return, the Nashashibis supplied the army with valuable intelligence about the identity and location of the rebels. The Nashashibi peace bands were a factor to be reckoned with in Palestine – but they never posed a real challenge to the Husayni gangs.

During the closing months of 1938, after London's retreat from partition and with the army on the offensive, Fahkri Nashashibi tried to promote himself as leader of the Palestinian Arabs. He published an open letter in the Palestine press and gave interviews to the foreign press. He expressed his satisfaction that partition had been abandoned and claimed to be the spokesman of the Arab moderates. He claimed that the Nashashibis' National Defence Party, together with those independent Arabs who opposed the Mufti, represented over 75 per cent of the country's economic interests and, together with their supporters, over half the Arab population of Palestine. But his claims were ruined by his uncle Ragheb, who denounced his letter in public. Any lingering doubts about Fahkri's standing were dispelled by the dozens of telegrams that poured into the High Commissioner's office, denying his right to represent anyone.[47]

It is impossible to quantify the extent of the Palestinian Arab opposition to the Mufti's camp – no figures are available. What *is* clear is that the Mufti retained absolute control of the Palestinian Arab mainstream – an estimated 70–80 per cent of the Arab population. Hillel Cohen "guesstimates" that apart from those Arabs involved in the sale of lands to the Zionists – the sellers and the various brokers and lawyers who acted as middlemen – there were no more than a few dozen Palestinian Arabs who collaborated actively with the Zionists. In addition, there was a wider circle of a few hundreds who were active sporadically. Those who sold their lands to the Zionists were accused by the nationalists of being traitors, even as many in the Mufti's own camp were also selling off their lands (see Chapter 6).

Some Arab collaborators told their Zionist operatives that they were acting from ideological motivation. Others claimed that they "saw no fundamental problem in selling land to Jews". Still others calculated that the Zionists could not be defeated, and therefore it was pointless to try fighting them. These claims must be treated with due circumspection. Hillel Cohen's narrative is one-dimensional, based largely on the Arabs' own narratives. Understandably, they tended to inflate their own importance and to maintain that they were acting out of principle. The Zionists were quite aware of this but they and their Arab collaborators shared a common goal, "to weaken the Mufti and undermine the legitimacy of his national leadership".[48]

It is difficult to maintain that those Palestinian Arabs who collaborated with the Zionists did so because they had not acquired any nationalist consciousness. From the very start of British rule in Palestine, the country had been racked by the tectonic changes generated by British rule and Zionist immigration. Before the rebellion of 1936–39, the country had already suffered three rounds of Arab rioting against the Jews (1920, 1921 and 1929). No Arab could have failed to notice the dramatic demographic increase of the Yishuv during the first half of the 1930s. This last development was one of the main reasons why the Arabs rebelled in 1936.

It is also difficult to maintain that by the mid-1930s, none of the Arabs who sold their lands to the Zionists was aware that they were part of a wider process that was helping the Zionists to acquire a territorial base for a future Jewish state. The Arabs' consciousness of the historical process taking place is reflected in the Arabic press in Palestine, which from 1930 to 1935 inveighed repeatedly against the sales. The press also attacked those Arab brokers who, to quote one article of May 1934, "are increasing every day among various classes of rich and poor people who have been dazzled by the Zionist gold". On 16 September 1932, the Palestinian newspaper *al-Jami'ah al-'Arabiyyah* published the following warning:

> There is no doubt that the question of the sale of lands is about one of the greatest dangers that threatens the future of the country.

One month later, the same paper blamed the Arabs "for assisting the establishment of the Jewish National Home by accepting the transfer of their lands to the Jews".[49] In 1933, a British official who had his finger on the Arab pulse expressed his empathy for their plight; on the one hand, their fear of being swamped by the Zionists, but on the other, clearly unable to resist the temptations of personal material benefit:

> ... Every year some Arab sells land to other Jews. No Jew ever sells his land to an Arab. The Jews are prepared to pay fantastic prices to get land so how can you expect the individual Arab, however "patriotic", to withstand the pressure to sell?[50]

Some of the opposition to the Mufti feared that it was futile to try to resist the powers that were ranged against the Arabs. When Ragheb Nashashibi was asked in 1943 why he was accused of being such a "loyal servant of the British" he replied: "Because, with the little power we have, the only rational line is to be friendly and conciliatory with the British. If we don't try to win the British over as allies, who will take our side against world Jewry?".[51]

For many Arabs, their reason for opposing the Husaynis was personal. Many had been killed, injured and humiliated by the Husayni terror. A strong desire for revenge entered the Palestinian Arab paradigm. Arab society in Palestine had no democratic tradition or institutions via which opposition could express itself with impunity. The terror campaign strengthened even further the kinship ties of those injured. In the words of one study of the Palestinian Arab opposition, during the 1936–39 rebellion, the opposition gained many new adherents – victims of "aggression and nepotism that characterized the national political leadership of the Husseinis".[52]

However, one reservation must be entered. Whereas many Arabs maintained friendly relations with their Jewish neighbours, none was willing to recognize Jewish sovereignty over Palestine. The same study concluded:

> the fear of takeover by the Zionists rendered overt political alliance with them unacceptable for the majority of the Palestinian population.[53]

The large majority of the Palestinian Arabs remained passive, desperately trying to stay out of trouble. Of those who collaborated with the Zionists, most if not all did so for material benefit, whether from the sale of their lands or from direct payments for information rendered (usually asked for in advance). Many Arabs even became dependent upon Zionist funding. Some owed their status within their own community entirely to their connections with the Zionists. But the Zionists were unable to live up to the Arabs' "hugely inflated impression of world Jewry's influence and wealth". Many Arabs became angry and disillusioned when the Zionists didn't give them all that they expected. The problem of inadequate funding was exacerbated by some collaborators who embezzled the funds they received and failed to produce the promised results.[54]

The Nashashibi-led opposition itself became debilitated by internal dissensions and personal arguments. Some of the notable families openly denigrated Fahkri Nashashibi. In September 1941, shortly before Fahkri's assassination in Baghdad, Suleiman Tuqan, an opposition notable, told his Hagana handler that Fahkri was:

> ... a British agent ... He chases after money and status and spends his time getting drunk, sleeping with women, and attending loud parties that do nothing at all for the Arab cause ... He brings disgrace upon himself and on anyone who joins him.[55]

The rebel gangs also suffered from internal dissensions. By the end of 1938, they had been beaten by the British army and were demoralized. The dozens of life sentences imposed by the military courts and the numerous executions had spread terror into the hearts of the general population. The gangs lost all internal cohesion and internal disputes spread like wildfire. Unable to resist British military pressure, many rebels left the gangs. Some fled to Syria, others returned home. This widened the schism between the political leadership, most of who lived in comfortable exile in Syria, and the commanders in the field.[56] Much of the friction resulted from the social divide between the poorer peasant leaders in Palestine and the wealthier notables in exile. In late 1938, a group of local Palestinian leaders formed their own "Bureau of the Arab Revolt", in protest at the Mufti's dictates.

Many of the internal disputes involved charges against the Mufti himself, who was accused of misusing and embezzling funds. The gang commanders accused him of misappropriating contributions to the rebellion, of misusing *waqf* funds, and of having been personally involved in the sale of Arab lands (including his own) to the Zionists.[57] In June 1939, a group of commanders protested his rejection of the May White Paper. They accused his henchmen of acts of wanton terror against Arabs from rival camps. Their manifesto asserted that had the Mufti devoted the funds at his disposal to the welfare of the Palestinians:

> the country would have had no room left for a single Jew, and there would not have remained any land for them to purchase.[58]

A certain degree of national identity had permeated Palestinian Arab society during the first two decades of the mandate. But by the end of the 1930s, it was in danger of being subsumed under the cruelties of intra-clan terror. Ragheb Nashashibi's biographer, his nephew, noted:

> It is true that family rivalries seemed to take precedence over the national interest.[59]

This is supported by the study of the Arab collaborators:

> As the rebellion deteriorated into corruption and crime, the national interest became more and more marginal and Jewish intelligence had greater success – not only in cooperation with opponents of the rebellion but also in recruitment of informers within the rebel bands.[60]

Having little sense of national solidarity, the gang leaders had treated their own countrymen with cruelty, and worse still, they had humiliated the village headmen (*mukhtars*) in front of their villagers. If only for these reasons, the Nashashibi peace bands enjoyed an ephemeral measure of rural support. The gangs' desperate need of food and supplies was the primary reason for their contact with the village population. In retrospect, the gang leaders expressed remorse about the fact that they had alienated so many villagers. Several of them, together with some Palestinian refugees in Syria, signed a manifesto that accused the Mufti of wanting to continue the rebellion for his own political ends. In the spring of 1939, one commander analysed their failure to revive the rebellion:

> We found that the spirit of the Revolt is waning. The behaviour of the fighters towards the villagers is extremely brutal and horrifying: cruel robbery, execution without prior investigation, conflicts without reason, disorder and inaction.[61]

Yet the defeat of the rebel gangs in Palestine did not change Britain's conviction that the Mufti was the Arabs' absolute ruler, if only due to his proven ability to terrorize and ultimately to eliminate all opposition. The Nashashibis never had any hope of matching or defeating the Husayni rebels. Their dependence upon Zionist funding – an open secret – hardly added to their prestige. Most of the Arabic press condemned Fakhri and the gangs, for "rebelling against the national consensus". This attitude of the press was not lost on the British, who had no interest in aiding the losing side in an internecine conflict between unequal protagonists.

In any case, once the British had crushed the rebellion, they had no further use for the Nashashibi peace bands, which they disarmed and dispersed. At the end November 1938, Ragheb Nashashibi gave vent to his frustration at a meeting with Ambassador Lampson in Cairo:

> Every outrage and misery which we moderates in Palestine have to suffer remains unchecked by the Palestine government ... consideration has often been given to the opinions and wishes of the Mufti who is allowed to be a real dictator from his Lebanon Headquarters, is allowed to organize assassinations, the smuggling of arms into Palestine ... and [maintain] friendly contacts with German and Italian propagandists who are continually active in Palestine on his behalf.[62]

But MacMichael wrote off the Nashashibis' Defence Party as a political force. On 13 December 1939, he wrote to MacDonald, the Colonial Secretary: "Its leader is a past number, its erstwhile secretary, Fahkri Nashashibi, has gone too far in the field of politics and morality alike for even the strongest stomachs". Six months later, in June 1940, he reported to Lord Lloyd, the new Colonial Secretary:

> ... the Defence Party commanded little respect and its following was small. Its figurehead, Ragheb Bey Nashashibi, is a past number, its Secretary and most energetic member, Fahkri Nashashibi, is a young blackguard whose energies are chiefly devoted to self-interest and who is believed to be in Jewish pay.[63]

Above all, the government had learned from its mistakes during the first stage of the rebellion in 1936. Faced with the very real prospect of a loss of control in Palestine, after the Munich crisis was resolved, they determined to crush the rebellion by force.[64]

In February 1939, only MacMichael's obdurate veto prevented the government from inviting the Mufti to the round-table conference in London. The decision was taken against the strong protests of Ambassador Lampson in Cairo.[65] But this was little more than an act of face-saving. From his residence near Beirut, the Mufti remained the final arbiter of Arab policy on Palestine. The Palestinian Arab delegation in London consulted with him constantly, using British telecommunications (which of course were read by the British). Initially, Jemal al-Husayni, the titular head of the Palestinian Arab delegation, refused to accept the Nashashibis as part of the official Arab delegation. He protested angrily at the inclusion of Fahkri as an advisor, claiming that he had acted "hand in glove with the British Military Intelligence Service and with the Zionists and ... [was] regarded by the people of Palestine as having stabbed the nation in the back". MacDonald retorted that he had already agreed to allow Ragheb to choose his own delegates, and could not go back on his word. The Nashashibi delegation, headed by Ragheb, numbered just two delegates, with Fahkri as its "advisor". Fahkri's expenses were covered by a Zionist subvention of P£4000.[66] (The round-table conference is dealt with in the following chapter.)

Fahkri's assassination in Baghdad in November 1941 delivered a fatal blow to the Nashashibi opposition. Fahkri was eulogized by his cousin as "a political animal, a fighter with a touch of the machiavellian in him". The Arab opposition was deprived of its most outspoken and courageous leader (even if his integrity and morals were questionable). Fahkri's loss of support within his own community was reflected by the composition of the crowd that paid its last respects at his funeral. Most of the 800 people who attended were British (represented officially by a minor official) and Jewish. Of the Arabs who attended, most were villagers. None of Jerusalem's Arab notables showed up. The already debilitated opposition had become "a shepherdless flock". Fakhri's death, together with the Mufti's successful escape from Persia and his warm reception in Berlin, strengthened the Husayni camp.[67]

The Palestinian Arabs were tired and resentful of being terrorized by the gangs. The bitterness and mutual hatred between the rival Arab factions remained an indelible stain on Palestinian Arab society. In April 1939, Ragheb Nashashibi told a Zionist contact:

> ... for fifty years the Arabs will kill one another to avenge what happened during the disturbances.[68]

Notes

1 Report by Lt General Haining, August–October 1938, in CO 733/379, 75528/74, NA.
2 cf. Michael J. Cohen, *Palestine: Retreat from the Mandate, 1936–1945*, London/New York: Paul Elek/Holmes and Meier, 1978, p. 71. Jewish immigrants did *not* arrive solely in British ships.
3 ME (O) 292, 24 January 1939, Cab 51/11, NA.
4 Bushire (or Bushehr) was the chief seaport and the administrative centre of the Bushehr province on the Persian Gulf, on the south-western coast of Iran.
5 Cmd 5479, *Report of the Palestine Royal Commission: The Peel Report*, London: HMSO, July 1937.
6 The report reserved for the British a strategic corridor running from Lydda airport to the Mediterranean sea at Jaffa, via the main British army base at Sarafand, as well as an area around Haifa port, and a British presence at Jerusalem.
7 On the formation of Arab labour unions after World War Two, one of which was sponsored by the Histadrut, cf. Hillel Cohen, *Army of Shadows: Palestinian Collaboration with Zionism, 1917–1948*, Berkeley: University of California Press, 2008, pp. 212–14; On Arab-Jewish labour relations in the Palestine Railways union, cf. Zachary Lockman, *Comrades and Enemies: Arab and Jewish Workers in Palestine, 1906–1948*, Berkeley: University of California Press, 1996.
8 Cohen, ibid, pp. 15–16.
9 ibid, pp. 21–26.
10 cf. Kenneth W. Stein, *The Land Problem in Palestine, 1917–1939*, Chapel Hill: University of North Carolina Press, 1984, pp. 82, 116, 216–20.
11 Yehoshua Porath, *The Palestinian Arab National Movement*, vol. two, *From Riots to Rebellion, 1929–1939*, London: Frank Cass, 1977, pp. 260 ff., and Mark Tessler, *A History of the Israeli–Palestinian Conflict*, Bloomington: Indiana University Press, 1994, pp. 239–41.
12 Porath, ibid, pp. 254–58, 301; Cohen, *Retreat*, pp. 51–52, 62–65. In November 1924, Egyptian extremists assassinated Sir Lee Stack, the British Governor General of the Sudan and Sirdar of the Egyptian army. In retaliation, General Allenby, the British High Commissioner, made a series of humiliating demands (including a £500,000 fine) of Saad Zaglul's government, that brought about his resignation.
13 Ormsby-Gore to William Battershill (Chief Secretary in the Palestine Administration, 1937–39), 8 September 1937, CO/733/352, NA.
14 Porath, *The Palestinian*, vol. two. pp. 235–36.
15 Harvard (British Consul, Beirut) to Colonial Office, 12 November 1938, CO 733/368/3, NA.

16 Porath, *The Palestinian*, pp. 242–43; Intelligence report by Col H.P. Rice (Acting Inspector General of Palestine Police), 27 October 1937, in CO 733/311/5; and MacMichael to Colonial Office, 12 May 1938, in CO 733/368/2; see also intelligence reports in KV 2/2084–85, NA.
17 Report of 12 November 1939, in FO 371/23241, NA.
18 Report of 22 October 1939, ibid.
19 Mustafa Kabha, *The Palestinian Press as a Shaper of Public Opinion, 1929–1939: Writing up a Storm*, London: Vallentine Mitchell, 2007, p. 205.
20 ibid, p. 210.
21 ibid, pp. 205–6.
22 Porat, *The Palestinian*, pp. 254–58.
23 Howard Sachar, *Europe Leaves the Middle East, 1936–1954*, New York: Allen Lane, 1972, p. 92. For a survey of the various estimates of how many Arabs were killed, see Cohen, *Army*, pp. 142–44.
24 Porat, *The Palestinian*, p. 269.
25 ibid, pp. 239–41.
26 Both quotes are from A.J. Sherman, *Mandate Days: British Lives in Palestine, 1918–1948*, New York: Thames & Hudson, 1998, pp. 108, 111.
27 Cohen, *Army*, p. 126.
28 Zionist intelligence report, 4 September 1937, in S25/10.097, Central Zionist Archives (CZA).
29 Cohen, *Army*, pp. 134–35, 137.
30 The first assassination attempt on Fahkri was made in Palestine in July 1937. Ragheb survived to serve as a minister in several Jordanian governments. After 1948, several other Palestinian notables took office under King Abdullah, not only Nashashibis but also Husaynis and members of the Istiqlal. See Ragheb's biography, written by his nephew, Nasser Eddin Nashashibi, *Jerusalem's Other Voice: Ragheb Nashashibi and Moderation in Palestinian Politics, 1920–1948*, Exeter: Ithaca Press, 1990, pp. 81–82, 86, 101, 123.
31 Cited in Sherman, *Mandate Days*, p.128. MacMichael was an Arabist and a classical scholar; he had served previously in the Sudan and in Tanganyika.
32 The Northern Fence was built by the Jewish construction company, Solel Boneh. Between April 1940 to November 1943, the British built 62 more fortified police stations, at the enormous cost, for those days, of £1¾ million. Personal communication from Dr Gad Kreuzer, Bar-Ilan University.
33 Sherman, *Mandate Days*, p. 114.
34 Battershill private diary, Mss British Empire s. 467, box 12, file 6, folios 24–29, The Bodleian Library, Oxford.
35 Report by Lt General Haining for August–October 1938, in CO 733/379, 75528/74, NA.
36 ibid, and Battershill private diary, supra.
37 cf. James Barker, "Monty and the Mandate in Palestine", *History Today*, January 2013; also: www.historytoday.com/james-barker/monty-and-mandate-palestine
38 ibid.
39 Sherman, *Mandate Days*, p. 117.
40 Edward Horne, *A Job Well Done: A History of the Palestine Police Force, 1920–1948*, Sussex: The Book Guild, 2003, p. 233.
41 General Haining to Generals Montgomery and O'Connor, undated, December 1938, from the papers of General O'Connor, cited by Simon Anglim, "Orde Wingate and the Special Night Squads: A Feasible Policy for counter-terrorism?" www.academia.edu/645942/Orde_Wingate_and_the_Special_Night_Squads_A_Feasible_Policy_for_Counter-terrorism.
42 Horne, *A Job*, pp. 417, 425–26.

286 *The Arab rebellion, II*

43 cf. Simon Anglim, *Orde Wingate and the British Army, 1922–1944* (*Warfare, Society and Culture*), London: Pickering & Chatto, 2010, and idem, "Orde Wingate and the Special Night Squads", supra.
44 It was explained to Churchill that General Haining had ordered Wingate back to England for being "too pronouncedly pro-Jewish and anti-Arab." Minute by J.M. Martin, Churchill's private secretary, 3 July 1944, in Prem 4/51/9, NA.
45 Cohen, *Army*, pp. 127–28.
46 ibid, pp. 132, 145–48, 150–51. The first assembly of supporters was reportedly attended by an unspecified number of notables from 45 villages, the second by some 3000 villagers. Dr Cohen's study must be treated with reservation, since his work is based almost exclusively upon the Hagana archives, on Arab testimonies and on the reports of the Zionist intelligence agents who handled them. He has not used the British archives; secret British intelligence assessments and articles from the British press cited have also been culled from the Hagana archives.
47 Cohen, *Retreat*, p. 62, and Nashashibi, *Jerusalem's Other Voice*, p. 88.
48 Cohen, *Army*, pp. 2–3, 7. Cohen notes that after the establishment of Israel, it was common for Arabs to "revamp their biographies and boast of their collaboration with the Jewish state". Likewise, Arabs applying to the new state of Israel for jobs commonly claimed that they were old friends of the Jews; idem, p. 248.
49 These and other articles are cited in Stein, *The Land*, pp. 18–84. *al-Jami'ah al-'Arabiyyah* was a Husayni newspaper founded in 1927. It led the public campaign against the Nashashibis.
50 Diary entry of Christopher Eastwood, one of Wauchope's private secretaries, 14 April 1933, cited in Sherman, *Mandate Days*, p. 88.
51 Nashashibi, *Jerusalem's Other Voice*, pp. 91–92.
52 Cohen, *Army*, pp. 261–62.
53 ibid, p. 26.
54 ibid, pp. 26, 182, and personal communications from the author.
55 ibid, p. 182.
56 The British hanged over 100 Arab rebels between 1937 and 1939; cf. Joseph Nevo, "Palestinian-Arab Violent Activity during the 1930s", in Michael J. Cohen, Martin Kolinsky, eds, *Britain and the Middle East in the 1930s*, London: Macmillan, in association with King's College, 1992, pp. 169–89.
57 In January 1937, Colonel Gilbert MacKereth, the British Consul at Damascus, told the Peel Commission that they need only to check the Tabu, the Palestine Land Register; Cohen, *Retreat*, p. 204, note 73.
58 ibid, p. 64. The manifesto was signed by section commanders from Jaffa, Lydda, Nablus, Ramleh and Tiberius.
59 Nashashibi, *Jerusalem's Other Voice*, p. 92.
60 Cohen, *Army*, p. 165.
61 Porat, *The Palestinian*, p. 266.
62 Lampson report of 30 November 1938, in FO 371/21869, NA; cited in Nashashibi, ibid, pp. 152–53.
63 Nashashibi, ibid, pp. 116, 160.
64 On the Arabic press, cf. Kabha, *The Palestinian Press*, p. 217; on British reservations about the Nashashibi "peace gangs", cf. Porath, *The Palestinian*, pp. 255–56.
65 Cohen, *Retreat*, pp. 62–63.
66 Nashashibi, *Jerusalem's Other Voice*, pp. 104–5, 156, and Cohen, *Army*, p. 133.
67 Nashashibi, ibid, p. 64, and Cohen, ibid, p. 203.
68 Sachar, *Europe Leaves*, p. 258.

13 Appeasement in the Middle East, 1937–39

> You were given the choice between war and dishonour. You chose dishonour, and you will have war.
>
> Churchill to Chamberlain on the Munich Agreement

British reservations about partition

The report of the Peel Commission was presented to the government in June 1937. Its major finding was that the mandate in Palestine was no longer workable. It recommended the partition of Palestine into separate Arab and Jewish states, leaving strategic enclaves in British hands.[1] It proposed that the Arab state be annexed to Trans-Jordan. It also recommended the restriction of Jewish immigration to a "political high limit" of 1000 per month during the interim period, pending the establishment of the independent Arab and Jewish states. For the Colonial Office, the Peel Plan appeared to offer an honourable exit from the Palestine quagmire, while guarding key British interests. At the end of the month, the Cabinet, chaired by Neville Chamberlain, approved the report "in principle".

As noted already, on the Zionist side Weizmann and Ben-Gurion favoured the Peel Plan, as a basis for negotiation. Weizmann used his contacts with British politicians in an effort to ensure parliamentary support for partition. On 8 June 1937, he convened a private meeting in London with a number of opposition MPs; those present included Clement Attlee (Labour), Archibald Sinclair (Liberal) and Churchill and Leo Amery (Conservative backbenchers). The meeting did not produce the result that Weizmann hoped for.

Churchill, who was somewhat inebriated, dominated the conversation. He fulminated against partition as a retreat from the Balfour promise to encourage Jewish settlement in all of Palestine west of the river Jordan. He called the government "a lot of lily-livered rabbits", but promised Weizmann that he would support partition – if that was what the Zionists wanted: "If you ask us to fight, we will fight like tigers". But Churchill proceeded to attack the government's weakness. He compared the partition proposal to the Germans' reoccupation of the Rhineland in March 1936; with the Germans, the government had acquiesced in a violation of the Treaty of Versailles; with Palestine, the Partition Plan was a violation of the Balfour Declaration. Churchill was adamantly against partition but concluded: "If Dr [Weizmann] told him to shut up when the time came, he would shut up".[2] Weizmann left the meeting encouraged. But he had not read the opposition's motives correctly.

Churchill revealed his true motives to Lord Melchett, his close friend, at a private dinner at the end of July. Churchill was moved by his own frustrated political ambitions, and by his concern for Britain's position in the Middle East. He feared that the creation of a Jewish state in Palestine would drive the Arab states into the arms of the Italians. Melchett reported back to the Zionists that Churchill had admonished: "the Jews must not rock the imperial boat" and warned that they must ensure that:

> Great Britain is not defeated in the Mediterranean ... he thinks our real danger in such an event would be the support which Italy might give the Arabs, and even if we could stand up to the Arabs, we certainly could not stand up to the Arabs and the Italians together.[3]

Churchill continued that the Jews had waited so long for a state of their own, they should have the patience to wait a few more years, until the looming world crisis had passed. Sovereignty must come in due course, "although it might take a century or two centuries". He then treated Melchett to his own "brainwave", a proposal that was in fact a harbinger of the 1939 White Paper:

> There may be times when it is impossible to allow immigration; there may be times when it is wise to restrict the sale of lands ... Things will then get better again.[4]

Melchett reported back to the Zionists that Churchill had shown "a complete absence of any sense of reality of the present situation". Melchett agreed with Baffy Dugdale's assessment that Churchill was "playing politics" with the Zionist cause, seizing upon any opportunity to attack the Chamberlain government. She accused the opposition of using the Zionists as a "cat's paw" of English politics.[5]

The House of Commons debated the Partition Plan on 21 July 1937. It received a cool reception. Prominent members of the opposition, including the elderly Lloyd George, seized the opportunity to attack the government. Churchill reneged on his promise to Weizmann to support the plan. He took no part in the debate itself but, together with Lloyd George, he lobbied behind the scenes to secure the passage of an amendment which deferred a Commons vote until after the plan had been considered by the League of Nations. Chamberlain's government enjoyed a comfortable majority in the House, and could have easily secured a majority for the Partition Plan. But during the 3 weeks that had elapsed since the Cabinet vote, he had evidently had his own second thoughts about the wisdom of setting up a Jewish state in Palestine. He directed that the vote would not be one of confidence, thereby allowing MPs to vote as they wished.

Churchill had his own agenda, and the Zionist cause was not high on the list of his priorities. Indeed, he went public with his rejection of partition, in an especially commissioned article for the *Jewish Chronicle*, published on 3 September 1937. He warned that partition would bring only war to the Eastern Mediterranean, providing the Italians with a golden opportunity to intervene, thereby embarrassing the British. He advised that the Zionists would do "far better to persevere along the old lines".

In May 1939, during the Commons debate on the Palestine White Paper, Churchill would vaunt his own role in shelving the 1937 Partition Plan:

> The House persuaded them not to force us into an incontinent acceptance of their partition plan, and within a few months, though they did not thank us for it, they had themselves abandoned and discarded it as precipitately as they had adopted it.[6]

Clearly, with the international horizon darkening, any delay could have only a deleterious effect. "Baffy" thought that the Commons debate of July 1937 had been a disaster. Many believed that the Zionists themselves were partly responsible for the failure. The Zionists' own reservations about partition – that the area proposed for the Jewish state was too small – also contributed to the Commons' delay. One member, Kenneth Pickthorne MP, claimed later:

> The Jews ... had overdone their case during the debate in Parliament after the Royal Commission's report ... the Government had been prepared at that time to carry out the Commission's proposals without much delay, but the Zionists and their powerful friends in Parliament had prevented it by their strong attacks during the debate.[7]

After the Holocaust, many of those Zionists who had opposed partition in 1937 would feel remorse and regret for having opposed the establishment of a Jewish state before the war.

The bureaucratic burial of partition

Inevitably, the Colonial and Foreign Offices clashed over the Peel Plan. From the restricted purview of the Colonial Office, partition appeared to offer the only honourable exit from what was now regarded as a colossal imperial blunder – the Balfour Declaration. Harold Downie of the Colonial Office noted:

> The falseness of our position hampered us at every turn; now at length we have a means of escape ... by which we can do substantial justice to both

parties and clean our conscience of the odious imputation of breach of faith. We are ... in sight of shore after a prolonged buffeting in heavy seas. Are we to scuttle the life-boat merely because the coast looks rocky and dangerous?[8]

But the Foreign Office was concerned primarily with retaining Britain's foothold in the Middle East. The ramifications of a hostile Arab world aligned with Britain's enemies outweighed any conceivable argument in favour of partition. Foreign Office policy on Palestine was determined by its *éminence grise*, George Rendel, head of its Middle East department. He adumbrated a new doctrine, which henceforth would underpin British policy in the region: Palestine must be treated as an integral part of the Arab Middle East; any false step there might lose for Britain the support not only of the Arab but also of the Moslem world. Given Britain's geo-strategic position after 1937, this left only one policy option – the appeasement of the Arab states.

The British were embarrassed further when during the summer of 1937, the Iraqi Prime Minister appealed to the Palestinian Arabs to reject the Peel Plan, and even more so at Geneva in September, when the Iraqi representative attacked partition during the debate at the session of the League's Permanent Mandates Commission. These attacks by Britain's supposed ally against a plan approved by the Cabinet did nothing to enhance her prestige in the Middle East, and served only to increase doubts about the government's sincerity about partition.[9]

Whether or not the Foreign Office had quietly encouraged the Iraqis, the Colonial Office suspected its hidden hand behind the declarations. Ormsby-Gore warned Foreign Secretary Eden that unless he supported him on partition, he, Ormsby-Gore, would have to tell the Prime Minister that he could no longer be responsible for Palestine. It was as if the departments involved were working for different governments. Rendel despaired; the Colonial Office would never consider an alternative to partition. General Haining, the GOC Palestine, regarded the renewed outbreak of violence in the country as a challenge to British rule by a band of unrepresentative criminals while the Air Ministry believed that the current disturbances were incited from Syria. But further statements by Arab leaders against partition only strengthened Rendel's conviction that Britain must abandon the Peel Plan.

It was evident that the goal of the second phase of the Arab rebellion, which began in September 1937, was to force Britain to retreat from partition. But the Foreign Office refused to contemplate the suppression of the Palestinians by force. In November 1937, Eden, briefed by Rendel, advised the Cabinet that the Arabs, both inside and outside Palestine, had rejected partition, and that its imposition by force would "bring Britain into a collision with the Arab countries and jeopardize British interests".[10] Rendel refused to treat the violence as anything other than "a political movement due to our Zionist policy" – to which the solution had to be political. This could happen only if they granted the Arabs' legitimate national demands, i.e. the early abandonment of partition and the grant of independence to a predominantly Arab Palestine.

Both the British Consul at Damascus and Zionist sources supplied the government with intelligence assessments of the scope of this second stage of the rebellion, and of the Mufti's role in managing it from Beirut. There was hard evidence that he was behind the renewed terrorist campaign in Palestine, aided by the connivance of the Syrian gendarmerie in smuggling arms to the terrorist bands in Palestine.

But Rendel adhered rigidly to his *ideé fixe*. He dismissed the Zionist report as "a Jewish document". He refused to treat the violence in Palestine as anything other than a political reaction to the government's Zionist policy. The only long-term, viable solution must be the granting of the Arabs' legitimate demands. The first, urgent step had be the removal of partition from the agenda. He also dismissed the Colonial Secretary's vilification of the Mufti:

> One can easily overrate the importance of the part which the Mufti personally plays in the Palestine-Arab national movement. The Colonial Office and the Zionists are very much inclined to attribute the whole of the Palestine trouble to the Mufti personally, and to Italian funds.[11]

Inevitably, the Foreign Office, as the senior department, prevailed. But the government could not simply abandon partition – which would be regarded universally as a capitulation to Arab violence. Therefore, a well-worn bureaucratic gambit was used: the Cabinet appointed another commission, a "technical" one, charged officially with working out a practical plan of partition. Unofficially, and in the strictest confidence, the Foreign Office ensured that the new Commission was authorized to recommend scrapping the whole idea.

In addition to the official, published terms of reference, the Colonial Secretary was instructed – at the insistence of the Foreign Office, backed up by the Prime Minister – to write a private letter to Sir John Woodhead, the Commission's chairman, informing him that he was also free to report that his Commission had been unable to find any practical scheme of partition. Ormsby-Gore was subjected to the humiliating condition of having his private letter vetted and approved by the Foreign Secretary, before he handed it over to the Secretary of the Cabinet. In the interim, the government tried to cool tempers in Palestine with an announcement that no action would be taken for a long time.

The mutual suspicions and scorn between the Colonial and Foreign Offices dissipated only in May 1938, when Malcolm MacDonald replaced Ormsby-Gore as Colonial Secretary. The latter, like some of his predecessors, was also broken by the Palestine *imbroglio*. His efforts to resist the Foreign Office earned him no points with the Zionists, and certainly did not endear him to the Arabs. In January 1938, he gave vent to his feelings of frustration and impotence in a private note to the Prime Minister:

The Arabs are treacherous and untrustworthy, the Jews greedy and, when freed from persecution, aggressive ... I am convinced that the Arabs cannot be trusted to govern the Jews any more than the Jews can be trusted to govern the Arabs.[12]

High Commissioner Wauchope had become too identified with the failed, lenient policies of 1936. When the rebellion broke out anew in September 1937, it was decided to remove him. In October 1937, the Cabinet confirmed the decision, and appointed in his place Sir Harold MacMichael, a seasoned colonial administrator. MacMichael did not take up his post until early March 1938.

Thus in the spring of 1938, two almost simultaneous changes in personnel occurred. The two key officials dealing with Palestine were removed – the Colonial Secretary and the High Commissioner. At first sight, the changes appear to be mutually exclusive, but they were not. The adoption of a tougher military line against the Palestinian Arab rebels, and the change of high policy in London to one of appeasement of the Arab states were entirely compatible in the government's purview. In view of the deterioration of the international situation, the government determined to appease the Arab states, while at the same time, in the breathing space afforded by the Munich Agreement, to reassert its control of Palestine.

The two dismissed officials had become identified with policies that were defunct. Wauchope's dismissal reflected the bankruptcy of his policy of appeasing the rebels in 1936. The determination to treat them with a firm hand required a new man. Ormsby-Gore was replaced because he had become too associated with the plan to partition Palestine into Arab and Jewish states.

The 1939 White Paper

The Palestine White Paper of 1939 was *not* a British surrender to Arab violence in Palestine. The Arab rebellion was crushed well before the new policy was approved by Parliament in May of that year. The new policy had been incubating since the summer of 1936 when, following the Italian conquest of Abyssinia, Britain had for the first time permitted Arab rulers – of Iraq, Saudi Arabia and Trans-Jordan – to intervene in the affairs of the Palestine. The new policy was the second link in a policy of securing quiet in the Middle East – the first was the so-called gentleman's agreements with Italy. In contrast to the attempts to appease Nazi Germany, the appeasement of Italy was supported by a wide consensus in the Commons, including Churchill. The government was determined to secure at least the acquiescence of the Arab states to its new policy in Palestine, thereby retaining their "benevolent neutrality".

At the beginning of 1938, with the Partition Plan on the shelf for at least a few months, the War Office was commissioned by the government to prepare a study of the military consequences if the Arab states turned hostile to Britain (a) when she was otherwise at peace, and (b) when she was at war with one or more of the major powers. The study concluded that it was unlikely that the Arabs would combine against Britain in peacetime. However, its warning of the consequences for Britain in wartime could not be ignored:

> The greater the delay in implementing a policy in Palestine, the greater will be the opportunity for foreign propaganda to consolidate Arab hostility to Britain and the more difficult it will be to control ... The dangers and extent of Arab hostility might be greatly increased should Britain be at war with any of the great powers. A serious reverse or signs that Britain might lose the war might lead to definite hostile action by some of the Arab governments. Guerilla attacks over a widespread area, attacks on isolated British posts, massacre of British and Jewish personnel, and sabotage of communications, possibly combined with an invasion of Palestine and Transjordan might be expected.[13]

However, the military did not believe that Arab hostilities against British positions in the Middle East would be a decisive factor:

> History shows that the Arabs are disinclined to take decisive action to support even their friends until they see evidence that the side they favour is in the ascendant ... Arab hostility might lengthen the war, but even if it extended to Egypt and Persia, it would not necessarily prove a decisive factor in its ultimate outcome.[14]

Lacy Bagallay, Rendel's successor at the Foreign Office from the end of 1938, commended the War Office, but asserted that they had understated their case. He warned of the grave political consequences if the Arabs came to hold Britain responsible for the establishment in Palestine of a Jewish state:

> There can be no doubt that if partition is enforced our prestige and reputation will never be the same again and that the Arab world will wait, if necessary for years, for the day of revenge upon us and the Jews, which any preoccupation on our part elsewhere will give them.[15]

Notwithstanding his "Zionist" past (see Chapter 10), Malcolm MacDonald, the new Colonial Secretary, was soon persuaded that even if the government had wanted to partition Palestine, none of the indigenous parties would agree to any specific plan. After an intensive study of the situation, including a 2-day visit to Palestine in August, he concluded that the Zionists would never agree to any reduction in the area proposed by the Peel Commission, whereas the Arabs rejected the very idea of a Jewish state in Palestine, whatever its size. He was soon converted to the Foreign Office line.

The government was now prevented from announcing the official burial of partition only by its own bureaucratic creation – the Woodhead Commission. Given the need to keep up appearances, the government could neither make concessions to violence, nor anticipate the report of the Commission, which carried out its investigation in Palestine during the spring and summer of 1938, at the height of the disturbances there.

Once back in London, the Commission was given every possible hint by the government that it was expected to do its "dirty work" for it – to take responsibility for burying partition. MacDonald took it for granted that the Commission would find against partition. In September 1938, with the Munich crisis at its peak, he met Woodhead privately, and pleaded with him to give an early indication of his Commission's findings, and asked him if he could not deliver the report earlier. MacDonald claimed to have evidence that the Arabs were planning a wide-scale insurrection for the third week of October, and told Woodhead that if he could issue his report before that date, and thereby signal the official demise of partition, it would ease the government's position considerably.

Woodhead not only refused, but also turned down MacDonald's request to be allowed to sound out the members of the Commission at an informal dinner. Ten days later, at the height of the Munich crisis, a joint meeting of Colonial and Foreign Office officials decided that in the event of the outbreak of war, partition would be suspended and all immigration to Palestine stopped, on the grounds of lack of shipping.

At the beginning of October, MacDonald recalled High Commissioner MacMichael and some of his senior officials to London, in order to assess the situation in Palestine. From 7 to 10 October, Colonial Office officials met with their Foreign Office counterparts, and with General Pownall of the War Office. All present were agreed that the Balfour Declaration had been a mistake and that Britain could not sponsor the establishment of a Jewish state, in any part of Palestine.

MacDonald advised that the entire security system in Palestine was on the point of collapse – the reinforcements requested by the Palestine authorities had been diverted to Egypt, for the defence of the Suez Canal. The Arab police had been disarmed due to their unreliability, and the British were reaching the "political limit" at which Jewish security forces could be used. There were already more Jews under arms in Palestine than all the British troops and police combined! MacMichael proposed that in order to defuse the situation, the government should issue an immediate statement to the effect that partition had been found to be impracticable. But MacDonald refused to pre-empt Woodhead.

On 19 October 1938 MacDonald told a Cabinet meeting that whereas partition remained official government policy, he himself had become convinced long ago that it was not the right one. Finally, in late October, the Woodhead Commission duly reported that they had been unable to recommend boundaries for "self-supporting Arab and Jewish States".[16] The government published a new White Paper that included the Commission's report, and its own rejection of partition. The government also announced its intention to convene a round-table conference of the parties concerned, in one final attempt to find a solution to the Palestine problem.

On 9 November 1938, the day after Crystallnacht,[17] the War Office circulated an intelligence assessment of the situation in the Middle East should Britain and France find themselves at war with Germany and Italy in April 1939:

> Had the European crisis of September 1938 developed into war, and had partition not been abandoned, we would probably have had to reckon with open rebellion in Palestine supplemented by contingents from outside and repercussions in other Arab countries. Whatever their wishes may have been, the Arab Governments would have found it extremely difficult to fulfil their treaty obligations ... Owing to the abandonment of partition and the prospects that **the rebellion in Palestine will have either been brought under control or will have subsided through appeasement by April 1939**, the feeling of hostility to Great Britain ... should be no greater, and may be much less than at present.[18]

On the day after the government's announcement, Chaim Weizmann lunched with two Conservative backbenchers – Winston Churchill and Leo Amery. Churchill was pleased that partition had been shelved, and reiterated his old proposal, now with a slight variation: that Jewish immigration should be limited to the extent of the Arabs' natural increase, plus an additional 10,000 per annum. Given the Palestinian Arabs' two-thirds majority, the scheme would have sentenced the Yishuv to permanent minority status. But according to Leo Amery's record of the meeting, Weizmann apparently jumped at the idea.[19]

There was virtually an all-party consensus in the British Parliament on the need to limit Jewish immigration. The elusive issue was to find the right formula, i.e. a maximum level that would still reassure the Arabs that they would retain their majority in Palestine. It was possibly on the basis of his impressions from his meeting with Weizmann that on 24 November 1938, Churchill announced in the Commons his own plan for a solution to the Palestine problem. He stated that if he were an Arab, he too would be alarmed by the "excessive rate" of Jewish immigration into Palestine:

> They [the Arabs] wonder whether a halt is ever going to be called to it, and they fear that it is going to be their fate in the land of their birth to be dominated by this energetic, new-coming people, dominated economically, politically, completely.[20]

Churchill added enigmatically that it was obvious that the "economic absorptive capacity formula" laid down by his own White Paper of 1922 would have to be conditioned and interpreted in regard to the "general political situation of the country". In regard to the rate of Jewish immigration, he proposed that the government determine a rate for the next 10 years at a figure that would not decisively alter the demographic balance between Arabs and Jews. He dropped the idea that he had broached with Weizmann – of an additional 10,000 above the Arab birth rate. His plan was almost identical to the principle that would guide the Chamberlain government's policy. The *Jewish Chronicle* commented acidly that Churchill's proposals "might well be regarded as a welcome success by many even of those who find themselves in the Mufti's camp".[21]

During the following months, British policy on Palestine proceeded along two parallel axes: the pursuit of a decisive military defeat of the Arab rebellion in Palestine and concurrently, the search for a political solution that would satisfy the Arab states. The general mood at the Foreign Office may be gauged by the following private telegram sent on 30 August 1938, by Charles Bateman, a minister at the Cairo embassy, to Sir Lancelot Oliphant, the Deputy Under-Secretary at the Foreign Office. His gratuitous Shylock reference reflects both a cynical recognition that in contrast to the previous World War, the Jews now had no bargaining position, and a general undercurrent of prejudice in the department:

> The Jews are anybody's game these days ... Britain should concentrate on placating the Arabs ... they [the Jews] have waited 2000 years for their "home" ... they can well afford to wait a bit more until we are better able to help them get their last pound of flesh ... especially as we are the only friends they have left in the world.[22]

After the scrapping of partition, the government went through the motions of convening one last conference between the Arabs and the Jews, in order to demonstrate that it had tried to reach an equitable compromise. In effect, the convening of the conference was a purely tactical move, to demonstrate that before taking its own decision, the government had done its utmost to reconcile the parties to the conflict. But the British showed their hand in advance, by inviting representatives of the Arab states to attend. It was *their* approval, not that of the Palestinians or the Jews, that the government sought.

The government appreciated that a solution to the Palestine problem favourable to the Arabs would expose it to Jewish charges of a breach of faith. However, it was also aware that the position of the Jewish people in 1939 was drastically different from what it had been in 1917, and during the 1920s. In the event of a conflict between Britain and Nazi Germany, the Jews would have no option other than to side with the former. The Arabs *did* have an alternative. In his August telegram to Oliphant, Bateman had suggested flippantly that they invite the Mufti to London, and promise him that Britain would "call off 'our Jew immigrants'", if he would call off "his thugs".[23]

The Colonial Office prepared contingency plans, for the likely event that the sides proved unable to reconcile their differences. When that happened, then Britain, as the responsible mandatory Power, would impose its own "equitable" settlement. The government's thinking was summed up accurately by Sir John Chancellor, the former High Commissioner (1928–31), who met MacDonald in September 1938:

> [He] doubted if [the conference] would result in any agreement – both Jews and Arabs must be relieved of responsibility of abandoning positions which they have taken up, and this could be done only through decisions of His Majesty's Government ... [he] appreciated incidental advantage of holding conference would be to show that, before taking their own decision, His Majesty's Government had gone to utmost limit to reconcile the opposing parties.[24]

In December 1938, the Colonial Office drafted two alternative proposals for the future regulation of Jewish immigration; the first would permit an annual rate that would bring the Jews up to 35–40 per cent of the total population within 10 years; in that case, subsequent immigration would be determined by another conference. If, as expected, the Arabs turned down this proposal, the government would add a "sweetener" – they would offer the same rate of immigration for 10 years, after which, any subsequent entries would be made conditional upon Arab assent. In that case, the government would insist on the higher ratio of 40 per cent. On 1 February 1939, the Cabinet approved this strategy.

The round-table conference was opened formally by Prime Minister Chamberlain at St James's Palace, London, on 7 February 1939. The Zionist delegation included Weizmann, Ben-Gurion and Moshe Shertok (Sharett) and two prominent Diaspora Jews – one from England and one from the United States.[25] The government released the members of the HAC incarcerated in the Seychelles, but proscribed the Mufti. However, the British accorded him the nominal title of head of the Palestinian delegation, and he agreed to remain "voluntarily" in Beirut. But the Palestinian delegation was dominated by the Mufti, even if he was not seated at the negotiating table. They consulted constantly with him – with full government cognizance – ensuring that he continued to determine the Palestinians' policy as effectively as if he had been physically present. After 3 years of Husayni terror, the Nashashibis were emasculated. They would have preferred a continuation of the British mandate, even if that meant some limited Jewish immigration. But their minority voice was irrelevant. The Arab states' delegation included the Emir Abdullah of Trans-Jordan, Nuri al-Said, the Iraqi Foreign Minister, Feisal, the Saudi royal prince, and some ranking Egyptian politicians, including Ali Maher Pasha, Prime Minister several times.

Since the Palestinian Arabs refused to sit in the same room with the Jews, MacDonald shuttled back and forth between the two delegations, conducting separate working sessions with each. This had the advantage for the British of enabling them to conceal from each side the gaps between the proposals that they brought to each side. The key developments at the conference will be reviewed here briefly.[26]

The Palestinian delegation refused to budge from their basic demands: an independent Palestinian state and a halt to all further Jewish immigration. After 3 years of Arab terrorist activity in Palestine, and against the background of Nazi expansion in Europe,[27] the Jews felt that they could not afford to compromise. They refused to contemplate any limitation on Jewish immigration except for economic considerations.

When Weizmann referred to Britain's moral duty to continue to fulfil the Balfour promise, MacDonald reminded him of her moral obligation to the Arabs, who had suffered due to the vagueness of the Declaration. In contrast to Weizmann, David Ben-Gurion, leader of the Yishuv since 1920, had read the "writing on the wall" at the time of the Munich Agreement. In the privacy of a closed meeting of the Jewish delegation to the conference, he referred presciently to Britain's cynical *realpolitik*:

> Did the question of consent apply only to those provisions of the Mandate which concerned the Jewish National Home or was the consent of the Arabs necessary also for the continuation of British rule in Palestine? Was the British Government ready to abandon Palestine if the Arabs did not consent to their remaining, or did they consider it necessary to remain in Palestine despite Arab opposition to foreign rule?[28]

Appeasement was not yet a disreputable word, certainly not in the Middle East. Indeed, MacDonald appealed to the Jewish delegation to help Britain to appease the Arabs. He explained the strategic importance of the Middle East for Britain, and admitted that her position there depended upon the co-operation of the Arabs. He warned that if Britain was "tried too hard", she would need to reckon with Arab hostility and her armed forces in the region would have to be increased. He asked rhetorically if the Jews' position in Palestine would be improved if Britain was forced out of the Middle East.

The Zionists tried in vain to persuade the British that half a million Jews in Palestine, with their superior skills and financial resources, would be able to look after British interests in the region. But the vaunted military and technological skills of the Zionists could never counterbalance the strategic assets that the British enjoyed in the Arab world – military bases and oil. Zionist arguments that the Arab danger was exaggerated and that the Jews made better soldiers fell on deaf ears.

Sensing the intransigent mood of both sides, MacDonald jettisoned his contingency plans, and began with a hybrid version of both of the pre-prepared contingencies: he offered the Arabs a limitation of Jewish immigration to a rate that would bring the Jewish population up to 35–40 per cent of the total within 10 years, together with an Arab veto on all subsequent immigration. He explained to the Jews that the 35 per cent estimate would allow them an annual immigration of 15,000; 40 per cent would double that figure (it will be recalled that Jewish immigration had peaked in 1935, at 62,000). Unsurprisingly, the Jewish delegation rejected the Arab veto out of hand, for it would have condemned the Yishuv to permanent minority status.

To the Arabs, MacDonald pleaded the case for allowing Jewish immigration into existing Jewish settlements, arguing that Jewish capital was necessary for the development of the country. The Arabs were unimpressed with this familiar argument, and insisted on a complete cessation of all Jewish immigration.

Any meaningful attempt to reach a compromise between the Arabs and the Jews came to an end over the weekend of 24–26 February. Due to a bureaucratic slip, the government sent by mistake to the Jewish delegation a copy of its proposals to the Arabs, thereby disclosing the government's double-dealing. The Zionists learned that under the constitutional proposals being advanced by the British, the original idea of equal representation for Arabs and Jews on the proposed executive council had been amended under Arab pressure to give the latter a 3–2 majority. The Zionists were also shocked to learn that the British had made a further, dramatic concession on immigration – the period of immigration before an Arab veto came into force had been cut from 10 to 5 years, after which the British would grant independence to Palestine. To make matters worse, these proposals were also sent to the Arab delegation and published in the Arab press in Palestine. Jewish extremists in Palestine reacted with a series of bomb outrages that claimed numerous Arab lives.

MacDonald tried to persuade the Jewish delegation that the draft proposals that they had received, due to a clerical error, were not final, and he offered to replace the Arab veto on further immigration with a decision to convene a further conference after 5 years. But the Jewish delegation, already disillusioned by MacDonald's lack of integrity, was hardly inclined to submit their people's fate to the whims of a further conference. The Palestinian Arabs were even less compliant. They already took for granted the idea of gaining independence after 5 years, and refused to contemplate yet another, British-sponsored conference to determine future immigration policy.

MacDonald tried in vain to persuade Weizmann not to walk out of the conference. But the latter, who was against breaking off the negotiations, was out-voted by the executive panel which determined the Jewish delegation's policy. A diplomatic sleight of hand was resorted to – the delegation agreed to allow MacDonald to announce that "informal discussions" would be continued.

The Arab states' delegates were the only ones who displayed any inclination to accept the government's proposals and they promised to try to persuade the Palestinians. But the Husayni-dominated majority of the Palestinian delegation held out for an independent state on the Iraqi model, within 3 years. On 2 March, MacDonald reported to the Cabinet that if nothing changed within the next few days, he would close the conference, leaving the government to declare its own policy, as anticipated.

On 7 March, MacDonald managed to arrange one final meeting – between the Jewish delegation and the representatives of the Arab states. It was a dialogue of the deaf. Weizmann and Ben-Gurion stated that the Zionists were the guardians of the entire Jewish people, and they could not forego their right to come to Palestine. Ali Maher Pasha of Egypt expressed his admiration for everything that the Jews had done in Palestine, but stated that it was impossible to bring in more than the 400,000 already there. He asked the Zionists themselves to declare that for the sake of peace, they would be willing to "stop immigration or at least to limit it".

Weizmann shocked his own colleagues when he tried to seize on the Egyptian "straw" of limiting immigration. He was over-ruled and corrected immediately by Ben-Gurion, who apologized cynically for "spoiling people's pleasure". He stated that the Zionists were indeed ready for "give-and-take negotiations", but there was no point in talking about any "slow-down", which was a one-sided concession. MacDonald tried in vain to persuade the sides to meet the next day. But the Arab-Jewish "negotiations" were at an end.

On the following day, MacDonald secured Cabinet approval for his own proposals, which, he declared, were the minimum that the Arab states would accept. The Arabs had demanded a maximum figure of 50,000 Jewish immigrants over 5 years. But MacDonald proposed they set the figure at 80,000. Only Walter Elliot, the Minister of Health, pointed to the gap between this figure and that originally approved by the Cabinet (150,000–300,000 over 10 years).

The Cabinet's only remaining concern was the perennial one – the risk that the new policy would provoke the Zionist lobby in the United States to stir up anti-British agitation. It was a sign of the times (one week before the Germans marched into Prague), that Prime Minister Chamberlain brushed aside this risk casually:

> If it was necessary to face an outbreak of anti-British feeling in the United States ... it was better that this should happen at a time like the present, rather than at a time of acute international crisis.[29]

As expected, at further meetings on 15 and 17 March, both the Jewish and the Palestinian delegations rejected the government's "final" offer.

In effect, all meaningful negotiations with the Jews and the Palestinians had ended on 8 March, but the London conference was not declared closed for another week. During this time, MacDonald and R.A. Butler of the Foreign Office held further meetings with the representatives of the Arab states, in an attempt to secure their agreement, or at least silent endorsement. A special Cabinet committee on Palestine met to discuss the additional concessions now demanded. At the Arabs' request, the ratio of Jews to Arabs on the proposed executive council was whittled down still further, from 3:2 to 2:1.

The Cabinet committee agreed also to establish an independent Palestine state after 10 years and, in the event of any postponement, to consult with the League of Nations and with the Arab states. The latter were thus granted a formal *locus standi* in Palestine.

The delegations of the Arab states left London, but further negotiations were conducted with them in Cairo, by Sir Miles Lampson, the British ambassador to Egypt. The Egyptians consulted the Mufti who, as feared by London, added new conditions, thereby effectively killing any chance of Britain securing the open approval of the Arab states. The Mufti demanded the formation of a Palestinian Cabinet once peace was restored to Palestine; a maximum of 75,000 Jewish immigrants, and a regular census to ensure that the Jews didn't exceed one-third of the total population; and finally, he demanded that the question of land sales to Jews be determined by mutual agreement between the High Commissioner and the Palestine Cabinet.

The British agreed to reduce their immigration proposal to 75,000 but refused to commit themselves to a regular census. In their own interests, they also rejected the demand to form a Palestinian Cabinet, since it might well expel the British themselves. Likewise, they refused to agree to any Arab control of the land market. Perhaps the most significant concession to the Arabs at Cairo was the deletion of the Jewish veto on the establishment of an independent state. This had been given to the Zionists in London as a quid pro quo for the Arab veto on all further Jewish immigration after 5 years.

On 20 April 1939, when the Cabinet committee confirmed the additional concessions to the Arabs, Chamberlain set the tone:

> We are now compelled to consider the Palestine problem mainly from the point of view of its effect on the international situation ... If we must offend one side, let us offend the Jews rather than the Arabs.[30]

The new White Paper was published on 17 May 1939. In its essentials, it followed the agreement reached between the British and the Arab states at Cairo. It contained three main proposals: the establishment of an independent Palestine state within 10 years, in treaty relations with Britain, and the appointment of Palestinians (two Arabs to each Jew) as heads of government departments, once peaceful conditions were restored to the country; the admission of 75,000 more Jews into Palestine over the next 5 years, subject to the economic absorptive capacity of the country, after which there would be no further immigration unless with Arab consent;[31] and third, it included new land regulations, restricting the sale of land to Jews to those areas where Jewish settlements already predominated, in order to consolidate these territorial blocs.

The new policy was criticized harshly in Parliament. The government's regular majority of 413 was reduced to 268, with 179 votes against, and an unprecedented 110 abstentions. Churchill joined the Labour and Liberal opposition in condemning the new policy. The Zionists were so impressed with his speech that they printed and circulated it. They found it convenient to forget that only the previous November Churchill had spoken in the Commons in favour of severe restrictions on Jewish immigration.[32] Now, in May 1939, Churchill asserted that the violation of Britain's public (Balfour) pledge would cause her potential allies to doubt if she could be relied upon.

A closer look at Churchill's speech shows that he did not in fact oppose the curtailment of Jewish immigration *per se*. For him, the "betrayal of the Balfour Declaration" lay in the veto given to the Arabs on all further immigration after 5 years:

> I select the one point upon which there is plainly a breach and repudiation of the Balfour Declaration – the provision that Jewish immigration can be stopped in five years' time by the decision of an Arab majority. That is a plain breach of a solemn obligation.[33]

True to form, Churchill seized the opportunity to attack the new policy as yet another one of Chamberlain's "shameful acts of appeasement":

> I could not stand by and see our solemn engagements into which Britain has entered before the world set aside for reasons of administrative convenience ... What will the world think about it? ... What will our potential enemies think? Will they not be encouraged by our confessions of recoil? Will they not be tempted to say: "They're on the run again. This is another Munich", and be the more stimulated in their aggression'?[34]

Leo Amery, another Conservative backbencher, thought that Churchill's speech was one of the best of his life. But he regretted the fact that the had "confined himself almost exclusively to rubbing in the one point that the complete stoppage of immigration was a breach of our pledges". Confirmation that the Arab veto was the only point that Churchill objected to is provided by MacDonald. In January 1940, he wrote the following private note to Chamberlain about Churchill's behaviour the previous May:

> I doubt whether, in his heart of hearts, he disagrees with the land policy; he certainly regards it as consistent with the Mandate, for he told me in the lobby that he would have supported us if it hadn't been for the Arab veto on immigration after five years.[35]

MacDonald's fate at the Colonial Office was similar to that of his predecessor, Ormsby-Gore, who fell from grace once he became the Minister responsible for Palestine. In a frank speech at the opening of the Commons debate on the 1939 White Paper, MacDonald stated:

> When the Prime Minister appointed me to the Colonial Office, a misguided friend of mine offered me warm congratulations. I replied that his

sentiments seemed hardly appropriate, since whatever policy the government pursued in Palestine, within twelve months I should be the most bitterly criticized Colonial Secretary of modern times. My calculation was wrong by two days.[36]

Not only the Zionists but Churchill too regarded MacDonald as a willing tool of Chamberlain's appeasement policies – and the symbol of their application in Palestine. When Churchill became Prime Minister in May 1940, he removed MacDonald from the Colonial Office, first to the Ministry of Health, and 9 months later, he "exiled" him to Canada, as the British High Commissioner.

In 1939, Britain's support for Zionism came full circle. After World War One, she had secured the mandate for Palestine largely by virtue of the Balfour Declaration. In 1939, on the eve of war, moral considerations were relegated to second place, behind *realpolitik*. The St James' conference was an exercise in colonial diplomacy and public relations, from which the Chamberlain administration knew exactly what it wanted, long before the conference opened.

During the course of the conference, when the government realized that it had miscalculated its ability to appease the Arab states, it simply compromised further – at the expense of the Zionists. The 1939 White Paper was a conscious, transparent act of appeasement, and with its publication Britain lost the moral and legal basis of her tenure in Palestine. The British Parliament and press condemned the government for its betrayal of past pledges – much as the Lloyd George and Baldwin governments had anticipated, less than 20 years before (see Chapter 7).

For the Zionists, timing was everything. The 1939 White Paper could not have come at a worse time for the Jewish people, on the eve of the greatest disaster ever to befall them. In a bitter public statement, the Jewish Agency lashed out at the government:

> It is in the darkest hour of Jewish history that the British Government proposes to deprive the Jews of their last hope and to close the road back to their Homeland. It is a cruel blow, doubly cruel; because it comes from a great nation which has extended a helping hand to the Jews, and whose position must rest on foundations of moral authority and international good faith ... The Jews will never accept the closing of the gates of Palestine nor let their national home be converted into a ghetto.[37]

MacDonald invited Weizmann to meet him, perhaps in the hope of calling on the credit of their warm relations in 1930–31. But Weizmann was blunt, to the point of being abusive:

> At least in Hitler one found the virtue of an absolutely frank brutality, whereas Mr MacDonald was covering up his betrayal of the Jews under a

semblance of legality ... [he] was handing over the Jews to their assassins.[38]

After the Commons vote on the White Paper, Weizmann was invited by Leo Amery to meet Harold Nicolson, an Independent Labour MP. Nicolson wrote the following account of their meeting to his wife, the novelist Vita Sackville-West:

> He [Weizmann] is more like Lenin than ever, but a Lenin who has been betrayed by those in whom he trusted. I fear our Palestine settlement is a terrible act of treachery and will do us great harm ... We are just handing the Jews over to the Arabs and giving up our mandate. That is what this amounts to ... We sat round feeing so helpless and ashamed.[39]

The League's Permanent Mandates Commission discussed the new policy in June 1939, and reported back that it was not consistent with its own interpretation of the mandate. The Commission's report required the approval of the League of Nations full Assembly. But World War Two began on 1 September 1939, before the League Assembly could pass judgement.

The Mufti vetoed the desire of the majority of the HAC to accept the White Paper, mainly since the British continued to insist upon his banishment from Palestine.[40] But the new policy was not designed to appease the Palestinians but the Arab states. Like that other instrument of appeasement, the Munich Agreement, it soon proved to be a broken reed. Although the 1939 White Paper remained the law of the land in Palestine for the duration of the war, it did not prevent the Mufti from collaborating first with the pro-Axis regime of Rashid Ali in Iraq, and from November 1941 with Mussolini, and with Hitler, whose guest he remained for the rest of the war. Nor did it prevent many Egyptians from regarding Nazi Germany as their saviour from British colonial rule.[41] The British concluded that the only way to ensure the Arabs' allegiance would be victories on the battlefield.

Notes

1 The strategic enclaves were the Haifa bay area, and a corridor running from the Lydda international airport to Jaffa, on the Mediterranean; the corridor included the main British army base in Palestine at Sarafand.
2 Michael J. Cohen, *Churchill and the Jews*, revised paperback edition, London: Frank Cass, 2004, pp. 173–75.
3 Melchett's record of dinner with Churchill, Z4/17121, Central Zionist Archives (CZA). On 2 January 1937, Britain and Italy signed the first "gentlemen's agreement", by which Italy recognized Britain's occupation of Egypt (of 1882) and the latter recognized Italy's conquest of Abyssinia (of 1936). In April 1938, the two countries signed a second "gentleman's agreement".
4 Melchett note, ibid.
5 Ms Dugdale agreed that Churchill had little or no idea of the issues involved; Dugdale diary, 9 June 1937, in Norman Rose, ed., *"Baffy": The Diaries of Blanche Dugdale, 1936 – 1947*, London: Vallentine Mitchell, 1973, p. 45.

Appeasement in the Middle East, 1937–39 305

6 Debate on 23 May 1939, *House of Commons Debates* (*H.C. Deb.*), 5th series, vol. 347, col. 2175.
7 Rose, "Baffy", p. 38. Pickthorne was the Unionist MP for Cambridge.
8 Minute by Harold Downie, 6 December 1937, CO 733/354, NA.
9 Iraq was granted nominal independence by Britain in 1930, and inducted as a member of the League of Nations, though Iraq continued to be regarded universally as a British vassal. Britain retained two strategic air bases in the country, at Habbaniya and Shaiba.
10 Cabinet memorandum of 17 November 1937, CP (37) 281, in Cab 24/273, NA.
11 Rendel minute, 11 February 1938, FO 371/21873, NA.
12 Ormsby-Gore to Chamberlain, 9 January 1938, FO 371/21862, NA.
13 War Office memorandum by Major Hawthorne, 9 February 1938, FO 371/2873, NA.
14 ibid.
15 Note by Bagallay, 21 March 1938, ibid. Rendel was appointed British Envoy Extraordinary to Bulgaria.
16 *Report of the Palestine Partition Commission* (Woodhead), October 1938, Cmd 5854, London: HMSO. Two of the Commission's four members recommended the creation of a Jewish state along a narrow coastal strip from Rehovot to Zichron Ya'acov, never more than 20 km wide, comprising just 5 per cent of Palestine; one member proposed an even smaller state, and one found that no practical plan of partition existed.
17 During the night of 8–9 November, the Nazis carried out a pogrom against German Jewry, which became known as Crystallnacht – the night of the broken glass. Over 90 Jews were killed and hundreds more injured; some 7500 Jewish shops and businesses and 177 synagogues were looted, destroyed and gutted. Some 35,000 Jews were arrested and sent to concentration camps. Insurance claims for lost and damaged property came to over $1.25 million. The House of Commons held a special debate on the pogrom on 21 November 1938.
18 MI 2A, 9 November 1938, in WO 106–1594B, NA. My emphasis.
19 Cohen, *Churchill*, p. 179.
20 Debate on 24 November 1938, *H. C. Deb.*, vol. 341, cols 1987–2017.
21 Cohen, *Churchill*, p. 180.
22 Bateman to Oliphant, 30 August 1938, FO 371/21881, NA.
23 ibid.
24 Chancellor–MacDonald interview of 17 September 1938, Prem. 1/352, NA.
25 Lord Reading, a former Chief Justice and Viceroy of India, and Rabbi Stephen Wise.
26 For details, cf. Michael J. Cohen, *Palestine: Retreat from the Mandate, 1936–1945*, London/New York: Paul Elek/Holmes and Meier, 1978, pp. 74–87.
27 On 12 March 1938, Nazi Germany annexed Austria, and on 15 March 1939, she marched into Prague, effectively annexing Czechoslovakia – thereby nullifying the Munich Agreement.
28 Cohen, *Palestine*, p. 75.
29 Meeting on 8 March 1939, ibid., p. 82. One week later, the Wehrmacht marched into Prague and turned Bohemia into a German Protectorate.
30 Cohen, *Palestine*, p. 84.
31 Gilbert Achcar writes mistakenly that the new policy provided for the immigration of 75,000 Jews *annually* for the next 5 years; *The Arabs and the Holocaust: The Arab-Israeli War of Narratives*, New York: Metropolitan Books/Henry Holt and Company, 2009, p. 143.
32 Churchill's speech was printed and published by the British Association for the Jewish National Home in Palestine.
33 Commons debate on Palestine White Paper, 22–23 May 1939, *H.C.Deb.*, vol. 347, col. 2168.
34 ibid.

35 Cohen, *Churchill*, p. 184.
36 Commons speech on 22 May 1939, in *H.C.Deb.*, vol. 347, col. 1937.
37 Wasserstein, *Britain and the Jews of Europe, 1939–1945*, London: Institute of Jewish Affairs/Clarendon Press, 1979, p. 20.
38 ibid, p. 21.
39 Letter of 17 May 1939, in *Harold Nicolson: Diaries and Letters, 1930–1964*, edited and condensed by Stanley Olson, New York: Atheneum, 1980, p. 150.
40 cf. Yehoshua Porath, *The Palestinian Arab National Movement, 1929–1939: From Riots to Rebellion*, London: Frank Cass, 1977, pp. 291–92, and Achcar, *The Arabs*, pp. 143–44.
41 Anwar Sadat, the future President of Egypt, spent most of the war either in British prison or as a fugitive.

14 World War Two
The Jews

> The emerging image of the great British leader [Churchill] appears to be more one of inspiration and determination than of leadership in detail.
> Gerhard Weinberg, *Germany, Hitler, and World War II*

Two seminal developments affected the Jewish people and the Zionists during World War Two: the Holocaust, the threatened physical elimination of European Jewry (some 12 million in 1939), and of the Yishuv in Palestine (some 450,000). In Europe, the Nazis murdered some 6 million Jews during the war; in Palestine, the threat of extinction hovered over the Yishuv for more than 2 and a half years. It was removed only during the winter of 1942–43, with the Allies' final defeat of Rommel's Afrika Korps.

The "lesson of the war" for the Jews and the Zionists was that they could not rely on the Great Powers to intervene on behalf of the Jewish Diaspora. All their appeals for operations to rescue Jews from Nazi-occupied Europe were met with either procrastination and/or rejection. In Palestine, the Yishuv could no longer rely on the mandatory Power, not even to furnish them with the elementary means for their own self-defence. The Zionists concluded that the fate of the remnants of the Jewish people now rested in their hands.

But first, we turn our attention to the military exigencies that confronted the British with the outbreak of World War Two.

Military exigencies

After World War One, strategic and political interests had sucked Britain into regions that lay outside its formal Empire. In the Middle East, both Egypt and Iraq were part of Britain's "informal" Empire – even if both states had formally been granted independence and neither had ever been technically part of the Empire. Both countries accommodated key strategic British air bases. Formally, British influence was provided for by treaty, but in practice it was guaranteed by the presence of British military forces. Until the Italian entry into the war, in June 1940, the Suez Canal served as a vital imperial artery on the short route to India. After Italy's entry, the Middle East became an active theatre of operations and the Mediterranean became hostile waters.

Egypt remained the theatre where Commonwealth forces (except Canadian) could most easily be concentrated.[1]

The defence of the Mediterranean and the Middle East was allotted a lower strategic priority than that of the British Isles and her Empire in the Far East. The Ten Year Rule and years of Treasury austerity had inflicted severe cuts on Britain's armed forces budget, leaving British naval bases and military installations in the Eastern Mediterranean devoid of the most basic of air defences. Most of the warships in the region were in need of modernization and barely operational. The scattered ground and air forces maintained in the region were equipped for colonial policing duties rather than for strategic defence.[2]

Until the very eve of World War Two, Britain had no plans for the defence of the Middle East. The Mediterranean was seen primarily as a staging ground and training centre for a fleet that would be needed to defend the Empire east of Suez. An attempt would be made to hold Egypt and the Suez Canal. The Canal Zone military base was still the largest in the world. Yet Italian air power and submarines had made control of the Mediterranean a difficult challenge. In 1938, the COS grudgingly agreed to a piecemeal solution – to build up British forces in Egypt to "self-sufficiency", in the hope that they would be able to withstand attacks for up to 2 months, until external assistance could arrive. But the Middle East might have to be abandoned, in the hope that victories in the major theatres of war would enable Britain to restore her position there later on.[3]

If the British could accept the temporary loss of the Middle East, the loss of Empire in the Far East might well be irretrievable. Moreover, the British were committed by repeated assurances to Australia and New Zealand that no interests in the Mediterranean would be allowed to interfere with the dispatch of a strong fleet to Singapore. These promises were given partly because Britain needed the ANZAC military forces to make up her own deficiencies.[4]

Palestine occupied a special place in Britain's Middle Eastern strategy. It was supposed to provide a reserve area and strategic depth, not only for the defence of Egypt and the Suez Canal, but for the Middle East as a whole. As noted already (in Chapter 12), the COS had determined in April 1938 that in the event of partition, Britain would retain a strategic corridor from Jerusalem to Jaffa, to include Sarafand, the main British army base in Palestine, and the airfields that it had built at Ramleh and Aqir.

By 1939, Palestine had also become a geo-strategic entrepôt, essential to Britain's air communications with India and the overland route to Iraq, the country through which Britain's vital oil supplies flowed. In wartime, in the event of the Suez Canal being closed to British shipping, the Baghdad-Haifa road would be needed to bring reinforcements to the Middle East from India. Haifa was the port through which any reinforcements for Palestine had to pass. Haifa was also a potential naval base for light vessels operating in the eastern Mediterranean – a wartime supplement to the main operations base at Alexandria – and the Mediterranean terminus of the oil pipeline from Iraq.

All of these interests depended upon stable security conditions in Palestine. Finally, in the event that the Egyptians refused to renew the 1936 treaty after its expiry in 1956, Palestine might become essential for holding an imperial reserve for the Middle East.[5]

Yet by the late 1930s, Palestine had become a serious strategic liability. The Arab rebellion fostered anti-British nationalism throughout the Middle East, at a time when Britain's prestige had sunk to a nadir, following Italy's conquest of Ethiopia and the significant build-up of her forces in Libya. In early 1938 the COS warned:

> The most probable cause of any Arab combination against the British Empire would be the thought that Italy was replacing us in the Middle East.[6]

As seen already, the Arab rebellion peaked during the summer of 1938, forcing the diversion of troops and equipment from Egypt to Palestine. For this reason, the unrest in Palestine was a source of constant concern for Sir Miles Lampson, the influential ambassador in Cairo. Anxious about the return of the strategic reserve from Palestine to the Canal Zone, he pressed the home government repeatedly to abandon its support of the Zionist cause. The prospect that Arab opposition might require the deployment of additional British forces to the region also had implications for Britain's ability to meet the German threat in Europe. In mid-September 1938, at the height of the Munich crisis, the COS warned:

> We regard with grave concern the possibility of the spread of disaffection to other Muslim Countries, involving us in a steadily increasing military commitment in the Middle East ... one which would be a most serious embarrassment to us in the event of war with Germany.[7]

Finally, the crises that confronted Britain during the summer and autumn of 1938 found her at her most vulnerable, militarily. In the summer of 1937, the Chamberlain government had decided on a £1500 million 5-year rearmament programme. As capital ships were taken out of service for refitting, the fleet passed through an extended period of weakness. The worst and most dangerous phase began in 1938 and was expected to end only in late 1939.[8]

Strategic dilemmas: the Jewish Division scheme[9]

It is impossible to understand British policy on Palestine during Churchill's first 2 years as wartime Prime Minister without monitoring closely the dire military crises that he faced on the battlefields of northern Europe and the Middle East. During this period, his every thought and effort were given to the very survival of the Empire, and of Britain herself as a sovereign state.

310 *World War Two: The Jews*

The conflicting priorities of the British and the Yishuv appeared at times to present zero-sum situations. From 1940 to 1942, the British government lived in constant fear of a German invasion of the British Isles. In the summer of 1940, Britain also faced a challenge to her hegemony in the Middle East – initially by Mussolini, whose forces outnumbered the British in that theatre, and from the spring of 1941, by Rommel's Afrika Korps. Facing the prospect of defeat in Egypt, the British drew up plans to evacuate their Middle East garrison. Their plans did not include the Jews who lived in the Arab Middle East. They would have faced the same fate as the Jews of Europe.[10] At the Arab-Jewish "round-table" conference in February 1939, the Colonial Secretary had warned the Zionist delegation that the fate of the Yishuv was linked to that of the British:

> If war broke out the Middle East might be the British Empire's "Achilles' Heel". The defeat of the British Empire ... would be a disaster as much for the Jews as for Britain.[11]

When the Germans invaded the Soviet Union in June 1941, Britain's future appeared to hinge upon the ebb and flow of the titanic clashes between the Wehrmacht and the Red Army. But the decisive battles between the German and Soviet armies were not fought until 1943.

On 10 May 1940, the very day that Churchill became Prime Minister, Hitler's Panzers began their blitzkrieg against the Low Countries and northern France. During the last week in May, it seemed inevitable that the bulk of the Anglo-French forces trapped by the Wehrmacht on the beaches of Dunkirk – some 224,000 British and 111,00 French troops – would either be killed or taken prisoner. Miraculously, the vast majority was rescued, although most of their equipment was abandoned on the beaches. The RAF lost 1000 aircraft over northern France, half of them fighters.[12] When Churchill celebrated the "miraculous deliverance" from Dunkirk in the House of Commons, he added the sober reservation: "but wars are not won by evacuations".

Churchill never again experienced such a profound and lasting shock as during those first weeks in office, when France was destroyed as a military power and the British were swept off the continent with apparent ease. British planning had assumed that her forces would fight the Wehrmacht alongside the French, albeit in a subordinate role – ten British to 94 French divisions. But within a few weeks at the end of May 1940, the main pillars of Britain's pre-war strategy collapsed. These disasters left an indelible impression on Churchill. For the rest of the war, he feared confronting a major German force on the battlefield. In October 1943 he and the COS would resist American demands to begin with the Normandy landings.[13]

The Royal Navy and the RAF saved the British from total defeat in 1940. British strategists planned to build up strength by sea power and to erode the Germans' strength by strategic bombing, in the hope that the German empire might implode from within, as it had done in 1918. The COS hoped that this would occur by 1942. But it would take 4 years before the Allied air campaign began to produce the results predicted by its advocates.[14]

Britain's strategic imperatives changed during the first 2 weeks of June 1940 – with the Italian declaration of war on the 10th and the French collapse on the 14th. Britain's first priority became preparations for the defence of the home islands against a German invasion. General Ironside, C in C Home Forces, predicted that the Germans would invade on 10 July 1940. The German invasion never happened. But on that day, 70 German aircraft bombed dockyards in Wales. The Germans had decided to precede a ground invasion with a punitive bombing campaign and the destruction of the RAF. The war for control of British skies had begun – the Battle of Britain. The turning point in the campaign came on 7 September, when Goering switched the Luftwaffe's attacks from RAF airfields to London and other cities. It was a monumental strategic error. England's urban population would pay a terrible price but the RAF survived, and kept Britain in the war in Europe.

Since July 1940, when Italy opened hostilities against the British in the Middle East, urgent calls went out for the services of the Palestine garrison – 11 battalions of well-trained and equipped British troops. The Middle East Command wanted the garrison to return to its primary strategic mission – the defence of the Suez Canal. Churchill insisted that the garrison return home, to help defend the shores of southern England against the anticipated German invasion. In order to relieve the British garrison in Palestine, he proposed that the Yishuv be armed and trained to take over the garrison's security duties. He expected that in the event of disturbances, the Jews would be able to cope easily with the Arabs. This prognosis rested in part on Churchill's contempt for the Arabs. Malcolm MacDonald reported one unguarded outburst in the late 1930s: "the Arabs were barbaric hordes who ate little but camel dung".[15]

In Churchill's private evidence before the Peel Commission in 1937, which he forbade the Commission to publish, he asserted that the "hordes of Islam" had "smashed up" Palestine, and the Arabs had left the country desert for "thousands of years".[16]

In October 1940, Churchill succeeded in pushing through the Cabinet a scheme to raise a Jewish Division, against the all but unanimous opposition of the ministers concerned. They warned that the Zionists had ulterior political motives, that the Arabs throughout the Middle East would rebel against the British. Guy Liddell, head of counter-espionage at MI5, articulated the position of the Whitehall establishment. In a private diary entry written in February 1941, on the eve of the first postponement of the Division scheme, he wrote:

> Although there may be considerable advantages in the scheme both from the point of finance in America and technical skill, I cannot help feeling it is a blunder, since the whole project will be used as propaganda against

us both by the Arabs and by the enemy. It will, moreover, pin us down to granting concessions to the Jews in Palestine after the war. It is one of those things which are done in time of strain and which are bitterly regretted afterwards.[17]

The Division scheme would be postponed repeatedly, and ultimately shelved in 1941 due to the veto of General Wavell, the hard-pressed C in C Middle East.

The Zionists were divided among themselves about the role to be assigned to the Jewish Division. The London-based Weizmann wanted it to fight in Europe against the Germans. He believed that a Jewish contribution to the Allied war effort would ensure the Zionists a seat at the peace conference, where this time, they would hold out for nothing less than a Jewish state. But Ben-Gurion, the Yishuv's leader, insisted that the Division was needed in Palestine, to ensure its physical survival. Ben-Gurion appreciated Weizmann's diplomatic assets, but believed that he had lost touch with realities in Palestine.

The passage of the 1939 White Paper had shocked the Zionists but until the entry of the Americans into the war in December 1941, they had no one else to turn to. Churchill's public opposition to the White Paper had rekindled the Zionists' hope. Once in the Cabinet, from September 1939, as First Lord of the Admiralty, Churchill assiduously kept the Zionists briefed about his efforts to block the implementation of the White Paper.

But once he became Prime Minister, Churchill's view of Zionist demands was subordinated to Britain's own strategic imperatives. Churchill was undoubtedly the dominant figure in British politics during the war, and rightfully earned a reputation as one of the strongest Prime Ministers in British history. He gave due warning to his Cabinet that he would abrogate the Palestine White Paper, but *after* the war. During his wartime ministry, he did nothing to abrogate it.

A rare, tantalizing glimpse of Churchill's views on Palestine and the Middle East is provided by the private diary of Henry Morgenthau Jr, the American Secretary of the Treasury, who visited London in August 1944. Morgenthau came for talks on his plan for "pastoralizing" Germany after the war. At one point in the discussion, with Foreign Secretary Eden present, Morgenthau raised the issue of saving Hungarian Jewry – a "problem" which the British feared might lead to a demand to allow large numbers of Hungarian Jews into Palestine. Morgenthau recorded Churchill's reply in his diary: "Churchill stated that he was against lifting the White Paper immigration quota in order to get the Hungarian Jews out, because he had promised the Arabs that while the war was on he would allow the [1939 White Paper] quota to stand".[18]

During the first crisis years of 1940–42, Churchill's Colonial Office rationed out the White Paper immigration quotas with extreme parsimony.[19] The department became obsessed with the alleged threat that the Germans would infiltrate Nazi agents among the new immigrants. In April 1940, the ubiquitous Shuckburgh, now Deputy Under-Secretary at the Colonial Office, wrote a paranoid internal memo, complaining about the Jews' lack of consideration for British interests:

> I am convinced that in their hearts they hate us and have always hated us; they hate all Gentiles ... So little do they care for Great Britain as compared with Zionism that they cannot even keep their hands off illegal immigration, which they must realize is a very serious embarrassment to us when we are fighting for our very existence.[20]

One year later, Harold F. Downie, head of the Palestine desk at the Colonial Office, added his own comment on the flight of Jewish refugees from Hitler's Europe: "This sort of thing makes one regret that the Jews are not on the other side of the war".[21] Ironically, some Foreign Office officials regarded comments like these as neurotic. One official proffered the following analysis of Downie's state of mind. It included the insinuation that the *Protocols of the Elders of Zion* were still alive and well inside the Colonial Office:

> One has ... to take into account Mr Downie's inward and spiritual conviction that illegal immigration is only the outward and visible sign of a world-wide scheme to overthrow the British Empire ... If one has a personal conviction that the Jews are our enemy just as the Germans are, but in a more insidious way, it becomes essential to find reasons for believing that our two sets of enemies are linked together by secret and evil bonds ... irrespective of the evidence we can produce ... The Foreign Office should, I submit, be careful not to tar itself with the brush of Mr Downie's curious and unprofitable beliefs.[22]

During the period 1939–42, the government twice banned all Jewish immigration for 6 months – notwithstanding the White Paper policy. The 5-year immigration quota of 75,000 certificates (of which 25,000 were earmarked for Jewish refugees) was rationed out so stringently that the full quota was not exhausted until December 1945.[23]

As seen already, since 1937, Churchill shared the British consensus that the establishment of a Jewish state in Palestine would drive the Arabs into the enemy camp. During the war, he was concerned about the Zionists primarily for two reasons: first and foremost, due to his enduring conviction about the power of the Zionist lobby in Washington to harm Anglo-American relations. This belief became critical during World War Two, due to his conviction that Britain could not prevail over Germany without the Americans. Since 1939 (in his secret correspondence with President Roosevelt),[24] Churchill laboured hard to persuade Roosevelt to join Britain in hostilities against Germany. On 7 June 1940, while he was still digesting the "miracle of Dunkirk", he called in Weizmann and asked him to leave as soon as possible for the United States, and to use his influence "in spurring Jewish public opinion to throw its whole weight into helping the Allies in the war". Four days later, Weizmann replied, asking for "some proof that Jewish effort ... will not be spurned, as it has been hitherto".[25]

Churchill's anxieties about securing American support had increased at the end of 1939, when the ambassador in Washington reported that the Zionist lobby was agitating against the Palestine White Paper, whose restrictions on land sales had not yet been promulgated. Churchill's Christmas Day Cabinet memorandum has been cited already in Chapter 2. It reminded ministers that in 1917 the government had not issued the Balfour Declaration "for light or sentimental reasons" and that now, at the end of 1939, they needed "to conciliate American Jewry and enlist their aid in combating isolationist anti-British tendencies in the United States" even more than they had in 1917.[26]

Churchill's warnings were countered by Shuckburgh, his own appointee to the Colonial Office back in 1921:

> The importance in present circumstances of retaining the goodwill of the United States needs no demonstration; but it is very doubtful whether the influence of the American Jews over the United States Government or over general opinion in American is really as potent as the Zionists and their supporters would have us believe ... There is evidence to show that Jewish stock in the United States is on the decline ... I doubt whether we need be unduly alarmed over the American bugbear. In any case we ought not to allow it to deflect us from the policy which we have deliberately adopted on the Palestine question.[27]

Churchill was virtually isolated inside the Cabinet on the Zionist issue. The new restrictions on land purchases by Jews were duly enacted in February 1940. Churchill's memorandum of Christmas Day 1939 remains of purely academic interest, an expression of one of his major motives for supporting the Zionists.

As noted already, Churchill's second interest in Palestine, until the threat of a German invasion had passed, was his obsession with the need to bring home the 11 battalions of the British garrison in Palestine. When the war began, Weizmann had offered Chamberlain the mobilization of the Jewish people for the Allied war effort. But the Whitehall officials were concerned above all not to repeat the "mistakes" of the First World War – giving wartime concessions or promises that would have to be redeemed after the war. The officials were alarmed when Weizmann's offer was accompanied by his hint that the differences between the British and the Zionists over the White Paper would now give way to "greater and more pressing necessities".[28]

Whitehall's opposition was due to its fear that if Britain raised a Jewish force, she would be accused by the Arabs of arming the Jews in order to take over Palestine. This would obviously be regarded as a betrayal of the promises given to them in the 1939 White Paper. In addition, it was feared that a Jewish force would resist any future political settlement not to the Zionists' liking. This contingency was particularly ominous given Britain's awareness of its own vulnerability in the region. Therefore, until May 1940, the stock reply to all Zionist offers of military aid was that any Jews wishing to fight in the Allied ranks could do so in established British units, commanded by British officers.[29]

Churchill had considered the possibility of arming the Yishuv since he first joined the Chamberlain Cabinet. At his first wartime meeting with Weizmann, in September 1939, he told the Zionist leader that he was very interested in the Jewish army project. In mid-October, he was given a memorandum on the project prepared by Captain Orde Wingate. On 3 September 1940, he again met with Weizmann to discuss Wingate's Jewish army scheme. The main appeal of the scheme was its promise that a Jewish force could be ready within 4 months to assume responsibility for internal security in Palestine. Wingate proposed the establishment of an entirely Jewish force of 20,000, to be trained by 1000 Jewish officers, and in addition, the establishment of a Jewish commando unit to fight in the Western desert.[30]

Brendan Bracken, one of Churchill's close advisors, warned him that Wingate's proposal was "desperately controversial" and likely to be strongly opposed by the Colonial Office. He added that the Jews were "unreasonably impatient" and that Weizmann was "pressing strongly for immediate and definite arrangements regarding this scheme for training officers".[31]

But Churchill dreaded to think of Washington's reaction if Britain should leave the Yishuv defenceless against either local Arab violence or an Axis invasion. In October 1939, he asked the Cabinet to approve his own revision of Wingate's scheme. However, in total disregard of the realities of intercommunal strife in Palestine, he vitiated the scheme by proposing a mixed force of Palestinian Arabs and Jews. His main argument was that a local military force would allow the British troops to return home. Predictably, Colonial Secretary MacDonald warned against doing anything to arouse Arab fears that they were arming the Jews to take over the country. But instead of rejecting Churchill's scheme outright, the Cabinet resorted to a worn bureaucratic device – it sent his proposal for investigation by a committee of officials from the Colonial and War Offices.[32]

The War Office warned that the arming of Palestinian units would inhibit the fitting out of the heavy British reinforcements that would be required the following spring for the Western Front. The department objected also that the Arabs could not be relied on, and proposed instead that if the garrison in Palestine had to be redeployed, they should concentrate a small rearguard in defence of strategic points such as Haifa, the main railway and possibly Jerusalem. The Colonial Office officials focused on the political implications of Churchill's scheme. They warned that the deployment of a Jewish military force to quell Arab disorders would set Palestine and the neighbouring Arab states ablaze. Shuckburgh warned that the Jews were pressing for a military force in order to be in a position to dictate their own terms for the ultimate political settlement in Palestine.[33] No one addressed the very real dangers facing the Yishuv.

The need to bring home the Palestine garrison was again on the Cabinet agenda on 12 February 1940, at the same meeting that took the final decision to enact the land regulations. MacDonald, supported by the Prime Minister, warned that any withdrawal of British troops from Palestine would lead immediately to a new outburst of the Arab-Jewish conflict. He conceded that if the security situation in Palestine improved, they might release the British forces stationed there, gradually. Churchill's response is worth citing in full, as a reflection of his total preoccupation with the defence of the home country:

> The sound policy for Great Britain at the beginning of the war would have been to build up ... a strong Jewish armed force in Palestine ... It was an extraordinary position that at a time when the war was probably entering its most dangerous phase, we should station in Palestine a garrison one-quarter of the size of our garrison in India – and this for the purpose of forcing through a policy which, in his judgment was unpopular in Palestine and Great Britain alike.[34]

Oliver Stanley, the Secretary of State for War, agreed on the need to bring the Palestine garrison home but he opposed the mobilization of either Arab or Jewish units in Palestine. The Foreign Secretary, Lord Halifax, reminded the meeting that the Palestine problem had wider ramifications, "extending throughout the Moslem world". The Cabinet dismissed the scheme.

The project to raise a Jewish military force had to wait on Churchill's appointment as Prime Minister, in May 1940. The Zionists hoped that the man who had attacked the government's Palestine White Paper when in opposition would now abrogate it, or at least mitigate its restrictions. But as noted, Churchill's arrival at Number 10 Downing Street coincided with a precipitous deterioration in Britain's military position – Dunkirk and Italy's entry into the war. The Middle East became an active war front. In the Western desert, the Italians had ten divisions facing two British. The physical threat to the Yishuv became immediate. In July 1940, the Italians began a series of bombing raids on Palestine, mainly but not only on Tel Aviv and Haifa (where the oil terminals and refinery were prime targets). One raid on Tel Aviv on 9 September 1940 left 137 dead.

The Arabs were impressed by Germany's early blitzkrieg victories over Belgium, Holland and France. They had not forgotten Britain's impotence in the face of Italy's conquest of Ethiopia (1935–36). They regarded Italy's entry into the war and the air raids on Palestine as presaging the end of the British mandate, together with her sponsorship of the Jewish National Home "experiment". At that juncture, in the summer of 1940, with the Battle of Britain about to begin, Britain's prospects in the Middle East did not appear to be at all promising.

The leaders of the Yishuv were no less sceptical. In 1939, Ben-Gurion had called on the Yishuv to fight the White Paper as if there were no war, and to join the British war effort against the Nazis as if there were no White Paper. With Rommel's arrival in North Africa in February 1941, the fate of the Jewish National Home now hung by a thread. The Jews feared that with the Afrika Korps menacing Egypt, the Palestinian Arabs, with help from their neighbours, would renew their rebellion.

Once at Number 10 Downing Street, Churchill placed the full weight of his position behind the demand that the British garrison be brought home from Palestine. On 18 May he pressed the COS:

> I cannot feel that we have enough trustworthy troops in England, in view of the large numbers [of German troops] that may be landed from air-carriers preceded by parachutists ... the transports which brought the Australians to Suez should bring home 8 battalions of Regular Infantry from Palestine, properly convoyed, even at some risk, by whichever routes is thought best.[35]

But the COS opposed the transfer, on both military and political grounds. They argued that the Mediterranean route was now too risky for troop transports, and if the troops were shipped via the Cape, they would not be available for fighting anywhere for several weeks. They warned that if Britain lost her imperial assets in the Middle and Far East, their own tiny island would in any case be unable to resist Germany. Not only that, but they argued that the evacuation of the Palestine garrison – their only reserve of trained, equipped troops in the Middle East – was likely to have a serious effect on their allies in the region, especially on Turkey, now wavering in her neutrality. Their allies would lose faith in Britain's ability to defend them, and the Italians would be encouraged correspondingly.

During the final stages of the retreat of the Allied armies to Dunkirk, Churchill focused exclusively on preparing for what he feared might be England's "last stand" – the defence of her coasts against a German invasion. His reply to the COS on 23 May indicates the depth of his fears:

> It is no use talking about a strategic reserve for the Middle East when we are in our present position at home. Even if these troops go round by the Cape they could be here in six weeks.

At the same time, Churchill was trying to persuade Lord Lloyd, his own appointee in place of Macdonald at the Colonial Office, to agree to a new Jewish army scheme, one he had just received from Ze'ev Jabotinsky, the Revisionist leader. Lloyd's reply, in which Shuckburgh's hand may be discerned, was a disappointment. He asserted that both the Arabs and the Jews of Palestine already had enough opportunity to contribute to the British war effort. He warned of the Zionists' ulterior political motives which, he claimed, Weizmann did not bother to conceal:

> It is clear that proposals of this kind, whether emanating from the New Zionists [Revisionists] or from the Zionists, have as their prime object the

recognition of the Jewish people as a nation, with a standing in the War Councils of the Allies and ultimately in the discussion of the terms of peace. In both cases the conversion of Palestine into a Jewish State as a reward for Jewish military assistance is the objective.[36]

Churchill was too preoccupied with the immediate and present danger facing Britain to give serious consideration to any long-term consequences of arming the Zionists. He brushed aside the inconvenient facts of the matter:

> I do not want Jewish forces raised to serve outside Palestine. The main and almost sole aim in Palestine at the present time is to liberate the 11 battalions of excellent Regular troops who are now tethered there. For this purpose the Jews should be armed in their own defence, and properly organized as speedily as possible. We can always prevent them from attacking the Arabs by our sea power which cuts them off from the outer world, and by other friendly influences. On the other hand, we cannot leave them unarmed when our troops leave, as leave they must at a very early date.[37]

On 25 May, as the situation of the Allied armies became yet more desperate, the COS circulated a memorandum to the war Cabinet entitled: "British Strategy in a Certain Eventuality". The eventuality referred to was the defeat of France, and Italy's entry into the war. The COS asserted that Britain would be unable to continue fighting Germany alone unless she received the "full economic and financial support" of the United States.[38] Churchill's demand to bring home the Palestine garrison was discussed briefly at a Cabinet meeting 4 days later. He reduced his demand that the entire garrison be shipped out of Palestine, insisting now that eight of the 11 battalions be brought home. But he did not attempt to over-rule the COS, who still protested. Within a few days, the unexpected safe evacuation of the Allied forces from Dunkirk reduced the urgency of bringing home the Palestine garrison.

Further, the rapidly changing war situation required changes in planning. In June 1940, the French surrender and the Italian declaration of war meant that in addition to the threat of a German invasion, Britain had to gird herself for an Italian attack against Egypt. No one in the Cabinet now questioned the need to transfer the garrison from Palestine to Egypt, and the consequent need to mobilize alternative security forces in Palestine. At the end of July, a special Cabinet committee decided to mobilize six indigenous battalions in Palestine to relieve the Palestine garrison: three Arab and three Jewish, 1000 men from each community. The new units were to be called the "Palestine Buffs". But the scheme faltered, due to the failure of the Palestinian Arabs to match the level of Jewish recruiting. At the end of August, Lloyd informed Weizmann that due to the low level of Arab recruitment, Jewish recruitment would have to be cut by half, to 500. He proposed that any Jews in excess of 500 might join a Jewish force to serve outside Palestine.

According to War Office sources, just 9041 Palestinian Arabs volunteered to serve in the British army during the whole course of the war.[39]

Following Italian advances into British Somaliland in early August 1940, Churchill again demanded that they arm the Yishuv, so as to allow the Palestine garrison to leave for the Canal Zone. On the 12th of the month he reprimanded General Wavell, C in C British Forces, Middle East, who opposed the proposal:

> I do not consider that proper use is being made of the large [British] forces in Palestine. The essence of the situation depends upon arming the Jewish colonists sufficiently to enable them to undertake their own defence, so that if necessary for a short time the whole of Palestine can be left to very small British forces.[40]

Four days later, Churchill issued a general directive to the War Office, ordering Wavell to transfer at short notice most of the Commonwealth forces, the Polish Brigade and a French volunteer unit from Palestine to the Nile Delta base.[41] But Wavell was reluctant to consider any wider scheme of Jewish recruitment until he had had a chance to assess the quality of the Palestinians already recruited into the "Buffs" scheme. The Colonial Office weighed in with its adamant opposition to any large-scale recruitment of Palestinian Jews.

On 3 September, Weizmann presented Churchill with a further plan: the mobilization of a Jewish Division of 10,000 and a "Jewish desert unit" to be commanded by Wingate. Churchill approved the plan, and authorized Weizmann to take it to the War Office.[42] The pace of negotiations increased in mid-September, influenced by the heavy Italian bombing raids on Palestine. British concern to defend the Suez Canal now outweighed all other considerations. On 13 September, Eden, the Secretary of State for War, advised Weizmann that the Jewish Division project had been accepted by all the departments concerned and it remained only for the Cabinet to give its formal approval.

The Jewish Division scheme not only aroused grave apprehension at Whitehall, but as noted already, it also caused a serious schism within the Zionist leadership. At a meeting of Zionist leaders in London on 18 September, Weizmann argued that a significant Jewish military contribution to the Allied war effort would bring the reward of a sovereign Jewish state. He chose to ignore Lloyd's demurral that recruits would not be allowed to demobilize and settle in Palestine after the war. But Ben-Gurion's first priority remained to arm the Yishuv for its own self-defence and only second, to join Britain's fight against Nazi Germany.

Weizmann reported that Lloyd feared Arab opposition to a Jewish force in Palestine. He asked rhetorically whether they should insist on the Division serving in Palestine – and thereby risk rejection – or accept what they could get now and ask for more later? Ben-Gurion conceded that they should take what they could get now, but insisted that the vital question was whether the Jewish units would be raised to fight anywhere or only in Palestine and the Middle East? He could not ask the Yishuv to join an army to fight outside Palestine. Weizmann warned:

> It was in the hands of Ben-Gurion to make or mar the scheme ... if they quibbled now, it would show lack of vision and confidence which in present circumstances would be deadly.[43]

The division between Weizmann and Ben-Gurion was never bridged. On 10 October 1940 the Cabinet agreed in principle to mobilize the Jewish Division. The project was forced through by Churchill who, as usual, dismissed the Arab factor. However, the Cabinet shackled the scheme with draconian conditions that were almost the antithesis of those sought by Ben-Gurion. The Division would number 10,000 men, of whom no more than 3000 could be mobilized in Palestine. Each recruit would be required to furnish a guarantee that he would be received back in his home country; the Division would be trained in Britain and no guarantee would be given about the theatre of war in which it would serve. Ever wary of the Zionist factor in American politics, the Cabinet decided to delay the official announcement until after the American presidential elections, due to take place on 5 November 1940. In the meantime, Weizmann was allowed to proceed with negotiations with the War Office on the administrative details of the scheme. At the end of the year, a commander of the proposed Division was appointed – Brigadier L.A. Hawes, the officer who had organized the shipment of the British Expeditionary Force to France.[44]

The delay in the official announcement gave the scheme's opponents at Whitehall the time to muster their arguments against it. During the winter of 1940–41, Britain suffered further military setbacks in the Balkans, which raised Turkey's neutrality to a premium and heightened fears of adverse Moslem reactions. All the departments concerned with Palestine and the Middle East remained fundamentally opposed to the scheme, especially to the inclusion of the word "Jewish" in the official announcement. In contrast to Churchill, they saw only the ramifications of the scheme, even in its present, emasculated version, for the Arab world. The following Foreign Office memo, written in January 1941, reflects Whitehall's total alienation from the Zionist cause, and its cynical approach to the Division scheme:

> The fundamental objection to the present scheme is that it is to be run by the Jewish Agency for *Palestine* ... It is to be operated by Dr Weizmann and his little clique of Palestine Zionists ... The fact that the Palestine Zionists are taking a lead in this matter will be regarded as evidence that the scheme has a direct connection with Palestinian affairs. The Arabs will believe that, somehow or other, the scheme is to benefit and strengthen the Jewish National Home in Palestine, presumably at the expense of Arab interests ... Dr Weizmann wishes to establish a claim on British gratitude in order that at the end of the war he may be in a

stronger position to induce HMG to relax their restrictions on Jewish immigration into Palestine.[45]

The officials argued also that the scheme might well boomerang against Britain. It would generate American expectations, if not demands, that they reward the Zionists with political concessions after the war. Not only that but they warned presciently of Zionist resentment if the Division was not allowed to fight in Palestine.

In January, a bitter dispute broke out between Eden and Weizmann. The latter was disillusioned when informed by Eden that the official announcement would make no mention of the Jewish Agency or of service in the Middle East. Weizmann also reacted violently to the demand that each recruit furnish a guarantee that after the war he would return to his home country. He felt humiliated by the insinuation that the Zionists intended using the Division as a "back door" into Palestine. He protested that millions would use the "front door".

In February 1941, additional opposition to the scheme came from Professor Rushbrook-Williams, director of Middle East propaganda at the Ministry of Information. He warned that the announcement of the Jewish Division now would be seized upon by Axis propaganda as proof of British subservience to the Jews. The Ministry urged further delay, warning that the "effect upon the Palestinian Arabs and upon the Middle East in general would be little short of disastrous".[46]

Opposition to the Division scheme peaked during the spring of 1941. General Wavell was under extreme pressure. Wavell's forces had been on the point of routing the last elements of the Italian army in North Africa when Churchill, using dubious means, secured a Cabinet decision ordering him to divert 20,000 troops from the operations in Tripoli to Greece. Churchill overrode the opposition of his top military advisors, who warned that they would be letting the Italians escape complete defeat, whereas a British intervention in Greece was bound to fail, as indeed it did.[47] At the end of February, with his troops already in transit to Greece, Wavell insisted that he could not accept the extra risk of Arab disturbances if the Jewish Division scheme were announced:

> It is vitally important that for the next six months at least I should be free as possible from commitments and anxieties in Palestine, Iraq and Syria.
>
> If this Jewish contingent is to be raised at all, I consider it essential that para 10 of the White Paper[48] on Palestine should be implemented first and that the raising of contingent should be dependent on Jewish acceptance and implementation of this.
>
> If any of the contingents are to be raised in Palestine they must be trained outside Middle East. In no circumstances must contingent be sent to Middle East ... It would however be much best not to raise contingent at all especially in view of general shortage of equipment.[49]

Churchill had yet to savour a major victory, and Wavell was now facing two campaigns simultaneously: in the Western desert and in Greece. Churchill did not feel able to over-rule his commander in the field, and he ceded ungracefully. On 1 March, he vented his spleen in a letter to the newly incumbent Colonial Secretary, Lord Moyne, yet another of his personal friends:

> General Wavell, like most British military officers, is strongly pro-Arab ... I am not in the least convinced by all this stuff. The Arabs, under the impression of recent victories [over the Italians], would not make any trouble now. However, in view of the *"Lustre"* policy [the Greek expedition] I do not wish General Wavell worried by lengthy arguments about matters of no military consequence to the immediate situation. Therefore, Dr Weizmann should be told that the Jewish Division project must be put off for six months, but may be reconsidered again in four months. The sole reason given should be lack of equipment.[50]

One month later, Churchill's comment about the docility of the Arab world turned out to be misplaced. On 1 April 1941, Rashid Ali staged a *coup d'état* against the pro-British Royal House in Iraq. On 2 May, with German help, he rebelled against the British.

When writing his memoirs after World War Two, Churchill conjectured that if only he had had a Jewish Division to keep order in Palestine, the "mass of fine troops" – British and ANZAC – tied down in Palestine might have prevailed over the Germans in Greece. In a vituperative first draft, written in 1948, he complained that his wish to arm the Jewish settlers had "encountered every kind of resistance" and asserted:

> All our military men disliked the Jews and loved the Arabs. General Wavell was no exception. Some of my most trusted Ministers like Lord Lloyd, and, of course, the Foreign Office, were all pro-Arab, if they were not actually anti-Semitic.[51]

One of his ghost-writers, Sir Norman Brook, Secretary to the Cabinet from 1947 to 1962, persuaded Churchill to delete the passage – not because he disputed its veracity, but because in the middle of the first Arab-Israeli war the comment might be taken out of context.

On 4 March 1941, Lord Moyne informed Weizmann of the decision to hold up the Jewish Division scheme. Disingenuously, he reassured him that it was not a reversal of the previous favourable decision. Weizmann was demonstrably incredulous, unable to believe the lack of equipment excuse. But on the eve of another of his long trips to the United States, he had no time to lobby against the decision.

Churchill agreed unwillingly to the delay of the scheme. But at this critical stage of the war, he was concerned more than ever to secure an early

American entry, and anxious to forestall any anti-British propaganda by the Zionist lobby in the United States. On 15 March, the day of Weizmann's departure for the United States, he called him in for a private meeting. He told the Zionist leader that they had no need of a long conversation, since their thoughts were 99 per cent identical. He added that each time they met, it gave him a "twist in his heart". He reassured Weizmann that although he had had to postpone the Jewish force, he would not let him down.[52]

Weizmann stayed in the United States for 4 months. Upon his return in July, he approached the War Office for a definite reply on the Division scheme. However, during his absence, several significant military developments had taken place. Not only had British armies suffered defeat at the hands of the Germans in Greece and consequently in Crete, but they had been required to deal also with Rashid Ali's pro-Axis rebellion. In addition, further to the Germans' dispatch of military aid to Rashid Ali, and intelligence warnings that the Germans planned to conquer Syria, the British launched a pre-emptive invasion. Rashid Ali's rebellion collapsed on 31 May. On 8 June, Anglo-Free French forces began the campaign against Syria. It took them some 5 weeks, until 14 July, to subdue the fierce resistance put up by the Vichy French forces.[53]

The events of May-June 1941 dictated yet another reassessment of British strategy in the Middle East. On the eve of their invasion of Syria, the British launched a propaganda campaign promising that they would grant its Arabs independence. This promise would involve the British in acute problems with de Gaulle's Free French, who had no intention of fulfilling the British promise.

The British Foreign Office appreciated that having promised independence to the Syrian Arabs, they would find it difficult to explain to the Palestinian Arabs why they were not to receive the same treatment. The British had no intention of relaxing their control over Palestine, but they could hardly announce that they were about to raise a Jewish Division – a step that the Arab world would regard as British collusion in a Jewish plot to take over the country. More than ever, Britain needed at least the benevolent neutrality of the Arab world. Rommel had landed in Libya, and the threat he posed to Egypt was manifested in his prolonged siege of Tobruk, since April 1941.[54]

Therefore, at the beginning of July 1941, when Weizmann approached David Margesson, the new Secretary of State for War, about the Jewish Division scheme, the latter was preoccupied with the situation in Syria, where the Vichy French had been defeated but were still haggling over peace terms.[55] In a private letter to Lord Moyne, Margesson wrote:

> The ostensible reason for delay [of the Jewish Division scheme] was the shortage of equipment, but the true reason was based upon political considerations, and it seems to me that the political dangers now are certainly no less than they were last March.
>
> The arrival of the Free French in Syria, and the apparent desire of General de Gaulle to take a large measure of control there, are new

factors complicating the Arab situation. If we are now to give the appearance of arming the Jews in bulk, I feel that we should land ourselves in a very pretty mess.[56]

Margesson proposed that they tell Weizmann that the Division would have to be delayed further, using the same pretext as before – the shortage of equipment. Weizmann was told that the shortage was now more acute than ever, further to the Soviet Union's entry into the war (in June) and the need to send arms and equipment to the Red Army.

It is unlikely that Weizmann had any clear idea about Britain's complex situation in the Middle East, nor of the added "complications" arising from the Anglo-French conquest of Syria. But by the same measure, the weaker Britain's position in the Middle East became, the greater the threat of a German conquest of Egypt and Palestine – and the more desperate the future prospects of the Yishuv. Therefore, Weizmann would not brook any further delay. On 10 September 1941, he sent an impassioned, personal appeal to Churchill. With the Americans yet to enter the war, he included his "trump card" – the Zionist lobby:

> Tortured by Hitler as no nation has ever been in modern times, and advertised by him as his foremost enemy, we are refused by those who fight him the chance of seeing our name and flag appear among those arrayed against him.
>
> I know that this exclusion is not your own intention or spirit. It is the work of the people who were responsible for the Munich policy in Europe and for the White Paper in Palestine. We were sacrificed in order to win over the Mufti of Jerusalem and his friends who were serving Hitler in the Middle East; whereas the only thing that can square the Arabs is British strength in the Middle East, as has been clearly shown in Iraq.
>
> But are the Jews so utterly unimportant as the treatment meted out to them suggests? I have spent four months in America ... closely watching the American scene. Forces over there are finely balanced; the position is uncertain. There is only one big ethnic group which is willing to stand, to a man, for Great Britain, and a policy of "all-out-aid" for her; the five million American Jews.
>
> It has been repeatedly acknowledged by British statesmen that it was the Jews who, in the last war, helped to tip the scales in America in favour of Great Britain. They are keen to do it – and may do it – again. But you are dealing with human beings, with flesh and blood, and the most elementary feelings of self-respect sets limits to service, however willing, if the response is nothing but rebuffs and humiliations. American Jewry waits for a word – a call – from His Majesty's Government. The formation of a Jewish Fighting Force would be that signal.[57]

There is no record of any reply from Churchill, but when he circulated Weizmann's letter to the Cabinet, it provoked a storm of protest, especially from the Foreign Office, many of whose officials had served during Chamberlain's premiership. They resented not only Weizmann's disparaging reference to the now discredited Munich Agreement, but also the fact that he had gone above their heads to the Prime Minister. Utterly consumed by their own anxieties and fury, the officials displayed an autistic indifference to the real dangers facing the Yishuv. Not a single official addressed this issue, at a time when British officers were putting the final touches to plans for their own evacuation of the Middle East. To the contrary, the internal debate within the Foreign Office generated not a few of the well-worn stereotypes about the Jews.

Eden protested that Weizmann's letter made him feel even less eager to help than before. Even J.M. Martin, Churchill's favourite private secretary, stated that the Zionists' motives were "frankly political". H.M. Eyres fumed that Weizmann had now opened "his mouth wider than before" and was now speaking of "our flag", i.e. of a separate Jewish army. Eyres accused the Jews of ingratitude, for having forgotten that they, the Jews, were the source of all Britain's troubles in the Middle East, and that for years the British had protected them against the Arabs. He asserted that had it not been for Britain's support of the Jews in Palestine, the Rashid Ali revolt in Iraq would not have occurred. With regard to the Division scheme, Eyres argued:

> Axis propaganda was now dinning into the Arabs that we are tied to the Jewish chariot, and every concession we make to the Jews merely confirms the Arab belief in the truth of those broadcasts.[58]

Eyres continued that American Jews were most sensitive to the accusation that they were trying to drag their country into the war, and he questioned if they would even welcome the announcement of a Jewish Division scheme. Neville Butler, head of the North American desk at the Foreign Office, went further still:

> There was just enough in Hitler's cry that America is run by a Judeo plutocracy to make the administration anxious that American Jews, as Jews, should not be leading the war party.

As will be seen in the next chapter, similar arguments were used when the Allies hesitated to mount operations to rescue Jews from Nazi-occupied Europe. R.A. Butler was the only official to add a word of caution – it would definitely be a mistake to snub the Jews gratuitously. But he concurred that Jewish feelings should not be a primary consideration when considering the Jewish Division. The Colonial Office officials agreed. Shuckburgh, evidently jaded by his two decades of dealing with the Palestine issue, insisted irritably that Britain's own interests must be the sole consideration:

> Dr Weizmann's letter to the P.M. is a typical production. I do not wish to enlarge upon it knowing, as I do, that I am regarded as prejudiced; but the whole thing seems to me to be put from a wholly imaginary angle. Dr Weizmann takes the ground that he is making us a generous offer, which we are brutally rejecting. The plain fact is that he is placing a pistol at our heads and is furious because we do not at once surrender. It is he, and not we who want this "Jewish Army", and the reasons for which he wants it are purely political and not military ... If we really want these reinforcements from the military point of view, by all means let us have them. If we do not, and if Dr Weizmann is merely pressing his point with a view to making political capital for the Zionists, then it seems to me not merely unreasonable, but wholly outrageous that we should be pestered with such a matter in such times as present.[59]

However, Churchill's anxiety about the Americans' contribution to the British war effort had been eased. Since the dark days of summer 1940, Britain's geostrategic position had been transformed. In August 1940, the Americans had agreed to loan 50 destroyers to Britain, in return for which the British leased to them a string of their overseas bases. In March 1941, the American Congress passed the Lend-Lease Bill, whereby supplies and military equipment were sold to Britain on preferential terms, with payment deferred, and in June 1941, the German invasion of the Soviet Union secured for Britain a desperately needed ally. Finally, on 14 August 1941, Churchill and Roosevelt had their first wartime meeting, at Placentia Bay, a fishing settlement on the south coast of Newfoundland. The two leaders signed the Atlantic Charter, defining joint goals and principles for the post-war world order. Churchill returned home with Roosevelt's promise that he would bring his country into the war as soon as he could.[60]

On 13 October 1941, the Cabinet cancelled the Jewish Division scheme, without any demurral from Churchill. The government departments concerned breathed an audible sigh of relief. Lord Moyne, the Colonial Secretary, reported to High Commissioner MacMichael the next day:

> You will appreciate what a relief it is to Ministers that a final decision on the main project for the creation of Jewish contingents should at last, after two years of discussions and negotiations, have been taken, and I feel sure that the news will be most welcome to you.[61]

The explanation given to the Zionists remained a lack of equipment. As noted, the real reasons were the dire risk that the Arabs would go over to the German side, and the fear of incurring a future political liability to the Zionists. The fate of the Yishuv should Rommel's Afrika Korps reach Palestine was not a consideration. The Zionists' euphoria following Churchill's appointment as Prime Minister had lasted less than 18 months.

The period of Rommel's advances across the Western desert between April 1942 and 3 November, when the second and decisive battle of El Alamein began, became known inside the Yishuv as the "200 days of anxiety". In the spring of that year, following Germany's crushing victories over the Soviets during the winter, and as Rommel advanced towards Egypt, the Hagana prepared the Carmel or Masada Plan. This plan, later blown up into mythical proportions, envisioned turning Haifa and the surrounding Carmel mountain range into a Masada-like fortress complex, from which those Jews who could get there would fight the Germans to the death. Jewish commando squads – the Palmach – trained and armed by the British from May 1941, were to have carried out guerilla raids against Rommel's forces.[62]

The fate of the Yishuv now hinged upon the ability of the British army to repel and defeat Rommel at the gates of Egypt. Only the British could save the Jews from the fate being visited upon those Jewish communities in Europe that had fallen under Nazi rule. On 17 April 1942, Moshe Shertok sent an appeal to General Claude Auchinleck, Commander of the Eighth Army in Egypt, asking that members of the Yishuv already mobilized into the Palestine Buffs be allowed to train as fighting battalions, from which the Jewish Division might be formed. His poignant appeal showed that the leaders of the Yishuv were well aware of the nature of Nazi barbarities in Eastern Europe:

> There can be no doubt that if the Nazis sweep across Palestine, all the Jews here will be annihilated. The destruction of the Jewish race is a fundamental element of the Nazi doctrine. The authorised news reaching us lately indicates that they are carrying out this policy with indescribable cruelty. Hundreds of thousands of Jews have died in Poland, in the Balkans, Roumania and in those Soviet provinces which the Nazis have invaded, as a result of mass executions, forced expulsions, and outbreaks of illness and starvation in the ghettoes and in the concentration camps. There is reason to believe that a much greater disaster will befall the Yishuv, if we fall into Nazi hands.[63]

At the end of June, Shertok repeated his appeal that the Jews be allowed to train a fighting force. From Washington, Weizmann added his own personal appeal to Churchill:

> Today again, the Jews of Palestine are facing a period of supreme danger. It is not only the annihilation of our work but the actual physical existence of nearly 600,000 Jews which is at stake ... if we go down in Palestine, we are entitled to go down fighting ... the refusal to grant this right will never be understood.[64]

Weizmann proposed the mobilization of 40,000 more Jews in Palestine, under Wingate's command. Churchill was still sensitive about the power of the

Zionist lobby in the United States. He forwarded Weizmann's request to the Colonial Secretary, adding some characteristically abrasive personal remarks:

> The strength of opinion in the United States is very great, and we shall suffer in many ways there by indulging the British military authorities' and the Colonial Office officials' bias in favour of the Arabs against the Jews. Now that these people are in direct danger, we should certainly give them a chance to defend themselves ... Wingate should not be put on one side, but given a fair chance and proper authority.[65]

Viscount Cranborne, the current Colonial Secretary, took personal offence at Churchill's charges. Even as the British themselves were making the final revisions of their plans for evacuating Egypt, he reiterated Whitehall's entrenched views about the Zionists' ulterior motives:

> I could not for a moment accept the suggestion that the officials of the Colonial Service are anti-Semite, any more than I am myself. We are all engaged in carrying out a policy which Parliament approved. Zionist leaders have never accepted that policy, and have been engaged, quite frankly, in pressing for a Jewish Army as a step toward a Jewish State. This could lead to serious trouble, as well as being inconsistent with British policy. This does not mean that I will not do all in my power to give the Jews of Palestine means to defend themselves against Nazi invasion.[66]

Weizmann's proposal was referred to the Middle East Command in Cairo. A conference of senior officials and military officers agreed to mobilize 10,000 new Jewish recruits, at the rate of 500 per month, to be incorporated into a Palestine regiment. But it rejected the Zionists' demand to recruit an additional 10,000 special police for the defence of Jewish settlements, arguing that the Hagana was already organized enough, in secret, for the defence of Jewish settlements. The conference asserted that in the event of a German invasion, no Jewish residual force, however well armed, would have any chance of defending the Yishuv. But such a force in Palestistine *would* constitute a political menace. The conference reduced the Agency's demand to an additional 1500 special rural police. It determined that none of the new units would be under Jewish command, or be allowed to use Jewish flags or insignia, or have any Zionist political objectives attached.[67]

After a row at Whitehall with the Foreign Office, on the role to be assigned to the new regiment, the Cabinet agreed that the official announcement about the regiment in Parliament would avoid all details of its duties. On 6 August, Cranborne announced the formation of the new regiment in the Commons. It was to serve in "Palestine or adjacent countries", for the defence of Palestine.[68]

Initially, the Jewish Agency gave the Palestine regiment plan its full support, believing that it would be trained as a combat unit. But disillusion soon set in, when the new GOC Palestine, General McConnell, told the Zionists that the regiment's duties would be similar to those of the existing Buffs – "defence of vital points and the provision of local mobile forces". Moreover, General Auchinleck, fully preoccupied with the pending battle against Rommel's forces, felt unable to equip the new unit as front-line troops. The War Office suggested that they salvage some of the plan's propaganda value by announcing that combat duties were not ruled out for the future:

> Object of Palestine Regiment was to sidetrack agitation for Jewish Army and unless we convince Jewish opinion here, in Palestine and in the United States that we are giving Palestinian Jews a real opportunity to fight in their defence of Palestine we shall not be better off than before.[69]

The Zionists realized that the regiment would be restricted to static guard duties. During the remaining, critical months before the second, decisive battle of El Alamein in November 1942, the Hagana was left to its own resources. The British triumph over Rommel in November marked the final turning point of the North African campaign. Although it was not apparent immediately, it ended Axis hopes of occupying Egypt, Palestine and the oilfields of the Middle East.

Those Whitehall officials who argued that Churchill was overstating the case about the influence of American Jews were given succour by an article written by the Jewish publisher of the *New York Times*, Arthur Suzlberger. Published in the *New York Herald Tribune* on 6 November 1942, the article told the Jews to drop the plan for their own army. He argued that Zionist calls for a Jewish army "created enmity among Moslems and added to the difficulties of the Allies ... [which] serves no useful purpose to continue ... which not only embarrasses the United Nations, but can be distorted by the Axis in the Arab world".[70]

By May 1943, all Axis forces had been cleared from North Africa but rumours about the Division scheme refused to die. The Arabs left no room for doubt about their reaction should the British arm the Jews. In January 1943, the indefatigable Nuri al-Said warned Richard Casey, the Minister of State in Cairo, that any move in that direction would be regarded by the Arabs as:

> ... a Jewish attempt to coerce the Allies into acceptance of a Jewish State, and the ultimate purpose of such an army as being to fight the Arabs for possession of Palestine.[71]

British officials shared Nuri's views, especially after the Zionists' Biltmore declaration in May 1942, demanding the establishment after the war of a "Jewish Commonwealth" in all of western Palestine (see Chapter 15). In June 1943, the military Command at Cairo sent to the Cabinet a warning about the dangers of an armed Jewish takeover of Palestine. It compared the Zionists to the Nazis – an accusation that would become a common theme among British officialdom:

> The principal danger lies in an endeavour on the part of the Jews, who are rapidly producing a highly organized military machine on Nazi lines, to seize the moment which is most favourable to themselves for the prosecution by force of their policy of establishing an exclusively Jewish State in Palestine.[72]

The Jewish Brigade

In September 1943, Moshe Shertok sent to the government a proposal to mobilize a Jewish brigade to fight the Germans in Europe. Churchill did not believe that a brigade would arouse the hostility of the departments concerned. In the background were the various appeals by the Jews and the Zionists to rescue Jews from the Nazis, and to bomb the Auschwitz death camp – all rejected. Churchill himself had been aware since 1941 of the mass murders of Jews by the Nazis during the first stages of the Holocaust.[73] If Weizmann's account is to be believed, in February 1944, Churchill told him, in florid terms:

> He would hand over Hitler to the Jews ... he intended asking for a Jewish Force, with a Jewish Flag, which would march across Europe with the armies of the United Nations, straight to Berlin.[74]

Churchill was concerned primarily with the symbolic aspect of the Jewish Brigade. On 3 July 1944, when he first raised the project in the Cabinet, he stressed:

> In view of the sufferings which the Jewish people were at present enduring there was a strong case for sympathetic consideration of projects in relation to them. He accepted the objections to a Jewish Division, but felt that we should not refuse to examine the possibility of a brigade group.[75]

But Churchill had again misjudged the Whitehall officials, who were now preoccupied with Palestine's fate after the war. The Colonial Office insisted that the Zionists' motives were political. The Zionists' claim that they wanted to help in the war effort was dismissed out of hand. The department asserted that a Jewish brigade could not make any contribution to the war effort. It estimated that it would take 12 months to train the brigade, whereas it was expected that the war would be over by January 1945. The War Office suggested that if a Jewish brigade were raised, it should fight the Japanese in the Far East, and objected to the brigade displaying a Jewish flag. But this time Churchill insisted. In a note to P.J. Grigg, the Secretary of State for War, he not only reiterated the symbolic and moral aspects of the scheme but, almost inevitably, reminded Grigg of "the American factor":

> I like the idea of the Jews trying to get at the murderers of their fellow-countrymen in Europe, and I think **it certainly would give a great deal of satisfaction in the United States**. I cannot conceive why this martyred race, scattered about the world and suffering as no other race has done at this juncture, should be denied the satisfaction of having a Flag.[76]

Grigg consulted the Colonial Office and the Middle East commanders. They raised the same objection that they had to the Jewish Division in 1941. Grigg replied to Churchill:

> ... all the official advice, military and civil ... is to the effect that the Jewish Agency are determined to place themselves in a position at the end of the war with Germany where they can force HMG to adopt a solution of the Palestine problem which is acceptable to them ... the appearance of a Jewish Force in Palestine will cause widespread riots.[77]

On 18 September 1944, Churchill over-ruled the officials' objections and drove the Jewish Brigade scheme through the Cabinet, albeit with "political" reservations: the brigade would not be allowed either to serve or to demobilize in Palestine and, in deference to Arab sensitivities, it would not be allowed to fly its own flag (with the Star of David insignia) in transit through Egypt but only upon its arrival in Italy.[78]

Notes

1 John Darwin, *Britain & Decolonisation*, London: Macmillan, 1988, p. 26; and Michael Howard, *The Mediterranean Strategy in the Second World War*, New York: Praeger, 1968, pp. 9–10.
2 Lawrence Pratt, "The Strategic Context: British Policy in the Mediterranean and the Middle East, 1936–39", in Uriel Dann, ed., *The Great Powers in the Middle East, 1919–1939*, New York: Holmes & Meier, 1988, p. 14.
3 ibid, pp. 19–20.
4 ibid, pp. 12–15.
5 ibid, pp. 20, 24.
6 COS report on the Strategic Aspects of Partition, CID paper, 467C, 14 February 1938, FO 371/21870, NA.
7 CP 199 (38), 14 September 1938, cited in Pratt, "The Strategic Context", p. 21.
8 Pratt, "The Strategic Context", p. 23. Between 1938 and 1939, the number of capital ships in active service declined by nearly one-third, from 13 to nine.
9 On the Jewish Division, cf. Michael J. Cohen, *Churchill and the Jews*, revised paperback edition, London: Frank Cass, 2003, Chapter 7.
10 Following the evacuation of Anglo-French forces at Dunkirk, the British prepared contingency plans for the evacuation of their forces from the Middle East; these were revised after the Germans' defeat of Britain in Greece in April 1941,

and Rommel's advances across the Western desert in May 1941. The plans made no provision for either the evacuation or the arming of the Jews in Palestine; see Ron Zweig, "British plans for the evacuation of Palestine", in *Studies in Zionism*, 8, Autumn 1983, pp. 291–303.
11 Cited in Bernard Wasserstein, *Britain and the Jews of Europe, 1939–1945*, London: Institute of Jewish Affairs/Clarendon Press, 1979, p. 17.
12 All but 5000 of the 335,000 Allied troops from Dunkirk were evacuated back to England between 26 May and 4 June. Hitler used the Luftwaffe, but not his Panzers against the evacuating forces. One hypothesis suggests that Hitler still hoped to make a peace deal with the British.
13 David Reynolds, *In Command of History: Churchill Fighting and Writing the Second World War*, London/New York: Penguin, 2004, p. 381.
14 Howard, *The Mediterranean*, pp. 7–8.
15 Malcolm MacDonald, *Titans & Others*, London: Collins, 1972, pp. 91–92.
16 Martin Gilbert, *Winston S. Churchill, 1922–1939*, vol. V, Boston: Houghton & Mifflin, 1977, pp. 847–48.
17 Diary entry for 13 February 1941, in Nigel West, ed., *The Guy Liddell Diaries*, vol. I: *1939–1942*, London/New York: Routledge, 2005, p. 132. The *post hoc* bitter regrets were quite evidently a reference to the Balfour Declaration.
18 Morgenthau record of London trip, *The Morgenthau Diaries*, book # 762, p. 205, Roosevelt Library, Hyde Park, New York State.
19 On 10 November 1943, after more than 4 of the 5-year period of the Palestine White Paper had elapsed, and more than 3 years after Churchill became Prime Minister, the Colonial Secretary informed the House of Commons that well under half of the White Paper's 75,000 immigration quota had been issued, just 31,078 certificates. By March 1944, the formal end of the 5-year immigration period, 20,000 immigration certificates remained unused.
20 Shuckburgh minute of 27 April 1940, in CO 733/426/75872/16, NA.
21 Downie minute of 15 March 1941, in CO 733/445, part 11, 76021/308, NA.
22 Minute by R.T. Latham, 27 April 1941, FO 371/27132, E1240/204/31, NA. No Nazi agents were ever discovered among the Jewish immigrants.
23 Churchill's directive to allow the survivors of the *Patria* disaster to remain in Palestine in November 1940 was an exception to the rule, which was not followed by any relaxation of the White Paper immigration restrictions. cf. Cohen, *Churchill*, pp. 279–85.
24 Roosevelt violated American neutrality laws by corresponding with Churchill; cf. F. Loewenheim and H. O. Langley, eds, *Roosevelt and Churchill: Their Secret Correspondence*, London: Saturday Review Press, 1975.
25 Weizmann to Bracken, 11 June 1940, in Z4/14.6961, Central Zionist Archives (CZA), also in *Weizmann Letters*, [*WL*] XIX, pp. 286–87.
26 Churchill's Cabinet memorandum, 25 December 1939, WP (39) 163, in Cab 67/3 and Cabinet debate on 27 December 1939, in Cab 65/2, NA. For the warnings of Lord Lothian, Britain's ambassador to the United States, and Churchill's views of the importance of American support and the influence of American Jewry, cf. Cohen, *Churchill*, pp. 186–203.
27 Shuckburgh minute, 7 February 1940, CO 733/426, 75872/14, NA.
28 Weizmann to Chamberlain, 29 August 1939, in the Weizmann Archives (WA). On the various negotiations for mobilizing Jewish military units, cf. Cohen, *Palestine*, pp. 98–124, and idem, *Churchill*, pp. 223–27.
29 By the end of 1940, 6500 Palestinian Jews had enlisted in the British army; by the end of 1942, the number had risen to 43,000; they were restricted mainly to guard and other defensive duties. cf. Yoav Gelber, *Jewish Palestinian Volunteering in the British Army During the Second World War*, vol. II, Jerusalem: Yad Yitschak Ben-Zvi, 1981 (in Hebrew).

30 On the September 1939 meetings, cf. Prem 4/51/9, NA; on the September 1940 meeting, see Weizmann report to General Dill, 3 September 1940, in WA.
31 Bracken note to Churchill, 31 October 1939, in Prem 4/51/9, NA.
32 Churchill-Weizmann interview in Prem 4/51/9 and minutes of Cabinet meeting on 19 October 1939 in Cab 65/1, NA.
33 Cohen, *Churchill*, pp. 204–5. In 1939, Shuckburgh was designated Governor of Nigeria, but because of the war he remained at the Colonial Office, retiring in 1942.
34 Cabinet discussion in Cab 65/5, NA.
35 For this and the following, see Churchill to COS correspondence in Cab 80/11, NA.
36 Note of 22 May 1940, ibid.
37 Churchill to Colonial Secretary Lloyd, 23 May 1940, ibid.
38 COS (40) 390, 25 May 1940, in ibid.
39 Notes in WO 201/185, NA, and Weizmann report of meeting with Lloyd on 27 August 1940, WA.
40 Churchill to General Ismay (for Wavell), 12 August 1940, in Prem 4/51/9, NA.
41 Winston S. Churchill, *The Second World War*, vol. 2, London: Cassell, 1949, p. 380.
42 Weizmann to General Dill, 3 September 1940, WA.
43 Meetings of 16 and 18 September in Z4/302/24, CZA.
44 Michael J. Cohen, *Palestine: Retreat from the Mandate*, London/New York: Paul Elek, 1978, pp. 107–8.
45 Minute by William Baxter, 29 January 1941, FO 371/27126, NA.
46 Cohen, *Palestine*, p. 109.
47 On 19 February 1941, Rommel began landing the first elements of the Afrika Korps in Tripoli. On 6 April, Hitler invaded Greece. On the same day, Wavell decided he was outflanked by Rommel's Panzers and began a 300-mile pullback to Tobruk. The British Expeditionary Force to Greece, which included hundreds of Palestinian Arabs and Jews, was totally outnumbered and outclassed by the Germans, and forced to withdraw to Crete, leaving many dead, wounded and prisoners behind. A daring German parachute-borne invasion of Crete routed the British forces there and took many more hundreds prisoner. Some 200 Palestinian Jews were killed in the Greece/Crete campaigns; some 1500 Palestinian Jews and 400 Palestinian Arabs were taken prisoner.
On Churchill's duplicity over the Greece campaign, see Reynolds, *In Command*, pp. 230–41.
48 This paragraph of the Palestine White Paper promised the appointment of Palestinian ministers, "once peaceful conditions were restored".
49 Wavell to Secretary of State for War, 24 February 1941, 26 February 1941, WO 193/68; forwarded to Churchill, in Prem 4/51/9, NA.
50 Churchill to Moyne, 1 March 1941, FO 371/27126, NA.
51 Reynolds, *In Command*, p. 191.
52 Cohen, *Churchill*, pp. 219–20.
53 On the Iraqi and Syrian campaigns, cf. F.H. Hinsley, *British Intelligence in the Second World War*, vol. one, London: HMSO, 1979, pp. 194–213, 410–14; also volume two, London: HMSO, 1981, and volume three, New York: Cambridge University Press, part I, 1984, part II, 1988. See also General Hellmuth Felmy, "German Exploitation of Arab Nationalist Movements in World War II", www.allworldwars.com/German-Exploitation-of-Arab-Nationalist-Movements-in-World-War-II.html.
54 The British garrison at Tobruk (comprising some 26,000 soldiers, the majority Australians) held out for 5 months, supplied by the Royal Navy. This first siege of Tobruk marked the first time that Rommel's Panzers had been halted. Its strategic importance lay in the fact that apart from Benghazi, Tobruk was the only major port on the African coast between Tripoli and Alexandria. German control would drastically shorten Rommel's supply lines. He could not attack Egypt while the

334 *World War Two: The Jews*

Tobruk garrison threatened his lines of supply. On 21 June 1942, following Rommel's victory at the battle of al-Gazala, the South African commander of Tobruk's 30,000-man garrison surrendered to Rommel, after a second siege of just 48 hours. Following the disastrous surrender of Singapore the previous February, the surrender of Tobruk marked one of the nadirs of the British war effort, and at the beginning of July, it led to a motion of no confidence in Churchill in the House of Commons.

55 The armistice between the British commander and the Vichy French was signed finally on 12 July 1941.
56 Margesson to Moyne, 4 July 1941, in Cohen, *Churchill*, p. 220.
57 Weizmann to Churchill, 10 September 1941, WA.
58 Memo by H.M.Eyres, 18 September 1940, in FO 371/27128, NA. On German propaganda in Arabic to the Middle East, see Chapter 18.
59 Shuckburgh to Parkinson, 22 September 1941, in CO 968 39/13117/15/11, NA.
60 Details in Cohen, *Churchill*, pp. 188–90.
61 Minutes of Cabinet meeting on 13 October 1941, in Cab 65/19, Moyne to MacMichael, 14 October 1941, CO 968 39/13117/15/11, NA.
62 In 1943, following the Allies' defeat of the Germans in North Africa, the British ordered the dismantling of the Palmach.
63 Shertok's memorandum is in: http://he.wikipedia.org/wiki/מאתיים_ימי_חרדה. His appeal was not found in the relevant file at the Central Zionist Archives, but specific reference to it is made in Shertok to Auchinleck, 22 June 1942, in S25/58-4t, CZA.
64 Weizmann to Churchill, 25 June 1942, in FO 371/31379, NA, copy in WA.
65 Churchill to Cranborne, 5 July 1942, in Prem 5.51.9, NA.
66 Cranborne to Churchill, 6 July 1942, ibid.
67 Minutes of Cairo conference in Cairo to Foreign Office, 21 July 1942, in FO 921/8, NA. Among those at the conference was Richard Casey, the Minister of State for the Middle East, High Commissioner MacMichael, General Auchinleck, C in C Middle East, and General Scobie, the GOC Palestine. For the opposition of the American General Staff and the US administration to mobilizing a Jewish army, cf. Richard Breitman, Allan J. Lichtman, *FDR and the Jews*, Cambridge, Mass: Harvard University Press, 2013, pp. 244–46.
68 Announcement in the Commons, House of Commons Debates (*H. C. Deb.*), 5th series, vol. 382, col. 1271.
69 War Office to the Minister of State, Cairo, 1 October 1942, in FO 921/8, NA.
70 Breitman, Lichtman, *FDR*, p. 244.
71 Nuri al-Said to Casey, 14 January 1943, in Cab 95/14, NA. On Arab protests, see also Chapter 18.
72 Resolutions of the Middle East War Council, 17 June 1943, WP (43) 247, Cab 66/37, NA. For conflicting British and Jewish estimates of the *Yishuv's* armed strength, cf. Cohen, *Churchill*, p. 248.
73 See details in the next chapter, and Keith Jeffrey, *The Secret History of MI6*, New York: Penguin, 2010, pp. 345–48.
74 Weizmann account to Zionist Political Committee, 23 February 1944, cited by Gelber, *Jewish Palestinian Volunteering*, p. 383.
75 Minutes of Cabinet meeting in Cab 65/47, NA. A brigade was one-third of the size of a division.
76 Churchill to Grigg, 26 July 1944, in Prem 4/51/9, part. 2, NA. My emphasis.
77 Grigg to Churchill, 8 August 1944, ibid.
78 Minutes of cabinet meeting on 18 September 1944, in Cab 65/47, NA.

15 The Allies, the Zionists and the Holocaust

> The great influence that anti-Semites everywhere always attributed to Jews had proved to be as imaginary as other constructs sick minds projected onto a group without help or power in the hour of its supreme peril.
> Gerhard Weinberg, *Germany, Hitler, and World War II*, p. 243

The history of the Palestine mandate cannot be understood without reference to the reactions to the Holocaust of the three principal "players" in the Palestine Triangle – the Arabs, the British and the Jews. This chapter deals with British and Jewish reactions. Chapters 17 and 18 will deal with the Arabs' affinities to Nazism in the 1930s, and with the Mufti of Jerusalem's collaboration with the Nazi regime during the war.

Over the last 15 years, the work of Richard Breitman has shown that the Allies knew far more about Nazi atrocities, from a much earlier stage of the war, than historians had previously believed.[1] The crescendo of reports reaching the West about the Nazis' wholesale slaughter of the Jews in Eastern Europe and the Soviet Union left no doubt about their unprecedented mass scale. The Allies' response was a cynical mix of spontaneous shock, followed by calculations of *realpolitik* and anti-Semitic recoil. Jewish appeals for aid and rescue were met with procrastination, disingenuousness and lies. The Allies' formal reply to all calls for help was that they could not divert military resources from operations against the enemy. But exceptions were made: the Allies mounted missions to rescue their own prisoners of war, and carried out operations that served their post-war political interests, notably the airlift of supplies and arms to the pro-Western Polish Home Army during their uprising against the Nazis in Warsaw in August 1944.[2]

The Allies' failure to divert resources against the Nazi death machinery was determined not only by military factors but also by their fear of domestic criticism, of accusations that they were fighting the war on the Jews' behalf. The British had an additional fear – losing the support of the Arabs, should successful rescue efforts in Europe lead to an irresistible flood of Jewish immigrants into Palestine.

The Biltmore Plan

The decision of Churchill's government to shelve the Jewish Division scheme in October 1941 effectively shattered the Zionists' faith in the British. Ben-Gurion blamed Weizmann for having "appeased" them, for not having insisted on the need for a Jewish military force in Palestine. But Weizmann refused to hold Churchill responsible for the cancellation of the Jewish Division scheme.

Nonetheless, in 1942 the Zionists switched their attentions from Britain to the United States. Their goal was to activate the Zionist lobby in the United States, which would press the American administration to bring pressure to bear on the British to implement a solution favourable to Zionism in Palestine. At the same time, they appreciated that they could not afford to alienate the British, whose armies were the only force standing between Rommel and Palestine in 1942. Weizmann explained to Rabbi Stephen Wise, the American Zionist leader, that they must preserve Churchill's friendship:

> As a British subject I have to be exceedingly careful not to contribute to the strain in Anglo-American relations ... We have one great friend in England, the Prime Minister ... I must be doubly careful not to do anything which might possibly make Mr Churchill's task more difficult.[3]

The Zionists determined to demand a sovereign Jewish state in Palestine as part of the new world order that would arise from the ashes of World War Two. In May 1942, an extraordinary meeting of the American Zionist Organization was held at the Biltmore Hotel in New York, attended by both Ben-Gurion and Weizmann. It resolved to change the movement's programme as formulated at the first Zionist Congress in 1897. What became known as the Biltmore Resolution demanded the formation after the war of a Jewish "commonwealth" in all of western Palestine. The Zionists still didn't dare to demand a sovereign Jewish state, given that the Yishuv numbered less than one-third of Palestine's total population.

The translation of the Biltmore Plan into a practical policy led to an open challenge by Ben-Gurion to Weizmann's leadership. The former, now at the height of his powers, believed that it was time for a changing of the old guard – time for Weizmann, now an ailing, elder statesman, to give way. Ben-Gurion advocated the move of 1 million Jews to Palestine after the war, in one single operation. But Weizmann, still committed to the 1937 Partition Plan, advocated a gradualist strategy, under the aegis of the British – an immigration of 100,000 Jews per year. The Biltmore programme, which gained the support of a majority of American Jews, greatly complicated Britain's position, both in the Middle East and in the United States. Henceforth, the British distinguished between the "moderate" Weizmann and the "radical" Ben-Gurion.[4]

The Biltmore Plan was conceived *before* news of Hitler's Final Solution was confirmed in August 1942, at first to the Jews and passed on by them to the West. No one could have imagined that by the end of the war in Europe, 6 million of Europe's 12 million Jews would have been murdered. These had been the Jews for whom the Jewish state had been designed.

What the Allies knew about the Holocaust

On 13 October 1943, Churchill defined his war strategy in the House of Commons:

> Everything for the war, whether controversial or not, and nothing controversial that is not *bona fide* needed for the war.[5]

It has been claimed that during the war itself, no one could have grasped the full scale and enormity of the Holocaust, that the mass extermination of the Jews was kept a tight secret by the Nazis. In his pioneering study of British policy towards the Jews during World War Two, Professor Wasserstein suggested a "psychological" explanation. Borrowing from a British psychiatrist, he hypothesized that the officials in Whitehall had perhaps suffered from:

> ... an imaginative failure to grasp the full meaning of the consequences of decisions, when those consequences were distant, unseen, and bore no direct personal relation to the actor ... distance need not be physical; it may simply be psychological ... The average British official lived in a different mental world from that of the Jewish refugee.[6]

However, Wasserstein (and Martin Gilbert, Churchill's official biographer) exempted Churchill from the accusation of Allied apathy, claiming that he was the only one in his administration who had understood the historical significance of the Holocaust at the time.[7] In 1981, Martin Gilbert, who had exclusive access to Churchill's private papers until the mid-1990s, claimed that information about the grim extermination process in the Nazi death camps remained a secret from the West until June 1944, when two Slovak Jews managed to escape from Auschwitz and brought to the West a detailed report on the camp's activities.[8] Other scholars, under the influence of Gilbert and of Churchill's own post-war professions of ignorance, claimed that the British had not understood that there had been a Nazi plan to exterminate all the Jews of Europe until after the liberation of the camps.[9] At the very least, these assertions are anomalous, given the Allied public Declaration of 17 December 1942, disclosing that they had learned of Hitler's Final Solution, the plan to murder all of European Jewry. In the Declaration, the Allies committed themselves to bringing to justice all of those involved in the crime – after the war.

In 1980, Professor Walter Laqueur published an appropriately titled study: *The Terrible Secret: An Investigation into the Suppression of Information about Hitler's Final Solution*. He concluded that the murder of Jews on a massive scale was common knowledge on the continent from the earliest stages of the war; it was leaked to the West by neutral journalists, by the intelligence services of the Polish Government-in-Exile (PGE), by various other governments-in-exile, and by embassies and escapees.[10] In June 1942, London's *Daily Telegraph* was the first major Western newspaper to report the extermination of the Jews on a massive scale. Further reports followed, on public radio and in the press, where they were usually relegated to the inside or back pages. Following Wasserstein, Laqueur suggested that perhaps the liberal democracies had been unable to understand the character of a regime so different from their own.

However, as will be shown here, the sheer mass of evidence about Nazi atrocities that accumulated from multiple sources, in real time, could not simply be discounted or dismissed by the Allies. Not only were they literally inundated by the amount of evidence, but they expressed their sheer horror at the extent of Nazi atrocities, not only in the privacy of government departments.

During the late 1970s and early 1980s, Professor Hinsley's multi-volume official history of British intelligence during World War Two appeared. It airbrushed the Holocaust out of the main body of its text. The volumes' indexes contain no references to the Jews, to Auschwitz, to the Holocaust, or to the concentration or extermination camps. Likewise, Keith Jeffrey's recently published history of the British secret intelligence service (SIS) refers just once, *en passant,* to the "terrible legacy of the Holocaust". Jeffrey states that he found "almost nothing" in the SIS archives "about the persecution of the Jews generally or the Final Solution". He explains that the service was constrained by "an acute shortage of funding," and had to narrow its focus.[11]

Jeffrey's conclusion about Bletchley Park's "narrow focus" is strange, to say the least, given that he also explains that the government's Code and Cypher School at Bletchley Park (GC & CS) was managed by MI6. Therefore, MI6 would have had access to the plethora of Signals Intelligence (SIGINT) about Nazi atrocities in Poland and the Soviet Union that was being deciphered from as early as 1940. Although Jeffrey made extensive use of Hinsley's magisterial work, he apparently missed the appendix tucked away at the end of volume two (not to mention the originals in the GC & CS files). This appendix reproduces extracts of GC & CS decrypts of the German Order Police reports on their activities during the summer of 1941:

> Between 18 July and 30 August 1941 ... at least seven occasions ... of mass shootings ... of victims described variously as "Jews", "Jewish plunderers", "Jewish Bolshevists" or "Russian soldiers in numbers varying from less than a hundred to several thousand". On 7 August ... 7,819 "executions" to date in the Minsk area, and on the same day ... 30,000 executions had been carried out since the police arrived in Russia. In the southern sector between 23 and 31 August the shooting of Jews, in groups numbering from 61 to 4,200 was reported on 17 occasions.[12]

But apart from the "official histories", the opening in the mid-1990s of Churchill's private archives, and of American and British intelligence and army files, following appeals to the courts by regular historians, has shattered former beliefs that the Allies did not discover Auschwitz-Birkenau's "terrible secret" until June 1944. The mass of material in the Allied intelligence files has changed our entire conception of what the Allies knew and when. In 1998, Professor Breitman concluded:

> Allied intelligence agencies were aware of even more detail concerning the eradication of Europe's Jews than was previously understood by historians.[13]

Since the intelligence staffs failed to decrypt a large number of the encoded transmissions, they knew that the number of people being killed was in fact much higher. As noted already, the British also received details of Nazi atrocities from other sources. The PGE was perhaps London's main source of information on Poland. For example, in 1943, a 19-page report on Auschwitz-Birkenau reached London, written by a "Polish Major", who for security reasons remained anonymous. The report was 19 pages long, three of which were devoted to the Jews. It estimated that 1.5 million Jews had already been gassed at Auschwitz-Birkenau since the spring of 1942. Gilbert refers to the report in his *Auschwitz & the Allies* but fails to note that it also reached Churchill's desk. As of 1999, the British archives had still not released this report.[14]

British analysts found the codes of the SS Order Police relatively easy to decrypt. By March 1940, they already had a good idea of these units' involvement in the atrocities being committed against the civilian populations of the areas conquered by the Wehrmacht.[15] From December 1940, British intelligence was able to decode and read details about the organization of Nazi concentration camps and of Nazi atrocities against Polish and Soviet civilians, primarily Jewish. Many of these decodes reached Churchill's desk.[16]

From May 1940, Britain had a Prime Minister who was an experienced, firm believer in the value of intelligence. A leading scholar of British intelligence concluded "No British statesman in modern times had a more passionate faith in the value of secret Intelligence than Winston Churchill". But at times his expectations of what intelligence might achieve were exaggerated, and at times, he used information impulsively. Once Churchill became Prime Minister, he brought about an unprecedented co-ordination of the various intelligence services. He insisted not only on receiving frequent intelligence summaries but also on seeing the raw data. He was persuaded that there were too many intercepts for him to cover, and he agreed to receive a daily "buff-coloured box of the best of them". He called them his "golden eggs".[17]

From the summer of 1941, with the German invasion of the Soviet Union, the German radio transmissions read by the British included dozens of reports on mass executions carried out by the special units charged with killing off the Jews in conquered territories – the Order Police and the Einsatzgruppe. The reports included frequent references to the mass executions of Jews. The SIS could not have failed to realize that atrocities on an unprecedented scale were being committed.[18]

On 24 August 1941, Churchill threw discretion to the winds and in one of his BBC radio broadcasts, he referred to the atrocities being committed by the Order Police. His purpose was to explain to the British people why he had allied the country to the hitherto vilified Soviets. After commending the Soviets on the magnificent fight they were putting up, he referred to Hitler's retaliation:

> ... by the most frightful cruelties. As his armies advance, whole districts are being exterminated. Scores of thousands – literally scores of thousands – of executions in cold blood are being perpetrated by the German police-troops upon the Russian patriots who defend their native soil.[19]

The German transmissions referred to the increasing numbers and percentages of Jewish victims, but Churchill did not mention the Jews. It has been argued that he could not have mentioned them without disclosing the success of British cryptographers in breaking the SS codes. But he would have given away less by mentioning Jews than he actually did by identifying the police units involved.[20]

The heads of the SIS were aghast at Churchill's broadcast, made without consulting them. They feared that it would tip off the Germans about their decoding successes. Their fears were well founded. On 12 September 1941, 3 weeks after Churchill's broadcast, Kurt Daluege,[21] chief of the Order Police, ordered senior SS officers to stop sending their reports by radio. On the same day, part of a British decode of a "German Police" report revealed:

> Special Action Staff Operating with Police Battalion 301 claims to have shot 4200 Jews without loss to themselves.[22]

The SIS decided that no further reports on German atrocities would be included in its reports to the Prime Minister, since no further proof of their activities against the Jews was required:

> The fact that the [Order] Police are killing all Jews that fall into their hands should by now be sufficiently well appreciated. It is not therefore proposed to continue reporting these butcheries specifically, unless so requested.[23]

Since the SIS could not control their impulsive Prime Minister, they controlled the flow of information to him. Nonetheless, many items on the mass executions of Jews continued to reach him.[24] A recent study of the Roosevelt administration's policy towards the Jews noted: "Reliable information obtained by American intelligence sources that could have confirmed Nazi atrocities remained buried within the bureaucracy".[25] The same may be said about British intelligence.

Throughout the entire course of the war, Churchill never made any public mention of Hitler's singling out of the Jews for mass extermination. One scholar noted that the consequence of Churchill's public silence "was to perpetuate ignorance among government officials in Whitehall and abroad".[26] However, news of Nazi atrocities against the Jews seeped out via many other sources.

At the end of 1941, the British Ministry of Information had opened a special file, in which it collected the many reports, from the press and from private sources, on the fate of European Jews. Its third report, dated 22 January 1942, written just 2 days after the Wansee conference, summarized information received from private letters and news items: "The Germans clearly pursue a policy of extermination against the Jews ... ". It next cited an official German document: "the only things Jewish that will remain in Poland will be Jewish cemeteries".[27]

Had the British government wished to react publicly to the extermination of the Jews, it could have done so without breaching security, merely by citing private and foreign press reports. American intelligence files give an additional indication of when and how much the British knew about the Nazi death camps. In May 1945, British Military Intelligence (MI14) handed over to its American counterpart a list of over 500 former German concentration and death camp officers, to be arrested on sight. The British stated that the list had been compiled over "a period of several years". Some 20 per cent of the officers on the list had served at Auschwitz.[28]

The SIS also learned about the working of the death camps from the German SS encoding machine, nicknamed Enigma, whose cypher they "broke" in December 1940. Enigma was used for administrative purposes. From the spring of 1942 until February 1943, its decodes revealed unusually heavy traffic along the railways lines to Dachau, Buchenwald, Auschwitz and seven other camps. The cryptographers calculated that the various columns of figures indicated the number of camp inmates at the start of the previous day, the new arrivals, and the number at the end of the day. It was simple to arrive at the number of fatalities, by deducting one column from the other. One military historian concluded that the German cryptographers made use of these columns to calibrate the new settings of the Enigma machine, which were changed daily.[29]

In January 1942, representatives of the entire Nazi bureaucracy convened at the Berlin suburb of Wansee, in order to plan the construction of special death camps, in which the Nazis planned to murder all of Europe's 12 million Jews. The executions of Jews by mass shootings and in gas vans had proved to be too laborious and inefficient.

Although Allied governments did not receive confirmation about the proceedings of the Wansee conference until the late summer of 1942, they learned of the mass murders carried out in the death camps well before then.

The British received information on Auschwitz (Oswiecim) from the PGE almost from the day of the camp's opening in late 1940. Foreign Office officials who read the reports on the atrocities being committed at the camp during the winter of 1940–41 confessed: "the description of the camp at Oswiecim is terrible". In July 1941, the government ruled that there should be no direct reference to or mention of the Jews in official publications. But the Jews were mentioned in the *Polish Fortnightly Review*, a publication of the PGE, each issue of which was vetted and approved by the government before going on sale in London. The issue of 15 November 1941 reported that no Jew left Auschwitz alive and the "three crematorium furnaces were insufficient to cope with the bodies to be cremated".

On 9 July 1942, the British and Polish Ministries of Information jointly published a booklet entitled "*Bestiality Unknown in any previous Record of History*". It noted that another camp close to Auschwitz (evidently Birkenau) had "a crematorium five times as large as the one in the main camp".[30] In line with a government ruling of the previous year, the booklet did not mention the Jews specifically. But at a joint press conference attended by Polish and Polish-Jewish representatives, held at the Ministry of Information on 9 July 1942, Brendan Bracken, the Minister of Information, did refer to the extermination of the Jews. He "expressed horror and indignation at Nazi crimes in Poland and particularly atrocities committed against Jews". He claimed:

> 700,000 Jews had already been murdered in Poland, which was the "beginning of the wholesale extermination of the Jews".[31]

But Bracken adhered to the standard Allied line – retribution would be taken after victory. He made do with proposing some preparatory steps: the collection of the names of those responsible, so that they might be brought to justice quickly, by punishments that suited the crimes. The BBC broadcast his statement the next day. Several of the BBC's home and foreign broadcasts from June-July 1942 also referred to the mass slaughter of Polish Jewry.[32]

At the end of July 1942, in reaction to the accumulated reports on Nazi atrocities, the Council of Polish Jews in London appealed to the government to find some means of stopping the mass slaughter of the Jews. Churchill asked the RAF to examine the feasibility of razing a German town, "as explicit retribution for Nazi atrocities". But although the "blanket bombing" of German towns was already part of the RAF's strategy, the Cabinet rejected the idea of announcing that a special operation would be mounted as a retribution for the Germans' extermination of the Jews.[33]

The December 1942 Declaration

In August 1942, a Breslau industrialist named Eduard Schulte, who had taken part in the Wansee conference, told a Swiss industrialist about its proceedings.

The latter passed on the news to Gerhard Riegner, the representative of the World Jewish Congress in Geneva. Via his diplomatic contacts, Riegner sent the following telegram to London and Washington:

> Received alarming report about plan being discussed and considered in Führer headquarters to exterminate at one fell swoop all Jews in German-controlled countries comprising three and a half to four million after deportation and concentration in the East thus solving Jewish question once and for all stop campaign planned for autumn methods being discussed including hydrocyanic acid stop.[34]

Riegner's news was not welcome to Allied officials, who wanted to focus solely on their own military goals. The British had already persuaded themselves that there was little they could do to help the Jews, and that any attempt to do so would prejudice the war effort. But as the officials pondered what to do – or how to explain their lack of action – new intelligence poured in, not only into London but also into Washington. By late November 1942, enough information from different sources had reached the US State Department to convince Sumner Welles, the Under-Secretary of State. On 24 November, he summoned Rabbi Stephen Wise, to tell him that his own worst fears had been confirmed; on the next day, the *New York Herald Tribune* published an interview with Wise headed "Wise Says Hitler Has Ordered 4,000,000 Jews Slain in 1942".[35]

On the very same day further evidence arrived in London, brought by Jan Karski, the code-name for a Polish Catholic underground courier. Karski's original report is still closed but on 2 December, he told his story to two Polish Jews resident in London – Szmul [Shmuel] Zygielbojm, a member of the Polish Socialist Bund, and Ignacy (Yitschak) Schwartzbart, a Zionist. They sent the following report of their meeting with Karski to the Polish embassy in Washington:

> Of the three and one half million Jews in Poland and the five to seven hundred thousand who were brought there from other Nazi-occupied countries only a small number remains alive. It is no longer a question of oppressing Jews, but of their complete extermination by all kinds of especially devised and perfected methods of pain and torture.[36]

Their report concluded with an anguished appeal:

> What is happening to us is altogether outside the imagination of civilized human beings. They [in the West] don't believe what they hear. Tell them that *we are all dying*. Let them rescue all those who will still be alive when the Report reaches them. We shall never forgive them for not having supplied us with arms so that we may have died like men, with guns in our hands.[37]

Zygielbojm had arrived in London in March 1942 and became a member of the Polish National Council, the Polish government-in-exile. He became an active lobbyist on behalf of Polish Jewry. He publicized the news of the mass exterminations of Polish Jews in BBC broadcasts (on 2 and 25 June, and 2 July), and in the *Daily Telegraph*, on 25 June 1942. He and other Polish Jews exiled in London lobbied the Labour Party, including some of its ministers in Churchill's coalition government. On 2 September 1942, the Labour Party organized the only public meeting ever held during the war to protest German atrocities, specifically those in Poland and Czechoslovakia. Herbert Morrison, the Home Secretary, made the key speech, which again held out hope only for some future date: "We Britons want to assure all Poles and all Czechoslovaks ... that we know well that protests are not enough ... We wait the day when the chance to strike home will present itself".[38]

On 15 December 1942, the Labour Party published a resolution entitled "The Massacre of the Jews". It appealed:

> "to the conscience of civilized mankind to arise in passionate protest against the bloodiest crime in history ... within a short time the Jewish people ... will have been exterminated ... We appeal to those who still have power and influence in Europe at least to make an effort to save the children.[39]

Two days earlier, on 13 December, Edward R. Murrow, the American, London-based CBS correspondent, spoke of the death camps in a radio broadcast listened to by millions. He spoke of:

> a horror beyond what imagination can grasp ... there are no longer 'concentration camps' – we must speak now only of 'extermination camps'.[40]

The flood of evidence, much of it published, about Hitler's Final Solution forced the Allies to break their veto on all publicity about the mass murder of the Jews. On 17 December 1942, the governments of Britain and the United States and nine other Allies issued a public condemnation of Nazi war crimes against the Jews. It stated that they had learned of Hitler's Final Solution to the Jewish Problem – his plan to exterminate all of Europe's 12 million Jews. The Declaration condemned Germany's "bestial policy of cold-blooded extermination" of the Jews, and warned that all those involved would be punished after the war. Members of the US Congress and the British Parliament stood for one minute in silence.

The standing tribute in the Commons at the end of Eden's statement was impromptu. Harold Nicolson, diplomat and MP, commented in his private diary:

> Eden reads out a statement about the persecution of the Jews, and to our shame and astonishment a Labour Member (having been deeply moved

by a speech by Jimmy Rothschild) suggests that we should all stand up as a tribute. The Speaker says "Such an action must be spontaneous", so everybody gets up including the Speaker and the reporters. It is rather moving in a way.[41]

The 1942 Declaration was the Allies' first official denouncement of the Nazis' mass murder of the Jews. It was made only as a result of the incontrovertible mass of evidence supplied by Jewish organizations and the PGE. These sources were not as detailed as the German Police and SS decodes that had been in Allied hands for over a year.[42]

On the eve of the December Declaration, James de Rothschild appealed to Churchill to receive a delegation of the Board of Deputies of British Jews. But Churchill had issued a directive that all appeals on behalf of European Jews should be referred to the Foreign Office. The Prime Minister's office duly referred Rothschild's appeal to the Foreign Office, with a request that they make it clear to the Board that they, the Foreign Office, would handle any further appeals.[43]

On the same day that the Declaration was read out in the Commons, Viscount Samuel, in a speech in the House of Lords, appealed to the government to do something to save Jewish lives. Two days later, Zygielbojm sent a personal appeal to Churchill, to act to save those Polish Jews still alive. He wrote that of a community numbering 3.5 million Jews, barely one half were still alive. No reply is on record.

The December Declaration was followed by a month of intensive radio broadcasts to Europe on the Jewish problem. However, as noted eloquently by Wasserstein:

> The relief and solidarity was soon transformed into bitter disillusion and accusations of betrayal, when it became plain ... that the encouragements held out by such broadcasts were as insubstantial as the ether through which they were transmitted.[44]

An insight into the attitudes of the British Parliament to the December 1942 Declaration is again supplied by Harold Nicolson. His attitude to the Jews might be defined as a "benign xenophobia". Many of his class would have agreed with his diary note of June 1945: "Although I loathe anti-Semitism I dislike Jews". On 9 December 9 1942, 8 days before the December Declaration, after a parliamentary committee meeting at which Jewish representatives gave details of Nazi atrocities against the Jews, he confided to his diary:

> I have a sense that my fellow Members [of Parliament] feel not so much "What can we do for such people?" as "What can we do with such people after the war?"[45]

The Foreign Office acted as if the December Declaration had been a move in the wrong direction, one that needed correction. But there were exceptions to the department's generally anti-Semitic attitude. A few days after the Declaration, one official minuted:

> How can we say that "we have every sympathy and willingness to play our part" when we refuse to take any positive steps of our own to help these wretched creatures? Why should anyone else do anything if we refuse?[46]

Eden's conscience did not apparently trouble him. On the contrary, he carped that the December Declaration had merely stimulated complaints about the inadequacy of the government's efforts to save the Jews. Again, Nicolson's diary gives an intimate insight of Eden. Nicolson was a friend and admirer of Eden, but he saw through the heavy layers of charm. In January 1944, Nicolson was one of a deputation that met with Eden to discuss "what could be done to rescue a few more Jews from Germany". After the meeting, Nicolson commented sardonically on Eden's subterfuge:

> It is true, of course, that Anthony is apt to hide behind his own charm. One goes away thinking how reasonable, how agreeable and how helpful he has been, and then discovers that in fact he has promised nothing at all.[47]

News of the Holocaust continued to pour in to Western capitals.[48] Shmuel Zygielbojm lobbied indefatigably. Apart from personal appeals to Allied leaders and his BBC broadcasts, he had addressed the annual Labour Party conference in May 1942. Late in the year, he sent personal appeals to Roosevelt and Churchill, warning that the entire Jewish population of Poland was being exterminated, that of the pre-war population of 3.5 million and the 700,000 Jews deported to Poland since the start of the war, only 300,000 remained alive. His appeal concluded: "The surviving Jews in Poland beg you to find the means to save the remnant of Polish Jews who remain alive".[49] His appeals were ignored.

Zygielbojm's appeals indicate that at the time, he was one of the few who appreciated the historical significance of the Holocaust. In a BBC broadcast on 13 December 1942 (4 days before the Allied Joint Declaration), he stated:

> It will be a shame to go on living, to belong to the human race, if steps are not taken to halt the greatest crime in human history.[50]

In a further BBC broadcast, he declared:

> If Polish Jewry's call for help goes unheeded, Hitler will have achieved one of his war aims – to destroy the Jews of Europe irrespective of the final military outcome of the war.[51]

After months of frustrating, fruitless attempts, Zygielbojm became depressed by his failure to move the Powers to intervene. On 12 May 1943, after learning of the deaths of his wife and of his 16-year-old son in the fall of the Warsaw ghetto, he decided to end his own life – the ultimate act of self-sacrificing protest. The note that he left behind was addressed to Raczkiewicz, the first Polish President-in-Exile, and to General Sikorski, the Polish Prime Minister-in-Exile. It remains one of the most poignant historical indictments of both the perpetrators and the onlookers ever written:

> Responsibility for the murder of the entire Jewish population lies primarily with the murderers themselves, but indirectly humanity as a whole is responsible – all of the Allied nations and their Governments, who to date have done nothing to stop the crime ... By their indifference to the killing of millions of hapless men, to the massacre of women and children, these countries have become accomplices of the assassins ... Of the three and a half million Polish Jews, no more than three hundred thousand remained alive in April 1943 ... And the extermination continues.
>
> May my death be a resounding cry of protest against the indifference with which the world looks at the destruction of the Jewish world, looks on and does nothing to stop it.[52]

One rescue opportunity did occur shortly after the December Declaration, in February 1943. The Romanian government offered to release 70,000 of its Jews, and to transport them to Palestine. The Foreign Office dismissed the offer, calling it a "piece of blackmail" that would become a precedent for Germany and her satellites to "unload" all of their unwanted nationals. The department also warned that the 29,000 immigration certificates still remaining out of the Palestine White Paper's 75,000 must be saved until the expiry of the 5-year deadline, in March 1944. The Allies' stock reply remained that the trapped Jews' best chance for survival lay in the quickest possible defeat of the Germans.[53]

The pressures generated by the December Declaration did spawn one Allied gesture, an initiative to deal with the large numbers of Jewish refugees who had found temporary shelter in neutral countries. From 19 to 29 April 1943, the Atlantic Allies convened in conference on the island of Bermuda, to discuss ways of helping the Jewish refugees. No Jews were allowed to attend the conference, not even as observers. Their meeting coincided with the final battle of the Jews of the Warsaw ghetto (19–23 April).

At the closed sessions of the conference, the Americans and the British each accommodated the other's "sensitive areas". The British wanted nothing that would upset Arab opinion, or any major rescue operation that would consume the remainder of the Palestine immigration quotas; no negotiations with Germany for the release of Jews, and no aid to be sent to the Jews, which would constitute a breach of the Allied blockade of Europe. The Americans wanted nothing that would put pressure on their own limited immigration quotas. Neither ally was prepared to assume any responsibility for the refugees who had found shelter in neutral countries. They agreed to keep their private agreement secret, in order to avoid criticism of its limited scope. Their official communiqué announced a vague agreement to "encourage humanitarian acts by neutral countries ... [and] called for a guarantee of repatriation of refugees by all the countries fighting the Axis powers".

Richard Law, the Foreign Office delegate to the conference, derived satisfaction from the achievement of what he considered to be the most important objective of the conference: "a joint agreement on what should not be done". The conference named a dozen nations and islands as possible refugee sanctuaries, but not Palestine. As noted by one scholar:

> Ultimately, Bermuda proved to be as much an exercise in futility as the Evian [refugee] Conference of 1938.[54]

The Churchill government's continuing failure to take any active measures to rescue European Jews was a cause of considerable embarrassment for Anglo-Jewry, not least for those who counted themselves among his personal friends. Several prominent English Jews, but not only Jews, wrote personal appeals to Churchill, asking him to intervene personally to rescue European Jewry. One was sent to him on 16 January 1943, by Eva, the Marchioness of Reading, Lord Melchett's daughter, a converted Jew and ardent Zionist:

> You know, better than any words of mine can describe to you, the horrible plight of the Jews at the mercy of the Nazis. I have said to myself what can I do, who can help? And the answer is clear, only Mr Churchill can help and I can at least write and beg him to do so ... Some [Jews] can still be saved, if the iron fetters of the red-tape can be burst asunder ... I learn with amazement that His Majesty's representatives in Turkey withhold certificates for Palestine and threaten deportation for those who have escaped, because they are "illegal". England cannot surely sink to such hypocrisy that her members of Parliament stand to show sympathy to the Jewish dead and meanwhile her officials are condemning these same Jews to die? You cannot know of such things. I do not believe that you would tolerate them. There are still some 40,000 certificates for Palestine even under the White Paper regulations. Mr Churchill, will you not say they are to be used now, for any one who can escape, man woman or child? Is it possible, is it really possible, to refuse sanctuary in the Holy Land?[55]

Her letter was routinely passed to the Foreign Office for reply. The department referred her to a speech in the Commons by Deputy Prime Minister Attlee on 19 January, stating that the government was giving its "urgent consideration to the whole vast problem of rescue and relief for both Jews and non-Jews under the enemy yoke". Attlee had explained the great logistical difficulties of transporting large numbers of people out of Nazi-occupied Europe, even if they were allowed to leave. Nearly all of the escape routes passed through war zones where Allied requirements were "predominantly military", and could not be dismissed as "fetters of red tape". The Foreign Office letter, to which Churchill appended his signature, concluded with the disingenuous reassurance that the Palestine government would continue to admit Jewish refugees "up to the White Paper limit".[56]

In May 1944, Melchett himself sent a personal appeal to Churchill:

> There is one psychological factor which I think ought not to be overlooked ... That is the feeling of frustration and exasperation which this policy has caused – coming as it does from a Government over which Mr Churchill presides. His wholehearted championship of our cause in the past has made our people turn to him as a saviour, and it has been extremely difficult to understand how some of these acts could be carried out by a Government under his leadership, unless it be either that the information was kept from him or that it was put forward in some perverted form.[57]

Melchett's appeal failed to move Churchill to intervene.

The Auschwitz bombing proposal

The most meaningful and the potentially most effective operation that might have saved many Jewish lives would have been the bombing and destruction of the gas chambers and incinerators at one or more of the German death camps. The prime target was the Auschwitz-Birkenau death camp, which because of its location became from 1942 "the central killing site for Jews deported from all across the continent". Yet most British officials with access to the wealth of intelligence on Auschwitz chose either not to examine it or not to believe it.[58]

The first request to bomb the camp was made as early as January 1941 by General Sikorski.[59] But the RAF did not yet have the range to reach the camp. The PGE made a second request in August 1943. This time, there was some support from the RAF air staff, but their bombers were still unable to reach the camp with adequate bomb loads.

The camp finally came within the range of Allied bombers in 1944, with the conquest of the Foggia air base in southern Italy. From 2 June 1944, Foggia was used for the "Frantic Shuttle" – a series of bombing raids by USAAF heavy bombers on Central Europe, using Soviet airfields for refuelling. The goal of the raids was to cripple Germany's war economy. The Upper Silesia area, where the Auschwitz-Birkenau camp was situated, contained several industrial complexes supplying the Nazi war machine, including Blechhammer, with its huge oil-refining complex, and Auschwitz town (5 miles from the death camp), where the I.G. Farben petro-chemical complex was situated. From 7 to 29 August these plants were the focus of heavy USAAF aerial bombings.[60] As will be seen, the RAF also flew missions to Eastern Europe.

In the spring of 1944, two Jewish prisoners, Rudolph Vrba and Alfred Wetzler, managed to escape from Auschwitz-Birkenau and brought to the West a report on the horrific scale of the killings there. Armed with this new information, Jewish representatives in Washington and London asked the Allies to bomb the camp and the railway lines leading to it.[61] The bombing of the railway lines was quickly ruled out, since these could be repaired easily within a few days.

The American response to the Jews' request was blunt – outright rejection. Inside the American administration, one of the most active lobbyists for helping the Jews trapped in Nazi-occupied Europe was Josiah Dubois, a young Protestant, who in 1943 was assistant general counsel at the American Treasury, in the department's Foreign Funds Control Division. He discovered that both the State Department and the British Foreign Office were secretly collaborating to block the grant of licences to send aid to Jews trapped under Nazi rule, because they feared that the rescue of large numbers of Jews would put pressure on the Allies to give them refuge. Dubois discovered also that the State Department had ordered US diplomats in Europe to refrain from sending to Washington information about the mass murder of Jews.[62]

On Christmas Day, 1943, Dubois sent to Henry Morgenthau Jr, the Treasury Secretary, an 18-page report entitled "The Acquiescence of This Government in the Murder of the Jews". It charged the State Department not only with "gross procrastination but also with attempts to prevent action being taken to rescue Jews". In January 1944, Dubois' report stirred Morgenthau to establish a War Refugee Board (WRB) charged with bringing succour to Jewish refugees. Dubois served as the Board's legal counsel. The WRB also examined the proposal to bomb Auschwitz. But it renounced any idea that American combat units might be used specifically to "rescue victims of enemy oppression". In the spring of 1944, the US War Department rejected any idea of "a military mission for humanitarian purposes".[63]

The British reaction to the proposal to bomb Auschwitz, Churchill's in particular, was more convoluted. The Whitehall bureaucrats kept the Zionists in play for nearly 2 months before officially turning down their request to bomb the camp. But Churchill's initially positive response, impulsive and emotional, misled historians for decades. On 6 July 1944, Eden reported the Jewish Agency's request to bomb Auschwitz to Churchill. The Prime Minister instructed Eden: "get what you can out of the RAF". This was an unusual procedure, since air strategy and operations were not within the purview of the Foreign Secretary. Moreover, Archibald Sinclair, the Secretary of State for Air, was an old friend of Churchill's, and he could have approached him directly.

Churchill's written reaction to the news of the mass murders at Auschwitz-Birkenau, set to paper 4 days after his meeting Eden, has been published extensively:

> There is no doubt that this is probably the greatest and most horrible crime ever committed in the whole history of the world, and it has been

done by scientific machinery by nominally civilized men in the name of a great State and one of the leading races in Europe.[64]

On the basis of this short memo, historians have claimed that Churchill was the only one in his administration who understood the unique character of the Holocaust. It has been claimed that his instructions were sabotaged by the Whitehall bureaucracy, while Churchill himself was abroad for much of July and August. A check on Churchill's movements reveals that from 6 July (the day on which he wrote his first directive to Eden) until the end of August 1944, he spent over half of the period – some 34 days – at the helm of government in London. As for "sabotage" by the officials behind his back, it is worth recalling Churchill's well-earned reputation as a Prime Minister who involved himself in the most minor details of government:

> There was no more visible aspect of Churchill's war leadership than his daily scrutiny of what was being done across the whole range of execution of war policy ... Churchill followed everything that was being done with a meticulous eye ... To get things done, to ensure that policies that had been decided upon were not only being implemented but carried out expeditiously and effectively, was at the centre of Churchill's daily work.[65]

For decades, historians believed that the Jews' request to bomb the Auschwitz-Birkenau death camp had *not* come within the purview of Churchill's "daily scrutiny". But with the opening of Churchill's private archives to the general public in the mid-1990s, two identical letters signed by him came to light, both dated 13 July 1944. They were composed less than a week after he had told Eden to get what he could out of the RAF. The letters were addressed to the Archbishop of Canterbury and to Lord Melchett. They were quite clearly replies to their appeals to bomb Auschwitz:

> There is no doubt in my mind that we are in the presence of one of the greatest and most horrible crimes ever committed ... I need not assure you that the situation has received and will receive the most urgent consideration from my colleagues and myself but, as the Foreign Secretary stated [in a speech in the Commons on 5 July] the principal hope of terminating it must remain the speedy victory of the Allied Nations.[66]

Churchill's letter, probably written for him by the Foreign Office, was in line with the Allies' obtuse policy towards the Jews of Europe, which turned its back on the known fact that the Jews were the only people living under a Nazi death sentence. In early September 1944, Richard Law of the Foreign Office gave the government's verdict to the Jewish Agency – they would be unable to bomb Auschwitz. One of the disingenuous reasons given was that RAF aircraft did not have the range. But in fact Auschwitz lay directly under the flight path of the more than 100 RAF aircraft that in August 1944 flew far greater distances, in order to drop food and military supplies to the Polish Home Army insurgents in Warsaw. The flight paths of the aircraft flying to Warsaw took them almost directly over the Auschwitz-Birkenau camp.[67]

Gilbert has compared Churchill's intensive campaign to save the Polish army from decimation in Warsaw in August 1944 to his reaction to the Auschwitz bombing proposal:

> [Churchill's] appeals [to Stalin, to help the Polish Home Army in Warsaw] ... show the extent to which a matter considered of importance could be tackled at the highest level. This was a level which the Hungarian deportations, the Brand proposals and the bombing of Auschwitz never reached.[68]

After the war, there was a tendency by those who had held power to deny any knowledge of what had happened to the Jews during the war. In a statement before the Commons on 1 August 1946, Churchill stated, with a remarkable display of "diplomatic amnesia":

> I must say I had no idea, when the war came to an end, of the horrible massacres which had occurred; the millions and millions that have been slaughtered. That dawned on us gradually after the struggle was over.[69]

In recent decades there has been some debate on whether the bombing of Auschwitz-Birkenau in 1944 was technically feasible.[70] A symposium held in Washington in 1993 concluded that the gas chambers and incinerators at Auschwitz-Birkenau *could* have been destroyed from the air, with little or no collateral damage. The *post hoc* claim that a bombing raid would have caused many fatalities among the camp's Jewish inmates was not an inhibiting factor in 1944. In any case, the risk of "collateral damage" shrinks to insignificance when compared to what the Allies knew about the camp at the time – that it had a capacity to put to death 10–12,000 human beings per day.[71]

The answer to the enigma of why the Allies never bombed Auschwitz lies in the Allies' higher priorities and, in the case of many policy makers, plain anti-Semitism. The Foreign Office's reputation for anti-Semitism was well earned. One example is Sir Alexander Cadogan, one of Britain's most distinguished and influential civil servants. From 1938 to 1946, he was the Permanent Under-Secretary of State at the Foreign Office. His private diary provides an insight into the private prejudices of the official mind. In January 1944, the Soviet newspaper *Pravda* printed a mischievous, entirely spurious story about British negotiations with the Nazis for a separate peace. Venting his spleen into his diary, Cadogan directed an entirely gratuitous gibe against the Jews:

> They [the Soviets] are the most stinking creepy set of Jews I've ever come across.[72]

We also have the evidence of Sir Isaiah Berlin who, as noted already, served as the eyes and ears of the Foreign Office in Washington from 1942 to 1945. He found Foreign Office intelligence assessments about the Yishuv both "anti-Semitic and nonsensical". His initial illusion that a British Jew might "work happily in the Foreign Office" was shattered by his experiences in Washington.[73]

Perhaps the outstanding example was Anthony Eden, Churchill's Foreign Secretary from December 1940 to July 1945. Eden was the man charged by Churchill with determining British policy towards those European Jews trapped in Nazi-occupied Europe.[74] Eden was the quintessential English aristocrat, possessed of an inflated, colonialist hubris, with all of the attendant class and race prejudices. He was by education (Oriental languages at Oxford University) and inclination a fervent Arabophile. By corollary, he was anti-Semitic, a prejudice that he was careful not to display in public. After the war, one of Eden's personal acquaintances, Morley Safer, the Canadian CBS news reporter, recalled:

> The real issue was passive anti-Semitism within the British establishment – sometimes not so passive. Anthony Eden made his and the British government's position clear early on in the war; any attempt to negotiate the rescue of some Jews might result in Hitler "wanting us to take all the Jews". His private memoranda were even more, shall we say, explicit.[75]

Lest Safer's judgement be dismissed as idle gossip, we also have the contemporary testimony of Oliver Harvey, Eden's private secretary. His diary entry for 25 April 1943 reads:

> Unfortunately A.E. is immovable on the subject of Palestine. He loves Arabs and hates Jews.[76]

No one will ever know how effective or successful Allied bombing raids on Auschwitz-Birkenau might have been, or how many Jews might have been saved. But we now know that such an operation *was* feasible and had a reasonable chance of success. The excuses given by the Allies to the Jews were in the main disingenuous subterfuge. Had Churchill been willing in August 1944 to divert to Auschwitz-Birkenau just a handful of the RAF planes that flew to Warsaw (under his personal orders and supervision), the moral history of World War Two would have been radically different.

Allied policy towards the rescue of Jews didn't change even when their military fortunes improved, from 1943. Their refusal to divert military resources to rescue Jews had more to do with a lack of political will than with military incapacity. It is a curious fact that for the entire duration of the war, neither Churchill nor Roosevelt ever spoke publicly about the mass murder of the Jews.[77]

The Zionists' conclusions

It remains only to note the Zionists' total disillusion with the Allies – something they took good care not to publicize. In 1945, the Jews were a decimated, embittered people. They were unable to "understand" the Allies' failure to follow up on their solemn declarations with action.

After Germany's surrender in May 1945, Weizmann wrote to Churchill, asking him to redeem the promise he had made to him on 4 November 1944, to establish a "generous" Jewish state in a part of Palestine after the war. But Churchill had been alienated from the Zionist cause in November 1944 by the assassination by Jewish terrorists of his personal friend, Lord Moyne, the Minister of State in Cairo.[78] Churchill replied laconically that any settlement of the Palestine problem would have to await the Peace Conference.

At a closed meeting of the Zionist Political Committee held in London on 17 June to discuss Churchill's reply, there was a general feeling of outrage and frustration. Ben-Gurion called Churchill's letter an insult to their intelligence. But the most bitter reaction came from Weizmann himself, long suspected by the Yishuv leaders of being too close to the British:

> The P.M., General Smuts, the late President Roosevelt, had all let them down, maybe not intentionally, but inadvertently. **They made promises which they did not carry out or mean to carry out**.
> He felt very bitter ... Nobody cared what happened to the Jews. **Nobody had raised a finger to stop them being slaughtered**. They did not even bother about the remnant which had survived.[79]

The Zionists realized that the Allies had treated all their appeals disingenuously, that they had prevaricated when asked to be allowed to send aid to Jewish communities in Nazi-occupied Europe, to mount rescue efforts or to bomb the Auschwitz-Birkenau death camp. Churchill was singled out for particular denigration. Rabbi Fishman of the Mizrachi movement urged the Zionists to organize mass demonstrations, to protest his record:

> The P.M. [Churchill] had done nothing for them during his period of office ... No people had been fooled as the Jewish People had been fooled by the British government.[80]

No one dissented from these sentiments, but wiser counsels – Zionist *realpolitik* – prevailed. A personal attack on Churchill would alienate him from their cause, something they could not afford to do. Whether he was re-elected as Prime Minister, as expected, or even if he lost the post-war elections, Churchill's services might still be needed.

It has been suggested that in November 1947, the United Nations Resolution to partition Palestine was given as some kind of a compensation for the Jews' suffering during the war. This claim has never been substantiated by hard evidence. On the contrary, one scholarly study was unable to "find evidence that the Holocaust played a decisive or even a significant role" in the establishment of the state of Israel.[81] The collective conscience of the West, while perhaps uneasy at times, was not sufficient to move a majority of the members of the United Nations to vote for the establishment of a Jewish state in Palestine.

A Mass Observation survey carried out in England in 1947, on "public attitudes to the Palestine conflict", found a general indifference to the issue, and concluded: "Jewish sufferings during the war are not mentioned as a reason for sympathizing with Zionism aims".[82]

Winston Churchill, the mythical champion of Zionism, made one of the most blatant rejections of the Zionists' hopes in a public debate in the Commons on 1 August 1946:

> No one can imagine that there is room in Palestine for the great masses of Jews who wish to leave Europe, or that they could be absorbed in any period which it is useful to contemplate. **The idea that the Jewish Problem can be solved or even helped by a vast dumping of the Jews of Europe into Palestine is really too silly to consume our time in the House of Commons this afternoon. I am not absolutely sure that we should not be in too great a hurry to give up the idea that European Jewry may live in the countries where they belong** ... It is quite clear, however, that this crude [Zionist] idea of letting all the Jews of Europe go into Palestine has no relation either to the problem of Europe or to the problem which arises in Palestine.[83]

The general consensus about the return of European Jews to their countries of origin was not apparently influenced by a pogrom against the Jews that had taken place at the Polish city of Kielce, on 4 July 1946, just 4 weeks prior to this Commons debate. The pogrom had been reported in the British press, and had been mentioned by Lord Nathaniel Rothschild, in a House of Lords debate the day before.[84] Polish Jews had been murdered sporadically, as soon as the Germans left the country, in late 1944. But on 4 July 1946, the deadliest post-war pogrom took place at Kielce. Incited by the Polish Communist armed forces, on the old charges of a medieval blood libel, the pogrom took the lives of 42 Jews and left another 40 wounded. For Polish Jewry, the Kielce pogrom was a breaking point, after which they realized that they had no future in Poland.

But the Allies continued to maintain that they had spilled much blood in defeating Nazi Germany, to make Europe liberal and free and therefore, the Jews of Europe should return to their countries of origin. But behind the Allies' pious statements lay the fact that Western interests required the retention of the Arabs' friendship, and secure access to their strategic assets. The imposition of a Jewish state on Palestine, against the will of the Arab majority there, would not serve those interests.

The Jews understood that much more could have been done to save their European brethren. They learned, in the most tragic of circumstances, that the Great Powers' own interests prevailed over humanitarian considerations. Therefore, the real nexus between the Holocaust and the establishment of Israel lay in the Zionists' bitter conclusion that the Allies could not be relied on any longer, and that they would have to fight for a Jewish state in Palestine, even before they had reached a majority. The Zionists took their struggle for a Jewish state to the United Nations. But at the same time, from the end of 1945, Ben-Gurion began to mobilize funds for the purchase of military equipment, in preparation for the inevitable war against the Arabs.

Notes

1 Richard Breitman, *Official Secrets: What the Nazis Planned, What the British and Americans Knew*, New York: Hill and Wang, 1998, and Richard Breitman, Norman Goda and Timothy Naftali, *U.S. Intelligence and the Nazis*, Cambridge: Cambridge University Press, 2005.
2 The airlift to Warsaw was essentially a political duel between Churchill and Stalin over whether Poland would fall into the Western or Soviet sphere of influence after the war; cf. Michael J. Cohen, *Churchill and the Jews*, revised paperback edition, London: Frank Cass, 2003, pp. 301–2.
3 Weizmann to Wise, 20 June 1942, WA, and Cohen, *Palestine: Retreat from the Mandate, 1936–1945*, London/New York: Paul Elek/Holmes and Meier, 1978, pp. 130–31, 134–37.
4 Halifax to Eden, 1 July 1942, FO 371/31379, NA. On the Biltmore Plan and the Ben-Gurion–Weizmann clash, cf. Cohen, ibid, pp. 130–35. The Foreign Office was encouraged to support Weizmann by his close friend, Isaiah Berlin, who was the department's "eyes and ears" in Washington from 1942 to 45; Berlin's weekly reports to the Foreign Office were held in high regard and read also by Churchill; cf. Michael Ignatieff, *Isaiah Berlin: A Life*, New York: Metropolitan Books, 1998, pp. 119–20.
5 *House of Commons Debates (H.C. Deb.)*, 13 October 1943 vol. 392, cols 920–1012. Reprinted in Winston S. Churchill, *Onwards to Victory: War Speeches by the Right Hon. Winston S. Churchill,* London: Cassell, 1944, p. 238.
6 Bernard Wasserstein, *Britain and the Jews of Europe*, London: Institute of Jewish Affairs/Clarendon Press, 1979 p. 356. The psychiatrist he cited was Anthony Storr.
7 ibid, p. 350, and Martin Gilbert, *Auschwitz and the Allies*, second edition, New York: Holt, Rinehart, 1981, p. 340.
8 Gilbert, ibid.
9 Tony Kushner, "Different Worlds. British Perceptions of the Second World War" in David Cesarani, ed., *The Final Solution: Origins and Implementation*, London: Routledge, 1994, p. 247; also Barbara Rogers, "British Intelligence and the Holocaust: Auschwitz and the Allies Re-examined", *Journal of Holocaust Education*, vol. 8/1, summer 1999, pp. 89–106.
10 Rogers, ibid, pp. 92–93; Walter Z. Laqueur, *The Terrible Secret*, London: Weidenfeld & Nicolson, 1980, pp. 73–75, 199, 206.
11 F.H. Hinsley, *British Intelligence in the Second World War: Its Influence on Strategy and Operations,* vol. two, London: HMSO, 1981, and Keith Jeffrey, *The Secret History of MI6*, New York: 2010, pp. xiii, 688.
12 Hinsley, ibid, appendix V, p. 671. The Order Police worked alongside the Einsatzgruppen, killing off the civilian populations of areas conquered by the Wehrmacht.

13 Breitman, Goda, Naftali, *U.S.* p. 444, also pp. 17–19, 21–27, 36–37; Breitman, *Official Secrets*, and Richard Breitman, Norman Goda and Timothy Naftali, *Hitler's Shadow: Nazi War Criminals, U.S. Intelligence and the Cold War*, www.archives.gov/iwg/reports/hitlers-shadow.pdf. Breitman secured the opening of the US intelligence files for his *Official Secrets* by a Freedom of Information request and negotiations with the National Security Agency. This set a precedent for appeals by British historians for the opening of British intelligence files.
14 Rogers, "British Intelligence", pp. 92–96, 103.
15 Breitman, *Official Secrets*, pp. 31, 34, 37–38, 40, 41, 91.
16 Rogers, "British Intelligence", p. 90.
17 Christopher Andrew, "Churchill and Intelligence", *Intelligence and National Security*, vol. 3/2, July 1988, pp. 181, 183, 192, and Martin Gilbert, *Churchill's War Leadership*, New York: Vintage, 2004, p. 30.
18 Rogers, "British Intelligence", p. 92.
19 Breitman, *Official Secrets*, pp. 92–93.
20 ibid, p. 94.
21 Deleuge was "overlooked" by the Nuremberg prosecutors, but he was finally prosecuted and executed by the Czechs in 1946, for his responsibility for the destruction of the village and the mass executions of the population of Lidice in June 1942 (in retaliation for the assassination of Heydrich).
22 Summary of Enigma decode, 12 September 1941, in HW1 series, NA, cited in Martin Kolinsky, *Britain's War in the Middle East*, London: Macmillan, 1999, pp. 214–15.
23 Breitman, *Official Secrets*, p. 96.
24 ibid, p. 94, and idem, *U.S. Intelligence*, p. 468. Since most of the MI6 intelligence documents are still closed to the public, it is still impossible to know exactly how much the British knew about the Nazis' killing programmes.
25 Richard Breitman, Allan J. Lichtman, *FDR and the Jews*, Cambridge, Mass: Harvard University Press, 2013, p. 196.
26 Kolinsky, *Britain's War*, p. 215.
27 Breitman, *Official Secrets*, pp. 100–101.
28 Breitman, *U.S. Intelligence*, pp. 36–37.
29 Cohen, *Churchill*, p. 263. On the calibrations of the Enigma machine, cf. Peter Calvocoressi, *Top Secret Ultra*, London: Sphere, 1980, p. 15.
30 Rogers, "British Intelligence", pp. 94–95.
31 ibid, p. 96.
32 Breitman, *Official Secrets*, pp. 140–41.
33 ibid.
34 Text in: http://en.wikipedia.org/wiki/Riegner_Telegram
35 Breitman, *Official Secrets*, p. 145.
36 ibid, pp.148–49. A copy of their account reached the OSS.
37 ibid, p. 149.
38 Isabelle Tombs, "Szmul Zygielbojm, the British Labour Party and the Holocaust", in Christine Collette, Stephen Bird, eds, *Jews, Labour and the Left, 1918–48*, Aldershot: Ashgate, 2000, pp. 123–26.
39 ibid, p. 127.
40 Breitman, *Official Secrets*, p. 157; also Henry F. Feingold, *The Politics of Rescue: The Roosevelt Administration and the Holocaust, 1938–1945*, New Brunswick: Rutgers University Press, 1970, and www.fdrlibrary.marist.edu/archives/pdfs/holocaust.pdf.
41 House of Commons Debates [H.C. Deb.] Vol. 385, col. 2087; also diary entry, 17 December 1942, in Harold Nicolson, *Diaries and Letters, 1939–1945*, edited by Nigel Nicolson, London: Collins, 1967, p. 268. Nicolson enjoyed a distinguished political and literary career. In 1931, he began a short spell with Oswald

Moseley's New Party, whose newspaper he edited. But in 1932, he dissociated himself from Moseley's British Union of Fascists. He was elected to Parliament in 1935, as a National Labour candidate. He served for a year in Churchill's coalition at the Ministry of Information. He published 20 books, including studies of British and French literary figures and works of history. He was married to the writer Vita Sackville-West.

42 Breitman, *Official Secrets*, pp. 153–54.
43 Correspondence in Cohen, *Churchill*, p. 269; on Churchill's instructions that the Foreign Office should handle all Jewish appeals, see Meier Sompolinsky, *Britain and the Holocaust*, Brighton: Sussex Academic Press, 1999.
44 Wasserstein, *Britain and ...*, pp. 302–3.
45 Nicolson, *Diaries*, entries of 13 June 1945, p. 469, and 9 December 1942.
46 Initialled minute of 22 December 1942, FO 371/32682, W17521, NA.
47 Diary entry, 11 January 1944, *Nicolson Diaries*, p. 344.
48 Breitman, *Official Secrets*, pp. 118, and idem, *U.S. Intelligence*, p. 27.
49 cf. Jerry Klinger, *Schmuel Zygielbojm: A Lost Cassandra, the Holocaust and Zionism*: www.jewishmag.com/155mag/schmuel_zygielbojm/schmuel_zygielbojm.htm
50 Tombs, Szmul Zygeilbojm, p. 127.
51 Klinger, *Schmuel Zygielbojm*.
52 ibid. It is unclear whether he committed suicide by taking poison, or by turning on the gas in his apartment.
53 Minutes in FO 371/32682, W17521, NA. The Foreign Office had its figures wrong. Nine months later, in November 1943, the Colonial Secretary announced that 31,078 immigration certificates still remained.
54 Breitman, *Official Secrets*, pp. 183–85, 194, and Sachar, *Europe Leaves*, p. 436.
55 Prem 4/51/8, NA. Lady Eva Violet Mond Isaacs (1895–1973), daughter of Alfred Mond (Lord Melchett) and an Anglican mother; she became Marchioness of Reading when her husband's father died in 1935; converting to Judaism in the 1930s, she took up her father's fervent commitment to Zionism, becoming Vice President of the World Jewish Congress and President of its British section.
56 Churchill to Lady Reading, 21 February 1943, Prem 4/51/8, NA.
57 Melchett to Churchill, cited in Jean Goodman, *The Churchill Legacy*, London: Weidenfeld and Nicolson, 1982, p. 192.
58 Breitman, *Official Secrets*, pp. 72, 113–16, 121.
59 Rogers, "British Intelligence", p. 94.
60 cf. Wyman, "Why Auschwitz was Never Bombed", *Commentary*, vol. 65/5, May 1978, p. 47.
61 The full Vrba-Wexler report: www.holocaustresearchproject.org/othercamps/auschproto.html
62 cf. Rafael Medoff, *Blowing the Whistle on Genocide: Joseph E. Dubois and the Struggle for a U.S. Response to the Holocaust*, Indiana/London: Purdue University Press, 2009, and www.wymaninstitute.org/americanhero.php. For the conduct of the US Consuls in Europe, see Bat-Ami Zucker, *In Search of Refuge: Jews and US Consuls in Nazi Germany, 1933–1941*, London: Vallentine Mitchell, 2001.
63 Breitman, *Official Secrets*, pp. 200–201, 207–8, and Medoff, *Blowing the Whistle*. The War Refugee Board gave loans that helped keep alive Jews in occupied Europe, and helped over 2000 Jews to escape from France to Switzerland and Spain.
64 Churchill to Foreign Secretary Eden, July 11, 1944, in FO 371/42809, also Prem 4/51/10, NA; reprinted in Winston Churchill, *Triumph and Tragedy: The Second World War*, vol. 4, London: Cassell, 1954, p. 597.
65 Gilbert, *Churchill's War Leadership*, pp. 49–50.
66 Churchill to the Archbishop of Canterbury and Lord Melchett, July 13, 1944, Char 20/138A, Churchill Archives, Churchill College, Cambridge University,

67 Cohen, *Churchill*, pp. 300–301.
68 Gilbert article, *The Jerusalem Post*, 7 March 1980.
69 Debate on 1 August 1946, in *H.C. Deb.*, 5th series, vol. 426.
70 This claim was made as recently as 2012; cf. Yehuda Bauer, "How to Misinterpret History: On '"The Holocaust, America and American Jewry" Revisited'", *Israel Journal of Foreign Affairs*, vol. six/3, 2012, pp. 137–50.
71 Michael J. Neufeld, Michael Berenbaum, eds, *The Bombing of Auschwitz: Should the Allies Have Attempted It?* New York: St Martin's Press, 2000.
72 Entry for 17 January 1944, David Dilks, ed., *The Diaries of Sir Alexander Cadogan, 1938–1945*, London: Cassell, 1971, p. 597.
73 Michael Ignatieff, *Isaiah Berlin: A Life*, New York: Metropolitan Books, 1998, pp. 117–18.
74 On the anti-Semitism of the Foreign Office during World War Two, cf. Gilbert, *Auschwitz*, p. 364, and Wasserstein, *Britain*, pp. 38–39, 350.
75 Private communication from Morley Safer to Richard Breitman, cited in *Official Secrets*, p. 243.
76 Harvey diary, 25 April 1943, cited in Wasserstein, *Britain*, p. 34.
77 Alexander J. Groth, *Accomplices: Churchill, Roosevelt, and the Holocaust*, New York: Peter Lang, 2011, p. 72. Groth notes that in all of his 400 press conferences during the war, Roosevelt spoke at far greater length about his pet dog Fala than he did about the fate of the Jews.
78 On Churchill's reactions to Moyne's assassination, cf. Michael J. Cohen, "The Moyne Assassination, November 1944: A Political Analysis", *Middle Eastern Studies*, vol. 15/3, October 1979, and Bernard Wasserstein, "The Assassination of Lord Moyne", *Transactions of the Jewish Historical Society of England*, vol. 27, 1982.
79 Minutes of meeting in Z4/302/29, CZA. My emphases.
80 ibid.
81 Evyatar Friesel, "The Holocaust and the Birth of Israel", *Wiener Library Bulletin*, vol. 32, nos. 49/50, 1979, pp. 51–60.
82 Paul Keleman, "Looking the Other Way: The British Labour Party, Zionism and Palestinians", in Christine Collette, Stephen Bird, eds, *Jews, Labour and the Left, 1918–48*, Aldershot: Ashgate, 2000, p. 143.
83 *H.C. Deb.*, 5th series, vol. 426, col. 1258. My emphasis.
84 The Kielce pogrom was reported on during the course of July by the *Manchester Guardian* (seven times) and in the *Times* (twice). Nathaniel Rothschild referred to "pogroms based on the old, old story of the Jews murdering Christian children. And Cardinals, in spite of the precepts of many Popes, who refuse to condemn such acts". House of Lords Debates, 31 July 1946, vol. 142, col. 1188.

16 World War Two
The British and the Arabs

> Until reinforcements can reach the Middle East, our whole position is rather in the nature of a gigantic bluff.
>
> Foreign Office note, July 1940

Two major developments affected the Palestinian Arab cause during World War Two; the first was the disintegration and discrediting of their leadership in British eyes, a process that reached its climax with the flight of the Mufti to Berlin in 1941, and his wartime collaboration with the Nazis. The second development was the appropriation of the Palestinians' cause by the Arab League in 1944.

From 1940 to 1942, the period of maximum British vulnerability in the Middle East, they sought to retain the goodwill of the Arab states at almost any cost. From mid-1943, after all Axis forces had been cleared from North Africa, the British began to plan for their post-war hegemony in the Middle East. Their main concern was the challenge expected from the Soviet Union, their current ally. By the summer of 1944, with Germany apparently defeated, the parameters of the Cold War were already taking shape, and with them, the threat of World War Three. The friendship of the Arab states rose to an even higher premium.

The Palestinian Arabs in disarray

In June 1939, the meeting of the HAC in Beirut rejected the 1939 White Paper by a bare majority (six out of ten), against the advice of Egypt and Iraq. However, once the HAC's decision became known, all the Arab states, including Trans-Jordan, fell into line and added their stamp of approval. As noted already, the Mufti vetoed the new proposals because the British refused to pardon him and allow him to return to Palestine. The Mufti had reason to fear that in his absence, the Nashashibis, with British support, would seize power. On 29 May 1939, the Nashashibis published their support for the White Paper and announced their willingness to co-operate with the British.

The HAC's decision ran counter to popular sentiment among the Palestinians. The Mufti tried in vain to wrest more concessions from the British – the release of 2000 detainees and the commutation of some of the sentences passed on others. When the British rejected any amnesty, the rebel commanders also rejected the White Paper. The Mufti and the unpardoned rebels shared a common interest in trying to revive the rebellion. But they miscalculated that another brief period of violence would secure further concessions, and their own pardons.

But not all Palestinians agreed with the Mufti's line. Some of the rebel section commanders – those of Jaffa, Lydda, Nablus, Ramleh and Tiberias – signed a manifesto accusing him of rejecting the White Paper due to personal motives. The manifesto listed acts of wanton terror by the Mufti's henchmen against their fellow Arabs, and condemned him for misappropriating *waqf* funds and for selling of parcels of his own lands to the Jews. As noted above, the British were well aware that the Mufti had acted as a broker for the sales of Arab lands to Jews.

However, the internecine terror that had marred the second and most violent stage of the rebellion had all but silenced the voices of moderation. Since 1938, support for partition had become tantamount to risking one's life. The terrorists had succeeded in intimidating all but a small minority of the Palestinian Arabs.

During the early stages of the war, years of military crises, the British imposed a ban on all Arab political activity in Palestine. The ban was lifted only in August 1943 (after all Axis forces had left North Africa). All charges against the exiled Arab politicians were dropped and everyone but the members of the defunct HAC was allowed to return to Palestine – on condition that they did not engage in anti-British subversive activity. Jemal Husayni, the Mufti's cousin and right-hand man, remained interned in Rhodesia. He was not allowed to return to Palestine until February 1946 and then, on condition that until a permanent political solution was reached, the Arabs would acquiesce in continued Jewish immigration at the rate of 1500 per month.

Although the HAC had rejected the 1939 White Paper, the Arabs took it for granted that it represented the sacrosanct policy of the government. Foreign Office officials were frustrated and exacerbated by the Arab states' failure to endorse the 1939 White Paper. However, they appreciated that Britain could not now retreat from that offer:

> They [the Palestinians] had their chances, at the time of the Conferences on Palestine, for an agreement between Great Britain and the Arab States which would have been binding on all future Governments. By refusing to accept the White Paper they missed their chance. But this does not mean that they would not regard it as a breach of faith if the present Government went back on the solution which they have indicated in the White Paper to be the most just which is possible in all circumstances.[1]

Many moderate Palestinians saw the benefits of the new policy, including the lucrative perquisites of office. Indeed, some rebel leaders claimed that the new policy was designed to create jobs for the *effendis*. Some of the land-owning opposition was interested in aligning with the government in order to destroy the political and financial influence of their rivals. But few dared to repudiate the decision of the HAC, which had been endorsed by the Arab states. Nor did any one dare to challenge the Mufti's authority, if only due to fear for his own personal safety. Finally, many would not commit themselves to the White Paper before being convinced of London's intention to implement its constitutional measures – the appointment of Palestinian ministers and concrete steps towards self-government.[2]

During the war, most of the Palestinian pre-war leaders who had not been killed were either exiled or imprisoned. The Nashashibi-led Defence Party ceased to be a political force. They were discredited due to their initial acceptance of partition, and between 1937 and 1938 their followers had been decimated by the Husayni terrorist bands.

Fakhri Nashashibi's attempt during the war to resuscitate the Defence Party failed miserably. As seen already, his November 1938 claim to represent over half of the Palestine Arab community was repudiated by his own uncle, Ragheb Bey. The British remained convinced that the Mufti was the only Palestinian leader who enjoyed national support.

In the words of one scholar, Palestinian politics during the war were characterized by "a plethora of competing organizations and the lack of central political leadership".[3] The pan-Arab Istiqlal (Independence) party tried to fill the political vacuum. The Istiqlal had been founded in 1932 by a younger, educated generation, alienated from traditional clan politics. It counted among its members bankers, businessmen, journalists, lawyers and teachers, as well as a few scions of the land-owning notability. It focused its efforts in the economic field, in an attempt to save Palestine from a Jewish takeover. It established an Arab agricultural bank, which opened several branches across the country, and it revived the Arab Chamber of Commerce.

But the Istiqlal had to contend with a general inertia and the ubiquitous jealousies of political rivals. Its advocacy of unity with Syria failed to address the immediate threats facing the Arabs in Palestine: the British mandate and its sponsorship of the Jewish National Home. The party's adoption of the 1939 White Paper discredited it as being too close to the British. In November 1943, it tried to convene a 15th Palestine National Conference, but the other clan-based factions, still riven by dissension and mutual suspicions, refused to attend. The Istiqlal itself became plagued by internal feuding and by financial problems. Unlike the Mufti's Palestine Arab Party, it failed to establish a nation-wide network of party branches. It failed to establish itself as a grass-roots national movement with claims to be the spokesman of the Palestinians.[4]

Although their leaders were in exile, the Husaynis still acted as if the Palestinian leadership was their prerogative. The Mufti's prestige and influence declined, especially after 1943, as he continued to work on behalf of the Nazi cause in Berlin. But he was never disowned, and Palestinian politics still orbited around his clan. The Palestine Arab party was resuscitated in November 1944, under the nominal presidency of Tewfiq al-Husayni, a relation of the Mufti. It was apparent that the activists in Palestine were merely deputizing until the return of their exiled leaders.

These political developments took place against a background of significant socio-economic change in Palestine. The increased demands of the British armies in the Middle East stimulated a rapid growth of local industries. World War Two jump-started the Palestinian economy. Its human resources were mobilized to supply the needs of the large British armies stationed in the region. Palestine became a huge British base, and its industrial infrastructure was expanded in order to reduce Britain's dependence on external supplies. Local industries manufactured not only military equipment and certain types of ammunition, but also consumer goods for the huge garrisons starved of American and European goods. Given that the Mediterranean route was closed to merchant traffic for much of the war, imports from within the Middle East grew from 18 per cent in 1939 to 60 per cent in 1943. During the first 5 years of the war, the nominal value of Palestine's foreign trade more than doubled, from P£20 million in 1939 to about P£50 million in 1944. A growing balance-of-payments deficit was covered by over P£100 million in British military purchases, and an import of Jewish capital in the region of P£38 millions. However, given the rate of inflation, the real value of imports – especially in manufactured goods – fell during the war by more than one half.

The major field of expansion was industry. Both the Arab and the Jewish industrial sectors expanded rapidly, and enjoyed a steep rise in revenue. Arab industries prospered, but not as much as those in the Jewish sector. From 1939 to 1942, Jewish industrial output increased by an estimated 200 per cent, that of the Arabs by 77 per cent. The numbers of those employed in industry rose from 40–50,000 to 70–80,000. Jewish industries offered greater productivity, especially in the more technically complex military fields. The Arabs were able to offer lower labour costs for less sophisticated goods. Due to Britain's burgeoning military demands, the number of Arab industries quadrupled between 1939 and 1942.

These developments stimulated a large-scale migration of hundreds of thousands of Arab villagers to the towns, where they found work in urban industries, either on a daily basis or for longer periods. Agriculture became isolated from foreign markets and suffered from a shortage of labour. By 1940, almost 80 per cent of the Christian Arabs lived in towns, compared with 30 per cent of the Moslems. One study has estimated that by 1945 fully one-third of the Arab work force was employed in wage labour.[5]

The mass migration of Arabs from villages to cities and work camps caused social and family dislocation, and the new problems of periodical unemployment and inflation. With the general rise in incomes there came shortages and rationing, which led to inflation and a black market. It took the British until July 1943 to establish a War Economic Advisory Council, whose task was to devise instruments for subsidizing a variety of necessities, and to harness inflation.

The exile and/or discrediting of many of the leaders of the old, land-owning ruling clans eroded the power base of the traditional elites, whose patronage system lost much of its power. The growth of an uprooted, landless peasantry aggravated the fissures already present inside the Arab community. The salaried, commercial elite, based largely in coastal towns such as Haifa, Jaffa and Gaza, expanded and sought power through new commercial institutions.

The implementation of the White Paper constitution

During the months of military crisis in 1940, Whitehall debated whether to concede the Palestinian Arabs' demand for the implementation of the constitutional steps promised in paragraph 10/4 of the 1939 White Paper. This clause provided for the appointment of indigenous Palestinian heads of departments – in the ratio of two Arabs to each Jew – as soon as "peaceful conditions" were restored. The Arabs appreciated that progress towards sovereignty held the key to their future. Even if Jewish immigration and land sales to the Jews were severely restricted by the White Paper (the Arabs were aware that the official restrictions were frequently circumvented), the Palestinians knew that if they did not secure sovereign control over their own future while they were still in a two-thirds majority of the population, no other measures would help. They had already experienced reversals of British policy, and feared that if the Zionists were allowed to build up their numbers by immigration, they were likely to take over the country by force.

From 1940 to 1941, the British gave some consideration to trading off the mobilization of the Jewish Division for some measures of constitutional progress in Palestine. The Palestinian Arabs made no demands of the British during the war – many of their leaders were exiled abroad, while those still in the country were fragmented by internal rivalries. The main agitators for constitutional advance were extraneous; not coincidentally, those who lobbied the British were also rivals for leadership of the Arab world: Nuri al-Said of Hashemite Iraq and Ibn Saud of Wahhabi Saudi Arabia.

Concerned as ever to preserve the benevolent neutrality of the Arab states, the Foreign Office gave serious consideration to their demands for constitutional progress in Palestine. It will be recalled that with the outbreak of war, the Zionists had offered to raise a military force, in return for which they proposed a freeze on all further implementation of the White Paper, including its constitutional clauses.

But Sir Harold MacMichael (High Commissioner from 1938 to 1944) was the main obstacle to implementing the constitutional clauses of the White Paper. He refused to relinquish his absolute control over the country. His opinion, as the man-on-the-spot, carried great weight and could not be ignored. MacMichael favoured the implementation of the White Paper's restrictions on immigration and on land sales to Jews. But he vetoed any measure that would reduce his own authority in the country, especially not in wartime. Above all, he objected to the transfer of any of his authority to the Palestinian Arabs, whose 3-year rebellion had been crushed not so long ago. In any case, as he pointed out to Whitehall, the Palestinians had no recognized leadership acceptable to the British. He argued that the current calm in Palestine, while the war was in progress, hardly constituted the peaceful conditions envisioned by the White Paper.[6]

The Foreign Office concurred that the present time was not propitious for any constitutional changes in Palestine. But the department had broader considerations in the region – British interests in the Arab states. While agreeing that Britain could not loosen her control of Palestine, the officials speculated whether, if only for the sake of expediency, they might not garner the propaganda value of a further declaration of the government's *intention* to implement the White Paper. The implementation of the White Paper Land Regulations in February 1940 was regarded by them as a temporary sop to the Arabs. On the eve of their publication, Lacy Bagallay, head of the Eastern department of the Foreign Office, noted:

> The issue of the Land Regulation in a few days ought to keep the Arab States and the Arabs of Palestine quiet for a while. After that, the demand for something to be done in the constitutional line may grow stronger, and unless some further sop can be found, e.g. some extensions of what has already been done in the way of pardoning offenders, or some further pressures to put down illegal immigration, we may have to press the Colonial Office to do something under the constitutional head.[7]

British policy towards Palestine during the first half of 1940 fluctuated wildly with every change in British fortunes on the field of battle. With the German triumphs in the Low Countries and northern France, Axis propaganda in the Middle East, promising independence to Palestine and Syria, assumed greater significance. On 25 May 1940, at the height of the Dunkirk crisis, Nuri al-Said of Iraq asked for a clear-cut statement from London guaranteeing self-government for Palestine and Syria.

Bagallay rejected making any further concessions beyond enacting the Land Transfers Regulations. The British had reached the conclusion that their hegemony in the Middle East depended upon their military strength in the region. The Arabs' friendship was contingent upon British victories against the Italians, and from 1941, against Rommel's Afrika Korps. Bagallay rejected the notion that any further political gestures might guarantee Arab loyalty:

> Great Britain and France will not help themselves ... by making further declarations about Palestinian Arab independence. Beyond an affirmation that the White Paper remains the policy of His Majesty's Government (if it does) there is no further declaration that they could sincerely and

honestly make, and if they did make one it would not really satisfy Arab aspirations. It might, on the contrary, merely confirm the Arabs in their own sense of their own importance and of the present opportunity. The only way in which the two countries can help themselves effectively is to re-persuade the Arabs that they are going to win the war. The best way of achieving this object is to have actual military success. The second best is propaganda about coming military success.[8]

But the logic of this argument collapsed after the military disasters of May-June 1940. Whitehall again became anxious about the consequences for Britain's standing in the Middle East. In late June, following the surrender of the French, Bagallay changed his mind and proposed that Britain should reassure the Arabs of the government's good intent. His note was now tinged with resentment at the yoke imposed by Britain's support for Zionism:

> The acceptance of the German armistice terms by France has made it more important than ever that we should leave no weak joints in our armour in the Middle East. Arab doubts about our Palestine policy is the weakest of all these joints ... It seems to me that the reiteration of our intention to abide by our policy is a small price for the Zionists to pay for the terrible risks we are now running as a result of establishing their national home.[9]

But "reiteration of intentions" was as far as London was prepared to go. In 1939, the Foreign Office had been the prime force behind the passage of the Palestine White Paper. The intention had been to appease the Arabs at the expense of the Zionists, *not* to grant independence or in any way to reduce Britain's own control over the country – certainly not during the war.

Foreign Secretary Halifax proposed that the government reassure the Arabs that the immigration and land sales restrictions provided for by the 1939 White Paper would be enforced – but to tell them that it would not be possible to proceed with the constitutional steps for so long as the war lasted, adding that the government expected to do so when it ended. At a Cabinet meeting held on 3 July 1940, ministers raised objections to Halifax's draft. Clement Attlee (Labour), the Deputy Prime Minister and Lord Privy Seal, stated that he had always opposed the 1939 White Paper. Prime Minister Churchill, who had also opposed the White Paper, saw no reason why they should send any reply at all to Nuri al-Said, seeing that so far, Iraq had done nothing for the Allied war effort. The Cabinet compromised on an anodyne statement, to the effect that it saw no reason to make any change in the policy laid down for Palestine in 1939, and it remained unchanged. If Middle Eastern ambassadors were pressed for clarifications, they were authorized to state that they hoped and expected that after the war, conditions in Palestine would permit the implementation of the various stages of constitutional progress as provided for by the White Paper.[10]

In July 1940, Colonel S.F. Newcombe, an Arabist who had served with T.E. Lawrence during World War One, made a Middle East tour, sponsored by the British Council. His mission was to improve Arab public opinion about Britain. The government agreed that he should stop over in Baghdad, to try unofficially, with the help of Nuri al-Said, to obtain the Mufti's endorsement of the White Paper. On his way, Newcombe was briefed in Jerusalem by the High Commissioner. He was instructed to meet only with Nuri al-Said and with two prominent Palestinians, Jamal Husayni, the Mufti's cousin, and Musa Alami, but not with the Mutfi himself. Newcombe stayed in Baghdad for 2 weeks.

Newcombe's mission failed. The Arabs blamed the failure on Churchill's pro-Zionist prejudices. Musa Alami, who believed wrongly that Newcombe had come on an official government mission, claimed that Haj Amin would have accepted the White Paper provided that its constitutional clauses were implemented immediately. This was supposed to have been part of a package deal whereby Nuri al-Said would agree to declare war on the Axis and place two Iraqi divisions at Britain's disposal. The failure of Newcombe's mission has been cited by some Arabs as having provided the final proof that "Britain was incurably Zionist". It has even been cited as a factor leading to the pro-Axis revolt of Rashid Ali al-Gaylani the following year.[11]

But British documents reveal that the deal proposed by Newcombe was rejected out of hand, not by Churchill but by the Foreign Office – a department that was never suspected of being pro-Zionist. Its officials believed that Newcombe had gone to Baghdad to "try and make the Arabs [i.e. the Mufti] see reason". They were furious when Newcombe exceeded his terms of reference.[12] Although he had ostensibly accepted government policy when briefed in Jerusalem – no pardon for the Mufti and no general amnesty for Arab terrorists – he had proceeded to do "everything that he said he would not do". Newcombe agreed to the HAC's maximum demands – the immediate implementation of the White Paper's constitutional clause. In umbrage, Bagallay commented acidly:

> If Colonel Newcombe is merely going to put forward as suggestions for improving public opinion in Iraq that we should accept all the Arab demands about Palestine, I suggest that the British Council should now be asked to recall him and give him an appointment somewhere where he would do less harm.[13]

As will be shown in the next chapter, the underlying cause of Newcombe's failure was that the Mufti had already committed himself to the Nazi cause, convinced that the Germans were going to win the war. As Britain suffered military reverses, his hopes appeared to be on the brink of fulfilment. The Mufti had approached German officials in Istanbul and Berlin with declarations of support for the Axis well before Newcombe's arrival in Baghdad. Shortly before his arrival, the Mufti had dispatched both his German-speaking private secretary and an Iraqi minister on secret missions to Berlin, to negotiate with the Germans (see Chapter 17).[14]

Following their spectacular victories on the battlefield, German influence in Iraq was growing. Nuri al-Said tried to hedge his bets, between his British patrons and his pro-German officers and Cabinet ministers. When the Mufti had arrived in Baghdad, Nuri had offered to help him establish contact with German officials. The Mufti rejected his advances, preferring instead to work directly with the pro-German officers of the "Golden Square".[15]

When he returned to London, Colonel Newcombe lobbied the Colonial Office on the Palestinians' behalf. On 24 October, at the request of the Colonial Office, Newcombe met with Dr Weizmann, in a misguided attempt to persuade him to agree to the immediate implementation of the constitutional clauses. Newcombe later sent Weizmann a written summary of his proposal. Weizmann replied:

> To please the Arabs, you invite us to accept the White Paper, a denial of all our rights ... Our foremost desire is to help Great Britain to win the war, but we do not consider that we can best accomplish this by committing suicide.[16]

In a memorandum of 2 November 1940, Newcombe wrote an official report of his mission. He argued that the only obstacle to the friendship of the Arab world was their mistrust of Britain over the Palestine question and the only way to restore their faith was the immediate implementation of paragraph 10/4 of the White Paper. Given the details of the Mufti's contacts with the Axis gathered by British Intelligence, the following paragraph must have drawn some wry smiles at Whitehall:

> ... they [the Arabs] fear our inaction to fulfil the White Paper means again that the Government is under the influence of Dr. Weizmann and the Zionists. The Arabs say further that historically they have always looked to Great Britain and would do so again, or as one Arab expressed it "We hate Germans and Italians, we dislike you because of Palestine and Syria: but we know we are in the British house: we can quarrel in our own house, but let us settle our quarrel".[17]

But the most influential and persistent advocate of the Palestinian cause during this period was Sir Miles Lampson, Britain's ambassador to Egypt. His Cairo-centred view of the Arab world was at times totally out of sync with the wider picture as seen from London. With an inflated view of his own importance, his outspoken, on occasion impertinent views ruffled feathers in the highest quarters. For instance, in November 1940, he protested that Churchill's decision to transfer military supplies from Egypt to Greece was "completely crazy". His telegram to the Foreign Office was forwarded to Churchill, who sent him the following reprimand:

You should not telegraph at Government expense such an expression as "completely crazy" when applied by you to grave decisions of policy taken by the Defence Committee and the War Cabinet after considering an altogether wider range of requirements and assets than you can possibly be aware of.[18]

In mid-July 1940, while Newcombe was in Baghdad, Lampson sent a long survey of Arab nationalist trends in the Arab Middle East. He appealed to London against the Cabinet's refusal to proceed with the White Paper's constitutional measures. He feared that the Arabs would conclude from Britain's recent military reverses that she was a spent, if not an already defeated power. He claimed to detect "a strong movement towards confederation in the northern Arabic world, i.e. in Iraq, Syria, Transjordan and Palestine". The French collapse had raised the Syrians' hopes that they would shortly gain their independence. The Middle East Command in Cairo had warned against weakening Vichy's hold on Syria, lest Britain herself be forced to fill the vacuum – something she was currently too weak to do. If concessions in Syria had to be ruled out, then something had to be done in Palestine, where Britain's reverses had also raised expectations of attaining independence soon. He concluded that since they could do nothing to help the Syrians, they must grant some concrete concessions in Palestine – the immediate implementation of paragraph 10/4 of the White Paper.[19]

MacMichael, with his Palestinian perspective, ridiculed Lampson's analysis:

> There is a vast nucleus of variegated intrigue afoot throughout the Arab countries. To speak of it as "a strong movement for some confederation of independent states" suggests a unity which is very far from existing ... I regard it as a fallacy to suppose that to give a few Heads of Departments to Palestinians is likely to turn the politicians of Egypt, Syria and Iraq into likely allies or do more than convince them that we are on the run. The only thing that will achieve the end desired is success in the field of war which will open their eyes to the fact that our friendship is worth cultivating.[20]

An interesting German opinion is provided by Rudolf Hahn, a seasoned diplomat who worked in Syria during the spring of 1941, purchasing arms for the Rashid Ali government. In July of that year, he sent to Berlin his assessment of the potential of the Arab national movement. His derisive, at times whimsical assessment confirmed that of MacMichael:

> After a brief stay in Syria, I found to my astonishment that there was, at all events, no Arab movement there. True nationalist sentiment is unknown to the Syria tribes, a wild and for the most part unlovely mixture of races and religions, spoiled by greed, intrigue and jealousy,

accustomed from olden time to bribery by rival powers ... Independence is the pretext for unbridled speculation – freedom, the shield for unrestrained exploitation of the worker by the ruling class ... I found nothing in Syria that would have been capable of militant action. At the moment of danger, the swaggering leaders of the Arab freedom movement all failed.[21]

The Foreign Office also rejected Lampson's plea. The officials were not impressed by Lampson's warnings. Arab nationalism would not necessarily serve British interests. The fulfilment of the Arabs' aspirations for independence would mean the end of Western colonial rule and Britain's own interests. For as long as modern society depended on oil and for as long as Britain retained its Empire, she would need to maintain her present position in the Arab world. Not only that, but Britain was handicapped by her international obligations to support the Jewish National Home in Palestine. Therefore, by definition, Britain had to be against Arab nationalist aspirations, and no attempts "to get round this hard fact by pleasant phrases or half measures" would help in the long run:

> If we had something really striking to offer the Arabs, such as some assurances regarding the future of Palestine going far beyond the terms of the White Paper, and saying that the Jewish National Home would never be greater than at present, or, better still, could join this with some promise about the independence of Syria, the propitiation might be real and the attempt worth making. But what Sir Miles Lampson's recommendations really boil down to is to bring about one bit of the White Paper, i.e. the constitutional proposals, into force even while the war is on.[22]

Not only that, but the Foreign Office feared that any political initiative by Britain at the present juncture would convince the Arabs of Britain's vulnerability. They might already be asking themselves:

> ... why, if Germany with Italy at her side is going to win the war anyhow, should we engage in a hopeless struggle for what are in the event not our interests, but the interests of Britain and France? Would we not do better to accept the inevitable and make the best terms we can with the conqueror?
> Until reinforcements can reach the Middle East, our whole position is rather in the nature of a gigantic bluff. That bluff to succeed must be consistent ... tinkering about with minor questions arising out of (the White Paper) policy is not going to have a decisive effect in the face of much greater issues upon which opinion in the Middle East will ultimately depend.[23]

Lampson returned to the charge, after yet another military defeat, this time at the hands of the Italians in British Somaliland in August 1940.[24] Lampson had been briefed by Newcombe on his mission to Baghdad. Once again, he appealed to London to implement the constitutional clauses of the White Paper, "in order to keep the Arab world quiet". He warned that failure to cede the Arabs' demands now risked increased demands in the future.[25]

If anyone in Whitehall had considered making concessions to the Palestinians, the idea was stifled by a fresh initiative by Nuri al-Said. Not for the first time, the Palestinian cause was subordinated to and compromised by Nuri al-Said's pan-Arab ambitions. He now proposed that the British appoint a Council of Ministers in Palestine, instead of just a few heads of departments, and that Palestine be granted a constitution on the Iraqi model, within an Arab federation. Of course, Nuri himself was to head the new union. When consulted, MacMichael again warned against the consequences of showing any weakness:

> Not only would the pan-Arab appetite be whetted but our action would be attributed to fear and uncertainty ... Palestine would exchange its present comparative placid preoccupation with domestic issues for intense political excitement.[26]

The Foreign Office again sided with MacMichael, not least because it feared that Palestine might soon become a theatre of war. In that event, the British would need absolute control of the country. This made any administrative or constitutional changes unthinkable, especially since no demand had come from the Palestinian Arabs themselves.

But in the autumn of 1940, another wave of appeals from the Arab states triggered yet another change of mind at the Foreign Office. Notwithstanding all the arguments it had employed to reject Lampson's pleas just 3 months before, the department now recommended implementing the constitutional clauses of the White Paper. A new element had now entered the Palestinian equation – the Jewish Division, agreed to by the Cabinet in October. The department now fretted over how they were going to explain to the Arabs the decision to mobilize the Division. It suggested that the constitutional concession might be presented as a quid pro quo. In a memorandum that rehearsed Lampson's arguments, the Foreign and Colonial Offices made a joint appeal to the Cabinet, arguing that in view of Britain's vulnerability in the Middle East, it was time to implement the constitutional clauses:

> The situation in Iraq, where there are no British troops, is particularly unsatisfactory, and the Chiefs of Staff fear that serious military consequences may result unless a better atmosphere is created. In Egypt too, there is sympathy with Arab discontent, which might at any time express itself in a manner highly inconvenient to us in the Nile Valley. The Arab leaders in Syria and Palestine are in close contact with those in Iraq ... but in spite of this tendency to turn towards the Axis there is still widespread dislike of Nazism and a bitter hatred of Italy and distrust of

Italian ambitions ... all our Arab friends, Ibn Saud in particular, are constantly urging us, in our own interests, to make a definite effort to rally Arab opinion to our side ... in view of the increased gravity of the situation, we feel bound to invite the Cabinet to reconsider their conclusion of last July. Until we implement paragraph 10 (4) our good faith will remain suspect in Arab and Muslim eyes, and their criticism will not be easy to rebut.[27]

The argument appeared to be irresistible, especially since General Wavell's forces were facing an Italian force in the Western desert that outnumbered them by more than six to one.[28] But before the Cabinet had a chance to discuss the volte-face, disaster struck in Palestine. On 25 November 1940, a Jewish refugee ship, the *Patria*, was shattered by a huge explosion in Haifa harbor and sank. Some 240 Jewish refugees and a dozen British policemen lost their lives. The Jewish Agency announced that in their desperation, the Jewish refugees themselves had blown up the ship. The British were blamed for the tragedy, for having driven the refugees to this extreme measure. Only much later was it revealed that the explosion had been caused by a Hagana miscalculation – the use of an explosive device which had been intended only to disable the vessel. In these circumstances, in the wake of the emotional backlash over the huge number of dead, the government was unable to go ahead with the constitutional initiative, which would have been seen as a further blow to the Zionists. The window of opportunity was missed.

Two military developments during the next 4 months served to rule out further discussion of constitutional advance in Palestine. The first was Wavell's triumph over the Italian army in the Western desert from December 1940 to January 1941.[29] The second was Rashid Ali's military *putsch* in April 1941, followed by his rebellion against the British in May. Nuri al-Said had been at the centre of external Arab intervention in Palestinian affairs since 1936. His unseating by Rashid Ali removed the main source of external agitation for an improvement of the Palestinians' lot. The events in Iraq were an uncomfortable reminder of a lesson that the Foreign Office had supposedly learned the previous summer – the allegiance of the Arabs was contingent upon victory on the battlefield.

The Arab League appropriates the Palestinian cause

The political vacuum resulting from the lack of any Arab representative institutions in Palestine was occupied by the Arab states. Internal divisions inside the Palestinians' leadership made it easier for the Arab states to assume control. Since 1937, the Nashashibis had aligned themselves with King Abdullah of Trans-Jordan. On the other hand, there was bad blood between the Mufti and the Iraqi Hashemites, headed by the perennial Nuri Pasha. This feud had its origins in the role played by the Mufti in the Rashid Ali *coup d'état* that drove out the monarchy and Nuri al-Said. The crushing of the rebellion by the British at the end of May 1941 forced the Mufti to flee Iraq via Teheran, for Rome and Berlin.[30]

The British attitude to Arab unity was one of opportunistic self-interest which, as usual, fluctuated with the tides of war. They refused to believe in the Arabs' ability to overcome their numerous political and religious schisms and dynastic feuds. An early assessment of pan-Arabism, sent to London in August 1936 by the British consul at Damascus, the cradle of Arab nationalism, was never seriously challenged by the various British experts on the Middle East:

> As an idea the Pan-Arab idea exists; as a vital force it is destroyed by the weakness inherent in a feudal patriarchal system, jealousy and distrust. The Syrian Arab regards the Iraqi as inferior to him in culture, in fact as little better than the Bedu whom he despises, except when he can make use of him for his own political ends. The Saudi Arab he considers a poor, unenlightened person to be treated with tolerant condescension. The one possible cementing factor – the Muslim religion – in itself provides elements of further disruption. Sunni hates Shiah, both despise the Ismaili, whilst the Wahhabi [Saudi] considers himself the only real true follower of the prophet.[31]

With the outbreak of war, a Foreign Office paper added some external obstacles to Arab unity: "French suspicion that federation represented a British ruse to oust France from the Levant, and ... the revival of Turkish ambitions in the area". The French, who had left the British in no doubt about their opposition, had adopted a traditional "divide and rule" policy towards the Arabs. Even in the unlikely event that Syria was not included at first in any Arab federation, the French suspected that it would be sucked into it sooner or later.[32] In Palestine, MacMichael shared the French view:

> It is arguable that the "Arabs" will be more susceptible of control and less dangerous if they remain divided into the comparatively small units which time may yet demonstrate their ability to manage decently for themselves.[33]

The British first addressed the question of Arab federation in public in May 1941. Once again, their military position, following the revolt in Iraq, prompted a stock taking of their "Arab policy". During the spring of 1941, British prestige in the Middle East sank to its lowest point during the entire war.[34] As noted in the previous chapter, when Vichy Syria collaborated with the Germans in aiding the Rashid Ali rebellion, the British decided to conquer Syria, to pre-empt a German conquest. In British eyes, the French had lost all remaining legitimacy for their colonial rule over Syria when the Vichy regime surrendered to Germany in June 1940.

With the British decision to conquer Syria, the propaganda war with the Germans for the hearts of the Arabs assumed the highest priority. Lampson returned to his plea that some gesture must be offered to the Palestinians. On 13 May 1941, on the day that the first German bombers landed at Damascus with supplies for Rashid Ali, he telegraphed an urgent plea to London:

> We here in Cairo have for years before the war been pointing out ... that our Arab policy, particularly with reference to Palestine, must end by driving the Arabs into the arms of the Axis ... The Mufti, and Shukri Quwatli, and other anti-British leaders in northern Arab lands, have been able to create an anti-British atmosphere in those lands.[35]

Lampson concurred with the general consensus about the practical obstacles to Arab unity. But he stressed that the situation in the Middle East had now become so serious that they all had to agree on the need to formulate an Arab policy that would "have some chance of countering German propaganda". The Germans, he claimed, were offering the Arabs all that they could possibly desire: "independence, federation, expulsion of the Jews, French and British". He concluded that any British statement would have to include guarantees of a cessation of Jewish immigration into Palestine, Arab administrative predominance in Palestine, Syrian independence, and "assurances of our practical sympathy with Arab Federation".

The Foreign Office agreed that their plans to conquer Syria made some initiative to counter German propaganda urgent. They knew that the Syrians hated the French, and that the latter would regard any British support for Arab federation as a "subtle attempt ... to rob France of her share of the spoils in the last war".[36] But before the department could compose a position paper, Churchill intervened with his own brainwave, the establishment of a new political order that would expunge France from the map of the Middle East. On 18 May he sent a "Prime Minister's personal minute" to the CIGS:

> The French having quitted the League of Nations, their Mandate for Syria is at an end, and we should proclaim quite soon our intention to set up an independent Arab State, permanently allied to Turkey and Great Britain ... It will have to be made clear to de Gaulle at an early stage that unless the French in Syria come actively on our side to do the job, their political connection with that country is forever at an end.[37]

Churchill instructed the CIGS to raise the issue again in "a month from today, by which time we shall probably be wiser, though I hope not sadder", i.e. after the Syrian campaign.

Eden brought the issue of the government's "Arab policy" to the Cabinet at the end of May. He informed his colleagues that he would not raise the Palestine question for the present, but reminded them that the government's policy in that country was "unhappily a part, and a vitally important part of the Arab problem", and that in due course, he would welcome "a decision to take the next steps to give effect to the Palestine White Paper".[38] For the present, he proposed making a general public statement offering British support for the Arabs' own aspirations. On 29 May (*before* he received the Cabinet's official imprimatur), Eden included the following declaration in a public speech he delivered at the Mansion House, the official residence of the Lord Mayors of London:

> Some days ago I said in the House of Commons that H.M. Government had great sympathy with Syrian aspirations for independence ... It seems to me both natural and right that the cultural and economic ties between the Arab countries, yes, and the political ties too, should be strengthened. His Majesty's Government for their part will give their full approval to any scheme that commands general approval.[39]

The Foreign Office asked all its Middle Eastern ambassadors and the High Commissioner for Palestine to send in their views on Eden's statement.[40] It also commissioned a study of Arab federation by the Royal Institute of International Affairs (RIIA). The Institute's report distinguished between internal and external obstacles to Arab unity, and the growth of economic and national interests in the successor states that had risen after World War One – with their economic and political weaknesses. In addition, there were the English and French mandates, and French, Italian and Spanish rule in North-West Africa. The report asserted that Syrian independence must be the first step towards any accommodation with Arab nationalism. It suggested that Arab and Zionist interests in Palestine might be reconciled within the frame of an Arab federation.[41]

Both Churchill and Roosevelt agreed that the Zionist problem might be solved along these lines. But this was a grave miscalculation of the willingness of either the Arabs or the Zionists to compromise. The Arabs never contemplated the establishment of a Jewish state in Palestine. On the Zionist side, the elderly, London-based Weizmann may have indulged in fantasies about a partitioned Jewish state taking its place inside an Arab federation. But there was never any chance that the leaders of the Yishuv would agree to a minority status in Palestine.[42]

Churchill proposed his own "solution" to the Palestine problem, within the frame of an Arab federation. He supported the so-called Philby scheme, named after St John "Abdulla" Philby, an Arabian scholar and traveller who resided for long periods in Saudi Arabia. Philby had first broached his idea to Weizmann in late 1939, and to Ibn Saud himself in 1940. The scheme was presented to Churchill in 1941. It proposed that Britain elevate Ibn Saud to a "general overlordship" over an Arab federation, comprising "Palestine, Iraq and the South". Under this arrangement, the Jews would receive an "autonomous state" in a part of Palestine. As part of the deal, the Zionists were supposed to have given to Ibn Saud a £20 million development "loan". Churchill took it for granted that Ibn Saud would:

... have to come to terms with us about the Jews, but this should not be impossible as part of the creation of a vast Arab confederacy under his control.[43]

Weizmann showed considerable interest in the idea, and told mediators that the Zionists would be able to raise between £15–20 million for the "loan" to Saudi Arabia. But the Philby scheme had no roots in reality, as Leo Amery, now Secretary of State for India, pointed out to Churchill. Although Amery shared what was becoming the consensus at Whitehall, that "some sort of Arab federation with a Jewish sub-division of Palestine as a unit in it" appeared to be the only possible solution to the Palestine imbroglio, he ruled out the candidacy of Ibn Saud:

> If it were possible to get all the Arab states under one umbrella that would be the best solution, and Ibn Saud is much more of a statesman than any other Arab. But I very much doubt your Levantine *effendis* of Baghdad, Damascus and Jerusalem submitting to the overlordship of what they regard as a mere "beduin".[44]

At the end of September 1941, the government commissioned a further study of the feasibility of Arab federation, this time by the CID, which was asked to devote special attention to the possibility that it might afford a solution to the Palestine problem.[45] The CID's report buried any remaining illusions about Ibn Saud ruling the Arab world. It advised that the Palestine problem must be settled first or it would serve as a bone of contention on which all the Arab states could agree. The report also warned, presciently, that the only issue on which the Arabs might possibly agree was their opposition to Anglo-French colonial rule:

> The Arab desire for a closer union ... is in effect a wish to form a bloc of Arab States which will be strong enough to secure what are considered Arab rights in Palestine and Syria, and to present a united front to foreign powers, especially Great Britain and France.[46]

In regard to the Arabian Peninsula, the CID concluded:

> Saudi Arabia, the Yemen and the other States of the Arabian Peninsula, are even more unsuited to participate in a scheme of federation than the less backward Arab countries further north.

With the defeat of Rommel during the winter of 1942–43, both Zionists and Arabs began lobbying the British about the post-war future of the Middle East. The reinstalled premier of Iraq, Nuri al-Said, still lobbying for some form of federation under an Iraqi hegemony, ran up against the rival ambitions of Egypt and Saudi Arabia. London was content to allow the Arabs to squabble among themselves, fearing that any "unified" Arab bloc would be reduced to discussing the only issue that they could all agree on – Palestine, a problem that London preferred to put off until after the war.

In March 1943, Nuri al-Said sent agents to Egypt to promote his Greater Syrian scheme, and from July to August he himself toured the Arab capitals. The Foreign Office was by now exasperated by his agitation. The government could not openly oppose any Arab initiative, but neither could it give the Arabs any satisfactory answer about what would happen in the Middle East after the war. Nuri's lobbying elicited some derisive remarks from the irritable officials whose thankless task it was to deal with the Middle East:

> His [Nuri al-Said's] past dabblings in Pan-Arabism and his desire to offer the Mufti asylum in Iraq should have taught him that he cannot control these sort of movements as he likes ... we should impress on Nuri that he is setting foot on a very slippery slope ... His manoeuvres will probably end in one more of his hurried departures to Amman by RAF plane.[47]

The sole interest the Egyptians had in Arab federation was to secure for their country a leading role in any union that might emerge. Ibn Saud told the British ambassador in Riyadh that he trusted none of the Arab leaders, and advised the British to do likewise, since they were all: "playing their own hands in order to strengthen their position in their own countries". He assured the ambassador that if an Arab conference did materialize, he would confer with the British about what position he should take, in particular, if the conference began to discuss Palestine in a manner detrimental to their interests.[48]

Ibn Saud's assessment dovetailed conveniently with Whitehall's own. London was hoping to "freeze" the Palestine issue until after the war but Foreign Office fears materialized in February 1944, when Nahhas Pasha, the Prime Minister of Egypt, announced the convention of an all-Arab conference in Alexandria, scheduled for September 1944. The official British attitude to Nahhas was similar to that felt for Nuri al-Said – both were British clients, who held power by the grace of British bayonets. Initially, the British reaction to the Egyptian initiative was the same as to that of Nuri al-Said – imperious cynicism:

> Nahhas' tendency to balance his internal instability by Pan-Arab stunts seems liable to become embarrassing. While it is we who keep him in power, we may hope that he will not shout too loud about official Palestine policy; but this is a tiresome tendency and may turn out awkwardly for us. We want *friendly* Arab leadership from Egypt, more like Ibn Saud – and more of his dignity and reserve too.[49]

During the summer months, British diplomatic efforts focused on persuading the Arab states not to discuss the Palestine issue, but to wait until after the war. On the eve of the Alexandria conference the complacent officials crowed over Arab disarray:

> The stage is now set. The Arab leaders are all at sixes and sevens. The Iraqis are jealous of Nahhas. Nahhas hates Nuri. The Amir of Transjordan wants to be King of Syria and has recently quarrelled with Shukri Quwatli, the President of Syria. Ibn Saud is backing Shukri because he hates all Hashemites ... The Palestinian Arabs can't agree on a delegation to represent them in the absence of their leaders in Germany, or under lock and key ... There are all the elements of an unedifying dog-fight, but we really dare not crash in and tell them to put it off – they would then at least agree about our opposition to Arab unity ... We have already got undertakings from those participating to the effect that they will treat any references to Palestine with special discretion in view of the importance of not increasing tension while the war lasts.[50]

The Alexandria conference lasted from 15 September to 7 October 1944. At its close, the delegates unanimously passed five resolutions, which became known as the Alexandria Protocol. The first four dealt with the establishment of an Arab League, and the economic, political and social relations between its members. The fifth dealt with Palestine. It stated that the rights of the Palestinian Arabs could not be infringed "without danger to the peace and stability of the Arab world". It asserted that the engagements assumed by Britain (in 1939) now constituted "the acquired rights" of the Arabs.[51]

In the last months of the war against Hitler, the Arab states had finally delivered what the British had struggled for in vain in 1939. Apart from Churchill, there was a general consensus at Whitehall that Britain must honour its obligations under the 1939 White Paper. But after the assassination of Lord Moyne on 6 November, Churchill retired from his thankless position as the lone sponsor of the Zionist cause inside his Cabinet.

One of the first assessments of the Alexandria Protocol was written by Sir Kinahan Cornwallis, the ambassador in Baghdad, a veteran Middle East hand. He warned that any retreat now from the 1939 White Paper would lose Britain the friendship of the Arab world. His advice became Foreign Office orthodoxy:

> This acceptance of Britain's last official statement of policy by and on behalf of the so-called extremist Palestine party, and its endorsement by the conference is very significant. It means on the one hand that the Palestinian Arabs are now committed to an acceptance of the White Paper, and that we have the general support of the Arab world for the policy enshrined. But, on the other hand, it means equally that any serious divergence from that policy will confront His Majesty's Government not only with the hostility of the Palestinian Arabs, but with that of all the signatories to the Alexandria Protocol.[52]

The Arab League was established formally in March 1945, notwithstanding British efforts to stifle it at inception. French and Zionist observers were convinced that the League was a cynical creation of Perfidious Albion. The League soon became a hotbed of intrigue and rivalry between the Arab states, quite beyond British control. As predicted, its member states divided along dynastic and religious lines. Various *ad hoc* alignments vied among themselves for the leadership of the Palestinian Arabs' cause. Broadly speaking, two coalitions faced each other inside the League. On one side there were the Hashemite monarchies of Iraq and Trans-Jordan, supported by loosely organized pan-Arabists who still hankered after the pre-World War One Greater Syria dream. On the other side were the Saudi and Egyptian royal houses, supported from 1946 by newly independent Syria and Lebanon.[53]

One astute historian, an employee of the Ministry of Information when the League was founded, later wrote the following retrospective:

> Both [the Jews and the Free French] saw it as a threat to themselves, but also as fresh evidence of the extent to which British partiality for the Arabs led to delusions about Arab feelings for Britain; in their eyes it amounted to digging a pit into which the British too would ultimately fall. And so it might have been, had not the Arab League ... allowed itself to become a chatter of shifting and quarrelsome cliques.[54]

The Foreign Office made a virtue of necessity. Since 1936, when Nuri al-Said had first been allowed to intervene in Palestinian affairs, the Middle Eastern wheel had revolved full circle. The Alexandria Protocol and the establishment of the Arab League provided manifest proof of the Foreign Office thesis that the Palestine mandate could not be treated in isolation, that Britain's every move there would generate repercussions throughout the Arab world.

Notes

1. Note by Lacy Bagallay, head of the Foreign Office Middle East department, 18 January 1940, FO 371/24563, NA.
2. Issa Khalaf, *Politics in Palestine: Arab Factionalism and Social Disintegration, 1939–1948*, Albany: State University of New York Press, 1991, pp. 66, 75.
3. Hillel Cohen, *Army of Shadows: Palestinian Collaboration with Zionism, 1917–1948*, Berkeley/Los Angeles: University of California Press, 2008, p. 206.
4. Khalaf, *Politics*, p. 86.
5. For this section, cf. Roger Owen, "Economic Development in Mandatory Palestine", in Roger Owen, ed., *Studies in the Economic and Social History of Palestine in the Nineteenth and Twentieth Centuries*, Carbondale: Southern Illinois University Press, 1982, pp. 27–32; also Cohen, *Army*, pp. 212–13, Khalaf, *Politics*, pp. 232–33, 236, and Ylana Miller, *Government and Society in Rural Palestine, 1920–1948*, Austin: University of Texas, 1985, pp. 163–67.
6. MacMichael reports of 31 December 1939 and 27 June 1940, FO 371/24563, NA. MacMichael was a veteran colonial career official; he had served in various positions in Egypt since World War One, and as Governor to Tanganyika from 1933 to 1937.

7 Bagallay note, 16 February 1940, FO 371/24563, NA. The Land Regulations were approved by the Cabinet on 28 February 1940, and announced in the House of Commons on the same day.
8 ibid.
9 Bagallay note of late June 1940, ibid.
10 Minutes of Cabinet discussion on 3 July 1940, Cab 65/8, NA.
11 Statement by Musa Alami, FO 921/151, NA; also Geoffrey Furlonge, *Palestine is my Country: The Story of Musa Alami*, London: John Murray, 1969, pp. 127–28.
12 The German documents and a post-war interview with the Mufti reveal that he opposed the Newcombe mission; cf. Lukasz Hirszowicz, *The Third Reich and the Arab Middle East*, London/Toronto: Routledge and Kegan Paul/Toronto University Press, 1986, pp. 80–82.
13 Minute by H.M.Eyres, 5 August 1940, FO 371/24549, NA.
14 ibid, also Philip Mattar, *The Mufti of Jerusalem: Al-Hajj Amin al-Husayni and the Palestinian National Movement*, New York: Columbia University Press, 1988, pp. 100–101.
15 Anthony R. de Luca, "'*Der Grossmufti*' in Berlin: The Politics of Collaboration", *International Journal of Middle East Studies*, 10/1, February 1979, p. 127.
16 Weizmann to Newcombe (copied to Lord Lloyd), 2 December 1940, Weizmann Archives (WA).
17 Copy of Newcombe memorandum in Weizmann Archives, ibid.
18 Martin Gilbert, *Finest Hour: Winston S. Churchill, 1939–1941*, London: Book Club Associates, in association with Heinemann, 1983, pp. 905–6.
19 Lampson to Foreign Office, 13 July 1940, CO 733/426, 75872/85, NA. Lampson, Lord Killearn from 1943, was a veteran Middle Eastern diplomat; he served as High Commissioner to Egypt from 1934, and as ambassador from 1936 to 1946.
20 MacMichael to Colonial Office, 22 July 1940, ibid.
21 Hahn report on the German mission in Syria, from May to July 1941, in *DGFP*, vol. 13, pp. 250–51, cited in Jeffrey Herf, *Nazi Propaganda for the Arab World*, New Haven/London: Yale University Press, 2009, pp. 68–69.
22 Bagallay note of 30 July 1940, CO 733/426, 75872/85.
23 ibid.
24 The Italian army conquered British Somaliland in a campaign that lasted from 3 to 19 August.
25 Lampson to Foreign Office, 19 August 1940, FO 371/24565, NA.
26 MacMichael to Colonial Office, 24 August 1940, ibid.
27 Joint memorandum of 21 November 1940, ibid.
28 The Italians had 220,000 troops in Libya, as well as 80,000 native troops, and 200,000 troops in East Africa. In September 1940, an Italian army of 200,000 drove some 50 miles into Egypt before being checked. General Wavell had about 36,000 troops at his disposal.
29 Wavell drove the Italians some 400 miles to the west, taking around 130,000 Italian prisoners.
30 cf. Walid Khalidi, "On Albert Hourani, the Arab Office, and the Anglo-American Committee of 1946", *Journal of Palestine Studies*, Vol. XXXV/1, Autumn 2005, pp. 60–79.
31 Report by Consul Ogden, 21 August 1936, in FO 371/20024, NA. The Ismailis were the second largest branch of Shia Moslems, found mainly in Iran and Pakistan.
32 Annex A to draft memorandum on "Arab Federation", by Bagallay, 28 September 1939, FO 371/23239, NA.
33 MacMichael memorandum on The Prospects of "Federation" as a solution of the Palestine Problem, 13 September 1941, CO 732/87/79238, NA.
34 By May 1941, Rommel's first offensive had driven British forces over 400 miles back to the Egyptian border; the British Expeditionary Force to Greece had been

routed and forced to retreat to the island of Crete. Rashid Ali seized the opportunity of British weakness to stage his revolt against the British. At the end of May, the British were again routed by the Germans on Crete.

35 Lampson to Foreign Office, 13 May 1941, FO 371/27043, NA. Quwatli was head of the anti-colonialist Syrian national bloc, and President of Syria from 1943–49.
36 cf. memorandum on "Arab Federation", by Lacy Bagallay, First Secretary, 28 September 1939, FO 371/23239, NA.
37 Churchill note of 18 May 1941, in Prem 3/422/2, NA.
38 Eden Cabinet memorandum, 27 May 1941, WP (41) 116, Cab 66/16, NA.
39 Text of Eden's speech in FO 371/27043, NA; also Michael J. Cohen, "A Note on the Mansion House Speech", *Asian and African Studies*, 11/3, 1977, p. 375. Eden's speech was approved by the Cabinet *post facto*, on 2 June. On the various conspiracy theories that grew up around Eden's statement, see idem, pp. 375–77.
40 Report on Arab Federation by Standing Official sub-committee of the CID for questions concerning the Middle East, 9 January 1942, Cab 95/1, NA.
41 RIIA report of 9 June 1941, FO 371/27044, NA.
42 For Churchill's and Roosevelt's views on Arab federation, see Michael J. Cohen, *Palestine: Retreat from the Mandate, 1936–1945*, London/New York: Paul Elek/Holmes and Meier, 1978, p. 143.
43 Churchill note to CIGS, 18 May 1941, in Prem3/422/2, NA.
44 Amery to Churchill, 10 September 1941, Prem 4/52/5, pt. 2, NA.
45 Eden to Churchill, 29 May 1941, Prem 4/52/5, pt 2, NA; also Cab 95/1, M.E. (0) (42) 4. NA.
46 For this and following, cf. the committee's report of 9 January 1942, Cab 95/1, NA.
47 Note of 21 March 1943, by H.M. Eyres, head of the Middle East department at the Foreign Office, FO 371/34956, NA.
48 Jedda to Foreign Office, 20 April 1943, FO 371/34957, NA.
49 Note by R.M.A. Hankey, 1 June 1944, FO 371/39988, NA.
50 Note by Hankey, 16 September 1944, FO 371/39990, NA. At the last minute, Musa Alami was chosen to represent the Palestinians. Alami, related to the Mufti by marriage, was one of his close advisors until 1941.
51 Cohen, *Retreat*, p. 148.
52 Cornwallis to Eden, 5 November 1944, FO 371/3991, NA. Cornwallis headed the Arab Bureau in Cairo during World War One; he spent the next 20 years in Iraq as advisor to King Faisal; on 2 April 1941, the day after the Rashid Ali *putsch*, he was named British ambassador, in a vain effort to keep Iraq inside the British fold.
53 On the Alexandria Protocol, the formation of the Arab League and its decisions on Palestine, cf. Cohen, *Retreat*, pp. 146–50.
54 Elizabeth Monroe, *Britain's Moment in the Middle East, 1914 – 1956*, London: Chatto & Windus, 1964, p. 92. Miss Monroe was Director of the Middle East Division of the Ministry of Information from 1940 to 1944.

17 The Arabs and Nazi Germany

> Palestinian Arabs in all social strata have great sympathies for the new Germany and its Führer ... [it] is probably so widespread because the Palestinian Arabs ... long for an Arab "Führer". And because in their fight against the Jews, they sense that they share a common single front with the Germans.
> Report to Berlin by Walter Döhle, German Consul in Jerusalem, March 1937

This chapter tries to assess the Arabs' (in particular the Palestinians') affinities to the Axis Powers, and to ascertain to what extent the British were justified in their fears that the Arabs would defect to the Axis in wartime. It will deal with the Mufti of Jerusalem's approaches to Fascist Italy and Nazi Germany during the 1930s; the next chapter will deal with his collaboration with the Nazis during his wartime stay in Berlin.

I will attempt first to answer the question: What verdict has history returned on the Mufti's collaboration with the Nazis and the SS?

The judgement of history

The contemporary historical debate over the Holocaust has fallen victim to the post-1948 propaganda wars between the Arabs and Israel. After World War Two, the Zionists publicized the Mufti's collaboration with Hitler, in an effort to delegitimize the Palestinians' claims to a national state in mandatory Palestine. For their part, Arab historians and apologists have tried to minimize the significance of the Mufti's role as leader of the Palestinians, and to airbrush his collaboration with the Nazis out of the Palestine narrative. Holocaust denial in the Arab world during the first decades after the rise of Israel served a political purpose – the claim that the Jews invented the myth of their own mass murder undermined the legitimacy of the Jewish state founded in its wake.

I have tried not to fall into the trap of "drawing conclusions about the contemporary world from past patterns".[1] But many historians, on both sides, each with their own political agenda, have been less cautious. One Jewish scholar has drawn a direct line between the Mufti's collaboration with the

Nazis during World War Two and the prevalence of anti-Semitism in the contemporary Arab world.[2] At the other extreme, in a total perversion of history, some Arab publications have tried to reverse the Arab and Jewish roles: "accusing Zionism of collaborating with the Nazis in exterminating European Jews ... presenting the Palestinians as the true victims of the Holocaust".[3]

Much of the debate has focused on the status of the Mufti as the Palestinians' leader: did he continue to lead and determine the Palestinian Arab narrative after his flight from Palestine in October 1937? Zionist publications on the Mufti's role in Nazi Berlin induced Arab apologists "to minimize the extent or significance of his collaboration". Some Arab historians have criticized the Mufti for harming the Palestinian cause, but hardly any have addressed the moral issues involved.[4]

Arab apologists claim that the Mufti fled to Berlin because British persecution endangered his life, and drove him into the arms of the Germans. A recent (Israeli) study of the Palestinian Arab opposition to the Mufti adopts the hypothesis that the Palestinians' support of Nazi Germany was due to Britain's cruel suppression of the 1936–39 rebellion, and to the Arabs' fear that Britain would continue to support the Jewish National Home.[5] While this argument contains an element of truth, it fails to take into account Britain's desperate attempts to mend her bridges with the Arabs on the eve of World War Two. The 1939 Palestine White Paper offered to set up an independent Palestinian state within 10 years, and guaranteed the Arabs that they would retain their two-thirds majority of the population. With the benefit of hindsight, the Mufti himself conceded later that his rejection of the British offer was the biggest mistake of his life.

Some of the Mufti's Arab biographers have focused on his efforts in Berlin to secure an Axis declaration of support for Arab independence. But they have expunged his wartime propaganda broadcasts on behalf of the Nazis to the Middle East and his efforts to sabotage initiatives to rescue East European Jews trapped under Nazi rule. One early biography by Philip Mattar, a Palestinian-born US resident, made the premature claim that the "thousands of captured German documents ... had failed to produce any evidence of the Mufti's direct involvement in the [Nazi] atrocities".[6]

In 1946, Jamal al-Husayni, the Mufti's cousin, argued in testimony before the Anglo-American Committee on Palestine that the Mufti's collaboration with the Nazis had been no worse than Churchill's wartime alliance with Stalin. He made the contorted case that the Mufti had not worked for a German victory but only for his own people, in order to "ensure political gains should the Germans win the war".[7]

In 1946, the *Palestine Encyclopaedia* noted cursorily that the Mufti had resided in Berlin for 4 years during the war, and that Allied governments sought to try him for war crimes after it. It made no mention of his war crimes. An obituary written after the Mufti's death in 1974 praised him for his support of the pro-Axis rebellion in Iraq in 1941 and for his work on behalf of the Palestinian cause after his return to Cairo in 1946. But again, it airbrushed out the Mufti's stay in Berlin.[8]

The Mufti was less lenient on himself than his later apologists. In his memoirs, he showed no remorse for what he had done during the war, and employed a thinly veiled euphemism to explain his goal:

> I was certain that a German victory would have completely saved our country from imperialism and Zionism ... that had Germany and the Axis been victorious, no remnant of Zionism would have remained in Palestine.[9]

One exception among the Arab apologia is a recent polemic by Gilbert Achcar, a Lebanese-born US resident. He too extrapolates from the past to the present, but he does concede that the Mufti's "anti-Semitism and collaboration with the Nazis is beyond all serious question". Achcar presumes not only to make an objective assessment of "the conflicting narratives" but also to analyse "their role in today's Middle East dispute".[10] He charges the Jews with "exploiting a tragedy while denying the tragedies of others" but dismisses the Mufti as a foolish villain, duped by the Nazis, whose activities were in any case ineffectual and insignificant. Without having visited the archives himself, Achcar dismisses out of hand the research of German historians on the Arabs' relations with the Nazis (see Chapter 18) as flagrantly prejudicial propaganda.[11]

Achcar asserts that the Mufti's propaganda from Berlin to the Middle East, urging the Arabs to kill the Jews and to rebel against the British, found only a "pitiably feeble echo". This claim is in conflict with the unanimous assessments and deep concern of Allied intelligence services across the Middle East about the effectiveness of the Nazi propaganda broadcasts in Arabic, and the dangers of widespread Arab support for Germany, should Rommel triumph in the Middle East (see Chapter 14).[12]

The historical evidence, both from the contemporary Arabic press in Palestine (see below), and from the voluminous British political and Intelligence files, refutes the claims that the Mufti ever ceased to be the Palestinians' leader.[13] The Mufti continued to dominate the Palestinian Arabs after his flight to the Lebanon in late 1937. The reign of terror that he unleashed in the summer of 1937, against any Arab who supported partition, shattered irretrievably all possibility of any national consensus or democratic opposition. As noted already, the Mufti's veto of the 1939 White Paper, against the majority opinion of the HAC, was responsible for the Palestinians' rejection of the British offer. Even during the Mufti's absence abroad, no rival camp managed to inherit the Husaynis' hegemony.

After the war, the Mufti was held by the French under house arrest in Paris. In 1946, he fled to Egypt, where he was received with all the accolades fitting an eminent Arab leader. He was greeted by waves of "sympathy and enthusiasm, manifested in numerous press articles and pilgrimages to his home".[14] It has been argued by some that the Egyptians, in "their anti-British and anti-colonial mood", welcomed the Mufti only in order to snub the British, whom they were trying to evict from their country. This unsupported assumption is intended to bolster the argument that after the war, the Mufti was no longer regarded as the Palestinians' leader. But this hypothesis rests on a misinterpretation of Yehoshua Porath's classic study of the Palestinian Arab national movement, which in fact ends in the year 1939. A closer look at Porath's text reveals that he states clearly that the Palestinians' preference of the Arab states over the Mufti to mediate between them and the Allies was a "tactical consideration", since the Mufti, a war criminal wanted by the Allies, was *persona non grata*. This logical tactic did not reflect the Mufti's status in the Arab world. Indeed, the Arab League openly supported him, and lobbied the British to allow him to return to Palestine.[15]

After World War Two, no Arab leader questioned whether the Mufti's wartime record should disqualify him from resuming his position as leader of the Palestinians. The Allies had hard evidence of the Mufti's war crimes (the Yugoslavs were the first to issue an indictment against him) but, fearing his prestige and status in the Arab world, neither the British nor the French dared to apprehend him.

Achcar's claim about the size of the Mufti's following was in fact preceded by Professor Mustafa Kabha, an Israeli Arab, in an article published first in Hebrew in 1999. Based on a selection of articles in the Arabic press, he concluded:

> The claim of wall-to-wall Palestinian support for Fascism and Nazism – from their rise to their demise – suffers from overgeneralization and is inaccurate, not to say absurd. Mufti Haj Amin al-Husayni's devotion to these two regimes and his activities in their service during the Second World War do not prove that the entire Palestinian movement held similar views.[16]

Of course, no one has ever claimed that "the entire Palestinian movement" shared the Mufti's views. However, Kabha himself, in a book he published in 2007, all but reverses himself! He shows that following the Mufti's flight to the Lebanon, all the Arabic press, even those known previously for their hostility towards him, now "competed at praising and extolling him":

> The mufti's distinction as exclusive leader of the Palestinian National movement intensified after he was deposed by the British and fled to Lebanon ... The traditional opponents of the mufti in the press, headed by the newspaper *Filastin*, which was long considered the mufti's opponent, displayed their support for him, stating that he was their sole leader and that his acts embodied the wishes of the Palestinian people.[17]

In late 1937, the editor of *Filastin* announced his resignation from the Nashashibi's Defence Party. Another opposition paper, *al-Jami'a al-Islamiyya*

(Islamic Unity), also modified its position towards the Mufti, and reduced its criticism of him.[18] As will be seen below, these "changes of heart" were not changes of mind, but the result of intimidation and violence by the Mufti's gangs.

There *have* been overgeneralizations and inaccuracies about the Mufti's role as leader of the Palestinians. Quite obviously, it is impossible to calculate exactly how many Palestinians continued to support him, nor their motives for doing so. But equally, it would also be quite wrong to dismiss him as a key player in the Palestinian narrative. The author of a sympathetic study of the Palestinian opposition to the Mufti, many of whom collaborated with the Zionists, estimated that approximately 70–80 per cent of the Palestinian Arabs continued to support the Mufti for the entire duration of the British mandate.[19]

Palestine in Hitler's grand strategy

The Nazis disparaged the peoples of Asia and Africa, including the Arabs, on grounds of their racial inferiority. Numerous Nazi leaders and officials expressed an aversion to their "character and political behavior, a disbelief in their state-forming capacity and their loyalty as allies".[20] In *Mein Kampf*, published in 1925, Hitler had expressed his scorn for all colonized peoples:

> I must recognize the racial inferiority of the so-called "Oppressed Nations", and that is enough to prevent me from linking the destiny of my people with the destiny of those inferior nations.[21]

Until 1939, Hitler's grand strategy remained to reach an agreement with Britain, whereby he would recognize her Empire – including her Middle Eastern hegemony – in return for which Britain would grant him a free hand in Central and Eastern Europe. Hitler determined that any large-scale German involvement in the Middle East would have to wait until after his conquest of Eastern Europe and the Soviet Union. He considered that the potential benefits of an alignment with the Arab national movements were not enough to risk a conflict with Britain.[22]

This strategy did not always serve Arab interests. The key example was the so-called Transfer (Heb. *Ha'avara*) Agreement, concluded between Germany and the Zionists in August 1933. By this agreement, German-Jewish emigrants to Palestine were required to deposit their money in one of Germany's transfer banks, and to buy with it goods and machinery manufactured in Germany, which they were allowed to take with them to Palestine. The agreement served several German goals. The first was to rid Germany of her own Jewish community (in 1933, there were about 500,000 Jews in Germany). The second was to boost German exports, by breaking the international Jewish boycott of her goods. Although German exports to Palestine remained a small fraction of her overall trade, by 1937 they had overtaken the British.

In that year their value soared to RM31.4 million, from RM1.25 million in 1933.[23]

Arab objections failed to persuade the Germans to cancel the Transfer Agreement. Their protests against the emigration of German Jews to Palestine were rebuffed with the argument that any reduction would be made up quickly by Jewish immigrants from Eastern Europe. In January 1938, Hitler added his own imprimatur to the Transfer Agreement, stating that Palestine was "a desirable destination in the emigration process".[24] The Zionist movement flourished in Germany under Hitler until late 1938.

In 1937, the Germans were alarmed when the British Cabinet approved the Peel Plan to partition Palestine into Arab and Jewish states. Even if Nazi doctrine posited that the racially inferior Jews were incapable of establishing a viable state of their own, the new plan raised the spectre of an independent Jewish power base in Palestine, from which world Jewry would pursue its global conspiracy. But by the autumn of that year, their fears abated, as it became clear that the Chamberlain administration was having second thoughts.[25] The Partition Plan was officially scrapped in November (see Chapter 13).

Although it was in Germany's interest to strengthen its position in the Arab world, for most of the 1930s, Berlin refused to intervene with the British, or to offer anything more than token support for the Arab national movements. Until 1939, the Nazis' first priority remained to do nothing in the Middle East that might spoil their relations with the British. Another factor limiting German policy in the region was the agreement signed in October 1936 by Hitler and Count Ciano, the Italian Foreign Minister, whereby Germany ceded the Middle East to the Italians as their sphere of influence. Hitler was content to leave the hegemony in Arab affairs to Rome until he had completed the conquest of the Soviet Union.[26] However, their agreement did not survive General Wavell's mauling of the Italian Army in the Western desert during the winter of 1940–41.[27] Hitler personally ordered the formation of the Afrika Korps, and appointed General Erwin Rommel as its commander. His strategy was to keep the British tied down in North Africa, as he put the final touches to Barbarossa, the plan to conquer the Soviet Union.

Until late 1937, all Arab requests for arms were rejected politely by Hitler, as were requests for meetings with Nazi officials in Berlin. German diplomats rebuffed all Arab protests against partition. The warnings of Germany's Middle Eastern envoys that Berlin was alienating the Arab world were discounted. However, there are indications that arms and money were passed to the Mufti via the Abwehr, German military intelligence (see p. 408).[28]

From 1939, the Transfer Agreement began to lose its relevance for Germany. After Hitler's violation of the Munich Agreement in March 1939, he abandoned the strategy of seeking a *rapprochement* with Britain. With his drive for *lebensraum* in the East, it became clear that not just Germany but all of Eastern Europe would have to be made *Judenrein*. Clearly, Palestine alone would be unable to accommodate the millions of Jews living in the East European territories that Hitler planned to conquer.

The reception of Fascism and Nazism in the Arab World: Egypt and Palestine

In the early 1930s, Nazi Germany's anti-Semitic policies evoked a widespread, positive response among Arab nationalists across the Middle East. One scholar has suggested that if the powerful German nation felt threatened by the Jews, "a suppressed Arab national could hardly accept their presence".[29]

During this decade, a plethora of political organizations and paramilitary youth movements modelled on Fascist and Nazi organizations sprouted up in the Arab world. In Iraq, there was the al-Futuwwa, a youth organization modelled on the Hitler Youth, and the influential, pan-Arab, Fascist al-Muthanna Club, both openly supportive of the Nazis.[30] In Syria, there were Fahkri al-Barudi's Iron Shirts and Antoun (Antoine) Sa'ada's Socialist National Party, founded in Beirut in 1932. Born to a Lebanese Greek Orthodox family, Sa'ada adopted the Fascist paradigm – the cult of the individual, emphasis on racial purity and mystical nationalism. He advocated the restoration of a Greater Syrian state. The party's rituals included a Hitler-style salute, an anthem set to the music of the Nazi anthem, and a flag with a curved swastika, called "the red hurricane".[31] In the Lebanon, a number of paramilitary youth organizations with clear Fascist leanings were formed between 1936 and 1937: the Najjada (a pan-Arab Moslem association), the "White Shirts" (Christian Maronites), and the Kataeb (Phalange), a Christian Arab party led by Pierre Gemayel, modelled after the Spanish Falange and the Italian Fascist Party.[32]

Egypt

At the turn of the twenty-first century, a "revisionist" narrative on Egypt has emerged, which challenges the previous historical consensus ("master-narrative"), that argued that during the 1930s, Egypt was receptive to Fascism and Nazism. Its authors claim that their own case study of Egypt, using "a much wider range of sources and with a more Arab-oriented perspective" than hitherto, "forms part of an emerging alternative narrative concerning the relationship of the Arab world to fascism". They assert that when their methodology is applied to the countries of the Fertile Crescent (Iraq, Lebanon, Palestine and Syria), it will produce a similar revision of the older narratives on those countries' receptiveness to Fascism and Nazism.[33]

The older consensus attributed the Egyptians' admiration of Nazi Germany to the resurgence of Islam and to the charge made by the influential Moslem Brotherhood that "western civilization was striving to destroy Islamic-Arab civilization in order to conquer and westernize it". The Moslem Brothers disseminated a negative image of the West, especially of Great Britain, due to its "shameful" 70-year occupation of Egypt and its support of Zionism in Palestine. The Brothers' charges were supported by "pan-Arab and pan-Islamic radical intellectual circles". This consensus claimed that militant pro-Nazi circles in Egypt had planned to betray Britain during the war, but had been prevented from doing so only by Lampson's ultimatum to King Farouk in February 1942.[34]

The "revisionist" school, led by Professor Israel Gershoni, rejected what he called the "crude Orientalist cliché ... that totalitarianism was ready-made for a country like Egypt". He posited that the scholars of the older narrative had been misled by the rewriting of history by the Young Officers movement in Egypt in the 1950s. The fault of the older school was that their conclusions were based on too narrow a sample of the available literature. The revisionists maintain that when this sample was "broadened to consider ... secondary intellectuals, journalists, political and religious activists", a totally different picture of the debate on the relative merits of democracy and Fascism emerged.[35]

Gershoni and Jankowski propose no less than "a new reading of the political and intellectual history of Egypt", that Egypt should be removed from the roll of those Arab states that expressed unreserved admiration for Fascist Italy and Nazi Germany. They adopted the "public sphere" theory (and revisions of it) of the German sociologist Jürgen Habermas, and transposed it from Europe to the Middle East. They argue that Egypt's "public sphere" was the *effendiyya*: a native, urban middle class of "professionally educated state servants". In their study of the Egyptian intellectuals' "liberal discourse", they give preference to "the analysis of local voices in the press over colonial archives and the voices of grand theoreticians". Without quantifying their numbers, they accredit the *effendiyya* not only with making "the press the major public means of communication in Egypt ... [with] literally hundreds of publications" but also with dictating "norms and expectations to broader segments of society".[36]

Gershoni and Jankowski concede that initially, some Egyptians were attracted to Fascism's "organizational strength, socio-economic restructuring, psychological self-confidence, and success in apparently achieving national revival". But they assert that the *effendiyya* ultimately rejected Fascism, since they were alienated by "the adverse effects of totalitarian rule and aggressive chauvinist nationalism ... [and] the pernicious consequences of internal dictatorship and external aggression".[37]

Gershoni and Jankowski have contributed significantly to our knowledge of the liberal disposition of Egyptian intellectuals in the 1930s. However, their claim that their work should lead to a new *political* history of Egypt – "with few exceptions politically involved Egyptians ... remained faithful to liberalism",[38] raises not a few problems.

First, can a sociological methodology related to Europe be transferred to the Middle East – not only to Egypt but also to the Fertile Crescent, whose peoples were subjugated for 400 years by the Ottoman Empire? Second, can the influence of the printed word in the largely literate states of Europe be compared to its influence on the overwhelmingly illiterate peoples of the Middle East? How does one even begin to measure the influence of the printed press even in developed democracies, during the first half of the twentieth century? Is it possible to do so in a largely illiterate, feudal society such as Egypt, where election results (and frequently, the press itself) were subject to the pressures of a landed aristocracy, royal intervention and, in the last resort, to British *diktat*?

The great majority of the Egyptian population, resident mainly in rural areas, took no part in the political life of the nation. Out of a total population of around 16 million in the mid-1930s, only 19 per cent (just over 3 million) of those aged 5 years and more knew how to read and write (lower than the 22 per cent rate for the Arab population of Palestine in the same period)! In comparison, the average literacy rate for France (with a population of 33 million in 1936) was 96.7 per cent and for Italy (with a population of 36 million in 1931) was 79 per cent.[39]

In 1937, *Al-Ahram,* the most influential Egyptian newspaper, with by far the largest circulation, sold an estimated 45,000–50,000 copies per day. It would have been read by less than 2.5 per cent of the urban elites of Egypt's two major cities, Cairo and Alexandria, which in 1937 had a combined population of over 2 million – considerably more than double the total Arab population of Palestine at the time! Even given the existence of many lower-circulation dailies, and even if Egyptian daily newspapers did become "the most influential medium of the interwar era",[40] does it necessarily follow that they set or determined the national agenda?

Even allowing for the Arab tradition of reading newspapers out loud in the local café and at other social venues, how many Egyptians, especially the illiterate *fellahin*, socialized on a regular basis? Of those who did, how many would have been interested in, much less able to comprehend the relative merits of democracy and totalitarianism?

But above all, there was a considerable dissonance between the *effendiyya*'s liberal discourse and the directions taken by Egyptian society during the 1930s. On the face of things, Egypt's socio-economic tribulations during this period provided a fertile breeding ground for authoritarian ideas, much as they had in Germany. Egypt suffered a painful backlash from the severe economic depression that swept the world after the Wall Street Crash. The hardships suffered by the Egyptian masses resulted in major socio-economic inequalities and political turmoil. Gershoni and Jankowski inform us that the Egyptian Parliament was taken over by a self-serving, corrupt class of large land-owners while political life was marred by "sterile and destructive factionalism" and "personalized power struggles". All this created an atmosphere of "political polarization, repression, and violence". From 1930 to 1933, King Fuad ruled through a "Palace-oriented dictatorship", and between 1938 and 1939, his son, the young, autocratic King Farouk, effectively took over the political system, together with "his coterie of conservative and/or opportunist advisers".[41]

All this turbulence occurred against a backcloth of Fascist and Nazi triumphs:

Fascist Italy and Nazi Germany seemed to be marching from political triumph to political triumph in 1938–39; the potential appeal of dictatorship as the way to achieve dramatic results was never stronger. Internally, the perceived shortcomings of the existing parliamentary system fed both the desire for and the prospect of fundamental reform centred round the then-popular figure of Egypt's monarch.[42]

Egypt spawned only one openly Fascist political party – Young Egypt. Founded in October 1933, the party was a relatively small, albeit influential political force. It had its own "storm troopers", the "Green Shirts", who held torchlight processions and adopted literal translations of Nazi slogans such as "One folk, one party, one leader". Many ordinary Egyptians took part in their rallies, many others watched them from the sidelines. Like the Nazis, Young Egypt called for a boycott of Jewish businesses and organized physical attacks against the Jews. A bevvy of other paramilitary youth organizations based on the Nazi model were formed in Egypt. The Wafd, Egypt's dominant political party, formed its own paramilitary youth organization, the "Blue Shirts" (built on the League of Wafdist Youth). Jankowski has called them "a major phenomenon in Egyptian public life".[43]

Right up until the outbreak of World War Two, Egypt's intellectuals pressed for parliamentary reform, for more education on the virtues of democracy, and the initiation of steps to ensure "a genuine, honest opposition" as an "essential barrier to the spread of fascist tendencies in Egypt". Their articles were written against the context of the "increasing street brawling of Egypt's paramilitary youth organizations".[44]

Gershoni and Jankowski dismiss or play down the contacts between Egyptian leaders and Nazi Germany as "the abortive efforts of a handful of Egyptians (the King and his associates; some army officers; the anti-imperialist activities of Young Egypt) to collaborate with the Axis powers". They also dismiss the post-war publication of "fragmentary German documentation" on secret Egyptian-German contacts during the war as "a way of discrediting the Egyptian parliament".[45]

It is apposite to recall that some of these army officers – mainly of peasant origin – formed the Free Officers movement after the war, and in 1952 toppled the *ancien régime* in Egypt (still under British occupation) by military *putsch*. Their charismatic, authoritarian leader, Colonel Gemal Abdel Nasser, soon captured the hearts and imagination of the Egyptian masses. He became one of the most popular, influential and towering figures not only of Egypt's but also of the Arab world's modern history.

Furthermore, since Gershoni's voluminous publications reach only up to the middle of 1940, we do not know if or how Egyptian public opinion changed once North Africa became a war front. In mid-1940, no one, not even Hitler himself, had any idea that in February 1941 the Afrika Korps, commanded by Erwin Rommel, one of Germany's most brilliant generals, would assume control of Axis forces in Libya. With each of Rommel's military triumphs in the Western desert, the most important question for many Egyptians (as for many Palestinian Arabs) was no longer whether to support "the enemy of my enemy", but which side was going to win the war.

Gershoni's and Jankowski's conclusion that British assessments before the war "concluded that Axis propaganda efforts in Egypt (and other parts of the Middle East) were largely ineffective"[46] – made without any source given – is not supported by the facts. Allied officials and intelligence agents across the Middle East did not have either the inclination, much less the leisure to study the Egyptian intellectuals' "liberal discourse" in the innumerable major and fringe newspapers and journals. They had to concern themselves with the words and actions of those who determined the country's political agenda – whether in the Parliament, the Royal Palace, the army barracks or the streets.

As seen in the previous chapter, by the summer of 1940, the British Foreign Office – the architect of the 1939 Palestine White Paper – had reached the conclusion that any further appeasement of the Arabs would be pointless, that only British victories on the battlefield might keep them loyal. If anything, the Americans were concerned even more than the British about the Arabs' loyalty. In November 1942, American forces landed in Morocco (Operation Torch), at the other end of the Mediterranean to Palestine, far removed from the "Zionist Problem". The American military was soon troubled by the "Jewish Question" in North-West Africa. The 330,000 Jews of Algeria, Morocco and Tunisia had suffered discrimination under the Vichy authorities from 1941 to 1942, and even worse treatment when the Germans arrived. On 17 November 1942, 8 days after the American landings, Roosevelt called for the "abrogation of all Nazi-inspired laws or decrees and the release of all anti-Nazi political prisoners in French North Africa".[47]

Roosevelt's call was enough to induce a state of near hysteria among senior American officers. Aware of the considerable influence of the significant Jewish minority in the United States, the army command was concerned about the Arab reaction. On 22 November 1942, General George Patton (General Eisenhower's deputy in Morocco) complained that the removal of the decrees would "provoke so much Arab unrest that he would need 60,000 Allied troops just to maintain order". He warned "American favoritism for Jews could provoke Arab violent reprisals":

> Arabs don't mind Christians but they utterly despise Jews. The French fear that the local Jews [,] knowing how high their tide is riding in the U.S.[,] will try to take the lead here. If they do the Arabs will murder them and there will be a local state of disorder ... I suggest that you write [Chief of Staff of the Army] Gen. Marshall and inform him of the situation so that if some State Department fool tries to foist ... Jews on Morocco, we will stop it at the source. If we get orders to favor the Jews[,] we will precipitate trouble and possibly civil war.[48]

On 28 November 1942, Adolph A. Berle, Assistant Secretary of State from 1938 to 1944, noted in his diary: "I gather only God could tell whether the Arab tribes would rise".[49]

The British were not at all sanguine about the support of the Arabs until the final retreat of Axis forces from North Africa, in mid-1943. Italian propaganda broadcasts from the island of Bari had worried them from 1934 until April 1938, when the Italians stopped them, temporarily, as part of the second "Gentleman's Agreement".[50] They were also concerned about the Arabs', especially the Iraqis' and the Palestinians', intensive contacts with Nazi and Italian representatives in the late 1930s, and their receipt of cash payments – in Baghdad, Beirut and in Jerusalem. Most of these contacts were monitored by British intelligence. (see Chapter 18).

Egypt never declared war on Nazi Germany. The Young Egypt Party did declare its support for Britain in August 1939, on the assumption that Italy would join Germany in the war. But when Italy remained neutral, the party changed its position to neutrality, in conformity with the position taken by the 'Ali Mahir government. But Young Egypt's public demonstrations against the Jews and their campaigns to boycott Jewish goods were not forgotten by the British. In January 1942, Lampson reported on the prevalence of anti-Semitism in Egypt. Apart from the general resentment of British support for the Jews in Palestine, there was a general belief in Egypt that the Jews controlled the black market.[51]

In May 1941, General Wavell, whose forces were already thinly stretched out across his Middle East Command, had been reluctant to send troops to crush the revolt in Iraq by force. When he did, the British took preventive measures in Egypt to avert any possibility of additional trouble there. They acted against Young Egypt, on the suspicion that its members had distributed pamphlets urging the Egyptians to sabotage the country's communications if the British retreated before Rommel's Panzers. The British shut down the party's paper, prohibited party meetings, arrested its leaders and retained them in custody until late 1944.[52]

During the fateful summer months of 1942, the American administration shared British concerns about their position in Egypt, and consequently in the entire Middle East. Both capitals were anxious not to take any step that might arouse Arab hostility. On 7 July 1942, one week into the first battle of El Alamein, Weizmann was received by President Roosevelt. His administration was under heavy pressure from the Revisionists' "Committee for a Jewish Army" which had organized a huge publicity campaign. When Weizmann asked Roosevelt "what about Palestine?", he replied:

> I always wanted to make a statement about the Jewish Army, which I think is a good thing, but the situation in Egypt is so dangerous that the British are frightened of the Egyptian Army turning against them, and therefore I would like to wait ten days or a fortnight.[53]

Gershoni and Jankowski claim that their "rereading of Egyptian history in the 1930s" can be applied also to Iraq, Palestine and Syria. It is appropriate therefore to turn now to Palestine, to see if any "substantial anti-Fascist and anti-Nazi voices" appeared in its Arabic-language press.[54]

Palestine

Egypt was *sui generis*. No historical or sociological comparison can be drawn between Egypt and the Arabs of the Fertile Crescent. The Moslems of Ottoman Syria had been ruled from Istanbul for 400 years, until the British and the French conquered the region during World War One. By contrast, in Egypt, Muhammad Ali and his son, Ibrahim Pasha, had challenged Ottoman rule during the first decades of the nineteenth century; although the Ottomans remained titular rulers of Egypt until World War One, *de facto*, the country was ruled by the British from 1882. Egypt was the only country in the Middle East that by 1914 had developed a clear, geographically delineated national identity.

The subjects of Ottoman Syria had never enjoyed either autonomy or any semblance of self-rule. Arab nationalism as a political force emerged only at the beginning of the twentieth century. Until then, the connotation "Arab" was reserved for the Bedouin of the Arabian Peninsula. Until mid-1920, the Palestinian Arabs aspired to be ruled from Damascus, as the southern province of what had been Ottoman Syria. After World War One, Greater Syria was "ruled" for less than 2 years by the Hashemite Emir Faysal, by the grace of British arms.

Among the former provinces of the Ottoman Empire, the political and social fabric of Arab society in Palestine was unique. Palestine's relatively small Arab community (just over 600,000 Moslem and Christian Arabs in 1920) was dominated by two feudal, land-owning clans – the Husaynis and the Nashashibis. The mandatory's policy of dividing the perquisites of power between the two clans in fact set them on a collision course. The British assured the Husaynis predominance, by awarding Haj Amin al-Husayni control of the considerable patronage at the disposal of the Supreme Moslem Council (SMC) in 1920, and by appointing him Grand Mufti of Jerusalem the following year.

The Arabs of Palestine also faced unique problems: not only the yoke of British colonial rule but the threat that under Britain's aegis, the Jewish National Home would be allowed to grow by Jewish immigration until the Jews became a majority. The Arabs feared that when that happened, Palestine would be converted into a Jewish state.

Palestinian Arab society never developed what has been called the "the temporizing compromises" that keep a political community safe from terror.[55] All British offers to establish institutions of self-rule (legislative or advisory councils) were rejected by the Arabs, since the British insisted on retaining a veto over all issues pertaining to the future development of the Jewish

National Home. With almost the inevitability of a Greek tragedy, the unstable *status quo* between the clans was shattered irrevocably in the summer of 1937, when Haj Amin unleashed a reign of terror against the supporters of the Peel Commission's plan to partition Palestine into Arab and Jewish states.

Dr Mustafa Kabha, a student of Professor Gershoni, has attempted to apply his "liberal discourse" paradigm to Palestine, in a study of the Arabic press. Kabha suggests the dubious hypothesis that the Arabic press in Palestine both shaped and reflected public opinion. Wittingly or not, his book refutes both of these claims!

Many new Arabic newspapers began publication in Palestine during the 1920s. After the 1929 crisis many papers began to appear as dailies. By the late 1930s, the Arabic press counted some 11 dailies, 14 weeklies and nine monthlies. But circulation was modest compared with the Egyptian or even the Lebanese press. The two largest-circulation papers, the Moslem-owned *al-Difa'* (the flag) and the Christian-owned *Filastin*, sold between 4000 and 6000 copies. At the height of the 1936–39 rebellion, their circulation rose on occasion to 8–10,000. The Moslem population, particularly in the rural areas, regarded *al-Difa'* "as a counterbalance to the Christian *Filastin*".[56] These figures reflect both the small size of Palestine's Arab population and, as has been noted already, their low literacy level – around 22 per cent in 1932.

Most of the influential Arab papers in Palestine were owned and controlled by rich urban families. They were conservative, and avoided printing articles that would harm their own class interests. For example, they were reluctant to print articles opposing land sales to the Jews. From the very first years of the mandate, most of the papers became pawns either of the Mufti's camp, the councillors (Majlisiyyun, i.e. the SMC), or of the opposition (Mu'aridin), headed by the Husaynis and the Nashashibis. Their papers reflected the power struggles between the two camps. Many journalists, including senior newspaper editors, switched camps according to their own personal interests, or according to who paid them more. One exception was *Al-Karmil*, an outspoken weekly, whose Lebanese-born owner, Najib Nassar, supported the peasants' interests against those of the large land-owners. The paper began publication in Haifa in 1908, but it was forced to close down in 1942, due to financial troubles.[57]

As noted, the Husaynis enjoyed a clear advantage over their rivals, with their control of the SMC funds. Only those who could afford the expense of publishing a newspaper without the Husaynis' financial support dared to criticize them. When an independent paper ran into financial difficulties, which sooner or later happened to most of them, the Husaynis came to the rescue, with the condition that the paper follow the Husayni line. The Husaynis also hired journalists to promote their views.[58]

The primary mission of the Arabic press in Palestine was to fight the political restraints imposed by the British, in particular, their sponsorship of Zionism. Kabha asserts that the Palestinians first turned away from Britain (and towards Fascism and Nazism) after her retreat from the 1930 White

Paper (see Chapter 10), and because of "the incompetence displayed by [the] democratic regimes during the global economic crisis".[59] But an earlier study by Professor Ayalon has shown that the Arabic press protested against Jewish immigration even before World War One, and from 1918, inveighed against the British occupation, for "permitting the growth of an alien entity [the Zionists] ... according to the principles of the Balfour Declaration".[60]

Another study of the Palestinian Arabic press, by Rene Wildangel, claims that there was a general "anti-fascist sentiment among the Palestinians".[61] This claim is not supported by Kabha's study. Some Palestinian Arabs, even those with anti-Jewish prejudices, did object to Nazi Germany's persecution of the Jews, on pragmatic grounds, since it generated sympathy for them and encouraged the emigration of more Jews to Palestine.[62] But Dr Kabha shows that during the 1930s, the Palestinian press displayed a widespread admiration for Fascist Italy, and even more so for Nazi Germany. Even if an occasional critical article did appear, "almost all the newspapers" displayed "sympathy and admiration towards the German regime". Kabha explains that a major factor that found support among the Arabs was Nazi Germany's "antagonism ... toward the Jews and the Zionist movement".[63]

The Palestinians' "antagonism towards the Jews" degenerated to plain anti-Semitism. Wildangel concedes that the Palestinians "adopted some elements of European fascist movements, such as military-party discipline and uniform shirts and forms of organization, including male youth groups that could be dispatched to project power and violence in the streets". However, he distinguishes between the Palestinians' brand of Fascism and that prevalent in Europe. However, Wildangel's claim that there was no "Führerkult" in Palestine, because of the antagonism between the "pro- and anti-mufti factions",[64] is erroneous.

No one seriously questions the Mufti's affinity for Nazi Germany. The Mufti *did* acquire many of the attributes of a Palestinian Arab Führer (this point will be elaborated upon below). He did so even if he never acquired the state powers of coercion enjoyed by the European dictators.

Although Kabha declares that the purpose of his first article (1999) was "to counter the prevalent concept of the Palestinian movement as supporter of the Fascist and Nazi movements", his book (2007) shows clearly that the Arabic press in Palestine had few if any reservations about Fascist or Nazi ideology, which "stressed national pride and its symbols as a way of redeeming the people from their difficulties". Not only that, but the enmity of the Central Powers to Britain was an asset, since the latter was "perceived by Palestinian Arabs at the time as their major and primary enemy".[65]

Initially, articles in the Arabic press spoke of the attractions of Mussolini's Italy for Palestinian Arab youth. But it also expressed reservations about the cruelty of Italian colonialism. *Filastin* and *al-Difa'* were especially critical of the "atrocious nature of Italian imperialism" in Libya and, from the end of 1935, of the ruthless conquest of Ethiopia.[66] In contrast, at least until the later 1930s, Nazi Germany could not be accused of brutal colonial expansionism, certainly not of an Arab population.

At a time when Egyptian intellectuals were deploring the Nazis' deprivation of the democratic rights of the individual, the Arabic press in Palestine continued (until 1937) to publish adulatory profiles of Hitler. The Palestinians were urged to emulate Nazi Germany's achievements. *al-Difa'*, the Mufti's paper, was the most sympathetic to Hitler. From June to July 1934, the paper ran a series of flattering articles on his life and achievements, urging its readers to emulate him. In July 1934, the paper's editor awarded Hitler the title "Redeemer of Germany from misery, poverty, and disgrace". *al-Difa'* had close links with the Germans and received from them financial subventions and pictures that were not available to other papers. The paper called on the Arabs to read the Nazi Party's platform ("the national pride programme") and to emulate it. *Filastin* also complemented Hitler. In an article of February 1932, it dubbed him "one of the great men of the new world".[67]

As Kabha explains, the Palestinian Arabs' reservations about Germany were pragmatic, rather than ideological. They protested Hitler's refusal to stop the emigration of German Jews to Palestine, and his failure to halt the transfer of German manufactured goods by German-Jewish immigrants. Typical was an article that appeared in *al-Jami'a al-Islamiyya* (Islamic Unity) on 9 January 1938: "German hostility towards the Jews has been detrimental to us as it led to the great Jewish immigration to Palestine". A second reason was Hitler's rejection of Palestinian requests for arms and funds during the 1936–39 rebellion.[68]

Whereas Arab anti-Semitism in Palestine never became as lethal as that of the Nazis, in many other senses it was not so different from the European brands. Many press articles attributed to the Jews extraordinary powers, echoing classical themes about world-wide Jewish conspiracies to seize control of the world. A few extracts from Dr Kabha's survey will be cited here (he does not reproduce any dissenting voices).

Kabha claims that many articles castigated the sale of Arab lands to Jews, and tried promote a "social and economic boycott of Jewish settlements". These articles described the Jews as "permissive, materialistic and corrupt", implying that any contact with them would lead to the "moral corruption of Arab society". This is somewhat inconsistent, as he also states that most of the Arabic newspapers were owned by the wealthy urban elites and did not campaign against the land sales, from which their class benefited.[69]

From 1932, the visible increase in the rate of Jewish immigration provoked a flood of anti-Semitic articles in the Arabic press. Some writers insisted that the Palestinians had their own, indigenous brand of anti-Semitism. In June 1934, an article in *Filastin* protested British and Jewish accusations that the Arabs had been influenced by the Nazis, insisting "Our loathing of Zionism has deep roots, originating many years before the emergence of Nazism".[70]

The Arabic press began to blame the Jews for "every misfortune or disaster" that befell the country. *Filastin* accused them of being responsible for a government increase in the customs tariff on flour, while *al-Jami'a al-Islamiyya* "credited" them with the devaluation of the pound sterling. The Jews were blamed for the series of natural disasters that befell the country at the beginning of the 1930s (drought and plague); in December 1932, *Sawt al-Sha'b* referred to them as "traitors to all rules, blood-thirsty and law evaders". Allegations about Jewish communism and heresy were common. In October 1933, a*l-Jami al-'Arabiyya* wrote about the "tens of hundreds of Jews" entering Palestine every day, "carrying the germs of communism, the seeds of heresy and other destructive ideas". In September 1932, a*l-Jami al-'Islamiyya* featured a cartoon depicting a Jew collecting money, not only for Jewish settlements in Palestine but also "in order to manage [their] world interest, such as combatting religion and faith, disseminating communism, and organizing world revolution".[71]

In August 1934, *al-Difa'* published an editorial that echoed a theme common in the British discourse of the 1920s, one that Churchill himself had espoused 1920 (see Chapter 1):

> The Jews were a people of intrigue and rebelliousness everywhere they went and in every period. They have always disrupted public security and caused tension and disturbances not only in foreign communities but also within their own community. This is a known fact about the Jews.[72]

In September 1933, *al-Difa'* called the struggle against the Zionists a jihad (holy war), and warned that anyone who did not take a part in this war was committing a sin. The Arabic press also featured cartoon caricatures of the Jews, in the best tradition of *Der Stürmer*, the Nazi anti-Semitic weekly. For instance, in September 1932, *Filastin* printed a cartoon depicting Zionism as an intimidating crocodile, opening its mouth wide to swallow two Arab peasants, while an armed British soldier stood by calmly.[73]

Mir'at al-Sharq (Mirror of the World) was the only Arab newspaper that dared to go against the trend. In April 1935 it urged Arab-Jewish co-operation, arguing that the Arabs and the Jews were cousins, and Palestine was the only safe haven for them. The paper was denounced by the rest of the Arabic press, and accused of collaborating with the Jews.[74]

The Zionists monitored the Arabic press closely, with mounting anxiety. They could not forget the pogroms carried out by the Arabs against the Jews in 1920 and 1921, especially not the savagery of the slaughter of Jewish men women and children in Hebron and Safed in 1929 (see Chapter 10).

All the press in Palestine was subjected to the British censor, who acted against papers that published inflammatory articles against the British. It suspended those Arabic newspapers that criticized the Peel Partition Plan or the alleged machinations of British rule. For example, *al-Liwa* was suspended for several months after it attacked the Peel Partition Plan. When it reappeared in January 1938, it featured an article asserting that the mandatory government was composed of "an English body and a Jewish mind", and claimed that it discerned an "English-Jewish plot aimed at disrupting the reliability and good reputation of Haj Amin". Other Arabic papers were suspended for "implying incitement or support of the gangs". The British censorship, imposed some times at the last minute, forced editors to leave blank spaces.[75]

As the rebellion gained momentum, the British also blocked the import of foreign Arabic newspapers. The number of foreign papers banned rose from six in 1936, to 28 in 1937, to a peak of 45 in 1938. In 1939, the year in which the rebellion was crushed, the number of banned papers fell to 18.[76] The outbreak of war in 1939 found the Palestinians exhausted from the rebellion. During the war, the British imposed tight controls over the Arabic press in Palestine, closing all but three newspapers, which they used for disseminating "closely censored news and commentary". The British also banned the import of Arabic newspapers, but only sporadically and intermittently. These steps did not prevent the arrival of news about developments in Europe, both about the battlefronts and about the Nazis' atrocities against the Jews.[77]

Freitag and Gershoni have argued that the appearance of Fascism and Nazism in the 1930s:

> ... triggered the emergence of lively public debates [in the Arab Middle East] on crucial issues: the very nature of a political system appropriate to Arab political culture – democracy vs. dictatorship; a liberal party government vs. authoritarian rule ... individual liberty and freedom of expression and organization vs. forms of totalitarianism.[78]

As noted, they have suggested that the Egyptian paradigm can be applied to Palestine. But even a cursory look at Kabha's book reveals that there was rarely if ever any "plurality of public opinions" in Palestine. One must bear in mind Kabha's own definition of public opinion: the "main elite groups in Palestinian society".[79] No body of Palestinian intellectuals condemned the tyrannical nature of the Nazi regime. This was due to the fact that quite apart from the restrictions imposed by the British censor, the Arabic press suffered from the even heavier hand of the Mufti. Few Palestinian Arabs dared to oppose him.

Once the Arab rebellion began in 1936, the Husaynis added physical threats and intimidation to the earlier financial control that they had exercised. In the words of Kabha:

> The leaders of the armed bands heading the revolt terrorized the various newspapers and dictated their moves.[80]

The Arabic press was frequently caught between the conflicting pressures of the British censor and the Arab gangs. Newspapers would prepare news items, which the censor forced them either to change or to retract. But on the morrow, they would be forced by the gangs to print the original version. The increasing frequency of these changes led to a decline in their readers' trust, and to public appeals for "a more reliable picture". In 1938, several editors simply packed their bags and fled the country, due to the intimidation of the armed gangs. They were unwilling to bow to peasant thugs whom they considered to be their social inferiors.[81]

Only one newspaper dared to take an independent line, but only once. On 27 November 1937, after the Mufti had fled to the Lebanon, *Sawt al-Sha'b* called for a new leadership to replace the HAC, most of whose members had by then either fled or been exiled. The Mufti's armed gangs reacted by attacking the paper's editor, who joined those who had fled to the Lebanon. He returned only in late 1939, after the rebellion had been crushed. The Arabic press either supported the Mufti or maintained silence on local affairs. Instead, they filled their pages with "international, literary or religious affairs".[82]

The internecine Arab violence in Palestine reached its peak during the summer of 1938, as the rebellion itself reached its apogee. Press appeals to the gangs to stop the internal violence had little or no effect. The gangs infiltrated urban centres (Jaffa, Haifa, Gaza and Majdal), and ordered people to wear the traditional peasant head covering (the kufiyha). Those who refused or were caught wearing the Turkish fez were "beaten and humiliated".[83]

Thus at a critical juncture in Palestinian history, whatever limited freedom had been retained by the Arabic press was smothered by the physical threats and violence of the Husaynis' armed gangs. Far from "shaping" or reflecting public opinion, it would be more accurate to say that henceforth, the Arabic press was gagged by Husayni terror. The Arabic press had ceased to determine the public agenda – the Mufti did. It is through this prism that one must assess the Arabic press.

Dr Kabha claims that from 1937, the Arabic press began to advocate working to improve relations with the British, despite their "actions in favor of the Jews and against the Arabs". But strangely, he makes no reference to the Palestine White Paper of May 1939 – Britain's overt attempt to appease the Arabs. The new policy declared that Britain considered that its sponsorship of the Jewish National Home was completed. Kabha makes no reference to the months-long debate about the new policy, fiercely opposed by the Zionists, which surely must have featured in the Arabic press. However, one article cited by him, in *al-Jami'a al-Islamiyya* on 27 June 1939, might indicate an indirect appeal by the Mufti to the British to improve the terms of the White Paper. The article called on the Arabs to "reach an arrangement with Britain and form an alliance, **on condition that this would help realize Arab national aspirations** (my emphasis)".[84]

Dr Kabha's claim that the Palestinians espoused the Allied cause during World War Two rests on just three articles published during the war itself. Of the three articles, only one bore any resemblance to the liberal high ground taken by the Egyptian intellectuals. In October 1939, Akram al-Khaldi, a "Palestinian author and journalist", published an article in *Filastin*, describing the war as: "a contest between truth and falsehood, between order and anarchy and between democracy and dictatorship [and warned] ... anyone who did not support democracy at this crucial time would later bear a mark of disgrace". The third and last article cited by Kabha, published in July 1940, also appeared in *Filastin*. It called upon the Palestinians to enlist in the British army.[85] But Kabha does not relate this article to its political context. As noted above, the British had initiated a plan to mobilize Palestinian Arabs and Jews into a new unit to be called the Palestine Buffs, 1000 from each community. The scheme was a limited success, due to the Arabs' failure to match the number of Jewish recruits. The British were forced to scale down the number of Jews enlisted to 500 (see Chapter 14).

Dr Kabha's study fails to relate the press articles he cites to the political history of the mandate: the periodical negotiations between all the parties concerned, the British White Papers that defined and changed policy and, most significant for our purpose, the Husaynis' intensive contacts with the envoys of Fascist Italy and Nazi Germany, which will be discussed below. Quite regardless of what the Palestinian Arabs read or heard about from the press, most chose the course that best suited their own personal interest. Of the minority who dared to oppose the Husaynis, most did so for purely personal reasons: some due to economic distress and/or the prospect of financial gain (land sales, money payments); some due to clan or village loyalties; and some as the result of personal injury or loss at the hands of the Husayni terrorist bands.

How much did the Arabs know about Nazi Germany's war activities?

From the spring of 1941, with the landing of Rommel's Afrika Korps in Libya, Zionist intelligence reports left them in no doubt that significant sections of the Arab population were awaiting Rommel's triumphant arrival eagerly, anticipating that the Germans would solve their "Jewish Problem" in Palestine.

The Palestinians received a plethora of information from the local Arabic press in Palestine. But the Palestine press remained something of a "literary satellite in the Egyptian and Lebanese cultural orbits". The major Egyptian newspapers were usually available in the main Palestinian cities on the day of publication. Many educated Palestinians took out subscriptions. Palestinian intellectuals:

> ... would impatiently await the arrival of [Egyptian journals]. They would read them thoroughly and critically split into thinking groups and parties, supporting one author or another and engaging in passionate debates of the ideas brought up in the journal.[86]

Newspapers in Arabic were sold in all of the major Palestinian towns and in the larger villages. Single copies were sent to the smaller villages, where traditionally, they were read out aloud in cafés and at other public meeting places.[87]

We also have the testimony of leaders such as Ragheb Nashashibi that he read translations of most foreign-language newspapers regularly.[88] Many Palestinians also read the English-language *Palestine Post*, which began publication in Jerusalem in 1932. Some of the Palestinian intelligentsia read the Hebrew press. News items about the first stages of the Holocaust first appeared in the Hebrew press in June 1941, with the German invasion of the Soviet Union. Items on Nazi atrocities appeared with more frequency in the Hebrew press from the beginning of 1942.

From the earliest stages of World War Two, readers of the Egyptian press learned not only about Nazi military successes but also about the atrocities they were committing against the Jews of Eastern Europe. Egyptian newspapers printed far more coverage of Nazi cruelties in Europe than the Palestinian press did.[89]

In February 1941 (as Rommel landed his first units in Libya), an opinion poll carried out for the American consulate in Jerusalem among hundreds of Palestinian Arabs found that 88 per cent supported Nazi Germany and only 9 per cent Great Britain. During the course of that summer and winter, the Mufti's camp was encouraged by his successful escape from Iraq and the warm welcome he received in Berlin. Combined with the looming threat of an invasion by Rommel, the reports of Zionist agents in the field confirmed their leaders' fears about the Palestinians' hostility.[90]

By the end of 1941, the murderous nature of the Nazi regime was common knowledge across the Middle East. One of the key Zionist intelligence agents was Ya'akov Cohen, a Samaritan who lived in Nablus. Cohen reported regularly to the Jewish Agency on the situation in Nablus, a centre of Arab nationalist activity. Nablus was home to some of Palestine's most prominent Arab nationalists: 'Awni 'Abd al-Hadi and Muhammad 'Izzat Darwaza, leaders of the Istiqlal Party, and Ahmad Shuqayri, the first chairman of the Palestine Liberation Organization (PLO, 1964). From time to time, Cohen also reported about trends in other major towns with large Arab populations (i.e. Haifa).[91] If we assume that Nablus and Haifa were representative of Arab nationalist feeling in Palestine, then Cohen's reports belie the contention that a majority of Arabs supported the Allies.

At the beginning of the war, Fahkri Nashashibi had published a lone pamphlet against Fascism. Given his record of taking Zionist subsidies (see Chapter 12), the suspicion arises that the pamphlet was paid for and possibly written by the Zionists (or even the British). In any case, this was an isolated event, which did not arouse any Arab reaction. Fahkri's assassination in Baghdad in November 1941 was applauded by Nazi propaganda transmissions.[92]

Cohen reported from Nablus that the Arabs had an up-to-the-hour knowledge of the ebb and flow on the war fronts, both in Europe and in the Western desert. Radio transmissions became a major source of information, even more important than the printed word. The Arabs listened to Radio Jerusalem, which began broadcasting in 1936, and to Egyptian and Lebanese stations. They listened also to Radio Bari, on which they would have heard the Mufti's broadcast from time to time. But they preferred Radio Ankara, whose news coverage was the most comprehensive. Ahmad Shuqayri left a graphic description in his memoirs of listening to foreign radio stations at night, following the conquests of the German army in Europe, and Rommel's advances in the Western desert.[93]

On 25 November 1941, Cohen reported from Nablus that the Mufti's supporters were holding nightly meetings, confident that Rommel would reach Palestine by the coming spring and "free the country of its Jews". They were spreading rumours that the democracies had promised to build the Jewish National Home not only in Palestine, but in Syria and Trans-Jordan too. There was a lot of talk about the revenge the Mufti would take on the Palestinian opposition, once the Germans arrived. On 13 April 1942, Cohen reported that the Mufti's supporters were congratulating themselves that it was only a matter of weeks before the Germans conquered Palestine, and liberated them from both the British and the Jews.[94]

On 2 July 1942, the second day of the first battle of El Alamein, the Mufti's supporters organized a public meeting in Nablus, in order to congratulate each other on the approaching victory and to wish the Mufti a long life. Cohen reported that the Mufti's supporters in Haifa had visited the local villages of Kabatia and Yabed, where they had met with his followers in order to plan the pillaging of Jewish villages in the Jezre'el valley, after the British retreat. By the same token, members of the opposition were filled with deep anxiety, convinced that in the event of a German victory they would be the first to suffer revenge at the hands of the Mufti's men.[95]

On the same day in July, Cohen reported that the Arabs had received news about the fate of the Jews in Europe with "open joy". They expressed the hope that the Germans would conquer Palestine and "liberate" them from their Jews. Some of the moderate minority refused to believe the news, arguing that it was merely Jewish propaganda designed to capture the sympathy of the world, that it was inconceivable that a country of Germany's cultural level could commit atrocities such as those being reported.[96]

Even after Rommel's defeat in the second battle of El Alamein, the Palestinians did not give up hope that the Germans would conquer the Middle East. On 28 November 1942, Cohen reported that the Mufti's supporters were spreading exaggerated news of Rommel's advances into Egypt, causing "great rejoicing". The Husaynis' support for the Mufti remained solid, and at times turned violent. In 1943, 'Abd al-Qader al-Muzaffar, a former Mufti supporter, was attacked with a Molotov cocktail after criticizing the Mufti's "alliance with the Nazi regime".[97]

The Mufti, Fascism and Nazism

The Husaynis' motives for persisting in their quest for an alliance with Nazi Germany proved to be stronger than their disappointment with Hitler after he refused to halt the emigration of German Jews. Porath's pioneering study of Palestinian Arab nationalism concluded:

> The Nazi leanings of the Husaynis were not coincidental. The bestial anti-Jewish attitude of the Nazis drew the attention of the Palestinian Arab nationalists who regarded the Nazis as natural allies in the struggle against the Jews.[98]

The fact that no Arab Nazi party was ever formed in Palestine was not because there was no local demand. It was due to Nazi reticence. A Nazi Party decree of June 1934 had denied membership of foreign Nazi parties to non-Germans. Not only that, but the Nazis considered the Arabs to be too politically unreliable and likely to leak Germany's involvement in local politics to London and Paris.[99]

In 1933, Joseph Francis, the Palestine correspondent of *al-Ahram*, wrote on behalf of a group of Palestinian Arabs to Heinrich Wolff, the German consul in Jerusalem (1933–35), asking for his aid in forming a local Arab Nazi party. Wolff (whose wife was Jewish) opposed the idea, fearing that it would ruin his good relations with the British. Berlin confirmed Wolff's decision not to offer official German sponsorship to an "Arab National Socialist movement". Wolff also received instructions to discourage any contact between Arab Nazi sympathizers and the various local branches of the Nazi Party among the German Templer community in Palestine (about 1800 strong).[100]

The Arab rebellion turned Palestine into a focus for pan-Arab and anti-West agitation. In March 1937, Wolff's successor, Walter Döhle (1936–39), sent to Berlin the following assessment of Arab public opinion in Palestine:

> Palestinian Arabs in all social strata have great sympathies for the new Germany and its Führer ... [it] is probably so widespread because the Palestinian Arabs, in their struggle for existence, long for an Arab "Führer". And because in their fight against the Jews, they sense that they share a common single front with the Germans.[101]

Later in the year, a large street demonstration took place, in which the Arabs displayed "hundreds of German flags and pictures of Adolf Hitler". The event caused acute embarrassment to Döhle, who reassured the British that the Germans had had nothing to do with the demonstration, nor had they supplied the flags and the posters of Hitler (as noted above, the Germans did in fact supply pictures and cash to the Mufti's newspaper, *al-Liwa*). In October 1938, a conference of Islamic parliamentarians was held in Cairo, "for the defense of Palestine". Anti-Semitic texts were distributed, including Arabic translations of *Mein Kampf* and the *Protocols of the Elders of Zion*.[102]

Hitler's strategy on the Middle East began to change from 1939. After his string of successful, bloodless coups in Europe, he was convinced that he could achieve his goals without an alliance with Britain. He began to refer in public to the plight of the Palestinian Arabs, and to give favourable consideration to Arab requests for arms.[103]

The Mufti of Jerusalem was arguably the Fascists' and the Nazis' most significant Arab collaborator. He had both personal and ideological reasons for his support of the two Central Powers. After his exile from Palestine in October 1937, he remained *persona non grata* with the British. A recent study of Mussolini's policies in the Middle East during the 1930s concluded:

> Italian sources, even when taken with a pinch of salt, expose a leader [the Mufti] who had placed himself firmly in the Fascist camp already in the 1930s.[104]

The files of the German Foreign Office and the royal treatment accorded to the Mufti once he arrived in Berlin both indicate the high regard in which he was held by the Nazis. Before the war, Allied intelligence services monitored every approach made by the Mufti to Italian and Nazi agents, every subsidy and arms shipment that the Arabs received from the Axis, and every public speech and propaganda broadcast made by him against the Allies during the war.

It is impossible to quantify the number of Arabs who listened to the Mufti's wartime propaganda broadcasts from Berlin and Bari. But we do know that Axis, especially Nazi, shortwave broadcasts to the Middle East caused the Allies grave concern. The American Consul at Cairo monitored all of the Nazi transmissions and sent transcripts to the State Department in Washington.

Until Rommel's landings in Libya at the beginning of 1941, Mussolini was more directly involved with the Middle East than Hitler. Mussolini's policies towards the Arabs were, like Hitler's, conditioned by his relations with the British. In 1934, as Mussolini began his challenge to the British hegemony over the Middle East, the Italian radio station at Bari, in southern Italy, began daily transmissions of anti-British propaganda in Arabic. His readiness to supply the Arabs with arms and money increased as he planned the conquest of Ethiopia (1935–36). His goal was to divert and tie down the British as much as possible with Arab disturbances in Palestine during his military campaign. In January 1936, the Mufti secretly approached the Italian Consul in Jerusalem to ask for money and arms. Rome agreed. Musa al-Alami became the conduit for the transfer of the funds. al-Alami, a Cambridge-educated lawyer, was the personal secretary to High Commissioner Sir Arthur Wauchope. He was connected to the Husayni clan via his brother-in-law, Jamal-al Husayni. The money was delivered in cash that was transferred in packages from Rome. When asked by Shertok of the Jewish Agency if the Palestinians were receiving Italian funds, al-Alami denied it.[105]

In September 1940, when the Italian Foreign Minister Ciano met von Mackenson, the German ambassador, in Rome, he lamented the huge sums he had wasted on the Palestinians:

For years he had maintained constant relations with the Grand Mufti, of which his secret fund could tell a tale. The return on this gift of millions [presumably Italian lira] had not been exactly great and had really been confined to occasional destruction of pipelines, which in most cases could quickly be repaired.[106]

The Italian records reveal that before World War Two, Italy transferred to the Mufti a total of some £157,578. In September 1936, al-Alami travelled to Rome to negotiate a shipment of arms via Belgium to the Palestinian rebels. The arms were to have been shipped to Saudi Arabia and thence smuggled overland to Palestine. But the Saudis backed out of the deal, either due to their fear of the British reaction or to fear of the influence that Italy might acquire in the Middle East.[107]

Iraq and Saudi Arabia also tried to establish closer relations with Rome, recognizing Mussolini's Italy as a Great Power and wishing to lessen their dependence upon Britain. Their main interest was to obtain military equipment, especially since Britain found it hard to meet all the Arabs' requests, needing to rearm herself against a resurgent Germany.

The Mufti identified ideologically more with Hitler's regime than with Fascist Italy, even if, as will be seen in the next chapter, Italy's Middle East strategy served the Mufti's interests better than that of the Nazis. Germany's military and industrial power, projected across Europe from 1936, was more alluring than that of Mussolini's Italy. But above all, the Nazis' virulent anti-Semitism contrasted with Mussolini's initially milder treatment of his Jews.[108] The Mufti hoped that Hitler's solution to the "Jewish Problem" in Europe would be applied by the Nazis to Palestine, to solve *his* "Jewish Problem".

Bernard Lewis has singled out the rise of the Jewish National Home in Palestine and the resulting conflict between Arabs and Jews as a seminal factor in Arab anti-Semitism. The Nazis themselves were only too aware of this, as noted by one SS official:

> The Arab Question is bound up insolubly with the Jewish Question. The Jews are the mortal enemy of the Arabs, as they are the deadly enemy of the Germans. Anyone in Germany who deals with Arab politics must be a convinced and uncompromising adversary of the Jews.[109]

Arab apologists, including the Mufti himself, have blamed the British for his collaboration with the Nazis. In 1946, the Mufti explained that the British had hounded him so much that Berlin became "the only alternative he had to arrest or exile".[110] One of his Arab apologists has asserted:

> Because the British really had no intention of carrying through with the [1939] White Paper, they pretty much destroyed any chance for a settlement with moderate elements. They also drove the Mufti, who might have accepted the White Paper if the British were willing to commit

themselves to it, towards the Axis and into anti-British propaganda and agitation during the course of the war.[111]

The truth is radically different. The Mufti believed that Islam and National Socialism shared a common *weltanschauung*. He tried to adapt the teachings of the *Koran* to Nazi ideology. He asserted that the office of the caliph also embodied the Führerprinzip, the underpinnings of a political, social, spiritual and military leadership. He mined the *Koran* in order to find verses that decreed obedience, order and discipline. He drew an analogy between the Islamic jihad and the Nazi *der kampf* – both calls "to engage in the struggle" against unbelievers. He asserted that Islam also revered the family as the basic social unit – the *Volk*. He preached that the vitality of the Nazi regime should serve as a model for all Moslems in their struggles.[112]

The Mufti's "romance" with the Nazis began in 1933, the year of Hitler's ascent to power. He was not "hounded" anywhere by the British until late 1937, when he was implicated in the assassination of Lewis Andrews, the Acting British District Commissioner for the Northern District. Until October 1937, he continued to enjoy the considerable perquisites of the presidency of the SMC and of the office of Grand Mufti of Jerusalem.

In March 1933, shortly after the Nazis' rise to power, the Mufti sent a congratulatory telegram to Hitler, expressing his admiration and his unconditional support for the Nazis, their boycott of Jewish goods, and their struggle against Jewish influence. Following a meeting with the Mufti in Jerusalem on 31 March 1933, Consul Wolff reported back to Berlin:

> The Mufti explained to me today at length that Moslems both within Palestine and without welcome the new regime in Germany and hope for the spread of fascist, anti-democratic forms of government to other countries ... Moslems are hoping for Germany to declare a boycott [of "Jewish" goods], which they would then enthusiastically join throughout the Moslem world.[113]

One month later, the Mufti had a second meeting with Wolff, this time accompanied by several Arab sheikhs. He asked for a halt to all emigration of German Jews to Palestine. Notwithstanding the rejection of the Mufti's request, Wolff's annual report for 1933 stated: "Hitler and the new Germany were accorded a high degree of popular enthusiasm and support".[114]

There was a certain symmetry between the options available to the Arabs and to the Jews. The Jews had no option but to support the British, due to the Nazis' anti-Semitism. Many Arabs, including the Mufti's camp, saw little option but to support Nazi Germany, due to Britain's support for Zionism.

In 1937, the Mufti lobbied the Germans to support his efforts to block the Peel Plan to set up a Jewish state in a part of Palestine. On 16 July, he asked Consul Döhle if the Germans would receive an emissary of his in Berlin. At a further meeting a month later, he asked the Germans to intervene with the

Polish government, to prevent the emigration of Polish Jews to Palestine. Döhle promised to forward the Mufti's requests to Berlin, but advised him that it would be best if German sympathy were kept discreet. Döhle was pronouncedly pro-Arab, and warned Berlin that Germany's indifference to the Arabs' cause would alienate them. On 16 July 1937 – the same day that the Mufti met Döhle in Jerusalem – two members of the HAC, Awni Abd el-Hadi and Muin el-Mahdi, met in Baghdad with Fritz Grobba, the German envoy. They too sought German support, and asked to be received in Berlin.[115] Although Grobba was also non-committal, some of the Mufti's agents *were* received by German officials in Berlin before the war.

Notwithstanding Berlin's official policy of non-involvement in Palestine, there are indications that the Abwehr by-passed official policy and transferred financial and material aid to the Palestinians before World War Two. One Abwehr report of early 1939 described in detail the financial aid given to the Mufti in Beirut for the rebellion in Palestine. Another report, of June 1939, claimed that the Mufti had been able to carry out the rebellion in Palestine only thanks to their funds. On occasion, Grobba visited Beirut and handed over funds to the Mufti, and once gave £800 in cash to Musa al-Alami. The Abwehr was also involved in the plans to send German weapons to Palestine via Saudi Arabia and Iraq. Allied intelligence monitored most of these activities.[116]

When the second stage of the Arab rebellion began in September 1937, the Nazis dispatched to Palestine a two-man mission – Herbert Hagen, head of the Jewish section of the SD (the elite intelligence section of the SS), and his deputy, Adolf Eichmann. Their assignment was to study the "organizational structure" of the Zionist movement, and to meet the Mufti. They missed the Mufti, who had already fled the country. But they did meet with a Hagana agent, Feivel Polkes, who showed them around Haifa and took them to visit a kibbutz. When the British discovered the Nazis' presence, they expelled them summarily to Egypt. Hagen's and Eichmann's report, laced with anti-Semitic rhetoric and contempt for the Arabs, concluded that the Palestinians were too primitive and self-seeking to be of much use to Germany:

> There was very little likelihood that the Arab countries, although united in their rejection of the Partition Plan, would actually do anything to help Palestine as they were, on the one hand, too afraid of the English, and, on the other, their leaders were corrupt and too busy lining their own pockets with money from Moscow, Rome and, possibly, Germany.[117]

Notwithstanding Germany's official reticence, the Mufti's agents were successful in securing meetings in Berlin with top Nazi officials. In November 1937, Dr Said Imam, an agent of the Mufti, arrived in Berlin with an offer to support German interests and trade in the Arab East, to disseminate Nazi ideology, boycott all Jewish goods, continue terrorist acts against the French in all of their colonial and mandated territories, and to "prevent by all possible means the establishment of a Jewish State in Palestine". The German reply was non-committal.[118]

With the outbreak of World War Two, the Mufti fled from the Lebanon to Baghdad. He was granted political asylum by the Iraqis, feted and accorded a status equivalent to that of a minister. He became Rashid Ali's ideological mentor, and was invited to his meetings with Axis representatives in Baghdad. During his stay there, from late 1939 until May 1941, the Mufti was in constant contact with Italian and German agents and with officers of the pro-Axis Golden Square. American intelligence estimated that while in Baghdad, the Mufti received some $400,000 from Italy and Germany, over $75,000 from the Iraqi administration, and in addition, a monthly allowance of $4000 from the Iraqi secret service. When Fritz Grobba arrived in Baghdad during the second week of May 1941, he disbursed "sums in gold to Rashid Ali and in dollars to the Mufti". Both men asked for more money, the Mufti claiming that he needed it for a "major action" in Palestine.[119] All these activities took place in a country under British rule.

Following the series of British military reverses in northern Europe during the spring and summer of 1940, the Mufti sent out feelers to German officials in Ankara and Berlin, declaring his support for the Axis and asking for more military aid. A veteran of broken British promises after World War One, the Mufti sought a declaration of Axis support for Arab independence. At the end of June 1940, Nuri al-Said and Naji Shawkat, the Iraqi Justice Minister, travelled to Ankara for talks with the Turkish Foreign Minister. After a week, Nuri al-Said returned home. Shawkat, whose mission was co-ordinated with the Mufti, stayed on and held talks with Franz von Papen, the German ambassador to Turkey (1939–44).[120]

Shawkat and his two brothers were prominent members of the pro-Nazi al-Muthanna Club. He told von Papen that he represented an Arab committee headed by the Mufti, which included among its members himself, the officers of the Golden Square, Shukri al-Quwatli of Syria and some Saudi notables, including Ibn Saud's personal adviser, Sheikh Yusuf Yasin.[121] Shawkat brought with him a personal letter from the Mufti, congratulating Hitler on his victories:

> ... on the occasion of the great political and military triumphs which [the Führer] has just achieved ... The Arab nation everywhere feels the greatest joy and deepest gratification ... The Arab people, slandered, maltreated, and deceived by our common enemies, confidently expect that the result of your final victory will be their independence and complete liberation, as well as the creation of their unity.[122]

Von Papen was duly impressed, but told Shawkat that Germany had traditionally left affairs in the Middle East to Italy. Shawkat replied that just as the Arab national movement had fought Anglo-French imperialism, it would also fight Italian imperialism. When von Papen asked Shawkat how the Arabs proposed to help Germany, he replied that when the time came, the Iraqi army would help the Germans against the British. British intelligence learned of Shawkat's meeting with von Papen, which served to confirm their suspicions of the pro-Axis leanings of prominent Iraqi figures.[123]

In the summer of 1940, the Mufti sent another envoy to Berlin, 'Uthman Kamal Haddad, a young Arab activist. Haddad remained there from late August until mid-October 1940. He presented himself to Grobba and to other senior officials of the German Foreign Office as a representative of "the Arab leadership". According to Grobba's notes, Haddad asked for a declaration recognizing the right of the Arab countries to independence and self-determination and proposed that they resolve the "question of the Jewish element" in the same way that the Axis had done. In return, Haddad promised that Iraq would not only esrablish diplomatic relations with the Axis, but would grant Germany and Italy preferred diplomatic status, and preferential rights to the exploitation of its mineral resources, including its oil reserves. He promised that the Iraqis would overthrow Nuri al-Said and set up a pro-Axis government. When that happened, the Arabs would also launch a rebellion against the British in Palestine, to which Iraq would contribute 10,000 troops. Haddad promised that if the Axis provided financial and military aid, the Arabs would be able to handle the 30–40,000 British troops in Palestine.[124]

This fanciful scenario was dismissed out of hand by the Axis, especially by the Italians, who had no intention of conceding to the Arabs any measure of autonomy within the revived empire that they planned to re-establish in the Middle East. Sobered by the poor returns on his investment in the Palestinians so far, Ciano told the Germans that the Arabs were too weak, that they had no experience in self-government, and therefore, a public declaration supporting their independence would not be "expedient" at present.[125] The declaration that the Axis ministers broadcast on 23 October 1940 was non-committal:

> Germany (Italy) ... has always watched with interest the struggles of the Arab countries to achieve their independence. In their effort to obtain this goal the Arabs can count upon Germany's (Italy's) full sympathy also in the future.[126]

Not to be put off, the Mufti wrote again to Hitler on 20 January 1941, expressing the Arabs' readiness to work with him against Britain, their common enemy. He volunteered to mobilize the Arabs to sabotage Britain's vital communications in the region, on condition that Germany provided arms. The Mufti's approach met with a mixed reception in Berlin. Not only did Hitler and the Foreign Office still defer to the Italians, but they did not want to upset the Vichy regime that now controlled Syria by making open-ended promises about Arab independence. The officials also declined to promise weapons, but Foreign Minister Ribbentrop suggested that Germany begin to send money payments to the Mufti. In April, a sum of RM100,000 was mentioned. In addition, it was proposed to improve German intelligence in the Middle East by supplying the Mufti's secretary with a short-wave radio transmitter.[127]

As Rommel's Panzers drove ashore in North Africa in February 1941, Berlin issued a new statement, recognizing the Arabs as an "old *Kulturvolk*" and indicated that Germany was prepared to send arms. The Mufti and the Iraqi military, knowing nothing of Barbarossa, were confident that the future of the Middle East lay with Nazi Germany.[128] But at the end of May 1941, 3 weeks before the Wehrmacht crossed the borders of the Soviet Union, Rashid Ali's rebellion against the British was crushed. German military aid, flown in via Vichy-controlled Damascus, was too little and arrived too late. After the war, Luftwaffe General Helmuth Felmy, who co-ordinated the German mission to help Rashid Ali, wrote in his report:

> The chief reason for the failure of the Germans to provide the Iraqis with adequate assistance in their struggle against the British was the lack of political foresight shown by the German Government. However, it would have been helpful if the Iraqis had tried to arrive at an arrangement with Germany before the start of the revolt … Such measures as were finally taken were completely overshadowed by the preparations for Operation Barbarossa.[129]

The collapse of the rebellion in Iraq was followed on 1 June by a pogrom against the Jews of Baghdad (the farhud). This was not a spontaneous event, but the "outcome of intense anti-Jewish propaganda in the [Iraqi] army, police and youth organizations". It was a revenge reprisal by pro-Axis elements (members of the al-Muthanna Club were prominent among them), against a defenceless Jewish community. According to British estimates, over 600 Jewish adults and children were killed, and a great deal of Jewish property was destroyed. Nine days after the pogrom began, the Italian legation in Baghdad reported that the Jews were still being attacked and their property still being looted. On instructions from London, Sir Kinahan Cornwallis, the British ambassador, refused to allow British troops to enter the city to protect the Jews and restore order. London's principal concern was that the Iraqi Regent should appear to be re-establishing himself "independently", without the aid of British bayonets. Saving Jewish lives was a secondary consideration. Evidently this was not an episode of British imperial history that the British took pride in. Neither the memoirs of the British officers involved, nor the official British history of the war make any mention of the pogrom.[130]

Notes

1 Israel Gershoni and James Jankowski, *Confronting Fascism in Egypt: Dictatorship versus Democracy in the 1930s,* Redwood City, CA: Stanford University Press, 2010, p. 281.

2 Jeffrey Herf, *Nazi Propaganda for the Arab World,* New Haven/London: Yale University Press, 2009, pp. 138–39.
3 Meir Litvak and Esther Webman, *From Empathy to Denial: Arab Responses to the Holocaust,* New York: Columbia University Press, 2009, p. 377; on the political manipulations of Arab and Zionist narratives, see also Ulrike Freitag and Israel Gershoni, "Politics of Memory: The Necessity for Historical Investigation into Arab Responses to Fascism and Nazism", *Geschichte und Gesellschaft,* vol. 37, 2011, pp. 311–331.
4 Litvak, Webman, ibid, p. 307.
5 Personal communication from Hillel Cohen, author of *Army of Shadows: Palestinian Collaboration with Zionism, 1917–1948,* Berkeley/Los Angeles: University of California Press, 2008. Cohen's study is based entirely on Arabic and Zionist sources. Even British intelligence reports are cited from Zionist intelligence reports.
6 Philip Mattar, *The Mufti of Jerusalem: Al-Hajj Amin al-Husayni and the Palestinian National Movement,* New York: Columbia University Press, 1988, cited in Litvak, Webman, *From Empathy,* p. 300. In the 1990s, Allied intelligence files and the German archives gave up a treasure trove of information on the Mufti's nefarious wartime activities in Berlin, and in Bosnia; see Chapter 18.
7 Litvak, Webman, ibid, p. 298. Jemal's testimony was belied by Allied recordings of his wartime propaganda broadcasts from Berlin to the Middle East, and by photographs they had obtained of his recruiting Bosnian Moslems for Waffen *SS* units.
8 ibid, p. 302.
9 ibid, p. 299. The Mufti first published his memoirs as a series of articles in the Egyptian paper *al-Masri,* in 1954. They were published as a book the same year, in Cairo; numerous editions have been published subsequently.
10 Gilbert Achcar, *The Arabs and the Holocaust: The Arab-Israeli War of Narratives,* New York: Metropolitan Books/Henry Holt and Company, 2009. Achcar's goals are set out on the inside of his front cover. On the Mufti's wartime collaboration with the Nazis, see also the extensive Wikipedia entry (210 footnotes, and massive bibliography): http://en.wikipedia.org/wiki/Haj_Amin_al-Husseini
11 ibid, pp. 158, 171. His 15-page bibliography contains no primary sources.
12 ibid, pp. 137, 147; see also Derek Penslar's review of Achcar's book, in *The Jewish Review of Books,* vol. 5, spring 2011. The Allies' monitoring of and concern about Nazi propaganda broadcasts to the Middle East are the focus of Jeffrey Herf's prize-winning book, published in the same year as Achcar's book.
13 See political reports in CO 537/1318, 2643, CO 733/439/12, 368/2, 311/5, FO 371/61834-35, FO 141/678, 1284; and intelligence reports in the KV 2 series, files 2084-2092, NA. The KV 2 Security Service files were opened in 1999.
14 Litvak, Webman, *From Empathy,* p. 297.
15 cf. Freitag and Gershoni, "Politics of Memory", p. 326, and personal communication from Professor Gershoni; also Yehoshua Porath, *The Palestinian Arab National Movement: From Riots to Rebellion,* vol. two, *1929–1939,* London: Frank Cass, 1977, pp. 302–3. On the Arab League's support for the Mufti, cf. reports in KV 2/2085-86, NA.
16 Kabha's article was published first in Hebrew in 1999 without footnotes: "The Palestinian National Movement and Its Attitude to Fascism and Nazism, 1925–45", *Zmanim* (Times), no. 67, 1999, Tel Aviv University, pp 79–86. He reproduced it in English, with footnotes in 2011: "The Palestinian National Movement and Its Attitude toward the Fascist and Nazi Movements, 1925–1945", *Geschichte und Gesellschaft,* vol. 37, 2011, pp. 437–50. All quotes here are from the English version. The quote is on p. 449.
17 Mustafa Kabha, *The Palestinian Press as a Shaper of Public Opinion, 1929–1939: Writing up a Storm,* London: Vallentine Mitchell, 2007, pp. 12, 209. The book is

an adaptation of Kabha's PhD thesis, written under the supervision of Professor Gershoni.
18 ibid, pp. 210–11.
19 Personal communication from Dr Hillel Cohen.
20 Achcar, *The Arabs*, p. 315.
21 Cited in ibid, pp. 137–38.
22 cf. Lukasz Hirszowicz, *The Third Reich and the Arab East*, London/Toronto: Routledge & Kegan Paul/University of Toronto Press, 1966, pp. 40–42.
23 Francis R. Nicosia, *The Third Reich and the Palestine Question*, London: I.B. Tauris, 1985, p. 43–49, 194–95, appendix 8, p. 213; Klaus Gensicke: *The Mufti of Jerusalem and the Nazis: The Berlin Years*, London: Vallentine Mitchell, 2011, pp. 26–27. For the debate for and against the Transfer Agreement within the German bureaucracy, cf. Hirszowicz, *The Third Reich*, pp. 31–33. Many of the items imported under the Transfer Agreement were bought by Arabs.
24 Nicosia, ibid; Andreas Hillgruber, "The Third Reich and the Near and Middle East, 1933–39", in Uriel Dann, ed., *The Great Powers in the Middle East, 1933–1939*, London/New York: Holmes & Meier, 1988, pp. 277, 280, and *Documents on German Foreign Policy, 1918–1945*, vol. V, Washington: US Government Printing Office, 1953, p. 786.
25 Hirszowicz, *The Third Reich*, pp. 29–33; Achcar, *The Arabs*, pp. 141–42, and note 141, p. 323.
26 Hirszowicz, ibid, p. 267.
27 For details of Wavell's rout of the Italian army, see p. 380, notes 28–9.
28 Hillgruber, *The Third Reich*, pp. 275–77, 280; Anthony R. de Luca, "'Der Gross-Mufti'" in Berlin: The Politics of Collaboration", *International Journal of Middle East Studies*, 10/1, February 1979, pp. 125–38; Nicosia, *The Third Reich*, pp. 101–2, 123–25, 197–99.
29 cf Götz Nordbruch, *Nazism in Syria and Lebanon*, London: Routledge, 2009, pp. 3–4, 138.
30 The al-Muthanna Club was established in Baghad in the late 1930s; it remained active until June 1941, when it played a key role in the Farhud, the pogrom of the Jews of Baghdad.
31 Sa'ada's party had a profound political influence on the twentieth-century history of Lebanon and Syria, even if the party itself was a political failure. Sa'ada himself was imprisoned by the French authorities several times and finally executed by the Lebanese in 1949. cf. Daniel Pipes, "Radical Politics and the Syrian Social Nationalist Party", *International Journal of Middle East Studies*, vol. 20/3, August 1988.
32 Nordbruch, *Nazism in Syria and Lebanon*, pp. 3–4, also Hirszowicz, *The Third Reich*, p.13.
33 Gershoni and Jankowski, *Confronting Fascism in Egypt*, pp. 273–75; among the prominent orthodox scholars they refer to are Nadav Safran and P.J. Vatikiotis, pp. 6–7.
34 ibid, pp. 214–18; also Israel Gershoni, "Rejecting the West: The Image of the West in the Teachings of the Muslim Brotherhood, 1928–39", in Uriel Dann, ed., *The Great Powers in the Middle East, 1919–1939*, New York/London: Holmes & Meier, 1988. pp. 370–90, and Israel Gershoni, "Beyond Anti-Semitism: Egyptian Responses to German Nazism and Italian Fascism in the 1930s", *EUI Working Paper RSC*, no. 32, 2001, pp. 4–5.
35 Gershoni, "Beyond Anti-Semitism", ibid, and Gershoni and Jankowski, *Confronting Fascism in Egypt*, p. 272.
36 Gershoni, Jankowski, ibid, pp. 13, 50–54; Gershoni, "Beyond anti-Semitism"; also Pieter Wien, "Coming to Terms with the Past: German Academia and

Historical Relations between the Arab Lands and Nazi Germany", *International Journal of Middle East Studies,* vol. 42/2, May 2010, pp. 311–21.
37 Gershoni and Jankowski, *Confronting Fascism in Egypt,* p. 265.
38 ibid, pp. 12, 271–72. Gershoni was in fact preceded by Professor Ayalon, who in 1988 noted both the attractions for the Arabs of the Fascist and Nazi regimes, and their reticence about their repressive and aggressive nature; Ami Ayalon, "Egyptian Intellectuals versus Fascism and Nazism in the 1930s", in Dann, *The Great Powers,* pp. 391–404
39 Israel Gershoni, *Redefining the Egyptian Nation, 1930–1945,* Cambridge: Cambridge University Press, p. 12; also UNESCO report: http://unesdoc.unesco.org/images/0000/000028/002898EB.pdf.
40 Gershoni, Jankowski, *Confronting Fascism in Egypt,* pp. 56–57. They add that "one estimate" (source not given) claims that the paper's circulation rose to 150,000 by 1944.
41 The world price of cotton, Egypt's major export, dropped by over 50 per cent between 1928 and 1931, and between 1928 and 1933, the total value of Egyptian exports dropped by one-third; cf. Gershoni, *Redefining,* pp. 1–7.
42 Gershoni, Jankowski, *Confronting Fascism in Egypt,* pp. 5, 272.
43 cf. James Jankowski, "The Egyptian Blue Shirts and the Egyptian *Wafd,* 1935–38", *Middle Eastern Studies,* vol. 6, No. 1, January 1970, pp. 77–95. The "Blue Shirts" were preceded in Egypt by the Italian community's Fascist "Black Shirts", by the so-called "rover squadrons" of the Muslim Brotherhood, and by Young Egypt's "Green Shirts".
44 Gershoni, Jankowski, *Confronting Fascism in Egypt,* p. 195.
45 ibid, p. 272; Israeli Gershoni, *Dame and Devil: Egypt and Nazism, 1935–1940,* two volumes, Tel Aviv: Resling, 2012 (in Hebrew), p. 288.
46 Gershoni and Jankowski, *Confronting Fascism in Egypt,* p. 278.
47 Richard Breitman and Allan J. Lichtman, *FDR and the Jews,* Cambridge, Mass: Harvard University Press, 2013, p. 247.
48 ibid, p. 248.
49 ibid, p. 247.
50 Under the so-called "Gentleman's Agreement", Britain recognized Italy's conquest of Ethiopia. Radio Berlin began its Arabic broadcasts to the Middle East in 1939.
51 Lampson report of 8 January 1942, in FO 371/31576, NA.
52 Gershoni and Jankowski, *Confronting Fascism in Egypt,* pp. 262–65.
53 Weizmann report of meeting with Roosevelt, *The Letters and Papers of Chaim Weizmann,* vol. XX, Michael J. Cohen, ed., Jerusalem: Israel Universities Press/ Transaction Books/Rutgers, 1979, p. 331. The first Battle of El Alamein ended in stalemate, on 27 July 1942.
54 Gershoni and Jankowski, *Confronting Fascism in Egypt,* pp. 273–74.
55 Michael Ignatieff, *Isaiah Berlin: A Life,* New York: Metropolitan Books, 1998, p. 24.
56 Ami Ayalon, *The Press in the Arab Middle East: A History,* New York/Oxford: Oxford University Press, 1995; and Kabha, *The Palestinian Press,* pp. 7, 201–6, 263. In December 1935, *al-Liwa,* a Husayni newspaper read mainly by the urban elite, sold only 200 copies in Jerusalem and 206 in Haifa, and just a handful of copies in smaller towns such as Qalqilya and Safed, Kabha; idem, p. 8.
57 Kabha, ibid, pp. 1–4, 16, 261.
58 ibid, pp. xv-xvi, 262.
59 Kabha, "The Palestinian National", pp. 438, 441.
60 Ayalon, *The Press,* pp. 96–101.
61 Rene Wildangel, *Zwischen Achse und Mandatsmacht: Palästina und der Nationalsozialismus,* Berlin: K. Schwarz, 2007. Wildangel was born in Germany, but has lived in Ramallah for several years, where he serves as director of the

Heinrich Boll Foundation. His internet site states that he is still struggling to make progress with his Arabic. I have had to make do with reviews of and references to his book, which is available only in German, a language that I do not know.
62 From the diaries of Sheqib Arslan, a notable pan-Arab Syrian, cited in Götz Nordbruch: "The Arab World and National Socialism: An Ambiguous Relationship", Centre for Mellemøststudier, Syddansk University, March 2011.
63 Kabha, *The Palestinian Press*, pp. 142–43.
64 Wien, "Coming to Terms", p. 318.
65 Kabha, "The Palestinian National", pp. 437–39, 442–43, and idem, *The Palestinian Press*, pp. 142–45.
66 Kabha, "The Palestinian National", p. 441. *Filastin* was owned by the al-Issa brothers, a wealthy, citrus-owning family; *al-Liwa,* the mouthpiece of the Husaynis, was a daily, edited by the Mufti's cousin, Jamal al-Husayni.
67 The Germans deposited funds directly into a special account of the manager of *al-Difa'*; Kabha, *The Palestinian Press*, p. 143. *al-Difa'* was the only Palestinian newspaper that presumed to rival Cairo's *al-Ahram*.
68 Kabha, "The Palestinian National", pp. 445–46; idem, *The Palestinian Press*, p. 253.
69 ibid, *The Palestinian Press*, pp. 266, 370.
70 ibid, p. 142.
71 ibid, pp. 131–33.
72 ibid. p. 132.
73 ibid, p. 133.
74 ibid, p. 134.
75 ibid, pp. 211, 228–29, 234–35. *al-Liwa* was suspended by the British from September 1937 until the beginning of 1938.
76 ibid, p. 249.
77 Ayalon, supra, and Kabha, "The Palestinian National".
78 Freitag and Gershoni, "Politics of Memory", p. 319.
79 Kabha, *The Palestinian Press*, pp. ix-x.
80 ibid, pp. 262–63.
81 ibid, pp. 4, 204–6. Among those who fled were 'Issa al-'Issa, editor of *Filastin*, and 'Issa al-Bandak, editor of *Sawt al-Sha'b*; this conflicts with Wildangel's claim, as reported by Wien, that the Arabic press remained "a genuine, in this case liberal, Arab voice, and retained some credibility"; cf. Wien, "Coming to Terms", p. 317.
82 Kabha, ibid, pp. 213, 236.
83 ibid, p. 216.
84 Kabha, "The Palestinian National", pp. 446–47.
85 *Filastin*, 28 October 1939, and 2 July 1940, cited in ibid, p. 447.
86 Ami Ayalon, *Reading Palestine*, Austin: University of Texas Press, 2004, pp. 51–53, and Chapter Five, "Collective Reading". Also personal communication from Professor Ayalon.
87 Litvak, Webman, *From Empathy*, pp. 28–30; also Kabha, *The Palestinian Press*, pp. 9, 80.
88 Nasser Eddin Nashashibi, *Jerusalem's Other Voice: Ragheb Nashashibi and Moderation in Palestinian Politics, 1920–1948*, Exeter: Ithaca Press, 1990, p. 93.
89 Personal communications from Professor Ayalon.
90 Cohen, *Army*, pp. 175, 179. The poll was never published.
91 All of Ya'akov Cohen's reports cited here are in file S25/4137 of the Central Zionist Archives, Jerusalem [CZA]. The Samaritans were a sect who regarded themselves as Jews, but were never accepted by the Orthodox Jewish mainstream. I am grateful to Dr Esther Webman for bringing these documents to my attention.

Cohen signed all of his reports "yud-kaf" (Y.C.) – I am grateful to Dr Hillel Cohen for identifying him for me.
92 Cohen, *Army*, p. 205.
93 I am grateful to Professor Ayalon for bringing Shukayri's memoirs to my attention: *Forty Years in the Arab and International Arena*, Beirut, 1969. Shukayri was a prominent Palestinian lawyer, a member of the Nashashibi Defence Party and from 1936 a member of the HAC.
94 Cohen's reports, 25 November 1941 and 13 April 1942, in S25/4137, CZA.
95 Report of 2 July 1942, ibid.
96 ibid.
97 ibid; also Cohen, *Army*, pp. 184–85.
98 Porath, *The Palestinian Arab*, p. 76.
99 cf. Nicosia, *The Third Reich*, pp. 90–91.
100 ibid.
101 Klaus-Michael Mallmann and Martin Cüppers (hereafter M-C), "Elimination of the Jewish National Home in Palestine: The *Einsatzkommando* of the Panzer Army Africa, 1942", *Yad Vashem Studies*, vol. 35/1, 2007, p. 16.
102 Nicosia, *The Third Reich*, pp. 15–16, 98–99. On the German supply of pictures and cash to *al-Difa'*, see note 67.
103 ibid, pp. 48, 201.
104 Nir Arielli, *Fascist Italy and the Middle East, 1930–40*, Basingstoke: Palgrave Macmillan, 2010, p. 191.
105 Hirszowicz, *The Third Reich*, pp. 14–15, 27; Arielli, ibid. al-Alami, regarded by the Zionists as a moderate, also held unofficial peace talks in the mid-1930s with Judah Magnes, the American-Jewish President of the Hebrew University in Jerusalem.
106 *DGFP* XI, cited in Howard Sachar, *Europe Leaves the Middle East: 1936–1954*, London: Allen Lane, 1974, p. 167. The exchange rate at the time was about 100 lira to the pound sterling.
107 cf. Arielli, *Fascist Italy*, pp. 72, 110–19. A RAF intelligence report of November 1936 estimated that the Italians had already spent £75,000 on the Palestinians; idem, pp. 118–20. The "Belgian" arms deal included over 4000 rifles with 7 million cartridges and 35 machine guns with 70,000 cartridges.
108 On the Mufti's meeting with Mussolini on 27 October 1941, see Daniel Carpi, "The Mufti of Jerusalem, Amin el-Husseini, and his Diplomatic Activity during World War II (October 1941-July 1943)", *Studies in Zionism*, vol. 7, Spring 1983, p. 106. Before the Second World War, Italy's Jewish population numbered between 35,000 and 45,000, just over 0.1 per cent out of a total population of 35 million. During the first period of Mussolini's rule, Jews continued to hold prominent positions in the army and inside the Fascist movement. After Italy joined Germany in the Second World War, Mussolini stepped up his anti-Jewish rhetoric. According to the Mufti, at his meeting with Mussolini in October 1941, the Duce had told him that "of Italy's 45,000 Jews, not more than 2,500 would be left".
109 Bernard Lewis, *The Jews of Islam*, London: Routledge and Kegan Paul, 1984, pp. 189–90, and intelligence estimate by Erwin Ettel, SS-Brigadeführer, a Middle Eastern expert at the German Foreign Office, undated, but some time at the end of 1942, in M-C, "Elimination", p. 19.
110 Interview given by the Mufti to the *New York Times*, 6 October 1946.
111 Issa Khalaf, *Politics in Palestine: Arab Factionalism and Social Disintegration, 1939–1948*, Albany: State University of New York Press, 1991, p. 66. The author makes no mention of the Mufti's anti-Semitism, or of his close collaboration with the SS.
112 cf. de Luca, "'Der *GrossMufti*'", pp. 136–38.
113 Hillgruber, *The Third Reich*, p. 276, and Geniscke, *The Mufti*, p. 29.

114 Gensicke, ibid; Nicosia, *The Third Reich*, p. 86.
115 On the Mufti's meeting with Döhle, cf. Gensicke, ibid, pp. 30–31, Hirszowicz, *The Third Reich*, p. 34, and Döhle to Foreign Office, 10 August 1937, in *DGFP*, V, pp. 786–87; on the Palestinians' visit to Grobba, and representations to the Germans by Iraqi, Saudi and Syrian envoys, see Hirszowicz, idem, pp. 34–36.
116 Gensicke, ibid, pp. 38, 48, and Nicosia, *The Third Reich*, pp. 185–86.
117 M-C, "Elimination", pp. 19, 22; Gensicke, ibid, pp. 32–34; also Klaus Polkehn, "The Secret Contacts: Zionism and Nazi Germany 1933–41", *Journal of Palestine Studies*, vol. 3/4, Spring 1976.
118 *DGFP*, V, pp. 778–79.
119 Martin Kolinsky, *Britain's War in the Middle East: Strategy and Diplomacy, 1936–1942*, London: Macmillan, 1999, pp. 157, 160; and Herf, *Nazi Propaganda*, p. 236.
120 Hirszowicz, *The Third Reich*, pp. 78–79.
121 Bashir M. Nafi, "The Arabs and the Axis: 1933–40", *Arab Studies Quarterly*, Spring 1977; Klaus-Michael Mallman, Martin Cüppers, *Nazi Palestine: The Plans for the Extermination of the Jews in Palestine*, New York: Enigma Books, 2010, pp. 35, 63-64.
122 *DGFP*, vol. X, pp. 143–44, Washington D.C., cited in Sachar, *Europe Leaves*, p. 165, Gensicke, *The Mufti*, pp. 41–43.
123 *DGFP*, ibid, and Nafi, "The Arabs and the Axis", p. 14, note 72.
124 *DGFP*, X, cited in Sachar, pp. 166–67, Gensicke, *The Mufti*, pp. 43–44, Hirszowicz, *The Third Reich*, pp. 82–84.
125 Hitler to Ribbentrop, 15 November 1942, in *DGFP*, vol. XIII, pp. 786–87.
126 *DGFP*, XI, in Sachar, p. 167, Gensicke, *The Mufti*, pp. 44–45, Hirszowicz, *The Third Reich*, pp. 86–91.
127 *DGFP*, XI. pp. 128–29, and *DGFP* XII, pp. 18–19, 121, 234–43, 241, cited in Kolinsky, *Britain's War*, p. 154, and Gensicke, ibid, pp. 45–47.
128 Kolinsky, ibid, and Gensicke, ibid, p. 40.
129 cf. General Hellmuth, "German Exploitation of Arab Nationalist Movements in World War II", RG 338, NAUS; available at: www.allworldwars.com/German-Exploitation-of-Arab-Nationalist-Movements-in-World-War-II.html.
130 Eli Kedourie, "The Sack of Basra and the *Farhud* in Baghdad", in *Arabic Political Memoirs and Other Studies*, London: Frank Cass, 1974; Kolinsky, *Britain's War*, p. 162, Mallman and Cüppers, p. 25, and Gensicke, *The Mufti*, pp. 51–52. Sami Michael, an Israeli writer of Iraqi origin, witnessed the Farhud. He testified later that anti-Semitic propaganda was broadcast routinely by the local radio and by Radio Berlin in Arabic. Anti-Jewish slogans, such as "Hitler was killing the Jewish germs", were written on walls on the way to school. Shops owned by Moslems had "Moslem" written on them, so that they would not be damaged during anti-Jewish riots.

18 The Mufti of Jerusalem in Berlin, 1941–45

> A majority of the Palestinian Arabs was "fiercely anti-Jewish" and saw in the approach of Rommel "an ideal opportunity to murder all Jews and seize their property"
>
> US intelligence report, August 1942

The Mufti's quest for an Axis guarantee of Arab independence

With the collapse of the rebellion in Iraq, both the Mufti and Rashid Ali fled to Iran. The Italians sent a special envoy to Teheran, Alberto Mellini, to help the Mufti evade arrest. The Mufti was sheltered in the Italian Legation in Teheran and, after shaving off his beard and dyeing his hair, Mellini escorted him out of the country through British and Iranian checkpoints and thence to Rome.[1]

The Mufti had prepared an imaginary cover story, with which he tried to impress both the Italians and the Germans. When he arrived in Rome on 11 October 1941, he told Italian military intelligence that he headed a secret organization, the "Arab Nation", which had branches in every Arab country. He met Mussolini on 27 October and asked for an Axis public declaration supporting Arab independence in Palestine, Syria, Lebanon and Iraq. According to the Mufti's own record of the meeting, he also demanded the "abolishment" of the Jewish National Home in Palestine and that the Jews in the Arab countries "should receive the same treatment ... as they do in the Axis countries". Mussolini expressed his general approval, and stated [falsely] that he had always opposed Zionism. As for the Italian Jewish community, Mussolini promised that "only a deserving few would remain". But Mussolini warned that he would have to consult first with the Germans about the public declaration that the Mufti wanted. The Italian Foreign Office advised that the Mufti should be given a positive reply and recommended giving him an initial sum of 1 million lira (about £10,000).[2]

The Mufti proceeded to Germany, arriving in Berlin on 6 November 1941. Rashid Ali arrived 2 weeks later. The Germans invested astronomical sums in the two Arab expatriates, treating them like demi-royalty. American intelligence learned that the Mufti was given a villa in Krumme Lanke, an affluent resort suburb of Berlin, and a paid staff of 20–30 people. He and Rashid Ali were each given the princely sum of RM80,000 per month for living expenses (at the time, a German field marshal received an *annual* base salary of RM26,500). From spring 1943 to spring 1944, the Mufti also received RM50,000 per month for "personal expenses", and Rashid Ali RM65,000 for "operational expenses". Apart from these payments, they each received substantial sums in foreign currency to support adherents living outside Germany.[3]

On 28 November, Hitler received the Mufti, with Ribbentrop and Grobba present. It was a meeting of hearts and minds – a shared hatred of the Jews and dedication to the idea of racial purity. The Mufti stated his goal of establishing "an independent, united Arab state" comprising Iraq, Syria, Lebanon, Palestine and Trans-Jordan. Hitler reassured him that Germany supported an uncompromising struggle against the Jews, including the Jewish National Home in Palestine, which was "nothing but a focal point for the destructive influence of Jewish interests". He avowed that his real aim in the Middle East was to eliminate all the Jews living in Arab territories under British rule.

But Hitler also made it clear that the Mufti's ambitions in the Middle East and the Axis declaration recognizing Arab independence would have to wait until after the Germans conquered the Caucasus and southern Russia:

> The moment Germany's tank divisions and air squadrons appeared south of the Caucasus, the public message that the Grand Mufti expected could be addressed to the Arab world.[4]

Hitler was confident that this would take only a few more months. He flattered the Mufti that when that time came, the Germans would be ready to declare their support for Arab independence and that he, the Mufti, would become "the most authoritative spokesman of the Arab world". The Nazis were impressed by the Mufti's red beard, blond hair and blue eyes and concluded that he had an Aryan heritage, from his mother's side, a Caucasian. Hitler remarked approvingly:

> [he was] a person who has among his ancestors more than one Aryan with probably the best Roman heritage.[5]

The Mufti thanked Hitler for his reassurances, adding that he had every confidence in the Germans since they had no territorial ambitions in Arab territories and they shared common enemies – the British and the Jews. The Mufti also offered to raise an Arab legion to help liberate Arab countries from British rule. One final effort by the Mufti to make his collaboration conditional on a German guarantee of Arab independence was brushed aside by Hitler. In any case, his Middle East experts disparaged the Arabs' military potential.[6]

The Mufti's ambitions to be recognized as leader of the Arab countries in the Fertile Crescent were thwarted by the arrival in Berlin of Rashid Ali, on 21 November 1941. He too sought Axis approval for Arab independence, in "Iraq and all the other Arab countries in the Fertile Crescent" but under his leadership. But in two meetings with Ribbentrop, on 16 and 22 December 1941, Rashid Ali succeeded only in obtaining a letter recognizing him as the Prime Minister of Iraq.[7]

At this juncture, during the second week of December 1941, the war was transformed from a European into a global conflict. On 5–6 December 1941, the Wehrmacht was forced to retreat for the first time, by a Soviet counter-offensive outside Moscow. On 7 December, the Japanese attacked Pearl Harbor and the US declared war on Japan. On 11 December, Germany declared war on the United States. The appearance of a land army (the Red Army) big enough to beat the Wehrmacht was of even greater significance than the American entry into the war. The Wehrmacht had failed to reach the Caucasus and was now confronted by the rigours of the harsh Russian winter. This meant that the war would be prolonged indefinitely,[8] as would German (and Italian) recognition of Arab independence.

Both Germany and Italy soon came to appreciate that the Mufti and Rashid Ali were concerned more about their own personal status as the recognized head of the "Arab Liberation Movement" than about guarantees of the Arabs' future independence. They were also aware that the two were trying to play off the Axis powers against each other. The mutual recriminations between the two Arabs also ignited intrigues and squabbles between their respective followers across Europe.[9]

The Mufti sought Axis support for his own dream of becoming the head of a Greater Syria, to include Palestine, Syria, Lebanon, Trans-Jordan and Iraq. In January 1942, he managed to obtain from Ribbentrop a written guarantee of Arab independence, although the document contained no guarantee of the Mufti's own future status.[10]

The Mufti also laid claims to the spiritual leadership of the Arabs, in effect, to a new caliphate. He repeated in Berlin his entirely fictitious claim that he was head of a "secret organization of the Arab Nation", based on the "Führerprinzip", which had "prepared and executed the revolutions in Palestine, Syria, and Iraq". He even claimed that Rashid Ali was a member of his organization, and had taken a personal oath of loyalty to himself. Rashid Ali denied the existence of any such organization, or that he had ever recognized the Mufti's authority. He tried to persuade the Germans that the Mufti was no more than a religious leader, with no real political status in the Arab world.[11]

The rivalry between the two Arab expatriates led to a feud between their respective sponsors in the German Foreign Office – Erwin Ettel, the Nazi official in charge of Arab affairs, who sided with the Mufti, and Dr Grobba, the Middle East envoy, who supported Rashid Ali. Ettel claimed that the Mufti had won the respect and admiration of a large majority of the Arabs, whereas Rashid Ali was merely "a typically successful parliamentary leader ... tainted by his previous association with the liberal democratic system". Grobba warned of the danger of becoming involved in the intra-Arab struggle; the Mufti should be regarded as a spiritual leader, but in contrast to Rashid Ali, he had yet to demonstrate his political usefulness. But Grobba cautioned that any encouragement of Rashid Ali would best wait until the Wehrmacht had conquered Iraq. The German Foreign Office was impressed more with the Mufti's acumen and took Ettel's advice. In December 1942, Grobba was "exiled" to Paris.[12]

At the end of April 1942, the Arabs' persistent lobbying for an Axis guarantee of Arab independence finaally produced an exchange of letters between the Axis foreign ministers, on the one hand, and Rashid Ali and the Mufti on the other. Ribbentrop and Ciano confirmed that:

> The independence of the Arab lands presently suffering under British suppression was a goal of the German and Italian governments and that both governments were prepared to provide "every imaginable form of support" to assist the liberation struggle and bring about the elimination of the Jewish National Home in Palestine.[13]

Conspicuously absent from the letters were the words "full" or "complete", before the word "independence". The Arabs were forbidden to publish the letters. At this stage of the war, neither Germany nor Italy was prepared to sponsor the establishment of a greater Arab state, or to commit itself to supporting full Arab sovereignty. For their part, the Arabs had few illusions about the limited nature of the "promises" given. All sides were quite aware that everything would depend on the military outcome of the war.

During his stay in Berlin, the Mufti repeatedly gave vent to his anti-Semitic views – all recorded faithfully by the Germans' bureaucratic machinery. The Islamic Central Institute in Berlin, reopened in December 1942, provided the Mufti with an ideal platform. At the opening ceremony, attended by Joseph Goebbels, the Propaganda Minister, the Mufti delivered a speech affirming that he was both "a National Socialist and Islamic fundamentalist". He stated that the Jews were:

> ... among the most bitter enemies of the Muslims, who for ages have professed their hostility and everywhere make use of spite and cunning in their encounter with Muslims.[14]

He continued with typical Nazi anti-Semitic stereotypes:

> In England and America, Jewish influence is dominant. It is the same Jewish influence that lurks behind godless communism, which is inimical to all religions and fundamental principles. That Jewish influence is what has incited the peoples, plunging them into this destructive war of

attrition, whose tragic fate benefits the Jews and only them. The Jews are the inveterate enemies of the Muslims, along with their allies the British, the Americans and the Bolsheviks.[15]

In April 1942, in a letter to Ribbentrop, the Mufti and Rashid Ali sought official German support for the "elimination of the Jewish National Home in Palestine". Ribbentrop had no problem in supplying the requested assurance. Once again, the Mufti noted their identity of views:

> Along with unity in the struggle against England and communism, there was agreement most especially with regard to fighting against the Jews. In this struggle of Germany against international Jewry, the Arabs felt a very close bond of solidarity with Germany.[16]

It is apposite to note that the Mufti repeatedly urged the Germans, in vain, to replace the term "anti-Semitism" with "anti-Judaism", for fear that hostile countries would accuse the Germans of lumping the Arabs and the Jews together.[17]

The Arab-German Battalion (Deutsch-Arabische Lehrabteilung, DAL)[18]

One of the Mufti's contributions to the German war effort was his work in mobilizing Arabs residing in Europe to volunteer for an Arab unit in the Wehrmacht, to be trained and officered by the Germans. As noted already, the Mufti had first raised the idea of mobilizing an Arab legion at his meeting with Mussolini and Ciano in Rome, in October 1941. Hitler agreed to the idea in December.

In fact, the nucleus of an Arab military unit already existed prior to the Mufti's arrival in Berlin. It comprised Arab students resident in Germany who had volunteered for service in the Wehrmacht at the time of the Iraqi rebellion in May 1941. After a 4-week training course in Germany, some 30 Arab volunteers were transferred to Cape Sounion, some 70 kilometres south of Athens, to train as officers for the Arab force. According to the Germans, Arab enrolment never exceeded battalion strength (500). The DAL attracted not only Arab students already in Europe but Arab prisoners-of-war – mainly Palestinians, from the battles of Greece and Crete – as well as refugees from Iraq and Syria. One prominent recruit was Fawzi el-Kaukji, a Syrian-born Arab, who in 1936 had commanded a 200-man guerilla band against the British in Palestine. Kaukji had risen to the rank of major in the Iraqi army but he spent most of the war in Berlin, where he married a German woman and enjoyed a life of indolent luxury.[19]

Hellmuth Felmy, a Luftwaffe General, was appointed the DAL's commander.[20] The DAL was supposed to remain a part of the Wehrmacht, until it entered Arab territory. But the Mufti and Rashid Ali differed over which theatre of war it should serve in. Their quarrel involved their own personal ambitions, which in turn were contingent upon the divergent strategies of the Germans and the Italians. The latter wanted to conquer the region from the West, from Libya to Egypt and thence to Palestine. But the Germans, who dominated the Axis, devoted their main effort to their *drang nach Osten*, to Eastern Europe and Russia. After that, as Hitler had told the Mufti, they would conquer the Middle East from the Caucasus, via Iran and Iraq. The Mufti favoured the Italian strategy, Rashid Ali the German.

Initially, the Germans considered deploying Arab troops in the Middle East, using Arab irregulars for guerilla warfare in the Syrian desert. But there were logistical and tactical obstacles. In the summer of 1942, they considered sending the DAL to Libya, but Allied air superiority over the Mediterranean made it too risky. Finally, the German High Command decided to send the DAL to the eastern front, to fight against the Red Army.

Rashid Ali favoured this strategy, believing that after the conquest of the Caucasus, Iraq would become the centre of Axis interest in the Middle East, with himself as the acknowledged Arab leader. The Mufti tried to insist that the DAL be deployed to North Africa, to fight alongside Rommel's forces, to conquer Egypt and then Palestine. He protested directly to Field Marshal Keitel, head of the Wehrmacht Supreme Command, insisting that the Arabs should fight only in Arab countries, with which they were more familiar. The German High Command, irritated by the dissensions between the "Arab Big Two", dismissed the Mufti's protests.

When Rommel captured Tobruk at the end of June 1942, the Mufti volunteered to travel to Egypt, to mobilize Arab collaborators. The Germans considered the journey too risky but the Mufti did serve as a conduit for Nazi communications with King Farouk of Egypt, who in April 1941 had expressed his interest in co-operation with the Axis. In March 1943, in reply to another message forwarded via the Mufti, Farouk expressed his hope for an Axis victory.[21]

The Mufti tried to further his own ambitions in talks with the Italians, in Rome. In a July 1942 meeting with Count Ciano, he proposed leaving for North Africa in order to set up an Arab centre that would gather intelligence and conduct sabotage behind the enemy lines. At a further meeting in September, with General Cesare Amé, the head of military intelligence, he repeated his proposal to travel to North Africa, to establish and lead a "centre for co-operation with the Axis powers". This body would be responsible for the "dissemination of written, oral and broadcast propaganda in Egypt and other Arab countries ... [and] the securing of Intelligence reports". He offered also to organize and command regular Arab units, to include those volunteers already in Italy, all deployed under an Arab flag alongside regular Axis units.[22]

At the same time, in August 1942, the Mufti sent a memorandum to the German High Command, in which he outlined his plan to destabilize the British position in the Middle East, in preparation for the German conquest. He offered to:

... set up bands of Arabs as a fighting force and equip them. They will march to Egypt and other Arab countries in order to disturb and harass the enemy by destroying roads, bridges and means of communication, and to promote uprisings in the interior ... such units will have a positive effect on morale in the Arab countries and will appeal to the [Arab] volunteers in the British army.[23]

On 16 September, the Mufti met in Rome with Admiral Canaris, head of the Abwehr, and with Generals Fehmy and Amé. But even though Mussolini himself had apparently approved his plan, he failed to move the Germans from their Caucasian strategy.[24] Later in the month, following the Wehrmacht's advances into the Caucasus, the DAL was deployed to Stalino in Russia. But in January 1943, following German reverses, it was transferred back to Palermo. Once back in Berlin, the Mufti persuaded senior German officials to send the DAL to Tunisia, to supervise the induction of Moslem volunteers. Admiral Canaris promised the Mufti to fly him out to Tunisia, "to help direct pro-Axis political and military activity". But the German Foreign Office vetoed the idea, noting:

... the Mufti's prestige in North Africa stems mainly from his position as a religious leader, whereas his political influence is virtually nil.[25]

The fact is that the Germans now had at their disposal a local Tunisian leader of far greater political significance than the Mufti – Habib Bourguiba, leader of the Destour (Constitutional) Party.[26] The Mufti soon found a new avenue for his energies – helping the German war effort in the Balkans.

The battles back and forth across the Western desert from 1941 to 1942 held different significances for the British and the Germans:

The British fought in the Middle East under the considerable disadvantage that, whereas any victories they were likely to achieve could only do indirect damage to German interests, an Axis victory which drove British forces from Egypt and the Persian Gulf might make it impossible for them to carry on the war at all – a situation which Hitler's naval and military advisers were, happily, quite unable to make him understand. At best, British victories in the Middle East could only compel the diversion of German troops to the Mediterranean – and that not in sufficient quantities to make possible an invasion of North-West Europe.[27]

The winter of 1942–43 saw yet another major turning point in the war. The Wehrmacht suffered major reverses on both the North African and East European fronts. In North Africa, the balance of forces was changed by Rommel's headlong retreat from El Alamein at the end of October, and the landings of Allied forces in Morocco and Algeria on the night of 7 November

1942. Although the Germans landed forces in Tunisia on 9 November, the Axis forces were now trapped in Tunisia and Tripolitania, between the British forces in Egypt and half of Libya to the east and Allied forces to their west. In May 1943, the last Axis forces were driven out of North Africa.[28]

On the Russian front, the surrender by Major General Paulus and his Sixth Army at Stalingrad in January 1943, and a major counter-offensive by the Red Army during the winter of 1942–43, that pushed the Wehrmacht back thousands of miles, signalled the final failure of Barbarossa. In the summer of 1942, the Red Army defeated the Wehrmacht in the battles for the Kursk salient, in the greatest armoured clashes ever known. The Red Army would retain the strategic initiative for the rest of the war.[29]

In November 1944, in reaction to Britain's formation of the Jewish Brigade, those Arab troops still in the Wehrmacht were formed into an Arab Brigade. The Arabs' service in the Wehrmacht was not a success story. The Arab ranks in the DAL were resentful of the superior attitudes adopted by many German officers. Discipline was poor and many Arab troops had refused orders to transfer to the eastern front. General Felmy's post-mortem recorded the Germans' disappointment with the Arabs' military skills and discipline and their inability to think independently.[30]

The Mufti and the "Final Solution" in Palestine: Einsatzgruppe Egypt

Soon after his arrival in Berlin, the Mufti had the first of several meetings with Heinrich Himmler, head of the SS, and Adolf Eichmann, head of Section IV B 4, the Jewish section of the RSHA (the Reich Main Security Office). Eichmann was impressed with the Mufti. He gave him a detailed review of the progress already made with the "Solution of the Jewish Question in Europe", illustrating his talk with statistics and maps. The Mufti told Eichmann that Himmler had already agreed to his request that after the Axis victory in the Middle East, one of Eichmann's advisors on Jewish affairs would go with him to Jerusalem in order to deal with outstanding problems.[31]

It appears that the basic questions pertaining to the "Jewish Question" in Palestine were clarified during the Mufti's first meeting with Eichmann. The Mufti was referred to Eichmann's associate, SS Obersturmbannführer Hans-Joachim Weise, to discuss practical matters in detail. The Mufti's contact in the German Foreign Ministry, as noted already, was Erwin Ettel.[32]

There is circumstantial evidence that by mid-May 1942, the Mufti had been shown some of the German concentration and death camps. Three members of Rashid Ali's staff and one of the Mufti's were given a 2-hour tour of the Sachsenhausen concentration camp, some 35 kilometres to the north of Berlin. The Arabs left with "a very favourable impression". There is also unsubstantiated testimony that Himmler took the Mufti on a tour of the Oranienburg concentration camp and the Auschwitz death camp. Again, the Mufti is reported to have been impressed, and expressed his support for the elimination of European Jewry.[33]

During the spring and summer of 1942, the Mufti's dreams of exterminating the Yishuv appeared to be on the verge of realization. After the fluctuations of the previous year, Rommel enjoyed a string of military triumphs. On 21 June, the strategically important fortress of Tobruk surrendered to him.[34] Hitler rewarded him with a field marshal's baton, and Rommel promised the Führer that his next stop would be Suez. During the next 8 days, Rommel's Panzers drove another 350 km to the east and on 29 June conquered the fortress of Mersa Matruh, on Egyptian soil. The Germans were convinced that the British were beaten. After the conquest of Egypt, the road to Palestine would be open. By early July, British forces had retreated to their final defensive position near El Alamein, just over 100 km from Alexandria. In the course of Rommel's advances, thousands of Arab soldiers had deserted from the ranks of the British army. By 1943, some 8000 Arabs, 7000 of them from Palestine, had disappeared into hiding with their weapons, waiting to join Rommel's advancing forces.[35]

It was at this juncture, in July 1942, in anticipation of Rommel's final triumph, that the Germans took the first steps in their plan for the extermination of the Jews of the Middle East. The method was to be the same as that which they had employed during the first stages of the Holocaust in Eastern Europe and the Soviet Union – with the Einsatzgruppe (they numbered between 600 and 800 men, and were usually divided into 4–6 smaller Einsatzkommando). The mission of these SS death squads was to murder entire Jewish communities in territories conquered by the army, typically by shooting.[36] In February 1941, when Rommel began his North African campaign, the German leadership, in consultation with Hitler himself, set up Einsatzgruppe Egypt, whose mission would be to carry out the mass murder of the Jews living in the Middle East, including the Yishuv in Palestine.

With the fall of Tobruk, the first Einsatzkommando Egypt was assembled in Berlin and sent to Athens to await further orders. Its mission was to escort Rommel's advancing forces, and to liquidate the Jews in their path. SS Lt Colonel Walter Rauff was appointed to command the unit. Rauff had already accumulated a wealth of experience in the mass murders of Jews.[37]

Rauff's kommando numbered a mere 24 men – seven SS officers and 17 non-commissioned officers and men. The Germans' experience in Eastern Europe had shown that the Einsatzgruppe could usually rely on local collaborators. Their intelligence indicated that large numbers of Arabs would be willing accessories. The unit was placed under the command of one of Rommel's staff officers. Once Egypt was conquered, the unit would be deployed to Palestine. Rauff's orders were to continue "the destruction of the Jews begun in Europe with the energetic assistance of Arab collaborators" in the Near East.[38]

There is no direct evidence about the Mufti's knowledge of or involvement with Einsatzgruppe Egypt, although it appears likely that he was aware of its existence (SS Colonel Weise, who had been appointed as the Mufti's liaison officer, became Rauff's assistant in the Einsatzgruppe).[39]

When Rommel launched his first attack against El Alamein (1–12 July 1942), 500 miles to the east of Tobruk, the Einsatzkommando Egypt was readied for action. As noted, although this first battle of El Alamein ended in stalemate, Rommel believed that the conquest of the Middle East was still within his grasp. On 20 July 1942, Rauff flew to Tobruk. As noted by the two German historians of Nazi policy in the Middle East:

> With the Einsatzkommando under Rauff and certain support that could be expected from the Arab side in Palestine, the mass murder of the Jewish population in mandatory Palestine could also have been put into high gear once that breakthrough occurred.[40]

But what Rommel had expected to be a short stopover at El Alamein dragged out over three long summer months. His defeat at the second battle of El Alamein (23 October–5 November), followed by his retreat all the way back to Tunisia, made it clear that at best, the German conquest of Egypt, and then Palestine, would take much longer than at first thought.

Rauff's kommando never joined him in Libya. In September 1942, it was ordered to return from Athens to Berlin. Two months later the unit was deployed to Tunis. Out of consideration for her Italian ally, Rauff was not allowed to eliminate Tunisia's Jewish community. Instead, he and his men rounded up the Jews as forced labour on the construction of German fortifications. On 13 May 1943, shortly before the final defeat of the Axis in North Africa, Rauff's unit was sent to Naples. From there it was transferred for security police duties to the island of Corsica.[41]

Plans for the physical elimination of the Yishuv were put on hold. But for as long as the Germans were still fighting, or at least until late 1944, they continued with the "industrial" mass murder of European Jews – all potential emigrants to Palestine. The Mufti continued to incite the Arabs over the airwaves to kill all the Jews of the Middle East.

In retrospect, Hitler's failure to conquer Egypt was one of his great missed opportunities. From 1941 to 1942, the Middle East was secondary in German strategy to the conquest of the Soviet Union. The Germans could have ousted the British from Iraq in May 1941, had they intervened earlier, with more force. The Wehrmacht's rout of the British in Greece and in Crete is ample testimony to that. Hitler's Middle East advisors tried in vain to persuade him that Rashid Ali's rebellion would spread to the entire region. Had he allotted Rommel more resources, Germany could have ousted the British from Egypt and the Middle East. At the time of Rommel's advances towards Egypt, some of the young Egyptian officers, who in 1952 would seize power, prepared plans for a *putsch* against the British.[42]

Germany's missed opportunities in the Middle East were also those of the Mufti and of Rashid Ali. Their dreams of returning home in the baggage trains of the Axis armies in order to liberate the Arabs from British rule sustained a fatal setback. The Mufti remained in Rome until the day of the Italian surrender – 25 July 1943. He then moved to Berlin, where he remained until Germany's surrender.

Nazi propaganda broadcasts in Arabic

Throughout his stay in Berlin, the Mufti broadcast Axis propaganda in Arabic to the Middle East. The broadcasts are arguably the most authentic and frank expression of the Mufti's personal *weltanschauung*. The Nazis appreciated the Mufti's services. They calculated that if the Arabs rebelled, Allied access to oil would be seriously prejudiced, forcing them to divert valuable resources from elsewhere.

Whereas Nazi propaganda in Europe reassured the Germans and the rest of Europe that they, the Germans, were liquidating the Jewish enemy, their propaganda transmissions in Arabic to the Middle East and to North Africa urged all Moslems to rise up against the British and to kill the Jews. The Nazis knew that "anti-Zionism and anti-Semitism were crucial points of entry to the hearts and minds of the Arabs".[43]

The transmissions repeated themes familiar from *The Protocols of the Elders of Zion* – of international Jewish conspiracies to control the world. During the winter of 1941–42, they constantly repeated the message that the Allies were controlled by the Jews, "the arch-enemies of Islam" and the real instigators of World War Two:

> They [the Jews] controlled American finance and forced Roosevelt to pursue a policy of aggression. Roosevelt and Churchill, though criminals themselves, were "playthings in the hands of Jewish fiends who are destroying civilization".[44]

At first, the broadcasts claimed that Roosevelt was the "tool and stooge" of the Jews. But in late 1942, they began to claim that he was a Jew after all, who had pushed the United States into a war that was directed "according to Jewish intentions and interests".[45]

The Mufti charged that in Palestine, the Jews were profaning the al-Aqsa mosque and that the establishment of the Jewish National Home – which would become the base for Jewish control of the world – was a major Allied goal:

> Chaim Weizmann was an "aspirant to the throne of Palestine ... [and] was determined that Palestine, Syria and Transjordan will be united as a pure Jewish centre that will control the whole of the Middle East and, eventually, the world".[46]

In August 1942, two American intelligence officers stationed in Egypt drew up an assessment of the impact of Axis propaganda in the Middle East. They warned that German propaganda was far superior to that of the Allies, that over 75 per cent of the Moslem world (including those in India) favoured the Axis – if only because they believed in a German victory and wanted to be on the winning side. The report noted that one of the main reasons for Moslem hostility to the Allies was British sponsorship of the Zionists in Palestine. They warned that with the arrival of Rommel's forces on Egyptian soil, the Palestine problem had become urgent, "heavy with the threat of open revolt with its stab in the back danger to a retreating Allied force".[47]

Their report warned that the Middle East was "brimming with hostility to the Jews". This included Persia and Iraq, where the Jews controlled "the small banking, money lending, commerce and export-import business ... as well as ... large blocks of desirable real estate in the cities". The report continued that a majority of the Palestinian Arabs was "fiercely anti-Jewish" and saw in the approach of Rommel "an ideal opportunity to murder all Jews and seize their property". It urged the Americans to take the initiative in calling a round-table conference to settle the Arab-Jewish conflict in Palestine to the satisfaction of all parties concerned. For all of its generalizations and its inclination to exaggeration, the report reflected the consensus among Western officials and intelligence regarding the depth and extent of Islamic hostility towards the Jews and Arab support for Nazi Germany.[48]

As noted above, the winter of 1942–43 marked a major turning point of the war, both on the Eastern Europe and the North African fronts. An Allied victory was still not a foregone conclusion, but some of the Nazis' more enlightened Arab supporters began to have second thoughts. But the Mufti had already "burned his boats". Even if he had to put on hold his hopes for the elimination of the Yishuv, the Germans were still helping to "solve" his "Jewish Problem"; so long as they were killing Jews, the Germans were reducing significantly the number of potential European Jewish emigrants to Palestine. In the summer of 1943, Himmler, for whom the Mufti "felt nothing but admiration and affection", told him that the Germans had "already exterminated more than three million Jews". The Mufti professed later to have been surprised by this figure.[49]

As the Wehrmacht retreated westward, the Mufti became obsessed with the fear that the Jewish National Home "experiment" would succeed after all. The language of his broadcasts became more toxic. In a talk he gave at the Islamic Institute in Berlin on 2 November 1943 (the anniversary of the Balfour Declaration), he unleashed a long tirade about the alleged Anglo-Jewish conspiracy that had led to the Balfour Declaration. He had no inhibitions about emulating Hitler's terminology:

> The world will never know peace until the Jewish race is exterminated. Otherwise wars will always exist. The Jews are the germs which have caused all the trouble in the world.[50]

In a propaganda broadcast transmitted by Radio Berlin 1 month later, he stated:

> ... the wiping out of what is called the "Jewish National Home" and the freeing of all the Arab countries ... is a principled [sic] part of the policy of mighty Germany which cannot be changed.[51]

At the beginning of 1944, rumours circulated about a post-war compromise on Palestine that would recognize the Jewish National Home. Nahhas Pasha, leader of the governing Wafd Party in Egypt, was cited as an Arab leader who favoured the plan. The Mufti made a series of broadcasts threatening excommunication and eternal damnation for any Arab willing to compromise on "Anglo-Jewish schemes" to set up a Jewish state in Palestine.[52]

In the same month, following further reports of massacres of Jews in Europe, Senators Robert Taft and Robert F. Wagner introduced a resolution into the US Senate calling for Palestine to be opened to unlimited Jewish immigration. Radio Berlin reacted with a tirade against the "criminal American senators", warning:

> ... a great tragedy is about to be unfolded, a great massacre, another turbulent war is about to start in Arab countries. Much fine blood will be shed and innocent and dear souls will be lost.[53]

On 1 March, the Mufti broadcast the following tirade in Arabic:

> ... wicked American intentions towards the Arabs are now clearer, and there remain no doubts that they are endeavouring to establish a Jewish empire in the Arab world. More than 400,000,000 Arabs oppose this criminal American movement ... **Arabs! Rise as one and fight for your sacred rights. Kill the Jews wherever you find them. This pleases God, history and religion. This serves your honour. God is with you** [emphasis in original].[54]

This may read today as hysterical hyperbole but persistent fears of Arab support for Nazi Germany led George Marshall, the US Chief of Staff of the army, to ask the Senate's Foreign Relations Committee to postpone the Taft-Wagner resolution, on military grounds. When the Secretaries of State and War and the President himself added their opposition, the resolution was withdrawn. On 3 December 1944, Roosevelt told Senator Wagner:

> There are half a million Jews there [in Palestine]. Perhaps another million want to go ... On the other side of the picture there are approximately seventy million Mohammadans [sic] who want to cut their throats the day they land. The one thing I want to avoid is a massacre.[55]

Even during the summer of 1944, by which time some senior SS officers were secretly seeking a deal with the Allies that would save their skins, the Mufti relentlessly pursued his goal of urging the Nazis and the Arabs to kill as many Jews as possible. But as it became ever more apparent that the Allies were winning the war, the Arabs were changing their allegiance to the victors. German propaganda broadcasts in Arabic rarely dwelt on the military side of the war, but more on Allied schemes to install the Jews as rulers of the Middle East.

German propaganda transmissions to the Arab world continued to cause grave concern among senior Allied military and diplomatic officials. Some senior American officials feared that its influence on the Arab world would force the Allies to transfer reinforcements from the European war fronts to Egypt. One trump card played incessantly by German propaganda was British sponsorship of the Jewish National Home in Palestine. Most Allied officials pressed for a solution of the Palestine question that would be acceptable to the Arab world.[56]

Blocking Jewish emigration from Eastern Europe

The Mufti did his best to sabotage the various schemes for the release of Jews from Eastern European countries, to prevent them reaching Palestine. He wrote numerous appeals to the foreign ministers of Romania and Hungary, urging them not to allow their Jews to leave for Palestine. Routinely, he recommended that they send their Jews to Poland, knowing well what fate awaited them there.

The Romanian dictator Antonescu, pressured by the Nazis to give up his Jews, "preferred to rob and persecute" them, rather than "turn them over to the Germans for killing".[57] In December 1942, he proposed the release of 75–80,000 of Romania's Jews, on condition that each paid a ransom of 200,000 Romanian lei. News of the proposal prompted the Mufti to write to the foreign ministers of both Romania and Hungary, urging them not to release their Jews to Palestine, the scene of a "long and bloody struggle between the Arabs and Jews". He repeated his suggestion that they send their Jews instead to Poland.[58] The Romanian proposal fell through, as the British refused to grant such a large number of immigration visas for Palestine.

In February 1943, the Mufti learned that Britain had agreed to the entry into Palestine of 4000 Jewish children with 500 adult companions from Bulgaria. On 6 May, he wrote to the Bulgarian Foreign Minister, asking him to cancel the scheme. He warned of a "Jewish danger for the whole world, especially for the countries where Jews live", and again recommended sending them to Poland, as a "rewarding deed vis-à-vis the Arab peoples". One week later, he appealed to Ribbentrop to force Bulgaria, Hungary and Romania to abort "this Jewish-English-American plot". The German Foreign Office promptly cabled the German ambassador in Sofia to block the rescue operation.[59]

A new British offer, sent via the Swiss – to exchange the 4500 Bulgarian Jews for 20,000 "fertile German internees up to the age of 40" – was considered seriously by the German Foreign Office. But Himmler had decreed that no Jewish children were to be allowed to emigrate from Eastern Europe, and he vetoed the transfer of any Jews to Palestine. He argued that the Reich could not tolerate that: "such a noble and courageous people as the Arabs be ousted by the Jews from their homeland".[60]

Bulgaria was aligned with Nazi Germany, but was not a belligerent and did not share her extreme ant-Semitism. Its government allowed some 12,000 Jews to be transported from its annexed territories – Thrace, Macedonia and Eastern Serbia – to Treblinka, but rejected German demands to send its own Jews to the death camps.[61]

In March 1944, the Germans occupied Hungary and the Mufti needed to concern himself no longer about the fate of its Jews. The Germans began to transport Hungarian Jews to Auschwitz-Birkenau, and within 3 months, they had put to death some 400,000 in this single camp.

In a memorandum he wrote after the war, Wilhelm Melchers, a German Foreign Office official who had served previously as German consul at Haifa, testified to the Mufti's frenetic lobbying to prevent the migration of East European Jews to Palestine:

> The Mufti kept cropping up all over the place and lodging protests; in the Minister's office, in the Undersecretary of State's waiting room ... the Home Office, the Press Office, the broadcasting service, and also the SS ... The Mufti was a sworn enemy of the Jews and made no secret of the fact that he would rather see them all killed.[62]

The Moslem Waffen SS units in Bosnia[63]

The Mufti's most concrete "contribution" to the Nazi cause was his work recruiting Balkan Moslems for the Waffen SS.

The Balkans had been racked by ethnic conflict for centuries, which bred internecine savagery, terror and massacre. The traditional method of killing was "slaughter by knife", sometimes known as "the cult of the knife".[64] One scholar has commented:

> Across Eastern Europe people were not simply anti-Semites who murdered their neighbours at the first opportunity, but locals who, in a desperately poor region, saw the "elimination" of the Jews as a chance to acquire some material goods.[65]

The Balkan Christians equated the Bosnian and Serbian Moslems with the hated Turks. From 1942 to 1945, a bloody civil war raged between Tito's communist partisans, Serbian monarchist Chetniks and the Croatian Fascist Ustashi. The Moslems were one of the main victims of Chetnik terror. When Hitler occupied Yugoslavia in April 1941, the bulk of the country was divided between Germany and Italy: Germany controlled Serbia, while Croatia, ostensibly an independent state, came under Italian influence, but was actually divided into German and Italian military control. By 1943, the Germans had virtually eliminated the Jewish community of Serbia.[66]

In Bosnia, Moslems and Croats seized the opportunity of the civil war to wipe out entire Jewish and Christian communities in the Sarajevo region. Old men, women and children were butchered. Even the Nazis protested the bestiality of the massacres. Between September and November 1941, great numbers of the Bosnian Jewish community were deported to concentration camps. Eventually, those who survived were transported to Auschwitz and executed.[67]

Confronted with wide-scale ethnic terror, the Bosnian Moslems were determined to secure political autonomy for Bosnia-Hercegovina. Their leaders approached the Mufti in Berlin, pleading with him to use his influence with Hitler to set up a Bosnian protectorate. The Mufti approached Himmler, who agreed to recruit the Bosnian Moslems into a Waffen SS division. Eventually, two Moslem SS divisions were raised: the 13th (1st Croatian), which earned notoriety as the Handjar (Sword) troopers and numbered some 20,000 Moslems, became the largest of all the Waffen SS divisions; a second Moslem division was formed in June 1944 – the 23rd or Kama (dagger). These were meant to become the armed forces of the projected Nazi protectorate of Moslem Bosnia-Hercegovina.

Palestinian Arab historians have left the impression that these divisions fought solely in their own self-defence, against Tito's communists and the Serbs.[68] The truth is more complex, and considerably less palatable. The Moslem SS divisions engaged not only in self-defence but in counter-terror against their fellow Slavs. In addition, inspired and incited by the Mufti and by Nazi ideology, they determined to use the opportunity to solve their own "Jewish Problem". They carried out the mass murder and ethnic cleansing of entire Jewish communities in Bosnia-Hercegovina. Of the roughly 14,000 Jews of this region, some 90 per cent, or 12,000, were murdered. Of the 10,500 Jews of Sarajevo, only about 800 survived. The Moslem SS divisions also murdered several hundred thousand Christian Bosnian Serbs and burned down countless numbers of their churches and villages. Numerous eyewitness accounts testified that they had committed the "worst atrocities".[69]

The Mufti established good relations with General Gottlob Berger, who handled the recruitment of all non-German forces into the Waffen SS units. In April 1943, Himmler sent the Mufti to Zagreb and Sarajevo to help recruit the Bosnian Moslems. At Sarajevo, he was greeted by cheering crowds and photographed with leading Moslem clerics. He spoke in various mosques, exhorting the faithful to join the new SS division. He also briefed prominent Bosnian Moslem clerics.

In January 1944, the Mufti visited Bosnia and spent 3 days with the Handjar Division. In one of his speeches to the men, he made the following declaration of principles, intended to guide the faithful everywhere:

> This division of Bosnian Moslems, established with the help of Greater Germany, is an example to Moslems in all countries ... National-Socialist

Germany is fighting against world Jewry. The *Koran* says: "You will find that the Jews are the worst enemies of the Moslems".[70]

Himmler agreed to assign the ideological guidance of the divisions to imams approved by the Mufti. In April 1944, the Mufti established an "Imam Institute" for training clerics for the division. In speeches to officers and imams of the divisions, he repeated the theme of the affinity and parallels between National Socialism and Islam, especially their joint crusade against the Jews. In October 1944, he stated:

> ... a victory for the Allies would constitute a victory for Jewry, and thus a greater danger for the Muslims and for Islam in general. Co-operation of four hundred million Muslims with their real friends, the Germans, can have a great influence on the war.[71]

The Handjar Division was not susceptible to discipline. In September 1943, when it was garrisoned in France, a group of Communist infiltrators staged a mutiny within the Pioneer Battalion. The rebels captured most of the German personnel and executed five German officers. The mutiny did not spread far and was suppressed quickly. Approximately 20 of the rebels were executed. In 1945, when rumours circulated that the division was to be transferred to fight outside Bosnia, entire companies deserted with their weapons. Again, the Moslems killed some of their German officers. During the winter of 1944–45, as the Red Army conquered Yugoslavia, the division disintegrated.[72]

Bringing the Mufti to justice after the war

After the war, cynical self-interest inclined Britain and the US to overlook the war crimes of former Nazis and their collaborators, especially when the suspects might be turned into "valuable assets" against the Soviet Union. Cold War political considerations, and the prospect of a new global conflict, inhibited the Allies from bringing many Nazi criminals to justice.

On 17 August 1945, the Yugoslav government was the first to place the Mufti on its official list of wanted war criminals and to demand his extradition, in connection with his activities with the Bosnian Moslem SS division. But on 28 August, Beirut Radio reported that Abd el-Rahman Azzam-bey, the Secretary-General of the Arab League, had made an official request to the Yugoslav embassy in Cairo, asking that Yugoslavia drop the Mufti's name from its wanted list. The Arab League also appealed to President Tito in person. He soon realized that neither the British nor the French were going to risk provoking the Arabs or the world's Moslems against themselves. Therefore, with a Moslem community in excess of 12 per cent of Yugoslavia's total population, Tito decided to drop charges against the Mufti.[73]

The atrocities committed by the notorious Handjar Division had not escaped the Allies' notice. The British would have been content for Yugoslavia to press charges against the Mufti, but they were soon disabused of this hope. British intelligence had acquired extensive evidence on the Mufti's collaboration with the Nazis, much of which they did not disclose to the Cabinet.[74]

After the German surrender, the Mufti escaped to Paris, arriving by car in May 1945. The French placed him under house arrest, but allowed him to receive visitors. The British twice asked the French to hand him over to the SHAEF authorities, but they refused.[75] In October 1945, when the British made a formal request for the Mufti's extradition, the French asked if they intended bringing him to trial as a war criminal. This forced the British to consider the wider ramifications of their policy towards the Mufti, beyond its criminal aspects. The Allies had more than enough evidence about the Mufti's wartime activities to indict him as a war criminal, but they feared negative repercussions in the Arab world if they acted against him. The British were no less fearful than the French.

In November 1945, the British Cabinet considered what action the government should take against those Palestinian Arabs who had collaborated with the Nazis, referred to euphemistically as "Palestine renegades" – 35 in all. George Hall, Labour's Colonial Secretary, advised his colleagues that the Palestine government was ready to deal with 14 of them, but there were 21 whom they did not want to see back in Palestine. The most prominent among the latter was the Mufti.[76]

Under British law, the Mufti was liable to charges of high treason. The Cabinet had before it a report of April 1945, sent by Viscount Gort, the Palestine High Commissioner. It contained evidence on the Mufti's propaganda broadcasts on behalf of the Nazis during the war. He had been supervisor of Axis propaganda broadcasts from their radio stations in Bari, Berlin, Athens and Rome. His broadcasts had been "violently anti-British and pro-German". (In January 1946, Lord "Haw-Haw", a British citizen, would be executed for doing exactly what the Mufti had done during the war – broadcasting anti-British propaganda from Berlin.) There were also photographs of the Mufti inspecting Bosnian Moslem Waffen SS troops.[77]

Under British Defence Regulations, section 2A, the Mufti was liable to a life sentence of hard labour. But under the more draconian Palestine Defence Regulations to which the Mufti was subject, he was liable to the death penalty. But Gort warned that the Mufti remained a hero in the eyes of the Arab masses. Even if they were aware of his wartime collaboration with Hitler, they were probably unaware of the full extent of his crimes:

> Haj Amin promised the Arabs freedom from Zionism and from British and French domination ... Among the Palestine fellahin there is an almost religious veneration of Haj Amin and any attack on him would be regarded as an attack on a good Moslem.[78]

This was evidently the consensus among many senior British officials in Palestine. In October 1945, Arthur Giles, head of the CID in Palestine, told the assistant American military attaché in Cairo that the Mufti might be the only force able to unite the Palestine Arabs and "cool off the Zionists". Giles concluded sardonically that although they couldn't accept the Mufti back in Palestine, "it might not be such a damn bad idea at that".[79]

Colonial Secretary Hall told the Cabinet that it was "very likely" that they could muster enough evidence to justify the Mufti's prosecution for aid given to the enemy during the war. But he repeated Gort's warning – the Mufti's reappearance in Palestine would be "a calamity". At the same time, the government did not want the publicity that a trial in London would arouse. Even if they secured a conviction and a sentence of penal servitude for life, his detention in the UK would present "a difficult problem". Hall concluded that for very "cogent reasons", it would be most unwise for the government to attempt to bring the Mufti to justice, or even to have him arraigned before a UN tribunal, due to his continuing high standing in the Arab world:

> The Mufti is still regarded with respect by Arab and Moslem peoples in many parts of the world and as a religious leader he retains a certain sanctity in their eyes. His actions are regarded by them as being those of an honest patriot inspired rather by anti-Zionist than anti-British intention, and it is certain that, should he be brought to trial either in Palestine or elsewhere, there would be political repercussions very damaging to us in the Middle East and other Moslem countries.[80]

Nonetheless, Hall warned that it was imperative that the Mufti should not be allowed to go free – not only because of his war record, but due to his "undoubted capacity for further mischief". The Cabinet supported the Colonial Secretary's recommendation to deport the Mufti and the Palestine "renegades" directly to the Seychelles, without bringing them first to trial in London. They could not afford to risk a suit of *habeas corpus*, and the negative publicity and protests that might attend a public trial in London. Hall reassured his colleagues that it would not be the first time that they had detained Palestinian political prisoners in the Seychelles.[81]

Five days after the Cabinet meeting, the respected *Manchester Guardian* printed a scathing critique of the government's failure to bring the Mufti to justice:

> There he is still, but well on the way to respectability. If the British Government recognizes him it will be a scandal and Nuremberg will become a mockery.[82]

One Arab historian congratulated the British on their "astute" judgement:

> Photographs, documents and quotations proving the Mufti's faith in the Nazi cause, would "unlikely do more than to remind the Arabs that their leader had made a mistake".[83]

British plans for deporting the Mufti came to naught and in May 1946 he fled Paris. Fearing either an Allied indictment or an assassination attempt by Jewish terrorists, he decided that it would be the better part of wisdom to seek refuge in an Arab country. He managed to evade French surveillance and reached Cairo on 8 June 1946. He was accorded a hero's welcome. His presence in a villa in the suburbs of Cairo, protected by two detachments of Egyptian police and regular army guards, was an open secret. At a time when the British were facing not only a Jewish rebellion and acts of terror in Palestine but also Egyptian demands to evacuate the Suez Canal base, their inclination to act against the Mufti on Egyptian soil was even less than that of the French to act against him in Paris.

Shortly after his arrival in Cairo, the Mufti embarked on a round of intensive political activity, meeting with Arab leaders and summoning the members of the defunct HAC to his house near Alexandria. This was in flagrant breach of his assurances to the Egyptian government, and of the Egyptian government's assurances to the British, that he would not engage in political activity. In December 1946, the Council of Arab Foreign Ministers, meeting at Alexandria, decided unanimously to ask the British to allow the Mufti "to enjoy his civil rights and ... to return to Palestine". Many Arabs believed that Britain's failure to act against him must be due to some secret agreement they had. The British were persuaded that a majority of Palestinian Arabs supported the Mufti, as the only one who could halt the Zionists' momentum. Thus they feared that any action they took against him would arouse a storm of Arab and Moslem protest. With Arab oil and strategic bases in the balance, the Mufti's record as a war criminal was a minor matter.[84]

The Mufti himself showed no remorse for his actions during the war. Dr Achcar cited the following passage from the Mufti's memoirs, in which he tried, disingenuously, to dissociate himself from the Holocaust:

> My intention was not to bring about the extirpation of the Jews, but rather to prevent a flood of aggressive Jewish immigration that sought to inundate Palestine and empty it of its native inhabitants.[85]

But the Mufti was less circumspect in a series of essays that he published in 1954, in *al-Misri*, an Egyptian newspaper affiliated with the Moslem Brotherhood. In one of them, he all but justified the Holocaust. He was not the first, nor the last to blame the Jews themselves for the calamities that had befallen them. He claimed that the Nazis' deadly hatred of the Jews was due to the fact that in return for the Balfour Declaration, the Jews had helped the British in their fight against the Germans during World War One. His essay contains echoes of the "stab-in-the back" theory put out by the German military after World War One, to explain why they had lost the war:

> In return for the [Balfour] Declaration, the Jews agreed to serve Britain and its policy and to provide all possible support for the war effort ...

This is the main reason for Hitler's war against the Jews ... Germany's revenge against the Jews was harsh, and it annihilated millions of them during the Second World War ... the Jews' aspirations in Palestine and their acts against Germany during the First World War ... became the reason for the disasters that befell them during the Second World War.[86]

Notes

1. Daniel Carpi, "The Mufti of Jerusalem, Amin el-Husseini, and his Diplomatic Activity during World War II (October 1941-July 1943)", *Studies in Zionism*, vol. 7, Spring 1983, p. 104.
2. ibid, pp. 106–7, and Klaus Gensicke, *The Mufti of Jerusalem and the Nazis: The Berlin Years*, London: Vallentine Mitchell, 2011, p. 69.
3. Richard Breitman, Norman Goda and Timothy Naftali, *Hitler's Shadow: Nazi War Criminals, U.S. Intelligence and the Cold War*, www.archives.gov/iwg/reports/hitlers-shadow.pdf.
4. Record of Hitler-Mufti meeting on 28 November 1941, in Jeffrey Herf, *Nazi Propaganda for the Arab World*, New Haven/London: Yale University Press, 2009, pp. 77–78, Gensicke, *The Mufti*, pp. 66–68, and *DGFP*, XIII, pp. 881–85, cited in Martin Kolinsky, *Britain's War in the Middle East: Strategy and Diplomacy, 1936–1942*, London: Macmillan, 1999, p. 198. The translated quotation is in Gensicke, p. 67.
5. Carpi, The Mufti, p. 114; also *Hitler's Table Talk, 1941–1942* (London, 1953), cited by Lucasz Hirszowicz, *The Third Reich and the Arab East*, London: Routledge and Kegan Paul, 1966, p. 263.
6. Gensicke, *Nazi Propaganda*, p. 68.
7. Carpi, The Mufti, p. 111.
8. Michael Howard, *The Mediterranean Strategy in the Second World War*, New York: Praeger, 1968, p. 15.
9. Gensicke, *The Mufti*, pp. 70, 72–73, 75–77, and Anthony R. de Luca, "*Der GrossMufti* in Berlin: The Politics of Collaboration", *International Journal of Middle East Studies*, 10/1, February 1979, pp. 125–38.
10. Gensicke, ibid, p. 73.
11. ibid, pp. 76–77, and de Luca, "*Der Grossmufti*", pp. 133–34.
12. Gensicke, ibid, pp. 88, 90–91, de Luca, ibid, pp. 133–35, and Hirszowicz, *The Third Reich*, pp. 252–53, 259–61.
13. e Luca, ibid, p. 131; Hirszowicz, ibid. pp. 227–28; Carpi, The Mufti, p. 113.
14. Klaus-Michael Mallmann and Martin Cüppers, "Elimination of the Jewish National Home in Palestine: The *Einsatzkommando* of the Panzer Army Africa, 1942" (hereafter, M-C), *Yad Vashem Studies*, vol. 35/1, 2007, p. 19; Geniscke, *The Mufti*, pp. 108–9.
15. M-C, ibid, p. 20.
16. ibid, p. 26.
17. Gensicke, *The Mufti*, p. 89.
18. On the DAL (Deutsch-Arabische Lehrabteilung), the Arab-German Battalion, cf. ibid, pp. 81–98, General Hellmuth Felmy, "German Exploitation of Arab Nationalist Movements in World War II": www.allworldwars.com/German-Exploitation-of-Arab-Nationalist-Movements-in-World-War-II.html (also in RG 338, The US National Archives, Maryland), and M-C, *Nazi Palestine: The Plans for the Extermination of the Jews in Palestine*, New York: Enigma Books, 2010, pp. 75–77.
19. Gensicke, *The Mufti*, pp. 82–83; M-C, ibid, p. 127. For a time, Kaukji helped General Felmy to train the DAL at Cape Sounion, and became head of Nazi

propaganda in Athens. He was promoted to the rank of colonel. During his stay in Berlin, he and the Mufti became fierce rivals.

20 For this and following, see Felmy, "German Exploitation", supra. Felmy had flown missions over the Sinai desert in World War One, and in May 1941 had commanded the Germans' abortive intervention on behalf of Rashid Ali.
21 Gensicke, *The Mufti*, pp. 79–81; M-C, *Nazi Palestine*, p.130.
22 Carpi, The Mufti, pp. 118–19.
23 August 1942 memorandum in M-C, *Nazi Palestine*, p. 132, and idem, "Elimination", p. 28.
24 Carpi, The Mufti, p. 120.
25 ibid, 129.
26 ibid. The Destour Party was founded in 1920 with the goal of ridding Tunisia of French colonial rule. Bourguiba repeatedly expressed his willingness to work for the Axis.
27 Howard, *The Mediterranean*, p.12.
28 The Allies' overwhelming superiority in equipment and troops led to the complete rout of the Axis forces in May 1943. Over 230,000 German and Italian troops were taken prisoners of war, including most of Rommel's Afrika Korps.
29 On 2 February 1943, General Paulus surrendered at Stalingrad with 90,000 officers and men; he and the German satellite divisions in his force had sustained between 500,000 and 850,000 casualties (killed and wounded). During the battles for the Kursk salient, in July-August 1943, Red Army casualties were about five times those of the Wehrmacht: 1.6 million to the Germans' 366,000 men.
30 Felmy, "German Exploitation", supra.
31 M-C, "Elimination", pp. 27–28. Eichmann and the Mufti first met some time at the end of 1941, or the beginning of 1942.
32 cf. Herf, *Nazi Propaganda*, p. 90. Sturmbannführer was a paramilitary rank in the Nazi Party equivalent to major; Obersturmbannführer was equivalent to Lt Colonel.
33 Sachsenhausen was a punishment and labour camp for political prisoners. It is estimated that 30–35,000 people were either killed or died there; cf. Gensicke, *The Mufti*, p. 169, note 54; also interview with a Dutch survivor of Auschwitz, Ernst Verduin, cited by Emerson Vermaat, "Haj Amin Al-Husseini – Nazi collaborator", in *Militant Islam Monitor. Org*, February 2008; also Simon Wiesenthal, *The Grand Mufti: Agent Extraordinary of the Axis*, Salzburg: Ried-Verlag, 1947 (in German).
34 Rommel took more than 30,000 prisoners, a large number of vehicles, and huge amounts of fuel and rations at Tobruk.
35 M-C, "Elimination", p. 18.
36 The Einsatzgruppe operated from September to October 1939 during the conquest of Poland; during the course of the German invasion of the Soviet Union, these units, together with the Order Police and local collaborators, murdered some 1 million Soviet Jews.
37 M-C, "Elimination", pp. 4–5, 9. Rauff was one of the pioneers and distributors of the gas vans used to asphyxiate victims. He had organized the logistics of the mass murder of the Jews in the Soviet Union.
38 ibid, pp. 6, 15.
39 Herf, *Nazi Propaganda*, pp. 125–26, and personal communication from Dr Martin Cüppers.
40 M-C, "Elimination", pp. 2, 30.
41 ibid, pp. 29–30; Richard Breitman, Norman J.W. Goda, Timothy Naftali and Robert Wolfe, *U.S. Intelligence and the Nazis*, New York: Cambridge University Press, 2005, pp. 456–57.
42 M-C, *Nazi Palestine*, p. 136.

43 Herf, *Nazi Propaganda*, pp. 87, 89.
44 ibid, p. 99.
45 ibid, p. 163.
46 ibid. p. 99.
47 ibid, pp. 138–39.
48 ibid, p. 140.
49 Gilbert Achcar, *The Arabs and the Holocaust: The Arab-Israeli War of Narratives*, New York: Metropolitan Books/Henry Holt and Company, 2009, p. 152.
50 Gensicke, *The Mufti*, pp.184–87. The talk was broadcast the next day on Berlin's Arabic service.
51 ibid, p. 190.
52 ibid, pp. 195–97.
53 ibid, p. 209.
54 ibid, p. 213.
55 Richard Breitman and Allan J. Lichtman, *FDR and the Jews*, Cambridge, Mass: Harvard University Press, 2013, p. 297.
56 Gensicke, *The Mufti*, p. 194.
57 Gerhard Weinberg, *Germany, Hitler, and World War II*, Cambridge: Cambridge University Press, 1995, p. 239.
58 Gensicke, *The Mufti*, pp. 124–25; also M-C, *Nazi Palestine*, pp. 98–99. On the Mufti's efforts to block the rescue of children from East European countries, see also Jennie Lebel, *The Mufti of Jerusalem and National Socialism*, Belgrade: Čigoja štampa, 2007,(translated from the Serbian by Paul Münch), pp. 262–66.
59 Gensicke, ibid, pp. 119–20.
60 ibid, p. 122. The British were prepared to accept the children anywhere within the British Empire except for Palestine or the Middle East; idem, p. 170, note 73.
61 ibid, p. 122–23; Weinberg, *Germany, Hitler*, p. 239; and essay by Dr Albena Taneva, Centre for Jewish Studies, Sofia University: www.hetireland.org/downloads/the_power_of_civil_society_the_fate_of_jews_in_bulgaria_during_the_holocaust.pdf
62 Gensicke, ibid, p. 122.
63 The Waffen SS were multinational, at times multi-ethnic military units.
64 For this and following, cf. Jozo Tomasevich, *War and Revolution in Yugoslavia, 1941–1945: The Chetniks*, Redwood City, CA: Stanford University Press, 1975, p. 260, and Gensicke, *The Mufti*, pp. 132–50.
65 Dan Stone, "Beyond the Auschwitz Syndrome", *History Today*, vol. 60/7, February 2012.
66 Weinberg, *Germany, Hitler*, p. 237.
67 For this and following, cf. Carl K. Savich, "The Holocaust in Bosnia-Hercegovina, 1941–45", www.serbianna.com/columns/savich/006.shtml
68 cf. Philip Mattar, *The Mufti of Jerusalem: Al-Hajj Amin al-Husayni and the Palestinian National Movement*, New York: Columbia University Press, 1988, p. 104, and Taysir Jbara, *Palestinian Leader Hajj Amin al-Husayni: The Mufti of Jerusalem*, Princeton: Kingston Press, 1985, p. 185.
69 Tomasevich, *The Chetniks*, pp. 258–60; also Emily Greble, *Sarajevo, 1941–1945: Muslims, Christians and Jews in Hitler's Europe*, New York: Cornell University Press, 2012.
70 Herf, *Nazi Propaganda*, p. 201.
71 Speech on 4 October 1944 by the Mufti to officers and imams of the Bosnian Waffen SS divisions, cited in ibid.
72 http://en.wikipedia.org/wiki/13th_Waffen_Mountain_Division_of_the_SS_Handschar_(1st_Croatian)
73 Documents from the Yugoslav government archives cited in Lebel, *The Mufti*; also Gensicke, *The Mufti*, pp. 74, 105.

74 In an interview given to the *New York Times* on 6 October 1946, Rabbi Dr Stephen Wise, co-chairman of the Zionist Emergency Council, claimed that the US State Department held thousands of documents in a file called "*Buro der Gross Mufti – Berlin*", containing evidence of his collaboration with the Germans and the Italians.
75 SHAEF (Supreme Headquarters Allied Expeditionary Force) was the headquarters of the commander of Allied forces in North-West Europe, from late 1943 until 14 July 1945.
76 For this and following, see Cabinet memorandum by the Colonial Secretary, "Palestine Renegades", 21 November 1945, CP (45) 294, Cab 129/4, NA.
77 UK Defence Regulation 2A, and Palestine Defence Regulation 24, annexes to CP (45) 294, ibid. "Lord Haw-Haw" was the nickname given to William Joyce.
78 Minutes of Cabinet discussion, 27 November 1945, CM (45) 56th, Cab 128/2, NA.
79 Breitman, Goda, Naftaki, *Hitler's Shadow*: www.archives.gov/iwg/reports/hitlers-shadow.pdf.
80 Colonial Secretary's memorandum, CP (45) 294, Cab 129/4, NA.
81 Minutes of Cabinet discussion, 27 November 1945, CM (45) 56th, Cab 128/2, NA.
82 "The Ex-Mufti", *Manchester Guardian*, 26 November 1945.
83 Issa Khalaf, *Politics in Palestine: Arab Factionalism and Social Disintegration, 1939–1948*, Albany, NY: State University of New York Press, 1991, p. 118, citing a telegram of 29 September 1945 from the Palestine administration to the Colonial Office.
84 On the Mufti's political activity in Cairo, cf. summary by Colonial Secretary Creech-Jones, 14 January 1947, in 371/61834, and reports in FO 141/678, 1062, 1284, 52586, CO 537/1318, and KV 2/2086–91, NA. On the Allies' need for Arab oil and strategic bases after the war, cf. Michael J. Cohen, *Fighting World War Three from the Middle East: Allied Contingency Plans, 1945–1954*, London: Frank Cass, 1997.
85 Achcar, *The Arabs*, p. 151.
86 "The Jewish Fifth Column in Germany", in Zvi Elpeleg, *Through the Eyes of the Mufti*, London: Vallentine Mitchell, 2009, p. 102.

19 Why the British left

> Suppose a lot of Arabs kill a lot of Jews or a lot of Jews kill a lot of Arabs, or a lot of Syrians kill a lot of French or vice versa, this is probably because they have a great desire to vent their spite upon each other.
>
> Winston Churchill, January 1945

Post-war decolonization

The process of decolonization after World War Two has been described as:

> ... a partial retraction, redeployment and redistribution of British and European influences in the regions of the extra-European world whose economic, political and cultural life had previously seemed destined to flow into Western moulds.[1]

World War Two brought about the demise of the old European colonial empires. France and Italy had been defeated, and victorious Britain was debilitated and bankrupt. Britain and Germany were the only belligerents who had been in the conflict from beginning to end. The war had been won by Soviet brawn and American industrial power. Britain had been humiliated in the Far East by the Japanese, and was now overshadowed by the two extra-European superpowers – the Soviet Union and the United States – the new arbiters of world affairs. The anti-colonialism of the two superpowers made it harder for Britain to reassert her authority without jeopardizing her all-important alliance with the Americans. However, two points need to be noted. First, in the context of their joint preparations for the possibility of a new world conflict, this time against the USSR, the Americans were dependent upon British strategic air bases, both in East Anglia and in the Middle East, for at least the first decade after World War Two. Second, the American insurance against Soviet aggression in Europe in fact gave Britain more security than she had enjoyed in the 1930s.[2]

Britain's involvement in the war had had economic, political and social consequences for her overseas territories, which inevitably affected the colonial relationship.[3] Her imperial prestige and authority had been undermined, and her dominions had transferred their fealty to the United States. Not only that, but the Labour Party, elected to power in 1945 for the first time in its history with a commanding majority (393 seats, against the Conservatives' 213), needed to fund the establishment of the welfare state that it had promised its voters. In 1918, Lloyd George had cut back the army's budget to pre-war levels, and insisted that the colonies must be self-supporting. This had patently not worked, due largely to unanticipated security expenses. After World War Two, few but a handful of die-hards believed that Britain could still afford the expense of Empire.

The performance of the British economy and Britain's status as the greatest trading and investing power had been in decline since the beginning of the twentieth century. Even at the turn of the century, Britain's industrial base was already dwarfed by those of Germany and the United States. By World War Two, the Soviet economy also overtook her. Britain's economic performance had declined progressively since 1918. After 1945, her growth relative to that of other powers was sluggish, and she was forced to cope with recurrent economic crises. The loss of her former imperial pre-eminence, the limited size of her industrial base compared to those of the United States and the Soviet Union, together with her failure to modernize after 1945, all reduced her international influence, and made the economic burden of defending a global empire insupportable.[4]

Nonetheless, the recognition that the post-war world would be dominated by the two superpowers did not bring about an immediate British renunciation of Empire. It was not easy for British statesmen, including some Labour ministers (in particular Ernest Bevin, Labour's dominant Foreign Secretary), to reconcile themselves to the fact that this time, victory would not guarantee the perpetuation of Britain's imperial hegemony. For many, the imperial mindset survived due to sheer inertia.

The question of how Churchill would have managed the Empire had he remained Prime Minister after 1945 must remain hypothetical. There are no indications that he was contemplating divesture during his last months in office. In January 1945, he treated the COS to his own *tour d'horizon* of Britain's position in the Middle East. One might mistake the following for his views on the "New Provinces" in the Middle East after World War One (see Chapter 3):

> As long as we keep our troops well concentrated, a certain amount of local faction fighting can be tolerated and we can march in strength against the evil-doers ... Suppose a lot of Arabs kill a lot of Jews or a lot of Jews kill a lot of Arabs, or a lot of Syrians kill a lot of French or vice versa, this is probably because they have a great desire to vent their spite upon each other. Our attitude should be one of concentration and reserve. We really cannot undertake to stop all these bloodthirsty people slaying each other if that is their idea of democracy and the New World. The great thing is to hold on to the important strategic places and utter

wise words in sonorous tones ... We are getting uncommonly little out of our Middle East encumbrances and paying an undue price for that little.[5]

These words reflect the hubris of an imperialist, nineteenth-century mind, unable to reconcile itself to the erosion of British power and status that had taken place during the war. For Churchill, Britain's only vital strategic holding in the Middle East had always been Egypt.

The Labour administration that succeeded Churchill's wartime coalition had an entirely different world outlook, a dual commitment to the welfare state and, by corollary, to the divestment of empire. However, Bevin believed initially that Britain could continue to act as a Great Power, by heading a Euro-African power bloc. The international influence of this bloc would have rested upon the mineral riches of Africa, especially on its uranium deposits, of which the United States had scarce supplies. For a time, Bevin deluded himself that he would soon have the Americans "eating out of British hands".[6]

However, domestic economic exigencies exerted an effective, even if delayed veto on lingering imperial aspirations. When President Truman abruptly terminated the Lend-Lease programme in August 1945, the Labour government sent Maynard Keynes cap in hand to Washington to plead for a $3.75 billion loan. The Americans granted the loan eventually, but it failed to solve Britain's underlying economic problems.[7] In 1949, an economic crisis and loss of confidence in sterling led to a devaluation of the British currency, and extinguished Bevin's delusions of economic autonomy. But it did not prevent Sir Oliver Franks, a senior diplomat who served as ambassador in Washington from 1948 to 1952, from declaring in 1954, in the BBC's annual Reith Lecture, that he had always, and still did take it for granted that Britain would continue to be a Great Power.[8] Even if Britain did remain the world's third strongest power for more than a decade after the war, she was mortgaged both economically and militarily to the United States. The writing was written plainly and clearly on the wall.

Decolonization was not as difficult for Britain as might have been feared. Contrary to Lenin's theories about imperialism as the highest state of capitalism, Britain's most important economic interests had never lain in her Empire. Valuable as colonial trade was, the major and increasing share of Britain's overseas investments was channelled to the United States, Europe and Latin America. By 1945, the imperial connection had lost whatever economic rationale it once had. Britain left India in August 1947, 12 months earlier than planned. It was the most significant and symbolic element in the devolution of Empire. However, not only did it arouse little reaction in Britain, but it also had little practical effect. Much of the British capital invested in Indian industry had already passed into Indian hands, and in any case, independent India remained tied to London for as long as the pound sterling remained an international currency. British governments made it difficult to convert sterling into other currencies.[9]

By 1947, Britain had already given up the greater part of her Empire, a process made easier by the fact that unlike the French, few of her citizens had settled permanently in her colonies. Apart from the protests of a minority of imperialist die-hards, the government enjoyed wide support in the Commons for its policy of decolonization.

But the Middle East – Palestine and Egypt in particular – were *sui generis*. During both world wars, Egypt had served Britain as a staging area for the transfer of British and colonial troops to various theatres of war. In 1945, the Egyptian base, with its 38 army camps and ten air bases, was the largest military base in the world. During World War Two it had accommodated the equivalent of 41 divisions and 65 aircraft squadrons.[10]

Many studies have failed to take into account the new strategic importance that both countries assumed after World War Two. Once the government gave up India, the traditional role of the Suez Canal – as an imperial artery to India and Singapore, and as a conduit for the transfer of Indian fighting forces to theatres of war in Europe and in the Middle East – did become defunct. One respected historian, who did not have access to the COS files, asserted that the retention of the Suez Canal after the evacuation of India was due to the anachronistic mindset of the British military.[11]

However, the crises and tensions generated by the Cold War drove the strategic planners in London and Washington to draw up contingency plans for the possibility of World War Three, this time between the Atlantic Allies and the Soviet bloc. In these plans, Egypt and Palestine (its strategic annex) were linked like Siamese twins. The Suez base was allotted a new role in these plans – as a staging post and launching platform for a strategic air offensive against the Soviet bloc. Given the Soviets' overwhelming preponderance in conventional air and land forces, the only way for the Allies to prevail in a war would be by strategic air attack, partly nuclear. Given that until the mid-1950s, the Americans did not have a heavy bomber with the range to deliver its payload from the continental United States to Soviet targets, the air attack would have to be launched from British-controlled air bases, overseas. Indeed, it might be argued that Britain's major asset for the Americans, at least until the mid-1950s, was her air bases in South-East England and in Egypt.

The Egyptian bases had clear advantages over those in East Anglia. Not only were they much closer to Soviet targets, but bombers flying from Egypt across the desert wastes of the Middle East would not be subject to the same volume of opposition (enemy fighters and anti-aircraft fire) as those flying from British bases across Soviet-occupied Europe. And finally, the clearer skies of the Middle East would permit many more flying sorties. Allied planning also allotted to Palestine a vital role: first, as a transit territory through which Allied armies would move north-east to block an anticipated Soviet offensive against Egypt; and second, since Palestine's coastal plain was designated as the site of Britain's final, last-ditch defensive position at which to stop a Soviet offensive.[12]

Palestine as an alternative base to Egypt

In retrospect, it is clear that at the end of World War Two, the Arab-Zionist conflict in Palestine was already intractable. On the one hand, in the emotion-laden aftermath of the Holocaust, it proved impossible to adhere to the immigration restrictions imposed by the 1939 Palestine White Paper – its 75,000 immigration certificates were used up by the end of 1945. But on the other hand, the Arab League had issued a clear warning that failure to adhere to the White Paper would lead to the denial of access to the Arabs' strategic assets – their air bases and oil.

Britain's evacuation of Palestine does not fit neatly into the general pattern of decolonization. It was complicated by two extraneous factors: first, by Palestine's close strategic connection with Egypt and second, by the growing encroachments of the United States, Britain's senior partner in the Atlantic alliance.

Whereas the Labour government was committed to giving up India, it was determined to hold on to Egypt, for the strategic reasons already given. Bevin liked to think that he would be able to persuade the Arabs that the new social-democratic regime in Britain could serve the interests of the Arab people. His approach would replace Britain's traditional collaboration with the pashas. His goal was to offer the Arab leaders independence, in return for the grant of base rights. Initially, he ran up against the objections of his own military, who objected that any loosening of control in the Middle East would jeopardize Britain's vital strategic interests. In March 1946, when the government first raised the option of evacuating the Egyptian base, the COS insisted that nothing be moved out until adequate, alternative bases were readied.[13]

In April 1946, British and Egyptian officials began to negotiate a new Anglo-Egyptian treaty, to replace that of 1936. On Bevin's instructions, the British side agreed to pull out its garrison, in return for an Egyptian agreement to allow British forces to return in the event of war or the imminent threat of one. As a gesture of goodwill, Britain evacuated its military forces from Cairo and Alexandria to the Canal Zone (which she had been required to do by the 1936 treaty). In May, further to the importuning of the COS, and following the acrimonious Commons debates on the draft treaty, Bevin insisted upon a strict guarantee of British re-entry in the case of imminent war.[14]

Rumour was rife that Palestine was under consideration as an alternative base to Egypt. This was due to the fact that for the first 2 years after the war, military stores were being moved about all over the Middle East, including to Palestine, simply because the government was unable to tell the military where their main base was to be. In May 1946, the Zionists warned the British that if they did not allow the 100,000 Jewish displaced persons (DPs) into Palestine, as recommended by the Anglo-American Committee, they would do all they could to hinder the transfer of British bases to Palestine.

At first sight, neighbouring Palestine appeared to offer a natural substitute for the Egyptian base. The British had developed useful road and rail networks and a number of army and air bases in the country; it was geographically close to Egypt, and under the League mandate, Britain enjoyed freedom of movement there. But the military pointed out that Palestine, with its limited communications and ports, would be unable to accommodate the huge amount of personnel and stores of the Egyptian base.[15]

Churchill, now leader of the opposition, was incensed by Labour's retreat from Empire, in particular, from Egypt and India, and equally incensed by the government's apparent determination to hold on to Palestine. Churchill had abandoned the Zionist cause in November 1944, following the assassination of Lord Moyne. It is unlikely that he was privy to the Allies' top-secret contingency plans for fighting World War Three, or aware of the new strategic roles allotted to Egypt and Palestine. Essentially, he had not changed his imperial *weltanschauung* since the end of World War One. He inveighed repeatedly against the government's readiness to abandon "mighty India" while clinging to "tiny Palestine".

Churchill was concerned that the negotiations with Egypt were holding up the evacuation of Palestine. On 24 May, during the Commons debate on the draft Anglo-Egyptian treaty, he warned that the use of Palestine as "a jumping-off ground for the re-occupation of the Canal Zone in time of an emergency" would increase American suspicions of Britain's imperialist intrigues, and "impair the prospects of American aid".[16]

The COS pressed the government to build extra garrison facilities in Palestine, in order to accommodate the extra troops from Egypt. One Foreign Office official commented presciently that it was far-fetched to expect the government to undertake the construction of a new base in Palestine, which would take 10–14 years to complete, when they could not be certain of remaining in the country for even the next 12 months. When the project came up for discussion at the Cabinet's Defence Committee in September 1946, there was still no sign of either an Anglo-American consensus on Palestine or any compromise between the Arabs and the Zionists. Attlee determined that the garrisoning of any forces in Palestine must depend on the the country's final political disposition. This did not preclude the eventual stationing of British troops in an independent, Arab Palestine. Whereas Bevin noted that the Arabs appeared to be amenable to granting them military facilities, he cautioned that any premature move might prejudice negotiations with them.[17]

In retrospect, some British generals confessed that they had been too slow to appreciate that overseas bases could not serve Britain's strategic goals if the garrison was forced to defend itself against a rebellious local population. In 1950, General Sir John F. Crocker, C in C of Middle East Land Forces (MELF) from 1947 to 1950, conceded with hindsight that because the military had grown accustomed to local hostility, they had been slow to appreciate that "unpopularity made a base too hot to hold".[18]

In 1947, the COS concluded that it was preferable to withdraw from Palestine rather than lose the Arabs' friendship. Any military or logistical advantage that might be gained by holding on to Palestine would be cancelled out by the risk of losing the friendship of the Arab states. In September 1947, on the eve of the UN Assembly debate on Palestine, the COS advised:

> In addition to the military requirements ... for the defence of Palestine, we have an overall strategic requirement to retain the goodwill of the Arab world in order that our interests throughout the Middle East shall not be jeopardized. Further, since any solution to the Palestine problem will involve the termination of our Mandate, we must be in a position to negotiate treaties with the Successor State or States if we are to retain our strategic requirements. We cannot, therefore, be a party to any solution of the Palestine problem in which the Arab world cannot be brought to acquiesce.[19]

Anglo-American diplomacy and politics

There were a number of reasons why the British decided to give up the Palestine mandate. But none was more significant than their failure to reach an agreement with the Americans on a settlement of the Arab-Zionist conflict.

Bevin believed that British interests dictated a resolution of the problem amenable to the Arabs. But they were prevented from imposing one by what became in effect an American veto. Although the British and the Americans had identical strategic interests in the Middle East, and they co-ordinated their planning for a possible future conflict with the Soviet Union, the American establishment was divided within itself over the Palestine question.

The Palestine problem had become an issue in American politics before the end of the war. During his last months in office, Churchill became so exasperated with American "meddling" that in January 1945, in an internal memo, he suggested that if it didn't stop, Britain should hand Palestine over to the United States. On 1 July 1945, just 4 days before the general election, he aired his frustrations in a rancorous note to the COS and the Colonial Secretary:

> I do not think that we should take the responsibility upon ourselves of managing this very difficult place while the Americans sit back and criticize ... I am not aware of the slightest advantage which has ever accrued to Great Britain from this painful and thankless task. Somebody else should have their turn now.[20]

On 12 April 1945, Harry Truman, hitherto a relatively minor figure in American politics, succeeded Roosevelt as President, by virtue of his position as Vice-President. The Democratic Party had solid reasons for seeking the goodwill of its Jewish voters. The Democrats did not enjoy the munificent donations from big industry that the Republicans received. A large amount of the funds they required to function came from wealthy Jews. The Democrats also enjoyed a near-monopoly on the Jewish vote – Roosevelt had received 90 per cent of it in the 1944 presidential elections.

In principle, Truman agreed with the State Department's position on the country's strategic interests in the Middle East – a mirror view of the stand taken by the British Foreign Office. But Truman's political advisors in the White House vetoed any move that might alienate the Democrats' Jewish constituency. Truman could not gainsay the advice of men whom he had hired to ensure that he would win the presidency in his own right. The political advisors determined Truman's Palestine policy, even if Zionist pressures, wielded frequently by members of his own administration and by Democratic members of the Congress, at times brought to the surface the President's innate anti-Semitism. On 19 November 1947, just 10 days before the crucial UN vote to partition Palestine into Arab and Jewish states, Clark Clifford, Truman's most trusted advisor inside the White House, presented him with a memorandum on the significance of the Jewish vote in presidential elections:

> The Jewish vote, insofar as it can be thought of as a bloc, is important only in New York. But (except for Wilson in 1916) no candidate since 1876 has lost New York and won the Presidency, and its 47 votes are naturally the first prize in any election.[21]

Candidates for the presidency needed 266 electoral votes to win. The difference between winning or losing New York alone was 94 votes. The Jews comprised just 3 per cent of the American population at the time, but a high percentage turned out to vote and in closely run elections, they could swing the vote in either direction; this was true not only for New York State (47 electoral votes), but also for Pennsylvania (36 electoral votes), Illinois (27 electoral votes) and Ohio (23 electoral votes).[22]

On 22 June 1945, Truman acceded to a Zionist initiative and agreed to dispatch Earle G. Harrison as his personal representative to Europe, to study the plight of the Jewish refugees in the DP camps there. Harrison's report recommended easing their plight by the immediate grant of an additional 100,000 immigration certificates for Palestine.[23] Truman forwarded Harrison's report to London, together with his own conclusion that the solution to the DP problem was "the quick evacuation of as many as possible of the non-repatriable Jews, who wish it, to Palestine". The British were certain that any significant additional Jewish immigration into Palestine, over and above the 1939 White Paper quota, would ignite an Arab-Jewish war. Bevin replied to Truman that if the President made a statement to this effect, he would declare in the Commons that he expected the Americans to send four divisions out to Palestine, in order to quell the disorders that would follow. Bevin knew very well that the Americans would not send any military forces to Palestine, not even in support of a policy favourable to the Zionists.[24]

Truman was persuaded to hold up his statement, but the ritual of Anglo-American friction over Palestine had been set. The British became convinced that the Zionists, confident of Truman's support, would never agree to any compromise acceptable to the Arabs that would also preserve the West's strategic interests in the Middle East.

Bevin's first step was to try to bridge the gap with the Americans by involving them responsibly in a joint study of the Jewish DP problem. In October 1945, he persuaded them to take part in a joint inquiry into the issue, hoping that this would relieve the pressure on Palestine, by finding other countries that would take the Jews in. But the Americans turned the tables on him. Whereas the British draft terms of reference did not include Palestine, the Americans insisted on adding a clause instructing the Committee "to make estimates of those who wish, or will be impelled by their conditions to migrate to Palestine or other countries outside Palestine".[25]

Richard Crossman MP, a British member of the joint Committee, who was converted to Zionism during his stay in Palestine, published a book on his experience the year after he returned to England. He expressed his exasperation with the Americans:

> As for the Americans, I suspect that about half of them don't care two hoots, while the other half, either for Zionist reasons or because they don't want any more Jews, back the Jewish case for immigration into Palestine.[26]

At the Americans' request, the announcement of the joint Committee was delayed until 13 November, in order to keep Palestine out of the ongoing election campaign for the mayoralty of New York. Lord Halifax, the British ambassador in Washington, explained to the Foreign Office that any public statement about the Committee, which would mean the indefinite postponement of any large-scale Jewish immigration into Palestine, would:

> ... inflame the million or so Jewish voters ... and altogether destroy the prospects of the Democratic candidate whose Republican rival for Mayor was ... a Jew.[27]

Bevin's evident frustration, both with the deteriorating security situation in Palestine (see Chapter 20) and with the "spoiling" Zionist lobby in the United States, led him to make an impromptu, tactless comment when he announced the appointment of the new Committee at a press conference:

> If the Jews, with all their sufferings, want to get too much at the head of the queue, you have the danger of another anti-Semitic reaction to it all.[28]

Bevin was repeating in public the kind of remarks that his colleagues reserved for behind-closed-doors meetings. The influential London *Times* complemented Bevin on his statesmanship:

> The policy enunciated by Mr Bevin, who is demonstrating a firm grasp of Middle Eastern affairs, deserves full support. It offers the best hope of a

plan of relief through international cooperation for the present plight of European Jewry.[29]

But his outburst effectively "burned his boats" with the Zionists. Not only did they regard the new Committee as an instrument of procrastination, again demonstrating the British government's betrayal of its election promises, but Bevin's outburst "proved" to them that he was motivated by anti-Semitism. In mid-December, Weizmann was quoted by the *Palestine Post* as remarking: "Is it getting too much at the head of queue if, after the slaughter of six million Jews, the remnant ... implore the shelter of the Jewish Homeland?". Crossman commented astutely that Bevin's remark "might go down in Britain", but "in Belsen it sounded like the mouthing of a rabid anti-Semite".[30]

The Anglo-American Committee's report, submitted to London and Washington in April 1946, adopted Harrison's recommendation to allow the immediate immigration of 100,000 Jews into Palestine. However, the report also ruled out statehood for either the Arabs or the Jews, stipulated that all the illegal underground organizations in Palestine should be disarmed, and recommended the indefinite continuation of the British mandate.

The British Cabinet was anxious about the Arabs' anticipated negative reactions to the report. But it agreed that securing the co-operation of the Americans must be Britain's highest priority. However, there was a British consensus that the report must be accepted *in toto*, i.e. that no new immigrants would be admitted into Palestine until the "illegal organizations" had been disarmed. The COS warned that a disarmament operation would require troop reinforcements, which might slow down the rate of demobilization. They estimated that absorbing the new immigrants and improving the Arabs' conditions, as recommended by the Committee, would cost an initial £100 million, and a recurrent annual charge of between £5 and 10 million. The British determined that a *sine qua non* of implementing the new plan would be American participation in the financial and military costs.[31]

The joint Committee's report was anathema to the Zionists. Ben-Gurion's initial reaction to it was one of rage and total rejection. Ever suspicious about the machinations of Perfidious Albion, he regarded the report as a perpetuation of the 1939 White Paper in disguise:

> The Americans had been caught in the trap set for them by the British Foreign Office and had helped to legitimize the "annihilation of Zionism"; instead of a Palestinian state as proposed by the White Paper, they now proposed a "British colonial-military state ... which would never become a Jewish State".[32]

But calmer Zionist councils prevailed. As a tactic, they proposed uncoupling the recommendation on the 100,000 immigration certificates from the rest of the report. In Washington, the Zionist lobby prevailed upon Truman to issue a public statement favouring the immigration of the 100,000, in return for which the Zionists would praise his "humane and constructive approach". James Byrnes, the US Secretary of State, phoned Truman from Paris, begging him not to make any public statement on the Committee's report. On 27 April, Bevin had told him that Britain was concerned that the Yishuv was accumulating large quantities of arms, bought mostly with funds supplied by American Jews. Bevin had warned him that the British were considering evacuating Palestine. But in Washington, domestic politics prevailed. Notwithstanding considerable pressure from the State Department, urging Truman not to speak out, he issued a statement on 30 April expressing his satisfaction that his own request for the immediate admission of the 100,000 Jews had been endorsed by the joint Committee, whose report also effectively cancelled the 1939 White Paper.

British hopes of American co-operation were dashed. Truman's unilateral step marked a new stage in what they regarded as the President's submission to the Zionist lobby. During the previous summer, in deference to London's request, he had at least delayed his public support for the Harrison report. This new display of the Zionist lobby's power all but threw the British into despair.

In fact, Truman had become a resentful hostage of the Zionist lobby. His statement in favour of the 100,000 was extremely embarrassing to the State Department but, as Halifax reported to London: "forces had been at work in the White House which the State Department had been quite unable to control".[33] Truman had intended endorsing the State Department's line, which favoured a joint Anglo-American endorsement of the Committee's report. This is confirmed by a private letter written by Truman in late 1947:

> Had it not been for the unwarranted interference of the Zionists, we should have had the matter settled a year and a half ago. I received about thirty five thousand pieces of mail and propaganda from the Jews in this country while this matter was pending. I put it all in a pile and struck a match to it.[34]

On 15 May 1948, the day after Truman granted official American recognition to the independent state of Israel, he wrote another private letter, in which he confirmed his belief that the unitary state proposed by the joint Committee had been the "correct solution". He added his belief that eventually they would "get it worked out that way".[35]

The British became obsessed with the effect that domestic politics was having on Truman's Palestine policy. But they had to be very cautious in their dealings with Washington, especially until Congress approved the British loan, which it did in July 1946. The British could take some comfort from the fact that they were winning points in the Middle East due to Truman's vacillations. American officials in the region reported that the British were telling the Arabs that they would have adopted a policy more favourable to them had it not been for American pressure. Secretary Dean Acheson recorded later:

Attlee had deftly exchanged the United States for Britain as the most disliked power in the Middle East.[36]

In the House of Commons, there was a growing, wall-to-wall consensus in favour of evacuating Palestine. Churchill for one believed that it was long overdue. In a disjointed speech in the Commons on 1 August 1946, he first claimed that had he won the general election the previous year, he would have "faithfully pursued the Zionist cause" but added enigmatically, "as I have defined it". However, his next comment showed that nothing had modified the jaundiced attitude to Palestine that he had developed during his last months in office:

> We should ... as soon as the war stopped, have made it clear to the United States that, unless they came in and bore their share, we should lay the whole care and burden at the feet of the United Nations organization; and we should have fixed a date by which all our troops and forces would be withdrawn from the country.[37]

One month after this speech, Colonial Secretary Hall warned Weizmann that there was wide support for Churchill's suggestion that Britain should return the mandate to the United Nations. It would take just 5 months more before the government did just that.

During the summer of 1946, further talks were held in London between American and British officials, aimed at devising practical ways to implement the Anglo-American Committee's report. The White House tried to make Jewish immigration the first point on the agenda, but the London talks were conducted in the shadow of grave warnings by the chiefs of staff on both sides of the Atlantic about the risks of alienating the Arab states. In a memorandum circulated on 10 July by the JCS to the President and all the senior government departments concerned, they warned that the guiding principle of the London talks must be:

> ... that no action should be taken which will cause repercussions that are beyond the capabilities of British troops to control ... The reappearance of American armed forces in the Middle East would unnecessarily risk such serious disturbances throughout the area as to dwarf any local Palestinian difficulties ... the implementation of the [Anglo-American] report by force would prejudice British and American interests in much of the Middle East, and the USSR might replace them in influence and power throughout the area, a development equivalent ... to outright conquest.

The JCS concluded with a cautionary reminder that "a great part of our military strength, as well as our standard of living, is based on oil".[38] Their warnings were echoed by the COS in London:

All our defence requirements in the Middle East, including maintenance of our essential oil supplies and communications, demand that an essential feature of our policy should be to retain the co-operation of the Arab States, and to ensure that the Arab world does not gravitate towards the Russians. [The oil] factor alone makes the retention of Arab friendship essential.[39]

The British Cabinet endorsed the COS report 2 days before the talks between American and British officials began in London. The Allies' political and military echelons were agreed that the Zionists' aspirations to a Jewish state in Palestine were in direct conflict with their own vital economic and strategic interests in the Middle East.

Once the London talks began, the American team readily agreed to a Colonial Office scheme of provincial autonomy – one that had been submitted anonymously to the Anglo-American Committee and rejected by it. The plan, christened "Morrison-Grady" after the titular heads of the Anglo-American teams, awarded both the Arabs and the Jews some measures of autonomous authority. But it left Britain in control of customs, defence, foreign relations, railways and communications – and initially, also of immigration and public security. Henry Grady, the head of the American team, thought that the new scheme could be presented as a step toward the Zionists' aspirations – partition. But most of all, Grady was relieved that the British had not asked for American military support, and that their financial demands were well within the parameters defined by Truman – $25 to 50 million.[40]

The plan also met two important British desiderata: first, it did not require the approval of the United Nations, where foreign, i.e. Soviet, intervention could be expected; and second, the British would continue to enjoy complete freedom of movement for her military forces in Palestine.

But the Morrison-Grady plan again fell foul of Truman's domestic political agenda – to provide immediate relief for the Jewish DPs in Europe. It stipulated that the movement of the Jewish DPs would begin only *after* the whole plan had been accepted in its entirety by all sides. Truman told Grady several times that he personally favoured the new plan. But the Zionist lobby secured a meeting with Truman for James MacDonald, a member of the Anglo-American Committee, together with senators Mead and Wagner, Democrats representing New York. The meeting degenerated quickly into a first-class row between Truman and MacDonald. The latter upbraided the President that if the sacrifice of the 100,000 was the price he was paying for the new plan, his name would go down in history as anathema. Truman exploded, and insisted that he not yet agreed to anything. Visibly irritated, Truman expostulated: "Well you can't satisfy these people ... The Jews aren't going to write the history of the United States or my history".[41]

MacDonald reported back to the Zionists that Truman's frustration was caused by his realization that there was no easy solution to the problem after all; he had hoped to redeem his political obligations (to his Jewish constituency) by securing the early immigration of the 100,000 Jews, at the cost of a $45 million grant from the Congress. But the Morrison-Grady plan ran into opposition, not only from Republicans and prominent Jewish leaders, but also from members of Truman's Cabinet and some Democratic members of the Congress.[42]

It was already mid-summer, well into the campaigning season for the Congressional elections, due to be held early in November. Paul E. Fitzpatrick, chairman of the New York State Democratic Committee, cabled Truman: "If this plan goes into effect it would be useless for the Democrats to nominate a state ticket for the election this fall". Loy Henderson, director of the Near Eastern division at the State Department, admitted ruefully to Ambassador Halifax that the Morrison-Grady plan would have been approved by the administration had it not been for the Zionists' objections.[43] This assessment was a true reflection of domestic politics in the US. But there had never been any chance that the Arabs would accept the new plan.

The Jewish Agency Executive, meeting in Paris in emergency session in August 1946, began to edge towards a compromise – especially when warned by an urgent phone call from a Truman aide that unless the Zionists came up with a "realistic plan", the President would "wash his hands" of Palestine. The Executive decided to agree to negotiations on the basis of the new plan, with the goal of seeking improvements: the immediate start of immigration, extensions to the boundaries of the Jewish province, and a stipulation that after an interim period the Jewish province would become a sovereign Jewish state.[44]

A further round of behind-the-scenes lobbying in Washington produced further misunderstandings, which would shortly blow up in Bevin's face. The Americans informed London of the Zionists' demands for immediate immigration and early statehood, and expressed the hope that further negotiations in London might produce a compromise between the Morrison-Grady plan and the Jewish Agency's proposals.

One cause for British hope was that temporarily, the moderates within the Jewish Agency – Weizmann and Nahum Goldmann – were left in charge of negotiations. But further talks with the Zionists in London at the end of August revealed that even the moderates insisted on partition being the basis of any tripartite talks with the Arabs. The British refused, knowing that the Arabs would never agree. The Zionists turned to their last resort – the lobby in Washington. They hoped that American pressure would force the British to revise their position. But Truman would not be moved. On 5 September, he announced at a press conference that the "federation plan" was still under consideration, as was a loan of $300 million to the Arabs.

Britain's principal concern now, as it had been in 1939, was to secure the approval of the Arab states. The British held another round of informal talks with the Arabs in September. Predictably, they rejected out of hand both the provincial autonomy plan – which they discerned was a step towards partition – and the immigration of the additional 100,000 Jews. The British adjourned the talks on 2 October, intending to resume them, together with the Zionists, in January – after the December sessions of both the UN and of the Zionist Congress.

But during the hiatus, one further, critical American intervention occurred. It had become an American tradition that politicians broadcast messages to their Jewish constituents on the eve of Yom Kippur (the Day of Atonement), the most solemn day in the Jewish calendar. In 1946, Yom Kippur fell on Saturday 5 October – just 1 month before the Congressional elections. The Zionist lobby went into action, to secure a presidential statement in favour of partition. The Republicans were glad to seize upon Palestine as an election issue. Yet again, Truman felt compelled by political exigencies to issue a public statement favouring the Zionist position.[45]

Truman had intended keeping Palestine out of the election campaign, but David Niles, his advisor on Jewish affairs, told him that Governor Dewey, the Republican leader, was going to make a statement favouring partition and large-scale Jewish immigration into Palestine. Niles lectured Truman that he was not just a statesman, but also the leader of a political party, and as such "was expected to help congressmen, senators and governors to get re-elected".

On 3 October, Dean Acheson, the Under-Secretary of State, gave the British ambassador, Lord Inverchapel, the text of the pro-Zionist statement that Truman was going to make the next day. Inverchapel cabled to London that Truman felt that he had no choice but to pre-empt Dewey's speech, "designed to catch whole Jewish vote in five major eastern states that tend to dominate Presidential elections".

The British received the text of Truman's speech during the early hours of 4 October. Bevin was furious, and threatened that if the speech provoked further disorders in Palestine, the government was likely to "throw in its hand". Attlee protested in a personal telegram to Truman that the President had refused "even a few hours grace to the Prime Minister of the country which has the actual responsibility for the government of Palestine", and warned Truman that his speech might result in the frustration of British conciliatory efforts and "the loss of still more lives in Palestine".[46]

But Truman went ahead with the speech. Ironically, it was misinterpreted at the time, and by several historians since. Truman had sent the original Zionist draft to the State Department for its approval. The officials there eviscerated it. Their draft, approved by Truman, sponsored a compromise between the Zionists' demand for partition and the Morrison-Grady scheme. The relevant section ran:

> I cannot believe that the gap between the proposals which have been put forward is too great to be bridged by men of reason and goodwill. To such a solution our Government could give its support.[47]

When the Zionists' envoy in Washington, Eliahu Epstein (later Eilath), complained to Niles the next day that the State Department had emasculated the

Zionist draft, the latter replied presciently that it did not matter, since the speech would be interpreted universally as American support for partition. Epstein conceded that not a single paper had picked up the "compromise" part of Truman's speech, and all of the press featured his speech under the headline: "Truman's support of a Jewish State".

At the beginning of November 1946, Bevin sailed to the United States for a 6-week visit. He received the impression that the administration was chastened and repentant and had retreated from its demand for the immigration of the 100,000. This was due largely to the fact that Truman's overt playing up to the Jewish gallery had not convinced the Jewish electorate. The Democrats were punished in the elections for New York State, and lost control of both houses in the Congressional elections. Their defeat in New York was especially painful. For the first time since 1928, the Republicans won New York City by a clear majority. Governor Dewey was returned by a majority of 650,000, and the Democratic candidate for senator, Irving Lehman, a Jew and a popular former governor, was defeated by nearly 250,000 votes.

On 8 December 1946, Bevin had a private meeting with Truman at the White House. The president told him "how difficult it had been for him with so many Jews in New York" and expressed the hope that now that the elections were out of the way, "it would be easier for him to help".[48]

But Bevin was not convinced that Truman would be able to push through a settlement in Palestine that would be unpalatable to the Zionists. Confident of the President's support, the Zionists would never compromise. The Yom Kippur statement marked a watershed in the evolution of the Arab-Zionist conflict in Palestine – the British abandoned their quest for an Allied consensus.[49]

One last round of talks in London, held from January to February 1947 between Arab, British and Zionist representatives, predictably failed to produce a compromise. The Zionists rejected British demands that the Arabs be offered some form of constitutional progress towards self-rule, and a veto on all subsequent immigration after the 100,000. Even the Colonial Office, which initially was prepared to consider partition, recoiled from the borders demanded by the Zionists. The Arabs refused to consider either a Jewish state or any additional Jewish immigration.[50]

Bevin decided to throw in the towel. The Cabinet decided to refer the Palestine issue to the United Nations, without recommendations. The decision coincided with two other major acts of decolonization. Within the same 8 days in February 1947, the government also decided to withdraw British forces from Greece by the end of the year, and to evacuate India by the summer of 1948 (the evacuation was brought forward by 1 year).

On 18 February 1947, Bevin announced the government's decision in the House of Commons:

> We have decided that we are unable to accept the scheme put forward either by the Arabs or by the Jews, or to impose ourselves a solution of

our own. We have, therefore, reached the conclusion that the only course now open to us is to submit the problem to the judgement of the United Nations ... We shall then ask the United Nations to consider our report, and to recommend a settlement of the problem. We do not intend ourselves to recommend any particular solution.[51]

One week later, Bevin opened the Commons debate on Palestine. He had never acquired the niceties of diplomatic protocol and in unprecedentedly blunt language, he chastized the president of Britain's senior ally:

> I begged that the statement [of 4 October] be not issued, but I was told that if it was not issued by Mr. Truman a competitive statement would be issued by Mr. Dewey. In international affairs I cannot settle things if my problem is made the subject of local elections.[52]

In the context of British hostility caused by the terms imposed by the Americans on their loan to Britain, this part of Bevin's speech was greeted by prolonged cheering.

On 29 November 1947, the UN General Assembly decided to partition Palestine into Arab and Jewish states, linked by an economic union, and to set up an "international state" of Jerusalem. In retrospect, it is clear that even as the British sent the Palestine imbroglio to the UN in February 1947, the stage was already set for the first Arab-Israeli war. The gap between the two communities was irreconcilable. As the High Commissioner foresaw, only a trial of arms on the battlefield might conceivably settle the issue.

In June 1948, barely a month after Britain's evacuation of Palestine, Bevin met with Harold Nicolson at a dinner held in his honour at the Persian Embassy in London. There was widespread international criticism of Britain's scuttle from Palestine, which had been invaded by five Arab states on the night of the High Commissioner's departure. Nicolson found Bevin "in good form – noisy and vulgar". Bevin treated him to a frank summary of his views on Palestine:

> He [Bevin] pays no attention to all the attacks of the American press. What do they matter? After all, it is the principle that counts, and nobody is going to tell him that in principle it does not pay better to remain friends with 200 million Moslems than with 200,000 Jews, "to say nothing of the oil".[53]

Notes

1 John Darwin, *Britain & Decolonisation*, London: Macmillan, 1988, p. 7.
2 ibid, pp. 21, 24, 32. On the Americans' need of British strategic air bases, cf. Michael J. Cohen, *Fighting World War Three from the Middle East: Allied Contingency Plans, 1945–1954*, London: Frank Cass, 1997.
3 Darwin, *Britain*, p. 23.

4 ibid, p. 19.
5 Minute in Prem 3/296/9, NA.
6 John Kent, "Bevin's Imperialism and the idea of Euro-Africa, 1945–49", in Michael Dockrill and John Young, eds, *British Foreign Policy, 1945–56*, New York: St Martin's Press, 1989, pp. 47, 66, 70.
7 President Truman signed the credit agreement in July 1946. The loan was for $3.75 billion, to be repaid with an annual interest rate of 2 per cent. The last instalment was repaid in December 2006.
8 Oliver S. Franks, *Britain and the Tide of World Affairs*, London: Oxford University Press, 1955, p. 6.
9 James Joll, *Europe Since 1870*, London: Penguin, 1983, pp. 469–70.
10 Michael J. Cohen, *Palestine and the Great Powers, 1945–1948*, Princeton: Princeton University Press, 1982, p. 34.
11 Philip Darby, *British Defence Policy East of Suez, 1947–1968*, London: Oxford University Press for RIIA, 1973.
12 On Allied contingency planning for the Middle East, cf. Cohen, *Fighting World War Three*, especially pp. 31, 95–123.
13 Cohen, *Palestine*, pp. 38–39.
14 William Travis Hanes, *Imperial Diplomacy in the Era of Decolonization*, Westport, Conn: Greenwood, 1995, pp. 46–47. Final agreement was reached in October, during direct talks between Bevin and Sidqi Pasha, the Egyptian Prime Minister. But the Egyptian Parliament rejected the treaty, and Sidqi resigned.
15 Cohen, *Palestine*, p. 38.
16 House of Commons Debates (*H.C. Deb.*), vol. 423, cols 771–72. After much heated debate, the US Congress approved the $3.75 billion loan in July 1946.
17 Cohen, *Palestine*, p. 39.
18 Interview between General Crocker and Elizabeth Monroe, 20 October 1950, Monroe papers, Middle East Centre, St Antony's College, Oxford.
19 Cohen, *Palestine*, pp. 39–40.
20 Churchill minute of 1 July 1945, FO 371/45377, NA; reprinted in Winston S. Churchill, *The Second World War*, vol. vi, *Triumph and Tragedy*, London: Cassell, 1954, p. 654.
21 On Truman's policies on Palestine, see Michael J. Cohen, *Truman and Israel*, Berkeley/Los Angeles: University of California Press, 1990; the citation is on p. 60; on Truman's anti-Semitism, see idem, pp. 7–10, 13, 135. Ironically, in 1948, Truman would become the first candidate since Wilson to win the presidency without winning New York.
22 ibid, pp. 60–69.
23 Cohen, *Palestine*, p. 56; Harrison was Dean of the University of Pennsylvania Law School; when he toured the DP camps during the summer of 1945 they contained some 50,000 Jews; by the following summer, their numbers had swelled to 250,000.
24 ibid, p. 57, and Richard Crossman, *Palestine Mission*, New York: Harper, 1947, p. 47.
25 Cohen, ibid, pp. 60–64.
26 Crossman, *Palestine Mission*, p. 38.
27 Halifax to Bevin, 27 October 1945, FO 371/45382, NA.
28 Cohen, *Palestine*, pp. 66–67.
29 The *Times*, 14 November 1945.
30 *The Palestine Post*, 14 December 1945; Crossman, *Palestine Mission*, p. 76.
31 Cohen, *Palestine*, pp. 112–13.
32 Ben-Gurion to AZEC, 22 April 1946, Ben-Gurion Archives (BGA).
33 Halifax to Foreign Office, 7 May 1946, CO 537/1759, NA.
34 Truman to Senator Claude Pepper, 20 October 1947, confidential file, box 59, Truman Archives (HST).

35 Truman to Bartley Crum, 15 May 1948, file 204D, box 776, HST.
36 Dean Acheson, *Present at the Creation,* London: Hamilton, 1970, p. 175.
37 *H.C. Deb.*, 5th series, vol. 426, cols 1252, 1257.
38 Memorandum of 21 June 1946, SWNCC 311, series 091, National Archives, United States (NAUS). At the time, Europe was totally dependent upon oil imports from the Middle East; cf. Cohen, *Fighting World War Three*, pp. 19, 36.
39 "The Military Implications of the Anglo-American Report". COS (46) 188, 10 July 1946, NA.
40 For details, cf. Cohen, *Palestine*, pp. 124–27.
41 MacDonald report to Zionists, 28 July 1946, BGZ, and Z4/20276, CZA.
42 Cohen, *Palestine*, pp. 128–30.
43 ibid, pp. 131–32.
44 ibid, pp. 142–45. The Truman aide who telephoned to Paris was David Niles, a Jew, Truman's (and Roosevelt's before him) aide on Jewish affairs.
45 Thomas Dewey was Governor of New York State from 1942 to 1954, and Republican nominee for president in 1944 and 1948. In fact, Dewey upstaged Truman on Yom Kippur, by demanding that several hundred thousand Jews be admitted into Palestine.
46 Cohen, *Palestine*, pp. 164–66.
47 Cohen, *Truman*, p. 144.
48 Note of Bevin-Truman meeting on 8 December 1946, in FO 800/513, NA.
49 Cohen, *Truman*, p. 145.
50 Cohen, *Palestine*, pp. 225–26.
51 *H.C. Deb.*, vol. 433, cols 985–94.
52 ibid, cols 1908, 1918, 1920.
53 Diary note of 17 June 1948, *Harold Nicolson, Diaries & Letters, 1930–1964,* edited and condensed by Stanley Olson, New York: Atheneum, 1980, p. 335. Nicolson, diplomat, author and diarist, was a National Labour MP from 1935 to 1945.

20 The British lose control in Palestine

> With its officials attempting to administrate from behind masses of barbed wire, in heavily defended buildings, and with those same officials (minus wives and children evacuated some time ago) living in pathetic seclusion in "security zones", one cannot escape the conclusion that the Government of Palestine is a hunted organization with little hope of ever being able to cope with conditions in this country as they exist today.
> Report by Robert Macatee, the US Consul in Jerusalem, May 1947

The Jewish Resistance Movement (JRM)

The Labour government's Palestine policy provides a classic case of a political party reneging on its election promises – all the more cynical since the party's ministers had sat in Churchill's coalition for 5 years and were quite familiar with the problems involved. In its 1945 election campaign, the party promised that it would rescind the 1939 White Paper, and gave "its solemn pledge" that it would not stop the Jews from becoming a majority in Palestine. At the party's annual conference in 1945, held on 24 May, shortly before the general election, Hugh Dalton, who would become Chancellor of the Exchequer, stated:

> It is morally wrong and politically indefensible to impose obstacles to the entry into Palestine now of any Jews who desire to go there. We consider that Jewish immigration into Palestine should be permitted without the present limitations.

Dalton went so far as to suggest that in consultation with the United States and the Soviet Union, Britain should take steps "to see whether we cannot get that common support for a policy which will give us a happy, free and prosperous Jewish state in Palestine".[1]

But once burdened with the responsibilities of office, the Labour government began to see things differently. On 14 September 1945, the Cabinet decided to continue with the 1939 White Paper policy until a permanent solution was found. It decided that when the 75,000 immigration quota was exhausted (at the end of 1945), it would continue to allow Jewish immigration at the rate of 1500 refugees per month. The decision was leaked by Reuters 2 days later. It was the first indication for the Zionists that Labour was going to renege on its election promises.[2]

While London and Washington engaged in a merry-go-round of futile diplomacy, marred by political machinations, the British progressively lost control of the situation in Palestine.

David Ben-Gurion, head of the Jewish Agency, decided that only a demonstration of the Yishuv's military potential might force the British to reverse their pro-Arab policy. In October 1945, he authorized the formation of a Jewish Resistance Movement (JRM), to co-ordinate joint insurgency operations by the three Jewish undergrounds – the Hagana, IZL and LEHI (known to the British as the Stern Gang). The strategic goal of the JRM was to sabotage British military and communications systems in Palestine, thereby demonstrating to the British that they could not control Palestine without the support and co-operation of the Yishuv. The JRM decided also to organize Aliya Gimmel, illegal immigration, with Hagana combat units on board, with orders to resist British attempts to apprehend them.

But the goals of the Hagana, under the orders of the Jewish Agency, were different from those of the other two groups. The Jewish Agency, which enjoyed the support of the overwhelming majority of the Yishuv, believed that military "demonstrations" carried out by the Hagana would wring political concessions from British. But the dissident terrorist undergrounds, following the Irish and Russian anarchist models, believed that terror and assassination would break Britain's will to remain in Palestine.

The Hagana mounted two major, nation-wide operations against the British – one during the last night of October 1945 and a second in June 1946 (see p. 465). Both operations were designed to demonstrate, with a minimal loss of life, that the Yishuv could disrupt Britain's hold on Palestine. The first operation, nicknamed the "Night of the Railways", sabotaged Palestine's railway system in 153 places, destroyed rolling stock and locomotives, and damaged or destroyed several British police launches, used for tracking the ships bringing in illegal immigrants. The next day, the London *Times* commented that the operation indicated a "large force of trained men and careful planning and timing", a "demonstration rather than a full-scale attack". Bevin called in Weizmann and Shertok the next day and asked them bluntly if the operation meant that the Zionists intended to settle the issue by force. They replied that while they deprecated violence, the events of the previous night had been provoked by the delay of any policy statement. Bevin blamed the Americans for the delay, caused by their domestic electoral considerations.[3]

The British dispatched huge reinforcements to Palestine. The garrison grew from 50,000 at end of the war to 80,000 by the end of 1945, to 100,000 by 1947. One of the units transferred to Palestine from Europe was the 6th Airborne Division. Its original mission was to serve as an imperial strategic reserve, positioned to respond quickly to trouble in any part of the Empire. But from 1945 to 1946 it became bogged down in operations against the JRM, and from 1946, when the JRM broke up, against the two Jewish terrorist organizations. Trained to be ruthless, the parachutists were nicknamed "poppies' by the Yishuv – a reference to their red berets and black hearts.

The British also extended the use of capital punishment. In January 1946, they amended the Palestine Defence Regulations, extending the death penalty (previously imposed only for carrying arms or ammunition) to "any member of any group or body committing an offence against the regulations". The Yishuv felt that the new, draconian regulations, together with Britain's measures to prevent Holocaust survivors from entering Palestine, had removed any lingering vestige of her moral claim to rule the country.

The British appreciated that the JRM was a popular revolt, supported by a majority of the Yishuv. At the end of 1945, General Sir Alan Cunningham, Britain's last High Commissioner to Palestine, informed London that as many as 50 per cent of the Yishuv were "definitely desirous of offensive armed action against us". This meant that the revolt could not be suppressed by force. Its grievances would have to be met by a political solution that also went to the heart of the Jewish refugee problem in Europe. As noted already, Bevin hoped that a solution might be found in collaboration with the Americans. However, once the Americans agreed to the Joint Committee of Inquiry, the British ceased to be free agents in Palestine.

During the winter of 1945–46, the Labour government became ensnared in a dilemma largely of its own making. Hoping that the Joint Committee would produce some political panacea, it repeatedly prevented the army from taking punitive action against the JRM. London feared that any extensive military operations against the Yishuv might escalate into widespread violence and bloodshed, which would lay the government open to charges of prejudicing, even sabotaging the Joint Committee's work. This would lead to a Zionist boycott of the Committee's proceedings and, worst of all, to an adverse American reaction.

Initially, the military command in Palestine advised that with the forces at its disposal, the army would find it difficult, if not impossible, to locate all the Jewish arms caches in the country and to disarm the Yishuv. But as troop reinforcements were brought in, Jewish acts of terror escalated during the winter of 1945–46, and as the Hagana posed a tangible threat to Britain's lines of communications between Egypt and Palestine, the Middle East Command in Cairo became more insistent in its demand for a punitive operation against the Hagana. As will be seen below, the government did permit one major operation against the Yishuv, in July 1946. But the unleashing of the army's full potential was never a real option, since its every move was transmitted to the international media by the Jewish Agency, threatening to turn British actions into a public relations disaster.

In addition to London's reticence, the army frequently found itself at odds with the High Commissioner, its nominal supreme commander. By the very nature of their different roles, the agenda of the high commissioners in Palestine was frequently in conflict with that of the army. The army's sole concern was to crush any insurgency as swiftly as possible, with minimum casualties. But the High Commissioner opposed the use of excessive violence, whether against the Arabs during the rebellion of 1936–39 or against the Jews after the war. As the head of the civil administration, he was concerned mainly with the smooth resumption of his rule after the disturbances. That would be impossible with a population that had been brutalized and alienated by harsh repressive measures.

British intelligence knew that the Jewish Agency, despite its denials, was behind the JRM operations. In January 1946, the army drew up a contingency plan to arrest and detain the leaders of the Hagana, to raid the Agency's offices and arrest its executive. But the Cabinet ruled out any move before the Anglo-American Committee delivered its report. By the spring of 1946, enraged and frustrated by constant terrorists attacks, the military command in Palestine was chafing at the bit. Strengthened by reinforcements, they now felt able to tackle the Jewish insurgency, and continued to press the government to lift its ban on military operations. The government finally did so when the Committee's report failed to produce the hoped-for Anglo-American consensus.

Tensions peaked on the night of 25 April 1946, when the IZL killed seven British soldiers in a series of attacks in Tel Aviv. Lt General J.C. D'Arcy, the GOC Palestine (1944–46), warned that unless "drastic and spectacular punitive action" was taken, he might lose control of his troops, who would go on the rampage. But the political situation was particularly delicate, just a few days ahead of the publication of the Anglo-American Committee's report. On 30 April, the COS, sensitive to the political factor, decided that the Cabinet must be the final arbiter of what action to take in Palestine, "in order to avoid the risk of alienating American opinion".[4]

The military's doubts about its ability to keep control of the troops developed into a major issue. On 4 May, General Sir Bernard Paget, the C in C Middle East, warned the COS that in the event of any further terrorist actions in Palestine, the troops were likely to take matters into their own hands. The COS asked the Prime Minister to allow the army to go on the offensive, on the basis that on purely military grounds it was "only right ... that the man on the spot should possess some latitude of action". But Attlee denied permission for any large-scale operation, insisting that in the event of any further outrages, the army must act only against the actual perpetrators and their collaborators.

On 15 May, General D'Arcy again pressed the COS for authority to go on the offensive, warning once again about the danger of a collapse of army morale and discipline. He warned that the price of inaction would be incalculable: his troops had reached breaking point, and he could not vouch for their reactions should another terrorist attack occur. D'Arcy introduced a new argument – what would be the Arab reaction? He warned that failure to act against the Jews might provoke the Arabs to take matters into their own hands. On the other hand, an operation to disarm the Jews and break up their illegal organizations, for which he now had sufficient troops, would be the best way to persuade the Arabs to compromise and concede further Jewish immigration. The cost of quelling a new Arab insurrection, he warned, would be far higher than that of disarming the Yishuv:

> Disarmament of the Jews was a limited liability which could be militarily calculated [provided the Arabs remained quiet]. On the other hand, if there was a general uprising amongst the Arabs, it was not possible to estimate the extent of the commitment or to foretell how long it would continue.[5]

As noted in the previous chapter, the Zionists' initial elation when Truman declared his support for the immediate emigration of 100,000 Jewish DPs to Palestine soon gave way to deep disillusion, when the British insisted that the Committee's report must be implemented in its entirety, beginning with the disarming of their underground militias. They concluded that American pressure alone would not make the British change their policy. Therefore, they planned one further large-scale "demonstration". Since they suspected that the British intended moving the Egyptian base to Palestine, their last operation – dubbed the "night of the bridges" – was designed to show the British that they would be unable to exploit Palestine as a strategic base without the co-operation of the Yishuv.

On 12 May, the Hagana's secret radio transmitter broadcast an advance warning of its intentions:

> Britain, in evacuating Syria, Lebanon and Egypt, intends to concentrate its military bases in Palestine and is therefore concerned to strengthen her hold over the Mandate ... But this double game will not work ... We would therefore warn publicly His Majesty's Government that if it does not fulfil its responsibilities under the Mandate – above all with regard to the question of immigration – the Jewish Resistance Movement will make every effort to hinder the transfer of British bases to Palestine and to prevent their establishment in this country.[6]

During the night of 16–17 June, the Hagana destroyed ten of the 11 road and rail bridges connecting Palestine to its neighbours. On the 17th, the LEHI attacked railway workshops at Haifa, and the IZL kidnapped five British officers, as hostages against two IZL men held by the British under sentence of death.

These operations, far from intimidating the British into adopting a pro-Zionist policy, provided the pretext for carrying out the nation-wide search-and-arrest operation planned the previous January. Following the latest rash of Jewish terrorist acts, the government in London was confident of receiving a sympathetic press. The British also felt confident that they could rely on American support for the disarming of the underground militias. This latest Hagana operation had merely underlined the urgent need to do so. From this point on, events in Palestine escalated out of control.

At 0445 on Saturday 29 June 1946, the British launched Operation Agatha, a 2-week, nation-wide manhunt (the Yishuv dubbed it the "Black Sabbath"). In a memorandum written 3 days before the operation, General Sir Evelyn Barker, GOC Palestine from March to October 1946, defined its goals:

> If law and order is to return to the country, action must be taken against those primarily responsible ... the extreme element of the Jewish Agency, GHQ *Hagana* and the whole of the *Palmach* force.

But the military command understood that the goal of the operation was limited to restoring British control over Palestine. They did *not* believe that military measures were an alternative to a political settlement. General Barker wrote:

> As a result of persecution of their defenceless people over a number of years, they [the Jews] are now determined to hold on to their arms for self-defence, and in this there is a certain degree of right on their side.

He agreed that military measures could only be palliatives: "The ultimate solution must depend on a satisfactory political answer".[7]

Some 17,000 British troops took part in Operation Agatha. The Jewish Agency's headquarters was raided and documents incriminating the Agency in the JRM were seized. The operation's main objective was to apprehend and neutralize the Palmach, the elite, combat arm of the Hagana.[8] The British knew that any attempt to disarm the entire Hagana would set the whole Yishuv against them. Even though Hagana intelligence had learned in advance of the operation, it caught them by surprise. A total of some 2700 Jews were detained, including members of the Jewish Agency executive and half of the Palmach corps – though apparently not its most senior officers.

Although the operation's main goal was not to search for arms, 15 secret caches ("slicks") were discovered during its course, including a huge one at a kibbutz near Haifa. These cordon-and-search operations exposed the troops to extremely tense situations. When a settlement was surrounded prior to the search, to ensure that no one entered or left it, hundreds, sometimes thousands of men, women and children would try to break the siege on foot. The troops were frequently faced with the impossible option of having to fire on unarmed women and children.[9]

The British indulged the illusion that Operation Agatha would restore the moderate Weizmann to the Zionist helm. Richard Crossman, an astute observer, commented later that the British had failed to appreciate that Weizmann was "very tired, very ill, too old and too pro-British to control his extremists".[10]

Weizmann had no intention of becoming a Jewish quisling. Even had he been willing to take on the role, there was no chance of him succeeding, since he had no constituency inside the Yishuv. He had not been a party to the planning of the operations carried out by the JRM. He supported all operations to foil British attempts to detain illegal immigrants, but he opposed all actions that might have detrimental political repercussions. Presciently, he had warned the Jewish Agency leaders that the Hagana risked provoking the British to go on the offensive to disarm the Yishuv. This would leave it helpless to confront the major challenge facing it, a war with the Arab states. In July 1946, Weizmann threatened to resign. This brought about the ostensible break-up of the JRM. But he told the British that any resumption of negotiations was contingent upon the release of the detained members of the Agency's executive.

Ben-Gurion (in Paris) and Moshe Sneh in Palestine, the political heads of the Hagana, were still at large, with warrants out for their arrest. The British set unrealistic terms for any resumption of negotiations: a cessation of all acts of violence, the disbanding of the Palmach, British control of the Hagana, and a halt to all propaganda against them. Agatha did not produce the alternative, moderate leadership that the British had hoped for but it did effectively end the JRM. From June 1946 to November 1947, the Hagana didn't carry out any further acts of sabotage, nor did it clash with the British.

But the terrorist dissidents refused to stop their operations. On 22 July 1946, the IZL blew up the entire south wing of the King David Hotel in Jerusalem, the headquarters of the British administration and its intelligence corps. The IZL claimed that it had given three advance telephone warnings to evacuate the hotel. But Henry Gurney, the Chief Secretary of the Administration, claimed later that the calls had come too late. In any case, he refused to take orders from the Jews to evacuate his headquarters. Some 92 men and women, including Arabs, British and Jews, were killed.

The disaster shocked the British and the Yishuv alike. No one had foreseen the unprecedented number of casualties. Apparently Sneh had approved the operation, even asking the IZL to reduce the warning time given for evacuation, so that the British would not have time to save the incriminating evidence seized from the Jewish Agency's offices during Operation Agatha. In fact, the relevant evidence was not kept at the King David Hotel.[11]

The disaster generated universal opprobrium and a convenient public relations setting for a further British crackdown on the Yishuv. General Cunningham warned London that unless "some immediate and striking action" was taken, the Arabs were likely to take the law into their own hands. He recommended the immediate suspension of all immigration until a political solution was found, and the sequestration of all Zionist funds. In London, the COS discussed what reprisals should be taken. Field Marshal Montgomery, the abrasive new CIGS (since June), proposed raiding several large Jewish arms dumps whose location the army knew of. Lord Tedder, Chief of the Air Staff, proposed a nation-wide arms search.

Ironically, the provincial autonomy plan, so vilified by the Zionists, which was under consideration in London and Washington, saved the Yishuv from harsh reprisals, either military or financial. The Cabinet vetoed all the options proposed by the military. The British still hoped, by now desperately, that a joint Anglo-American political solution would redeem them.

Since the Palestine problem had become internationalized, its public relations aspect became a vital weapon in the struggle for public opinion. After Agatha, the British published a special White Paper, containing selections from the confiscated Jewish Agency documents, proving its involvement in the JRM.[12]

Apart from considerations of high policy, British action against the Yishuv was also impeded by the tensions between the civil and military branches of government, both in London and in Palestine. As the situation in Palestine deteriorated, these tensions intensified. The refusal of both the Cabinet and the High Commissioner to give the army a free hand generated a crescendo of frustration among the troops. The rank and file enjoyed the sympathy of their officers, who were just as frustrated with the civilians for not allowing them to "get on with the job".

Many of the officers who served in Palestine came to resent what they felt was Jewish ingratitude – after the British had saved them from the Arabs during the 1936–39 rebellion and from Rommel during World War Two. Some of the army units arrived in Palestine sympathetic to the Jews, after what they had witnessed in Europe, especially those who had liberated the concentration and death camps. General Barker had commanded the force that liberated the Bergen-Belsen death camp in April 1945. He and his men had been appalled by the horrors they had seen. But once in Palestine, many of the troops turned anti-Semitic, after suffering at the hands of the Jewish terrorists.

The army's resentment of the Jews and their sense of betrayal were expressed by many officers, at times in public, in defiance of military discipline. For example, Lt Colonel Richard Webb was relieved of his command for anti-Semitic statements he made to foreign correspondents. In October 1946, after two of his soldiers had been killed, he summoned a press conference in Jerusalem at which he lashed out against the Jews. He called them "a despicable race" and added: "These bloody Jews – we saved their skins in Alamein and other places and then they do this to us". Webb left Palestine on 1 November 1946.[13]

But the most significant example was General Barker himself, following the King David outrage. Shortly after his arrival in Palestine, Barker, a married man, began to frequent the Jerusalem salon of Katie Antonius, widow of George Antonius, author of the classic *The Arab Awakening*. Very shortly after they met, he and Katie became lovers. Rumours of their affair circulated Jerusalem. Barker's anti-Semitism pervaded his numerous love letters to Katie, which he continued to write from England for several years after his premature departure from Palestine. He assured her repeatedly that he sided with the Arabs, and shared with her military secrets, including classified information on the army's fight against the Yishuv. In April 1947, back in England, he ventilated his venom about the Jews:

> Yes I loathe the lot – whether they be Zionists or not. Why should we be afraid of saying we hate them? It's time this damned race knew what we think of them.[14]

Barker was in his office in the King David Hotel when the IZL charges destroyed its south wing, burying many under the rubble. He emerged unscathed, but he totally lost his sang-froid, and brought about his own fall from grace. Within minutes of the explosion, he rushed to his office in an incontrollable rage, and wrote an impulsive order of the day to the entire British garrison in Palestine. In the worst of anti-Semitic traditions, and going way beyond his mandate as GOC, he ordered his officers to have their troops ostracize the entire Yishuv, both socially and economically:

> The Jewish community of Palestine cannot be absolved from responsibility for the long series of outrages culminating in the blowing up of a large part of the Government offices in the King David Hotel causing grievous loss of life. Without the support, active or passive, of the general Jewish public the terrorist gangs who actually carried out these criminal acts would soon be unearthed, and in this measure the Jews in this country are accomplices and bear a share of the guilt. I am determined that they shall suffer punishment and be made aware of the contempt and loathing with which we regard their conduct ... I have decided that with effect on receipt of this letter you will put out of bounds to all ranks all Jewish establishments, restaurants, shops, and private dwellings. No British soldier is to have social intercourse with any Jew ... these measures ... will be **punishing the Jews in a way the race dislikes** as much as any, by striking at their pockets and showing our contempt of them.[15]

No one minimized the scale of the King David atrocity, but the British authorities, both in London and in Palestine, were quite aware of the divisions inside the Yishuv, and experienced enough to recognize the imprint of one of the dissident terrorist groups on the King David outrage. But Barker had lashed out at the entire Yishuv.

Barker's aide, Brigadier Sale, gave the order of the day a low secrecy classification and it was leaked. The Zionists seized upon it as a propaganda bonanza, and promptly disseminated it to the world's media. The text was transmitted to the Western media before the army had time to revoke the order. The resulting universal odium soon matched and overshadowed the revulsion caused by the King David atrocity itself. Barker's action became a major public relations disaster for the British. One British newspaper carried a caricature of Barker holding *Mein Kampf*. The Zionists earmarked him as their hated enemy, second only to Bevin.

The government relieved Barker of his command, with almost immediate effect, just a few months after his arrival in Palestine. In October, the government announced that Barker would be "promoted" to a new command in Britain. Strangely, notwithstanding Barker's disgrace, he was allowed to stay on in Palestine until the following February – presumably for "personal reasons".

In reaction to the King David outrage, the government allowed the army to carry out one further operation against the terrorists. With information that the IZL ring responsible for the outrage was hiding in Tel Aviv, the army organized a search operation in the city – code-name Shark. But the operation had only a very limited success. One weapons cache was uncovered, and Yitschak Shamir, the LEHI leader, was apprehended. But Menahem Begin, leader of the much larger IZL, which had carried out the King David bombing, was in fact hiding in the city but eluded the British.

In fact, there was some basis to General Barker's charge that the majority of the Yishuv had become the silent accomplices of the dissident terrorists. The Yishuv *was* horrified by and recoiled from the terrorists' numerous assassinations and murders, and was profoundly shocked by the huge loss of life at the King David hotel. But every perceived anti-Semitic outburst, whether by Bevin in London or by Barker in Jerusalem, reinforced the Jews' post-Holocaust trauma about the apathy of the Allies to their plight. Not only had the Allies not lifted a finger to save the Jews from Hitler's clutches during the war, but they were now indifferent to the fate of the survivors. Each British deportation of Jewish refugees, would-be immigrants who had reached Palestine's shores, increased the Yishuv's alienation still further.

During the last months of 1946, after the JRM had been officially dismantled, Jewish terrorist acts in fact escalated. The IZL reached British targets outside Palestine. On 31 October, IZL saboteurs penetrated and blew up parts of the British Embassy in Rome, causing extensive damage. Panic headlines in the British press predicted assassinations in Britain itself. On 17 November, the IZL blew up a police vehicle in Palestine, killing four soldiers. In reaction, British troops and police went on the rampage in Tel Aviv, wrecking cafés and assaulting Jewish passers-by. A total of 33 cases of British assaults were reported. Two days later, the IZL blew up the British central income tax office in Jerusalem, destroying most of its records. On 26 November, the violent resistance of some 3900 would-be immigrants to forcible deportation at Haifa resulted in two Jewish fatalities, 45 hospitalizations and 30 British soldiers injured.

During the periodical disturbances that wracked Palestine from the 1930s on, the GOCs complained habitually that no major operation could be undertaken without the High Commissioner's authority. More often than not, he turned down their requests for offensive actions, as being politically inexpedient. At the end of November 1946, the new CIGS, Field Marshal

Montgomery, paid a flying visit to Palestine. Before his departure, he met with the Defence Committee in London, hoping to secure its authority for "taking the gloves off" in Palestine. Not only did the political factor still inhibit the government, but Prime Minister Attlee reminded Montgomery pointedly that at the time of Operation Agatha the previous June, the Cabinet had authorized the High Commissioner to arrest the heads of the Jewish Agency executive and of the illegal Jewish militias. At the time, the army had assured the Cabinet that they could break the illegal organizations – but apparently they had not![16]

On 29 November, Montgomery met in Jerusalem with Cunningham and General Charles Dempsey, General Barker's replacement as GOC. Cunningham insisted that they allow the Jewish Agency and the Hagana to weed out their own dissidents. He warned that if the army acted against the terrorists, it "would merely annoy the Jews and make matters worse". Montgomery and the army were enraged at what they regarded as Cunningham's appeasement of the Yishuv. However, all agreed that only a clear-cut political solution might restore order. Only if no political solution were forthcoming would strong military action be required. As if to underline Britain's impotence, in late December, 1 month after Montgomery's visit, after the British had imposed a sentence of 18 years in jail and 18 lashes of the whip on two IZL members for their involvement in a bank robbery, the IZL retaliated by kidnapping and whipping a British major and three sergeants. The British never used the whip again in Palestine. While the army ranks in Palestine became ever more frustrated and furious, public opinion in Britain was enraged by the constant news of their troops' mounting casualties and humiliation.[17]

With the perspective of hindsight, the author of the official history of the Palestine Police wrote later:

> Quite half the military had not the slightest idea of the great political issues at stake in Palestine or why they were not being used to stop Jews from entering the country if they wished, or taking such parts of the land as they wanted for settlement. To most, Palestine was a land of Wogs and Yids, each in their different ways as tiresome as the other.[18]

General Montgomery, whose tunnel vision saw only the military aspect of the Palestine problem, persisted in his belief that he could eradicate the Jewish terrorists by force. Inevitably, his views clashed with those of the majority of the Cabinet, who were convinced that the only long-term solution to Palestine's problems was political. At times, this led the government into paradoxical situations.

At the beginning of January 1946, back in London, Montgomery secured the Cabinet's authorization for a large-scale military operation in Palestine. A majority of the Cabinet agreed with him that the restoration of order was critical to the rebuilding of British prestige in the Middle East. He was authorized, if necessary, to bring over yet more reinforcements from Germany. Yet the Cabinet left the final decision to Cunningham, who, with the Colonial Secretary, opposed Montgomery's proposal! Cunningham warned presciently that a major offensive would create anarchy in the country, force the evacuation of British women and children, and wreck any chances of a political solution.[19]

By the beginning of 1947, the writ of British law had ceased to run in Palestine. Nothing symbolized this more than the kidnapping of two British citizens by the IZL on 26 and 27 January 1947: in Jerusalem, Major Collins, a retired intelligence officer, and in Tel Aviv, Ralph Windham, a British judge, who was abducted while sitting at the Bench of the Tel Aviv District Court. The two men were held hostage against Dov Gruner, an IZL member, under sentence of death for his part in a raid on a police station 7 months previously. Gruner was persuaded to appeal against his sentence to the Privy Council, and with the stay of his execution, the IZL released the two hostages. However, these kidnappings were merely the prelude to the worst IZL outrage, 6 months later.

The government decided to execute a contingency plan drawn up the previous July, after the King David atrocity. All non-essential British personnel and women and children were evacuated from Palestine. Within 4 days, by the end of January, some 2000 British adults and children had left the country. A second step in the plan was Operation Cantonment – the relocation of all remaining civilian staff and troops into security compounds protected by barbed wire, in sequestrated blocks of residential areas. The Jews promptly nicknamed these so-called "safe areas" the "Bevingrads". Most of the remote areas in Palestine were abandoned, left to the mercies of either Arabs or Jews. The crews of armoured vehicles were given a new, limited role – to escort convoys from one place to another.[20]

In theory, Montgomery had been authorized to go on the offensive against the dissident terrorists. But yet again, political developments in London precluded any large-scale military crackdown. At the very time that the IZL carried out its kidnappings, the government began to go through the motions of one final effort to achieve an Arab-Zionist compromise. It convened the last Palestine conference, from 27 January to 13 February 1947. When this failed to produce any meeting of Arab and Zionist minds, the government referred the Palestine mandate to the United Nations.

IZL terrorist attacks reached new peaks during the spring of 1947, culminating in March with an attack on a British officers' club in which they killed 12 officers. The British imposed a curfew on Tel Aviv and Jerusalem, but failed to unearth any terrorist leaders. In any case, they were unable to enforce the curfew for more than a couple of weeks. Between 1938 and 1947, the British sentenced to death 12 members of the IZL and the Lehi. Ten were executed by hanging, the other two committed suicide in prison. These measures had no deterrent effect on the two terrorist undergrounds. But the Jewish resistance was exhausting British resources.

By March 1947, Cunningham was deeply concerned about whether the army could even defend is own men. He advised the Colonial Office that the dual burdens of coping with the terrorists' attacks, with the sporadic imposition of martial law, and of stopping illegal immigration were growing beyond his ability to cope with:

> The Palestine budget is already overburdened by the cost of the deportations and now faced with considerable losses due to martial law. It is extremely doubtful if it could continue to bear the increased charges on account of immigration and enable even a semblance of good administration to remain in unaffected parts of the country.[21]

In May 1947, the American consul in Jerusalem sent home a doleful report on Britain's loss of control of the country:

> With its officials attempting to administrate from behind masses of barbed wire, in heavily defended buildings, and with those same officials (minus wives and children evacuated some time ago) living in pathetic seclusion in "security zones", one cannot escape the conclusion that the Government of Palestine is a hunted organization with little hope of ever being able to cope with conditions in this country as they exist today.[22]

Illegal immigration

The other rock upon which the British mandate in Palestine was shipwrecked was the Zionists' illegal immigration campaign. Initially, some Whitehall officials deluded themselves that an improvement in Europe's economic situation might ease the pressure on Jews to emigrate from Europe, that if the government could only gain time, many Jews might "seek their personal rehabilitation ... and forget the Zionist dream".[23]

Such hopes displayed a mental chasm between the British official mind and that of a people who had survived the traumas of the Holocaust, only to suffer what the majority of them perceived as the Allies' indifference. Not only that, but the DPs were being educated by Zionist agents that only a Jewish state could offer them permanent salvation.

Britain's fight against the would-be immigrants not only earned her universal odium, but it also offset the Yishuv's natural alienation from its terrorist minority. Each time that the British navy towed into Haifa a ramshackle ship with its load of wretched Jewish refugees and forcibly dragged them ashore, the spectacle induced emotional mass demonstrations on Mount Carmel. In February 1947, Cunningham reported that the "scenes of emotion and violence" that had become a regular feature of the forced deportations plunged the entire Yishuv into "an intense state of hysterical emotional tension ... making any move by the Jewish Agency against the terrorists more difficult".[24]

Logistically, the Zionists' attempts to break the British blockade on Palestine's coasts became a heavy charge on the resources of the Mediterranean fleet. The navy's attempts to track the *Exodus* during the summer of 1947 tied up four ships for nearly 2 months, disrupted its training programme, and exhausted a considerable part of the Mediterranean fleet's annual fuel allocation. Even if the British did succeed in tracking down and intercepting over 70 per cent of the would-be immigrants, they never solved the problem of what to do with them. The government's fond hopes of releasing the "illegals" in monthly batches of 750 against the official immigration quotas of 1500 proved pitifully inadequate. At first, the British held the DPs in a makeshift detention camp at Atlit, just south of Haifa, whose capacity was a mere 1500. By August 1946, the camp had filled up. The government decided to deport future would-be immigrants to new camps in Cyprus. But within 12 months of their opening, the Cyprus camps were also bursting at the seams This led to an ill-considered, *ad hoc* decision to deport the refugees back to their ports of departure.[25]

In February 1947, British intelligence learned that the Zionists planned to escalate the illegal immigration campaign – to increase substantially the number and size of ships, and to arrange for several to arrive off the coasts of Palestine simultaneously. The military advised Cunningham that they would be unable to cope with this new development. Nor was the navy able to guarantee the interception of every ship that reached Palestine's 3-mile territorial limits. In fact, the whole interception system was breaking down. The navy had the capacity to transport from Palestine to Cyprus only 3000 Jews per month – the rest had to await deportation in the Atlit camp. The navy depended on RAF spotter planes in order to intercept the illegal transports, but the RAF was unable to send up its planes for more than half of the days of each month.[26]

In April 1947, with the Cyprus detention camps filled to overflowing, the government decided to deport all future illegal immigrants back to their ports of embarkation. The situation became critical when in May 1947, British intelligence reported that a relatively large ship, the *President Warfield* – renamed *Exodus* by the Zionists – thought to be capable of carrying 5000 passengers, was due to leave a European port for Palestine. The saga of the *Exodus* does not need retelling here in detail: its interception by the Royal Navy when 30 kilometres off the coast of Palestine, at 3.00 a.m. on the morning of 18 July; the bloody fight on its decks, leaving three Jewish fatalities, all broadcast live to the world by Hagana radio transmitters; the forced transfer of the wretched Holocaust survivors to British ships at Haifa, witnessed by members of the UN Committee on Palestine (UNSCOP); the refusal of the deported Jews to disembark voluntarily when the British transported them back to their French port of origin; and their final transfer back to the British-occupied zone of Germany. The whole episode translated into yet another public relations disaster.[27]

The British were outmanoeuvred at every step by the Zionists. The *Exodus* episode demonstrated the impossibility of overcoming the political and humanitarian problems of enforcing the immigration restrictions in the emotion-charged aftermath of the Holocaust. When the government's legal experts prepared learned papers arguing the judicial propriety of Britain's struggle against illegal immigration, F.B.A. Rundall, the British consul in New York, commented cynically that Britain could "produce all the international law in the book and it will count for little against the Jewish vote in the next election".[28]

As always, the American reaction was critical. Bevin had been warned in advance by Ambassador Inverchapel against trying to deport the *Exodus* refugees back to Germany:

> I feel bound to point out that the forcible return of these people to the country which was so recently the scene of the worst anti-Semitic atrocities would almost certainly cause a wave of American indignation ... which might have unfavourable repercussions at a delicate stage of Anglo-American relations.[29]

As usual, the public relations aspect and the reaction of 5 million American Jews were everything. President Truman's own personal feelings were irrelevant. It is nonetheless apposite to note exactly what Truman, in his heart of hearts, did feel at the time. We now know, due to the discovery in 2003 of Truman's private desk diary, that as the 4500 Jewish refugees from the *Exodus* were being transported against their will back to Europe, in British ships, the Zionists mobilized Henry Morgenthau, President Roosevelt's Secretary of the Treasury, to lobby Truman. In a short phone call, Morgenthau asked him to intervene with the British, to have them either relax or abandon their policy of deporting Jewish illegal immigrants. This 10-minute call prompted Truman to write the following anti-Semitic diatribe in his diary, a ventilation of his pent-up resentment of the Zionist lobby:

> He'd no business, whatever to call me. **The Jews have no sense of proportion nor do they have any judgment on world affairs ... The Jews, I find are very, very selfish.** They care not how many Estonians, Latvians, Finns, Poles, Yugoslavs or Greeks get murdered or mistreated as DPs as long as the Jews get special treatment. **Yet when they have power, physical, financial or political neither Hitler nor Stalin has anything on them for cruelty or mistreatment to the underdog.**[30]

Bevin knew nothing of Truman's personal feelings, or the extent to which his Palestine policy was dictated by his political advisors. And if he had, it would not have helped. Bevin was now trapped in a cul-de-sac. With no British accommodation left for the Jewish refugees in the Cyprus camps, and fearful as ever of adverse Arab reactions, Bevin proceeded with the deportations. The *Exodus* episode, and its denouement, convinced UNSCOP as much as anything else that the British were not fit to administer the mandate and that the Jews deserved a state of their own.

The *Exodus* was only the start of a new Zionist strategy – the dispatch of larger ships to Palestine, each capable of carrying 5–6000 passengers. In October 1947, the British learned that two more large ships, the *Pan Crescent* and the *Pan York*, with an estimated total complement of 16,000, were due to sail for Palestine from Bulgaria and Romania. By this date, the British had already announced their intention of leaving Palestine by May 1948. The option of mortgaging in advance several months of immigration quotas was discussed, as a desperate last-ditch resort. Cunningham warned that if they tried to deport the refugees, the costs would have to fall on the British taxpayer, since the liabilities of the Palestine administration already exceeded its assets. He was inclined to wash their hands of all responsibility and allow the immigrants to enter Palestine "quietly". But Trafford Smith, the chair of the interdepartmental Illegal Immigration Committee, reminded his colleagues that if they allowed in the 16,000 refugees, it would "appear to the world in general, and in particular to the Arabs, as ... a capitulation in favour of the Jews".[31]

The Foreign Office, anxious about the reactions of the Arab states, insisted that the government must carry out its obligations to the full until the legal termination of the mandate. The State Department intervened and mediated a compromise solution. The Jewish Agency agreed to delay the sailing of the two *Pans* until after the passage of the UN Partition Resolution at the end of November. The Zionists agreed to send the two ships direct to Cyprus. The ships arrived at Cyprus with their complement of Jewish refugees on Christmas Day 1947. The refugees disembarked peacefully and allowed themselves to be interned. They were allowed to sail for Palestine after the State of Israel declared its independence. The entire agreement was carried out "without any formal announcement and without the knowledge of the Arabs".[32]

At the end of July 1947, the illegal immigration campaign and terrorist acts by the dissident underground groups both peaked. On 30 July, shortly after the denouement of the *Exodus* affair, the Jewish terror campaign reached its grisly climax. The IZL hanged two British sergeants, in retaliation for the hanging of three of its own members the day before. The IZL had held the sergeants hostage against the lives of its own men. After executing them, the IZL suspended the men's corpses from a tree in a nearby wood, with booby-trap charges attached. When the army found the bodies, their comrades' attempts to cut them down set off the charges, blowing the first corpse to pieces and injuring the army captain involved.

On the same evening, British police and troops again went on the rampage in Tel Aviv, assaulting Jewish passers-by and smashing the windows of buses and shops. Young Jews formed self-defence groups and retaliated by stoning the British forces. The British were forced to withdraw all foot patrols from Tel Aviv. When the troops returned to base with their stories of being attacked, the men returned spontaneously to Tel Aviv in armoured vehicles. This time, they fired at random at pedestrians, shops and cafés. Five Jews were killed and ten injured. The long-feared, worst-case scenario had materialized. An army court of enquiry was duly appointed. The identities of those involved was known, but none of their officers was prepared to divulge them. Disciplinary action was taken against seven constables, but no criminal charges were pressed.[33]

In England, the hangings seared the national psyche, provoking universal outrage and disgust. They ignited anti-Semitic riots in London and in many of the depressed cities of northern England. They also crystallized an all-party consensus in Parliament that Britain must evacuate Palestine. Five days after the outrage, Churchill again supplied the roar of the British lion. At a Conservative Party fête at Blenheim Palace, before an enthusiastic crowd of 60,000, he attacked Labour's colonial policy:

> While we had blithely cast away mighty India and Burma ... the Government had at all costs clung to tiny Palestine. Nearly 100,000 soldiers had been kept in Palestine, and £30,000,000 or £40,000,000 a year of our hard-earned money had been cast away there ... No British interest is involved in the retention of the Palestine Mandate. For nearly 30 years we have done our best to carry out an honourable and self-imposed task. A year ago I urged the Government to give notice to the United Nations that we could and would bear the burden of insults and injuries no longer. But the Ministers only gaped in shameful indecision, and they are only gaping still.[34]

In one of the more moderate reactions in the British press to the hangings, a *Times* editorial stated:

> They [the two sergeants] were kidnapped unarmed and defenceless; they were murdered for no offence. As a last indignity their bodies were employed to lure into a minefield the comrades who sought to give them a Christian burial. The bestialities practised by the Nazis themselves could go no further.[35]

In view of the nation-wide outcry at home, the Colonial Office urged the High Commissioner to take "extraordinary measures" against the terrorists. But the British had run out of options in Palestine. After consulting with the military, Cunningham reported back that the security forces had already taken all conceivable measures open to them apart from blowing up houses. The imposition of martial law was under consideration, but he did not believe that this alone would stop terrorism – although it would mean the delay of troop reductions and possibly require reinforcements. The public mood in Britain had made it quite clear that such measures were no longer acceptable. Even so, Cunningham urged that the troop withdrawals then under way should be delayed, since he was not sure that he could continue to keep the civil administration working under present conditions.

Cunningham discussed the imposition of martial law with General Sir John Crocker, the C in C MELF. Crocker was vigorously against. He thought it inadvisable on political grounds, on the eve of the UNSCOP report, which might still provide the basis for an agreement. Crocker also believed that there was a growing body of Zionist moderates now prepared to co-operate, even if not openly. But Crocker's main objection was on military grounds. Martial law would operate against Arabs and Jews alike, and might provoke extremist Arab elements to act against them. Above all, with Britain's position in Egypt uncertain and vulnerable, the MELF was unable to tie down large forces in Palestine. Both the CIGS and the War Office confirmed Crocker's decision. In Palestine itself, the troops were ordered not to leave their security zones unless armed and accompanied by at least three other men. All vehicles were required to travel with at least one other armed soldier next to the driver.[36]

Evacuation

In retrospect, the events of January 1947 – the IZL kidnappings, the British evacuation of all non-essential personnel, and the confinement of all troops to barbed-wired compounds – all clearly marked the break point of British morale and their loss of control. At the beginning of February 1947, Henry Gurney wrote in a private letter to J.M. Martin, now Assistant Under-Secretary of State at the Colonial Office:

> I must say that the strain has been pretty heavy and now that the remaining British are all behind barbed wire we are beginning to wonder how long it will be possible to carry on civil administration here at all – I don't know whether any of our colleagues in the F.O. appreciate how it feels not to be allowed out of your home without an escort in British territory.[37]

The Colonial Office, inundated with reports on the deteriorating situation in Palestine, wanted to divest itself of this troublesome problem as soon as possible. On the other hand, the Foreign Office was desperately anxious to find a solution that would retain for Britain the friendship of the Arab world. The conflicting agendas of the two departments sparked high tension between their officials. In another letter to Martin, Gurney referred to what he considered to be the total divorce of the Foreign Office from reality:

> They [the Foreign Office] don't seem to know the answer to anything or to pay any attention to our views or indeed to anything except what comes from the Foreign Office, who seem singularly ill-informed. Secondly, if as we do regard the (UN) Commission's job as virtually impossible, why do we not say so instead of letting the Commission find out for themselves, after which they will merely accuse us of making it impossible. I have been greatly tempted to go there [to the UN in New York] myself, but with what we have now to do here it is impossible.

> I find it hard to believe that anyone in New York ... has the slightest idea of what the Palestine Government and its present problems look like from the inside.[38]

Gurney's jaundiced views reflect the growing demoralization of the civilian officials and the security forces in Palestine. The police ranks felt impotent and a growing sense of impending chaos, as Jewish terrorist outrages continued. Not even the increasingly punitive measures adopted by the British, including capital punishment, appeared to deter them. During the course of the mandate, from 1920 to 1948, over 550 Palestine Police were killed.[39]

By 1947, as at the height of the Arab Rebellion in the summer of 1938, the British realized that the Arabs and the Jews were losing faith in their ability to preserve law and order in the country:

> Both Arabs and Jews were aware that British morale, the essential ingredient to upholding the Mandate's authority, was eroding under the strain of prolonged warfare with shadowy opponents, on behalf of a policy that commanded little respect and less enthusiasm.[40]

The hanging of the two sergeants in July 1947 served as the straw that finally broke Britain's back. It generated a national consensus that not even the Foreign Office could ignore. In the Commons debate on the outrage on 12 August, Arthur Creech-Jones, the Colonial Secretary, tried to pass off the hangings as something the authorities had anticipated but, echoing Churchill's public speech of the previous week, he conceded "[a]mong the British public there is fierce questioning as to the burden and cost to Britain, and the tragedy involved by Britain continuing to shoulder this international liability".[41]

When Creech-Jones briefed the British delegation to the UN General Assembly, scheduled for September 1947, he instructed them to take into account: "the strong feeling now apparent in the country and the House of Commons in favour of British withdrawal from Palestine". The IZL's draconian methods, morally repugnant as they were, had proved decisive in transforming the evacuation option of the previous February into a firm resolve.[42] Many observers (including the Zionists) did not believe the Colonial Secretary's first announcement at the UN on 18 September that Britain intended to evacuate Palestine. Therefore, to ensure that the members of the UN and the inhabitants of Palestine should have no doubts about Britain's resolve, he was instructed by the government to repeat the same declaration on 16 October "[m]y government desire that it should be clear beyond all doubt and ambiguity that not only is it our decision to wind up the mandate but that within a limited period we shall withdraw".[43]

John Beith, the Foreign Office official charged with the thankless job of trying to stop illegal immigration, commented with evident relief:

> Our decision to withdraw from Palestine has regained us our freedom of manoeuvre *vis-à-vis* both sides. As regards the Arabs, it has absolved us

from any responsibility for imposing a pro-Zionist solution while retaining Arab goodwill ... we must avoid any signs that we might hang on in Palestine. The Arabs will interpret any such sign as an indication that we were preparing to propose a Zionist solution.[44]

On 29 November 1947, the UN General Assembly passed by the required two-thirds majority the resolution to partition into Arab and Jewish states, with an independent, internationally supervised state of Jerusalem. The UN set 30 June 1948 as the date of the British evacuation, and the end of October 1948 for the establishment of the Arab and Jewish states, and the international state of Jerusalem.

Britain abstained from the vote, in the hope that the Arab world would not hold her responsible. The Foreign Office noted with satisfaction that the Arabs believed, with some justification, that the Americans were responsible for the UN partition vote.[45] Once the British were convinced that no compromise solution acceptable to Arabs, Jews and Americans was possible, they determined to get out of Palestine as quickly as possible. On 11 November, the COS advised the Cabinet that the military withdrawal from Palestine could be completed by 1 August 1948. Two days later, Sir Alexander Cadogan, the British representative to the UN, passed this information on to the relevant UN committee. The civilian administration, headed by the High Commissioner, would leave Palestine on 14 May, leaving behind a small force to complete the removal of military stores.[46]

Britain's strategy was to withdraw with as few British casualties as possible, without being blamed by the Arabs for helping to set up a Jewish state in Palestine. To this end, Harold Beeley, Bevin's right-hand man at the Foreign Office, urged that the evacuation be speeded up, even at the cost of leaving military stores behind:

> It seems to me we should now make it our first concern to consolidate the goodwill we have gained in the Arab world, at least by contrast with the other great powers, and to avoid any incident in Palestine which might destroy this asset. The longer we remain in control of the country, the greater would be the risk of some such incident ... Surely the military stores are of less consequence than our future relationship with the Arab States.[47]

While it was universally believed that in the event of an Arab-Israeli war, the Arabs would "push the Jews into the sea", the British military did not share this view, and it was *not* the reason for Britain's hasty evacuation. To the very last day in Palestine, Britain's official policy was to treat the Arabs and the Jews with strict impartiality, lest she be accused of favouritism. There were many exceptions to this rule – a number of soldiers and officers favoured the Arabs and/or sought revenge against the Jews. But the British refused to hand over or sell any British property to either side, whether army camps, air bases, Tegart police forts, armoured cars, blankets, drill jackets or toothbrushes. Police posts were simply evacuated, and usually fell into the hands of whichever side – Arab or Jewish – was closest. Those posts that were not in either an Arab or Jewish area were fought for. Military equipment, ordnance and classified files that could not be taken were destroyed or burned; vehicles that could not be shipped out were run over cliffs.[48]

The process of winding up the mandate was thankless and demoralizing. British civilian and military staff left by sea, from Haifa. The administrative staff withdrew during the spring of 1948 from east to west, to an enclave round Haifa harbour. During the final weeks of the mandate, the administration virtually ceased to function. All British judges were sent back to England in March and British courts ceased to function; the Post Office shut down in April, the prisons ceased to function and most of the prisoners escaped. The secretaries left at the beginning of April, leaving senior officials and officers to write their letters by hand. The theft of British cars became so common that by the time the administration finally left Jerusalem, they had only two left.

Sir Henry Gurney's private diary reflects the tribulations of a stranded colonial regime forced by high policy to wind itself down. On 20 April he wrote:

> We are staying now merely to get out, and by staying on making getting out more difficult ... whereas until recently we were staying on to help the Army to get out, now the Army is staying on because for political reasons we are not allowed to go, although the Army wants us to. It is quite clear that the situation in Jerusalem is not appreciated in London.

Four days later, he commented morosely on his personal sense of humiliation: "the Government's authority is being flouted right and left by both sides, and what good this prolongation of these humiliating conditions does to anybody is hard to see". On 29 April, 16 days before evacuation, Gurney noted cynically that the administration's task now was "to cut off the branch on which it was sitting. The branch must hold until May 15th but must fall exactly on that day".[49]

It is perhaps fitting to leave the final word to William James Fitzgerald, the last Chief Justice of Palestine. On 8 November 1947, 3 weeks before the passage of the UN Partition Resolution, he wrote the following graphic observation, in a private letter to Sir Harold MacMichael, the former High Commissioner:

> I find myself a participant in what I can only regard as a retreat we may find it somewhat hard to justify in history. There is no doubt about it – we are going. The decision undoubtedly has the concurrence of 99% of

the British people and I accept *vox populi*: it is the manner of our leaving that worries me ... Whatever one may think of the rights and wrongs of either side, it surely is a new technique in our imperial mission to walk out and leave the pot we placed on the fire to boil over.[50]

Notes

1 Richard Crossman, *Palestine Mission*, New York: Harper, 1947, pp. 52–54, and Fritz Liebrich, *Britain's Naval and Political Reaction to the Illegal Immigration of Jews to Palestine, 1945–1948*, London: Routledge, 2005, pp. 20–21.
2 For this and the following, cf. Michael J. Cohen, *Palestine and the Great Powers, 1945–1948*, Princeton: Princeton University Press, 1982, Chapter 4.
3 ibid, pp. 72–73.
4 ibid, pp. 78–80
5 General D'Arcy to COS, 15 May 1946, FO 371/52525, NA.
6 Printed in *Palestine: Statement of Information Relating to Acts of Violence*, Cmd 6873, London: HMSO, July 1946.
7 Barker memorandum of 22 June 1946, in the Cunningham papers, box 5, file 5, The Middle East Center, St Anthony's College, Oxford University.
8 The Palmach was mobilized and trained by the British in 1941, following Rommel's first advances across the Western desert.
9 cf. the series of interviews with British officers and officials by an Israeli journalist, Hadara Lazar, in *Out of Palestine*, London: Atlas, 2011, published first in Hebrew in 1990, by Keter, Jerusalem.
10 Crossman, *Palestine Mission*, p. 123.
11 Cohen, *Palestine*, pp. 90–91. The Zionists were apparently not aware that police and intelligence files very rarely left the police headquarters compound, housed in its own independent building. cf Edward Horne, *A Job Well Done: A History of the Palestine Police Force, 1920–1948*, Sussex: The Book Guild, 2003, p. 300.
12 Cmd 6873, July 1946.
13 www.jta.org/1946/11/01/archive/palestine-high-commissioner-retires-from-army-service-lt-col-webb-leaves-palestine.
14 Tom Segev, *One Palestine, Complete*, New York: Metropolitan Books, 2000, p. 468. In late 1947, the Hagana blew up Katie's house and took a large number of documents, including nearly 100 of the general's love letters to her, all written on official army stationery and delivered by hand by Barker's army driver. The Jewish Agency chose not to publish the letters, possibly because with the UN Partition Resolution and the British decision to evacuate Palestine "in their pockets", they thought it the better part of wisdom not to antagonize further those British forces still in the country.
15 Cohen, *Palestine*, p. 94, my emphasis.
16 Meeting of the Defence Committee, 20 November 1946, FO 371/52565, NA.
17 Cohen, *Palestine*, pp. 232–33.
18 Horne, *A Job Well Done*, pp. 560–61.
19 Conference at Colonial Office, 3 January 1947, Cunningham papers, box 5, file 4, The Middle East Centre, St Anthony's College, Oxford (MEC), and Cabinet meeting of 15 January 1947, in WO 32/10260, NA. General Cunningham retired from the army in October 1946, and relinquished the role of Commander-in-Chief Palestine but he retained the post of High Commissioner until the end of the mandate.
20 Cohen, *Palestine*, pp. 236–37; Horne, *A Job Well Done*, p. 568.
21 Cunningham to Colonial Secretary, 9 March 1947, CO 537/2333, NA. At the end of 1948, the Palestine administration estimated that it had spent some LP3, 335,000 in combating Jewish illegal immigration; CO 733/481/2, NA.

22 Robert Macatee to Marshall, 22 May 1947, 501 BB Pal/5–2247, box 2181, NAUS.
23 Fritz Liebrich, *Britain's Naval and Political Reaction to the Illegal Immigration of Jews to Palestine, 1945–1948*, London: Routledge, 2005, p. 27.
24 Cunningham to Colonial Office, 16 February 1947, CO 733/2333, NA.
25 Between the end of the war and May 1948, the Mosad, the Jewish Agency's illegal immigration organization, sent 69,878 Jews without certificates to Palestine, in 70 ships; only 13 of the ships evaded detention and arrest; some 51,500 Jews were intercepted and detained. The majority of the Cyprus detainees were freed and made their way to independent Israel after May 1948; Cohen, *Palestine*, pp. 250–52; Liebrich, *Britain's Naval*, pp. 232–33, 254–55.
26 Cunningham to the Colonial Office, 9 March 1947, CO 537/2234, NA.
27 During the fight on board the *Exodus*, three Jews were killed, 28 required hospitalization and over 200 required first aid; cf. Cohen, *Palestine*, pp. 250–57, Nicholas Bethell, *The Palestine Triangle*, New York: Putnam, 1979, pp. 318–43, and Aviva Halamish, *The Exodus Affair*, London: Vallentine Mitchell, 1998.
28 Rundall minute of 11 July 1947, cited in Liebrich, *Britain's Naval*, p. 105.
29 Lord Inverchapel to Bevin, 14 August 1947, FO 371/61822, NA.
30 Diary entry of 21 July 1947, www.trumanlibrary.org/diary/page21.htm, my emphases; also Michael J. Cohen, "A New Look at Truman and 'Exodus 1947'", *Israel Journal of Foreign Affairs*, vol. 3/1, 2009, pp. 93–100.
31 Liebrich, *Britain's Naval*, pp. 236–37.
32 ibid, pp. 171, 194, 250–51.
33 Cunningham to the Colonial Office, 15 November 1947, CO 733/477, 75156/151a, NA.
34 Report in *The Times*, 5 August 1947.
35 *The Times*, 1 August 1947.
36 Cunningham to Colonial Secretary, 4 and 7 August 1947, Cunningham papers, box 2, file 2, and General Crocker to Cunningham, 13 August, idem, box 5, file 4, MEC.
37 Gurney to Martin, 8 February 1947, in CO 967/102, NA. At the end of the mandate, the ill-fated Gurney was appointed High Commissioner to Malaya. In October 1951, he was shot and killed by Communist guerillas.
38 Gurney to Martin, 24 January 1947, ibid.
39 Horne, *A Job Well Done*, p. 100, n. 36.
40 A.J. Sherman, *Mandate Days: British Lives in Palestine, 1918–1948*, New York: Thames & Hudson, 1998, pp. 113–14.
41 Debate in House of Commons Debates (*H.C. Deb.*), vol. 441, cols 2306–88.
42 Cohen, *Palestine*, p. 247, and author's interview with General Sir Gordon MacMillan, the last GOC Palestine, 20 July 1978.
43 British UN delegation to Foreign Office, 16 October 1947, FO 371/61882, NA.
44 Note by Sir John Beith, 22 October 1947, in FO 371/61883, NA.
45 For details of the machinations, lobbying and bribery that preceded the passage of the UN Partition Resolution, cf. Cohen, *Truman and Israel*, Chapter 9.
46 Cohen, *Palestine*, pp. 287–88.
47 Beeley to Burrows, 2 December 1947, E11513, FO 371/61891, NA.
48 Horne, *A Job Well Done*, pp. 576–78. A black market for military equipment developed, but this was on the private initiative of individual soldiers or policemen susceptible to lucrative money deals.
49 Sherman, *Mandate Days*, pp. 228–36, 241; Gurney diary entries for 20, 24 and 29 April 1948, on p. 231.
50 Fitzgerald to MacMichael, 8 November 1947, cited in ibid, p. 210. Fitzgerald, just 53 years old at the time, had reached the peak of his career. He was unable to find a suitable judicial position in England.

Conclusion

> The P.M., General Smuts, the late President Roosevelt, had all let them down, maybe not intentionally, but inadvertently. They made promises which they did not carry out or mean to carry out.
>
> Chaim Weizmann, June 1945

No history of the British mandate in Palestine is complete without reference to the anti-Semitism endemic in British society. It was never legislated into law, as on the continent, but resentment of and prejudice against the Jews, in all strata of British society, pervade the entire period covered by this book. It was not confined to the fringes of the right wing, to the street brawls provoked by Mosley's British Union of Fascists in the 1930s, or to the anti-Semitic riots of the unemployed in 1946. In the 1920s, it pervaded the public discourse, both in Parliament and in the press. It appeared in the works of some of Britain's most respected writers. It was in the genes of many Cabinet ministers and senior army officers. It was ubiquitous in the internal correspondence of all the government departments that dealt with Palestine, not least during the Holocaust, when Whitehall officials griped about the ingratitude of the Jews. Anti-Semitism was present in London's exclusive gentlemen's clubs (many of which didn't accept Jews as members), as it was in at least one of the holiest of holies of the British Academy – Oxford University. It was not until 1932 that All Soul's College elected a Jew (Isaiah Berlin) to its staff. At the upper levels of the British establishment, anti-Semitic sentiment was usually kept "below the radar", confined to private letters and diaries, or to the smoking rooms of their London clubs.

It is with this context in mind that one must assess Britain's issue of the Balfour Declaration in November 1917, and her 28-year long tenure of the League of Nations mandate for Palestine. Britain's support of Zionism was not an altruistic enterprise. It lasted until other, higher interests superseded those of the 1920s. The 1917 Declaration was a military exigency, which at the same time also served Britain's imperial interests. With the aid of Zionist diplomacy, the British finessed the French out of Palestine (the Sykes-Picot Agreement) and persuaded President Wilson to agree to Britain's acquisition of another colony. During the 1920s, the windfall of Jewish capital mobilized by the Zionists enabled the British to maintain and develop Palestine, and to help pay for other imperial projects in the region, all at little or no cost to the British taxpayer.

After World War One, many right-wing British politicians, as well as the right-wing press, protested that the Declaration did not oblige the British to take on the mandate for Palestine. None other than Arthur Balfour, the Declaration's namesake, proposed in 1919 that the Americans take on the burden. The level of the opposition's anti-Zionist rhetoric in Parliament prompted Leo Amery MP to refer to the existence of an "anti-Semitic" party in the House of Commons.

Had there been any doubts about the Palestinian Arabs' opposition to Zionism, they were swept away in 1921 by the second round of Arab riots and pogroms. These could not simply be dismissed as the product of the military regime's ill-willed negligence, as had happened the year before. Nonetheless, when the Conservatives came to power in October 1922, they realized that if the government ended its commitment to Zionism, it would have to return the mandate to the League of Nations. Not only would the breaking of the Balfour promise cause an international loss of face, but Britain would lose a strategic asset, financed largely by Zionist-imported capital. As Lord Curzon told an imperial conference in October 1923: "Palestine needs ports, electricity, and the Jews of America were rich and would subsidize such development".

The role played in Palestine by Zionist-generated capital was demonstrated in 1925, when the government published a tender for a concession to exploit the minerals of the Dead Sea. Of the four offers submitted, only the Zionist consortium stayed the course. The British noted that unlike their competitors, the Zionists were not motivated primarily by the desire to turn a quick profit, but by their vision of a Jewish state.

Arab opposition to the Yishuv was held at bay during the 1920s, with the classic colonial tactic of "divide and rule". The leaders of the two major Palestinian clans, the Husaynis and the Nashashibis, were bought off with the perquisites of local self-government, religious and municipal. Although the Yishuv enjoyed an economic surge during the first half of the decade, it lapsed into recession during the second half. In 1927 and 1928, more Jews left Palestine than arrived. Many observers concluded that the Zionist "experiment" had spent itself.

But in August 1929, the superficial quiet was shattered by the "Wailing Wall" riots. Any lingering illusions that Arabs and Jews might co-exist peacefully in Palestine were dispelled. There was a general consensus in Whitehall that the Jewish National Home experiment must be curbed, or even terminated. Those charged with the administration of Palestine concluded that the Balfour Declaration had been a huge mistake, and that British interests in Palestine, and in the Middle East in general, required its abrogation. In October 1930, the Labour government issued a new statement of policy (a White Paper) that would have brought an indefinite halt to all further Jewish immigration and severely curbed Zionist land purchases.

The Yishuv would have been "frozen" at around one-fifth of the Arab population.

The new policy marked a "crossroads" in the history of the mandate. But it was conceived prematurely, 9 years before its natural progeny, the 1939 White Paper. A unique combination of political and economic factors led the Labour minority government to retreat. The 1930 White Paper was the only one of the three major policy statements on Palestine (the others were voted into law in 1922 and 1939) that was not even put to the vote in Parliament. During a period of deep economic depression, the government feared the potential of the Zionist lobby in the United States to incite the American administration against Britain. The recession made Britain even more dependent on the import of Jewish capital to finance its administration in Palestine, and the Treasury refused to invest the huge sums required to reform the Arab agricultural sector.

Fearing the loss of face that would follow a formal withdrawal from its own published policy statement, the government stumbled into a clumsy way to by-pass it. In February 1931, Prime Minister MacDonald issued a "reinterpretation" of the new policy in a private letter to Dr Weizmann. The letter was accorded the status of official policy when MacDonald read it into the protocols of the House of Commons. His letter remained the law of the land in Palestine until 1939.

Commenting bitterly on the government's retreat, Sir John Chancellor, the High Commissioner, wrote to his son in 1931: "MacDonald had been intimidated by the Jews ... The world economic crisis required special caution; who wanted at this junction to get into trouble with 'world Jewry'?"[1]

The government still felt able to ignore the protests of the Palestinian Arabs. Hitler and Mussolini had yet to threaten the European *status quo*, and Britain had not yet allowed the Arabs states a *locus standi* in the affairs of Palestine.

From 1931 to 1936, the year in which the Arab rebellion erupted in Palestine, the Yishuv more than doubled in size, from 180,000 to nearly 400,000 souls. The Arab rebellion was subdued by the British army at the end of 1938. But since 1936, with the Germans and the Italians threatening British interests in both Europe and the Middle East, Britain's first priority became to find a Palestine settlement that would be acceptable to the Arab states. The Foreign Office usurped the Colonial Office's fiefdom over Palestine, on the hypothesis that Britain's policy there had a critical effect on her position in the Arab and Moslem worlds.

During the 1920s, Palestinian Arab society was fissured between the rival camps of the traditional, land-owning elites, the Husaynis and the Nashshibis. The Husaynis prevailed and their leader, Haj Amin el-Husayni, effectively dominated the Palestinian Arabs throughout the mandate. Haj Amin's meteoric rise began in 1921, when with British help he was appointed Grand Mufti of Jerusalem; in 1922, the British appointed him President of the Supreme Moslem Council. The Nashashibi-led opposition was a significant sociological factor in Palestine but it failed to present a viable alternative to the Husayni clan. Notwithstanding the external challenges of foreign rule by a Western, Christian power, which gave special privileges to Jewish immigrants, the Palestinians failed to develop a national culture able to rise above parochial, feudal and personal ties.

During the first half of the 1930s, a younger, more educated, Arab urban middle class developed, which formed new political parties. But from mid-1937, Palestinian Arab society was traumatized by the internecine terror campaign that the Husaynis launched against any Arab who agreed to the Peel Plan to partition Palestine into Arab and Jewish states. Wide sections of the rural peasantry were alienated from their traditional leaders. The extensive migration of the *fellahin* from village to town during World War Two exacerbated internal divisions further, leaving the fabric of Arab society weak and vulnerable. The Mufti's legacy to his people was a culture of internal dissension and internecine terror.

In the 1939 White Paper, Britain declared that she had fulfilled her obligation to sponsor the Jewish National Home in Palestine. In their vain effort to appease the Arab states, the British offered the Palestinian Arabs more than they could possibly have expected – shortly after they had crushed their 3-year long rebellion. The new policy promised them an independent state within 10 years and government by majority rule; 5 more years of Jewish immigration, guaranteed to preserve the Arabs' two-thirds majority of the population, after which the Arabs would enjoy a veto on all further Jewish immigration. A majority of the Higher Arab Committee, the Palestinians' ruling executive body, favoured accepting the new offer. But Haj Amin rejected it, since the British refused to allow him to return to Palestine. Despite widespread criticism of the new policy, the outbreak of World War Two prevented the League from discussing whether it infringed the terms of the mandate.

After the war, the Mufti conceded that he had missed a historic opportunity in 1939. But it is unclear whether his main regret was that he had chosen the losing side in the war. The Mufti had committed himself to the Nazi camp long before 1939. He admired and followed Hitler's diplomatic and military triumphs from the early 1930s. He sought and found parallels between Nazi doctrine and verses in the *Koran*. Quite evidently, he aspired to a similar style of absolutist rule for himself in Palestine.

British attempts to appease the Arab states proved no more successful than had Chamberlain's attempt to appease Nazi Germany at Munich. In July 1940, following Italy's entry into the war, the Foreign Office – the architect of the 1939 White Paper – concluded that the only way to ensure the Arabs' allegiance would be by British victories on the field of battle. When he became Prime Minister, Churchill, who had attacked the 1939 White Paper in Parliament, warned his Cabinet that he did not regard himself as committed to it. But he also made it clear that any change in the *status quo* in Palestine would have to wait until after the war. In November 1944, with the assassination in Cairo of his good friend, Lord Moyne, Churchill abandoned the Zionist cause.

In 1939, the British knew that the Jews had no alternative but to side with them during the coming war. The first 3 years of the war were a traumatic experience for the Yishuv in Palestine. During the spring of 1940, when news arrived of the German rout of the Allies in northern Europe, and of Italy's declaration of war, the Yishuv became concerned about Britain's vulnerability in the Middle East. Their anxieties increased after Rommel's Panzers landed in Libya in February 1941. The Yishuv leaders feared that the Palestinian Arabs would seize the opportunity of British weakness to renew their attacks against them. In the context of the twin Arab and German threats, the final rejection by Churchill's government of the Jewish Division scheme in October 1941 burned deeply into the Zionist psyche. The scheme had held out the hope of securing the elementary right of self-defence against the Arabs and, if worst came to worst, to die fighting the Germans, with dignity.

In September 1940, the general public could have learned of the mass atrocities being committed by the Nazis from Churchill's BBC broadcast. By the spring of 1942, the mass slaughter of the Jews in Eastern Europe by the Nazis was common knowledge, in the Middle East too. In April 1942, before Rommel reached El Alamein, Moshe Shertok, head of the Jewish Agency's political department, sent the following telegram to General Auchinleck, the GOC of British Middle East Land Forces:

> There can be no doubt that if the Nazis sweep across Palestine, all the Jews here will be annihilated. The destruction of the Jewish race is a fundamental element of the Nazi doctrine. The authorised news reaching us lately indicates that they are carrying out this policy with indescribable cruelty. Hundreds of thousands of Jews have died in Poland, in the Balkans, Roumania and in those Soviet provinces which the Nazis have invaded, as a result of mass executions, forced expulsions, and outbreaks of illness and starvation in the ghettoes and in the concentration camps. There is reason to believe that a much greater disaster will befall the Yishuv, if we fall into Nazi hands.[2]

But the British turned down all of the Yishuv's appeals to give them arms and combat training. With the exception of mobilizing some small Jewish commando units (the Palmach), to help them in their own emergencies, the British refused to train the Jews for anything beyond static guard duties. They prepared detailed plans for evacuating the Middle East, which did not include the Jews of the Middle East.

The Mufti's standing as leader of the Palestinian Arabs and his wartime collaboration with the Nazis have been reviewed in detail (Chapters 17 and 18). Arab historiography on the Palestinian Arabs' loyalties during World War Two is confused. Many historians, including the Mufti himself, claim that British cruelty to the Arabs during the 1936–39 rebellion and

Britain's personal vendetta against the Mufti drove him into the arms of the Nazis. This is not accurate. The Mufti did not suffer personally from British cruelty, nor was he a reluctant fugitive in Berlin. His support for the Nazis was based upon an ideological affinity and a shared anti-Semitism. He hoped that the Nazis would apply their "Final Solution" to the "Jewish Problem" in Europe to *his* "Jewish Problem" in Palestine. Not only the Allies but the Zionists also listened to the Mufti's short-wave propaganda broadcasts to the Middle East from Berlin, inciting the Arabs to kill their Jewish neighbours.

At the turn of the twenty-first century, a "revisionist" school of Middle East historians and sociologists emerged, claiming that Egyptian intellectuals had not been as receptive to Fascist and Nazi ideas as had been claimed hitherto. They claimed not only that their discovery required a revision of the political history of Egypt, but that a similar examination of the printed publications in Iraq, Palestine and Syria would reveal similar liberal discourses, which would also require the rewriting of their histories.

But there is a wide chasm between the academic studies of Egyptian liberal intellectuals and the political realities in Egypt and the Middle East during the 1930s and 1940s. Only on very rare occasions have intellectuals changed the course of their country's history. This has yet to happen in the Middle East.

The most reliable study of the Palestinian Arab press during the mandate, by Dr Kabha, an Israeli Arab, did not reveal any "liberal discourse". On the contrary, many articles expressed admiration for Hitler and his achievements. Dr Kabha concluded his book with what he termed an "interesting paradox":

> On the eve of the Second World War almost all the Palestinian newspapers supported Britain and the democracies ... [this] support of the democratic camp created an interesting paradox. On the one hand, the deportation of Haj Amin from Palestine ... led to press sympathy for [him] ... Even the opposition newspapers declared their loyalty to his leadership and his struggle against the British. On the other hand, this identification did not lead to support for Haj Amin's activities in the international field. Each side ... supported a different camp, but they almost never attacked each other.[3]

But neither Kabha nor anyone else has yet made a reliable study of the Arabs' allegiance during World War Two. Kabha's conclusion about the Palestinian Arabs' allegiance to the Allies during the war is based on just four wartime newspaper articles, the last one dated July 1940, before the Middle East became a theatre of war. From the spring of 1941 until the end of 1942, Zionist intelligence reports from urban centres of Arab nationalism indicated a widespread hope that Rommel would conquer Palestine, and "relieve" the Arabs of both the British and the Jews.

Zionist fears were shared by Allied diplomats and intelligence agents in the region. They were unanimous in their warnings about the dangers of an Arab "stab in the back". The allegiance of the Palestinian Arabs was never tested, because Rommel never reached Palestine. During the summer of 1943, the Axis armies were driven from North Africa. Hitler's failure to conquer the Middle East was one of his great missed opportunities. But for Hitler, the conquest of the Middle East was always second to conquering *lebensraum* in the East. His missed opportunity was also the end of the Mufti's dream of physically eliminating the Yishuv (for which the Nazis had organized a special SS unit). The Mufti continued to collaborate with the Nazis until the end of the war in Europe. Every European Jew murdered by the Nazis meant one less potential emigrant to Palestine.

Some scholars have dismissed the Mufti's wartime activities in Berlin as marginal and ineffective. However, both sides in the war, the Nazis and the Allies, treated him with great respect, as an important Arab leader. The Germans rewarded him handsomely, believing that he performed a key role in their propaganda transmissions to the Arab world. Allied intelligence services in the Middle East were seriously concerned about the effects of his radio transmissions in Arabic to the region. No Arab leader ever repudiated the Mufti, not before, during or after the war.

After the war, Allied officials continued to warn that the West's continued support for the Jewish National Home in Palestine would turn the Arab world against them. This consensus, even when account is made for prejudice, cannot simply be dismissed as groundless, collective paranoia. The Mufti fled Paris for Cairo in June 1946. His immediate reassumption of the leadership of the Palestinian Arabs may be verified by the British diplomatic and intelligence files cited in the body of this book. The Mufti remained a respected figure in the Arab world until his death in 1974.

There is a direct connection between the Palestine mandate and the Holocaust. But it is not the conventional wisdom that sees the UN Partition Resolution as an expression of the world's conscience – that more had not been done to save the Jews from Hitler's "Final Solution". The speech of Andrei Gromyko, the Soviet Foreign Minister, at the UN in May 1947 might be seen as a lone public expression of conscience. He stated that since no European state had been able to defend the Jews during the war, it was impossible now to deny them a state of their own. But Gromyko added that his own preferred solution, "the one deserving most attention", was a single, binational state, with equal rights for Arabs and Jews. We also know that the Soviets' main objective in voting for the Partition Resolution was to undermine Britain's position in the Middle East.[4]

Popular Zionist historiography (promoted by the best-selling book and box office hit film) transformed the *Exodus* incident into a defining episode in the Zionist struggle for a Jewish state. The *Exodus* may well have helped to convince the UN Committee on Palestine that the British must return their mandate and evacuate Palestine. But it did *not* persuade any Western leader that the Jews should have a state of their own in Palestine (see Chapter 20 for Truman's reaction).

Ernest Bevin, the British Foreign Secretary, has been singled out as the principal, anti-Semitic enemy of the Zionist cause. But Bevin represented a popular consensus in the British Parliament, one that included most of the Conservative opposition. They argued that after the Allies had liberated Europe from Nazism and Fascism, the Jewish survivors of the Holocaust should return to their countries of birth. It is worth recalling Churchill's deprecatory remarks on this issue in the House of Commons, on 1 August 1946: "[t]he idea that the Jewish Problem can be solved or even helped by a vast dumping of the Jews of Europe into Palestine is really too silly to consume our time".[5]

Churchill's statement was made just 4 weeks after the notorious pogrom of Jews at Kielce, Poland, an atrocity that had received ample publicity in the British media during the previous weeks (see Chapter 15).

Underlying the Allies' reluctance to allow the Jewish DPs into Palestine lay their material interests in the Arab world – strategic bases and oil. After the war, the Middle East assumed a new significance in the Allies' grand strategy. The ailing economies of Western Europe were absolutely dependent upon the region's oil reserves and in the feared event of World War Three, the Americans planned to use British air bases in Egypt as a launching pad for strategic air strikes against Soviet targets. More than ever before, the appeasement of the Arab states was a categorical imperative. Britain finally gave up Palestine in 1947, only when forced to by her failure to reach agreement with the US about the solution to the Arab-Zionist conflict.

The British mandate provided the aegis under which the Zionists laid the foundations of the state of Israel. Without the protection of British arms during the Arab rebellion of 1936–1939, it is doubtful if the Yishuv could have survived as a viable entity. But in 1939, Britain ruptured the Zionists' belief in her as a trustee. Their hopes that Prime Minister Churchill would revoke Chamberlain's appeasement of the Arabs were dashed within a little over 1 year. In the summer of 1944, the Jews realized also that their appeals to the Allies to bomb the Auschwitz-Birkenau death camp had been turned down on specious grounds. They emerged from the war disillusioned and traumatized, their faith in the Western democracies shattered.

From January to February 1947, the British convened one final Arab-Zionist conference in London. When that failed to produce a compromise, they referred the mandate back to the UN, without recommendations. When the UN decided to partition Palestine into Arab and Jewish states – a decision that the British warned would lead to an Arab-Jewish war – the British felt no obligation to assume responsibility for establishing a Jewish state. They had no intention of placing British soldiers in harm's way, in order to execute a plan that would jeopardize the support of the Arab states.

In September 1947, 2 months before the passage of the UN Partition Resolution, Britain announced that she was evacuating Palestine. The Labour government decided to do what it had done with India – to remove her personnel from the line of fire and leave the protagonists to fight it out on the field of battle. Britain focused on one goal – to withdraw from Palestine with the fewest possible casualties.

The Zionists felt that they had no alternative but to fight for a Jewish state – even against an Arab population twice the size of the Yishuv, and the armies of five Arab states. For the overwhelming majority of Arabs, a Jewish state in Palestine was not an acceptable option. On the morrow of the UN Partition Resolution the Palestinians made their first attacks against the Yishuv, thereby igniting the first Arab-Israeli war.

Notes

1 Tom Segev, *One Palestine, Complete*, New York: Metropolitan Books, 2000, p. 337.
2 See S25/58–4t, Central Zionist Archives, Jerusalem. Shertok's appeal is cited in: http://he.wikipedia.org/wiki/מאתיים_ימי_חרדה.
3 Mustafa Kabha, *The Palestinian Press as a Shaper of Public Opinion, 1929–1939: Writing up a Storm*, London: Vallentine Mitchell, 2007, p. 269.
4 On Gromyko's speech and analyses of Soviet intentions, cf. Michael J. Cohen, *Palestine and the Great Powers, 1945–1948*, Princeton: Princeton University Press, 1982, pp. 261–62, 283.
5 *House of Commons Debates*, 5th series, vol. 426, col. 1258.

Bibliography

Unpublished primary sources

National Archives (formerly the PRO), Kew, London.
Weizmann Archives, Rehovot, Israel.
Central Zionist Archives, Jerusalem.
Churchill Archives, Churchill College, Cambridge University.
Imperial War Museum Archives, London.
Digital Library of the London School of Economics, London.
Bodleian Library of Commonwealth and African Studies, Rhodes House, Oxford.
Middle East Centre, St Anthony's College, Oxford University.

Published primary sources

Daily Express
Daily Mail
Manchester Guardian
The Times
Hansard: Debates of the British Parliament*:*
The Houses of Lords and Commons, 5th series.
The Foreign Relations of the United States, Washington DC.
Documents on German Foreign Policy, 1918–1945, vol. V, Washington: US Government Printing Office, 1953, series D, vol. 13, London: HMSO, 1964.
The Letters and Papers of Chaim Weizmann:
vol. VII, Leonard Stein, ed, Jerusalem: Israel Universities Press, 1975
vol. XIII Pinhas Ofer, ed., Jerusalem: Rutgers University, Transaction Books, 1978
vols XIV, XV, Camillo Dresner, ed., Jerusalem: Israel Universities Press/Transaction Books/Rutgers, 1978.
vol. XX, Michael J. Cohen, ed., Jerusalem: Israel Universities Press/Transaction Books/Rutgers, 1979.
Winston S. Churchill: companion volumes to the official biography, Martin Gilbert:
vol. IV/2, 1917–22, Boston: Houghton Mifflin, 1978.
vol. IV/3, 1917–22, Boston: Houghton Mifflin, 1978.
The Israel-Arab Reader: A Documentary History of the Middle East, Walter Laqueur and Barry Rubin, eds, New York: Penguin Books, 1984.

Online sources

Simon Anglim, "Orde Wingate and the Special Night Squads: A Feasible Policy for counter-terrorism?" www.academia.edu/645942/Orde_Wingate_and_the_Special_Night_Squads_A_Feasible_Policy_for_Counter-terrorism.

Richard Breitman, Norman Goda and Timothy Naftali, *Hitler's Shadow: Nazi War Criminals, U.S. Intelligence and the Cold War*, www.archives.gov/iwg/reports/hitlers-shadow.pdf.

Hellmuth Felmy, "German Exploitation of Arab Nationalist Movements in World War II", www.allworldwars.com/German-Exploitation-of-Arab-Nationalist-Movements-in-World-War-II.htm. (also in RG 338, The US National Archives, Maryland).

George Orwell, "Anti-Semitism in Britain," *The Contemporary Jewish Record*, London: April 1945. http://orwell.ru/library/articles/antisemitism/english/e_antib

Truman's desk diary for 1947. www.trumanlibrary.org/diary/page21.htm

The Vrba-Wexler report on Auschwitz-Birkenau, 1944: www.holocaustresearchproject.org/othercamps/auschproto.html

Memoirs, diaries

Charles Robert Ashbee, *A Palestine Notebook, 1918–1923*, New York: Doubleday/Page and Company, 1923.

Norman and Helen Bentwich, *Mandate Memoirs, 1918–1948*, London: Hogarth Press, 1965.

Charles Edward Callwell, ed., *Field Marshal Sir Henry Wilson, Bart, His Life and Diaries*, vol. II, London: Cassell, 1927.

Roger Courtney, *Palestine Policeman*, London: Jenkins, 1939.

David Garnett, ed., *The Letters of T. E. Lawrence*, London: Jonathan Cape, 1938.

E.C. Hodgkin, *Letters from Palestine, 1932–36*, Thomas Hodgkin, ed., London: Quarter Books, 1986.

Edward Keith-Roach, *Pasha of Jerusalem*, London: Radcliffe Press, 1994.

Norman and Jeanne MacKenzie, eds, *The Diary of Beatrice Webb*, vol. 4, *1924–1943*, "The Wheel of Life", London: Virago, in association with the LSE, 1985.

Nigel Nicolson, ed., *Harold Nicolson, Diaries and Letters, 1939–1945*, London: Collins, 1967.

Chaim Weizmann, *Trial and Error*, New York: Shocken Books, 1949.

Nigel West, ed., *The Guy Liddell Diaries*, vol. I: *1939–1942*, vol. II, *1942–1945*, London/New York: Routledge, 2005.

Books

Gilbert Achcar, *The Arabs and the Holocaust: The Arab-Israeli War of Narratives*, New York: Metropolitan Books/Henry Holt and Company, 2009.

Nir Arielli, *Fascist Italy and the Middle East, 1930–40*, Basingstoke: Palgrave Macmillan, 2010.

Ami Ayalon, *Reading Palestine*, Austin: University of Texas Press, 2004.

——, *The Press in the Arab Middle East: A History*, New York/Oxford: Oxford University Press, 1995.

Deborah Bernstein, *Constructing Boundaries: Jewish and Arab Workers in Mandatory Palestine*, Albany: State University of New York Press, 2000.

Nicholas Bethell, *The Palestine Triangle: The Struggle for the Holy Land, 1935–1948*, New York: Putnam, 1979.

Gideon Biger, *An Empire in the Holy Land, 1917–1929*, New York: St Martin's Press, 1994.

Eugene C. Black, *The Social Politics of Anglo-Jewry, 1880–1920*, Oxford: Blackwell, 1988.
Humphrey Bowman, *Middle East Window*, London: Longmans, Green & Co., 1942.
Richard Breitman, *Official Secrets: What the Nazis Planned, What the British and Americans Knew*, New York: Hill and Wang, 1998.
Richard Breitman and Allan J. Lichtman, *FDR and the Jews*, Cambridge, MA: Harvard University Press, 2013.
Richard Breitman, Norman Goda and Timothy Naftali, *U.S. Intelligence and the Nazis*, Cambridge: Cambridge University Press, 2005.
David Cesarani, ed., *The Making of Modern Anglo-Jewry*, Oxford: Basil Blackwell, 1989.
Hillel Cohen, *Army of Shadows: Palestinian Collaboration with Zionism, 1917–1948*, Berkeley/Los Angeles: University of California Press, 2008.
Michael J. Cohen, *Strategy and Politics in the Middle East, 1954–1960: Defending the Northern Tier*, London: Frank Cass, 2005.
——*Churchill and the Jews*, London: Frank Cass, first edition, 1985, revised paperback edition, 2003.
——*Fighting World War Three from the Middle East: Allied Contingency Plans, 1945–1954*, London: Frank Cass, 1997.
——*Truman and Israel*, Berkeley/Los Angeles: University of California Press, 1990.
——*The Origins and the Evolution of the Arab-Zionist Conflict*, Berkeley/Los Angeles: University of California Press, 1987.
——*Palestine and the Great Powers, 1945–1948*, Princeton: Princeton University Press, 1982.
——*Palestine: Retreat from the Mandate, 1936–1945*, London/New York: Paul Elek/Holmes and Meier, 1978.
Michael J. Cohen and Martin Kolinsky, eds, *Britain and the Middle East in the 1930s*, London: Macmillan, in association with King's College, 1992.
——*Demise of the British Empire in the Middle East: Britain's Responses to Nationalist Movements, 1943–1955*, London: Frank Cass, 1998.
Richard Crossman, *Palestine Mission*, New York: Harper, 1947.
John Darwin, *Britain & Decolonisation*, London: Macmillan, 1988.
——*The End of the British Empire*, Oxford: Blackwell, 1991.
Isaac Deutscher, *The Non-Jewish Jew*, London: Oxford University Press, 1968.
Douglas V. Duff, *Bailing with a Teaspoon*, London: John Long, 1953.
——*Palestine Unveiled*, London/Glasgow: Blackie & Son Limited, 1938.
——*Palestine Picture*, London: Hodder & Stoughton, 1936.
Blanche E. Dugdale, *Arthur James Balfour*, two volumes, London: Hutchinson, 1936.
Zvi Elpeleg, *Through the Eyes of the Mufti*, London: Vallentine Mitchell, 2009.
Todd M. Endelman, *Broadening Jewish History: Towards a Social History of Ordinary Jews*, Oxford/Portland: The Littman Library of Jewish Civilisation, 2011.
——*The Jews of Britain, 1656 to 2000*, Berkeley: University of California Press, 2002.
John Fisher, *Curzon and the British Empire in the Middle East, 1916–1919*, London: Frank Cass, 1999.
Geoffrey Furlonge, *Palestine is My Country: The Story of Musa Alami*, London: John Murray, 1969.
T. R. Fyvel, *George Orwell: A Personal Memoir*, London: Weidenfeld & Nicolson, 1982.
Yoav Gelber, *Jewish Palestinian Volunteering in the British Army During the Second World War*, vol. II, Jerusalem: Yad Yitschak Ben-Zvi, 1981 (in Hebrew).

Klaus Gensicke, *The Mufti of Jerusalem and the Nazis: The Berlin Years*, London: Vallentine Mitchell, 2011.

Israel Gershoni, *Dame and Devil: Egypt and Nazism, 1935–1940*, two volumes, Tel Aviv: Resling, 2012 (in Hebrew).

Israel Gershoni and James Jankowski, *Confronting Fascism in Egypt: Dictatorship versus Democracy in the 1930s*, Redwood City, CA: Stanford University Press, 2010.

Martin Gilbert, *Winston S. Churchill*, vol. IV, Boston: Houghton Mifflin, 1975.

——*Churchill and the Jews*, London: Simon & Schuster, 2007.

——*Auschwitz and the Allies*, New York: Holt, Rinehart, 1981.

Joseph Gorny, *The British Labour Movement and Zionism, 1917–1948*, London: Frank Cass, 1983.

Richard Griffiths, *Patriotism Perverted: Captain Ramsay, the Right Club and British anti-Semitism, 1939–40*, London: Constable, 1998.

Vasily Grossman, *Life and Fate*, London: Vintage Books, 2006.

Max Hastings, *Winston's War: Churchill 1940–1945*, New York: Alfred A. Knopf, 2010.

Jeffrey Herf, *Nazi Propaganda for the Arab World*, New Haven/London: Yale University Press, 2009.

Edward Horne, *A Job Well Done: A History of the Palestine Police Force, 1920–1948*, Sussex: The Book Guild, 2003 (first published in 1982 by the Palestine Police Force).

Michael Howard, *The Mediterranean Strategy in the Second World War*, New York: Praeger, 1968.

Sahar Huneidi, *A Broken Trust: Herbert Samuel, Zionism and the Palestinians*, London/New York: I.B. Tauris & Co., Ltd, 2001.

Albert M. Hyamson, *Palestine Under the Mandate, 1920–1948*, London: Methuen, 1950.

Michael Ignatieff, *Isaiah Berlin: A Life*, New York: Metropolitan Books, 1998.

Amitzur Ilan, *Bernadotte in Palestine*, London: Macmillan, 1989.

Taysir Jbara, *Palestinian Leader Hajj Amin al-Husayni: The Mufti of Jerusalem*, Princeton: Kingston Press, 1985.

Keith Jeffrey, *The Secret History of MI5, 1909–1949*, New York: Penguin Press, 2010.

J.M.N. Jeffries, *Palestine: The Reality*, Westport, CT: Hyperion Press, 1976 (first published by Longmans, 1939).

Mustafa Kabha, *The Palestinian Press as a Shaper of Public Opinion, 1929–1939: Writing up a Storm*, London: Vallentine Mitchell, 2007.

Sharman Kadish, *Bolsheviks and British Jews*, London: Frank Cass, 1992.

Charles S. Kamen, *Little Common Ground: Arab Agriculture and Jewish Settlement in Palestine, 1920–1948*, Pittsburgh: University of Pittsburgh Press, 1991.

Issa Khalaf, *Politics in Palestine: Arab Factionalism and Social Disintegration, 1939–1948*, Albany: State University of New York Press, 1991.

Aaron Kleimann, *Foundations of British Policy in the Arab World: The Cairo Conference of 1921*, Baltimore: Johns Hopkins Press, 1970.

Martin Kolinsky, *Law, Order and Riots in Mandatory Palestine, 1928–35*, London: Macmillan, 1993.

——*Britain's War in the Middle East: Strategy and Diplomacy, 1936–1942*, London: Macmillan, 1999.

Jennie Lebel, *The Mufti of Jerusalem Haj-Amin el-Husseini and National-Socialism* (translated from the Serbian by Paul Münch), Belgrade: Čigoja štampa, 2007.

Mark LeVine and Gershon Shafir, *Struggle and Survival in Palestine/Israel*, Berkeley: University of California Press, 2012.
Fritz Liebrich, *Britain's Naval and Political Reaction to the Illegal Immigration of Jews to Palestine, 1945–1948*, London: Routledge, 2005.
Meir Litvak and Esther Webman, *From Empathy to Denial: Arab Responses to the Holocaust*, New York: Columbia University Press, 2009.
Zachary Lockman, *Comrades and Enemies: Arab and Jewish Workers in Palestine, 1906–1948*, Berkeley: University of California Press, 1996.
John Lord, *Duty, Honor, Empire: The Life and Times of Colonel Richard Meinertzhagen*, New York: Random House, 1970.
Klaus-Michael Mallman and Martin Cüppers, *Nazi Palestine: The Plans for the Extermination of the Jews in Palestine*, New York: Enigma Books, 2010.
Philip Mattar, *The Mufti of Jerusalem: Al-Hajj Amin al-Husayni and the Palestinian National Movement*, New York: Columbia University Press, 1988.
Jacob Metzer, *The Divided Economy of Mandatory Palestine*, Cambridge: Cambridge University Press, 1998.
Ylana N. Miller, *Government and Society in Rural Palestine, 1920–1948*, Austin: University of Texas Press, 1985.
Elizabeth Monroe, *Britain's Moment in the Middle East, 1914–1956*, London: Chatto & Windus, 1964.
Moshe Mossek, *Palestine Immigration Policy under Sir Herbert Samuel: British, Zionist, and Arab Attitudes*, London: Frank Cass, 1978.
Nasser Eddin Nashashibi, *Jerusalem's Other Voice: Ragheb Nashashibi and Moderation in Palestinian Politics, 1920–1948*, Exeter: Ithaca Press, 1990.
Francis Emily Newton, *Fifty Years in Palestine*, Wrotham: Coldharbour Press, 1948.
Francis R. Nicosia, *The Third Reich and the Palestine Question*, London: I.B. Tauris, 1985.
Götz Nordbruch, *Nazism in Syria and Lebanon*, London: Routledge, 2009.
Roger Owen, ed., *Studies in the Economic and Social History of Palestine in the Nineteenth and Twentieth Centuries*, Carbondale: Southern Illinois University Press, 1982.
Yehoshua Porath, *The Emergence of the Palestinian-Arab National Movement, 1918–1929*, London: Frank Cass, 1974.
——— *The Palestinian Arab National Movement: From Riots to Rebellion*, vol. two, *1929–1939*, London: Frank Cass, 1977.
Jehuda Reinharz, *Chaim Weizmann: The Making of a Statesman*, New York/Oxford: Oxford University Press, 1993.
James Renton, *The Zionist Masquerade: The Birth of the Anglo-Zionist Alliance, 1914–1918*, Basingstoke/New York: Palgrave Macmillan, 2007.
Yaacov Reuveni, *The Mandatory Administration in Palestine: 1920–1948, A Historical Political Analysis*, Ramat-Gan: Bar-Ilan University, 1993.
David Reynolds, *In Command of History: Churchill Fighting and Writing the Second World War*, London/New York: Penguin, 2004.
Norman A. Rose, *The Gentile Zionists: A Study in Anglo-Zionist Diplomacy, 1929–1939*, London: Frank Cass, 1973.
———ed. *"Baffy": The Diaries of Blanche Dugdale, 1936–1947*, London: Vallentine Mitchell, 1973.
———*A Senseless, Squalid War: Voices from Palestine, 1945–1948*, London: The Bodley Head, 2009.

Howard Sachar, *Europe Leaves the Middle East: 1936–1954*, London: Allen Lane, 1974.

Tom Segev, *One Palestine, Complete*, New York: Metropolitan Books, 2000.

Nadav G. Shelef, *Evolving Nationalism: Homeland, Identity and Religion in Israel, 1925-2005*, Ithaca, NY: Cornell University Press, 2010.

A.J. Sherman, *Mandate Days: British Lives in Palestine, 1918–1948*, New York: Thames & Hudson, 1998.

Barbara J. Smith, *The Roots of Separatism in Palestine: British Economic Policy, 1920–1929*, Syracuse: Syracuse University Press, 1993.

Meir Sompolinsky, *Britain and the Holocaust: The Failure of Anglo-Jewish Leadership*, Brighton: Sussex Academic Press, 1999.

Kenneth W. Stein, *The Land Problem in Palestine, 1917–1939*, Chapel Hill: University of North Carolina Press, 1984.

Leonard Stein, *The Balfour Declaration*, London: Vallentine Mitchell, 1961.

Ronald Storrs, *Orientations*, London: Nicholson & Watson, 1937.

Richard Toye, *Lloyd George & Churchill: Rivals for Greatness*, London: Macmillan, 2007.

Barbara Tuchman, *The Bible and the Sword: England and Palestine from the Bronze Age to Balfour*, London: Alvin Redman, 1956.

Bernard Wasserstein, *Herbert Samuel: A Political Life*, Oxford: Clarendon Press, 1992.

——*Britain and the Jews of Europe, 1939–1945*, London: Institute of Jewish Affairs/ Clarendon Press, 1979.

——*The British in Palestine: The Mandatory Government and the Arab-Jewish Conflict, 1917–1929*, London: Royal Historical Society, 1978.

Martin Watts, *The Jewish Legion and the First World War*, Basingstoke/New York: Palgrave Macmillan, 2004.

Josiah C. Wedgwood, *The Seventh Dominion*, London: Labour Publishing Company, 1928.

Gerhard Weinberg, *Germany, Hitler, and World War II*, Cambridge: Cambridge University Press, 1995.

Mary C. Wilson, *King Abdullah, Britain and the Making of TransJordan*, Cambridge: Cambridge University Press, 1987.

R.D. Wilson, *Cordon and Search*, Aldershot: Gale & Polden, 1949.

David Wyman, *The Abandonment of the Jews*, New York: Pantheon Books, 1984.

Journal articles and chapters in books

Ami Ayalon, "Egyptian Intellectuals versus Fascism and Nazism in the 1930s", in Uriel Dann, ed., *The Great Powers in the Middle East, 1919–1939*, New York/ London: Holmes & Meier, 1988, pp. 391–404.

Daniel Carpi, "The Mufti of Jerusalem, Amin el-Husseini, and his Diplomatic Activity during World War II (October 1941-July 1943)", *Studies in Zionism*, vol. 7, Spring 1983, pp. 101–31.

Michael J. Cohen, "Zionism and British Imperialism II: Imperial Financing in Palestine", *Journal of Israeli History*, vol. 30/ September 2011, pp. 115–39.

——"Was the Balfour Declaration at risk in 1923? Zionism and British Imperialism", *Journal of Israeli History*, vol. 29/1, March 2010, pp. 79–98.

——"Churchill and Auschwitz: End of Debate?", *Modern Judaism*, vol. 26/2, May 2006, pp. 127–40.

―――"British Strategy in the Wake of the Abyssinian Crisis, 1936–39", in Michael J. Cohen and Martin Kolinsky, eds, *Britain and the Middle East in the 1930s*, London: Macmillan, 1982, pp. 21–40.

―――"Why Britain Left: The End of the Mandate", *Wiener Library Bulletin*, 1978, vol. xxxi, nos. 45/46, pp. 74–86.

―――"British Strategy and the Palestine Question, 1936–39", *Journal of Contemporary History*, vol. 7/3–4, July-October 1972, pp. 157–83.

Anthony R. de Luca, "'*Der Grossmufti*' in Berlin: The Politics of Collaboration", *International Journal of Middle East Studies*, 10/1, February 1979, pp. 125–38.

Ulrike Freitag and Israel Gershoni, "The Politics of Memory: The Necessity for Historical Investigation into Arab Responses to Fascism and Nazism", *Geschichte und Gesellschaft*, vol. 37, 2011, pp. 311–31.

Evyatar Friesel, "British Officials on the Situation in Palestine, 1923", Middle Eastern Studies, vol. 23, no. 2, April 1987, pp. 194–210.

Israel Gershoni, "Rejecting the West: The Image of the West in the Teachings of the Muslim Brotherhood, 1928–39", in Uriel Dann, ed., *The Great Powers in the Middle East, 1919–1939*, New York/London: Holmes & Meier, 1988, pp. 370–90.

―――"Beyond Anti-Semitism: Egyptian Responses to German Nazism and Italian Fascism in the 1930s", *EUI Working Paper RSC*, 2001/32.

Andreas Hillgruber, "The Third Reich and the Near and Middle East, 1933–39", in Uriel Dann, ed., *The Great Powers in the Middle East, 1919–1939*, New York/London: Holmes & Meier, 1988, pp. 274–82.

Sahar Huneidi, "Was the Balfour Declaration Reversible? The Colonial Office and Palestine, 1921–23", *Journal of Palestine Studies*, vol. 27/2, Winter 1998, pp. 23–41.

Mustafa Kabha, "The Palestinian National Movement and its Attitude toward the Fascist and Nazi Movements, 1925–1945", *Geschichte und Gesellschaft*, vol. 37, 2011, pp. 437–50.

Paul Keleman, "Zionism and the British Labour Party", *Social History*, vol. 21/1, January 1906, pp. 72–87.

Klaus-Michael Mallmann and Martin Cüppers, "Elimination of the Jewish National Home in Palestine: The *Einsatzkommando* of the Panzer Army Africa, 1942", *Yad Vashem Studies*, vol. 35/1, 2007, pp. 1–31.

Jacob Metzer, "Economic Structure and National Goals: The Jewish National Home in Interwar Palestine", *Journal of Economic History*, 38/1, March 1978, pp. 101–19.

George Orwell, "Anti-Semitism in Britain", *Contemporary Jewish Record*, London: April 1945, pp. 332–41.

Mayir Vereté, "The Balfour Declaration and its Makers", *Middle Eastern Studies*, January 1970, pp. 48–76.

Peter Wien, "Coming to Terms with the Past: German Academia and Historical Relations between the Arab Lands and Nazi Germany", *International Journal of Middle East Studies*, vol. 42, 2010, pp. 311–21.

Index

6th Airborne Division 462–63
7th Dominion League 22, 25
'Abd al-Hadi, 'Awni 43, 402, 408
'Abd al-Qader al-Muzaffar 403
Abd el-Rahman Azzam-bey 434
Abdullah, Emir of Trans-Jordan: ascension of 29, 46; Churchill on 179; at London conference 297; Nashashibi alliance with 372; and Arab rebellion 251, 256; and Frances Newton 206; and Peel partition plan 267–68
absentee landlords 135
Abwehr 387, 408, 424
Achcar, Gilbert 305n31, 384–85, 437
Acheson, Dean 452, 456
Afrika Korps: defeat of 307; formation of 387; threat to Egypt 310, 317, 391–92; Yishuv anxiety about 326
agrarian reform 142, 223, 227
Air Ministry 91, 290
Al-Ahram 390, 404
al-Alami, Musa 367, 381n50, 405–6, 408
al-Aqsa mosque 215, 269, 428
al-Barudi, Fahkri 388
Al-Difa' 138, 395–98, 415n67, 416
Alexandria, all-Arab conference in 377–78
Alexandria Protocol 378–79
al-Faruqi, Muhammad 45
al-Futuwwa 388
Aliens Act 1905 5–6
Ali Maher Pasha 297, 300
al-Jami'ah al-'Arabiyyah 138, 279–80, 385–86, 397, 400
Al-Karmil 137–38, 145n266, 395
Allenby, Edmund 75, 84–85, 89, 117, 166, **Plate 3**
al-Liwa 398, 404

al-Muthanna Club 388, 409, 411
Amé, General Cesare 423–24
American Jewry: Churchill on 188; fundraising from 167; and Jewish Legion 92n22
American Zionists: and 1939 White Paper 314; British wariness of 52, 187–91, 226, 229–31, 300, 327–28, 486; and Dead Sea minerals concession 204; lobbying Truman 451–52, 475; opposition to Weizmann 240; as Weizmann's trump card 324; in World War Two 325, 328–29, 336
Amery, Leo: on anti-Semitism 485; as Colonial Secretary 170, 174–76, 178, 187–91; as Gentile Zionist 22; influence over Palestine 192; letter to Carson 11; meeting with Churchill and Weizmann 295; on Philby scheme 376; and Dead Sea minerals concession 201; and Peel partition plan 287; and White Paper of 1930 230, 233–34; and White Paper of 1939 302
Andrews, Lewis 268–69, 407
Anglo-American Committee on Palestine 383, 446, 450–54, 463–65
Anglo–Egyptian Treaty of 1936 45, 161n25, 446–47
Anglo-Jewry: funding of Zionist project 168; and the Holocaust 348; Montagu on 50; political influence of 78; and Russian immigrants 27–29, 31–32; in Samuel's administration 100; as voting bloc 235, 238
anti-Judaism, Mufti's use of term 422
anti-Semitism: and the Allies in World War Two 352–53; analyses of 19–21; in Arabic press 137–38; and Arab Nazi sympathies 383; and British

politics 2, 5–10, 16, 29, 68–69, 171–72, 203; in British society 5, 33, 193, 484; in Egypt 393; and English literature 11–12; and Gentile Zionism 24; in Hope-Simpson's letters 222; and Jewish "separateness" 13–14; in Palestine 397
anti-Zionism: among British in Palestine 103; and anti-Semitism 68, 428; in British politics 70, 127, 203
Antonescu, Ion 431
Antonius, George 58, 103, 112, 115, 162n57, 468
Antonius, Katie 112, 468, 482n14
anxiety, 200 days of 327
ANZAC military forces 308, 322
Arab Agency 158
Arab Blood Society 141
Arab Brigade 425
Arab Bureau 79
Arab Executive: on "black letter" 239; Chancellor on 214; and land sales to Zionists 136, 144n70; Zionist protests against 266
Arab Federation: proposals for 258, 371, 373–77; RIIA report on 375
Arab-German Battalion (DAL) 422–25
Arabic press in Egypt 390, 402
Arabic press in Palestine: anti-Semitism in 397–99; and Arab rebellion 101, 136, 271, 299; Christian Arabs in 101; and Fascism 394, 396; and general strike 250; on Jewish immigration 396–97; and land sales 136–37, 279; and Mufti of Jerusalem 384, 399–400; ownership of 395–96; readership of 401–2; stance on World War Two 400–401, 489
Arab–Jewish conference of 1939 see London conference
Arab labour: after Arab rebellion 262n119; in Dead Sea minerals concession 206; Zionist boycott of 199, 223, 233, 237
Arab labour movement 284n7
Arab land sales: beginnings of 136; compensation for 227, 239; opposition to 136, 279–80; press articles on 397; social effects of 140–41; in White Paper of 1930 228
Arab League: establishment of 378–79; and Mufti 434; and Palestinian cause 360, 372; and White Paper of 1939 446
Arab Nation (organisation) 418, 420

Arab nationalism: British views on 52, 373; and civil service 101; emergence of 394; German views of 369–70; Lampson's survey of 369; and Nazi Germany 386–87, 409–10; Samuel's neutralisation of 112; Zionist denial of 266
Arab rebellion of 1936: Arab states' intervention in 255–59; beginnings of 248–49; British reactions to 245, 254; end of 259–60; and Foreign Office 97; general strike in 249–50; and land sales 137, 140; in rural areas 250–51; suppression of 239
Arab rebellion of 1937–38: and anti-British nationalism 309; areas controlled by 272; and British counterinsurgency 274–77; damage caused by 263–64, 270, 277; German reactions to 404, 408; internal disputes in 281–82; and Peel partition plan 290–91
Arab riots of 1920 24, 81, 86–87, 111
Arab riots of 1921: outbreak of 116; Samuel's response to 98
Arabs: attempted negotiations with British 45–46; British attitudes to 42–43; see also Palestinian Arabs
Arab states: and Anglo-American Committee 453–55; appeal to HAC 260; British appeasement of 3–4, 159, 240, 264–65, 273, 290, 487; British negotiations with 255–56; delegation to Arab–Jewish conference 297, 299–301; during World War Two 360, 371; intervention in Palestine 97, 245, 253, 255, 292; mediating with Allies 385; and Peel partition plan 268; post-war lobbying of 376–78; rulers named by British 46; war with Israel 492; and White Paper of 1939 362, 364–65
Arab United Bureau 266
Armenians, Turkish massacre of 48
Arnold, Lord 174
Asefat Nivcharim 102
Ashbee, Charles 82–83, 98, 104–5, 118–19, 149
Atatürk, Mustafa Kemal 63–64, 66, 72n7, 152
Atlit camp 474
Attlee, Clement: as Deputy PM 348, 366; and Anglo-American Committee 456; and Palestine garrison 447; and

Index

Peel partition plan 287; and Zionist uprising 464, 471
Auchinleck, General Sir Claude 327
Auschwitz-Birkenau: Allied knowledge of 337, 339, 341–42; Mufti's visit to 425–26; proposed bombing of 349–54, 491
Australia: Jewish refugees transported to 35n63; military role in World War Two 308
Axis powers: guarantee of Arab independence 418, 420–21; *see also* Italy; Nazi Germany

Bagallay, Lacy 293, 365–66
Baghdad: pogrom of Jews in 411, 417n130
Baldwin, Stanley 149, 172, 180n28, 191, 222, 230
Balfour, Arthur **Plate 3**; on colonialism 39; death of 209n18; as Gentile Zionist 22–24; on Jewish refugees 6; on League of Nations mandate 485; on Palestinian Arabs 55–56; role in Declaration 44; Weizmann's lobbying of 123; on Zionism 11, 45; and Hebrew University 79; and Morgenthau's mission 48; and Zionist loan 187–91
Balfour Declaration: American support for 49–51; Arab rejection of 127; British campaign against 146, 149; Chancellor on 214, 218; clarification of 131; commitment to 157–58; consequences of 56–57, 159; Devonshire on 53; Edwin Montagu on 31, 68; motivations of 5, 32–33, 44, 67–68, 484; Mufti's conspiracy theory of 429, 437–38; possible abrogation of 70–71, 122, 126; post-war opposition to 68; as promoting British interests 5, 44, 67–68; publication prohibited 78; as reward for Jews 46–47; Weizmann on 71
Barker, General Sir Evelyn 466, 468–70
Bateman, Charles 296
Battershill, William 275
Beaverbrook, Lord 29, 69, 73n27, 146
Bedouin 42–43, 108, 197, 269, 394
Beeley, Harold 480
Begin, Menahem 470
Beith, John 479–80
Bell, Gertrude 197
Belloc, Hilaire 9–10, 20

Ben-Gurion, David **Plate 6, Plate 10**; on 1930 White Paper 244n69, at London conference 297–98, 300; challenge to Weizmann's leadership 336; during World War Two 316–17; on Jewish Division 312, 319–20, 336; post-war role of 354, 356; and Anglo-American Committee 451; and Arab rebellion 278; and JRM 462, 467; and Peel partition plan 265, 287
Bentwich, Norman 103–5, 119, 214
Ben-Zvi, Yitschak 103
Bergen-Belsen death camp 468
Berger, Gottlob 433
Berlin, Isaiah: on anti-Semitism 19–21, 353; description of Palestine 113; election to All Soul's College 484
Bevin, Ernest: negotiations with US over Palestine 449–50, 452, 455–57; reputation as anti-Semite 2, 244n73, 450–51, 491; and decline of Empire 443–44; and deportation of refugees 475; and Middle East 446, 448; and relinquishment of mandate 457–58; and trade union caucus 226, 234–35; and Zionist uprising 462–63
Bicknell, R. H. 200
Biltmore Plan 329, 336–37
Black and Tans 213, 240n1
Blake, George Stanfield 200
Blue Shirts 391
Board of Deputies of British Jews 32, 345
Boer War 8, 10
Bols, Louis 77, 84–85, 87, 89
Bolshevism: Churchill's antipathy to 121; Jewish conspiracy theory of *see* Judeo-Bolshevik bogey; and League of British Jews 32
Bonar Law, Andrew 146, 149, 160n16, 172
book debts 173
Bosnian Jews 433
Bosnian Moslems, in Waffen SS 412n7, 432–34
Bourguiba, Habib 424
Bowman, Humphrey 107, 109, 130, 253
Bracken, Brendan 315, 342
Brandeis, Louis 49–51, 59n46, 204, 226, 231
Breitman, Richard 335, 339
Britain: 1926 General Strike in 174; anti-Semitic organisations in 16–19; anti-Semitic riots in 477, 484; Arab

public opinion of 367–68; attitudes to Palestine in 355; during World War Two 310–11, 314, 317–18, 326; Great Depression in 226–27, 229; history of Jews in 5 (*see also* Anglo-Jewry); imperial mission of 38–39, 42, 94; "Jewish problem" in 12–14; Jewish refugees to *see* Jewish refugees; in League of Nations 97
British Arabophiles 42, 108, 197
British armed forces: anti-Semitism in 79–85, 468–69; Arab desertions from 426; attitude to Middle East 61–63, 76; and Balfour Declaration 76, 79–80, 91; pro-Arab attitudes of 81, 85, 90–91; on strategic value of Palestine 150–53; and Ten Year Rule 246
British capital: and development of Palestine 168, 172, 175; and economic concessions in Palestine 195
British Commonwealth, Palestine joining 22, 25
British Empire: and colonial self-reliance 164–65, 174; end of expansion 61; German and Italian threat to 245–48; "informal" 307; military force behind 41; new territories in Middle East 41–42; political instruments in 40; post-war disintegration of 442–43, 445; supposed Jewish conspiracy against 313
British evacuation of Palestine: announcement of 479–80; criticism of 458; and decolonization 446; discussion with US on 452; and Egypt 447; and India 4, 491–92; post-war consensus on 453; process of 480–81; public clamour for 477
British forces in Palestine: and Anglo-Egyptian Treaty 161n25; and Arab rebellion 251–52, 259, 272, 275–76; Churchill's desire to repatriate 314, 316–17, 319; during World War Two 311; numbers of 41, 212–13, 217; political knowledge of 471; post-war increase in 447, 462–63; and Wailing Wall riots 216–17; and Zionist uprising 463–64, 468
British General Staff 43, 76, 150–52
British in Palestine: and Arab rebellion 253, 274–75; attitudes to Yishuv 101–2; demoralisation of 148; failure to protect Arabs 141–42; preference for Arabs 102–5, 107–8; social lives of 95–96, 112
British Military Intelligence Service 283
British Palestine administration: appointing Arabs to 364; area of control 263; budget of 166, 173–74, 239; end of 481; establishment of 96–97; and Jewish Agency 77, 127; on land ordinances 138; loss of control 472–73, 478–79; security forces of 91, 170, 276–77, 294 (*see also* Palestine police); and Zionists 125, 132, 170
British Union of Fascists (BUF) 13–14, 16, 358n41, 484
The Britons 29
Brook, Sir Norman 85, 322
Bulgarian Jews 431–32
Bureau of the Arab Revolt 281
Burr, Sidney 274
Bury, Howard 202
Butcher, Sir John (the first Baron Danesfort) 194–95
Butler, Neville 325
Butler, R. A. 300, 325
Byrnes, James 452

Cadogan, Sir Alexander 352, 480
Cafferata, Raymond 213
Cairo: anti-Zionism and anti-Semitism in 79–80; Foreign Office officials in 52; Middle East Command in *see* Middle East Command; Moyne's assassination in 23
Carson, Sir Edward 11
Central Committee for the Jihad 269
cereals, overproduction of 136
Chamberlain, Austen 189, 230, 236
Chamberlain, Neville: as Chancellor 180n28, 191, 247; Churchill's attacks on 302–3; negotiations with Germany 263; rearmament programme of 309; and Arab–Jewish talks 297, 301; and Peel partition plan 287–88
Chancellor, Sir John **Plate 5**; on future of Palestine 297; as High Commissioner in Palestine 97, 103, 214; on Jewish immigration 219, 225; resignation of 237; and elective bodies 216; and Wailing Wall riots 217–20; and White Paper of 1930 235, 486
Chatfield, Admiral Sir Ernie 248
chemical industry, in Palestine 193
Chesterton, A. K. 16–17

Chesterton, G. K. 9, 13, 16, 20
Churchill, Winston **Plate 2**; alienation from Zionism 354–55, 378, 488; on American Jewry 52; on American meddling in Palestine 448; on Arabs 108–9, 311; on Balfour Declaration 157; as Chancellor of the Exchequer 170, 173–78, 184–85; as Colonial Secretary 118, 120–22, 131; correspondence with Roosevelt 313–14; defending Rutenberg concession 195–96; feud with Leo Amery 191; as Gentile Zionist 22–24; imperialism of 62–63, 443–44, 447; on Indians 39; influence over Palestine 64, 192; on Jewish refugees 491; on Jewish "separateness" 14–15; Nazi propaganda about 428; as Prime Minister 303, 309, 312, 316, 326; on White Paper of 1939 162n53, 301–2, 366, 487; on White Paper of 1939; and anti-Semitism 2, 13, 84–85; and civil service appointments 100–101; and Duke of Westminster 18; and evacuation of Palestine 64, 477; and Gallipolli 72n7; and intelligence services 339; and invasion of Syria 374; and Jewish Brigade 330–31; and Jewish Division 321–23, 327–28; and "Judeo-Bolshevism" 28; and Miles Lampson 368–69; and OETA 84; and Peel partition plan 287–89; and Philby Plan 375; and repatriation of Palestine garrison 311; and Russian intervention 26; and separation of Transjordan 29, 179; and Ten Year Rule 246; and the Holocaust 337, 340, 348–52; and Zionist loan 187–88, 190
Ciano, Count 387, 405–6, 410, 421–23
CID (Committee of Imperial Defence): on Arab states 264–65, 376; on defence of Suez 43; on Far East 248; Field's remarks to 246; on importance of Palestine 43–44, 71; on Middle East 263
CIGS (Chief of Imperial General Staff): Wilson as 39, 61, 63, 66, 81, 84; in World War Two 374
civil service, ethnic balance of 100–101
Clayton, Gilbert 72, 79–80, 106–7, 151, 153–54
Clifford, Clark 449
Cohen, Leonard 170

Cohen, Ya'akov 402–3, 416n91
Cold War 360, 434, 445
colonialism, new form of 96–97
Colonial Office: and Arab rebellion 255–57, 268–69, 275; attitude to Arabs 109–10, 328; attitude to Zionists 225; case for Balfour Declaration 153–55; Churchill at 66; and economic concessions 192–93, 200–201, 206–7; and evacuation of Palestine 478; and immigration quotas 132–33; influence on Passfield 221, 225; interventions in Palestine 53, 124–25; on Jewish Brigade 330; on Jewish Division 315; and Jewish immigration 297, 312; Meinertzhagen at 25; and Morrison-Grady plan 454; opposition to Zionist loan 186; and Palestine loan 170–71; and Peel plan 287, 289–90; responsibility for Palestine 97, 120, 122, 166; on Samuel's democratic reforms 99–100; and Wailing Wall riots 218–19; and White Paper of 1930 230–33, 235
colonial rule, indirect 40
Congreve, General 39, 75, 81, 83–84, 91, 122
Conjoint Committee of British Jews 22
Conservative Party: anti-Semitism among 16, 18; opposition to Zionism in 29, 68, 128, 150, 171; press aligned with 69; reassessment of Palestine policy 72, 146–47
Cornwallis, Kinahan 378, 411
COS (Chiefs of Staff): on 1920 riots 216; on Arab states 453–54; budgeting by 246; on defence of Egypt 308; and disarmament of illegal organizations 451; on Italian threat 247, 263, 309; on Normandy landings 310; on Palestine garrison 317; on withdrawal from Palestine 151, 447–48; and Zionist uprising 464
Cousinhood, Anglo-Jewish 30, 32
Cranborne, Viscount 328
Creech-Jones, Arthur 479
Crocker, General Sir John 477–78
Crossman, Richard 112, 450–51, 466
Cunningham, Alan 463, 467, 471–74, 476–77, **Plate 16**
Curzon, Earl: expressing support for Zionism 33, 44; on financing of Jewish colonisation 155, 207, 485; objections to Balfour Declaration 50;

world outlook of 67–68; and dismissal of OETA 88–90; and Palestine policy 72, 149, 153, 158
Cyprus, detention camps in 474
Czechoslovakia: crisis in 263–64, 305n27; Nazi atrocities in 344

Daily Express 73n27, 146, 155
Daily Mail 29, 69, 146–47
DAL (Deutsch-Arabische Lehrabteilung) *see* Arab-German Batallion
Dalton, Hugh 461
Danesfort, Lord 204–5
D'Arcy, J. C. 464–65
Dardanelles campaign 45, 72–73n19, 126
Dead Sea: minerals concession 193, 199–201, 207, 485; Newton's oil exploration at 206–7
December 1942 Declaration 342–47
decolonization 442, 444–46, 457
Deedes, Wyndham 117–19, 124–25
Defence Party 267, 278, 283, 362, 385
de Gaulle, Charles 323, 374
de Haas, Jacob 51, 59n53
Democratic Party (US) 448, 450, 454–55, 457
Dempsey, General Charles 471
Department of Education, Arabs in 100
Department of Public Works, ethnic balance of 100
de Rothschild, Edmund 183
de Rothschild, James 92n14, 202, 211n68, 345
Deutscher, Isaac 27
Dewey, Thomas 456–57, 460n45
Diaspora Jewry, emancipation of 21
Dill, John 252, 260
Disraeli, Benjamin 6
Diston, Adam 14
Dizingoff, Meir **Plate 2**
Döhle, Walter 404, 408
Dome of the Rock 104, 215
Domvil, Sir Barry 16
Downie, Harold 289–90, 313
DPs (displaced persons) 446, 449, 459n23, 473–75
Dubois, Josiah 350
Duff, Douglas 58, 108, 213
Dugdale, Blanche "Baffy": on Churchill 288–89; support for Zionism 22; as Zionist informant 189–90, 262n33; and White Paper of 1930 230
Duke of Buccleuch 203

Duke of Devonshire 148, 150, 156–59
Duke of Westminster 17–18
Dunkirk 310, 313, 316–18, 332n12

Earl of Birkenhead 203–4
Earl of Lytton 206, 211n75
Earl of Plymouth 205–6
Eastern European Jews, in World War Two 431–33
Eastwood, Christopher 140, 286n50
economic absorptive capacity principle: in 1922 White Paper 127, 129–30; in 1930 White Paper 228; in 1939 White Paper 301; application of 132, 134; in "black letter" 237; Churchill on 295–96; Hope-Simpson on 223; replacement by Peel Commission 265
Economic Board for Palestine (EBP) 170, 201
Eden, Anthony: anti-Semitism of 2, 353; as Foreign Secretary 246–47, 290, 312; as Prime Minister 42; resignation from Chamberlain's government 261n7; in World War Two 374–75; and Jewish Division 319, 321, 325; and proposed bombing of Auschwitz 350; and the Holocaust 344–46
Eder, David 119, 142n11
effendis: absentee landowning 135, 137, 139, 266; in Egypt 389; and White Paper of 1939 362
Egypt: after World War Two 445–46; and Arab Federation 377; British garrison in 3–4, 261n6, 247, 308; evacuation of 161n29; Fascist sympathies in 388–93, 489; in "informal empire" 307; Italian attack on 318; Mufti of Jerusalem in 437; national identity of 394; Nazi plans for 426–27; negotiations with Arab states in 301; Palestine as strategic buffer of 67, 153–54, 446; reinforcements for 263; volatility of 151
Egyptian Expeditionary Force (EEF) 76, 79, 122, 161
Eichmann, Adolf 408, 425
Einsatzgruppe 340, 425–27, 439n37
Eire (Irish Free State) 120
electrification: and Arab communities 196–97; British opposition to 198; concession for *see* Rutenberg electricity concession
el-Mahdi, Muin 408
Emery, E. P. 109

Enigma machine 341
Epstein, Eliahu 456–57
Ethiopia, conquest of 212, 245–46, 309, 316, 396, 405, 414n50
Ettel, Erwin 420, 425
European Jews: Allied policy towards 353–56; appeals for rescue of 307, 325, 345, 348–50; Arab attitudes to 403; British intelligence on 341; extermination of 336–38, 342–44, 383, 425, 429, 489–90 (*see also* Holocaust)
Exodus incident 474–76, 490
Eyres, H. M. 325

Fabian Socialists 47, 221
Faisal, King of Syria 85
Far East: air communications to 45; strategic priority of 246, 248, 308
farmers' parties 266
Farouk, King of Egypt 389–90, 423
Fascism: F. Nashabibi's pamphlet against 402; influence on Arab world 388–91, 396, 399, 404, 414n38; Mufti's attempted adaptation to Islam 407
Fawzi el-Qawukji 251, 260, 273, 422, 438n19
Faysal, King of Iraq 46
Fehmy, Helmuth 424
fellahin: agricultural methods of 139; and Arab rebellion 250; British attitudes to 108; land sales by 135, 137; proletarianization of 136; revolt of 272; and Zionism 266
Felmy, Helmuth 411, 422, 425
Field, Frederick 246
Filastin 271, 385, 395–98, 400–401, 415n66
Final Solution *see* European Jews, extermination of
Fitzgerald, William James 481–82
Foggia air base 349
Foreign Office: and Arab nationalism 370, 392; concerns on Jewish immigration 255; and constitutional proposals 361, 365–67, 371; and the Holocaust 345–47, 350–52; inquiry into 1920 riots 87; on Jewish Division 320–21, 325; and Jewish refugees 476; and negotiations with Arab states 255–56, 258–59, 478; and OETA 76; and Peel plan 289–91; responsibility for Palestine 97, 166, 231, 236, 245; on Syrian invasion 374

France: defeat in World War Two 311; sheltering the Mufti 269–70; *see also* Free French forces; Vichy France
Francis, Joseph 404
Franks, Sir Oliver 444
Free French forces 323, 379
Free Officers movement (Egypt) 391
Frontier Force (Arab Legion) 176–77, 419, 422
Fuad, King of Egypt 390
Fuller, J. F. C. 16
Fyvel, T. R. 12

Galilee 96, 145, 267–68
GC 22; and anti-Semitism 24, 27, 30; and Bolshevik Revolution 26
Gentlemen's Agreements 292, 304n3, 393, 414n50
German Jews: and Balfour Declaration 54; Bolsheviks categorised as 27, 69; immigration to Palestine 249, 386–87, 397, 407
Germany: exports to Palestine 386–87; Nazi regime in *see* Nazi Germany; potash monopoly of 202–3, 205; Zionist approaches to 52
Gershoni, Israel 389, 395; and James Jankowski 389, 391–92, 394
Ghazi, King of Iraq 257
Gilbert, Martin 14, 337, 339, 352
Giles, Arthur 435–36
GOC (General Officer Commanding) Palestine: High Commissioner veto over 97; inquiry into 1920 riots 87
Goebbels, Joseph 421
Golden Square 368, 409
Gold Standard 174, 227
Gort, Viscount 435–36
Gosling, Harry 234
"government gangs" strategy 277
Grady, Henry 454
Grattan Bushe, Henry 103–4
Greater Syria: Abdullah's ambition for 268; after World War Two 394; British conquest of 75; British military support for 85, 87; and Fascist movements 388; Mufti's ambition for 420; Turkish possession of 48–49
Greece: British backing against Turkey 61–65; during World War Two 321–23, 368, 457
Green Shirts 391
Grey, Sir Edward 24
Grigg, P. J. 331

Grobba, Fritz 408–10, 419–21
Gromyko, Andrei 490
Gruner, Dov 472
Gurney, Henry 467, 478–79, 481

Ha'am, Ahad (Asher Ginsberg) 130, 143n42
HAC (Higher Arab Committee): and Arab rebellion 252, 259–60, 400; Defence Party resignation of 267; Fawzi's flouting of 251; and London conference 297; and MacDonnell 254–55; meetings with German representatives 408; and Nuri al-Said 258–59; post-war meeting of 437; and second phase of rebellion 268–69; setting up of 249; and White Paper of 1939 304, 360–62, 384, 487
Haddad, 'Uthman Kamal 410
Hagana: agents of 281, 408; bombings by 482n14; counter-insurgency against 464; foundation of 102; nationwide operations by 462, 465–66; and *Patria* disaster 372; representatives of 86; supplying weapons to Nashashibi 278; and Zionist terrorists 471
Hagen, Herbert 408
Hague Convention 76
Hahn, Rudolf 369
Haifa: in Arab rebellion 272; electrification of 197; Italian air raids on 316; in Masada Plan 327; oil refineries at 45, 181n49
Haifa port: development of 151, 167, 179n10, 184; during Arab general strike 253; strategic value of 25, 152, 161–62n33; in World War Two 308
Hailsham, Lord 230
Hailsham/Simon letter 230, 234
Haining, General Robert 264, 275, 277, 290
Haj Amin el-Husayni **Plates 11–12**; 1920 pardon of 110; appointment as Mufti of Jerusalem 105, 110–12; and Arab-German Battalion 422–24; and Arab rebellion 251–52, 268–70, 281–82, 291, 395; in Baghdad 409; and Bentwich 104; and Bosnian Moslems 433–34; collaboration with Nazi Germany 3, 367–68, 382, 396, 405–9, 487–89; conflict with Hashemites 372; and Eastern European Jews 29, 431–32; escape to Berlin 284, 360, 373, 383, 402, 418–19; and the Holocaust 425–27, 437; and Ibn Saud 256; influence over press 399–400; 145n70, as land broker 361; as leader of Palestinian Arabs 279, 362, 383–86, 486; and London conference 297, 301; memoirs of 384; Newton's admiration of 197; and Nuri al-Said 377; patronage of his clan 215; pause from anti-British activity 240; on Peel partition plan 271; president of HAC 249; propaganda broadcasts of 428–30, 490; Rendel on 291; rivalry with Rashid Ali 420–21; and SMC 265, 394; supporters of 403; and Wailing Wall riots 215–16, 219, 266; as wanted war criminal 434–37
Hajjar, Bishop 138
Haldane, Aylmer 62
Halifax, Lord 316, 366, 450, 452, 455
Hall, George 435–36, 453
Handjar Division 433–34
Haram as-Sharif 215, 269
Harding, A. J. 185
Harmsworth, Esmond 69
Harris, Arthur 84
Harrison, Earle 449
Harvey, Oliver 353
Hashemites: in Arab League 379; British support for 46; Devonshire on 53; goal of Arab Federation 258; Ibn Saud's opposition to 268, 378; Lawrence on 43
Hashemite–Wahhabi rivalry 256, 258
Hawes, L. A. 320
Hebrew press in Palestine 402
Hebrew University in Jerusalem 79
Hebron, Arab attacks in 216, 225
Henderson, Loy 455
High Commissioner of Palestine: and armed forces 463–64, 471; first 88–89; powers of 127; role of 97–98
Himmler, Heinrich 425, 429, 431–33
Hinsley, Professor Harry 338
Histadrut 102, 167, 221, 284n7
Hitler, Adolf: Arab support for 404; on colonized peoples 386; meeting Mufti 419; Mufti's congratulations for 407, 409; Palestinian press coverage of 397
Hoare, Samuel 152
Hobson, J. A. 8
Holocaust: Allied knowledge of 335, 337–39, 341–43; and establishment of Israel 355–56; impact on Jewish people 3; news in Palestinian press

402; Palestinians as victims of 383; public information about 344–45; survivors of 491; and the Zionists 307; and Zygielbojm's suicide 346–47
Holocaust denial 382
Holy Basin in Jerusalem 111
Homer, Annie 200
Hoofien, Siegfried 103
Hope-Simpson, John: on Arab land sales 139–40; on "black letter" 237–38; on Malcolm MacDonald 231; on Passfield 232; report of 222–24, 226–28, 235–36; on Zionism 233
Horne, Edward 87, 213; on 1921 riots 116
House of Lords: anti-Zionism in 55, 128, 147, 150; and Dead Sea minerals concession 203–6
Hungarian Jews 312, 352, 431–32
Husayn, Sharif of Mecca 45–46, 52–53, 159
Husayni, Jemal 283, 361, 367, 383
Husayni, Tewfiq 363
Husayni clan: Arab opposition to 277–80; and Arab rebellion 112, 270–71; contacts with Axis 401; control of SMC funds 111, 395; dominance of 394; and Fawzi el-Qawukji 251; opposition to 266; and Peel partition plan 265, 267–68; pre-eminence among Palestinians 362–63; Samuel's patronage of 110; support for Mufti 403; terrorism by 270–71, 280, 297, 362, 400–401, 487
Hyamson, Albert 37n118

Ibn Saud: and Arab Federation 377; as Arab leader 364, 375–76; British support for 58n37; feud with Hashemites 258, 268; negotiations with British 256; payments to 265; war with Husayn 46, 262n28; in World War Two 372
Imam, Said 408
Imam Institute 434
immigration labour certificates 132
India: Churchill and Wilson on 63; evacuation of 4, 457
Indian Moslems 215
international Jewry: Arab perceptions of 280; British attempts to sway 54; British ideas of power of 10, 33, 47, 51–52; conspiracy theories of 7–10, 26, 85, 197–98, 397, 428; Hope-Simpson on 237

IPC oil pipeline 250, 258, 270, 277
Iraq: 1920 rebellion in 62, 91; British payments to 265; collaboration with Italy 406; Fascist organisations in 388; German influence in 368; in "informal empire" 307; intervention in Arab rebellion 256–57; links with Mediterranean 152; opposition to partition 267; Rashid Ali's rebellion in 322, 411; writing off debt of 187–88, 190
Ireland 62, 70, 126
Iron Shirts 388
Isaacs, Sir Rufus 9
Islam, Mufti's pro-Nazi interpretation of 407, 421–22, 434
Islamic Central Institute in Berlin 421, 429
Islington, Lord 203–4
Israel (State of): Arabs applying for jobs in 286n48; Berlin on 21; foundations of 491; and the Holocaust 355–56, 382; and Suez Crisis 42; US recognition of 452
'Issa al-'Issa 271, 415n81
Istiqlal (Independence Party) 285n30, 362, 402
Italy: aid to Mufti 269, 406, 409, 416n107, 418; attitude to Arabs 410; British appeasement of 246–47, 261n7, 292; Churchill on 288–89; conquest of Abyssinia *see* Ethiopia, conquest of; entry into World War Two 307, 311, 316, 318; fighting in North Africa 263, 321, 372; invasion of Somaliland 319, 370; invasion of Somaliland 380n24; Jewish population of 416n106, 418; and Nazi Germany 387; propaganda broadcasts by 393, 405; support in Arabic press for 396
IZL (Irgun Zwai Leumi): attacks on British soldiers 464–65, 471; execution of members 472; hangings by 476–79; and JRM 462; kidnappings by 472; terrorist bombings of 467, 470
'Izzat Darwaza, Muhammad 402

Jabotinsky, Ze'ev 86–87, 93n58, 240
Jaffa: Arab rebellion of 1936 in 250; demolitions in 250, 254; electrification of 197; martial law in 116–17
Jaffa–Petach Tikva road 209n12
Jaffa port 253

Jarallah, Hussam al-Din 278
Jarallah family 110
JCS (joint chiefs of staff) 453
Jeffrey, Keith 338
Jeffries, J. M. N. 146–47, 149, 197–99
Jerusalem: 1920 riots in 86; in Arab rebellion 275; demographic balance in 99; as "international state" 458, 480; Jewish majority in 252; mayors of 110–11; sewage problems in 82–83; world Islamic congress in 240
Jewish Agency: and 1939 White Paper 303; and Arab rebellion 278; authority of 225; enlarged 191, 226, 229; and Jewish Division 328; and JRM 462–64; proposals to Anglo-American Committee 455; raids on 466; and refugee ships 476; and SMC 266, 273; Weizmann's warnings to 467; and Zionist terrorists 471
Jewish Brigade 330–31, 425
Jewish capital: British Empire's dependence on 2, 165, 184, 186, 192, 196; conspiracy theories of 197; and Dead Sea minerals 200–202; and immigration 133; import into Palestine 42, 98, 155–57, 167, 484–86; and Jewish enterprise 167–69; and Palestine loan 170–71
Jewish Colonial Trust 206
Jewish community in Palestine *see* Yishuv
Jewish Division: attempted formation by Yishuv 327–29; Churchill's proposal for 311–12, 315, 322; end of scheme 326, 336; and implementation of White Paper 364, 371; opposition to 320–21, 323–25, 488; Weizmann's proposal for 319
Jewish enterprises 165, 167
Jewish immigration to Palestine: and 1922 White Paper 127–29; 1930s increase in 249; and 1930 White Paper 228, 234; Anglo-American negotiations on 449, 453, 457; Arab opposition to 99, 112, 135, 162n56, 220; and Arab rebellion of 1936 253–56, 260; and Arab riots of 1921 87; "black letter" on 237; British curbs on 2–3, 117–19, 134, 301; Churchill's proposal on 295–96; during Great Depression 134; during World War Two 312–13; in early years of Mandate 131–32, 173; and economic booms 136, 182, 184; and elective institutions 124–25; Hope-Simpson on 223; illegal 462, 473–76; and Labour government 461; and OETA 78; political implications of 134–35; reversing process of 182–83; Shaw Commission on 221–22; suspension of 117–18; US Senate resolution on 430
Jewish labour: and Dead Sea minerals concession 202, 206; and electricity concession 199; Histadrut campaign for 167; and public works 184–85, 237; Zionist preference for 228
Jewish labour movement 221; *see also* Histadrut
Jewish Legion 36, 80, 92n22
Jewish National Fund 141, 145n87
Jewish National Home: in 1922 White Paper 129–30; Arab acquiescence to 101, 117–18; and Arab anti-Semitism 406; Arab opposition to 141, 217; British patronage of 99–100, 102, 113; and Churchill 23; end of British support for 1; financial assistance to 227; fundraising for 167–68; investment in 165, 169–70; in League of Nations mandate 125; military attitude to 76; Trans-Jordan removed from 29, 36n98; Zionist Commission responsibility for 78
Jewishness: flight from 7; liberal critique of 7
Jewish refugees: after World War Two 446, 450, 454, 465, 491 (*see also* DPs); from Axis-occupied Europe 313, 347–50; British deportation of 470, 473; conscription of 80; from Germany 35n63; and *Patria* disaster 372; political opposition to 16; from Russia and Eastern Europe 6–7; ships of 476; violence against 10; and Zionism 31
Jewish terrorists: and anti-Semitism in British forces 468; in Arab rebellion 274; assassinations by 23; British offensive against 471–72; in JRM 462–63, 465, 476; response to Arab–Jewish conference 299
jihad 398, 407
Joyce, William (Lord Haw-Haw) 17, 435
Joynson-Hicks, William 128, 160–61n17, 171–72, 175, 180n27, 193–94
JRM (Jewish Resistance Movement) 461–63, 465–68, 470

Judeo-Bolshevik bogey 26–28; in 1920s 68–69; in Arab press 138; and Balfour Declaration 54; and British in Palestine 88, 106; and British military 84; Churchill's belief in 23, 121; in World War One 51

Kabha, Mustafa 385, 395–97, 399–401
Karski, Jan 343
Kaukji, Fawzi *see* Fawzi el-Qawukji
Kent, Tyler 17
Kenya White Paper 223
Kerr, Philip 124
Keynes, John Maynard 444
kibbutzim 221
Kielce pogrom 355, 491
King David Hotel, IZL bombing of 467–70, 472
Kipling, Rudyard 10–11
Kirkuk–Haifa oil pipeline 167, 178, 180n10, 181n49, 190
Kisch, F. H. 110

Labour Party: and the Holocaust 344, 346; Palestine policy of 461–62, 485; post-war government of 443–44, 446; and Zionism 220–21, 230, 235
Lampson, Miles 248, 301, 309, 368–71, 373–74
lands administration, in Palestine 136–39, 208n9, 225
Laqueur, Walter 337–38
Laski, Harold 226, 229, 231, 242n47
Law, Richard 348, 351
Lawrence, T. E. 10, 42–43, 197
League of British Jews 32
League of Nations: British campaign against Italy at 246; Permanent Mandates Commission 97, 242n35, 290, 304
League of Nations mandate for Palestine: Baldwin government retaining 171–72; and Balfour Declaration 23, 485; Britain's surrender of 453; Churchill on 126; concept of 96–97; delayed ratification of 67, 88–89, 121; and economic development 169; fourth article of 77, 127; and Wailing Wall riots inquiry 218
Lebanon: Fascist organisations in 388; Haj Amin's asylum in 269–70, 273, 283
Lees, Aubrey 17
LEHI (Stern Gang) 462, 465, 470, 472
Lend-Lease programme 326, 444

The Letter of the Ten 32
liberalism, and anti-Semitism 7
Liberal Party: eclipse of 191–92, 232; supporting Labour minority governments 220, 226, 229
Libya, Axis forces in 425
Liddell, Guy 311–12
The Link 16–17
Lloyd, T. K. 134, 184, 186
Lloyd George, David **Plate 1**; dismissal of OETA 88; fall of government 73n19, 147; as Gentile Zionist 22; on Jewish question 14–15; meeting with Passfield 222; on military spending 61, 165; on Peel plan 288; press opposition to 69; on White Paper of 1930 230, 232–33, 235; and Balfour Declaration 44, 46–47, 123, 126; and Herbert Samuel 89–90; and Mandate in Palestine 24–25; and Marconi scandal 9; and post-war Middle East 63–64, 67; and the Bolsheviks 27; and Zionism 26, 47–48, 124
London conference of 1939 296–300, 303, 310
Lugard, Lord 223

MacDonald, James 454–55
MacDonald, Malcolm: as Colonial Secretary 291–94, 302–3; at London conference 298–300, 310; on Palestine garrison 316; as "point man" for father 231–32; and Jewish Division 315; and White Paper of 1939 302
MacDonald, Ramsay: "black letter" of 235–39, 486; and Passfield 223; and Shaw Commission 218, 222; and White Paper of 1930 220, 229–32, 234–35; and Zionism 221
MacDonnell, Michael 97–98, 254–55, 262n24
MacDonogh, General George 119, 142n11
Mack, Julian 204
MacKereth, Gilbert 144–45n70
MacMahon, Sir Henry 45–46, 52–53
MacMahon–Husayn correspondence 45–46, 146–47, 158, 218
MacMichael, Sir Harold **Plate 14**; appointment as High Commissioner 273–74, 292; Fitzgerald's letter to 481–82; on Haj Amin 270; on Lampson 369; on Nashashibis 283; recall to London 294; and Arab

rebellion 264, 272, 275; and constitutional proposals 364-65, 371
March of Folly 52
Marconi scandal 8-9
Margesson, David 323-24
Margolin, Eliezer 80, 92n24, 116
Marquess of Reading 231
Marshall, George 430
Martin, J. M. 325, 478
Masada Plan 327
Mavrogordato, Arthur 217
Maxe, Leo 10
McDonnell, Michael 103, 114n32
Mediterranean, strategic deprioritisation of 248
Meinertzhagen, Richard 24-25, 124
Melchers, Wilhelm 432
Melchett, Lord, see Mond, Alfred
MELF (Middle East Land Forces) 447, 477-78, 488
Mellini, Alberto 418
MI5 17, 311
MI6 35, 338
MI14 341
Middle East: Anglo-French partition of 49, 88; Britain's unplanned conquests in 164-65, 307; British status in 248, 263, 290, 298; disorders of 1936 in 247; during World War Two 307-8, 310, 316; impact of Axis propaganda on 428-29; Nazi German strategy in 387, 404-5, 423, 427, 490; post-war importance of 491; War Office analysis of 295; World War Two battles in 424
Middle East Command in Cairo: and Hagana 463; and Jewish Division 328; and Palestine garrison 311; and reinforcement of Egypt 263; separation of Palestine from 127; on Syria 369
Middle East Reserve 263-64, 275
military courts 270, 272, 276, 281
Milner, Lord 95
Mir'at al-Sharq 398
Mond, Alfred (Lord Melchett): and 1930 White Paper 229; and Churchill 288; and Dead Sea minerals concession 201-2, 205; and Palestine loan 170-71; and the Holocaust 349, 351; and Wailing Wall riots inquiry 218; and Zionist loan 183
Money, General Arthur 81-83
Montagu, Edwin 7, 30-31, 49-51, 68

Montagu, Samuel 9
Montgomery, Field Marshal Sir Bernard Law 275-76, 467, 470-72, **Plate 15**
Moody, Sydney 59n66, 148, 156
Morgenthau, Henry 48-49, 312, 350, 475
The Morning Post 29, 32, 146
Morocco, Allied forces in 392, 424
Morrison, Herbert 16, 344
Morrison-Grady plan 454-56
Moslem Brotherhood 388, 437
Mosley, Oswald 12-17, 484
Mosul-Haifa oil pipeline *see* IPC oil pipeline
Moyne, Lord: assassination of 23, 354, 378, 447, 488; as Colonial Secretary 322; on Jewish Division 326; yacht of 179
Mufti of Jerusalem: elections for 105, 110; Haj Amin becoming 104; *see also* Haj Amin el-Husayni
Munich Agreement: effect on Zionists 298; Hitler's violation of 387; White Paper of 1939 compared to 162n53, 304
Munich crisis 275, 283, 294, 309
Murrow, Edward R. 344
Mussolini, Benito: British attitudes to 246-47; invasion of North Africa 310; Mufti's collaboration with 304, 418; and the Arabs 405

Nablus: Arab nationalists in 402; and Arab rebellion 250; Palestinian national congress at 130
Nahhas Pasha 377-78, 430
Naiditch, Isaac 202
Najjada 388
Nashashibi, Fahkri 273, 278, 281-84, 362, 402; anti-Fascist pamphlet 402
Nashashibi, Ragheb **Plate 13**; on the British 280, 282; conflict with Fahkri 278; on Husayni hit-list 278; in Jordanian government 285n30; as mayor of Jerusalem 111, 265; and Haj Amin 110; and Peel partition plan 267-68; and SMC 273
Nashashibi clan: alliance with Hashemites 372; and Arab rebellion 251, 271; British attitudes to 278; dominance of 394; exclusion from SMC patronage 215; opposition led by 486-87; and Peel partition plan 265; Samuel's patronage of 110; Zionist funding of 282-83

Nashashibi peace bands 278, 282
Nassar, Najib 395
Nasser, Gemal Abdel 391
Nazi Germany: Arab support for 304, 374, 383, 388, 396, 402, 429; atrocities by 3, 335, 338–39, 341–42, 345, 402, 488; attitude to Arabs 404, 406, 410; British sympathisers of 16–17, 25; Chamberlain's negotiations with 263; funding of Mufti 409–11; grand strategy of 386–87; interventions in Palestine 408; Jewish genocide by 307, 327, 330, 336–37 (*see also* Holocaust); Jews as forced labour under 427; reoccupation of Rhineland 245, 287–88; threat to Palestine 212; war victories of 310, 316, 391
Nehru, Jawaharlal 14
Newcombe, S. F. 367–69, 371
Newton, Frances 90, 195, 197–99, 206–7
New Zealand 308
Nicolson, Harold: career of 357n41; meeting Weizmann 304; and Ernest Bevin 458; and the Holocaust 345–46
Niemeyer, Otto 209
Night of the Railways 462
Niles, David 456–57
Nordic League 16–17
Norman, Frances 210n47
Northcliffe, Lord 29, 69–70, 73n27, 143n20, 146–47, 160n3
North-West Africa, Jewish population of 392
Novomeysky, Moshe 193, 199–207, **Plate 8**
Nuri al-Said: as Arab leader 364; and Arab rebellion 258–59; contacts with Germany 368; on Jewish Division 329; at London conference 297; and Palestine constitutional proposals 365, 367, 371; proposals for Arab federation 268, 376–77; travel to Turkey 409; unseating of 372, 410

OETA (Occupied Enemy Territory Administration): and 1920 riots 86–88; British community support for 82; dismissal of 88; establishment of 75–76; and official British policy 85; racial prejudice among 81–82; and Zionist Commission 78
officers' clubs 95
oil: Arab states' resources of 298, 370; discovery near Dead Sea 206

Oliphant, Sir Lancelot 296
Operation Agatha 466–68, 471
Operation Barbarossa *see* Soviet Union, German invasion of
Operation Cantonment 472
Operation Torch 392
Oranienburg concentration camp 425
Ormsby-Gore, William: on anti-Semitism 69, 128–29; as Colonial Secretary 255; on Dead Sea minerals concession 202; on Muslims 107; replacement of 292, 302; Weizmann's letter to 166; in Zionist Commission 92n14; and Arab rebellion 256–59, 269; and "black letter" 236; and Peel plan 290–92; and subsidy for Trans-Jordan 177–78; and Zionist loan 183
Orthodox Jews 146, 216
Orwell, George: anti-Semitic stereotypes of 11–12; on colonialism 40; writings on anti-Semitism 19–20; on Zionism and colonialism 224
Ottoman Empire: British nostalgia for 109; demise of 41; granting commercial concessions 192; Morgenthau's attempted negotiations with 48–49; partition of 64; Russian threat to 22
Ottoman Syria 61, 75, 166, 394

Paget, General Sir Bernard 464
Palestine: Arab–Jewish conference in London on *see* London conference of 1939; Isaiah Berlin's reminiscences of 113; border fortifications of 274; Britain's duplicitous stance on 158–59, 299; British administration in *see* British Palestine administration; British attitudes to people of 38–39; British economic interests in 155; British imperial mission in 94; British press reports on 146–47; Cabinet sub-committee on 149–50, 157–58; Churchill's comments on 42, 125–29, 312; considered as military base 446–47; constitutional progress in 364–66, 372; debts of 165–66, 171–73, 175, 187, 209n24; economic concessions in 207–8; economy of 165, 168–69, 173–74, 184, 363; elective institutions in 99–100, 123–24, 149, 216; electrification of *see* Rutenberg electricity concession; English and Hebrew press in 402

(*see also* Arabic press in Palestine); industrialisation of 165, 197–99, 363; Italian air raids on 316, 319; judiciary of 97–98, 254; legislative council proposal for 127–28, 130–31, 226, 228, 237; loans for *see* Palestine loan, Zionist loan; in Middle East strategy 308–9; military administration in *see* OETA; military command of 213, 259; Nazi plans for 328, 426; pan-Arab conferences on 268; parliamentary debates on 69, 129, 232; peace as a strategic imperative in 264; political pluralism in 399; population of 132–33, 150, 203, 296; press regulations in 398–99; recent research on Arab–Zionist relations 1; as refugee sanctuary 348–49; Royal Commission of Inquiry into *see* Peel Commission; strategic value of 2, 43–47, 67–68, 71–72, 150–55; trade volumes of 182

Palestine Arab Executive *see* Arab Executive
Palestine Arab party 362–63
Palestine Buffs 318–19, 327, 329, 401
Palestine conference of 1947 472, 491
Palestine Currency Board 185, 209n13
Palestine Defence Regulations 435, 463
Palestine Economic Corporation 206
Palestine gendarmerie 176, 213
Palestine loan: British guarantee of 170, 172, 174; and development 166–67; increasing 172–73; raising 168–71
Palestine Mining Syndicate 200
Palestine municipal elections of 1927 215–16
Palestine police: and 1920 riots 86–87; in Arab rebellion 276; Arab section of 264; British Section of 213; killings of 479; subordinated to army 274
Palestine Post 258–59, 402
Palestine Potash Company 206
Palestine Railway Union 1
Palestine Regiment 328–29
Palestine Zionist Executive 77–78, 87, 91–92n14, 106, 110, 119, 127
Palestinian Arabs: and 1922 White Paper 130; in Alexandria Protocol 378; Arab kings' appeal to 252; and Arab League 379; in Arab Revolt 59n62; ban on political activity 361; and "black letter" 239; and British administration 103–4; British attempts to control 52–53, 485; British attitudes to 53–55, 108–9, 112, 154; Christian 100–101, 103, 145, 267, 363, 394; Churchill on 42, 62, 196; collaborators with Nazis among 396–97, 404–5, 435–36; collaborators with Zionism 279; delegation to London conference 283, 297–300; during World War Two 360, 488–90; and economic concessions 196–97, 208; economy of 253, 363; Gentile sympathy for 15; and growth of Yishuv 121–22, 138–39; institutions of 101; internecine conflict of 271–73, 280–82, 284, 400, 486–87; and Jewish enterprises 167–68; as land brokers 135, 141; land sales by *see* Arab land sales; leadership of 365, 372; Lawrence on 43; Meinertzhagen on 88; Newton's support for 199; and OETA 77; opposition to Mufti 266, 277, 279–80, 383, 386; and Peel partition plan 265, 267; political parties of 267; and *Protocols of the Elders of Zion* 29; social structure of 267, 394–95; sources of information 402–3; as tenants 136; urbanisation of 140, 363; in World War Two 318–19; Zionist attitudes to 109–10; and Zionist Commission 78
Palestinian Jews *see* Yishuv
Palestinian pound 165
Palin, General P. C. 87, 93n61
Palmach: British counterinsurgency against 466; British mobilisation of 488; in Masada Plan 327
pan-Arabism 373, 377, 379
Passfield, Lord *see* Webb, Sidney
Patria disaster 332, 372
Patton, General George 392
Peel Commission: and Arab rebellion 256–57, 259; Churchill's private evidence to 311; and Jewish immigration 143n22, 287; and land sales 142; on political high ceiling 134–35; publication of report 265; on SMC 112, 269
Peel partition plan: Arab responses to 251, 267–68, 271; British response to 287–89; burial of 294; Eden's opposition to 247; German reaction to 387, 407; and Zionist land purchases 140

PGE (Polish Government-in-Exile) 338–39, 342, 344–45, 349
Phalange (al-Kataeb) 388
Philby, St John 42, 197, 375
Philby scheme 375–76
Pickthorne, Kenneth 289
Plumer, Field Marshal, Viscount Herbert 175–79, 182–83, 185, 192, 201, 213–14, **Plate 4**
Poalei Zion 234
Poincaré, Raymond 183
Polish Jews: emigration to England 80; emigration to Palestine 133, 173, 182, 408; Nazi atrocities against 342–44, 346; post-war pogroms against 355
"political high level" 135, 143, 265
Polkes, Feivel 408
Porath, Yehoshua 385, 404
Poston, Ralph 112
potash 193, 199–200, 202–3, 205–6, 211n60
Protocols of the Elders of Zion: and Balfour Declaration 54; and Bolshevism 26–27; and British in Palestine 29, 81; in Nazi era 404, 428; publication in England 7, 9–10, 36n88
public schools, jargon of 96
public sphere theory 389

Radio Ankara 403
RAF (Royal Air Force): and Auschwitz 349–51, 353; and defence of Britain 310–11; and the Holocaust 342; and illegal Jewish immigration 474; rise in prominence of 150
Rafah 151
railways, in Palestine 462
Ramle, jackal hunting at 96
Ramsay, Archibald 16–18
Rashid Ali: Axis support for 304, 373–74, 427; coup d'état of 322–23, 325, 372; defeat of 411; escape to Berlin 418–20; and Mufti of Jerusalem 372, 409, 420–23; and Newcombe's mission 367
Rauff, Walter 426–27
Red Book 17, 35n52
Rendel, George 290–91, 293
Revisionist Party 240
Ribbentrop, Joachim von 410–11, 419–22, 431
Richmond, Ernest 104–7, 217–18
Riegner, Gerhard 343
Right Club 16–18

RIIA (Royal Institute of International Affairs) 375
road construction, in Palestine 180n11, 185
Romania 161, 347, 431, 476
Rommel, General Erwin: Arab approval for 401, 403; defeat at El Alamein 376, 426–27; landing in Africa 323, 333n47, 488; military successes of 327; Yishuv defence plans against 329
Roosevelt, Franklin: on European Jews 359n77; Jewish vote for 448; meeting with Churchill 326; Nazi propaganda about 428; on Palestine 393, 430; secret correspondence with Churchill 313; and North-West Africa 392
Roosevelt, Franklin. on Zionism 375
Rothschild bank 171, 180n23
Royal Navy: and Dunkirk 310; in Eastern Mediterranean 245–46
Rundall, F. B. A. 475
Russia, British intervention in 26–27
Russian Jews: and Bolshevism 30, 32, 54; as refugees in Britain 31
Russian Revolution *see* Bolshevism
Rutenberg, Pinhas **Plate 7**; electrification and Zionist project 199; Melchett's testimony of 205; opposition to Weizmann 231; personal attacks on 195; representing Haganah 86; in Russian Revolution 210n45
Rutenberg electricity concession: Colonial Office offering 125, 127–28; and Dead Sea minerals concession 204; granting of 125, 127; opposition to 128, 167, 172, 193–99, 201

Sa'ada, Antoun 388, 413n31
Sachsenhausen concentration camp 425
Safed, Arab–Jewish violence in 216
Safer, Morley 353
Samaria 250–51
Samaritans 402, 415n91
Samuel, Sir Herbert **Plate 1, Plate 3**; defence of Balfour Declaration 70–71; on future of Palestine 154; High Commissioner of Palestine 87, 89–90, 97–102; on Jewish state in Palestine 24, 43; King's Birthday speech by 120–23; meeting with Passfield 222; Montagu's letter to 68; and 1921 riots 116–19; and conscription 31–32; and development of Palestine 165, 168–69;

and Ernest Richmond 105–6; and Jewish immigration 120–22, 132; and Marconi affair 9; and Palestinian Arabs 110–12, 212
Sarafand 284n1, 304n1, 308
Saudi Arabia: CID on 375–76; collaboration with Italy 406; opposition to partition 267
Sawt al-Sha'b 398, 400, 415n81
security zones 461, 473, 478
Sephardi Jews, assimilation of 7
Serbian Jews 433
Seychelles 436
Shamir, Yitschak 470
Shaw, Walter 218
Shaw Commission 139, 219–22, 235, 266
Shawkat, Naji 409–10
Shertok, Moshe **Plates 9–10**; at London conference 297; on Nazi Germany 488; and Jewish Brigade 330; and Jewish Division 327; and Musa al-Alami 405; and Ragheb Nashahibi 273; and Zionist violence 462
Shibli, Abd al-Qadar 266
Shiels, Drummond 236
Shuckburgh, John: on Arabs 109; on Balfour Declaration 54–56, 159; demoralisation of 148; on electrification 167; on Jewish Division 325–26; Meinertzhagen on 124; on Palestine question 52–53; Weizmann's influence over 71; in World War Two 312–15; and "black letter" 237; and Chancellor's proposals 219; and draft constitution 127; and Zionist loan 183
Shukri al-Quwatli 374, 378, 409
Shuqayri, Ahmed 402–3
SIGINT (Signals Intelligence) 338
Sikorski, General 347, 349
Simon, John 230
Sinai Peninsula 43, 68, 151
Sinclair, Archibald 287, 350
SIS (Secret Intelligence Service) 338, 340–41
SMC (Supreme Moslem Council): and Arab rebellion 249; dissolution of 112; establishment of 110; Haj Amin as leader of 111, 215, 240, 269; and land sales to Zionists 136; Nashashibi's bid for leadership of 273; successor to Haj Amin 278; Zionist action against 266
Smith, Trafford 476
Smuts, Jan 222, 234

Smyrna 61, 63–67, 73n19
Sneh, Moshe 467
Snell, Harry 219
Snowden, Philip 226–27
SNS (special night squads) 277
Socialist National Party 388
Sokolov, Nahum 44, 91n14
Soviet Jews 439n37
Soviet Union: defeat of Germany 420, 427; German invasion of 310, 326, 339–40, 402, 411, 439n37; Nazi atrocities in 335, 338; on Palestine 490; Western conflict with 4, 442, 445, 491
SS Order Police 339–40, 439n37
Stalingrad 425
Stanley, Oliver 316
Stein, Kenneth 135
Stein, Leonard: on Gentile Zionism 26; on Herbert Samuel 98–99, 119
Stevenson, Frances **Plate 1**
Storrs, Ronald: on Arab rebellion 260–61; on OETA 75, 77–79; and 1920 riots 86; and Ernest Richmond 104
Suez Canal: after World War Two 4, 445; defence of 41, 43, 151, 311; military base in 308, 445; Palestine as buffer to 23–25, 33, 43–45, 67–68, 152–53; in World War Two 307
Sunday Express 147
Suzlberger, Arthur 329
Sydenham, Lord 147, 157–58
Sykes, Sir Mark 10
Sykes–Picot Agreement 10, 44, 49, 484
Syria: British and Free French invasion of 323–24, 373–75; Fascist organisations in 388; partition of 135; *see also* Greater Syria
Syrian Arabs 133, 144n56, 251, 323, 373

Taft, Robert 430
Tannous, Afif 139
taxation, in Palestine 208n9
Tegart, Charles 274
Tel Aviv: British troops rampage in 470, 476–77; construction boom in 133–34, 173–74, 182; Italian air raids on 316; Jewish majority in 252; Tweedy on 103
Templeton, Viscount 204–5
temporizing compromises 394
tennis 95, 102
Ten Year Rule 246, 261n3, 308
TGWU (Transport and General Workers Union) 234

Thomas, J. H. 168, 255
Tito, Josip Broz 432–34
Tobruk, siege of 323, 333–34n54, 423, 426–27
Tottie, W. H. 200
Tottie-Bicknell group 200–201
Transfer Agreement 386–87
Trans-Jordan: annexation of Arab Palestine 265, 287; British slush fund in 265; and Dead Sea minerals concession 203; electrification of 125, 127; Palestine subsidising 176–79, 181n46; self-government in 124; severance from Palestine 130
Treaty of Lausanne 152
Treaty of Sèvres 63
Trenchard, Hugh 216–17
Trotsky, Leon 27–28
Truman, Harry 444, 448–49, 451–52, 454–57, 475
The Truth 18
Tulloch, Thomas 200, 203–4
Tulloch-Novomeysky group 202
Tunisia 392, 424–25, 427
Tuqan, Suliman 278, 281
Turkey: British relations with 151–52; Churchill's moves against 63–67, 120; post-war nationalism in 63–64, 66–67; *see also* Ottoman Empire
Tweedy, Owen 102–3, 218, 237

Ukraine, Jewish refugees from 117
UN Committee on Palestine (UNSCOP) 474–75, 478, 490
unemployment, in Palestine 184
United Nations: Palestine referred back to 457–58, 472; partition plan of 354–55, 458, 480, 490–91
United States: and Arab–Zionist conflict 448–50, 452–53; British and French propaganda towards 54–55; British debt to 164; closure of immigration to 133; forces in North-West Africa 392; and the Holocaust 340–41, 350; and Jewish Brigade 331; Jewish influence in 48 (*see also* American Zionists); post-war dominance of 442–44, 446; Wall Street Crash in 226; Weizmann in 183, 323; and World War Two 313–14, 420
UNSCOP (UN Committee on Palestine) 474–75, 478, 490

Va'ad Leumi 102, 119, 216, 231
Vansittart, Robert 23
Versailles Peace Conference, and Arab independence 46
Vichy France 323, 369, 373, 392, 410–11
von Papen, Franz 409–10
Vrba, Rudolph 350

Wafd (Egypt) 391, 430
Wagner, Robert 430
Wailing Wall: as holy site for Judaism and Islam 215; Tweedy's visit to 103
Wailing Wall riots of 1929: British reactions to 485; and Chancellor's resignation 97; gains for Mufti from 240; inquiries following 2, 218 (*see also* Shaw Commission); and Jewish immigration 134; origins of 214–16; outbreak of 216
Wansee conference 341–43
waqf lands 110
Warburg, Felix 229, 231, 243n54
Warburg, Otto 199, 211n58
War Office: analysis of Arab states 292–93; and Arab rebellion 257, 275; on Jewish Brigade 330; and Jewish Division 320; on Jewish Division 315; and OETA 76; and security in Palestine 91
Warsaw ghetto 347
Wasserstein, Bernard 70–71, 337–38, 345
Wauchope, General Sir Arthur **Plate 9**; as High Commissioner in Palestine 97, 109, 249; and Arab rebellion 250, 254, 257–60, 269, 273; removal of 292
Wavell, General 319, 321–22, 372, 387, 393
Webb, Beatrice: diaries of 221, 242n29; on MacDonald government 229, 235; on Montagu 31; on motivations of Balfour Declaration 47, 224; pro-Arab sympathies of 107–8; on Weizmann 225; and future of Palestine 56–57
Webb, Richard 468
Webb, Sidney (Lord Passfield): as Colonial Secretary 56, 221; on East Africa 223; on population of Palestine 133; and East Africa 224; and Norman Bentwich 104; and post-Wailing Wall riots inquiries 218, 222; and White Paper of 1930 232–33, 235–36; and Zionism 224–25
Wedgwood, Josiah 22, 25, 202

Weise, Hans-Joachim 425
Weizmann, Chaim **Plate 1**, **Plate 10**, **Plate 16**; arrival in Palestine 77; defence of Balfour Declaration 71; diplomatic activity of 48–52; during World War Two 318; on future of Palestine 143n40; lobbying of Balfour and Lloyd George 123–24; at London conference 297–300; meeting with Faysal 10; Nazi propaganda on 428; Nicolson on 304; on Palestinian Arabs 109–10; on Peel partition plan 265; as political Zionist 130; press campaign against 146; scientific discoveries of 58n41, 83; sidelined by extremists 466–67; Zionist rivals of 240; and appointment of High Commissioners 119; and Balfour Declaration 46–47; and Blanche Dugdale 22; and Colonial Office 125; and Dead Sea minerals concession 202, 206; and Ernest Bevin 451; and Franklin Roosevelt 393; and Herbert Samuel 90, 102, 122–23; and Jewish Division 312, 314, 319–25, 327–28, 336; and Jewish immigration 336; and Malcolm MacDonald 303–4; and negotiations after Arab rebellion 259; and Newcome 368; and Palestine sub-committee 149–50; and Passfield 224–26, 232; and Peel partition plan 287; and Philby plan 375–76; and Ramsay MacDonald 2, 226, 229–31, 235–36, 239; and role of Jewish capital in Palestine 166–67; and Winston Churchill 123–24, 315, 336, 354; and Zionist loan 183–84, 187–88, 190–91; and Zionist violence 462
welfare payments, in Palestine 184–85
Welles, Sumner 343
West Bank, Jordan's annexation of 268
Wetzler, Alfred 350
White, Arnold 7
White Paper of 1922: and Balfour Declaration 131; Clayton on 153; on Jews in Palestine 129–30; passing into law 172; and Samuel's speech 122; and Shuckburgh's outline 127–28
White Paper of 1930: Chancellor's role in 225; retreat from 111, 229–31, 234, 237–38; revisions to 228
White Paper of 1939: as appeasement 303, 383; and Arabic press 400; British commitment to 378; Churchill blocking implementation of 312; Commons debate on 289; constitutional measures in 364–69, 374; immigration quotas under 332n19, 347, 446; Labour Party on 461–62; Land Regulations 141, 365; Mufti's veto of 304, 360–61, 367, 384; origins of 292, 295; Palestinian reaction to 360–62; publication of 301; purpose of 2–3
White Shirts 388
Wickham Steed, Henry 26–28
Wilson, Field Marshal Sir Henry (CIGS) 61–63, 66, 81
Wilson, Woodrow 27, 46, 48–51, 88, 96, 484
Windham, Ralph 472
Wingate, Orde 277, 315, 319
Wise, Stephen 336, 343, 441n74
Wolf, Lucien 22, 30–31
Wolff, Heinrich 404, 407
Woodhead Commission 291, 294–95, 305n160
World War One: American Zionists in 48–49, 51–52; British Empire expansion due to 164; costs for Britain of 41; debts to US from 226; Jewish immigrants to Britain during 10; Margolin during 92n24; Rutenberg in 193
World War Two: American Zionists in 313–14; British intelligence during 338; British priorities in 310; decolonization after 442; and Palestinian economy 363–64
WRB (War Refugee Board) 350

Yemen 256–57, 376
Yishuv: and Arab rebellion 278; Arab violence against 250, 274; arms supply of 452; blamed for King David Hotel bombing 469; British attempts to limit 261; British protection of 491; Chancellor's antipathy to 225; Churchill's proposals to arm 311, 315, 319 (*see also* Jewish Division); delegation to London 90; disarming 464–65, 467; during World War Two 307, 310, 312, 324–27, 488; enlistment in British army 332n29; Foreign Office assessments of 353; German plans for annihilation 427–28; growth of 132–35, 238, 249, 279, 486; institutions of 102; as part of Arab

Federation 375–76; on Peel partition plan 265; perceived influence of 106–7; political institutions of 101; support for armed struggle 463, 470; tax burden on 139; vulnerability of 112–13; and Zionist Commission 78, 127

Yishuv economy: autonomy of 252–53; crisis of late 1920s 187, 212, 485; industrial sector of 169, 363; and Tel Aviv construction boom 133–34, 174, 176, 182

Yishuv leaders: attack by Hope-Simpson on 223; language skills of 112

Yom Kippur 215–16, 456–57

Young, Hubert 118, 124

Young Egypt Party 391, 393

Yugoslavia: Axis occupation of 432–33; indictment of Mufti 385, 434

Zaghlul, Saad 80, 151

Zionism: and anti-Semitism 11, 15, 197; Arab collaborators with 149, 266–67, 279–82; Arab opposition to 76, 89, 266, 485; Balfour on 55; and Bolshevism 26, 28, 84, 106; Britain's retreat from 212, 219, 303; British commitment to 2–3, 33, 44, 55, 224, 366; British opposition to 69–70, 118–19, 128, 155; Churchill's lack of sympathy to 64–65; cultural 130; Jewish opposition to 29–32; Lampson on 248; Orwell's opposition to 20; Protestant empathy for 25; as self-funding 2, 42, 94, 98

Zionist Commission *see* Palestine Zionist Executive

Zionist Congresses: 16th 208n7; 17th 240; 20th 265, **Plate 10**

Zionist labour movement 103, 221–22, 234, 266

Zionist loan: British guarantee for 185–87, 189–91; raising 182–84

Zionist Mule Corps 93n58

Zionists: and 1922 White Paper 130; and 1930 White Paper 229, 231–32; and 1939 White Paper 303; accusation of collaboration with Nazis 383; and Anglo-American Committee 451–52, 454–55; appeal to League of Nations 97; and Arab Federation proposals 375; and Arabic press 398; Berlin on 113; Churchill's attitudes to 313; in civil service 104; compared to Nazis 329–30; co-operation with Germany 48, 386; disillusion with the Allies 336, 354, 356, 465; economic concessions granted to 192–93; and economic development 156; and Evelyn Barker 469–70; and Herbert Samuel 119–20, 122; and industrialisation 197–98; intelligence agents of 402; and Jewish division 312, 319; and Jewish immigration 118, 132–33; land purchases by 135–37, 139–41, 222, 227–28, 239–40, 314; meetings with Colonial Office 124–25; and Mufti of Jerusalem 215, 382; negotiations with British 52; and OETA 76–77; and Peel partition plan 140–41, 289; and Rutenberg concession 199

Zygielbojm, Szmul 343–47

Printed in Great Britain
by Amazon